BUSINESS and the CITIES

a book of relevant readings

edited by
Neil W. Chamberlain

BASIC BOOKS, Inc. Publishers
New York/London

301.24
C355b

© 1970 by Basic Books, Inc.
Library of Congress Catalog Card Number: 71-110767
SBN 465-00778-3
Manufactured in the United States of America

Preface

There has always been a grudging respect, even among professional President-baiters, for the laconic commonsense of Calvin Coolidge, a kind of New England Will Rogers without the wit, whatever quality that may leave him. But even that image has been subject to erosion in recent years. One of his most widely known aphorisms was that "the business of the United States is business." Today there are a dwindling few, even in business, who would quote that Coolidgeism with approval. The United States has become very much preoccupied with nonbusiness business.

The change has come with something of a rush. In the 1930's, to be sure, under the punishment visited on society by the blackest depression in American history, the inherited philosophy of business society underwent much criticism and some revision. The most profound departure from the economic scriptures occurred in the area of labor relations. Prior to that time the creed had always read that business performed its social responsibilities by turning out a good product at a fair price and by creating new products and making them more widely available. It had its specialized role to play, and as long as it played that role well, no one could properly ask for more. In the 1930's, in the face of widespread unemployment and distress, people came to ask for more, sometimes expressing their demands improperly—as in the sitdown strikes.

When the tide of New Deal legislation had subsided with the coming of World War II, one important landmark left on the beach was labor legislation, which, among other things, gave workers the right to organize into unions in order to gain some control over the conduct of corporate affairs, imposing a correlative duty on the part of management to bargain with their employees in a good-faith effort to reach a mutual accommodation. An important new chapter had been written in business philosophy. No longer was it sufficient that business govern its conduct by how well it could please the customer. It had to satisfy its employees too, not just keeping them happy enough to remain on the payroll and produce but also giving them some say about how the plant should be run.

Still, by the time of the Eisenhower 1950's the unions had been taken in stride. Collective bargaining had revised the rules of the game but it had not changed the game. In the President's "businessman's cabinet" the Secretary of Defense, a former chief executive of General Motors, could remark that "what is good for General Motors is good for the United States," a kind of free translation of Calvin Coolidge's code. Granted that the public response was largely disapproving, and that the remark itself had a certain ambiguity, the incident nevertheless suggested that at least some businessmen in high places still held a rather clear and unconfused view of the role of business in society. With whatever hindrances the unions supplied, the business of business was to get on with the production of America's goods and services. A number of conservative academic economists echoed that faith.

That view has not wholly gone out of fashion, but it now hardly represents dominant business or academic thinking. Events of the 1960's have precipitated new social crises in which business has, against its will and for better or for worse, become involved. The greatest of these has been the confrontation of the races in the United States, beginning with the civil rights movement in the early years of the decade and coming down through the Kerner Commission and black power right on to such present movements as the Black Panthers and black capitalism. But along with this most dramatic and perhaps decisive social struggle have gone other developments in quick succession, involving "confrontations" with consumers over product quality and safety, with youth over life styles, with communities over air, water, and sound pollution.

Business firms are being asked to redefine their relationships to groups in society other than their own consumers and employees. The confusion attending these new pressures lies in the fact that there is no clear indication of what relationships are to be freshly structured, or how. Business firms are currently experimenting and floundering in this new territory, just as they did in the industrial relations areas a few decades back. Precisely because there is no clear directive as to what is wanted, many firms are picking their way through this uncharted territory with caution; a few, however, are exhibiting some daring.

At least a major part of business's new responsibilities can be subsumed under the general heading of community relations. What is new is that these cannot be discharged simply by general programs such as donations to summer camps for children or sponsorship of public concerts—however laudable these may be. The relationships now demanded are with specific segments of society—young dropouts who need special training which a company can provide, neophyte black businessmen who require indoctrination in business techniques and perhaps some financial assistance or guarantee, neighborhood groups whose housing is being rehabilitated. In effecting such programs, the business firm must establish working relationships with a number of other organizations. There are, of course, the government agencies, such as the Office of Equal Opportunity, which are charged with special programs. But the new voluntary organizations—the several national and local associations, which have been set up to promote the interests of blacks; the neighborhood groups, whose organization is usually unstable and sometimes chaotic; even the youth organizations, with their own patterns of leadership and discipline—probably present the greatest challenges to business management.

In earlier years, relationships with such organizations would have been regarded as charitable activities undertaken unilaterally by those companies which chose to become involved. That conception has been violently shattered in recent years. Today's voluntary organizations pattern themselves after the labor unions of the 1930's. They draft demands to present to managements; they expect to negotiate those demands; in fact, they marshall their bargaining power to back them—whether through enlisting the support of government officials and influential public citizens, or through publicity, demonstrations, or disruptive tactics, or through organized boycotts.

Business experience is still too limited to determine the extent and effect of such pressures. It is impossible to say with any certainty whether they, like union pressures, are something which can never be "satisfied" but will be subject to the continuing escalation, the "more, more, more" syndrome, which has characterized the labor movement since the days of Strasser and Gompers. It is also too soon to say whether these are pressures which business will learn to take in stride, like the unions, with the effect of changing the rules of the game a bit but leaving the game intact in its essentials.

There is some slim basis for believing that there are rule changes pending which may have profounder effects. One after another president of a major corporation has publicly testified that profits and efficient production are no longer sufficient objectives for their organization. Professor Harold Leavitt has suggested that corporate executives, now reaching the top rungs of the business ladder at younger years than their predecessors, sometimes find themselves bored with just more of the same. "The company president," he headlined an article in the *Harvard Business Review,* "is a Berkeley rebel."

The real determinant of business's future is not the psychological state of the businessman himself but what his society demands—*effectively* demands —of him. It would appear that the efficient production of goods and services to satisfy individual material wants is no longer the highest order of social priority. The quality of our social life is rapidly moving up the scale of want preferences. The prolonged period of military preoccupation, now going into its third decade, constituted the first major break in that consumer orientation. It now appears for a variety of reasons that need not occupy us here that we, as a nation, are unwilling to postpone the attack on social needs in order to continue military adventures. In the process of reassessing our national priorities—however painfully and confusedly—and in the process of our social evolution, society is passing into a new stage.

A number of major problems are raised in the process. How does a firm combine profit and nonprofit activities, and in what proportions? Are such diverse programs even compatible? Does extension into new and perhaps inappropriate fields jeopardize successful continuity of the traditional forms of corporate behavior? What standards operate in the newer areas? The questions could be extended at length.

Not all—perhaps not many—of these deeply significant questions are answered in the following pages. Business involvement in urban problems on any scale is of recent date; indeed, most observers would maintain that business involvement on a substantial scale has not even begun. In part for that reason the amount of hard analytical thinking which has gone into the changing role of the firm in society, particularly with respect to its relation to the urban setting, has been slight.

Some of the materials reproduced deal more with the background of the problems which business confronts than with the business role, but such background information is essential. Some of the writings are more descriptive than analytical, but these contribute to our knowledge of what is going on. The range of the subject matter is in one sense very broad, running from poverty to education, but even so it does not encompass certain major areas such as housing and transportation. At the same time one thread of thought which runs through virtually all the subjects examined is the necessity of finding some workable and equitable accommodation of minority interests with those of the dominant white citizenry.

It is difficult to escape a feeling of despair in contemplating the plight of cities in the contemporary American scene. But each problem also presents an opportunity. The question which underlies all the materials in this book is the extent to which business will recognize it as such.

Neil W. Chamberlain
September 1970

Contents

Part I THE NATURE OF BUSINESS INTERESTS IN THE CITY

A *What Business Is Doing*
   1 The Role of Business in Public Affairs   5
      NATIONAL INDUSTRIAL CONFERENCE BOARD

B *How Much Can Business Do?*
   2 The Public Role of Private Enterprise   13
      E. SHERMAN ADAMS
   3 Private Initiative for Profit   19
      A. WRIGHT ELLIOTT
   4 Apply Our Systems Analysis   20
      ARJAY MILLER

C *Institutional Realignment*
   5 Business Wrestles with Its Social Conscience   25
      ROBERT C. ALBROOK
   6 A New Co-Aim for Business   29
      HENRY G. PEARSON
   7 Management Incentives for Social Action   35
      GARY F. JONAS
   8 The State of Business and the Business of the State   41
      CARL MADDEN
   9 The Public Side of Private Business   47
      NEIL W. CHAMBERLAIN

Part II THE DEMOGRAPHIC DATA

   10 The Challenge of America's Metropolitan Population Outlook—1960 to 1985   57
      PATRICIA LEAVEY HODGE and PHILIP M. HAUSER

Part III BUSINESS AND RACIAL RELATIONS

A Background

11 Excerpts from Report of the National Advisory Commission on Civil Disorders — 87
12 Racism — 104
   JOINT ECONOMIC COMMITTEE OF CONGRESS
13 Importance of the Job — 108
   ELLIOT LIEBOW
14 The Struggle for Employment — 112
   RUSSELL A. NIXON
15 Minorities and Apprenticeship — 121
   GEORGE STRAUSS
16 The Place of Political Protest — 128
   BAYARD RUSTIN

B The Business Reaction

17 The Kerner Report Should Be Required Reading — 132
   ELI GOLDSTON
18 Major Employers and Their Manpower Policies — 133
   BETTYE K. EIDSON
19 Toward Understanding the Hard-Core — 149
   NATIONAL ASSOCIATION OF MANUFACTURERS
20 In the Matter of Allen-Bradley Company — 152
   OFFICE OF FEDERAL CONTRACT COMPLIANCE
21 Help Wanted . . . Or Is It? — 172
   U.S. EQUAL EMPLOYMENT OPPORTUNITY COMMISSION
22 Implementing Equal Employment Policy Throughout a Large Corporation — 178
   NATIONAL CITIZENS COMMITTEE FOR COMMUNITY RELATIONS

Part IV BUSINESS AND THE POVERTY SECTOR

A The Urban Poor

23 Where Are the Poor? — 186
   JOINT ECONOMIC COMMITTEE OF CONGRESS
24 Who Are the Poor? — 188
   SENATE COMMITTEE ON LABOR AND PUBLIC WELFARE

B *Approaches to Alleviating Poverty*

    25 Policy Issues 194
          ANTHONY DOWNS

    26 Creating Employment Opportunities 196
          SENATE COMMITTEE ON LABOR AND PUBLIC WELFARE

    27 Minimum Wage Legislation: A Limited Tool 206
          SAR A. LEVITAN

    28 Private Enterprise Participation in Antipoverty Programs 207
          STEPHEN KURZMAN

    29 The Negative Income Tax 213
          MARTIN SCHNITZER

    30 The "Poor" and the "Broke" 220
          ELI GOLDSTON

    31 "In a Welfare Center on Eighth Avenue": A Welfare Recipient's View of Welfare 220
          JULIUS HORWITZ

    32 Poverty or Planning 223
          LEON KEYSERLING

Part V BUSINESS AND MANPOWER DEVELOPMENT

A *The Need for Jobs*

    33 The Need for Jobs 228
          JOINT ECONOMIC COMMITTEE OF CONGRESS

B *Business Response to Government Stimulus*

    34 The Job Corps and Manpower Development and Training Programs 236
          STEPHEN KURZMAN

    35 The Job Corps—A Cost-Benefit Analysis 260
          OFFICE OF ECONOMIC OPPORTUNITY

    36 Jobs Corps Evaluation 262
          COMPTROLLER GENERAL OF THE UNITED STATES

    37 Report of the Secretary of Labor on Restructuring the Job Corps (1969) 264

C *Experience under Private Manpower Programs*

    38 Transferability of Manpower Programs 268
          ARNOLD NEMORE

    39 Employing the Disadvantaged: Inland Steel's Experience 298
          RALPH CAMPBELL

40	Private Industry and the Disadvantaged Worker E. F. SHELLEY AND COMPANY	309
41	A Look at the Disadvantaged Employer FRANK CASSELL	315

D A Skeptical View

42	Toward Greater Industry and Government Involvement in Manpower Development SAMUEL M. BURT and HERBERT E. STRINER	324
43	The Nature of the Job Problem and the Role of New Public Service Employment HAROLD L. SHEPPARD	330

Part VI BUSINESS AND EDUCATION

A Working with the Public Schools

44	Bridging the Gap from School to Work MANPOWER REPORT OF THE PRESIDENT	336
45	Uplifting Vocational-Technical Education U.S. CHAMBER OF COMMERCE	345
46	Business Involvement in Public Education—the Detroit Experience MICHIGAN BELL and CHRYSLER CORPORATION	347
47	Business Amid Urban Crisis NATIONAL INDUSTRIAL CONFERENCE BOARD	356

B Education within Industry

48	Innovation in Education A. WRIGHT ELLIOTT	358
49	Remedial Education E. F. SHELLEY AND COMPANY	358
50	Basic Education: Case Studies NATIONAL CITIZENS COMMITTEE FOR COMMUNITY RELATIONS	361
51	Upgrading Manpower—Whose Responsibility, What Responsibility? NEIL W. CHAMBERLAIN	365
52	Don't Ask the Employer . . . SAMUEL M. BURT and HERBERT E. STRINER	373

Part VII BUSINESS AND URBAN ECONOMIC DEVELOPMENT

A The City as a Market

53	The Private Side of Public Business NEIL W. CHAMBERLAIN	380
54	Does Business Have a Future? J. WILSON NEWMAN	384
55	Subsidies Are Needed ANTHONY DOWNS	387
56	Good Housing Can Be Good Business ELI GOLDSTON	388
57	The Opportunity in Rehabilitation UNITED STATES GYPSUM COMPANY	392
58	The Business of Education NATIONAL INDUSTRIAL CONFERENCE BOARD	394

B Economic Development of the Ghettos

59	Developing Business and Entrepreneurs in the Ghettos SAR A. LEVITAN and ROBERT TAGGART III	396
60	A Million Tiny New Businesses HAROLD F. CLARK	401
61	The Resources Aren't There BERTRAM M. BECK	402

C Promoting Black Capitalism

62	An Entrepreneurial School BERKELEY G. BURRELL	406
63	The Opportunity Industrial Center Program REV. LEON H. SULLIVAN	408
64	Discussion of the Statements of Berkeley G. Burrell and Rev. Leon H. Sullivan JOINT ECONOMIC COMMITTEE OF CONGRESS	412

D Governmental Encouragement of Small Business Enterprise

65	Small Business Loan Program STEPHEN KURZMAN	420
66	Promoting Small Business Through Government Procurement SENATE SELECT COMMITTEE ON SMALL BUSINESS	423

xiv | Contents

    67 GHEDIPLAN (Ghetto Economic Development and Industrialization Plan) 434
        DUNBAR S. MC LAURIN

E *Private Encouragement of Ghetto Business Enterprise*

    68 Rochester Business Opportunities Corporation 444
        U.S. CHAMBER OF COMMERCE
    69 Restoration: A Profile of Economic Development 452
        ALVIN N. PURYEAR

Part VIII BUSINESS AND THE FUTURE OF THE CITIES

    70 The Younger Generation 463
        ELI GOLDSTON
    71 Nongovernmental Leadership 464
        JOHN W. GARDNER
    72 The Social Environment of Private Enterprise 468
        NEIL W. CHAMBERLAIN
    73 Goals for Urban Development 473
        LYLE C. FITCH
    74 We Are the "Power" Group 496
        IRWIN MILLER
    75 What Business Can Do for the Cities 501
        Fortune Magazine
    76 How Deep Is the Private Sector's Involvement? 503
        CHESTER HARTMAN
    77 The Corporation in Larger Terms 505
        NEIL W. CHAMBERLAIN
    78 What Is to Be Done? 510
        GORDON P. SHERMAN

    Index 515

Part I THE NATURE OF BUSINESS INTERESTS IN THE CITY

We tend to take for granted *now* that business should be involved in the problems of the city. The only questions seem to be "How?" and "How much?" This general impression is one of relative recency, however. The private business firm is basically a profit-making enterprise. It is not always easy to justify as profitable and therefore appropriate to a business what seem to be essentially eleemosynary activities.

The apparently platitudinous statements of businessmen, perhaps (even probably) struck off by a company's public relations department, are often genuine efforts to make an undeniable need for change consistent with past principles which were radically different and a practical reality which is still constraining. The materials in this part explore these issues.

A *What Business Is Doing*

The variety of forms of business participation in community affairs is suggested in the following reading. The variation in company attitudes toward participation is likewise evident.

1
The Role of Business in Public Affairs
NATIONAL INDUSTRIAL
CONFERENCE BOARD

To what extent does a company have a social responsibility? This question has been brought into sharper focus than ever within the past year as demands arise from many sides for increased action by private enterprise—especially the business sector—to help meet the urban challenges facing the nation.

There are two conflicting viewpoints concerning the corporate role in society. One holds to a legalistic view of the corporation as a "limited liability" organization, existing solely for the purpose of investment-for-profit; as such, it is not considered a person and, therefore, should have no social conscience. In the words of one chief executive adhering to this concept, "our business is to manufacture and sell our products, not to solve the problems of the nation."

Upholding the opposite viewpoint, the policy statement of an auto manufacturer endorses a broad social involvement for the corporate enterprise:

> The Company will maintain an active interest in the general welfare of our society and participate in programs and citizen efforts concerned with social and civic improvement. The Company is particularly interested in the social, civic and physical betterment of the communities in which it operates . . . The Company regards itself as a citizen of the communities in which it maintains facilities and employs people. . . .

In between these opposing positions, as the survey reveals, there is a wide spectrum of attitudes toward corporate citizenship, most of them acknowledging at least some degree of social responsibility.

AREAS OF CORPORATE INVOLVEMENT

Two areas of company activity included in The Conference Board's definition of "public affairs" have a primarily social orientation, as compared with the political or economic emphasis of other areas. One is *community service*—characterized by financial contributions and other corporate aids and by encouragement of employee participation in the affairs of the locality. The second is *environmental problem solution*—involving corporate efforts to

---

From National Industrial Conference Board, *Studies in Public Affairs*, No. 2 (1968), pp. 25–28.

alleviate problems of a socioeconomic nature, such as air pollution, unemployment, mass transportation, crime, and urban renewal.

The survey attempted to discover how actively companies are concerned with community service and environmental matters as one measure of the scope of their public affairs involvement.

CONTRIBUTING TO THE COMMUNITY

One of the most concrete measurements of a company's social concern is its financial contributions, not only to the needs of the immediate community in which it operates but also to the larger social community, which may often be national in scope.

Nine out of ten respondents say they made a financial contribution to community betterment during the two-year period preceding the survey. Eight out of ten say they made a contribution in kind, either in lieu of or in addition to financial support. Such contributions include donations of equipment to schools, provision of office space for community organizations, and executive time and talent for civic projects (see Table 1–1).

EMPLOYEE PARTICIPATION IN COMMUNITY AFFAIRS

In addition to making corporate financial contributions, it is common company practice to invite employees to donate to worthwhile charitable causes as well, usually through at least one annual community fund drive conducted in-plant by employee volunteers.

A large number of firms (87 per cent) also urge employees to volunteer their time and effort to community groups of a social service, civic, and cultural nature. And three out of four look favorably on employee membership on school and library boards, and on law enforcement and other commissions. The practice of encouraging active participation is fairly uniform among companies regardless of size or industry classification.

Some companies endorse the concept of community service in their written policy statements. Others promote participation more informally. The president of an Eastern firm remarks that "It is a matter of general policy that the employee is encouraged to participate in community affairs. . . ." The chairman of a Boston bank comments, "Several hundred of our staff are engaged in a broad spectrum of political and public service activities. It is encouraged by company policy, which is well understood, but is entirely individual and unsupervised."

One lumber producer advises employees, however, that while it advocates service to the community, it "wants to be sure that the activity undertaken is performed well enough to reflect credit upon the Company as well as the individual." This firm, as well as others, often underwrites individual membership costs in approved organizations.

TABLE 1-1 Corporate Citizenship Practices

	TOTAL RESPONDENTS	BY SIZE			BY INDUSTRY	
		SMALL	MEDIUM	LARGE	MANUFACTURING	NONMANUFACTURING
Number of Companies	(1,033)	(146)	(494)	(393)	(683)	(350)
Company financial contributions to education, health, welfare, and so on	91.7	87.7	91.1	93.9	89.6	95.7
Company gifts of equipment, talent, and so on to community betterment	82.6	78.8	82.8	83.7	81.7	84.3
Encouragement of employee participation on community service organizations	86.5	85.6	84.0	90.1	84.3	90.9
Encouragement of employee service on local boards and commissions	75.1	78.1	73.7	75.8	73.2	78.9
Recognition for employee public service	60.3	58.9	58.3	63.4	54.3	72.0

TABLE 1-2 Company Willingness to Initiate Action on Environmental Problems

		PER CENT OF COMPANIES					
	TOTAL RESPONDENTS	BY SIZE			BY INDUSTRY	
		SMALL	MEDIUM	LARGE	MANUFACTURING	NONMANUFACTURING
Number of Companies	(1,033)	(146)	(494)	(393)	(683)	(350)
Improvement and expansion of local school facilities	55.6	59.6	54.9	55.0	56.4	54.0
Improvement of local school curriculum	48.5	50.7	49.4	46.6	48.8	48.0
Problems associated with school dropouts	53.9	58.9	52.2	54.2	52.7	56.3
Improvement of work/career opportunities for minority groups	69.2	69.2	65.2	74.3	67.9	71.7
Retraining of workers rendered unemployed by automation	72.6	73.2	70.6	74.1	74.1	69.7
Construction or improvement of medical facilities	62.1	63.7	60.9	63.1	62.8	60.9
Medical care for the aged	35.9	37.7	34.8	31.6	31.6	44.3
Provision for, or improvement of, low-income housing	31.3	37.0	30.8	29.8	25.6	42.3
More and better cultural facilities and activities	59.1	61.6	57.7	59.8	57.1	62.9
Purification and improvement of water supply	68.3	67.8	65.7	72.0	72.8	59.7
Reduction and control of air pollution	73.5	74.0	71.3	76.1	78.6	63.4
Improvement of urban and interurban transportation	60.4	61.6	50.1	60.6	57.1	66.9
Development of community recreational facilities	55.6	59.6	55.1	54.7	55.9	54.9
Improvement of law enforcement at local levels	61.4	67.8	61.7	68.5	60.9	62.3

Some companies permit the performance of occasional civic and community activities on company time. An insurance underwriter's policy declares:

> Employees are strongly urged to devote a portion of their time away from the company participating in such [community] activity. The company will be glad to consider requests for reasonable absences from work in cases where an employee's services are urgently needed by a religious, charitable, or educational organization during normal working hours.

Recognition for Service

Three out of five companies think well enough of employee participation in community activities to accord some form of recognition, with nonmanufacturing concerns most likely to take cognizance of such service. While respondents were not asked to describe the nature of such recognition, some mention that community service is entered on the employee's performance evaluation record and others report that "some recognition is given by publicity in company publications."

SOLVING SOCIOECONOMIC PROBLEMS

A majority of surveyed companies indicate that they are concerned with problems of an environmental—or socioeconomic—nature to the extent that they would be willing to initiate action to help solve many of them.

When presented with a list of fourteen specific problem areas (Table 1–2), more than half of the respondents said that in eleven of the areas companies should take the initiative in helping to find solutions. Matters receiving the highest percentage of affirmative responses are those most closely related to business interests, for example, air pollution and vocational training of displaced and unskilled workers. The least amount of concern is shown for low-income housing and medical care for the aged. Nonmanufacturers, however, express more willingness to advance solutions in these two areas than manufacturers.

A number of respondents who do not favor company initiative say, however, that they are willing to cooperate in solving such problems. Some prefer to work through trade associations or other business organizations. Others feel that "businessmen should participate, but companies, as companies, should not." "Solutions require an expertise not possessed by companies," comments one executive, and another remarks, "It is difficult to take the initiative when a paid public official is charged with this. We try to give constructive help."

While socioeconomic matters arouse less corporate concern than issues of a strictly political or economic nature on the national and state levels,[1] the survey shows that in the opinion of respondents such problems will constitute the primary area of local concern for companies during the coming decade.

NOTE

1. For a recent report on company attitudes toward national, state, and local issues, see "Business Defines Its Social Responsibilities," *Conference Board Record* (November, 1967).

B *How Much Can Business Do?*

One question over which many businessmen have been puzzling in recent years is how much initiative and responsibility business can and should take in improving the quality of urban life. To undertake too much responsibility is to invite business frustration and public disillusionment, but disillusion can also come from business not undertaking enough. How much is too much, and what is enough? How does the urban preoccupation fit into business's traditional preoccupation with profits? These questions are considered in the following statements by three business leaders.

2
The Public Role of Private Enterprise

E. SHERMAN ADAMS
Senior Vice President, First National City Bank, New York

In what ways and to what extent can private enterprise help with the urgent social problems that confront our society? Will it be able to achieve miraculous results here as it has in the field of production? Or will its participation continue to be much as it has been in the past—largely subordinate, aside from paying taxes? Or does the answer lie somewhere in between?

• • •

PROSPERITY AND POVERTY

The author is quite aware of the shortcomings of capitalism, especially in the past, but must confess to being impressed by its achievements. Never before has such a large proportion of the citizenry of a great nation enjoyed such a high standard of living, and American industry can certainly claim some credit for this tremendous accomplishment. Without a prosperous, growing economy, our social problems would today be far worse than they are.

Nevertheless, some poverty persists—and more than just a little. Approximately thirty million Americans exist in poverty today. About two-thirds are whites and one-third are nonwhites. This means that by widely accepted standards poverty afflicts 12 per cent of our total white population and appallingly 41 per cent of all nonwhites.

For years, most businessmen and many others believed that expanding prosperity would steadily shrink poverty until it disappeared. But it is now clear that continuing economic growth alone will not wipe out poverty. The realization has been spreading in the business community and elsewhere that additional approaches are needed.

THE CATS WITH THE BREAD

Until recent years, social problems were generally regarded as being of concern primarily to government and nonprofit agencies. Bankers and businessmen, in their role as individual citizens, have traditionally supported and worked for many charitable organizations. However, *corporate* involvement, as distinct from the part played by individual businessmen as citizens, has been largely restricted to making donations and paying taxes.

From an address at the 69th Annual Meeting of the New York State Welfare Conference, New York, November 20, 1968.

But within the past several years, the conviction has been growing that private enterprise must become more directly involved in these problems. Indeed, some regard business as the last best hope for the future. In the vernacular of the inner city, we're the cats with the bread. Whitney Young recently stated: "There is little doubt in my mind, or in the mind of anyone in the ghetto community, that the institution that can do most to turn America around is the business community. . . ."

On the other hand, it is plain that private enterprise cannot do this job alone. There are, to be sure, some things that certain companies can do in this area on a profitable basis entirely on their own, without any help from government. But the possibilities of this kind are really quite limited, whereas the problems are immense. Government must continue to perform a major role in providing funds and offering incentives to induce business to get more deeply into the act.

THE MOTIVATION OF BUSINESSMEN

Let us examine the incentives and the motivation of businessmen. Are businessmen concerned solely with profits? When we say that incentives are needed to induce business to do more on social problems, does this imply that business will become more involved only if it can make a lot of money by doing so? Is hope for profit the real reason why so many businessmen have now become interested in these problems?

In the first place, it can be stated with assurance that, aside from the construction industry, very few businesses expect to derive much, if any, immediate benefit from this involvement in terms of increased sales or improved profits. Rather, they are motivated primarily by the realization that the future welfare of their companies would be impaired by further social decay—or, to put it the other way around, that their companies will eventually benefit, along with the rest of the community, if social problems can be alleviated.

A certain number of businessmen are motivated in part by a sense of public responsibility, but it is not always easy to disentangle this motive from awareness of the interdependence of business with its environment. It is interesting that banks and public utilities so frequently take a leading part in community programs. One reason for this is that it is so crystal clear to the managers of these businesses that their future growth and prosperity are closely and inextricably tied to the future well-being of the communities in which they are located—their main markets and the source of their work force. A New York City bank cannot just up and move itself to Blue Mountain Lake.

Moreover, many businessmen are now convinced that if social problems are to be brought under control, they must pitch in and help. In their view, government has demonstrated its inability to deal with many of these problems effectively and it is imperative that the talents and experience of business be brought to bear on them.

Briefly, the motivation of businessmen in this area can be viewed as being largely a matter of long-range, enlightened self-interest. This is an overworked phrase, to be sure, but it is most appropriate. Moreover, the author has written to the public affairs officers of a number of leading corporations throughout the country, asking them for their candid, off-the-record opinion of this assessment. An overwhelming majority replied that they were in agreement with it.

INCENTIVES ARE ESSENTIAL

Even though businessmen realize that they have a stake in their communities, and even though they are not trying to profiteer on poverty, nevertheless there must be adequate incentives if the resources of private enterprise are to be mobilized to help with these problems on a sufficiently large scale. In a competitive market economy, profit-oriented companies simply cannot devote a sizable portion of their resources to unprofitable or even relatively low-profit activities.

Various special programs have been undertaken by individual companies on a philanthropic basis. But the hard fact is that these do not add up to much considering the magnitude of the problems with which we are faced. In this perspective, they amount to little more than tokenism. It would be naïve to expect private enterprise to mount and sustain the massive offensive that is needed without adequate financial incentives.

This does not mean, of course, that business will not be paying a large part of the costs of social programs. It has been doing so in the past, and will doubtless continue to do so. (For the fiscal year 1967, income taxes of United States corporations amounted to over $36 billion, and individuals who derive their income from business paid taxes of many billions more.) However, the cost of social problems is far too great to be financed by charitable contributions. Clearly, the most effective way to tackle many of them is to permit business to earn a fair return for doing much of the work and, at the same time, let it pay much of the cost through taxation.

EFFECTIVE PUBLIC-PRIVATE COLLABORATION

How can we achieve really effective collaboration of business, government, and other groups concerned with social problems? The collaborative approach has, of course, already been employed in a number of programs—urban renewal and public housing are the most conspicuous examples. But the potentialities of this approach have been by no means exhausted. In New York State, new plans based on this concept are being developed by the New York State Urban Development Corporation. At the federal level, various new proposals have been put forward by such public officials as Senator Javits, Senator Percy, and the late Senator Robert Kennedy. These differ considerably in specifics, but all of them envision new institutional arrangements to promote the cooperation of the public and private sectors.

Opinions differ as to what kinds of inducements should be employed. Some believe it may be necessary to resort to widespread use of tax incentives. Others strongly oppose this device, but the question remains as to whether, as a practical matter, less objectionable methods would be effective enough. Some programs utilize intricate combinations of tax incentives, credit guarantees, and direct subsidies. Also, there are certain fields where government can enlist the help of private enterprise on a contract basis.

The whole problem of incentives is urgently in need of greater attention. Business, government, and other interested groups should work together to produce sensible solutions.

DIFFERENT ROLES IN DIFFERENT AREAS

The role of private enterprise will obviously differ considerably in different areas. In some, such as housing and job training, business can and should take a leading part. In others—public education, for example—its role should be significant but essentially subordinate. In secondary schools, for example, businessmen could make a valuable contribution to the revitalization of the vocational curriculum.

In a field such as public welfare, business cannot feasibly participate in actual administration. However, we all know that there are glaring defects in the present welfare system, and businessmen should assist in achieving reforms and seeing to it that public assistance programs are wisely conceived and adequately funded. Just how helpful they can actually be remains to be seen.

At the far end of the spectrum is family planning. It should be obvious that one of the fundamental reasons why so many persons in our society are poverty-stricken is the high birthrate among the poor. In the United States, 38 per cent of all poor families with children have four children or more. Children constitute 42 per cent of all poor persons, and 63 per cent of these 12,500,000 children who exist in poverty are in families with four children or more. Family planning is a basic problem; government and social workers can help enormously, but banks and business firms can hardly be expected to do much in this area.

In contrast, consider job training. This is a field in which business has acquired considerable expertise over a long period. It makes sense for business to utilize their know-how to help solve one of our most urgent social problems, namely, the fact that so many persons are not qualified for the jobs that are available.

EMPLOYING THE UNEMPLOYABLES

At this point, let me discuss one case example which illustrates several key points. The bank I am with (The First National City Bank) has for years been hiring young people who have no skills and giving them on-the-job instruction. We have not been insisting on high school diplomas but we have been employing only those whom we thought could become productive employees without too much cost. Specifically, the bank has felt that it was justified in making an investment of several hundred dollars in training a potential employee but that this was about as much as it could reasonably afford. Thus, we employed grade A dropouts but not grades B or C.

However, today our policy has changed. In July, 1969, we inaugurated a new training center in a renovated loft building on Canal Street, New York City, where we are giving not only vocational training but also basic academic education, orientation, and counseling to 200 individuals who have been certified by the New York State Employment Service as being hard-core unemployed. These people are now on our payroll and will remain there as long as they wish if they become useful employees after sixteen to twenty-two weeks of intensive education and training. These are not grade A dropouts; they are seriously disadvantaged persons who are lacking in skills, have educational deficiencies, and need special help to enable them to adjust to a working society. The cost of giving them the treatment they require will be not just a few hundred dollars each, but several thousand dollars each.

SOCIETY BENEFITS MORE

This new training operation has come into existence because early in 1969 the National Alliance of Businessmen was formed to enlist banks and businesses in a determined assault on the problem of the hard-core unemployed. This program is making remarkable progress in dealing with this stubborn problem. One reason for its success is that it includes incentives. The Department of Labor stands ready to reimburse firms for the extraordinary costs incurred in providing remedial education and job training for so-called unemployables. Thus, First National City Bank now has a government contract which calls for the education, training, and special counseling of 700 such individuals. Reimbursement of the bank for the extraordinary costs of this program will probably come to around $1,500,000. Without such reimbursement, the bank simply could not have afforded to undertake such an extensive and expensive program.

Note that the First National City Bank is not the only, or even the chief, beneficiary of this operation. The greatest beneficiary (aside from the individuals involved) is society as a whole. Of the 200 trainees presently enrolled, 111 are on public welfare and 95 are heads of households. This program should enable most of these people to get off the welfare rolls and stay off permanently. These are individuals who might otherwise be on welfare the rest of their lives but who can now become self-supporting, productive citizens. I leave it to you to estimate the aggregate benefits that should accrue over a period of years, not just to the individuals concerned, but to the taxpayers who would otherwise be supporting them on relief.

In short, private firms are now providing effective education and training to many of the hard-core unemployed because the federal government is offering to share the cost. Business benefits, to be sure, but the community benefits even more. The same principle is applicable elsewhere.

WHERE ARE WE HEADED?

Let us summarize. What evaluation can be placed on what private enterprise has done to date? On this question also the author polled the views of public affairs officers of several dozen major corporations, specifically, the members of the Public Affairs Research Council of the National Industrial Conference Board, a knowledgeable, realistic group. The great majority of these corporate officials were in agreement that the contributions that private enterprise have made to date in helping to ameliorate social problems could *not* be characterized as being "really substantial." Indeed, the consensus was that (aside from some notable exceptions) these efforts have actually been quite spotty. In general, actions thus far do not possess the scope or reflect the urgency that the crisis requires.

What about the future? There was almost complete unanimity that over the years ahead private enterprise will become considerably more involved in social problems than it is today. However, there was much less confidence that business will make "far greater contributions" than it has to date. Several officials stressed the key importance of adequate incentives. As one person stated, "Business cannot afford to spend the money that will be necessary to change our social problems without having some incentive or income from these actions."

So there you have it. The task ahead is enormous, and it would be dangerous to expect too much of business. Miracles are definitely not in the cards. On the other hand, many businessmen sincerely want to help, and private enterprise unquestionably *could* contribute substantially more than it has toward alleviating social problems. However, this will not come about automatically. It will not happen unless we adopt realistic and far-sighted policies to bring it about. It will not happen unless all segments of society—people in business, government, and community organizations—all of us—pull together to make it happen.

3
Private Initiative for Profit

A. WRIGHT ELLIOTT
Vice President, National Association of Manufacturers

Why must we focus so heavily upon the efforts of the private sector? Primarily because the growing sense of urgency that prevails has activated the deep concern of businessmen across the nation. It is fair and accurate to state that in this national problem-solving effort national progress depends strongly on our ability to mobilize effectively both the economic and creative resources of the private sector on a totally unprecedented scale.

However, by way of caution, I have two real concerns with the concept and implementation of private-sector involvement. My first concern is that we are making the mistake of overstating what can and should be relegated to business, that is, to the private sector. For to state that the private sector is becoming increasingly engaged and that its efforts are seemingly having a high payoff, and further, that we must support an intensified effort to seek massive involvement must not be interpreted as saying that the whole job should be relegated to the private sector. This would admittedly be a dangerous operational assumption. However, my second concern is an even more dangerous overstatement that has been made consistently, namely, that the efforts of the private sector are doomed to failure. It is extremely distressing to note that there are already many "prophets of doom" who, even before the race has really begun, are declaring the private sector a loser.

Many of these statements are made out of a spirit of defensiveness by people whose ideologies (and even institutions) are severely threatened by the prospect of testing the private sector's ability to combat the grave problems of the cities. I would simply say, in this regard, that the task before us is too great and the stakes too high to prejudge an effort whose impact may be great for reasons that are less than objective.

There are two additional comments that I would make about private-sector efforts. First, it is extremely important to reexamine the very rationale underlying private-sector action. We are convinced that there are numerous important and largely unexplored opportunities that exist for the private sector to take part in urban problem-solving on a *profit-making* (and I would stress profit-making) basis. We must be ingenious enough in our deliberations to convert social problems into market opportunities if we are to activate the total resources of business in this crucial effort. Economic interest can and must be tied to and wholly compatible with social concern for urban im-

---
From an address before the Congress of American Industry, New York, December 4, 1968.

provement. We should not be embarrassed—indeed, to the contrary, we should be proud—if the problem of low-income housing could be solved by a process of creating a significant market opportunity.

Finally, with regard to the private sector, we must be ingenious enough, again, to formulate solutions which stress *initiative* by private industry. This means that industry can, should, and even must be more than a "reacting agent." I would go so far as to suggest that industry even attempt *consciously* to develop a series of competitive models to traditional public agencies and programs, for through such vigorous competition one would hope that durable and meaningful solutions will be produced.

4
Apply Our Systems Analysis

ARJAY MILLER
Former President, Ford Motor Corporation

The traditional view that corporate management is responsible solely to its shareholders must be enlarged. Under current conditions, I think that we in management cannot discharge our long-run responsibilities to shareholders unless we also behave responsibly with regard to customers, employees, government, education, and the press. Acceptance of this broader responsibility is good business as well as good citizenship.

Apply now our systems-analysis approach in this area: what are the broad social objectives of our society? Fortunately, we're in general agreement on objectives: we all want, for every citizen possible, health, safety, economic well-being, and dignity of person. This agreement permits us to concentrate on identifying and alleviating the problems that stand in the way of achieving our broad objectives.

We must clearly recognize that in this time of rising expectations all around the world, active planning *will* take place on how to solve the problems confronting society. The only real question, therefore, is the role that we as business play in that planning. If we sit back and take no part at all, we can be certain that others—most of them will have little or no business experience—will come up with schemes and plans. We can also be fairly certain that in those schemes there will be a major role for business to play.

From "A Fortune Forum on the Changing Business Scene," *Fortune Magazine* (March, 1967), p. 154. © 1967 Time Inc.

Business will do the work, and you can almost be sure that the planners will expect us to pick up the check. And since we are going to be involved anyway, I suggest that we participate in the planning and that in so doing we will come out with a better plan at lower cost.

The potential for human progress is virtually unlimited. For the first time, we have an opportunity to improve on a massive scale the well-being of mankind. The only real question is whether we will apply as much imagination and skill in using our discoveries as has been applied in making those discoveries.

C *Institutional Realignment*

Justifying or rationalizing business involvement in social programs, such as upgrading the physical and social urban environment, is not just a matter of personal predilection. It involves institutional realignment. The readings which follow grapple with this issue.

5
Business Wrestles with Its Social Conscience

ROBERT C. ALBROOK
Fortune Magazine

For many of the corporate executives involved, the intense new efforts by American business to deal with the problems of the cities are a baffling phenomenon. It seems clearer every week that quite a few corporations are taking on something for which they have no real precedent and no entirely satisfactory rationale. After all, corporations are profit-seeking enterprises, and many problems of the cities just don't look profitable. How can Alcoa or the Chase Manhattan Bank—to mention two that are heavily involved—rationalize the investment of stockholders' funds in ventures that do not (at least, not directly) benefit the stockholders?

Decisions to locate a plant or branch in an urban ghetto, for example, or to create jobs for the hard-core unemployed, seem, on the face of it, to be uneconomic. It is true that society itself may be healthier for such decisions and that Alcoa and Chase Manhattan will be better off in a healthy society, as their top executives have frequently argued. "It's going to take money to train the hard-core unemployed," President John Harper of Alcoa said recently. "But any time we can turn people into producers, they'll become consumers too. That increases the market; therefore it's profitable." However, there remains a stubborn difficulty: the expanded profit potential is available to all companies in an industry or area, not just to those that invest in training the unemployed. As Harper acknowledges, "If you try to relate it to a specific company, it's more difficult."

Even where everyone in an industry is pushing resources into the cities, there is some confusion as to just how far this process may be extended. How much pressure on earnings can a "socially responsible" company accept? At what point might there be a disclosure problem, that is, a legal requirement to disclose to stockholders the extent to which operations were being affected by noneconomic considerations? How many jobs should a company be prepared to create? For that matter, could it create any at all in a loose labor market?

With unemployment rates of below 4 per cent recently, job creation on a big scale may have been rational and profitable for a big company. But if the rate moved back up toward 5 per cent, hiring the hard-core ghetto unem-

---
Reprinted from the August 1968 issue of *Fortune Magazine* by special permission; © 1968 Time Inc.

ployed might mean turning away experienced workers. This would be expensive and would strike many Americans, no doubt including those experienced workers, as irresponsible. Yet it would also seem irresponsible to abandon aid to the ghetto unemployed when the going gets rough. Companies might elect (some, in fact, have elected) to make a kind of "contribution to society" by keeping on workers that they don't actually require. In effect, this is a form of featherbedding, an economically ruinous practice businessmen have long denounced.

In casting about for some precedents for their social involvement, some businessmen have cited philanthropic contributions. And it is true, of course, that profit-seeking public corporations have for quite a few years been reducing their profits deliberately by making donations to certain civic causes. However, the questions raised by these donations are much less vexing than those raised by programs for the cities. They can be cut back fairly easily when profits are under pressure. The amounts involved are generally modest; at present, all United States corporations donate only about $900 million to groups concerned with education, health, and so on, a figure that works out to roughly 1 per cent of pretax profits. And at any one company the amount given is at least known, which may not be true of the cost of programs for the cities. And, most important, donations do not affect the *operations* of the company; they do not require any managers to feed noneconomic considerations into decisions about, say, hiring or plant location.

A CHANGE IN ORATORY

In trying to solve the "rationale problem," businessmen have pretty much abandoned one familiar old formulation that used to be very popular: the view that corporations do the most good for society when they just stick to business and maximize their own profits. In this view, which was a staple of businessmen's after-dinner oratory for several decades, profits are basically incompatible with "good works," and those who ask companies to perform them are undermining the system that created the American standard of living. Today, it seems, only the critics of business argue that it cannot and should not do anything for the cities. Professor John Kenneth Galbraith doubts the seriousness of the business commitments. Michael Harrington, author of *Toward a Democratic Left* . . . , argues that the outburst of corporate conscience is menacing because "satisfying social needs and making money are two distinct and often antagonistic undertakings" and that businessmen should not play the dominant role in aid to the cities because "whatever other qualifications they may have, businessmen are not competent to design a new civilization . . . [and] have no democratic right to do so."

Not many executives would accept the imputation that the programs being pushed by the Urban Coalition and the National Alliance of Businessmen . . . constitute interference in other people's lives. In general, businessmen have come to define and justify their role in the urban crisis in several different ways. The arguments are not exclusive of one another, and some businessmen have used more than one of them.

Some view the programs as only a temporary expedient. In the words of Robert C. Richardson, a systems consultant based in Arlington, Virginia, they constitute "a one-time, short-term effort to correct an adverse situation. It should not be envisioned as a permanent solution . . . since involvement is clearly motivated more by social concern than good management considerations and is, therefore, basically incompatible with the profit orientation of corporations. Business should promote, and make, a one time maximum effort to implement solutions that will eventually eliminate the ghetto problem. . . ."

A second argument is that the programs for the cities, while tending to reduce profits in the short run, will increase them in the long run, that is, by improving the business climate. This is the basic position of John Harper, who has said, "I would hope that most people are at least farsighted enough to realize that any corporation, big or little, can't disassociate itself from its surroundings." Sometimes the formulation is more defensive: there may not *be* any profits—there may not even be a profit system—unless business moves vigorously now to generate new hopes and create new opportunities in the city slums. Speaking to Ford Motor Company stockholders in May, Henry Ford II made this grim observation:

> Your company and members of its management are engaged in such activities because we believe that business and industry have an obligation to serve the nation in times of crisis, whether the danger is internal or external. It is clear, moreover, that whatever seriously threatens the stability and progress of the country and its cities also threatens the growth of the economy and your company. Prudent and constructive company efforts to help overcome the urban crisis are demanded not only by your company's obligations as a corporate citizen but by your management's duty to safeguard your investment.

A BROADER VIEW OF PROFITS

Sometimes in arguing that there are long-term profits in the problems of the cities, businessmen come close to redefining "profits." Ford, for example, has suggested that it is time to rethink our understanding of that word. In a speech given in early 1966, he said:

> There is no longer anything to reconcile—if there ever was—between the social conscience and the profit motive. . . . It seems clear to me that improving the quality of society—investing in better employees and customers for tomorrow—is nothing more than another step in the evolutionary process of taking a more farsighted view of return on investment.

Some businessmen have argued that despite appearances to the contrary their investments in the city *are* profitable—that is, profitable in the conventional meaning of the term and in the short as well as the long run. They contend that the investments have some immediate payoffs that are hard to measure but are probably substantial. For example, Caterpillar Tractor has developed its own program to train hard-core unemployed in Peoria (it got some Labor Department money to support the program) and now wants to keep the trained men working even in periods when demand is soft. President W. H. Franklin of Caterpillar obviously does not view the program as featherbedding. He suggests that it helps the company to stabilize employment and that it would be close to a breakeven proposition if the accounting could adjust for all the direct and indirect costs of unemployment in Peoria and for the improvements in employee morale, loyalty, and productivity (at periods of peak demand) that flow from the policy.

Furthermore, such programs do a lot for the morale of *management*. Better educated, inclined to be more intellectual and at home with abstractions than their predecessors, younger managers are often seeking in their careers a greater identification with society and its needs. Not a little of the "enlightened self-interest" that corporations see in their programs for the cities lies in their appeal to the college-trained managerial candidates that are being actively courted. Robert D. Blasier, a Westinghouse vice president who is himself deeply involved in the National Alliance of Businessmen, observed in a recent speech: "If those who have the job to do get more than ordinary personal satisfaction from their work—because they're helping people right in their own towns—that's an extra dividend without a price tag."

• • •

BEYOND ECONOMICS

It may not seem terribly important that business has had trouble working out a rationale for its new role. With or without a rationale, business is *there,* which is presumably what counts. . . . And yet the lack of any agreed-upon rationale does seem to make a difference. One of its consequences is a fairly wide-ranging pessimism among businessmen. They are concerned that the programs under way may not have enough impact and staying power. . . .

Without a rationale, furthermore, it is quite unclear at many companies just how to proceed. Until that does become clear, each call for "action" will continue to be hedged and business will continue to invite suspicion that private enterprise remains as private as ever, concerned mainly with expedients to fend off threats of violence. And a great deal of the "action" itself will consist mainly of high-level meetings between businessmen. Alfred C. Neal, President of the Committee for Economic Development, has warned:

> When corporate executives can't rationalize something well enough to delegate it, to make it part of the ongoing, workaday business of the company, not a great deal is going to happen. As long as business looks on these new challenges as something akin to traditional philanthropy, which has always been a matter for the top officials and directors, business will not and cannot be fully engaged. This way lies only death.

L. W. Moore, president of American Oil, has complained, "Those levels of company management that hold the responsibility for actually managing the work—who operate where the action is—have not really become involved in the search for solutions to social ills."

THE EXITS ARE CLOSED

Eventually, it seems likely, middle management will become entangled in the problems of the cities. It is almost impossible to imagine a real turnabout—a decision that the cities, after all, are not the business of business. Any such turnabout would be a disaster, not only for the cities, but for private corporations, whose relevance to the modern world and "legitimacy" in that world would be cast in doubt.

Businessmen, more than most Americans, know very well that our society can no longer run away from its problems. Not long ago, the rivers would carry the wastes away, the suburbs offered the amenities and security that the city could not sustain, the South offered a haven from the unions, the West relief from congestion, when the forest was leveled or the mine stripped, there were new acres to conquer. Now most of the old exits to a simpler life have been closed off and America is obliged, for the first time on a massive scale, to address itself to the more difficult challenges of repair and renewal. Business has so much of the talents and resources needed to meet these challenges that it would be irresponsible to shirk the job.

6

A New Co-Aim for Business

HENRY G. PEARSON
Manager, Career Development, Polaroid Company

When you ask me as a businessman what my social purpose is in life I am at a disadvantage compared with the educator, lawyer, doctor, minister, or civil servant. Their purposes are easier to name and obviously social. Educators teach youth, lawyers defend clients, doctors heal the sick, ministers inspire their parishioners, and civil servants serve the public.

From *MSU Business Topics* (Spring, 1968). Reprinted by permission of the publisher, the Bureau of Business and Economic Research, Division of Research, Graduate School of Business Administration, Michigan State University.

My difficulty is that I cannot convincingly state my social purpose concisely. To produce a product and make a profit does not sound like a social purpose. I have to explain that my purpose is to convert materials and human energy into a product, distribute it at a price to those who want it, and also bring myself a reasonable financial return.

But even this explanation may not satisfy the doubters. If I manufacture X-ray equipment, they question *my* social value but not that of the hospital that uses it. If I make chalk, they ascribe social value to the teacher who uses it but not to me. They can see the librarian has social purpose but not the bookstore clerk. Why do we X-ray and chalk makers feel challenged and defensive about our social purposes in life? If society wants everything from sundaes to spacecraft, why are we not performing a social service in providing them?

Probably the answer is that we are. Supplying goods and services to people is a social activity in itself and therefore has social value. But the point is that for the most part these goods and services are material, while the question-raisers are looking for a purpose beyond the material. Arnold Toynbee observes that "material progress as a national goal has led to stagnation, boredom and moral decay." [1] Former Dean Donham of Harvard Business School asks us to "recognize a social function which characterizes other professions." [2] His colleague, the late Professor Selekman, stated unequivocally, "What business needs is the conviction that its function is morally justified." [3]

In this article I shall try to point out (1) that our two principal aims—to provide goods and services and to keep healthy (popularly known as making product and profit)—are too limited to be construed as having social purpose; (2) that social purpose cannot be had simply by participating in non-business "social" activities; (3) that an intrinsic social purpose already lies within our grasp and we should elevate it to a status equal to product and profit.

• • •

A TANGENTIAL SOLUTION

A tangential solution to finding our social purpose is currently dangling before us. It is that the business administrator should also digest the humanities, support education, uphold the arts, embrace poverty programs, sponsor uplift TV, and involve himself in the community. All of these can make him a better manager, offset the stigma, and identify him with social purpose. Now there is no doubt that the businessman is qualified to help solve urban problems. He can indeed use his management talents in organizing fund drives. His skills in finance, procurement, distribution, and salesmanship are dearly sought by the professional world. But are these efforts anything more than evidence of good citizenship? Are they not ancillary to our main purpose, which is to give intrinsic social purpose to making product and profit? This temptation to look for solutions elsewhere is one we have all fallen for as parents. To make ourselves good family men we join PTA, umpire Little League, and drive kids to Sunday school, while the real spadework still needs doing on location—at home. If charity begins at home, should not social responsibility also? And if we businessmen are convinced we must exercise it, then why not find a way to exercise it within our own plants and offices?

NEW CO-AIM FOR BUSINESS

Yet all the time the makings of an intrinsically social and moral purpose lies within our grasp. This purpose involves a component as critical as materials, machinery, buildings, computers, and balance sheets. It is present in time and space—for eight hours a day and in every facility. It obviously must focus on people. Our new social purpose, coequal with making product and profit, should be the *development of people*. Dr. Edwin H. Land, president of Polaroid, told us at an annual employees' meeting that the function of industry is the development of people. That, he said, is what industry ought to be for.[4] Charles H. Percy, president of Bell & Howell, in 1952 stated, "Our basic objective is the development of individuals."[5] This aim of helping the individual to grow as far as his talents allow and the company's needs permit [6] certainly matches that of parent, teacher, minister, doctor—all of whom are involved in the same process. As they are instrumental in the growth of people, so can the business employer be, too.

BUSINESS CAN DEVELOP PEOPLE

Without usually saying so specifically, many businessmen have been either wittingly or unwittingly moving towards this goal for the last fifty years. They grant that the employer should treat his employees with some of the respect he gives product and profit. Morale counts as well as machinery, materials, and money.

These employers are using several policies to move people toward equal status with product and profit. One is to furnish employees with such benefits as holidays, vacations, cafeterias, lounges, decor, clinics, bonuses, premiums, and escalating pay. "These do not necessarily make the man satisfied," says psychologist Frederick Herzberg, "they merely keep him from being dissatisfied."[7] They are a kind of hygiene like a disinfectant that holds disease in check. But keep spraying it on!

Another policy is to provide the vital shelter like seniority rights and pensions that care for man's security needs. Seniority systems protect the employee who has been employed the longest. If he has to be displaced, he has bumping rights over his juniors. If he has sufficient seniority when he retires, he receives a pension. To be sure, unions once had to push these ideas on management, but regardless of origin, they do represent a modest attempt at an old Judeo-Christian principle—the brother's keeper.

These employers are also trying to meet man's need for belongingness and participation. They foster suggestion systems, profit sharing, newspapers, and advisory committees. Off-hours they encourage recreation clubs, bowling leagues, art classes, and credit unions.

But most pertinent of policies to "grow" people is the use of the real "satisfiers." These meet man's need for self-fulfillment and self-actualization, and for realizing his potential. They are the opportunities to grow and advance in rewarding jobs that evoke recognition and bestow esteem. The employer must provide the work opportunities in which to grow and the education and training opportunities to grow with. Probably the most significant discovery in the field of human relations in the last fifteen years is that personal growth and development are the real satisfiers in the world of work.

An Ultimate "People's Aim"

But all of these policies and techniques seem to lack a keystone for a "people's aim." They are either mundane like lounges, paternalistic like pensions, or individualistic like promotion. They lack a central purpose that transcends others and that unites the combined purpose of corporation, employee body, and individual. This central purpose should involve the common belief that there is something sacred about man; that the relationships between men, therefore, have a sacred quality. As Martin Buber says, *I* and *Thou* are not just two people speaking and listening to each other, perceiving or even understanding each other. *Thou* is not just a person with certain characteristics. You cannot say *Thou* without saying with it the *I* of the combination *I-Thou*.[8] Others call this relationship the kind of love you bestow on everyone whether you like him or not. It accepts him as another human being like yourself. You love him unconditionally and undemandingly. Thus there develops a force that binds you to him.

Now, whether the businessman means to be or not, he is involved in his own little corporate society. If there is something sacred about man, then there is something sacred about this society of his. It is full of potential, limitless *I-Thou* relationships. It is a society in which every member can practice his own form of unconditional love.

Here then lies the opportunity for making a corporate aim about people come to life. It is a policy that works for the giant corporation or job shop; for the boss or bossed. Both Old and New Testament tell how: Love your neighbor as yourself. This command does not require you to like, help, hire, promote, look after, or be nice to everyone. It is really a minimum requirement. It simply asks that, just as you take your own interests for granted, you should take others' as much for granted as you do your own. And yet in so doing, you do everything for everyone; you are bound to everyone as yourself.

Fulfilling this aim may take hours, days, months, years, or forever. More likely, it will never be fulfilled. But it does not need to wait on an inner light, a prayer, consultant, or training program. It applies through the work day to vice president or clerk, to director or carpenter, to an eager staff assistant or a balky union agent. It applies to the good performer or the bad, the guard or the pilferer. It can pervade relationships in interviews, meetings, conferences, and coffee breaks. It can ride out the conflicts and pressures produced by competition, cost reduction, automation, negotiations, mergers, failures, layoffs, and boredom. It lies at the root of eliminating bias raised by sex, color, and age. As a working principle, it can be used to tackle prejudices against women bosses, Negro salesmen, and aging applicants. It is a principle which, if practised by the boss and emulated down the line, can permeate the company. It can develop the people making a product and a living into a community in which men treat men with the respect and dignity God gave them.

Four of these policies, then, that is, benefits, security, belonging, and self-fulfillment, have already been partially or totally accepted by business—solid evidence that the overall development of people makes sense as a co-aim for business. Adding the concept of unconditional acceptance of fellow employees is simply to adopt as a business policy an idealistic aim of our Western civilization. Together these five policies can create a corporate aim that is entirely analogous to that of the employee. He expects to work, make a living, and further his own development. The company likewise expects to make a product (work), to make a profit (a living), and to further the development of its employees. When the aims of the company and employees are so comparable, why are we reluctant to make growth of people an admitted corporate aim coequal to product and profit?

Two Reasons for Our Reluctance

One reason is that stockholders do not like (or directors think stockholders do not like) too much emphasis placed on the care, feeding, securing, and growing of employees. The annual report mentions people mainly as serving the ends of product and profit. People are supplementary to carloadings and dollars, not complementary. This concept, however, is profane. If man is sacred, he cannot be made subsidiary to carloadings. He demands a category of his own; he demands a purpose in his own right.

The other reason is that many managers are reluctant to make a new policy statement which they fear they cannot live up to. This is a common misconception about a policy statement. Those who make it or hear it tend to think that if it is not followed to the letter it becomes a broken promise. Quite the opposite. A policy is an aim, sometimes unachievable. It needs to be idealistic to have strong appeal, says Paul Pigors, Professor Emeritus of industrial relations at M.I.T.[9] Statements of belief always sound idealistic, states Xerox President Joseph C. Wilson.[10] Says another authority, Chris Argyris of Yale, "If I have become convinced of anything in my work with people, it is that idealistic dreams are excellent goals to have in front of us." [11] The fact that the aim cannot always be fulfilled makes it no less valuable.

The doctor's purpose in life is to save lives, but of course some patients die. Nevertheless, his purpose stays valid.

And if the doctor, teacher, lawyer, hospital, school, and government are not always able to achieve their ideals and make their purposes come true, why should we businessmen declare ourselves ineligible to make the attempt? We are not exempt just because we work under the private enterprise system. We live in a culture that subscribes to these principles about people, and we should openly subscribe to them, too.

Thus we shall not only have to overcome the aversion of our stockholders to being "soft" with people, but also our own reluctance to pronouncing an ideal which we know we may not always fulfill. Yet if we do not state it, how is anyone to know it *is* our purpose?

But once we decide to identify the development of people as a corporate aim—coequal to product and profit—then our own ultimate purpose will begin to clarify. As ours clarifies, so will that of the people who work with us, for it can become theirs as well. Together we shall find our social purpose is as well-defined as that of the doctor, lawyer, teacher, and one we can identify with.

NOTES

1. Arnold J. Toynbee, *Harvard Business Review* (March–April, 1959), p. 113.
2. Wallace B. Donham, *Administration and Blind Spots* (Boston: Harvard Graduate School of Business Administration, 1952), p. 11.
3. Ralph J. Sturkey, Jr., "Review of *Ethics in Business,* by W. A. Spurrier," *Management Review* (March, 1963), p. 77.
4. Edwin H. Land, speech at annual business meeting of employees, Polaroid Corporation, Cambridge, Mass., Jan. 20, 1956.
5. Stewart Thompson, *Management Creeds and Philosophies* (New York: American Management Association, 1958), p. 82.
6. *Polaroid Handbook* (Cambridge, Mass.: Polaroid Corporation, 1966), p. 1.
7. Frederick Herzberg, *Work and the Nature of Man* (New York: World Publishing Co., 1966).
8. Martin Buber, *I and Thou* (New York: Charles Scribner's Sons, 1958), pp. 3, 4, 11.
9. Paul Pigors, *Effective Communication in Industry* (New York: National Association of Manufacturers, 1949), p. 57.
10. Joseph C. Wilson, "Social Responsibility of the Businessman," *Personnel* (Jan.–Feb., 1966), p. 24.
11. Chris Argyris, "We Must Make Work Worthwhile, *Life* (May 5, 1967), p. 68.

7
Management Incentives for Social Action

GARY F. JONAS
Fry Consultants, Washington, D.C.

If the corporation can be a vehicle for social change, it does not necessarily mean that it will; for the latter depends significantly on the attitudes which managers have about their role in social issues.

THE STUDY

During the spring of 1968, a questionnaire was submitted to three groups at the Harvard Business School: top managers in the Advanced Management Program (AMP), middle managers from the Program for Management Development (PMD), and graduate students pursuing the Masters in Business Administration degree (MBA). Although these groups do not represent a cross section of American management, they are a good sample of present and future leaders of private enterprise. The alumni of Harvard's programs are found in all industries and most functional disciplines. Consequently the data from this study can be used to infer the direction and extent of management thinking on contemporary issues.

BUSINESS INVOLVEMENT

The questionnaire was designed to disclose the attitudes of the above outlined groups on the issue of the "social responsibility role of business." Twenty activities appropriate for expressing this role were listed. These ranged from traditional business endeavors, such as "contributing to the arts" and "hiring college students during the summer" to more revolutionary proposals such as "building plants in ghetto areas" and "buying only from suppliers who practice equal opportunity employment." A few *avant garde* ventures were also listed. These include such ideas as "providing free lunches for school children" and "hiring workers who are not needed just to help relieve the unemployment problem." The respondents were asked to rate each activity according to the following criteria: (1) Businesses have a responsibility to participate in this activity. (2) Business should engage in this activity but only

---
From *The MBA* (February, 1969). © 1969 by MBA Enterprises, Inc.

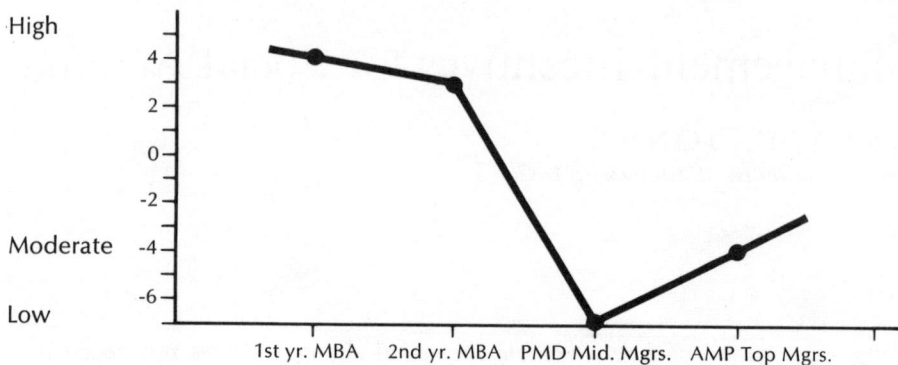

Fig. 7–1. Median Scores for All Groups on Social Responsibility Role of Business

if it is economically justifiable. (3) This is not a proper activity for a business to be involved in.

The three groups of respondents expressed significantly different attitudes on the issue of social responsibility. The median score of each group is plotted in Fig. 7–1. As might have been expected, the students felt that business should have a greater social commitment than either group of managers did. This difference in attitude could be attributed to several factors. One may be the exposure to social issues that students have in a number of their courses. Another may be the generational difference—today's students have grown up with the problems of race relations and urban decay. Thus, although graduate business students are far from a radical group, they still have an exposure to these problems which older managers lack. A third distinguishing characteristic of the student group is the security of their position. The students have nothing to lose by being in favor of social responsibility—it costs them nothing and it satisfies their benevolence needs. The survey further substantiates this last distinction; students who had spent two or more years in business before continuing their education were more reluctant to allocate corporate resources for social purposes. But even this group of older students expressed more concern for social issues than either of the management groups. This difference implies that future managers will sustain a greater commitment to social involvement than their predecessors did.

A comparison of the responses of top and middle managers provide some important insights. Top managers were willing to appropriate more corporate resources for social causes than the middle managers were. There are several possible explanations for this difference, each of which substantiates Galbraith's contention that managers are most concerned with their self interest—their status and power.

1. *Top managers receive public acclaim.* When a corporation makes a do-

nation or announces a social program, it is top management that receives the public recognition and acclaim:

> Mr. X., President of the ABC Company, announced that his organization was donating $500,000 to the local university for the purpose of studying the problems of hiring the handicapped. Mr. X's picture appeared in the daily papers and he was interviewed on several television shows. A month later, the university elected Mr. X to its Board of Directors.

Since top managers often receive the direct rewards for their organizations' social programs, it should not be surprising that they would be more willing to appropriate more corporate resources for this cause than the middle managers. An additional fringe benefit which often accrues to socially responsible top managers is increased political influence. Politicians enjoy mingling with the leaders of the business community and when they are both working for a common social cause their affinity increases. Hence, the top manager stands to gain both social and political influence when his firm is sensitive and responsive to social needs. Top managers may also be drawn to social consciousness by what has been called a "need for power." [1] Studies have shown that this "need" increases with age; such needs can find easy outlets in public welfare activities. It seems reasonable to conclude that the attitude of top managers is related to the direct rewards which they receive when their organization is socially responsive. Similarly, middle managers do not receive these benefits and, therefore, cannot be expected to have an equally strong social commitment.

2. *Middle managers are judged by economic performance.* Most top managers have their positions in the corporation firmly established. On the other hand, middle managers, whose compensation and promotion are much more sensitive to financial fluctuation, are still vying for the positions at the top of the corporate structure. This suggests that a middle manager should be more reluctant to allocate resources for which he is responsible to non profit-maximizing ventures than his top management colleagues. The problem which results is crucial for it is the top manager who designs and announces plans for community improvement but the middle manager who must implement them.

> Mr. J., the President of a leading automobile company has announced a plan to employ more hard-core unemployed in his organization. Mr. A, a middle manager in the company, endorses the president's plan and thinks about how he can help. He remembers that a position as a mechanic's aide is available in his department and feels that this job might be suitable for an untrained individual. Before searching for a new employee, he thinks of the risks involved in hiring a hard-core unemployed person. If the new employee is irresponsible or leaves, the performance of the department might suffer. He wonders whether he should risk part of his bonus on this venture. Finally, he decides not to hire a hard-core unemployed individual.

As the case of Mr. J. points out, reward systems must be redesigned to obtain middle management's support for social programs. Even though many corporate leaders might agree with Joseph Wilson of Xerox that "a corporate sense of social responsibility has become a reality and is essential for survival," [2] it takes more than top management commitment to make plans work. Top management should not expect to see such plans successfully executed until it can provide more tangible rewards for middle management's cooperation. It is folly to rely on the altruism of middle managers; clearly the recognition that top management receives for support of social programs must be transferred down to the lower levels of the organization. In addition, methods of rewarding middle managers for social sensitivity must be found.

The results of the questionnaire were also analyzed to discern which of the twenty proposed activities were most preferred. Ten activities were favored by all groups; they are listed in Table 7–1.

The activities listed are the type to which businessmen are inclined to give careful consideration. A high rating of the item "taking precautions above the legal requirements to prevent pollution" indicates that management is highly sensitive to this issue. Responsibility for inaction in this area apparently can-

TABLE 7–1 *Activities Preferred by All Groups*

ACTIVITY	NET PER CENT FAVORING *
1. Taking precautions above the legal requirements to prevent pollution.	81
2. Arranging for job placement of employees in the case of work shortage or close down.	78
3. Paying for the advanced education (part time) for employees.	69
4. Paying managers to take leaves of absence while working for the government on social problems.	47
5. Giving preference to the training of minority groups for jobs available within the company.	43
6. Hiring college students during the summer.	38
7. Giving preference in training of the hard-core unemployed for jobs available within the company.	14
8. Buying only from suppliers who practice equal opportunity employment procedures.	11
9. Building plants in ghetto areas.	2
10. Contributing to community libraries.	1

* Net per cent is determined by taking the per cent who responded "business should *not* engage in this activity" and subtracting it from the per cent who said "business should engage in this activity." All four groups are included in this calculation with equal weighting given to each group. The activities (ten) which are *not* included in this list received more "business should not engage" than "business should engage."

not be solely placed on businessmen. Possibly the government has failed to come forward with a definite corporate-oriented pollution-prevention program. This would substantiate a common complaint of managers that, although they are willing to make efforts in the social realm, they sometimes do not know how or what they should do. Identification of opportunities and encouragement of private efforts must be contributed by the public sector, if we are to benefit from the social consciousness of business leaders.

The contention that managers are most concerned with self-interest was verified by the second analysis of the data from part one of the study. For example, 85 per cent of the managers supported corporate sponsorship of advanced education for employees, but only 60 per cent of the students gave the same response. The obvious explanation is that all of the managers, who were benefiting from that program, were enthusiastic about the proposal. Students, on the other hand, see themselves as neither obtaining nor desiring more formal training. Consequently, their response was less favorable. For a second example involving the proposal "hiring college students during the summer," 32 per cent of the first year students, who were soon to be searching for summer work, thought companies should hire students, but less than 20 per cent of the second year class favored the same plan.

A comparison of managers' attitudes towards the hiring and training of minority groups and the hiring and training of the hard-core unemployed reveals a marked preference for the former. When managers were asked to explain this preference a common response was the following:

> The law of the land (Civil Rights Act) says that we must have equal opportunity for all races and ethnic origins. However, it does not specify that we must hire the hard-core unemployed. Moreover, many minority groups, particularly Negroes, have used social pressure against firms which did not employ a sufficient number of people from their race. It is just good business to be an equal opportunity employer.

Certainly businessmen seem to be responsive to legal pressure, but as Professor Levitt [3] pointed out they have a Pavlovian resistance to the passage of those laws. History shows that, when business fails to fulfill its social responsibilities (for example, in the areas of air pollution, civil rights, price fixing), the government intercedes and legislates this social role. Perhaps it is time for businessmen to follow Arjay Miller's advice: "The corporation must also go beyond its traditional role of business enterprise and seek to anticipate rather than simply react to social needs or problems." [4] Unless it does, continued opposition to legislation will have to increase in intensity. Undoubtedly a more constructive application of business resources can be found.

The recent attention given to the poor and the unemployed should be a signal to business that programs in this area are vital. The data from the survey (see also Table 7–2) indicates that business will respond to the needs of the hard-core unemployed but only if it is economically justifiable. But this is one activity in which economic justification is difficult, or impossible, to establish.

TABLE 7–2 *Activities with High Percentage of Responses "Business Should Engage in This Activity but only if It Can Be Justified Economically"*

ACTIVITY	PER CENT GIVING ECONOMICALLY JUSTIFIED RESPONSIBILITY
1. Building plants in ghetto areas.	70 (9) *
2. Hiring college students during the summer.	60 (6)
3. Giving preference in training to hard-core unemployed for jobs available within the company.	48 (7)
4. Training of minority groups for jobs outside the company.	45 (15)
5. Training of hard-core unemployed for jobs outside the company.	45 (15)
6. Sponsoring public cultural events.	37 (12)
7. Giving preference in training to minority groups within the company.	35 (5)

* Numbers in parenthesis indicate the ranking of this activity on the net social responsibility scale (Table 7–1). All four groups are included in this calculation with equal weighting given to each group. Note: a high ranking on this list and Table 7–1 indicates considerable concern for the activity. However, since this list consists of the responses which are not included in the other exhibit, it is impossible for an activity to be at the top of both lists.

If business wants to prevent government intervention, it will have to make a sincere commitment; this may mean setting up programs which will not give an optimal economic return.

Attention is now directed to the activities of the questionnaire which were most often given the response "Businesses should engage in this activity but only if it can be justified economically." They are listed in Table 7–2. For some of these activities, economic viability can be demonstrated; for others, government help through tax incentives, or other schemes, would be needed to make them financially feasible. The significance of this list is that it indicates potential areas for business action. The overwhelming support for "building plants in ghetto areas" is encouraging. One of the most socially destructive trends today is the relocation of industrial plants in suburban areas. This practice eliminates an important source of funds and jobs in urban centers. Some government leaders have been attempting to reverse this trend. According to this survey, these efforts will gain the support of businessmen, but only if their financial feasibility can be demonstrated.

CONCLUSIONS

Businessmen have found that involvement in the solution of urban problems is often consistent with the long term objectives of their organizations. However, although many top managers are committed to social action programs, middle managers have been found to be more reluctant to allocate corporate resources for such causes. In discussions with managers, it was discovered that reward systems were not geared to acknowledge a middle manager's social contribution. In addition, areas for future business participation were noted. When business has taken initiative in social problems, it has prevented government intervention. To assure proper participation in the future, middle management must be motivated and business-government cooperation assured.

NOTES

1. D. C. McClelland, *The Achieving Society* (Princeton, N.J.: D. Van Nostrand Company, Inc., 1961).
2. The John Diebold Lectures, Harvard Business School, April 23, 1968.
3. "Why Business Always Loses," *Harvard Business Review* (March–April, 1968), pp. 81–90.
4. "The Corporation and Social Responsibility," *Business World* (1968), p. 12.

8
The State of Business and the Business of the State

CARL MADDEN
Chief Economist, U.S. Chamber of Commerce

It is, indeed, as Big Daddy that the federal government presents its most puzzling face to business. Big Daddyism—or paternalism—means different things to different people. At best, it means a "helping hand" of protection to fairly well-defined groups in society. Business is, at least, on common ground with government as a customer or a competitor. But business lacks a fixed

From *Washington World* (May, 1966).

frame of reference in trying to adapt itself to a paternalism that operates outside the pushes and pulls of the marketplace. . . .

Here, as scholar George Stigler of The University of Chicago points out,[1] the debate between liberals and conservatives is seldom joined; there is no useful dialogue between them because they start from different assumptions. The liberals, as Stigler sees them, are highly person-oriented. They see the poorly housed, the poorly clothed, the poorly-educated, for example, as special groups needing the paternalistic care of the government. The conservatives see the economy as a system of impersonal forces which, through competition, offers opportunity to individuals.

Yet the debate may well have never been joined because liberals and conservatives may never have been talking to each other. The main issue may well be that both the liberals and conservatives have suffered from a cultural lag. Along with such changes as the revolutionary shift in the role of business and government over the past thirty years, the swift and accelerating pace of technology, and the increasing urbanization of the society, we have witnessed the obsolescence of some machines, some skills, some businesses, and some government programs. Likewise, the content of well-worn words, such as "individualism," "competition," "freedom," and "responsibility" has been subtly changed by the forces of science.

BUSINESS AND THE TECHNOLOGICAL REVOLUTION

The amazing predominance of technology as a unique feature of modern life has become almost a cliché. Even so, the age of technology is only at an early stage. It has been said that of all the scientists who have ever lived 90 per cent are alive today and that half the expenditures on research and development in the history of the United States have been made in the last decade. The recently issued Report of the National Commission on Technology, Automation, and Economic Progress [2] found that technological progress "has played a major role in bringing this nation the highest standards of material welfare more broadly disseminated throughout its population than has ever before been achieved in the history of the world." On the other hand, the report warns that "Our society must do a far better job than it has in the past of assuring that the burdens of changes beneficial to society as a whole are not borne disproportionately by some individuals."

Business, of course, is a major executor of technological change. Through the market system, we have developed a process of natural selection by which technologies are tested by performance. Business, as the major agent of technological change, bears a real responsibility for both its benefits and disruptions.

Yet how is the technological revolution now accelerating to be interpreted by liberals and conservatives of George Stigler's "unjoined debate"? A computer-programmed conservative from the above input might produce national policy prescriptions calling for greater incentives to business to generate more and better jobs and incomes. A computer-programmed liberal might yield an agenda such as the one proposed by the Commission: (1) government guarantee of a floor under family income; (2) government guarantee of jobs as the employer of last resort; (3) government matching of jobs through a national computerized job-matching system; (4) government relocation assistance to workers and their families; (5) "elimination of all social barriers to employment"; (6) "a federal executive in each (Federal Reserve) District" to coordinate federal programs for each region, and so on.

Issues that are likely to develop in tomorrow's highly urbanized, high-income, high-leisure society are certain to be oversimplified by traditional liberal and conservative views. Indeed, it may be well to recognize that perhaps the first task in addressing such issues is to demand far higher standards of discussion. Our society, which spends billions to place a man on the moon, knows little and studies little about what goes on in its cities. While the systems concept in engineering sciences forges ahead and operations research is widely applied to defense, there is scarcely a decent interdisciplinary research center in the range of social studies. It will remain difficult to rethink key concepts such as individualism, competition, freedom, and responsibility without higher standards of fact-gathering and analysis. Studies are still too few comparing results and intentions of government programs over a wide field. Where significant studies have been made of results, as in urban renewal, grave doubt has been cast on earlier simplistic assumptions.

● ● ●

The general business view supports the constitutional system of diffused political power and federal checks and balances. Likewise, the business ideal is the principle of a government of laws and not of men—of rules and not authority—to assure equal treatment and predictable scope and impact as against wide discretionary latitude. Business thus favors as an ideal legislation by Congress rather than discretion by the Executive. Finally, business as a group supports localism—a preference for government action nearest the people, but a recognition that the central government should act promptly and effectively when really needed.

BIG DADDY OR BIG BROTHER?

Business as a group thus faces a grave dilemma in respect to certain aspects of the Great Society. To be sure, businessmen sigh with relief that government now focuses on enlarging the economic pie rather than bickering over how to divide up a fixed pie. Businessmen respect the willingness of government today to entertain new ideas and examine the role of business in an open-minded way. Some, indeed, are candidly disappointed that tax cuts and investment credits, which had been pressed on government in the 1950's, were so long in coming. And at some levels of problem-solving businessmen have a natural and sincere respect for the pragmatic approach to political problems, as distinguished from the inflexible approach of ideology that marks today's government at the federal level.

Yet the principle of government action reflected in the "guidepost approach"—informal controls over economic activity—is disturbing to the business community for technical, economic, and philosophical reasons. Technically, the guidepost approach freezes past patterns, discriminates against the new, subverts the classic function of price in allocating resources, and thus promotes results akin to monopoly. Now embracing wage-price decisions, international investment decisions, and domestic investment decisions, these so-called "voluntary" controls shift the burden of government responsibility to business through self-enforcement that penalizes the conscientious and blunts the forces of competition.

It is philosophically, however, that the informal controls have their most important and disturbing possibilities. They pit the immediate interests of businessmen in face-to-face negotiations against their long-range interest in the existing framework of business-government relations. The danger in substituting discretionary consensus for the rule of law is not only constitutional. The danger is also, as the *Washington Post* has pointed out editorially, "that accommodations may be reached which are contrary to the interest of consumers and other groups." [3] The *Post* points out further:

> "The essential French view," writes Andrew Shonfield in his *Modern Capitalism*, "is that the effective conduct of a nation's economic life must depend on the concentration of power in the hands of a small number of exceptionally able people exercising foresight and judgment of a kind not possessed by the average successful man of business."

The threat of rule by elite groups implicit in the guidepost approach of informal controls is surely fraught with grave long-range implications. The solution to concentrations of power, as we have learned by examples both in Russia and Germany, is surely not further concentrations of power. The entire issue of informal controls, as the *Washington Post* properly emphasizes, "ought to be subjected to a searching analysis" by Congress. The legislative branch is especially appropriate as an agent for such a study because the issue of lack of legal sanction goes to the prerogative of the Congress to make laws.

The ideas behind the new welfare state and the new federalism likewise pose dilemmas for business and our society. As old as Bismarck and as new as Sweden's middle way, the new welfare state, starting from the present-day base of big government, would now add on comprehensive federal social welfare programs. The basic rationale, insofar as it can be inferred, is to achieve equality of security against economic risk and national standards of welfare levels. The new federalism seeks through escalated federal programs to expand assistance to localities and regions in order to apply national standards in education, health, and welfare; to promote regional and metropolitan community planning; to influence the location of industry; and to promote the growth of backward regions.

Arguments for these new federal initiatives are hardly unfamiliar. The country is being drawn together by the ties of technology as time and space have been foreshortened; increasing mobility among regions and vast rural-to-urban migrations convert the poorly educated of Mississippi into social problems for eastern cities; technical possibilities for health care should be more equally applied as an extension of basic public health; and, we are told, states are ineffectually governed and local government structure is obsolete.

But the arguments, while identifying problems, do not necessarily justify the premise of federal initiative. They define a politics of problems, not of issues. For those in the society who close their eyes to such problems, federal action is likely always to be traumatic in its shock potential. More and more businessmen, while recognizing better the politics of problems, are also beginning to question the strategy of federal solution. To this extent the promise becomes greater that a genuine debate will be joined. This promise is being expressed by business as a search for "constructive alternatives."

THE STRATEGY OF CONSTRUCTIVE ALTERNATIVES

The advance of technology has seen management education shift from a narrow professional or vocational base to deeper study of technical fields, the scientific method, and the content of the social sciences. Peter Drucker has pointed out the rise in business of the highly educated, technically competent young scientist and manager, secure in his postwar employment options, highly mobile and knowledgeable, and concerned locally in the main about the quality of life and not the status quo. Today, such young businessmen of the new breed, in Drucker's view, are themselves pragmatists, of modern mind. And, as Alfred North Whitehead pointed out, "The new tinge to modern minds is a vehement and passionate interest in the relation of general principles to irreducible and stubborn facts."

Such pragmatism of the scientific method is to be sharply distinguished from the improvised pragmatism of the New Deal—now the Old Deal to more and more people. It is the confident but painstaking method of the scientist, capable of application of principles with imagination and a sense of organization. It is, by and large, one step removed from the era of the tired old liberal or conservative, although often it is biased toward risking old slogans for the adventure of new solutions. It asks such audacious questions as these: Why can't metropolitan government in some form be developed? Why do we tolerate illiteracy? Why should not education be life-long and continuous? Why can't slums be rehabilitated by private industry? Why can't states be better governed? Why are teenagers unemployed when jobs are going begging? Why can't medical care be better organized?

The strategy of the constructive alternative is still being worked out. It calls for business recognition of and participation in solving social problems. In response to "creative federalism" it proposes in some areas "creative competition" between business and government to serve the national interest. George Champion of The Chase Manhattan Bank put the issue this way: "Just imagine what could be accomplished if some of this competitive zest were channeled into public service. Think of the good that could be done if business were to launch an all-out campaign of creative competition with government in developing imaginative new approaches to economic and social problems."

The guidelines Champion recommends for business are concentration of energy into areas of specialized knowledge, selection of areas where the tendency is especially strong to look to government for help, and personal involvement. He cites the case of United States Gypsum, which renovated a block of six apartments in Harlem at $9,000 unit cost, less than half the unit cost of new public housing. Another example is the superior technology that West Virginia Pulp and Paper applied to stream pollution and sewage disposal in Maryland and Pennsylvania. Still another example is the aerospace companies of California, which developed long-range plans using systems analysis to cope with California problems of transportation, crime, pollution, and data communication. These examples could be multiplied many times over.

CONCLUSION

Business is reacting positively in a modern context to the growth of government. Business has seen government take responsibility for the level of employment without dire postwar results. But it also sees government, already big, growing bigger. It sees at the federal level the disturbing growth of informal executive power and the gathering strands of the new welfare state and the new federalism. Whether these new initiatives impose a federal government blueprint, whether government becomes the junior partner in a renaissance of local initiative or a senior partner on the way to control, whether Big Daddy becomes Big Brother remains to be seen.

Yet, as the unjoined debate of liberal and conservative gives way to the politics of problems, it becomes clearer that the technological age of today and tomorrow requires a higher and different standard of public discussion. One business proposal is to strive competitively with government to solve social and economic problems. It is a hopeful proposal. Its philosophical roots lie in a characteristic of the modern mind, the interest in the relation between general principle and brute and irreducible fact. Such a modern mind might well question, coolly and objectively, the gap between government intentions and results and the wisdom today of much further government growth and social consumption relative to private consumption.

If modern minds are likewise attuned to meaningful up-dating of local government structure, to raising embarrassing questions about our low demands of performance in much public spending, and to an innovational push into hard-core social and economic problems, these things are all to the good. Indeed, they may be a harbinger of what Daniel Moynihan has called the "growing professionalizing of reform." Moynihan asks why shouldn't reform be subject to the same patient analysis and imaginative prescription as we bring to industrial innovation? If during the last five years the politics of prosperity has shifted our perspective from issues to problems, it has then moved the United States another step down the historic road of nationhood toward melding its varied and heterogeneous population into a unity of vision, its pluralistic society into a commonality of goals. The thing lacking now, as some businessmen would argue, is a politics to move into the age of science, a politics to redefine for that age the ancient wisdom of individualism, competition, freedom, and responsibility.

NOTES

1. George Stigler, "The Unjoined Debate," *Chicago Today* (Winter, 1966).
2. Report of the National Commission on Technology, Automation, and Economic Progress.
3. Editorial, *The Washington Post* (April 11, 1966).

9
The Public Side of Private Business
NEIL W. CHAMBERLAIN

A few years ago the *Harvard Business Review* published an article under the prosaic-enough title, "The Appointment Book of J. Edward Ellis." The author, Gilbert H. Clee, himself a businessman, followed his hypothetical executive through an exhausting schedule of meetings and conferences of what was presumably a typical day. The point of the piece was that virtually every decision he had to make was somehow related to Washington.

It will come as no revelation to even the least sophisticated layman that government is continually watching over the business shoulder. There are few aspects of corporate activity to which the law does not at some point relate:

From *Challenge* (January–February, 1966).

the quality of a product, pricing policy, advertising practices, wages, hours and working conditions, relations with labor unions and trade associations, finance and accounting, mergers and acquisitions, and, more recently, such considerations as a firm's part in air and water pollution—all of these matters and many others make government a constant participant in business decision making.

Such government regulation may be expanding—in fact, it is expanding—but it scarcely can be looked on as novel. In recent years economic historians have made quite a point of the extent to which government at all levels was actually meddling in business affairs, even in the springtime of this nation—a period we tend to think of as characterized by classical laissez-faire politics. The familiar category of "regulated industry" can be separately identified primarily because such an industry requires government permission before it can engage in certain actions; but as a matter of fact, despite the distinction the term implies, there is no unregulated industry.

However, government restrictions on business freedom, designed to safeguard the public interest, are surely the least interesting "public" aspect of private enterprise. A far more intriguing phenomenon is the extent to which business managers, in the course of their day-to-day operations, are guided by their own conception of the public interest without prodding by law. At least this is the case in business firms which are large enough to require professional management.

Of course, public-mindedness does not necessarily imply public-spiritedness—it may be social consciousness more than social conscience. What it does involve is the making of judgments, as part of the normal process of making business decisions, as to where public interest may be thought to lie. The decision may not follow directly from the judgment—a conflict between public and private interest is not always resolved by businessmen in the former's favor! And one can admittedly exaggerate the role of public interest considerations in business decisions. But the phenomenon is a real one and has been noted by numerous expert observers.

Reactions to this relatively recent development have been mixed. It is always dangerous to attribute attitudes to classes of people, but the following points of view are probably broadly representative.

First, on the part of business itself, there appears to be, as just noted, a widening acceptance of the necessity of taking the public interest into account. A look at the syllabus of almost any executive training program will confirm that this is recognized as an almost inevitable new dimension in decision making, and discussions around executive tables will suggest that it is probably desirable; it is certainly the "sophisticated" thing to do now. In the current popular jargon, "public responsibility" is "in." But this on one proviso—that it remain a discretionary matter, and thus sharply distinguished from regulation. The businessman expects to be regulated under law. He does not want social responsibilities imposed on him by fiat.

The historic encounter between President Kennedy and Roger Blough of United States Steel in 1962 nicely illustrates what can probably be taken as prevailing business attitude. On that occasion, Blough announced an increase in steel prices only a few days after a collective agreement had been concluded with the steelworkers union. The union had settled on terms that were generally regarded as "modest," that is, in line with the Administration's anti-inflationary "guideposts." The premise for such a settlement—never made explicit, but "understood" by both the union and the Administration—was that the steel industry would hold the price line, and also conform to the government's "guideposts." (Indeed, Kennedy had sent telegrams to both parties complimenting them on their economic statesmanship.) When the price increase broke only hours later, the Administration took this as a gross breach of faith and mobilized the government's not-inconsiderable weapons to pummel United States Steel until it rescinded the increase.

To the extent that any business opinion can be said to have crystallized, it was probably a "pox on both your houses." Blough was criticized by some for having ignored "legitimate" public interest by having instituted a price increase at all, at a time when balance-of-payments problems were sharply to the fore and would be exacerbated by any loss of steel export markets due to higher prices. Others, more lenient, nevertheless chastised him for his timing, which suggested an almost intentional flaunting of public interest or, at the least, to use a phrase much quoted at the time, an "incredible shortsightedness." Public interest could not be so willfully ignored.

But the business community was at least as solidly agreed that President Kennedy's reaction had been in error. Blough had committed an act of bad judgment, but not an illegal act. His exercise of discretion was faulty, but discretion implies the privilege of error. For Kennedy to have hit United States Steel with threats of new and renewed antitrust actions, of fine-combing for tax liabilities, of loss of government contracts and accelerated depreciation, and other such penalties, was, in effect, to convert a matter of judgment into a matter of law, and a presumed voluntary regard for public interest into a regulated requirement.

In general, in terms of this example, even though business did not then and does not now agree in principle with the Administration's wage-price guideposts, the latter are tolerated as long as they remain guides to a discretion retained rather than an attempt to deny discretion. More recently, that attitude was again revealed, clearly if less dramatically, in the contentious stands of the Administration and the aluminum industry over the government's release of aluminum ingots from its stockpile. The Administration somewhat ambiguously justified the timing of its action by referring to the "out-of-guideline" increase in the price of aluminum, while the industry condemned such "precipitous" retaliation for a price movement which it regarded as both reasonable and discretionary.

So much for business' attitude toward the role of public interest in private affairs. Government and the public are perhaps more inclined to be skeptical but hopeful. They are not so sure that business weighs the public interest enough in its judgmental scales. (Some are sure it does not.)

But at least business is pointed in the right direction. It is learning. An occasional episode, such as the 1962 steel pricing, raises suspicions and doubts, but the fact that at such times the business community is capable of being self-critical is at least reassuring. Business response to President Johnson's plea for voluntary restraints on overseas investment, while not all that was hoped for, is further evidence that managements can put public welfare ahead of maximum profit. If the poor devils sometimes stumble over their lines, at least give them encouragement for learning a new role.

Professional economists have a more divided opinion. While some join in cheering the "new" business ethic, others believe that government should exert a stronger influence to identify and achieve the public interest, and a middle group is thoroughly suspicious of the whole thing. They dislike the notion that any actions which are of importance to society should be left to the discretion of management. Social policy should be determined by representative government. The businessman's business is to look out for his own interests, not to try to decide in his own fumbling and inexpert way what is good for the public. He should concentrate his attention on getting as good a profit as he can, within the traditional governmental regulations which, as we earlier noted, are specifically designed to safeguard and advance society's welfare. If the economic system is functioning properly, business profits will depend on its serving the public well within its own sphere of competence. No more should be asked—or allowed.

This point of view, which, despite the lack of unanimity noted above we might appropriately label the economist's attitude, arises in part from the difficulty in defining the public interest. The public interest is not such an objective entity that it dictates specific actions. Can we, then, leave it to each individual to define it for himself, with the danger of all sins of omission and commission which would inescapably follow? Is not the only logical procedure to leave with representative government the gradual spelling out, in law, of those public interests which businessmen—like others—must respect, on pain of penalty?

There are two principal difficulties with this proposition. To begin with, we might equally well argue that when it comes to large-scale business activity, what is "private interest" is not so clearly definable either. The big corporation is the focus of widely dispersed, fragmented and contending interests. It almost takes on the character of a public concern—something which is appropriately enough recognized when we describe companies whose stock is traded on the exchanges as public corporations. Such companies are, in fact, public, not only with respect to numbers of stockholders, but numbers of workers, suppliers, dealers and customers. This is recognized by the phrase General Electric uses to express its policy toward the many parties to whom it feels some sense of responsibility—the "balanced best interests" of all.

Thus if the economist is worried about the vagueness of the public interest concept, he might be—and in many cases is—equally worried about the "private interest" concept which he presumes to be a sufficient guide for management of our giant corporations. If vagueness is allowed in the one domain, why not in the other?

But a more telling answer to economists who argue that government or the economic system, and not businessmen, should be the sole judges of the public interest is that this might well require a degree of regulation which would jeopardize the whole notion of private initiative. The belief that the "system" can so constrain business behavior as to rob it of any abusable discretionary content is at best wishful thinking, deriving in part from preoccupation with paper models where that result can be obtained because the model is engineered with that in mind. But the real economic system is another matter. It has been put together, over time by many hands and heads, for diverse purposes; economic power has become dispersed in ways which make it impossible to "constrain" all private discretion, leaving those decisions affecting the public only to government.

Nor is it clear that we would want to limit business discretion to such a degree even if we could. Giving business managers a right of initiative probably requires that we allow them a freedom of action which at times, unfortunately, can be abused. But to attempt to root out the abuse by further regulation and restriction may quite conceivably kill the genius of our economic system. Is it not, then, preferable to meet the needs of the situation by encouraging and quickening a sense of public consciousness?

Of course this does not mean that the government cannot enlarge, as necessary, its own regulatory powers to secure such ends as can best—or only—be secured through regulation. But in Western liberal societies, regulation can never empty the system of all private pools of discretion. It is with respect to the discretion which—inevitably—remains in business' hands that the development of a business attitude of public-mindedness can be called a step forward.

The more we talk about public interest in this broad and admittedly amorphous sense and sharpen our sensitivities to what that might imply by discussions, occasional confrontations, proddings of conscience, yes, and even academic courses in business school curricula, the less likely may be the need for direct government regulation and intervention. Governmental initiatives to secure public goals may be served to a greater degree by "indicative" actions, to borrow the French term. While the results will never be as neat and tidy as in a directed economy, neither will they stifle the spontaneity and freewheeling behavior which give buoyancy to our system.

The fact of the matter is that the relationship between firm and society has always been vague, and must remain so in an open economy. Does the former exist for the benefit of the latter, or at its sufferance? Does it have rights independent of the latter? Does it owe responsibilities to the latter? Does it have power over the latter? We would probably have to answer "yes" to all these queries, but the way these several parts are orchestrated, where the stresses are placed and the nuances provided will vary among individuals and over time. There is no universal answer, no neat guiding formula.

Let us turn now to another strand in this complex relationship between private and public. Business firms these days have been drawn increasingly into a network of public contractual responsibilities. Private business works for public ends—for a profit, to be sure.

At first encounter this may seem an innocuous enough proposition, scarcely worth noting. Companies, after all, have been selling supplies to the government ever since governments were formed. Firms that sell pencils and automobiles to government—supplies out of stock—are engaged in nothing more than a prosaic business relationship without much more significance than if the sale had been made to another business firm.

But what is happening now is that government is increasingly calling on the expertise of private business to assist it in the planning and executing of complex projects for public ends. It is joint public and private enterprise, a collaborative activity, which for some time now has been building the Great Society.

We need not dwell on the well-publicized operations of the Department of Defense to illustrate this phenomenon. It would be pointless to try to catalog the growing number of cases where government has relied on business to assist it in exploring, pioneering, experimenting and effectuating projects which are directed to the collective public good, in contrast to private consumer welfare; but a few examples are always helpful. Even before the new transportation bill was signed by President Johnson, the Budd Company was advertising that it was capable of putting a 125-mile-an-hour train into operation between Washington and Boston, and that it stood ready to make use "of its railway know-how recognized everywhere in the world, to come to grips with the problem of mass transportation." The billion-dollar Bay Area Rapid Transit System now under construction is the product of a public-private cooperation so complex that it would baffle an economic or political sleuth to draw lines of demarcation between the two sectors. COMSAT (Communications Satellite Corporation) is an even more spectacular illustration.

In California the state government put up for competitive bidding contracts for research studies intended to facilitate solution of four major problems it was facing—a rising crime rate, waste and pollution, a data processing system for the state's informational needs, and a state-wide transportation system that would not be obsolete before it was completed. The successful bidders were the Aerojet-General Corporation, Space-General Corporation, Lockheed, and North American Aviation, all of which had pools of trained talent which they could put to work on such projects. *Business Week,* in reporting the matter, commented that all the companies involved stood to take a loss on the particular project, but they—and fifty other bidding companies—had been attracted by the chance to show that they could handle "broad, nontechnical" studies for the government.

General Electric recently took an entire issue of its *Forum* to deal with the complex problems of our rapidly expanding cities. Its introductory statement noted that the issue is "not so much an appraisal of urban *problems* as it is a look at urban *opportunities,* for business, the professions, education, science, the individual—all elements of society." One of the authors, David Rockefeller, President of The Chase Manhattan Bank, urged that "urban redevelopment requires an active partnership between private enterprise and government agencies at all levels."

Can this "flowering" of private and public collaboration be dismissed with the cynical observation that such public interest is in fact only good dollar-earning, profit-increasing business-as-usual, with a little added public relations glamor? I for one do not think so. It is perfectly true that such collaboration *is* good business—but is that all that can be said? Along with such corporate involvement in the nation's public business—for a profit—there inevitably goes an interest in the successful completion of the project itself. The company's reputation is at stake, for one thing. But over and above that, businessmen get drawn into the spirit of the project itself, and this increases their appreciation of the public interest in what they are doing.

I don't want to press this point too far. Like many of my fellow academicians I am distressed by the narrowness of the point of view which one repeatedly encounters in major business leaders. The antigovernment phobia still runs strong. But then who expects changes in attitude to take place overnight? I myself am convinced that time is tending to push private and public welfare objectives into a closer and more compatible relationship.

It takes no careful reading to discern that there have been two quite separate strands of thought running through the above comments. On the one hand, we have commented on business' increasing awareness of the impact of its action on the public—a recognition by business that (as one of my students at Yale expressed it, in commenting on the 1962 steel pricing episode), "Let's face it—there *is* a public interest." On the other hand, we have noted the way in which business firms get drawn into the public's business, in an operational sense.

These two strands, separate though they can be made analytically, actually serve to reinforce each other. Business recognition of a public interest predisposes it to put its special capabilities in the partial service of society, even when the profit return may not be great. And business involvement in a growing number of projects which are expressly labeled "for the collective good" helps to strengthen in business an appreciation that the public interest is real even if not always easily identified.

Of course, the millennium is not at hand, and there will continue to be sickening instances of business flouting an all-too-obvious public interest. After all, the number of businessmen is large enough to guarantee that there will be no uniformity of conduct, good or bad. But the general direction in which business attitude is flowing—glacier-like though it may sometimes seem in its movement—is certainly toward a closer amalgam of public and private interest.

Part II THE DEMOGRAPHIC DATA

In order to understand the problems of the cities, one must first look at their people: How many are there? What is their composition in terms of age and race? How do they locate themselves within the metropolitan areas? What has been their rate of growth? What is the projection of urban population? These questions are examined in the following excerpts from a research report prepared for the National Commission on Urban Problems.

10

The Challenge of America's Metropolitan Population Outlook—1960 to 1985

PATRICIA LEAVEY HODGE AND
PHILIP M. HAUSER
Population Research Center, University of Chicago

METROPOLITAN AREA PROSPECT FOR THE UNITED STATES—1960 TO 1985

Recent and Current Population

In 1960, the population of the United States numbered 179.3 million. Of this number 112.9 million persons resided in Standard Metropolitan Statistical Areas (SMSA) [1] and the remaining 66.4 million in nonmetropolitan territory. Thus, slightly less than two-thirds of the American people (63 per cent) had become concentrated in metropolitan areas. The rapidity with which this nation has become metropolitanized is indicated by the fact that metropolitan areas between 1900 and 1960 absorbed 78 per cent [2] of the total population growth of the United States. In the decade from 1950 to 1960, while the population of the country increased by 18 per cent, metropolitan residence increased by 26 per cent, whereas nonmetropolitan residence increased by only 7.1 per cent (see Table 10-1).

There was considerable variation among the major regions of the nation in the concentration of the population in SMSA's. In the Northeast, the oldest industrialized part of the nation, almost four-fifths (79 per cent) of the population resided in metropolitan areas. In the West, the most rapidly growing region, 72 per cent resided in SMSA's. In the North Central region, containing the heartland of America's agriculture, exactly three-fifths (60 per cent) of the people lived in SMSA's. Finally, in the South, the least industrialized part of the nation, less than half of the population was metropolitan (48 per cent).

Although the South was the least metropolitanized region, the proportion of the population in SMSA's there increased the most rapidly between 1950 and 1960—by 7 per cent. The West, which, among the regions, experienced

---

From Research Report No. 3, prepared for the consideration of The National Commission on Urban Problems, U.S. Government Printing Office, Washington, D.C.

TABLE 10–1 Metropolitan* and Nonmetropolitan Population by Region, 1950 and 1960

REGION AND METROPOLITAN STATUS	POPULATION		CHANGE 1950–1960		PER CENT OF REGION		CHANGE 1950–1960
	1950	1960	AMOUNT	PER CENT	1950	1960	
United States	151,326	179,323	27,997	18.5	100.0	100.0	
Metropolitan	89,317	112,884	23,567	26.4	59.0	63.0	+4.0
Nonmetropolitan	62,009	66,439	4,430	7.1	41.0	37.0	–4.0
Northeast	39,478	44,678	5,200	13.2	100.0	100.0	
Metropolitan	31,267	35,350	4,083	13.1	79.2	79.1	–0.1
Nonmetropolitan	8,211	9,328	1,117	13.6	20.8	20.9	+0.1
North Central	44,461	51,619	7,158	16.1	100.0	100.0	
Metropolitan	25,075	30,963	5,888	23.5	56.4	60.0	+3.6
Nonmetropolitan	19,386	20,656	1,270	6.6	43.6	40.0	–3.6
South	47,197	54,973	7,776	16.5	100.0	100.0	
Metropolitan	19,418	26,436	7,018	36.1	41.1	48.1	+7.0
Nonmetropolitan	27,779	28,537	758	2.7	58.9	51.9	–7.0
West	20,190	28,053	7,863	38.9	100.0	100.0	
Metropolitan	13,557	20,135	6,578	48.5	67.1	71.8	+4.7
Nonmetropolitan	6,633	7,918	1,285	19.4	32.9	28.2	–4.7

* 1960 boundaries of SMSA's used.
SOURCE: U.S. Bureau of the Census, *U.S. Census of Population, 1960*, vol.I, *Characteristics of the Population*, part 1, U.S. Summary, Table Q; and ibid, *Selected Area Reports, Type of Place*, Final Report PC(3)-1E, Table 1.

the most rapid growth rates—both in metropolitan and nonmetropolitan population—ranked second in increased proportion of metropolitan population—the proportion increasing by 4.7 per cent. The proportion of the metropolitan population in the North Central region increased by 3.6 per cent during the decade, while the proportion of metropolitan population in the Northeast actually diminished by 0.1 per cent.

There were also important variations among the regions in the extent to which the metropolitan population was concentrated in a relatively small number of very large SMSA's or dispersed in a relatively large number of moderate or small SMSA's. Thus, in the Northeast, for one extreme, 69 per cent of the metropolitan population was concentrated in seven metropolitan areas of one million or more. In the South, at the other extreme, only 27 per cent resided in the five SMSA's of one million or more. In the North Central

TABLE 10–2 Regional Distribution of Number and Average Size of Metropolitan* Areas, 1960

REGION	NUMBER OF AREAS	AVERAGE POPULATION SIZE OF SMSA'S
Total	212	532,472
Northeast	47	752,128
North Central	59	524,797
South	77	343,325
West	29	694,310

* 1960 boundaries used for SMSA's.
SOURCE: U.S. Bureau of the Census, *U.S. Census of Population, 1960, Selected Area Reports, Type of Place*, Final Report PC(3)–1E, Table 1; and Bureau of the Budget, *Standard Metropolitan Statistical Areas, 1961.*

region 60 per cent of the SMSA population lived in the eight SMSA's of one million or more, and in the West 58 per cent of the SMSA population lived in four SMSA's of one million or more. In the Northeast the average metropolitan areas contained 752,128 inhabitants, in the South only 343,325 persons. In the North Central the average SMSA contained 524,797 inhabitants and in the West 694,310 (see Table 10–2).

The federal government through the United States Bureau of the Budget redefined SMSA's as of January, 1967, increasing the number of SMSA's from 212 to 228 in 1967, and redefined the boundaries of many of them. To present as updated a picture as possible of the metropolitan prospect, the population projections to 1985 which are presented below (see pp. 61–68) are based on the 1967 definition of SMSA's.[3] To provide a comparable 1960 base for the projections, the 1960 data have been adjusted to match the redefined 1967 boundaries.

TABLE 10–3 Metropolitan and Nonmetropolitan Population by Region, 1950 and 1960, Using 1967 Defined Boundaries of SMSA's

REGION AND METROPOLITAN STATUS	POPULATION		CHANGE 1950–1960		PER CENT OF REGION		CHANGE 1950–1960
	1950	1960	AMOUNT	PER CENT	1950	1960	
United States	151,326	179,323	27,997	18.5	100.0	100.0	
Metropolitan	94,000	118,968	24,968	26.6	62.1	66.3	+4.2
Nonmetropolitan	57,326	60,355	3,029	5.3	37.9	33.7	−4.2
Northeast	39,478	44,678	5,200	13.2	100.0	100.0	
Metropolitan	32,698	37,196	4,498	13.8	82.8	83.3	+0.5
Nonmetropolitan	6,780	7,482	702	10.4	17.2	16.7	−0.5
North Central	44,461	51,619	7,158	16.1	100.0	100.0	
Metropolitan	26,479	32,795	6,316	23.9	59.6	63.5	+3.9
Nonmetropolitan	17,982	18,824	842	4.7	40.4	36.5	−3.9
South	47,197	54,973	7,776	16.5	100.0	100.0	
Metropolitan	20,662	27,954	7,292	35.3	43.8	50.9	+7.1
Nonmetropolitan	26,535	27,019	484	1.8	56.2	49.1	−7.1
West	20,190	28,053	7,863	38.9	100.0	100.0	
Metropolitan	14,161	21,023	6,862	48.5	70.1	74.9	+4.8
Nonmetropolitan	6,029	7,030	1,001	16.6	29.9	25.1	−4.8

Source: U.S. Bureau of the Census, *Current Population Reports*, Ser. P-23, No. 23, October 9, 1967; and Bureau of the Budget, *Standard Metropolitan Statistical Areas, 1967*.

Under the 1967 definitions, the metropolitan population in 1960 would have been 119.0 million as compared with the 112.9 million for the 1960 definition (see Table 10–3). The proportion of the total population resident in SMSA's under the 1967 definition increases to 66 per cent from 63 per cent. The concentration of population in metropolitan areas in the Northeast increases to 83 per cent from 79 per cent; in the West to 75 from 72 per cent; in the North Central states to 64 from 60 per cent; and in the South to 51 from 48 per cent. The adjusted data are shown in Table 10–3, which also contains similarly adjusted date for 1950.

In general, it may be observed that the adjustment is relatively small and has no significant import for the growth patterns shown in the projections. Because the characteristics of the metropolitan population by age and color are readily available only for 1960 defined SMSA's, the 1960 base will be used in analyzing projected trends.

Projections to 1985

It is projected that the total population of the United States in 1985, under the assumptions employed, will be 252.2 million—with a possible range of from 240.7 to 263.6 million. Of the 252.2 million persons anticipated in the United States by 1985, it is estimated that 178.1 million, or 71 per cent of the total population, will reside in metropolitan areas (see Table 10–4). Then, the metropolitan population of the nation by 1985 may well be as large as the total population was in 1960. This projection indicates that the metropolitan population will increase by some 65.3 million or by 58 per cent during the twenty-five years from 1960 to 1985.[4] In contrast nonmetropolitan United States will increase by only 7.6 million persons, or 12 per cent.

Although the Northeast will show the smallest metropolitan increase both in rate of population growth and the proportion of the metropolitan population, the population residing in metropolitan areas in this region, at 47.3 million, will exceed its total population of 44.7 million in 1960. By 1985 the Northeast will have lost its position as the most metropolitanized region in the nation, with 81 per cent metropolitan, to the West which will have become 82 per cent metropolitan. The West will have achieved this status as the most metropolitanized region by reason of almost doubling its metropolitan population between 1960 and 1985—an increase of 99 per cent.

The North Central states will retain their rank as the third most metropolitan region, with 68 per cent of the population concentrated in SMSA's in 1985. The metropolitan population of this region will increase by 44 per cent.

The South will continue to experience the greatest relative increase in the proportion of the metropolitan population. This proportion will increase to 58 per cent in 1985, from 48 per cent in 1960—a 10 percentage point increase. Metropolitan population in the South will increase by 75 per cent.

TABLE 10-4 Metropolitan* and Nonmetropolitan Population by Region, 1960 and Projected 1985 (Numbers in thousands)

REGION AND METROPOLITAN STATUS	POPULATION		CHANGE 1960–1985		PER CENT OF REGION		CHANGE 1960–1985
	1960	1985	AMOUNT	PER CENT	1960	1985	
United States	179,323	252,185	72,862	40.6	100.0	100.0	
Metropolitan	112,884	178,138	65,254	57.8	63.0	70.6	+7.6
Nonmetropolitan	66,439	74,047	7,608	11.5	37.0	29.4	−7.6
Northeast	44,678	58,517	13,839	31.0	100.0	100.0	
Metropolitan	35,350	47,328	11,978	33.9	79.1	80.9	+1.8
Nonmetropolitan	9,328	11,189	1,861	20.0	20.9	19.1	−1.8
North Central	51,619	65,723	14,104	27.3	100.0	100.0	
Metropolitan	30,963	44,642	13,679	44.2	60.0	67.9	+7.9
Nonmetropolitan	20,656	21,081	425	2.1	40.0	32.1	−7.9
South	54,973	78,910	23,937	43.5	100.0	100.0	
Metropolitan	26,436	46,156	19,720	74.6	48.1	58.5	+10.4
Nonmetropolitan	28,537	32,754	4,217	14.8	51.9	41.5	−10.4
West	28,053	49,035	20,982	74.8	100.0	100.0	
Metropolitan	20,135	40,012	19,877	98.7	71.8	81.6	+9.8
Nonmetropolitan	7,918	9,023	1,105	14.0	28.2	18.4	−9.8

* 1960 boundaries of SMSA's used for 1960; 1967 boundaries of SMSA's used for 1985.
SOURCE: U.S. Bureau of the Census, *U.S. Census of Population, 1960, Selected Area Reports, Type of Place,* Final Report PC(3)-1E, Table 1; and Appendix A, Table A-1.

TABLE 10–5 *Average Annual Change, Per Cent Change and Equivalent Annual Growth Rates for Metropolitan* Area Population of Regions, 1950–1960, 1960–1965, 1960–1985, and 1965–1985*

REGION	CHANGE 1950–1960				CHANGE 1960–1965				CHANGE 1960–1985				CHANGE 1965–1985			
	AMOUNT	AVERAGE ANNUAL	%	RATE †	AMOUNT	AVERAGE ANNUAL	%	RATE †	AMOUNT	AVERAGE ANNUAL	%	RATE †	AMOUNT	AVERAGE ANNUAL	%	RATE †
Total	24,968	2,497	26.6	2.4	11,025	2,205	9.3	1.8	59,170	2,367	49.7	1.6	48,145	2,407	37.0	1.6
Northeast	4,498	450	13.8	1.3	2,165	433	5.8	1.1	10,132	405	27.2	1.0	7,967	398	20.2	0.9
North Central	6,316	632	23.9	2.2	2,151	430	6.6	1.3	11,847	474	36.1	1.2	9,696	485	27.7	1.2
South	7,292	729	35.3	3.1	3,361	672	12.0	2.4	18,202	728	65.1	2.0	14,841	742	47.4	2.0
West	6,862	686	48.5	4.0	3,347	669	15.9	3.0	18,989	760	90.3	2.6	15,642	782	64.2	2.5

* 1967 defined SMSA's used for each period.
† Compound interest formula: $P_z = P_o(1+r)^z$ where P_z = population at the second point of time, P_o = population at the first point of time, r = equivalent annual rate of growth, z = number of years between the two points.
SOURCE: U.S. Bureau of the Census, *Current Population Reports*, Ser. P-23, No. 23, October 9, 1967, and Ser. P-25, No. 371, August 14, 1967; Bureau of the Budget, *Standard Metropolitan Statistical Areas, 1967*; and Appendix A, Table A-1.

It is clear that each region of the nation must be prepared for great metropolitan population increases by 1985. Of the total metropolitan increase of 65.3 million in the United States, the West will absorb 19.9 million additional metropolitan inhabitants, the South 19.7 million, the North Central States 13.7 million, and the Northeast 12.0 million.

The annual growth rate of SMSA population between 1960 and 1965 was considerably below that between 1950 and 1960, 1.8 as compared with 2.4 per cent (geometric). This reduction in rate of growth was evident in each region and is, of course, reflected in the projections to 1985 (see Table 10–5).

Between 1960 and 1985 the metropolitan population of the nation as a whole will increase at a rate of 1.6 per cent (geometric) per annum. The annual growth rate of the population resident in SMSA's in the West will be 2.6 per cent; in the South, 2.0 per cent; in the North Central states, 1.2 per cent; and in the Northeast, 1.0 per cent. The annual growth rate anticipated in the West is one that will double the population about every twenty-seven years, whereas that of the Northeast will require about seventy years for a doubling.

TABLE 10–6 *Regional Percentage Distribution of Population by Metropolitan* Status, 1960 and Projected 1985*

METROPOLITAN STATUS AND YEAR	UNITED STATES	NORTHEAST	NORTH CENTRAL	SOUTH	WEST
1960					
Total population	100.0	24.9	28.8	30.7	15.6
Metropolitan	100.0	31.4	27.4	23.4	17.8
Nonmetropolitan	100.0	14.0	31.1	43.0	11.9
1985					
Total population	100.0	23.2	26.1	31.3	19.4
Metropolitan	100.0	26.5	25.1	25.9	22.5
Nonmetropolitan	100.0	15.1	28.5	44.2	12.2

* 1960 boundaries of SMSA's used for 1960; 1967 boundaries of SMSA's used for 1985.
SOURCE: U.S. Bureau of the Census, *U.S. Census of Population, 1960, Selected Area Reports, Type of Place,* Final Report PC(3)-1E, Table 1; and Appendix A, Table A-1.

The effect of the anticipated changes described on the regional distribution of the metropolitan population is given in Table 10–6. The West will have increased her proportion of the total metropolitan population of the United States from 18 to 22 per cent, and the South from 23 to 26 per cent. In contrast, the North Central states will show a decline from 27 to 25 per cent of the total metropolitan population of the United States, and the Northeast will show a relatively great decline from 31 to 26 per cent.

SATURATED CENTRAL CITIES: EXPANDING SUBURBAN RINGS

Central City and Ring—1960

In accordance with standard statistical usage central cities and SMSA ring (SMSA minus the central city) [5] data are presented to enable an analysis of central city and suburban population distributions.

In 1950, 52 million persons lived in the central cities of 1960 defined SMSA's, constituting 59 per cent of the SMSA population. Central city population grew by 5.6 million during the decade from 1950 to 1960, but the 58 million central city residents of 1960 central cities constituted only 51 per cent of the total metropolitan population (see Table 10-7). That the movement toward decentralization was even more pronounced is seen if adjustment is made for central city annexations during the decade; for if 1950 central city boundaries had remained constant from 1950 to 1960, only 47 per cent of the SMSA population of 1960 would be resident in central cities.

There was considerable regional variation both in 1950 and 1960 in the extent to which metropolitan area population was concentrated in central cities. In the Northeast 57 per cent of the 1950 metropolitan area population was contained within the central cities, while by 1960 less than half of the SMSA residents—49 per cent—lived within the central city. In one other region, the West, less than half of the SMSA population—45 per cent—resided in the central cities; whereas in 1950, 51 per cent of the population lived within these areas. The effect that large scale central city annexation in the West had on these figures is reflected in the percentages adjusted for annexation; for if the 1950 central city boundaries had remained constant, only 39 per cent of the SMSA population in the West in 1960 would have resided in central cities. In the North Central states 53 per cent of the SMSA population lived within central cities by 1960, compared with 63 per cent in 1950; and in the South 57 per cent of the 1960 population resided within the central cities compared with 60 per cent in 1950.

Projections to 1985

The projections reported herein assume that 1960 central city boundaries will remain unchanged between 1960 and 1985. It is further assumed that the proportional growth from 1950 to 1960 within the 1950 central city boundaries will occur within the 1960 central city boundaries between 1960 and 1985. Specifically the proportion of SMSA population in central city boundaries in 1950 was computed, as was the proportion of SMSA population in 1960, within the *1950* boundaries. The change in this proportion was pro-

TABLE 10-7 Population Growth in and outside Standard Metropolitan Statistical Areas* for the United States by Region, 1950–1960†

REGION AND METROPOLITAN OR NONMETROPOLITAN RESIDENCE	1960	1950	INCREASE 1950 TO 1960		PER CENT BY RESIDENCE WITHIN SMSA's		
			NUMBER	PER CENT	1960 UNADJUSTED	1960‡ ADJUSTED	1950
United States	179,323	151,326	27,997	18.5			
In SMSA's	112,885	89,317	23,568	26.4	100.0	100.0	100.0
Central cities	58,004	52,371	5,633	10.8	51.4	47.1	58.6
Outside central cities	54,880	36,946	17,935	48.5	48.6	52.9	41.4
Outside SMSA's	66,438	62,009	4,429	7.1			
Northeast	44,678	39,478	5,200	13.2			
In SMSA's	35,347	31,267	4,079	13.0	100.0	100.0	100.0
Central cities	17,322	17,881	−560	−3.1	49.0	48.9	57.2
Outside central cities	18,025	13,386	4,639	34.7	51.0	51.1	42.8
Outside SMSA's	9,331	8,211	1,120	13.6			
North Central	51,619	44,461	7,158	16.1			
In SMSA's	30,960	25,075	5,885	23.5	100.0	100.0	100.0
Central cities	16,511	15,837	674	4.3	53.3	50.3	63.2
Outside central cities	14,449	9,238	5,211	56.4	46.7	49.7	36.8
Outside SMSA's	20,659	19,386	1,273	6.6			
South	54,973	47,197	7,776	16.5			
In SMSA's	26,447	19,418	7,030	36.2	100.0	100.0	100.0
Central cities	15,062	11,721	3,341	28.5	57.0	46.6	60.4
Outside central cities	11,386	7,697	3,689	47.9	43.0	53.4	39.6
Outside SMSA's	28,526	27,779	746	2.7			
West	28,053	20,190	7,863	38.9			
In SMSA's	20,131	13,557	6,574	48.5	100.0	100.0	100.0
Central cities	9,110	6,932	2,178	31.4	45.3	39.4	51.1
Outside central cities	11,021	6,625	4,396	66.4	54.7	60.6	48.9
Outside SMSA's	7,922	6,633	1,289	19.4			

* 1960 boundaries of SMSA's used for both 1950 and 1960 figures.
† Number in thousands; not adjusted to add to independently rounded subtotals; minus sign (−) denotes decrease.
‡ Adjusted for annexations to central cities 1950–1960; uses 1960 population residing within 1950 limits of central cities.
SOURCE: U.S. Bureau of the Census, *U.S. Census of Population: 1960*, vol. I, *Characteristics of the Population*, pt. 1, Tables Q. 9 and 10.

jected to 1985 by five-year intervals, assuming that the change would gradually approach zero by 1985. The assumption that 1960 central city boundaries will remain unchanged is probably unrealistic, at least, for some areas of the country—particularly where there are young and rapidly growing central cities. It is exceedingly difficult, however, to predict future levels of annexation. By staying with fixed boundaries, it was felt that the results would at least be interpretable. The assumptions governing the distribution of population by color were somewhat more complex.

Between 1960 and 1985, the projections indicate that while SMSA populations in the nation as a whole will increase by about 58 per cent, the population in central cities will increase by only 13 per cent whereas that in suburbia, the ring, will more than double. The population in nonmetropolitan areas will grow at almost the same level as that in central cities, some 12 per cent (see Table 10-8).

In the West while SMSA population will almost double between 1960 and 1985, that in central cities will increase by about one-third, whereas that in suburbia will considerably more than double, increasing by 153 per cent. In the South, while SMSA population will increase by three-fourths, central city population will grow by 22 per cent whereas suburbia will considerably more than double, increasing by 144 per cent.

In the North Central and Northeastern states where SMSA growth rates will be lower than in the West and South, the pattern of more rapid suburban growth will also be evident. Moreover, central city population in these regions will remain almost constant, indicating that by reason of earlier rapid growth and boundaries which have remained relatively fixed for some time, central cities in these regions can absorb very little more population without drastic changes in land-use patterns. In the North Central states SMSA population will increase by 44 per cent while central city population will remain constant and ring population will almost double. Similarly in the Northeast, SMSA population will increase about one-third, while central city population will increase by only 5.7 per cent and suburban population by 61 per cent.

By 1985, then, under the assumptions used in these projections, 37 per cent of metropolitan residents in the nation will live in central cities and 63 per cent will reside in the ring. These figures would constitute a 15 percentage point decrease from 1960 for the central city and a corresponding increase in the ring (see Table 10-8).

By 1985, in each region less than half of the metropolitan area population will reside in the central cities. In the Northeast, the proportion residing in the central city will be down 10 points from 49 to 39 per cent. The proportional decline will be sharper in the North Central region—16 percentage points, with 37 per cent living in central cities by 1985 compared with 54 per cent in 1960. In the South 40 per cent of metropolitan residents will live in the central cities by 1985 as compared with 57 per cent in 1960, a decline in central city concentration of 17 percentage points. The West will show the smallest proportion of inhabitants residing in the central cities of any region,

TABLE 10–8 Projected Growth in and outside Metropolitan Areas* for the United States by Region, 1960–1985 †

REGION AND METROPOLITAN OR NONMETROPOLITAN RESIDENCE	1985	1960	INCREASE 1960 TO 1985 NUMBER	INCREASE 1960 TO 1985 PER CENT	PER CENT BY RESIDENCE WITHIN SMSA'S 1985	PER CENT BY RESIDENCE WITHIN SMSA'S 1960	CHANGE
United States	252,185	179,323	72,862	40.6			
In SMSA's	178,138	112,884	65,254	57.8	100.0	100.0	
Central cities	65,581	58,208	7,373	12.7	36.8	51.6	−14.8
Outside central cities	112,557	54,676	57,881	105.9	63.2	48.4	+14.6
Outside SMSA's	74,047	66,439	7,608	11.5			
Northeast	58,517	44,678	13,839	31.0			
In SMSA's	47,328	35,350	11,978	33.9	100.0	100.0	
Central cities	18,318	17,324	994	5.7	38.7	49.0	−10.3
Outside central cities	29,010	18,026	10,984	60.9	61.3	51.0	+10.3
Outside SMSA's	11,189	9,328	1,861	20.0			
North Central	65,723	51,619	14,104	27.3			
In SMSA's	44,642	30,963	13,679	44.2	100.0	100.0	
Central cities	16,643	16,642	1	0.0	37.3	53.7	−16.4
Outside central cities	27,999	14,321	13,678	95.5	62.7	46.3	+16.4
Outside SMSA's	21,081	20,656	425	2.1			
South	78,910	54,973	23,937	43.5			
In SMSA's	46,156	26,436	19,720	74.6	100.0	100.0	
Central cities	18,374	15,063	3,311	22.0	39.8	57.0	−17.2
Outside central cities	27,783	11,373	16,410	144.3	60.2	43.0	+17.2
Outside SMSA's	32,754	28,537	4,217	14.8			
West	49,035	28,053	20,982	74.8			
In SMSA's	40,012	20,135	19,877	98.7	100.0	100.0	
Central cities	12,247	9,180	3,067	33.4	30.6	45.6	−15.0
Outside central cities	27,765	10,955	16,810	153.4	69.4	54.4	+15.0
Outside SMSA's	9,023	7,918	1,105	14.0			

* 1960 boundaries of SMSA's used for 1960; 1967 boundaries used for 1985.
† Numbers in thousands; not adjusted to add to independently rounded subtotals; minus sign (−) denotes decrease.
SOURCE: U.S. Bureau of the Census, U.S. Census of Population, 1960, Selected Area Reports, Type of Place, Final Report PC(3)-1E, Table 1; and Appendix A, Table A-2.

with only 31 per cent as compared with 46 per cent in 1960—a decline of 15 percentage points.

CHANGING COLOR COMPOSITION
• • •
Projections for the Nation and Metropolis by Region

Between 1960 and 1985, it has been indicated that total population of the nation will increase by 41 per cent. The nonwhite population, however, by reason of relatively high fertility while mortality is diminishing, will increase by 68 per cent, whereas white population increase will be only 37 per cent. In absolute numbers, nonwhites in the United States will increase by 14.0 million, while whites will increase by 58.9 million. The more rapid rate of growth of the nonwhite population will raise their proportion of the total population to 14 per cent in 1985, from a level of 11 per cent in 1960 (see Table 10–9).

The projections indicate considerable variation in the growth rates of whites and nonwhites by region. In the West, the nonwhite population will more than double, increasing by 118 per cent, while the white population increases by 71 per cent. By 1985 then, the nonwhite population will constitute 9.9 per cent of this region, as compared with 7.9 per cent in 1960. In the Northeast the nonwhite population will almost double, increasing by 98 per cent, whereas the white population will increase by only 26 per cent. Nonwhites will thus constitute 11 per cent of this region in 1985, as compared with 7.1 per cent in 1960. Next in rate of nonwhite population growth will be the North Central states with an increase of 80 per cent; the white population of this region will increase by only 23 per cent. The slowest growth rate of nonwhite population, reflecting continued although dampened out-migration, will be in the South. In this region nonwhites will increase by 47 per cent, as compared with a 43 per cent increase for whites. The South will still have the largest proportion of nonwhite population, 21 per cent in 1985 as in 1960.

Despite the fact the South will experience the lowest nonwhite growth rate, it will have the greatest absolute increase in nonwhite population between 1960 and 1985—some 5.4 million—or 39 per cent of the total nonwhite increase in the United States. Next will be the Northeast states, which will absorb 3.1 million nonwhites, the North Central states 2.9 million, and the West with 2.6 million. By reason of these changes, nonwhite population in the South by 1985 will have shrunk to 49 per cent of the total nonwhite population, from a level of 56 per cent in 1960.

Because of continued although slackened migratory flows to metropolitan America as well as relatively high natural increase, the growth of nonwhite population in metropolitan areas will considerably exceed their rate of total

TABLE 10–9 *White-Nonwhite Population by Region, 1960 and Projected 1985*

REGION AND COLOR	POPULATION		CHANGE 1960–1985		PER CENT OF REGION		CHANGE
	1960	1985	AMOUNT	PER CENT	1960	1985	1960–1985
United States	179,323	252,185	72,862	40.6	100.0	100.0	
White	158,832	217,714	58,882	37.1	88.6	86.3	−2.3
Nonwhite	20,491	34,471	13,980	68.2	11.4	13.7	+2.3
Northeast	44,678	58,517	13,839	31.0	100.0	100.0	
White	41,522	52,269	10,747	25.9	92.9	89.3	−3.6
Nonwhite	3,155	6,248	3,093	98.0	7.1	10.7	+3.6
North Central	51,619	65,723	14,104	27.3	100.0	100.0	
White	48,003	59,228	11,225	23.4	93.0	90.1	−2.9
Nonwhite	3,617	6,495	2,878	79.6	7.0	9.9	+2.9
South	54,973	78,910	23,937	43.5	100.0	100.0	
White	43,477	62,016	18,539	42.6	79.1	78.6	−0.5
Nonwhite	11,496	16,894	5,398	47.0	20.9	21.4	+0.5
West	28,053	49,035	20,982	74.8	100.0	100.0	
White	25,830	44,201	18,371	71.1	92.1	90.1	−2.0
Nonwhite	2,223	4,834	2,611	117.5	7.9	9.9	+2.0

SOURCE: U.S. Bureau of the Census, *U.S. Census of Population, 1960, Selected Area Reports, Type of Place,* Final Report PC(3)-1E, Table 1; and Appendix A, Table A-1.

national growth. In the nation as a whole, while nonwhite population will increase by a little over two-thirds, the metropolitan nonwhite population will more than double, increasing by 105 per cent (see Tables 10–10 and 10–11). In contrast, the nonwhite population in the nonmetropolitan areas of the nation will increase by only 2.7 per cent. The white population will in general follow the same pattern of growth but at a lower level. Whites in metropolitan areas will increase by 52 per cent, compared with a growth rate of 37 per cent for the nation as a whole and a growth rate of only 13 per cent in nonmetropolitan areas.

Among the regions, the largest growth rate of nonwhites in metropolitan areas will be in the West, where they will increase by 150 per cent, while the white population will almost double, increasing by 94 per cent. In metropolitan areas of the West, nonwhites will rise to 11 per cent of the population by 1985—from 8.6 per cent in 1960. In the South, reflecting the continued metropolitanization of the region and decreasing out-migration, the nonwhite population in SMSA's will also more than double, increasing by 106 per cent. During the same period the white population will increase by two-thirds —67 per cent. In this region the proportion of nonwhites in SMSA's will rise to 23 per cent in 1985, from 20 per cent in 1960.

In the Northeast nonwhites in metropolitan areas will almost double, increasing by 99 per cent, whereas the whites will increase by only 28 per cent. In consequence, in this region nonwhites will increase to 12 per cent of the total population from a level of 8.4 per cent. In the North Central metropolitan areas nonwhite population will increase by 83 per cent, as compared with 40 per cent for whites. The nonwhites will make up 13 per cent of the population in 1985, as compared with 10 per cent in 1960.

Again, the greatest absolute increase in metropolitan nonwhite population will be in the South, with an increase of 5.5 million. It is to be observed this is a greater increase than the total increase of nonwhites in the South, because nonwhites in the *non*metropolitan South will actually diminish by 143,000. Needless to say, this projected decrease is subject to considerable error of estimate.

Next in order of numerical increase in metropolitan nonwhite population will be the Northeast with 2.9 million, the North Central states with 2.7 million, and the West with 2.6 million.

In accordance with the population projections, despite the decreased proportion of total nonwhites in the South by 1985, the percentage of the total nonwhite metropolitan population in the nation which resides in the South will remain about the same in 1985 as in 1960—at a level of about 40 per cent. This will reflect both the increasing metropolitanization of the South and her increasing ability to absorb her own population increase, including nonwhites, in addition to actually becoming an area of in-migration of whites.

The white and nonwhite population changes between 1960 and 1985 in the nonmetropolitan areas of the United States by region are shown in Table 10–11. In general, it may be observed that nonwhites outside metropolitan

TABLE 10-10 White–Nonwhite Metropolitan* Population by Region, 1960 and Projected 1985 (Numbers in thousands)

REGION AND COLOR	POPULATION		CHANGE 1960–1985		PER CENT OF REGION		CHANGE 1960–1985
	1960	1985	AMOUNT	PER CENT	1960	1985	
United States	112,884	178,138	65,254	57.8	100.0	100.0	
White	99,672	151,164	51,492	51.7	88.3	84.9	−3.4
Nonwhite	13,192	26,974	13,782	104.5	11.7	15.1	+3.4
Northeast	35,350	47,328	11,978	33.9	100.0	100.0	
White	32,388	41,423	9,035	27.9	91.6	87.5	−4.1
Nonwhite	2,962	5,905	2,943	99.4	8.4	12.5	+4.1
North Central	30,963	44,642	13,679	44.2	100.0	100.0	
White	27,718	38,698	10,980	39.6	89.5	86.7	−2.8
Nonwhite	3,245	5,944	2,699	83.2	10.5	13.3	+2.8
South	26,436	46,156	19,720	74.6	100.0	100.0	
White	21,183	35,362	14,179	66.9	80.1	76.6	−3.5
Nonwhite	5,253	10,794	5,541	105.5	19.9	23.4	+3.5
West	20,135	40,012	19,877	98.7	100.0	100.0	
White	18,403	35,682	17,279	93.9	91.4	89.2	−2.2
Nonwhite	1,732	4,330	2,598	150.0	8.6	10.8	+2.2

* 1960 boundaries of SMSA's used for 1960; 1967 boundaries of SMSA's used for 1985.
SOURCE: U.S. Bureau of the Census, U.S. Census of Population, 1960, Selected Area Reports, Type of Place, Final Report PC(3)-1E, Table 1; and Appendix A, Table A-1.

TABLE 10–11 *White–Nonwhite Nonmetropolitan* * *Population by Region, 1960 and Projected 1985 (Numbers in thousands)*

REGION AND COLOR	POPULATION		CHANGE 1960–1985		PER CENT OF REGION		CHANGE 1960–1985
	1960	1985	AMOUNT	PER CENT	1960	1985	
United States	66,439	74,046	7,607	11.4	100.0	100.0	
White	59,160	66,550	7,390	12.5	89.0	89.9	+0.9
Nonwhite	7,299	7,497	198	2.7	11.0	10.1	−0.9
Northeast	9,328	11,189	1,861	20.0	100.0	100.0	
White	9,134	10,846	1,712	18.7	97.9	96.9	−1.0
Nonwhite	193	343	150	77.7	2.1	3.1	+1.0
North Central	20,656	21,081	425	2.1	100.0	100.0	
White	20,285	20,530	245	1.2	98.2	97.3	−0.9
Nonwhite	372	550	178	47.8	1.8	2.7	+0.9
South	28,537	32,754	4,217	14.8	100.0	100.0	
White	22,294	26,654	4,360	19.6	78.1	81.4	+3.3
Nonwhite	6,243	6,100	−143	−2.3	21.9	18.6	−3.3
West	7,918	9,023	1,105	14.0	100.0	100.0	
White	7,427	8,518	1,091	14.7	93.8	94.4	+0.6
Nonwhite	491	504	13	2.6	6.2	5.6	−0.6

* 1960 boundaries of SMSA's used for 1960; 1967 boundaries of SMSA's used for 1985.
SOURCE: U.S. Bureau of the Census, *U.S. Census of Population, 1960, Selected Area Reports, Type of Place,* Final Report PC(3)-1E, Table 1; and Appendix A, Table A-1.

TABLE 10–12 Projected Growth 1960 to 1985 within Component Parts of Metropolitan* Areas by Color, by Region
(Numbers in thousands)

REGION, COLOR AND RESIDENCE	1985	1960	INCREASE 1960 TO 1985		PER CENT BY RESIDENCE WITHIN SMSA'S		
			NUMBER	PER CENT	1985	1960	CHANGE
United States							
White	151,164	99,692	51,472	51.6	100.0	100.0	
Central city	45,435	47,852	−2,417	−5.0	30.1	48.0	−17.9
Ring	105,730	51,840	53,890	104.0	69.9	52.0	+17.9
Nonwhite	26,974	13,192	13,782	104.5	100.0	100.0	
Central city	20,146	10,356	9,790	94.5	74.7	78.5	−3.8
Ring	6,827	2,836	3,991	140.7	25.3	21.5	+3.8
Northeast							
White	41,423	32,388	9,035	27.9	100.0	100.0	
Central city	13,485	14,925	−1,440	−9.6	32.6	46.1	−13.5
Ring	27,938	17,463	10,475	60.0	67.4	53.9	+13.5
Nonwhite	5,905	2,962	2,943	99.4	100.0	100.0	
Central city	4,833	2,398	2,435	101.5	81.8	81.0	+0.8
Ring	1,072	564	508	90.1	18.2	19.0	−0.8
North Central							
White	38,698	27,718	10,980	39.6	100.0	100.0	
Central city	11,326	13,793	−2,467	−17.9	29.3	49.8	−20.5
Ring	27,372	13,925	13,447	96.6	70.7	50.2	+20.5
Nonwhite	5,944	3,245	2,699	83.2	100.0	100.0	
Central city	5,318	2,849	2,469	86.7	89.5	87.8	+1.7
Ring	627	396	231	58.3	10.5	12.2	−1.7

TABLE 10–12 (continued)

REGION, COLOR AND RESIDENCE	1985	1960	INCREASE 1960 TO 1985		PER CENT BY RESIDENCE WITHIN SMSA'S		
			NUMBER	PER CENT	1985	1960	CHANGE
South							
White	35,362	21,183	14,179	66.9	100.0	100.0	
Central city	11,236	11,144	92	0.8	31.8	52.6	−20.8
Ring	24,126	10,039	14,087	140.3	68.2	47.4	+20.8
Nonwhite	10,794	5,253	5,541	105.5	100.0	100.0	
Central city	7,137	3,918	3,219	82.2	66.1	74.6	−8.5
Ring	3,658	1,335	2,323	174.0	33.9	25.4	+8.5
West							
White	35,682	18,403	17,279	93.9	100.0	100.0	
Central city	9,388	7,990	1,398	17.5	26.3	43.4	−17.1
Ring	26,294	10,413	15,881	152.5	73.7	56.6	+17.1
Nonwhite	4,330	1,732	2,598	150.0	100.0	100.0	
Central city	2,859	1,190	1,669	140.3	66.0	68.7	−2.7
Ring	1,470	542	928	171.2	34.0	31.3	+2.7

* 1960 boundaries of SMSA's used for 1960; 1967 boundaries used for 1985.

SOURCE: U.S. Bureau of the Census, *U.S. Census of Population, 1960, Selected Area Reports, Type of Place,* Final Report PC(3)-1E, Table 1; and Appendix A, Table A-2.

areas will diminish in proportion for the nation as a whole and in the West and in the South. In the latter region, as has been noted, there may be an actual decrease in the number of nonmetropolitan nonwhites. In the North Central and Northeast regions, however, the projections indicate some increase outside metropolitan areas in the proportion of the population that is nonwhite. This number would, however, remain relatively small.

The Central City and the Ring

In respect to changes in central city and suburban residence, there will be great differences between whites and nonwhites according to the projections. White metropolitan population will increase by 51.5 million, or 52 per cent, between 1960 and 1985; however, the white population residing within central cities will experience a decline of 2.4 million, or −5.0 per cent (see Table 10–12). White population residing within suburbia will increase by 53.9 million, a gain of 104 per cent.

The nonwhite population will double in metropolitan areas, growing by 13.8 million or 104 per cent. Within central cities nonwhites will almost double, growing from 10.4 million in 1960 to 20.1 million by 1985—a gain of 94 per cent. The rate of nonwhite growth in suburbia will be even more pronounced—141 per cent—but the numbers of nonwhites in the ring will still be relatively small. The nonwhite ring population will increase by 4 million from 2.8 million in 1960 to 6.8 million in 1985. In consequence, the dramatic rate of suburban growth not withstanding, 75 per cent of nonwhites residing in SMSA's in 1985 will be living in the central cities, a decline of only 3.8 percentage points over the 1960 per cent—78. In contrast, only 30 per cent of white metropolitan residents will live in central cities by 1985, a decline of 18 points from the 1960 level of 48 per cent. Thus, more than two-thirds—70 per cent—of white persons living in SMSA's will reside in suburbs, compared to 25 per cent of nonwhite metropolitan residents.

In the Northeast white central city population will drop by 1.4 million between 1960 and 1985, while white suburban population will increase by 10.5 million during the same period. Thus, while whites in the city will decline by 9.6 per cent, white population in the ring will grow by 60 per cent. The 4.8 million nonwhite residents of central cities in the Northeast in 1985 will experience an increase of 2.4 million over the 1960 figure of 2.4 million—or a doubling. The 90 per cent increase of nonwhites in the ring would mean that a half million more nonwhites will be suburban residents in 1985 than in 1960, the 1985 figure being 1.1 million.

In the North Central states the decline of white population in central cities will be even more marked than in the Northeast. The 11.3 million whites living in these central cities in 1985 will represent a decline of 2.5 million or 18 per cent under the 13.8 million in 1960. In contrast, the population of whites in the ring will almost double—97 per cent—growing from 13.9 million to 27.4 million. As in the Northeast, nonwhite central city population will show a large increase, rising by 87 per cent or 2.5 million persons. Thus, by 1960, nonwhite population in central cities of the North Central states will be 5.3 million. In contrast, the suburban population of nonwhites will remain relatively small, rising from 396,000 in 1960 to 627,000 in 1985, a gain of 58 per cent.

The white population of central cities in the South will remain essentially the same in 1985 as in 1960. The 92,000 more white persons in these central cities will represent a gain of less than 1 per cent. In contrast, white suburban population will grow by 140 per cent—from 10.0 million persons in 1960 to 24.1 million in 1985. Nonwhites in central cities will increase by 3.2 million —from 3.9 million to 7.1 million by 1985—a gain of 82 per cent. Nonwhite suburban population will grow even faster at a rate of 174 per cent—from 1.3 million in 1960 to 3.7 million in 1985.

The West is the only region in which white population in central cities will increase significantly. In 1960 whites in these cities numbered 8 million and they will grow by 1.4 million to 9.4 million by 1985—a growth of 18 per cent. White population growth in the suburbs, however, will greatly outstrip central city growth, for white ring population will grow by 152 per cent, rising from 10.4 million in 1960 to 26.3 million in 1985. Nonwhite metropolitan population in the West will also show impressive gains. The 2.9 million nonwhites in these central cities by 1985 will represent a gain of 1.7 million or 140 per cent over their 1960 number. The per cent gain of nonwhites in the ring will also be large—171 per cent—representing an increase of 928,-000 over the 1960 level of 542,000.

The patterns of change just described will result in population redistribution of whites and nonwhites in respect to central city and ring residence. As was mentioned above, by 1985 only 30 per cent of white metropolitan residents will live in central cities, whereas 75 per cent of nonwhites will. In the Northeast one-third of white persons in SMSA's will live in central cities, a drop of 13.5 percentage points over 1960. The ring-central city residence patterns of nonwhites, however, will change very little, with 82 per cent living in central cities by 1985 compared with 81 per cent in 1960. In the North Central states less than three-tenths (29 per cent) of white metropolitan residents will be in the ring by 1985, a drop of 20.5 percentage points over the 1960 level of 50 percent. In contrast, nonwhite residential concentration in central cities will increase slightly (by 1.7 percentage points) and by 1985, 89 per cent of nonwhite persons living in SMSA's will reside in central cities. In 1960, 53 per cent of Southern metropolitan whites resided in central cities, but, by 1985, this will have dropped by 21 percentage points to 32 per cent, with 68 per cent residing in the ring. Nonwhite concentration in central cities will also decline but not as dramatically. In 1960, 75 per cent of nonwhites in Southern metropolitan areas resided in central cities; by 1985, 66 per cent will reside there. In the West 43 per cent of white SMSA inhabitants lived in central cities in 1960; by 1985, 26 per cent, the smallest per cent for any region, will be central city residents. Nonwhite SMSA residents in the West were least concentrated in central cities of any region in 1960—69 per cent of them lived in central cities in 1960; 66 per cent will live there in 1985.

TABLE 10–13 Percentage of Population of Region Residing in SMSA's* and Residing in Central Cities by Color, 1960 and Projected 1985

REGION	1960						1985					
	SMSA's			CENTRAL CITIES			SMSA's			CENTRAL CITIES		
	TOTAL	WHITE	NONWHITE	TOTAL	WHITE	NONWHITE	TOTAL	WHITE	NONWHITE	TOTAL	WHITE	NONWHITE
Total	63.0	62.8	64.4	32.5	30.1	50.5	70.6	69.4	78.3	26.0	20.9	58.4
Northeast	79.1	78.0	93.9	38.8	35.9	76.0	80.9	79.2	94.5	31.3	25.8	77.4
North Central	60.0	57.7	89.7	32.2	28.7	78.8	67.9	65.3	91.5	25.3	19.1	81.9
South	48.1	48.7	45.7	27.4	25.6	34.1	58.5	57.0	63.9	23.3	18.1	42.2
West	71.8	71.2	77.9	32.7	30.9	53.5	81.6	80.7	89.6	25.0	21.2	59.1

* 1960 boundaries of SMSA's used for 1960; 1967 boundaries used for 1985.
SOURCE: U.S. Bureau of the Census, *U.S. Census of Population, 1960, Selected Area Reports, Type of Place,* Final Report PC(3)-1E, Table 1; and Appendix A, Table A-2.

CHANGING AGE STRUCTURE: RISE IN YOUNG WORKERS AND ELDERLY

Age Projections for the Nation and Metropolis by Region

For planning social policy projected changes in the color composition and in the age structure of the metropolitan population and *its* components are of fundamental importance. Projections were made of the age structure of the metropolitan population in terms of the following broad age classifications: youth (under fifteen years of age); labor force (fifteen to sixty-four years of age) further composed of youthful labor force (fifteen to forty-four years of age) and older labor force (forty-five to sixty-four years of age); elderly (sixty-five years and over). These broad age classes are analytically important in terms of stages in the life cycle, dependency burdens, education, assimilation of youthful workers into the labor force, the size of the older labor force, and provision of services for the aged population.

While it might be desirable to have the youthful labor force group further divided so as to separate high school and college age populations, these groupings will provide a picture of the magnitude of new workers that will need to be absorbed into the working force. . . . Since focus here is on the relative changes, Table 10–14 shows the percentage change in each age class by region for metropolitan and nonmetropolitan population.

While the total population will increase by 41 per cent during the twenty-five-year period, the largest proportionate increase will occur in the young labor force ages (fifteen to forty-four), which will increase by 57 per cent (see Table 10–14). The next largest increase will take place in the aged population, which will increase by 51 per cent. Reflecting the assumption of lowered fertility, persons under fifteen will increase by 30 per cent; and reflecting the aging of the small cohort born during the depression of the 1930's, the older labor force ages will increase by 19 per cent.

All ages combined in the metropolitan population will increase by 58 per cent. Persons aged fifteen to forty-four and those aged sixty-five and over will increase by about the same degree—74 and 76 per cent. The population of youth will increase by 49 per cent and the older labor force ages (forty-five to sixty-four) will increase by 31 per cent. The total nonmetropolitan population, in contrast, will increase by only 11 per cent, and the increases will be uneven for the various age groups.

There will be practically no change in the population under fifteen years of age (0.6 per cent). The labor force ages will increase by 17 per cent, but this will be the net result of an increase of 27 per cent in the young labor force ages and a decrease of 3.1 per cent in the older labor force ages. Persons over sixty-five will increase by 16 per cent.

The Northeastern and North Central states will show the smallest percent-

TABLE 10–14 Projected Per Cent Change in Population 1960–1985 by Broad Age Groups, for Total United States and Regions by Metropolitan* Status

REGION AND METROPOLITAN STATUS	ALL AGES	UNDER 15	AGE 15–64 TOTAL	15–44	45–64	65 & OVER
United States	40.6	30.5	44.3	57.2	19.0	50.8
Metropolitan	57.8	49.1	59.7	74.0	31.4	75.5
Nonmetropolitan	11.4	0.6	16.6	26.7	−3.1	16.4
Northeast	31.0	25.7	31.5	44.9	7.8	42.5
Metropolitan	33.9	30.1	33.4	47.9	8.4	47.7
Nonmetropolitan	20.0	10.1	23.9	33.6	5.2	25.6
North Central	27.3	17.7	31.7	45.5	5.4	31.9
Metropolitan	44.2	33.9	47.1	61.5	18.5	62.2
Nonmetropolitan	2.0	−6.8	7.4	19.4	−14.4	−0.3
South	43.5	29.5	48.2	58.5	26.2	65.6
Metropolitan	74.6	60.1	77.2	87.9	53.2	116.8
Nonmetropolitan	14.8	2.1	19.8	28.9	1.6	28.6
West	74.8	62.9	80.6	93.8	52.3	78.3
Metropolitan	98.7	88.3	103.1	117.7	71.8	105.5
Nonmetropolitan	13.9	3.1	20.1	29.1	1.2	15.0

* 1960 boundaries of SMSA's used for 1960; 1967 boundaries used for 1985.
SOURCE: U.S. Bureau of the Census, *U.S. Census of Population, 1960, Selected Area Reports, Type of Place,* Final Report PC(3)-1E, Table 1; and Appendix A, Table A-3.

age increases. In the metropolitan areas of the Northeast the population will increase by 34 per cent, but there will be considerable variation by age. Young persons will increase by 30 per cent, and persons of labor force age will increase by 33 per cent. The young labor force ages will show large gains, increasing by 48 per cent; whereas the older labor force will expand by only 8.4 per cent. The number of older persons will increase by 48 per cent. Nonmetropolitan population in the Northeast will increase by 20 per cent, and the *pattern* of changes by age will be similar to those in the metropolitan population although the increases will be less. Persons under fifteen, however, will increase by only 10 per cent.

Metropolitan population in the North Central states will increase by 44 per cent. The youngest age group will increase by about one-third (34 per cent), while the labor force ages will increase by almost one-half (47 per cent). As in the Northeast, however, this increase will be composed of a large increase in persons aged fifteen to forty-four (62 per cent) and a moderate increase (18 per cent) in persons forty-five to sixty-four. The population over sixty-five will rise by almost two-thirds (62 per cent). In contrast, the nonmetropolitan population in the North Central states will change very little, growing by only 2 per cent over the twenty-five-year period. Decreases will take place in three of the four age groups—persons under fifteen decreasing by 7 per cent, persons forty-five to sixty-four decreasing by 14 per cent, and persons sixty-five and over decreasing by 0.3 per cent. Only the young working ages will show an increase, with persons fifteen to forty-four increasing by 19 per cent.

The total population in the South, between 1960 and 1985, will increase by 44 per cent, while metropolitan population in the South will increase by 75 per cent. The oldest age group will show the largest percentage increase —more than doubling in size (117 per cent). Young persons will increase by 60 per cent, the youthful labor force ages by 88 per cent, and older workers by 53 per cent. Nonmetropolitan population in the South will increase by 15 per cent, but the increase will be quite uneven by age. Young persons and persons forty-five to sixty-four will remain about the same, growing by 2.1 and 1.6 per cent, respectively. Persons of labor force age, however, will grow by 20 per cent, reflecting largely the 29 per cent increase in persons aged fifteen to forty-four. Persons sixty-five and older will also increase by 29 per cent.

TABLE 10–15 *Projected Per Cent Change in Population 1960–1985 by Broad Age Groups, by Color for Total United States and Regions*

REGION AND COLOR	AGE					
	ALL AGES	UNDER 15	15–64			65 & OVER
			TOTAL	15–44	45–64	
United States	40.6	30.5	44.3	57.2	19.0	50.8
White	37.1	25.9	40.7	52.7	17.5	49.8
Nonwhite	68.2	59.5	74.6	91.8	33.5	63.4
Northeast	31.0	25.7	31.5	44.9	7.8	42.5
White	25.9	18.8	26.8	39.8	4.3	39.5
Nonwhite	98.0	103.9	93.0	104.2	65.1	120.9
North Central	27.3	17.7	31.7	45.5	5.4	31.9
White	23.4	12.5	28.1	41.3	3.1	29.5
Nonwhite	79.6	75.3	81.5	97.9	41.8	89.0
South	43.5	29.5	48.2	58.5	26.2	65.6
White	42.6	27.9	46.0	54.0	29.3	71.7
Nonwhite	47.0	34.5	57.4	77.3	12.1	36.4
West	74.8	62.9	80.6	93.8	52.3	78.3
White	71.1	57.6	77.4	90.5	50.1	76.0
Nonwhite	117.5	115.4	117.7	129.5	84.6	131.1

SOURCE: U.S. Bureau of the Census, *U.S. Census of Population, 1960, Selected Area Reports, Type of Place,* Final Report (PC(3)-1E, Table 1; and Appendix A, Table A-3.

The West will show the largest total population increase, with the regional population increasing by 75 per cent and the population in metropolitan areas almost doubling (99 per cent). The population under fifteen will grow by 88 per cent, while the number of persons fifteen to forty-four and the elderly will more than double, growing by 118 and 106 per cent, respectively. As in the South, the metropolitan areas of the West will also show sizeable gains in persons in the older labor force ages. Nonmetropolitan population in the West, as in the South and Northeast, will show moderate increases in the fifteen to forty-four and elderly age groups and essentially no change in the youth and forty-five to sixty-four year old groups.

In the country as a whole and in each region, the percentage growth of nonwhite population will exceed that of the white population. This differential will hold for each age group, in each region, with only two exceptions, which will occur only in the South. Here the growth in white persons forty-five to sixty-four and the elderly will exceed that in comparable ages among nonwhites (see Table 10–15).

For the population under fifteen years of age, the white-nonwhite differences in growth will be marked. For the country as a whole, white youth will increase by 26 per cent while nonwhite youth will rise by 60 per cent. In the Northeast young whites will increase by 19 per cent whereas nonwhites will increase by 104 per cent. In the North Central states young whites will increase by 12 per cent and nonwhites by 75 per cent. In the South white youths will increase by 28 per cent and nonwhites by 34 per cent. Finally, in the West, young whites will rise by 58 per cent while nonwhites under fifteen will more than double, growing by 115 per cent.

NOTES

1. *Standard Metropolitan Statistical Areas.* The terms metropolitan area and Standard Metropolitan Statistical Area (SMSA) are used interchangeably in this report. It has long been recognized that for many types of analysis it is necessary to consider as a unit the entire population in and around a city, the activities of which form an integrated economic and social system. Prior to the 1950 Census, areas of this type had been defined in somewhat different ways for different purposes and by various agencies. Leading examples were the metropolitan districts of the Census of Population, the industrial areas of the Census of Manufactures, and the labor market areas of the Bureau of Employment Security. To permit all federal statistical agencies to utilize the same areas for the publication of general-purpose statistics, the Bureau of the Budget has established "standard metropolitan statistical areas" (SMSA's). (In the 1950 Census, these areas were referred to as "standard metropolitan areas.") Every city of 50,000 inhabitants or more according to the 1960 Census is included in an SMSA. (From Appendix D of the Report.)
2. This is using 1960-defined SMSA's at both 1900 and 1960.
3. Except for New England, in which State Economic Areas are used for the 1967 boundaries.
4. The projection of metropolitan population trends has taken into account the slowdown in rate of metropolitan population growth estimated by the Bureau of the Census between 1960 and 1965.
5. Since the SMSA definition is based on whole county units, the SMSA ring portion does contain some rural population as well as urban population not contiguous to the suburbs of the central city(s).

Part III BUSINESS AND RACIAL RELATIONS

The one central issue from which all discussion of urban problems in the United States must take its departure is the question of whether and how a viable accommodation can be effected between the racial groups composing our cities. For the most part this means whether and how whites and blacks (to use those polarizing and nondescriptive terms) can learn to live with each other in close compass; however, in some cities other racial groups (the Puerto Rican immigrants in New York and Mexican immigrants in Los Angeles, for example) have become important enough to broaden the racial problem. Business cannot stay aloof from the problems of race. It is involved as employer, seller, landlord, community resident, and taxpayer.

While this part focuses on problems of racial relations, most of the succeeding parts will also contain related materials.

A Background

Following the race riots of 1967, which seared a number of the major cities in the United States, President Johnson appointed a special National Advisory Commission on Civil Disorders, which quickly became known as the Riot Commission and the Kerner Commission, after its chairman, Governor Otto Kerner of Illinois. The report of that Commission was released in 1968. Some of its findings are given in this section.

11

Excerpts From

Report of the National Advisory Commission on Civil Disorders

By 1967, whites could point to the demise of slavery, the decline of illiteracy among Negroes, the legal protection provided by the constitutional amendments and civil rights legislation, and the growing size of the Negro middle class. Whites would call it Negro progress from slavery to freedom toward equality.

Negroes could point to the doctrine of white supremacy, its widespread acceptance, its persistence after emancipation, and its influence on the definition of the place of Negroes in American life. They could point to their long fight for full citizenship, when they had active opposition from most of the white population and little or no support from the government. They could see progress toward equality accompanied by bitter resistance. Perhaps most of all, they could feel the persistent, pervasive racism that kept them in inferior segregated schools, restricted them to ghettos, barred them from fair employment, provided double standards in courts of justice, inflicted bodily harm on their children, and blighted their lives with a sense of hopelessness and despair.

In all of this and in the context of professed ideals, Negroes would find more retrogression than progress, more rejection than acceptance.

Until the middle of the twentieth century, the course of Negro protest movements in the United States, except for slave revolts, was based in the cities of the North, where Negroes enjoyed sufficient freedom to mount a sustained protest. It was in the cities, North and South, that Negroes had their greatest independence and mobility. It was natural, therefore, for black protest movements to be urban-based—and, until the last dozen years or so, limited to the North. As Negroes migrated from the South, the mounting strength of their votes in Northern cities became a vital element in drawing the federal government into the defense of the civil rights of Southern Negroes. While rural Negroes today face great racial problems, the major unsolved questions that touch the core of Negro life stem from discrimination embedded in urban housing, employment, and education.

Over the years the character of Negro protest has changed. Originally it was a white liberal and Negro upper class movement aimed at securing the constitutional rights of Negroes through propaganda, lawsuits and legislation. In recent years the emphasis in tactics shifted first to direct action and then

Washington, D.C.: United States Government Printing Office, 1968.

—among the most militant—to the rhetoric of "Black Power." The role of white liberals declined as Negroes came to direct the struggle. At the same time the Negro protest movement became more of a mass movement, with increasing participation from the working classes. As these changes were occurring, and while substantial progress was being made to secure constitutional rights for the Negroes, the goals of the movement were broadened. Protest groups now demand special efforts to overcome the Negro's poverty and cultural deprivation—conditions that cannot be erased simply by ensuring constitutional rights.

The central thrust of Negro protest in the current period has aimed at the inclusion of Negroes in American society on a basis of full equality rather than at a fundamental transformation of American institutions. There have been elements calling for a revolutionary overthrow of the American social system or for a complete withdrawal of Negroes from American society. But these solutions have had little popular support. Negro protest, for the most part, has been firmly rooted in the basic values of American society, seeking not their destruction but their fulfillment.

THE FORMATION OF THE RACIAL GHETTOS

Throughout the twentieth century, and particularly in the last three decades, the Negro population of the United States has been steadily moving from rural areas to urban, from South to North and West.

In 1910, 2.7 million Negroes lived in American cities—28 per cent of the nation's Negro population of 9.8 million. Today, about 15 million Negro Americans live in metropolitan areas, or 69 per cent of the Negro population of 21.5 million. In 1910, 885,000 Negroes—9 per cent—lived outside the South. Now, almost 10 million, about 45 per cent, live in the North or West.

These shifts in population have resulted from three basic trends: (1) A rapid increase in the size of the Negro population; (2) A continuous flow of Negroes from Southern rural areas, partly to large cities in the South, but primarily to large cities in the North and West; (3) An increasing concentration of Negroes in large metropolitan areas within racially segregated neighborhoods.

Taken together, these trends have produced large and constantly growing concentrations of Negro population within big cities in all parts of the nation.

● ● ●

Statistically, the Negro population in America has become more urbanized, and more metropolitan, than the white population. According to Census Bureau estimates, almost 70 per cent of all Negroes in 1966 lived in metropolitan areas, compared to 64 per cent of all whites. In the South, more than half the Negro population now lives in cities. Rural Negroes outnumber urban Negroes in only four states: Arkansas, Mississippi, North Carolina, and South Carolina.

Basic data concerning Negro urbanization trends . . . indicate that:

Almost all Negro population growth is occurring within metropolitan areas, primarily within central cities. From 1950 to 1966, the United States Negro population rose 6.5 million. Over 98 per cent of that increase took place in metropolitan areas—86 per cent within central cities, 12 per cent in the urban fringe.

The vast majority of white population growth is occurring in suburban portions of metropolitan areas. From 1950 to 1966, 77.8 per cent of the white population increase of 35.6 million took place in the suburbs. Central cities received only 2.5 per cent of this total white increase. Since 1960, white central-city population has actually declined by 1.3 million.

As a result, central cities are steadily becoming more heavily Negro, while the urban fringes around them remain almost entirely white. The proportion of Negroes in all central cities rose steadily from 12 per cent in 1950, to 17 per cent in 1960, to 20 per cent in 1966. Meanwhile, metropolitan areas outside of central cities remained 95 per cent white from 1950 to 1960, and became 96 per cent white by 1966.

The Negro population is growing faster, both absolutely and relatively, in the larger metropolitan areas than in the smaller ones. From 1950 to 1966, the proportion of nonwhites in the central cities of metropolitan areas with one million or more persons doubled, reaching 26 per cent, as compared with 20 per cent in the central cities of metropolitan areas containing from 250,000 to one million persons, and 12 per cent in the central cities of metropolitan areas containing under 250,000 persons.

The twelve largest central cities (New York, Chicago, Los Angeles, Philadelphia, Detroit, Baltimore, Houston, Cleveland, Washington, D. C., St. Louis, Milwaukee, and San Francisco) now contain over two-thirds of the Negro population outside the South, and one-third of the total in the United States. All these cities have experienced rapid increases in Negro population since 1950. In six (Chicago, Detroit, Cleveland, St. Louis, Milwaukee, and San Francisco), the proportion of Negroes at least doubled. In two others (New York and Los Angeles), it probably doubled. In 1968, seven of these cities are over 30 per cent Negro, and one (Washington, D. C.) is two-thirds Negro.

UNEMPLOYMENT AND UNDEREMPLOYMENT

The Critical Significance of Employment

The capacity to obtain and hold a "good job" is the traditional test of participation in American society. Steady employment with adequate compensation provides both purchasing power and social status. It develops the capabilities, confidence, and self-esteem an individual needs to be a responsible citizen and provides a basis for a stable family life. As Daniel P. Moynihan has written:

The principal measure of progress toward equality will be that of employment. It is the primary source of individual or group identity. In America what you do is what you are: to do nothing is to be nothing; to do little is to be little. The equations are implacable and blunt, and ruthlessly public.

For the Negro American it is already, and will continue to be, the master problem. It is the measure of white bona fides. It is the measure of Negro competence, and also of the competence of American society. Most importantly, the linkage between problems of employment and the range of social pathology that afflicts the Negro community is unmistakable. Employment not only controls the present for the Negro American but, in a most profound way, it is creating the future as well.

For residents of disadvantaged Negro neighborhoods, obtaining goods jobs is vastly more difficult than for most workers in society. For decades, social, economic, and psychological disadvantages surrounding the urban Negro poor have impaired their work capacities and opportunities. The result is a "cycle of failure"—the employment disabilities of one generation breed those of the next.

Negro Unemployment

Unemployment rates among Negroes have declined from a post-Korean War high of 12.6 per cent in 1958 to 8.2 per cent in 1967. Among married Negro men, the unemployment rate for 1967 was down to 3.2 per cent.[1]

Notwithstanding this decline, unemployment rates for Negroes are still double those for whites in every category, including married men, as they have been throughout the postwar period. Moreover, since 1954, even during the current unprecedented period of sustained economic growth, unemployment among Negroes has been continuously above the 6.0 per cent "recession" level widely regarded as a sign of serious economic weakness when prevalent for the entire work force.

• • •

THE LOW-STATUS AND LOW-PAYING NATURE OF MANY NEGRO JOBS

Even more important perhaps than unemployment is the related problem of the undesirable nature of many jobs open to Negroes. As Table 11–1 shows, Negro workers are concentrated in the lowest-skilled and lowest-paying occupations. These jobs often involve substandard wages, great instability and uncertainty of tenure, extremely low status in the eyes of both employer and employee, little or no chance for meaningful advancement, and unpleasant or exhausting duties. Negro men in particular are more than three times as likely as whites to be in unskilled or service jobs which pay far less than most.

• • •

Even given similar employment, Negro workers with the same education as white workers are paid less. This disparity doubtless results to some extent from inferior training in segregated schools, and also from the fact that large

TABLE 11–1

TYPE OF OCCUPATION	PERCENTAGE OF MALE WORKERS IN EACH TYPE OF OCCUPATION —1966		MEDIAN EARNINGS OF ALL MALE CIVILIANS IN EACH OCCUPATION —1965
	WHITE	NONWHITE	
Professional, technical, managerial	27	9	$7,603
Clerical and sales	14	9	$5,532
Craftsmen and foremen	20	12	$6,270
Operatives	20	27	$5,046
Service workers	6	16	$3,436
Nonfarm laborers	6	20	$2,410
Farmers and farm workers	7	8	$1,699

numbers of Negroes are only now entering certain occupations for the first time. However, the differentials are so large and so universal at all educational levels that they clearly reflect the patterns of discrimination which characterize hiring and promotion practices in many segments of the economy. For example, in 1966 among persons who had completed high school, the median income of Negroes was only 73 per cent that of whites. Even among persons with an eighth-grade education, Negro median income was only 80 per cent of white median income.

• • •

Growth of the Young Negro Population

We estimate that the nation's white population will grow 16.6 million, or 9.6 per cent, from 1966 to 1975, and the Negro population 3.8 million, or 17.7 per cent, in the same period. The Negro age group from fifteen to twenty-four years of age, however, will grow much faster than either the Negro population as a whole, or the white population in the same age group.

From 1966 to 1975, the number of Negroes in this age group will rise 1.6 million, or 40.1 per cent. The white population aged fifteen to twenty-four will rise 6.6 million, or 23.5 per cent.

This rapid increase in the young Negro population has important implications for the country. This group has the highest unemployment rate in the nation, commits a relatively high proportion of all crimes, and plays the most significant role in civil disorders. By the same token, it is a great reservoir of underused human resources which are vital to the nation.

The Location of New Jobs

Most new employment opportunities do not occur in central cities, near all-Negro neighborhoods. They are being created in suburbs and outlying areas—and this trend is likely to continue indefinitely. New office buildings have risen in the downtowns of large cities, often near all-Negro areas. But the out-flow of manufacturing and retailing facilities normally offsets this addition significantly—and in many cases has caused a net loss of jobs in central cities while the new white collar jobs are often not available to ghetto residents.

Providing employment for the swelling Negro ghetto population will require society to link these potential workers more closely with job locations. This can be done in three ways: by developing incentives to industry to create new employment centers near Negro residential areas; by opening suburban residential areas to Negroes and encouraging them to move closer to industrial centers; or by creating better transportation between ghetto neighborhoods and new job locations. All three involve large public outlays.

The first method—creating new industries in or near the ghetto—is not likely to occur without government subsidies on a scale which convinces private firms that it will pay them to face the problems involved.

The second method—opening up suburban areas to Negro occupancy—obviously requires effective fair housing laws. It will also require an extensive program of federally-aided, low-cost housing in many suburban areas.

The third approach—improved transportation linking ghettos and suburbs—has received little attention from city planners and municipal officials. A few demonstration projects show promise, but carrying them out on a large scale will be very costly.

Although a high proportion of new jobs will be located in suburbs, there are still millions of jobs in central cities. Turnover in those jobs alone can open up a great many potential positions for Negro central city residents—if employers cease racial discrimination in their hiring and promotion practices.

Nevertheless, as the total number of Negro central city jobseekers continues to rise, the need to link them with emerging new employment in the suburbs will become increasingly urgent.

• • •

CHOICES FOR THE FUTURE

The complexity of American society offers many choices for the future of relations between central cities and suburbs and patterns of white and Negro settlement in metropolitan areas. For practical purposes, however, we see two fundamental questions: (1) Should future Negro population growth be concentrated in central cities, as in the past 20 years, thereby forcing Negro and white populations to become even more residentially segregated? (2) Should society provide greatly increased special assistance to Negroes and other relatively disadvantaged population groups?

For purposes of analysis, the Commission has defined three basic choices for the future embodying specific answers to these questions:

The Present Policies Choice

Under this course, the nation would maintain approximately the share of resources now being allocated to programs of assistance for the poor, unemployed and disadvantaged. These programs are likely to grow, given continuing economic growth and rising federal revenues, but they will not grow fast enough to stop, let alone reverse, the already deteriorating quality of life in central-city ghettos.

This choice carries the highest ultimate price, as we will point out.

The Enrichment Choice

Under this course, the nation would seek to offset the effects of continued Negro segregation and deprivation in large city ghettos. The Enrichment Choice would aim at creating dramatic improvements in the quality of life in disadvantaged central-city neighborhoods—both white and Negro. It would require marked increases in federal spending for education, housing, employment, job training, and social services.

The Enrichment Choice would seek to lift poor Negroes and whites above poverty status and thereby give them the capacity to enter the mainstream of American life. But it would not, at least for many years, appreciably affect either the increasing concentration of Negroes in the ghetto or racial segregation in residential areas outside the ghetto.

The Integration Choice

This choice would be aimed at reversing the movement of the country toward two societies, separate and unequal.

The Integration Choice—like the Enrichment Choice—would call for large-scale improvement in the quality of ghetto life. But it would also involve both creating strong incentives for Negro movement out of central-city ghettos and enlarging freedom of choice concerning housing, employment, and schools.

The result would fall considerably short of full integration. The experience of other ethnic groups indicates that some Negro households would be scattered in largely white residential areas. Others—probably a larger number—would voluntarily cluster together in largely Negro neighborhoods. The Integration Choice would thus produce both integration and segregation. But the segregation would be voluntary.

Articulating these three choices plainly oversimplifies the possibilities open to the country. We believe, however, that they encompass the basic issues—issues which the American public must face if it is serious in its concern not only about civil disorder, but the future of our democratic society.

THE PRESENT POLICIES CHOICE

Powerful forces of social and political inertia are moving the country steadily along the course of existing policies toward a divided country.

This course may well involve changes in many social and economic programs—but not enough to produce fundamental alterations in the key factors of Negro concentration, racial segregation, and the lack of sufficient enrichment to arrest the decay of deprived neighborhoods.

Some movement towards enrichment can be found in efforts to encourage industries to locate plants in central cities, in increased federal expenditures for education, in the important concepts embodied in the "War on Poverty," and in the Model Cities Program. But congressional appropriations for even present federal programs have been so small that they fall short of effective enrichment.

As for challenging concentration and segregation, a national commitment to this purpose has yet to develop.

Of the three future courses we have defined, the Present Policies Choice —the choice we are now making—is the course with the most ominous consequences for our society.

The Probability of Future Civil Disorders

We believe that the Present Policies Choice would lead to a larger number of violent incidents of the kind that have stimulated recent major disorders.

First, it does nothing to raise the hopes, absorb the energies, or constructively challenge the talents of the rapidly-growing number of young Negro men in central cities. The proportion of unemployed or underemployed among them will remain very high. These young men have contributed disproportionately to crime and violence in cities in the past, and there is danger, obviously, that they will continue to do so.

Second, under these conditions, a rising proportion of Negroes in disadvantaged city areas might come to look upon the deprivation and segregation they suffer as proper justification for violent protest or for extending support to now isolated extremists who advocate civil disruption by guerrilla tactics.

More incidents would not necessarily mean more or worse riots. For the near future, there is substantial likelihood that even an increased number of incidents could be controlled before becoming major disorders, if society undertakes to improve police and National Guard forces so that they can respond to potential disorders with more prompt and disciplined use of force.

In fact, the likelihood of incidents mushrooming into major disorders would be only slightly higher in the near future under the Present Policies Choice than under the other two possible choices. For no new policies or programs could possibly alter basic ghetto conditions immediately. And the announcement of new programs under the other choices would immediately generate new expectations. Expectations inevitably increase faster than performance: in the short run, they might even increase the level of frustration.

In the long run, however, the Present Policies Choice risks a seriously greater probability of major disorders, worse, possibly, than those already experienced.

If the Negro population as a whole developed even stronger feelings of being wrongly "penned in" and discriminated against, many of its members might come to support not only riots, but the rebellion now being preached by only a handful.

If large-scale violence resulted, white retaliation could follow. This spiral could quite conceivably lead to a kind of urban *apartheid* with semi-martial law in many major cities, enforced residence of Negroes in segregated areas, and a drastic reduction in personal freedom for all Americans, particularly Negroes.

The same distinction is applicable to the cost of the Present Policies Choice. In the short run, its costs—at least its direct cash outlays—would be far less than for the other choices.

Any social and economic programs likely to have significant lasting effect would require very substantial annual appropriations for many years. Their cost would far exceed the direct losses sustained in recent civil disorders. Property damage in all the disorders we investigated, including Detroit and Newark, totalled less than $100 million.

But it would be a tragic mistake to view the Present Policies Choice as cheap. Damage figures measure only a small part of the costs of civil disorder. They cannot measure the costs in terms of the lives lost, injuries suffered, minds and attitudes closed and frozen in prejudice, or the hidden costs of the profound disruption of entire cities.

Ultimately, moreover, the economic and social costs of the Present Policies Choice will far surpass the cost of the alternatives. The rising concentration of impoverished Negroes and other minorities within the urban ghettos will constantly expand public expenditures for welfare, law enforcement, unemployment and other existing programs without arresting the decay of older city neighborhoods and the breeding of frustration and discontent. But the most significant item on the balance of accounts will remain largely invisible and incalculable—the toll in human values taken by continued poverty, segregation and inequality of opportunity.

Polarization

Another and equally serious consequence is the fact that this course would lead to the permanent establishment of two societies: one predominantly white and located in the suburbs, in smaller cities, and in outlying areas, and one largely Negro located in central cities.

We are well on the way to just such a divided nation.

This division is veiled by the fact that Negroes do not now dominate many central cities. But they soon will, as we have shown, and the new Negro mayors will be facing even more difficult conditions than now exist.

As Negroes succeed whites in our largest cities, the proportion of low-income residents in those cities will probably increase. This is likely even if both white and Negro incomes continue to rise at recent rates, since Negroes have much lower incomes than whites. Moreover, many of the ills of large central cities spring from their age, their location, and their obsolete physical structures. The deterioration and economic decay stemming from these factors have been proceeding for decades and will continue to plague older cities regardless of who resides in them.

These facts underlie the fourfold dilemma of the American city:

1. Fewer tax dollars come in, as large numbers of middle-income taxpayers move out of central cities and property values and business decline.
2. More tax dollars are required, to provide essential public services and facilities, and to meet the needs of expanding lower-income groups.
3. Each tax dollar buys less, because of increasing costs.
4. Citizen dissatisfaction with municipal services grows as needs, expectations and standards of living increase throughout the community.

These are the conditions that would greet the Negro-dominated municipal governments that will gradually come to power in many of our major cities. The Negro electorates in those cities probably would demand basic changes in present policies. Like the present white electorates there, they would have to look for assistance to two basic sources: the private sector and the federal government.

With respect to the private sector, major private capital investment in those cities might have ceased almost altogether if white-dominated firms and industries decided the risks and costs were too great. The withdrawal of private capital is already far advanced in most all-Negro areas of our large cities.

Even if private investment continued, it alone would not suffice. Big cities containing high proportions of low-income Negroes and block after block of deteriorating older property need very substantial assistance from the federal government to meet the demands of their electorates for improved services and living conditions.

By that time, however, it is probable that Congress will be more heavily influenced by representatives of the suburban and outlying city electorate. These areas will comprise 40 per cent of our total population by 1985, compared with 31 per cent in 1960, Central cities will decline from 32 to 27 per cent.[2]

Yet even the suburbs will be feeling the squeeze of higher local government costs. Hence, Congress might resist providing the extensive assistance which central cities will desperately need.

Thus the Present Policies Choice, if pursued for any length of time, might force simultaneous political and economic polarization in many of our largest metropolitan areas. Such polarization would involve large central cities—mainly Negro, with many poor, and nearly bankrupt—on the one hand, and most suburbs—mainly white, generally affluent, but heavily taxed—on the other hand.

Some areas might avoid political confrontation by shifting to some form of metropolitan government designed to offer regional solutions for pressing urban problems such as property taxation, air and water pollution and refuse disposal, and commuter transport. Yet this would hardly eliminate the basic segregation and relative poverty of the urban Negro population. It might even increase the Negro's sense of frustration and alienation if it operated to prevent Negro political control of central cities.

The acquisition of power by Negro-dominated governments in central cities is surely a legitimate and desirable exercise of political power by a minority group. It is in an American political tradition exemplified by the achievements of the Irish in New York and Boston.

But such Negro political development would also involve virtually complete racial segregation and virtually complete spatial separation. By 1985, the separate Negro society in our central cities would contain almost 21 million citizens. That is almost 68 per cent larger than the present Negro population of central cities. It is also larger than the current population of every Negro nation in Africa except Nigeria.

If developing a racially integrated society is extraordinarily difficult today when 12.1 million Negroes live in central cities, then it is quite clearly going to be virtually impossible in 1985 when almost 21 million Negroes—still much poorer and less educated than most whites—will be living there.

Can Present Policies Avert Extreme Polarization?

There are at least two possible developments under the Present Policies Choice which might avert such polarization. The first is a faster increase of incomes among Negroes than has occurred in the recent past. This might prevent central cities from becoming even deeper "poverty traps" than they now are. It suggests the importance of effective job programs and higher levels of welfare payments for dependent families.

The second possible development is migration of a growing Negro middle class out of the central city. This would not prevent competition for federal funds between central cities and outlying areas, but it might diminish the racial undertones of that competition.

There is, however, no evidence that a continuation of present policies would be accompanied by any such movement. There is already a significant Negro middle class. It grew rapidly from 1960 to 1966. Yet in these years, 88.9 per cent of the total national growth of Negro population was concentrated in central cities—the highest in history. Indeed, from 1960 to 1966, there was actually a net total in-migration of Negroes from the urban fringes of metropolitan areas into central cities.³ The Commission believes it unlikely that this trend will suddenly reverse itself without significant changes in private attitudes and public policies.

THE ENRICHMENT CHOICE

The Present Policies Choice plainly would involve continuation of efforts like Model Cities, manpower programs, and the War on Poverty. These are in fact enrichment programs, designed to improve the quality of life in the ghetto.

Because of their limited scope and funds, however, they constitute only very modest steps toward enrichment—and would continue to do so even if these programs were somewhat enlarged or supplemented.

The premise of the Enrichment Choice is performance. To adopt this choice would require a substantially greater share of national resources—sufficient to make a dramatic, visible impact on life in the urban Negro ghetto.

The Effect of Enrichment on Civil Disorders

Effective enrichment policies probably would have three immediate effects on civil disorders.

First, announcement of specific large-scale programs and the demonstration of a strong intent to carry them out might persuade ghetto residents that genuine remedies for their problems were forthcoming, thereby allaying tensions.

Second, such announcements would strongly stimulate the aspirations and hopes of members of these communities—possibly well beyond the capabilities of society to deliver and to do so promptly. This might increase frustration and discontent, to some extent cancelling the first effect.

Third, if there could be immediate action on meaningful job training and the creation of productive jobs for large numbers of unemployed young people, they would become much less likely to engage in civil disorders.

Such action is difficult now, when there are about 585,000 young Negro men aged fourteen to twenty-four in the civilian labor force in central cities —of whom 81,000 or 13.8 per cent, are unemployed and probably two or three times as many are underemployed. It will not become easier in the future. By 1975, this age group will have grown to nearly 700,000.

Given the size of the present problem, plus the large growth of this age group, creation of sufficient meaningful jobs will require extensive programs, begun rapidly. Even if the nation is willing to embark on such programs, there is no certainty that they can be made effective soon enough.

Consequently, there is no certainty that the Enrichment Choice would do much more in the near future to diminish violent incidents in central cities than would the Present Policies Choice. However, if enrichment programs can succeed in meeting the needs of residents of disadvantaged areas for jobs, education, housing and city services, then over the years this choice is almost certain to reduce both the level and frequency of urban disorder.

The Negro Middle Class

One objective of the Enrichment Choice would be to help as many disadvantaged Americans as possible—of all races—to enter the mainstream of American prosperity, to progress toward what is often called middle-class status. If the Enrichment Choice were adopted, it could certainly attain this objective to a far greater degree than would the Present Policies Choice. This could significantly change the quality of life in many central city areas.

It can be argued that a rapidly enlarging Negro middle class would also promote Negro out-migration, and thus the Enrichment Choice would open up an escape hatch from the ghetto. This argument, however, has two weaknesses.

The first is experience. Central cities already have sizable and growing numbers of middle-class Negro families. Yet only a few have migrated from the central city. The past pattern of white ethnic groups gradually moving out of central-city areas to middle-class suburbs has not applied to Negroes. Effective open-housing laws will help make this possible. It is probable, however, that other more extensive changes in policies and attitudes will be required—and these would extend beyond the Enrichment Choice.

The second weakness in the argument is time. Even if enlargement of the Negro middle class succeeded in encouraging movement out of the central city, it could not do so fast enough to offset the rapid growth of the ghetto. To offset even *half* the growth estimated for the ghetto by 1975 would call for the out-migration from central cities of 217,000 persons a year. This is eight times the annual increase in suburban Negro population—including natural increase—which occurred from 1960 to 1966. Even the most effective enrichment program is not likely to accomplish this.

A corollary problem derives from the continuing migration of poor Negroes from the Southern to Northern and Western cities.

Adoption of the Enrichment Choice would require large-scale efforts to improve conditions in the South sufficiently to remove the pressure to migrate. Under present conditions, slightly over a third of the estimated increase in Negro central-city population by 1985 will result from in-migration—3.0 million out of total increase of 8.2 million.

Negro Self-Development

The Enrichment Choice is in line with some of the currents of Negro protest thought that fall under the label of "Black Power." We do not refer to versions of Black Power ideology which promote violence, generate racial hatred, or advocate total separation of the races. Rather, we mean the view which asserts that the American Negro population can assume its proper role in society and overcome its feelings of powerlessness and lack of self-respect only by exerting power over decisions which directly affect its own members. A fully integrated society is not thought possible until the Negro minority within the ghetto has developed political strength—a strong bargaining position in dealing with the rest of society.

In short, this argument would regard predominantly Negro central cities and predominantly white outlying areas not as harmful, but as an advantageous future.

Proponents of these views also focus on the need for the Negro to organize economically as well as politically, thus tapping new energies and resources for self-development. One of the hardest tasks in improving disadvantaged areas is to discover how deeply deprived residents can develop their own capabilities by participating more fully in decisions and activities which affect them. Such learning-by-doing efforts are a vital part of the process of bringing deprived people into the social mainstream.

Separate but Equal Societies?

The Enrichment Choice by no means seeks to perpetuate racial segregation. In the end, however, its premise is that disadvantaged Negroes can achieve equality of opportunity with whites while continuing in conditions of nearly complete separation.

This premise has been vigorously advocated by Black Power proponents. While most Negroes originally desired racial integration, many are losing hope of ever achieving it because of seemingly implacable white resistance. Yet they cannot bring themselves to accept the conclusion that most of the millions of Negroes who are forced to live racially segregated lives must therefore be condemned to inferior lives—to inferior educations, or inferior housing, or inferior status.

Rather, they reason, there must be some way to make the quality of life in the ghetto areas just as good—or better—than elsewhere. It is not surprising that some Black Power advocates are denouncing integration and claiming that, given the hypocrisy and racism that pervade white society, life in a black society is, in fact, morally superior. This argument is understandable, but there is a great deal of evidence that it is unrealistic.

The economy of the United States and particularly the sources of employment are preponderantly white. In this circumstance, a policy of separate but equal employment could only relegate Negroes permanently to inferior incomes and economic status.

The best evidence regarding education is contained in recent reports of the Office of Education and Civil Rights Commission which suggest that both racial and economic integration are essential to educational equality for Negroes. Yet critics point out that, certainly until integration is achieved, various types of enrichment programs must be tested, and that dramatically different results may be possible from intensive educational enrichment—such as far smaller classes, or greatly expanded pre-school programs, or changes in the home environment of Negro children resulting from steady jobs for fathers.

Still others advocate shifting control over ghetto schools from professional administrators to local residents. This, they say, would improve curricula, give students a greater sense of their own value, and thus raise their morale and educational achievement. These approaches have not yet been tested sufficiently. One conclusion, however, does seem reasonable: any real improvement in the quality of education in low-income, all-Negro areas will cost a great deal more money than is now being spent there—and perhaps more than is being spent per pupil anywhere. Racial and social class integration of schools may produce equal improvement in achievement at less total cost.

Whether or not enrichment in ghetto areas will really work is not yet known, but the Enrichment Choice is based on the yet-unproved premise that it will. Certainly, enrichment programs could significantly improve existing ghetto schools if they impelled major innovations. But "separate but equal" ghetto education cannot meet the long-run fundamental educational needs of the central-city Negro population.

The three basic educational choices are: providing Negro children with quality education in integrated schools; providing them with quality education by enriching ghetto schools; or continuing to provide many Negro children with inferior education in racially segrated school systems, severely limiting their life-time opportunities.

Consciously or not, it is the third choice that the nation is now making, and this choice the Commission rejects totally.

In the field of housing, it is obvious that "separate but equal" does not mean really equal. The Enrichment Choice could greatly improve the quantity, variety, and environment of decent housing available to the ghetto population. It could not provide Negroes with the same freedom and range of choice as whites with equal incomes. Smaller cities and suburban areas together with the central city provide a far greater variety of housing and environmental settings than the central city alone. Programs to provide housing outside central cities, however, extend beyond the bounds of the Enrichment Choice.

In the end, whatever its benefits, the Enrichment Choice might well invite a prospect similar to that of the Present Policies Choice: separate white and black societies.

If enrichment programs were effective, they could greatly narrow the gap in income, education, housing, jobs, and other qualities of life between the ghetto and the mainstream. Hence the chances of harsh polarization—or of disorder—in the next twenty years would be greatly reduced.

Whether they would be reduced far enough depends on the scope of the programs. Even if the gap were narrowed from the present, it still could remain as a strong source of tension. History teaches that men are not necessarily placated even by great absolute progress. The controlling factor is relative progress—whether they still perceive a significant gap between themselves and others whom they regard as no more deserving. Widespread perception of such a gap—and consequent resentment—might well be precisely the situation twenty years from now under the Enrichment Choice, for it is essentially another way of choosing a permanently divided country.

THE INTEGRATION CHOICE

The third and last course open to the nation combines enrichment with programs designed to encourage integration of substantial numbers of Negroes into the society outside the ghetto.

Enrichment must be an important adjunct to any integration course. No matter how ambitious or energetic such a program may be, relatively few Negroes now living in central-city ghettos would be quickly integrated. In the meantime, significant improvement in their present environment is essential.

The enrichment aspect of this third choice should, however, be recognized as interim action, during which time expanded and new programs can work to improve education and earning power. The length of the interim period surely would vary. For some it may be long. But in any event, what should be clearly recognized is that enrichment is only a means toward the goal; it is not the goal.

The goal must be achieving freedom for every citizen to live and work according to his capacities and desires, not his color.

We believe there are four important reasons why American society must give this course the most serious consideration. First, future jobs are being created primarily in the suburbs, while the chronically unemployed population is increasingly concentrated in the ghetto. This separation will make it more and more difficult for Negroes to achieve anything like full employment in decent jobs. But if, over time, these residents began to find housing outside central cities, they would be exposed to more knowledge of job opportunities. They would have to make much shorter trips to reach jobs. They would have a far better chance of securing employment on a self-sustaining basis.

Second, in the judgment of this Commission, racial and social-class integration is the most effective way of improving the education of ghetto children.

Third, developing an adequate housing supply for low-income and middle-income families and true freedom of choice in housing for Negroes of all income levels will require substantial out-movement. We do not believe that such an out-movement will occur spontaneously merely as a result of increasing prosperity among Negroes in central cities. A national fair housing law is essential to begin such movement. In many suburban areas, a program combining positive incentives with the building of new housing will be necessary to carry it out.

Fourth, and by far the most important, integration is the only course which explicitly seeks to achieve a single nation rather than accepting the present movement toward a dual society. This choice would enable us at least to begin reversing the profoundly divisive trend already so evident in our metropolitan areas—before it becomes irreversible.

CONCLUSIONS

The future of our cities is neither something which will just happen nor something which will be imposed upon us by an inevitable destiny. That future will be shaped to an important degree by choices we make now.

We have attempted to set forth the major choices because we believe it is vital for Americans to understand the consequences of our present drift.

Three critical conclusions emerge from this analysis:

1. The nation is rapidly moving toward two increasingly separate Americas.

Within two decades, this division could be so deep that it would be almost impossible to unite: a white society principally located in suburbs, in smaller central cities, and in the peripheral parts of large central cities; and a Negro society largely concentrated within large central cities.

The Negro society will be permanently relegated to its current status, possibly even if we expend great amounts of money and effort in trying to "gild" the ghetto.

2. In the long run, continuation and expansion of such a permanent division threatens us with two perils.

The first is the danger of sustained violence in our cities. The timing, scale, nature, and repercussions of such violence cannot be foreseen. But if it occurred, it would further destroy our ability to achieve the basic American promises of liberty, justice, and equality.

The second is the danger of a conclusive repudiation of the traditional American ideals of individual dignity, freedom, and equality of opportunity. We will not be able to espouse these ideals meaningfully to the rest of the world, to ourselves, to our children. They may still recite the Pledge of Allegiance and say "one nation . . . indivisible." But they will be learning cynicism, not patriotism.

3. We cannot escape responsibility for choosing the future of our metropolitan areas and the human relations which develop within them. It is a responsibility so critical that even an unconscious choice to continue present policies has the gravest implications.

That we have delayed in choosing or, by delaying, may be making the wrong choice, does not sentence us either to separatism or despair. But we must choose. We will choose. Indeed, we are now choosing.

NOTES

1. Adjusted for Census Bureau undercounting.
2. Based on Census Bureau Series D projections.
3. Although Negro population on the urban fringe of metropolitan areas did increase slightly (0.2 million) from 1960 to 1966, it is safe to assume an actual net in-migration to central cities from these areas based upon the rate of natural increase of the Negro population.

12
Racism

JOINT ECONOMIC COMMITTEE OF CONGRESS

[*The Kerner Commission Report was the subject of hearings before the Joint Economic Committee of the United States Congress (90th Congress, 2nd session, 1968), from which these excerpts are drawn. The following is a colloquy between Representative Donald Rumsfeld (Illinois), a member of the Joint Economic Committee, and Representative James C. Corman (California), a member of the Kerner Commission.*]

REPRESENTATIVE RUMSFELD. Mr. Corman, could you define "racism" for us in [the] sense that it is meant in this whole discussion?

REPRESENTATIVE CORMAN. Yes, I would be glad to do my best. And this isn't the first time I have had the question asked. We had much discussion in the Commission when that phrase was first proposed. I was apprehensive about it, because the word means what the listener thinks it means, not what the speaker thinks it means.

And I was apprehensive, because I do not believe that America suffers from the same kind of white racism that we think of in Rhodesia or South Africa where we have this absolute separatism and a conscious, active feeling of superiority over Negroes. Rather, our white racism is evidenced in our institutions, and this is true throughout our society in every part of this land.

It is harsh. It is easier to see in some parts of our country than others. But an example which I think is the least justifiable of all is in my own Protestant denomination where we have one whole organization of Methodism for Negroes and another for almost all whites.

That's the kind of institutionalism that reflects white racism that we have tolerated in this country, we have been plagued with by our history.

REPRESENTATIVE RUMSFELD. Well, what does it mean? Does it mean a distaste, or does it mean a lack of understanding or a fear based on ignorance or on something else? Is there any way you can more precisely tell us what [the] word means in the sense that the Kerner Commission report talks about it and which we have talked about it?

REPRESENTATIVE CORMAN. Well, I suppose what the report is trying to say is that we just have different rules for people, based on color alone.

REPRESENTATIVE RUMSFELD. For whatever reason.

REPRESENTATIVE CORMAN. That's right. And those rules show up in a great number of ways.

For instance I visited Mississippi in 1963, and I discovered Negroes were not permitted to drive garbage trucks. They could ride on the back and dump the garbage, but under the mores of 1963 in Jackson, Miss., they weren't qualified to drive the truck.

Now, in Los Angeles I am led to believe—if we look at our institutions out there—that only Negroes are qualified to drive garbage trucks. Both of those are examples of white institutions.

REPRESENTATIVE RUMSFELD. So you would say that racism in the sense that this report uses the word means a conscious difference of treatment, based on color alone?

REPRESENTATIVE CORMAN. That is correct. And I think that white racism, to the degree it is a sin of each of us, is not so much in having created the institutions but, rather, in tolerating them and perpetuating them. It is the way we have always done it, and we kind of like to keep it this way, because we are a little bit fearful and apprehensive about what might happen if we changed.

Now, we can all support great and vast change in other parts of the country to bring standards up to where we think we are, but when we look within ourselves, within our own neighborhoods, within our own ranks of employment and our own schools, and we start thinking about, how do we dismantle this institution of racial segregation, it gets to be very difficult.

[*Senator William Proxmire (Wisconsin), Chairman of the Joint Economic Committee, joins in the exchange.*]

SENATOR PROXMIRE. How about a lot more publicity on this? For instance, I go into Milwaukee, I shake hands at the plant gates throughout the area, and I find similar plants where 20 per cent of their employment may be Negroes.

In other plants there's not a black face, not one, not one; 3,000 or 4,000 or 5,000 people employed. There's no Negro.

Now, this is true of a number of plants. We know there's that discrimination, and somehow I think that the publicity would help greatly. There's some way that this kind of fact could be brought to public attention.

REPRESENTATIVE CORMAN. Yes, sir; when we think of the Government as a purchaser, we have a lot of pretty good mechanisms to try to bring about fairness in employment, but that doesn't meet all of the problem at all.

SENATOR PROXMIRE. We haven't used that very rigorously, either.

REPRESENTATIVE CORMAN. We have used it very modestly, it seems to me, and we ought to do better than we are doing. An awful lot of it, so far as the business community, I think, is concerned, is what they think their customer wants. I have a lot of people ask me, for example, "What can I as a housewife in Van Nuys do?" And one of the things I have always suggested is wherever you trade, look and see whether or not they follow a fair employment practice. And if they do not, suggest that unless they do, you may change your place of doing business. I think that would do wonders, at the local level, the retail markets. In industry and construction there are sometimes union problems.

[*Representatives Thomas B. Curtis (Missouri) and Martha W. Griffiths, also members of the Joint Economic Committee, participate in the discussion with Representative Corman.*]

REPRESENTATIVE CURTIS. I am worried about the use of the term "white racism." I was happy to see some definition of what that term means brought out in Congressman Rumfeld's examination. . . . the task force studies on the riots themselves, I thought, were very good. Subsection 3 deals with the riot participants, and I am going to read what your own task force said, if I have the right place.

Yes. This is entitled the "Profile of a Rioter": "He is extremely hostile to whites but his hostility is more apt to be a product of social and economic class than of race. He is almost equally hostile toward middle-class Negroes."

Now, this is similar to my own personal observation from working in this area a lifetime. But if this is so, then, you see, this widely publicized statement of the Commission that white racism is the root cause is not true. Not that it isn't important, but to treat it as basic distracts us from what the real problem is.

I could illustrate it in this way, because I want to say something good about labor leaders. In our building trade unions we have probably the worst example of what are called lily-white unions. But, upon analysis, isn't that really the historical development of the guild system, where the father was passing on the skill to his son, rather than racism? I know I couldn't be a bricklayer in St. Louis because I don't have an uncle or a father or some relative who is a bricklayer. That doesn't mean that racism doesn't enter the picture and aggravate it. But I think the oversimplification of saying that the labor leaders are motivated by racism distracts our attention from what I think is really the core of the problem.

REPRESENTATIVE CORMAN. Yes, as someone periodically seeking public office, if I implied that, I would like to correct the record at this point.

REPRESENTATIVE GRIFFITHS. Well, believe me, it is implied and your labor leaders do resent it, because they feel in their hearts that they are not racially motivated, and yet the fact remains that Negroes, by and large, at least in St. Louis, Mo., have a difficult time getting into the building trades occupations—even though some are admirably suited to fill those jobs.

REPRESENTATIVE CORMAN. There is substantial evidence before our Commission, also before our Judiciary Committee when we were drafting what became the 1964 Civil Rights Act that this is an area which badly needed correction and the reason which led to the creation of the FEPC in the omnibus bill. My only comment about labor is that I was pleased to have testify before our committee in 1963 several of the most prominent labor leaders in the country urging that kind of discrimination be made against the law. I was terribly distressed to see that the National Association of Real Estate Boards did not take a similar position when we were grappling with the problem of open housing.

REPRESENTATIVE CURTIS. I think that is a proper observation. One final point, then. . . . A problem is that so much of this racism charge is interpreted to apply to all our institutions. I think we have to recognize, at least I hope that most of our institutions in our society are human institutions, not "white" institutions. The Ten Commandments weren't developed by white people. You can call the Ten Commandments the law of "whitey," but they aren't. They were developed by contributions from all colors and varieties of races. And I hope that the institutions—the bulk of those—that we are developing in our society aren't white, but human. This is so important because I think there is the tendency for any Negro who does move up to be called an Uncle Tom, because he is working with these human institutions. And there is also the tendency to talk about the mores of our society as being the mores of white culture. I hope this is not so, and I don't believe that it is so. So I think this becomes important in furthering this dialog.

13
Importance of the Job

ELLIOT LIEBOW
National Institute of Mental Health

[*The Kerner Commission's emphasis on the importance of employment in improving the lives of the disadvantaged black minority is reinforced by the following statement of Dr. Elliot Liebow of the National Institute of Mental Health before the Joint Economic Committee.*]

Day by day we seem more and more to be a nation in trouble. Race, class, and even generational differences are hardening into battlelines. There are those among us who find comfort in taking a larger view of things, as in pointing out that we have by far the highest standard of living ever achieved by any society, that we have come a long way in race relations, and that even the worst off among us is probably far better off than the great mass of people around the world. We must not let such a viewpoint obscure the dangers and the issues, since it is by our own standards of measurement that our society has failed a large number of our citizens. It is by our own standards of measurement that large numbers of our citizens are living in deep and degrading poverty, and it is by our own standards of measurement that we have failed to build cities and towns in which a fundamental decency pervades the relationship between citizen and citizen and in which a minimal amount of social peace and good order prevails.

Perhaps the poor, rural and urban, the unemployed and underemployed, the handicapped, the aged, the welfare recipient, are the largest single group that we have failed. But it is the ethnic poor in our cities—the Negroes, Puerto Ricans, and Spanish-speaking poor—who see no way out of their condition through traditional avenues of self-improvement, that are most vigorous and articulate in expressing their discontent in protest and violence. College students and teenagers are other major carriers of discontent.

The problem of each of these different groups is radically different, of course, but the groups are all alike in at least one respect: their members are, for the present at least, not gainfully employed. In our society, this commonplace observation takes on enormous significance, because it is principally through engaging in socially useful work that an individual participates as a valued member of society. In large part, it is through such participation, through investment of ourselves and our energies in enterprises deemed useful by our fellows, that we earn our livings, gain respect from others, and learn to respect ourselves.

The failure to be valued as full participants in our society is a central fact of life for American Negroes, especially for poor Negroes in our inner cities. It is as if they have been the victims of a giant lockout which has opened up —with pitifully few exceptions—only to those willing to do the dirty, menial, underpaid jobs that need to be done in every society. This, I believe, is an example of what the National Advisory Commission on Civil Disorders identifies as white racism, one of the principal causes of last summer's riots.

There are many practical hardheaded men and women who are willing to accept the Kerner Commission's analysis of the riots and of Negro discontent and even willing to accept some responsibility for what happened. But being practical, hardheaded men, they do not—properly—want to dwell on the past. "Where do we go from here?" they want to know. "What can we do to help the Negro into full participation in our national life?"

Typically, we locate the problem in the Negro himself. We say, for example, that Negroes are lazy, irresponsible, and don't want to work. Then we offer them the most menial, the dullest, the poorest paid jobs in our society and, sure enough, there are some of them that don't want to work.

We say that Negroes are less intelligent than whites, that they learn slower and learn less. Then we give them poorly equipped, overcrowded schools and the poorest trained, least experienced teachers, and, sure enough, on the average they seem to learn slower and learn less.

We say that Negroes cannot be trusted, that they will steal anything not nailed down. Then, in the midst of an affluence never before achieved by any society, we force large numbers of men, women, and children to live in deep and degrading poverty and, sure enough, some of them steal.

For a beginning, then, let us stop locating the problem in the Negro and let us face some important facts. The one most central fact is that most Negroes, like everyone else in our society, do want to work. Indeed, most Negroes have been working all along. Here in Washington, for example, the garbage does get picked up, the trash gets collected, streets are swept, hotel rooms are cleaned, office building floors and halls are mopped and polished, cars and restaurant dishes get washed, ditches get dug, deliveries are made, orderlies attend the sick and mentally disturbed, and so on. And, if the cities in your home states are even remotely like Washington and New York and Baltimore and Philadelphia, then most of the people whose job it is to do these things are black.

But, if most Negroes have jobs, what, then, is the problem? It is mainly that most of these jobs pay from $50 to, say, $80 per week. The man with a wife and one or two children who takes such a job can be certain he will live in poverty so long as he keeps it. The longer he works, the longer he cannot live on what he makes.

This apparent paradox is closely linked up with another assertion—a false one, I believe—that the Negro family structure, with its absent father and female-headed household makes for illegitimacy and dependency, emasculates the male and deprives young boys of acceptable male models. The fact is that most Negro children are raised in two-parent households, and the fact is that, if the Negro male has indeed been emasculated, it is not his family structure or his women who are responsible, but rather the larger society which has taken away his manhood by making it so difficult—often impossible—for him to earn a living and support a family and be the head of it. For that is what it means to be a man in our society, and perhaps in all other societies as well.

Given these facts, it is not surprising that there are a number—a very small proportion of the total but a substantial number, nevertheless—of Negro men who seem to neither have jobs nor want them, who work a day, a week or a month and quit, who won't follow up a job referral or stick with a training program.

Perhaps a majority of these are youths who dropped out of school physically in the ninth or tenth grade and psychologically five or more years earlier. Although most of them probably went to poor schools, not all of them would have profited commensurately from going to better schools. Learning —at least the kind we mean when we talk about formal education—is peculiarly dependent on will and desire. It is a volitional act or process that cannot be forced. Child, youth, or adult must want to learn in order to learn; he must have a reason or purpose; he must believe that it will make a difference in his life and that this difference will be to his benefit. But to hold such a belief requires an act of faith, and it is precisely this act of faith—this belief that education, academic or vocational, will eventually pay off and prove to have been worth the time and trouble—that many Negro youths in our cities are incapable of. Thus, it is that many young men in their late teens or early twenties who submit to remedial programs and teachers trying to teach them what they should have learned in the fourth, fifth, or ninth grade do little better the second time around than they did the first. Indeed, why should we expect it to be different? What has the passage of a few years done to change things? The young men have no more reason to trust the system and its promises of future rewards at the age of nineteen or twenty than they did at the age of nine or fifteen. If anything, they trust it less, for what they only suspected when they were nine or fifteen has been confirmed by personal experience and observation by the time they are nineteen or twenty. From his perspective, the black youth has few choices to make. He can forget about getting an education and become a busboy or janitor who cannot read or write, or he can work hard at getting an education and become a busboy or janitor who can read and write. In either event, if he becomes a busboy or janitor and works hard, he becomes—after a few years—a hard-working busboy or janitor.

A great many Americans, Negro as well as white, would argue that the young man is wrong, that even if that was the situation in the past, it is no longer the situation today. These different perceptions of social reality are one of the principal sticking points in Negro-white relations. Most whites and some Negroes believe that the Negro's situation has been improved dramatically since World War II, and that civil rights and other legislation have removed institutional discrimination and brought him to equality of opportunity and equality before the law. Negroes look at the same world and see a different reality. From the point of view of the Negro youth in a big city, things have changed very little if at all, and maybe they've gotten worse.

The weight of the evidence, I believe, supports the latter point of view. Negro unemployment has been running at about double that of whites; the dollar gap between white and Negro average family income has widened while the ratio of Negro to white average family income has remained relatively constant. And in the crucial area of education, there are more children attending segregated schools today than there were at the time of the Supreme Court's desegregation decision almost fifteen years ago.

We cannot hope to change the attitudes and beliefs and hostility of the Negro youth in our cities until we change the reality on which these attitudes are based. Promises of a better future are no longer sufficient. We must change the reality and let him experience it before we can expect him to believe in it and trust it. And without that belief and trust, the system simply doesn't work. He will continue to do poorly in school, to drop out or be pushed out, to be passed on from the wary eye of the teacher to the wary eye of the policeman on the street. Then he or his friends will further overload our court facilities, crowd our jails, add to the ranks of the unemployed and the dependent women and children, and so on and so on until the National Guard and the Army are called in.

How do we "change the reality and let him experience it?" If having a job and earning a living is, as I believe it is, the linchpin of full and valued participation in our society, then every able-bodied man must have a right to a job doing socially useful work which pays a decent wage. This will only be possible, I suspect, if the federal government acts as employer of last resort.

The negative income tax and other income supplement proposals, I believe, are focused on the wrong end of the employer-employee relationship. If a man does an honest day's work, whether it be sweeping the floor or simply guarding a gate, he has earned a right to a living wage. If a commercial or industrial enterprise cannot afford to pay the worker enough to live on, the failure lies with them, not with the employee, and it is the employer who needs to be subsidized, not the worker. In other words, enterprises which through inefficiency or for other reasons cannot afford to pay their workers enough to live on must leave the field or, if they are deemed socially useful and necessary, must be subsidized by the government so they can pay a living wage to their workers. In this way, the stigma and obligations that go with being the recipient of public assistance is removed from the worker (where it didn't really belong in the first place) and placed on the employer, where it does belong. Moreover, business and industry have already demonstrated that they can carry the burden of receiving public assistance—that is, subsidies —fairly lightly.

I am not an economist so I must leave to others to say how much public money will be needed or where it should come from. I know priorities must be established, but of one thing I am morally certain: That a job-rights program or its equivalent is more important to our national security and national purpose than all other programs, one by one or all together. I honestly believe that our experiment in democracy is at stake.

14
The Struggle for Employment

RUSSELL A. NIXON
New York University Center for Study of the Unemployed

[*Continuing the interest in the role of unionism in discriminatory practices affecting the employment of Negroes, the Joint Economic Committee heard from Russell A. Nixon, Associate Director of the New York University Center for Study of the Unemployed. His testimony deals only with a very limited problem—discrimination in apprenticeship programs. It should not be read as representative of union practices generally (a subject too broad for treatment here) but only as indicative of some of the difficulties confronting Negroes in securing "good jobs" and employers in hiring Negroes even when they are disposed to do so.*]

I will be addressing my attention to the construction industry—perhaps the most important employment area at issue, because of its huge size, because of its crucial central role in our economy, because of its special significance for the ghettos and minorities, and because of its enormously growing potential in our society.

I would start out by summarizing three facts which I think characterize the present situation and are relevant to this particular hearing addressed to the question of racial discrimination and employment.

These three facts are very simply stated.

First. As a result of a complex pattern of past and present discrimination and exclusion, minority workers are generally barred from most construction work—except in very marginal circumstances, and in the unskilled categories, the construction industry labor force on June 6, 1968, is lily white.

Second. No programs are underway, and no changes are in the works at the present time which will result in a balanced construction labor force with appropriate proportions of minority workers in the years immediately ahead.

Current antidiscrimination agreements and declarations by building trades, union, and employers, legal enforcement actions and special apprenticeship programs are highly laudable, but they are inadequate to change significantly the basically white makeup of the construction labor force.

Third. The continuing failure to create a minority worker construction labor force is leading to an intolerable impasse which threatens to result in drastic and often violent confrontation whenever building and construction is undertaken in our cities. It is unrealistic—and you here in Washington are sitting in the middle of an example of this, in the question of the stalemated cleanup work following the violence of some weeks ago—it is unrealistic to expect that white work crews are going to be permitted peacefully to rebuild our slums, rehabilitate and build new low-income housing, construct schools and hospitals, in the Negro, Puerto Rican, and Mexican-American neighborhoods of our country.

The comprehensive housing plan just approved by the Senate, the model cities program, government public works at all levels, are all put in jeopardy by the failure to integrate the construction labor force.

Finally, to shift from what I think is a statement of facts to an opinion and a recommendation.

A drastic crash program on a new level and a new scale is needed to bring Negroes, Puerto Ricans, and Mexican Americans quickly into the construction industry, and to avoid the dangers and troubles inherent in the present situation.

New routes and standards for entry into construction jobs, rationalization and restructuring of jobs, new programs of on-the-job training, with realistic ladders for occupational advancement must be developed.

I would emphasize to you that impressive steps are being taken by many employers at the present time, through the National Alliance of Businessmen, and the Urban Coalition, to do just this in major sections of industry.

It is high time that the construction industry made the same effort.

Since we are dealing here with extremely difficult and complex problems, and an issue which involves very seriously vested interests, I would suggest that a special blue ribbon commission be established to design and recommend a realistic program for the full and immediate integration of the Nation's construction labor force.

Dr. Beck has mentioned the special experience at Mobilization for Youth, and I think that this is significant, because Mobilization is a high-quality youth program, a pioneer in this field, in the Lower East Side of New York City, and its experience confirms the observations I have just made.

To put it very simply to you—in five years of rather sophisticated and very serious effort, Mobilization for Youth has been completely unable to channel its trainees, primarily Puerto Rican and Negro youth—into jobs in the construction industry.

Mobilization for Youth is aided in its job development efforts by a volunteer group of employers, union representatives, and other concerned individuals who comprise the Mobilization for Youth Committee on Employment Opportunities. The committee chairman is Herbert Bienstock, the Regional Director of the United States Bureau of Labor Statistics. A year ago, Mr. Bienstock appointed a Special Subcommittee on Employment in the Construction Industry, and named me as chairman with Holmes Brown, vice president of American Airlines, Donald Armiger, assistant vice president of the First National City Bank, Ed Corwin of the New York Board of Trade, and Harold Wolchok, Teamsters Union official, as other members. Aided by the Mobilization for Youth staff we have worked during the past year canvassing all avenues of approach to the development of jobs for MFY youth in the construction industry. These efforts are continuing, but as of now we have failed to place a single MFY Puerto Rican or Negro youth in construction work.

In the course of our efforts we have had conferences with all the principal groups concerned—with Government officials responsible for enforcement of nondiscrimination laws, with the head of the New York City Building Trades Council, with the chief employers, with civil rights representatives, with the personnel director of New York City, with the leaders of the Bureau of Apprenticeship Training, and with Workers Defense League apprentice training project leaders.

We have been impressed in our discussions with the unanimous and vigorous affirmation of hostility to all forms of racial discrimination in the construction industry. We do not question that. At the same time, we have been impressed with our inability to develop through these impressive and authoritative contacts any concrete program or process for the employment of MFY trainees in construction jobs in the city of New York.

We are concerned because we think that this reflects a generalized situation throughout the country as far as minorities are concerned.

Viewed from the frame of reference of the Kerner report, "national action on an unprecedented scale" to eliminate the roots of racial discrimination, it is completely inadequate merely to state that from now on, overt racial discrimination will be ended in the construction trades. This is true for at least two reasons.

First. De facto discrimination is part and parcel of the present apprenticeship and hiring system of the construction industry. Without far-reaching changes in the industry's job entry processes, that system will perpetuate a racist labor force, regardless of antidiscrimination avowals by employers, unions, and Government.

Second. The racist distortion of the present construction labor force composition is so extreme that "time" cannot be left to solve the problem and drastic balancing action, remedial actions, are immediately required. The estimate of the NAACP that "given a continuation of the present rates of advance, it will take Negroes 138 years, or until 2094 to secure equal participation in skilled, craft training and employment" is well founded.

The present policies of exclusion practiced by the construction trade unions is an admixture of racial discrimination and a tactic of limiting the supply of labor for advantage in the establishment of wages and working conditions for construction union members. This concern for wages and economic security is a thoroughly legitimate objective, but it cannot any longer be pursued at the price of racial exclusiveness, whether achieved by overt discrimination or by artificial hiring standards unrelated to job performance, discriminatory occupational tests, and an exaggerated and one-dimensional training procedure.

To continue to permit the misuse of the apprenticeship system and the craft standards to bar minorities is not only socially intolerable today, but it also jeopardizes the legitimate and socially desirable values of the apprenticeship and craft systems themselves.

The lessons of the developing manpower programs for the hard-core unemployed make clear that new employment policies to "screen in" rather than to "screen out" the disadvantaged are necessary. Industry, business and government generally are increasingly recognizing the need to redefine, redesign, and restructure jobs to create new job opportunities for the disadvantaged, to pursue special programs of recruitment in the ghettos and of in-service training and supportive services are necessary to make possible fruitful employment of hitherto excluded workers. Valuable new resources of labor are being uncovered. New careers in nonprofessional and subprofessional jobs in the public service are opening new opportunities for people who desperately need them and meeting serious manpower needs at the same time. These are manpower efforts that go far beyond simply refraining from illegal acts of discrimination or even of token and symbolic integration. They are in the spirit of the Kerner report. The construction industry has not yet made similar efforts.

The New York State Commission for Human Rights has recently completed a survey of the minimum qualification for apprentices in fifty-seven Building Trades Joint Apprenticeship Committees in New York City. These standards, summarized in Table 14–1, indicate the widespread exclusionist character of the apprentice system in New York.

When you add the less visible barriers and exclusion devices you can readily understand how this exclusion process perpetuates itself. I won't detail the

TABLE 14–1 *Minimum Qualifications, Fifty-Seven Building Trades Joint Apprenticeship Committees, New York City (as of January 11, 1968)*

Require high school graduation	30
Three years or more residence	22
Below twenty-six years of age	43
Police clearance or police record report	22
Minimum point score	23

SOURCE: "Building Trades Analysis of Apprenticeship Selection Standards in the New York City Area," New York State Commission of Human Rights (March, 1968) mimeo.

table—it is in the testimony. But out of the fifty-seven building trades joint apprenticeships, thirty of them require high school graduation for even applying to get into the industry. Twenty-two of them require police clearance before they can even apply to get into the industry. And twenty-three of them have "minimum point scores," which is a ready formula for exclusion.

The consequences of this type of practice is represented beyond any question in the facts of participation in the construction industry in the city of New York. It is within this framework that we have had our so far unsuccessful experience at mobilization in placing our youngsters in the construction industry.

Table 14–2, which was prepared by the Commission on Human Rights in New York City, on the basis of extensive hearings, and updated from 1963 to 1967. Just let me highlight a couple of points. These are symbolic.

The Elevator Construction Union Local No. 1, approximate total membership 2,300 people, has ten Negro and Puerto Rican journeymen. This is in a city with 35 per cent Negro and Puerto Rican population.

Plumbers Union Local No. 2, that is the home local of the president of the AFL–CIO, 4,100 members, twenty-one minority journeymen and two or three apprentices.

TABLE 14–2 *Estimated Union Membership and Apprentice Programs, Nonwhite Journeymen and Apprentices*

UNION	APPROXIMATE TOTAL MEMBERSHIP	NEGRO AND PUERTO RICAN JOURNEYMEN	APPRENTICES
Elevator Construction Union, Local No. 1	2,300	10	([1]) 5
Plumbers Union, Local No. 1	3,000	24	2
Plumbers Union, Local No. 2	4,100	21	2 or 3
Operating Engineers Union, Local No. 14 and 14A	1,600–1,750	23–50	0
Operating Engineers Union, Local No. 15 (A, B, C, D)	4,700	[1] 407	0
Sheetmetal Union, Local No. 28	3,300	([1])	([2])([3])
Ironworkers Union, Local No. 40	1,050	([1]) 7	14
Metallic Lathers Union, Local No. 46	1,600–1,750	5	5
Steamfitters Union, Local No. 638	6,800	—	14
A	4,000	0	—
B	2,800	200	—
Total	28,450	697	54

[1] Uncertain status.
[2] Zero Negroes.
[3] Twelve Spanish speaking.
SOURCE: "Bias in the Building Industry," an updated report, 1963–67, the city of New York, Commission on Human Rights (May 31, 1967), pp. 14–17.

In the Steamfitters Local 638, 6,800 members, 200 minority journeymen and fourteen minority apprentices.

On an overall basis the New York City Human Rights Commission estimates that less than 2 per cent of the skilled craft unions are Puerto Ricans and Negroes.

Let me repeat again—this is the situation in a "progressive" city—in a state and city that have pioneered in the enactment and application presumably of antidiscrimination legislation, in a city in which 30 to 35 per cent of our population are Negro and Puerto Rican, and in a city in which we are spending a billion dollars in the next year for school construction, and contemplating model cities programs, and rebuilding of slums, and the building of more hospitals. I suggest to you that these two purposes—or this purpose, and this situation, or condition, are completely at odds.

The conclusion of the New York City Human Rights Commission report is simply this. It says:

> The pattern of exclusion in a substantial portion of the building and construction trades, which was revealed in its 1963 hearings, still persists. . . . To a considerable degree, this exclusionary pattern is attributable to racial bias, but regardless of what the other underlying causes may be, there is no doubt that the import of this pattern of exclusion is racially discriminatory, and its victims are the non-whites. . . . The unions continue to maintain almost insurmountable barriers to non-white journeymen seeking membership. They continue to be lily-white. . . . The employers continue to shirk their responsibility to include the non-white journeymen in their work force. . . .[1]

I would suggest that this situation is at least as bad as in all of the other major cities of our country.

THE SPECIAL IMPORTANCE OF THE CONSTRUCTION INDUSTRY

This is important—and I come to the concluding point—because of the very particular importance of the construction industry. It is not just a by-the-way example, in my opinion. This is in the center of the employment and economic system of our country. The pattern of racial exclusion in the construction industry is of special significance because of a number of reasons:

1. *It is a large industry.* Total new construction expenditures in March, 1968 were at an annual rate of $81 billion. In that month this year, 3,425,000 wage and salary workers were employed in contract construction.

2. *It is an industry with especially large growth prospects.* On the logical assumption that social and employment programs of the future will emphasize urban redevelopment, slum clearance, housing, hospital, school and other public facility construction, the potentiality for growth in the construction industry is enormous. The conservatively based estimates of the United States

Department of Labor foresee an increase of 1 million workers in contract construction between 1965 and 1975. If the economic proposals of the Kerner Report are implemented, the growth of construction employment will be even greater.

3. *The Construction industry is extraordinarily dependent on public funds.* Between 50 and 60 per cent of new construction projects are federal, state, and local public works. With new programs, this proportion could rise substantially.

4. *Construction is highly visible and especially related to the low-income and minority population.* Everybody watches construction production. Much of it now and in the future will emphasize slum needs, be located in slum areas and be the result of special programs to meet the needs of minority groups.

5. *Construction jobs are good jobs and consequently important to minority workers whose complaint is low paid menial work as much or more than it is unemployment.* This is true on two counts.

(*a*) In 1967 average construction wages were $4.09 an hour, and $154.19 a week. Total private industry wages in 1967 were $2.67 an hour and $101.99 a week. Plumbers average weekly wage in 1967 was $170 and that of electricians was $190.42.

(*b*) Construction jobs are male jobs, both in the sense that they are filled by men and in the highly important symbolic sense that they are manly jobs. Thus this work has special meaning for the Negro male whose manhood has been demeaned by menial work.

The importance of construction suggests not only that racial exclusion from that work is particularly damaging, but that realization of equal rights in this industry would have enormous positive implications. Much of the test as to whether the Kerner report will have real meaning will be decided in the construction industry.

● ● ●

DISCUSSION

SENATOR PROXMIRE. Mr. Nixon, you discussed the mobilization for youth effort, and you said that you were unable to place a single Puerto Rican or Negro youth in construction jobs.

Precisely whom did you see? Was it local union people, employers, both? Where did you find your principal difficulty, and what did you do to try and move them?

MR. NIXON. The answer is that we talked with the leading construction employers in the city, and we talked with both Mr. Peter Brennan, who is the head of the Building Trade Council, AFL–CIO, New York City and New York State, and we talked with individual union officials. We have not been able to break through the apprenticeship entry route and the requirements which they have set up.

We have sent people to apprenticeship programs, tried to get them through, but without any exception they have been excluded by a variety of standards which are pretty well known—high school graduation, passing of tests at a certain level.

SENATOR PROXMIRE. Did you have any Negroes or Puerto Ricans who met these standards who were excluded—that is, who were high school graduates, got police clearance?

MR. NIXON. I am very glad you asked that, because that makes the point.

There is a tendency to turn off now and say "Well, there is no discrimination, anybody that can meet these standards can get in without discrimination." I think there is a great deal of truth in this statement. But the standards have now been set at such a level that whether or not there is racial discrimination as such, the consequence is excluding minority people from those jobs.

I would suggest that they are standards that are not related to performance, they are not related to what is required to do the job, they are excessive, they are designed basically to limit the supply of entry of labor into the trades.

SENATOR PROXMIRE. Do you get any cooperation in this viewpoint from employers? After all, employers are anxious to hire people to do the job. They often have a dearth of people who are available, especially in the construction trades, where you sometimes have a big demand, and they have to wait for people to meet it. Do you get any cooperation from any employer on this?

MR. NIXON. Let me just say that from employers and unions we are getting sympathy in a way we never got it before. But basically—

SENATOR PROXMIRE. How are you getting it in a way you never got it before? Are they suggesting ways in which there can be exceptions? What concrete measures are there?

MR. NIXON. They are much more open in their statements of hostility to discrimination. They are more open in their efforts to make sure that there is no overt discrimination practices. But they insist that the standards be maintained just as they are, and that they do not really change the requirements for high school graduation, no police record and so on.

SENATOR PROXMIRE. What proportion of Negroes have a high school diploma in this area, who are unable to find jobs?

MR. NIXON. Sixty or 70 per cent do not have, Senator.

SENATOR PROXMIRE. That single qualification excludes them. In addition, if they have any kind of police record, even if they are picked up on the basis of suspicion for something, they are out?

MR. NIXON. That is right. There are variations in this. Also beyond these specific requirements, there are the less definite requirements of a verbal test, an evaluation by an administration group.

There has been an effort, as you know—the Workers Defense League, financed by the Department of Labor—to try to get by the barriers that are set up through tutoring specially selected Negroes and Puerto Ricans and helping them to pass the tests by intensive efforts. I think this is a laudable effort. But I would suggest to you this highly publicized program is only aiming at the entry into apprenticeship throughout the country of 375 minority people in two years. This is not the route by which we can expect to achieve an integrated labor force to clean up Washington, D.C., right today, or to build new schools in the Bedford Stuyvesant area, the Lower East Side, or in Harlem, N.Y.

• • •

SENATOR PROXMIRE. Around our house I could not fix anything—my wife has to do all the work. I think that is common with many of us—no matter how much we have gone to school, or what evidence we have of formal education. A pragmatic examination of some kind—do you have this manual dexterity, do you have a way of being able to fix things—being able to work intelligently with your hands and so forth.

MR. NIXON. Senator, those standards and descriptions do not exist in the building trades. I say that categorically. I think they are not known for very good reasons, because if you found them out, you would find many of these standards are excessive, and even perhaps regressive in the sense that you set requirements which damage the likelihood of a worker staying on that work, and doing it properly.

It should be noted that when the civil rights movement began to develop, and the pressure against overt discrimination and against the "father to son" line began to develop, there began to be a substitution of higher standards in the building trades industry which did not exist before. These are new historical developments.

If you ask the plumbers' union or the carpenters' union in New York "How many of your members are high school graduates," they will look away in embarrassment, they do not know, except they do know most of them are not, and yet they set such a standard for entry.

Now, just one other point.

We have learned a great deal in the last few years, and industry has been learning and maybe teaching a great deal about this, and they have found that it is possible to use hitherto excluded people in very productive ways. They have found that their standards were excessive. One of the characteristics of the development as industry is trying to meet the demands for job opportunities of the disadvantaged is to lower the entry standards of requirement. That is happening in major corporations. It is a general lesson that we have learned in the labor market in the past years. I am just repeating myself to say to you that none of this has been translated into the construction industry in this country.

NOTE

1. New York City Human Rights Commission, *Bias in the Building Trades*, p. 44.

15

Minorities and Apprenticeship

GEORGE STRAUSS
Institute of Industrial Relations, University of California, Berkeley

Apprenticeship is not a major port of entry into the labor force. In a typical year only 30,000 youths complete registered apprenticeships and enter journeyman status. And yet apprenticeship has assumed symbolic status for Negro action groups, particularly when white skilled construction groups enter the Negro ghettos. "The elimination of racial discrimination from all apprenticeship training programs involves the economic life and death of the black laboring masses," observed A. Philip Randolph, then president of the Brotherhood of Sleeping Car Porters. And Sir W. Arthur Lewis, the noted black economist, suggests that "Perhaps the greatest contribution to black advancement would be to break up the trade unions' barriers which keep people out of apprenticeships in the building and printing trades, and prevent our upgrading and promotion in other industries."

Such feelings are easy to understand. Blacks, after all, are used to outdoor work, the skilled construction trades do not require a high degree of education, and they seem easy to learn. Further, prospective shortages of skilled craftsmen have been widely advertised. Finally, the practice of discrimination by unions seems particularly immoral, given union claims to be engines of democracy on the work front.

Thus it was especially galling to black pride that, in the early 1960's, in such progressive states as California and New York, only 2 per cent of apprentices were Negroes. Ironically, too, the prospect in the early 1960's was for fewer Negro apprentices rather than more. Negro population had declined in the South, which traditionally had been the training ground for Negro craftsmen (where, since before the Civil War, they had worked in segregated crews). Further, the limited amount of black apprenticeship was concentrated mainly in low-status occupations such as carpentry, painting, molding and core-making, and the mud trades (cement mason, plasterer, and, to a lesser extent, bricklayer). Throughout the country the elite "mechanical trades" (electricians, plumbers, and sheetmetal workers) were largely lily-white, as were the ironworkers (except for a large contingent of Indians) and the operating engineers. It was these elite trades which were expanding; the trades in which blacks were represented were contracting.

Blacks were largely absent too from apprenticeship programs in the manu-

---

Portions of this paper have been adopted from George Strauss and Sidney Ingerman, "Public Policy and Discrimination in Apprenticeship," *Hastings Law Journal*, XVI (February, 1965), 285–331.

facturing industry, even though they were frequently well represented in the unskilled and semiskilled occupations. Despite the strong antidiscrimination policies of the United Auto Workers, there were almost no Negro apprentices at General Motors.

MINIMAL EARLY SUCCESS

Not surprisingly, the first major civil rights demonstrations in the North—in 1963—were designed to obtain employment for Negroes on construction projects. For a while apprenticeship hit the front pages. A brief flurry of government activity ensued: states passed antidiscrimination laws; the federal government stepped in with regulation 29 C.F.R. 30 which required the "selection of apprentices on the basis of qualifications alone"; Title VII of the federal Civil Rights Act of 1964 specifically forbids discrimination in apprenticeship; Apprenticeship Information Centers were set up in a number of cities to provide information on how to apply for apprenticeship; state and governments, governors, mayors, and human relations committees all got into the act. Particularly in New York, many construction union leaders made firm promises to provide equal employment.

Early efforts were disappointing. A thorough study made in late 1965 and early 1966 revealed a picture which was quite spotty: [1] black apprenticeship had increased quite substantially in manufacturing, particularly in the auto industry. Negro carpentry apprentices had been employed in fair numbers in a number of cities. But significant progress in the four elite trades had been made in only one of the ten cities included in the study—New York. In that city Electricians Local 3 alone admitted 260 black apprentices. The Ironworkers, Sheetmetal Workers, and Pipe Trades, under various degrees of governmental and private pressure (including a court order in the case of the Sheetmetal Workers) admitted another eighty.

Outside New York progress was more modest. In Cleveland, after much turmoil, only seven Negroes were admitted; in Philadelphia and Oakland, five each; in Pittsburgh, but two; in Cincinnati, only one; in Atlanta and Houston, none at all. Detroit had a slightly better record: nine Negroes (compared to 1,210 whites). In Washington, the headquarters of many international unions, a city with a Negro majority, where much of the building is done for the federal government, the record for the four trades was less than 3 per cent—twenty-one Negroes out of 846.

Since 1965 progress has been more substantial, though many apprenticeship programs still have only token Negro representation or none at all. By 1968, the percentage of nonwhites in apprenticeship had increased to 7.2 (up from 2.5 in 1960), while 9.4 per cent of those newly enrolled in the first half of 1968 came from minority groups. In Cleveland, for example, Negro representation in the elite construction programs increased from seven in early 1966 to eighty-nine in late 1968. In San Francisco, of forty-four new electrical apprentices placed on the job in the beginning of 1969, four were

Negro, two Chinese, one Japanese, and four Mexican-American. These experiences are somewhat typical.

This progress was the result of a number of factors. Among others, (1) the governmental emphasis changed from concern with nondiscriminatory selection *procedures* to checks on the *actual presence* of Negroes on the job, that is, from methods to results, and (2) the union movement itself began to cooperate with programs such as Operation Outreach which trained blacks to pass apprenticeship entrance examinations. We will look at these developments in a moment, but first it will be useful to examine why blacks found it so hard to enter apprenticeship in the past.

NOT JUST DISCRIMINATION

Undoubtedly there has been a good deal of discrimination *against* Negroes as such in apprenticeship. Perhaps equally, if not more important, has been the discrimination in *favor* of friends and relatives. Until recently many trades frankly restricted their ranks to sons or at least gave them preference for openings. "It has been historic over the years," C. J. Haggerty, president of the AFL–CIO Building and Construction Trades Department, told a Congressional committee, "that you become an apprenticesboy in a given trade . . . by being a brother or a son or a cousin of a member, or of the employer or management. . . . ." Building tradesmen do not believe that family favoritism is immoral. Quite the contrary. They believe that the right to work in a trade is a property right that a man should be able to pass on to his children as part of his legacy. The point has been made in a number of building trades journals by coupling a quotation from the Talmud, "A father who does not give his son a trade steals from him," with a quotation from Ben Franklin, "He that hath a trade hath an estate." (In addition, by tradition, many trades have been reserved for specific ethnic groups, such as Italians.)

Even without preference sons have an advantage. They know how and where to apply for jobs. They have contacts among employers and business agents. They have learned the nomenclature of the trade and many have actually worked with its tools. Even those who look for jobs elsewhere at first always keep the trade in mind as a possible source of employment.

Negroes have none of these advantages. Rarely do they aspire to occupations which traditionally have been closed to them. They do not know of the existence of apprenticeship vacancies or where to apply to fill them. They receive little help in this regard from either their school counselors or from the employment service. In recent years better-qualified black youths have been channeled into colleges or into white-collar jobs.

In many trades, selection procedures have been quite informal, allowing all sorts of opportunities for favoritism and discrimination. But even in those trades which have formal selection procedures, the Negro is at a disadvantage. Too often he is a high school dropout—and so not considered for the better trades. Or he does poorly on entrance examinations, perhaps because his ghetto school gave him inadequate training. Or he has little worthwhile experience to bring the employer. Often, too, the standards for admission include irrelevant criteria.

Thus, union leaders have considerable justification when they complain that few qualified Negroes apply for apprenticeship. A much publicized effort in the New York City printing trades opened apprenticeship to all unskilled workers in the industry on the basis of written tests supervised by an impartial agency. Of 1,000 eligible workers, one-third were members of minority groups. A much smaller percentage of minority group members than of whites took the test, and of the seventy-one individuals who passed it, only two were Negro and one a Puerto Rican. Fifty of the 340 applicants for a court-ordered New York Sheetmetal examination were minority group members. The highest ranking Negro was *sixty-eighth* on the list. (In later examinations, as we shall see, tutoring by the Workers' Defense League yielded dramatically improved results.)

Similar evidence is offered which demonstrates that Negroes show little patience with lengthy selection procedures, even when these procedures have been shortened in "show" programs set up as a result of civil rights group pressures. For example, in New York, as a result of an intensive drive during the late summer of 1963, 1,600 Negroes and Puerto Ricans expressed interest in apprenticeship. About one-third of them were eliminated because of age, education, or residence requirements. Of those scheduled to be interviewed by a special building trades committee, 39 per cent failed to show up. Eventually forty-three youths were selected for apprenticeship by the carpenters. Of these forty-three, only six reported and were employed. The remaining thirty-seven either declined membership or did not report for interviews or placement.

Equivalent stories are reported from other areas. Pressures from civil rights groups lead unions to announce nondiscriminatory selection procedures. Opportunities are publicized, but few people show interest. Of those who show interest, few show up at the union hall and fewer still take the exam. In Pittsburgh, sixty Negro recent high school graduates were contacted regarding apprenticeship; thirty-seven showed interest and promised to apply. Only five actually applied, and only four took the exam. As psychologists have suggested, the Negro ghetto teaches youths to take a "short time perspective." They lack the Puritan "stick-to-itiveness" of white youths. Instead they have learned that initiative does not pay off; they expect a "run around" and avoid situations where they anticipate being humiliated.

This combination of lack of patience and inability to pass examinations tends to make the usual recruitment efforts quite discouraging. In Cincinnati, for example, a major effort, involving radio announcements, public meetings, and a city-wide rally, netted four Negro apprentices. Clearly something more than passive nondiscrimination and mass publicity is required if substantial numbers of Negroes are to be recruited for apprenticeship.

EQUAL EMPLOYMENT ACTIVITIES

Efforts to get Negroes into apprenticeship have been of three sorts: (1) regulations designed to reduce actual discrimination *against* minorities; (2) measures designed to improve the *supply* of qualified minority applicants; and (3) *affirmative action* requirements which judge employer efforts in terms of the proportion of minorities employed (and, in effect, require reverse discrimination on occasion).

Antidiscrimination Regulations

By 1964 most major industrial states had laws barring discrimination in employment. These laws had some effect in manufacturing and the service industries, but almost none in construction, the single largest employer of apprentices.

The procedures of state fair employment practice commissions are tremendously time consuming, relying on individual complaints (which few Negroes know how to file) and requiring proof of actual discrimination in each case (the absence of Negroes is usually not enough). Furthermore, the commissions' principal forms of leverage are conciliation and threat of unfavorable publicity. These methods are fairly effective with companies. But with unions, which control most apprenticeship programs, they have often led to stubborn resistance since for unions freedom to choose their members is as much a symbolic issue as discrimination in apprenticeship is for civil rights groups. Finally, since there were few black applicants for apprenticeship, there were in fact few cases of discrimination. Only recently have state commissions and the new federal Equal Employment Opportunities Commission begun to find that the absence of minority apprentices is itself evidence of discrimination even though no overt discriminatory acts have been proven.

State and federal apprenticeship agencies also have rules against discrimination in the programs under their jurisdiction. But such agencies look upon their functions as primarily promotional rather than regulatory. Most state and federal apprenticeship "consultants" have a background in the very trades they seek to regulate; they find it hard to develop enthusiasm for the elimination of practices with which they have grown up.

More effective than general strictures against discrimination have been specific rules, such as 29 C.F.R. 30 at the federal level, and equivalent or even stronger rules in some states. Generally these rules require that applicants be selected on the basis of formalized objective standards which permit review. The New York regulations specify selection procedures in considerable detail, restrict the weight of the interview given to applicants to 25 per cent of the total score, require that tests be limited to those "developed and administered by competent [outside] organizations," and (as observed) are interpreted with considerable strictness.

The principal impact of these rules has been to formalize selection procedures and to raise standards. An increasing number of trades use tests and require high school graduation for admission. The effect, as I have observed it, has been more to reduce nepotism than to increase Negro participation. In fact, it can be argued that the new standards have made it harder for Negroes to win admission. Color blindness may not be enough if rapid integration is our goal.

Nevertheless, antidiscrimination regulations have had some effect. By making clear the public condemnation of discrimination and by providing sanctions in the extreme case, these regulations have established a climate in which volunteer programs can be more effective.

Improving Applicant Qualifications

Another approach is to increase the supply of qualified apprentices. As we have seen, mere publicity as to the existence of apprenticeship openings is not enough. An example of what can be done, however, is the very successful program of the Workers' Defense League (WDL) in New York City. This organization carefully selects men whom it grooms to pass apprenticeship admission tests (it finds its best candidates among graduates of academic high school programs rather than vocational schools, and among those employed at low-paid jobs rather than among those completely unemployed). WDL guides its candidates through the apprenticeship selection maze (one union has a nine-page application form; many require high school records, and so on) and puts them through a six-week cram school designed to improve their test-passing and interview-taking proficiency. A measure of their success is the Sheetmetal admissions examination. In 1965 the highest ranking Negro scored sixty-eighth; two examinations later nine of the ten highest men were Negroes trained by the WDL (the union unsuccessfully tried to have the test rerun).

Recently, with United States Department of Labor financial backing, WDL programs or those similar to it (some are run by the Urban League, for example) have been extended to over forty industrial areas. By spring 1969 Operation Outreach, as it is called, helped with admission to apprenticeship for over 2,000 minority youth.

Affirmative Action

Measures to eliminate overt discrimination and to improve applicant qualifications alone do not fully explain the recent improvements in apprentice color-mix. Much of the progress to date is the result of pressures from government and civil rights groups for the establishment of "affirmative action" or de facto quota systems. Government contracting agencies (and a heavy percentage of the construction firms work for one branch of the government or another) have increasingly insisted that work crews be integrated in fact. The test of compliance with "affirmative action programs" is no longer absence of discrimination; it is the actual presence of Negroes on the payroll. In effect, the method of selection is secondary as long as it leads to black faces on the job. Union officials at times call this "blackmail." In the past, however, it was standard practice, in many of the apprenticeable trades, to give preference to sons and relatives; it might be justified today to give equal preference to blacks until the present imbalance is somewhat redressed.

Affirmative action has also called into question present admission standards, such as high school graduation or absence of a police record. Some of these are too stringent. In many trades excessive emphasis is being placed on "objective" standards, such as test results. The selection tests currently used are poorly validated, if at all. Of course, the trades argue, with considerable justification, that the basic criterion for selection should be getting the best man. But since we are not sure that present practices in fact do lead to selecting the best man—and we do know they tend to weed out Negroes—perhaps these practices should be suspended, at least for the current "civil rights emergencies."

APPRENTICESHIP IS NOT ENOUGH

Finally, the problem should be placed in perspective. Even if blacks were admitted to apprenticeship in proportion to their numbers in the population, there would be only about 10,000 openings each year, hardly enough to dent the ranks of the black unemployed. A high percentage of journeymen enter their trade through the "back door," by-passing formal apprenticeship. In many communities there are significant numbers of black nonunion craftsmen, some of whom can already meet union journeymen standards and others of whom might be trained to meet such standards fairly easily. Government insistence on "results," that is, quotas, would provide an incentive for unions to admit these craftsmen, perhaps temporarily lowering their standards (as occurs frequently in some trades in times of peak employment, for example, during World War II). Along the same lines, during wartime, "upgrader" programs were established in many manufacturing firms. These programs were designed to transform semi- and unskilled workers into craftsmen in a hurry. Similar crash programs could be developed to upgrade construction laborers and hod carriers, many of whom are now black.

Some of this is occurring already. The AFL-CIO Building Trades Department has agreed that under the Model Cities program special preference shall be given to "residents of the area" being redeveloped. Qualified journeymen will be permitted to work at journeymen rates on union projects even though they are not currently members of the union. Less qualified "residents" will be employed at lower rates. Some agreements already provide for "trainee" and "advanced trainee" categories by-passing normal apprenticeship procedures.

NOTE

1. Ray Marshall and Vernon Briggs, *The Negro and Apprenticeship* (Baltimore: The Johns Hopkins Press, 1967).

16
The Place of Political Protest

BAYARD RUSTIN

[In the following paragraphs, the Executive Director of the A. Philip Randolph Institute raises the question as to the relative importance of individual self-help and organized self-help on the part of Negroes. He concludes, in effect, that the former is important in making one's place within the existing system, but that the second is more important in changing the present system to provide expanded opportunities.]

It is only when the black ghetto of the North, which has yet to be organized massively by *any* civil rights group, comes to conscious political life that the full impact of the Negro revolution will be felt. But first of all, the economic and social setting in which such organization becomes possible and even probable has to be created. Just as the semiskilled factory workers did not create the CIO at the bottom of the Depression in 1932, but only when times were getting better a few years later, so the black masses require some tangible signs of hope and success before they are going to move.

For that matter, the white immigrant groups from Europe, which are so often held up as images of the "self-help" process, benefited from massive government intervention. The great advance made by the first and second generation workers took place, of course, in the 1930's, and the most important new institutions they created were precisely the industrial unions. But this did not happen in a vacuum. There was the Wagner Act, which, if it did not immediately guarantee collective bargaining rights, put the moral and psychological authority of the government on the side of the labor movement ("Mr. Roosevelt wants you to join," John L. Lewis said in those days). And there were the various programs—the climate of economic hope. Some Negroes participated in this progress; most were excluded because racism had kept them out of the factories, where the decisive events occurred.

From "Why Don't Negroes . . . ," *America* (June 4, 1966). © *America*, National Catholic Weekly, 106 West 56 Street, New York, New York 10019

In short, the CIO had to organize itself, but it did so under circumstances of federal intervention that made the momentous task easier to perform. Negroes have to organize themselves. And the Freedom Budget, which is their New Deal thirty years late, will not simply provide full and fair employment and lay the basis for the destruction of the physical environment of poverty. Like the Wagner Act and the social investments of the New Deal, it should also evoke a new psychology, a new militancy and sense of dignity, among millions of Negroes, who will see something more concrete and specific than a promise of eventual freedom.

But secondly, when I talk of the self-organization that the Freedom Budget should make possible, I am not talking about "self-help" in the neighborhood improvement sense. In *Dark Ghetto,* Kenneth Clark tells of how one New York block got together to clean up the street. In the doing, Clark rightly remarks, these Negroes gave tacit assent to the charge that it was their *fault* that the street was dirty, thus accepting one more of the white man's stereotypes about the Negro (that is, he is guilty of noncleanliness). What is more, the energy was misdirected. It should have been directed to City Hall as a demand that the city clean up the streets of Harlem the same way it cleans up the streets of the white middle class.

From the time of the American Revolution until the rise of the NAACP in the first decade of this century, Negroes have followed the advice of the self-helpers. When Negroes were thrown out of the Methodist Church in the 18th century, they established the African Methodist Episcopal Church. When they were not allowed to attend white universities, they set up Wilberforce University in Ohio. When insurance companies would not insure Negroes, fraternal organizations and social clubs took on the task. The history of the Negro people in the United States is a history of attempting to build separate self-help organizations. At the end of World War II, the Urban League and the National Council of Negro Women formed "Hold Your Job Committees." The committees conducted educational campaigns in the factories and the Negro community to urge Negroes not to give employers any excuse for discharging them after the war.

More recently, Black Nationalists and Muslims have believed that if Negroes would only follow the Protestant ethic and "Buy Black" (while a number of confused whites have said: "Be frugal"), they could end their economic dependence. But the fact is that if millions of Negroes are to change the conditions of their life, it will be not by becoming shopkeepers or by cleaning up their block, but by winning full and fair employment for black men as well as white.

Negroes should be individually virtuous—and so should whites. But the Negro movement's future does not lie along the line of making over millions of black personalities, one by one. The European immigrants and their children ceased being rude peasants not because they got religion or psychology, but because they got economic opportunity and hope. The Negro movement must now struggle against economic injustices that are more deeply rooted in the management and structure of our technology than anything the immigrants ever faced. And it can win this perilous fight only by way of militant political organization and through national programs.

B *The Business Reaction*

17

The Kerner Report Should Be Required Reading

ELI GOLDSTON
President, Eastern Gas and Fuel Associates

I was dismayed this morning to read the results of a poll taken at the annual meeting of the Chamber of Commerce of the United States. When asked to indicate the most important cause of civil disorder and riots in the American cities, 63 per cent of the businessmen in attendance listed "agitation from outsiders." A child psychologist reported some months ago that when he showed a picture of a teddy bear to Negro youngsters in the ghetto, two-thirds of them—almost the same 63 per cent—identified the teddy bear as a rat. Is it possible that our colleagues in the United States Chamber of Commerce regard these rats as "outside agitators"? Certainly the business community will make no progress in solving the social problems of our day until we acquire better understanding of easily available and indisputable facts. The report of the National Advisory Commission on Civil Disorders—the Kerner Commission Report—should be required reading for a modern business manager. No one has more to lose than the American business system if we permit America to become two societies—one black and one white, separate, unequal, and hostile.

From an address at the Harvard Graduate School of Business Administration, May 16, 1968.

18
Major Employers and Their Manpower Policies

BETTYE K. EIDSON
Department of Social Relations, The John Hopkins University

[*In addition to issuing its own report, the Kerner Commission sponsored a number of supplemental studies. One study, "Between Black and White—the Faces of American Institutions in the Ghetto," was undertaken by the Department of Social Relations of Johns Hopkins University under the general direction of Peter H. Rossi. He and his collaborators conducted extensive interviews in fifteen American cities to identify the attitudes and images that are held by policemen, educators, social workers, merchants, political party workers, and major employers with respect to Negroes in their city generally, and with respect to Negroes with whom they deal as clients, customers, students, and potential employees specifically. The following article is taken from this study.*]

Unlike the other occupational groups studied, the major employers in each of our fifteen cities are not necessarily located in the ghetto. Their connection with the Negro community is through the operation of the labor market, a metropolitan-wide system. The days have long gone by when workers lived close to their jobs and firms sought to locate within walking distances of their labor forces. Blue-collar and white-collar employees commute to work in the typical metropolitan area, freeing the business firm to locate itself considering other criteria.

Major employers were included in our study because business enterprises constitute one of the central institutions of the local community. Big business provides enough of the community's personal and collective income to make it a major force in a variety of ways.

From the point of view of a ghetto resident, getting and holding down a job is another way in which he is connected with the larger community. Whether or not he can participate in community life as a full-fledged member depends in very large part on whether the doors to this central institution are open. In our society man may be more than his occupation, but if he does not have an occupation, he is not much of a man.

The major employers were chosen from among the largest firms in each of

---

From "Between Black and White—the Faces of American Institutions in the Ghetto," by Peter H. Rossi and others, in *Supplemental Studies for the National Advisory Commission on Civil Disorders* (Washington, D.C.: U.S. Government Printing Office, 1968).

the fifteen metropolitan areas studied. Samples were drawn from a listing of such firms. In each firm we sought to interview the management official who either administered directly the labor recruitment of the firm or who set policy in that respect. We tried to interview thirty such persons in each city, almost achieving that objective, but ending up with a total sample of 434 respondents.

CHARACTERISTICS OF EMPLOYERS

If any occupational group in the survey could be expected to typify the sort of "white racism" alluded to in the Report of The National Advisory Commission on Civil Disorders, it would be without doubt the employers. This is so not because the employers reportedly engage in overt acts of repression against Negroes, nor even because they hold attitudes which would predict or condone such acts. They do not. It is rather the case that the men represent, as a group, institutions whose doors are open but whose thresholds are too high.

In a near literal sense, employers are the litmus papers which test the degree to which preparatory institutions function for groups which face ultimately the prospect of having the worth of that preparation evaluated in the marketplace. Employers (and merchants) differ from the other occupational groups in the survey in that they are involved with Negroes in exchange relations, as distinguished from relations based upon the provision of protective or of supportive services. As such, employers might reasonably be expected of all our groups to cast the most dispassionate and objective eyes upon the product of other institutions. Employers themselves put it succinctly, "After all, we're in business to make a profit."

Why, then, look at employers at all? Why not concentrate upon agencies and institutions which prepare people for work and assume that the return to labor will be commensurate with either the needs of the economy or the productivity of the worker, or both? A formal reason for not making this assumption is that the social structure and the occupational structure of a society are interlocked: the return one receives in exchange for his labor depends in part upon impersonal factors like supply and demand but also on custom, notions of equity, and the balance of power between groups and classes. A less formal, but not unrelated, reason for questioning the assumption (that virtue in the job market is automatically rewarded) is the growing political emphasis in the United States on the responsibility of the private sector to alter the existing social hierarchy by providing "meaningful" work for unemployed and underemployed members of minority groups.

Hence, we note two competing ideas about what can be done to upgrade Negroes: one idea is that the occupational structure *reflects* the existing social structure, and the other that the occupational structure *determines* or strongly influences the social structure, so that changes in the occupational structure can be wrought independently of changes in "customs or notions of equity" outside it. This contrast has some practical import, for if one takes the position that the occupational structure is independent of the social structure, one (in a policy role) would advise increased preparation for Negroes—more and better training or retraining—in order to fully incorporate Negroes into the economy. On the other hand, if one holds that the occupational structure influences or determines social arrangements outside it, the emphasis would logically be upon correcting imperfections in the job search, on illuminating and eliminating practices which screen out suitable personnel, on redesigning jobs, and so on. To state it simply, one would put his money on changing employers.

The employers with whom we have talked overwhelmingly (86 per cent) accept the proposition that they "have a social responsibility to make strong efforts to provide employment to Negroes and other minority groups." The finding which makes our stress upon the practical implications of competing ideas about how work is distributed more than academic is the following: in almost identical numbers (83 per cent), employers feel that very few Negroes are now qualified for white-collar or professional level jobs. Sixty-nine per cent state few Negroes are qualified for skilled level jobs. Twenty-three per cent share this view of the qualifications of Negroes for bottom-level jobs. Eventually, we will want to discover whether the employers' conceptions of the Negro labor market influence their actual hiring practices or whether their actual hiring practices are, in fact, a basic determination of these conceptions. In regard to the upgrading of the Negro occupational force, the two hypotheses indicate quite different public employment policies.

The men with whom we have discussed private employment policies contrast most markedly with the other occupational groups in the survey by virtue of their race. They are the whitest (100 per cent), the most affluent (66 per cent with annual incomes in excess of $15,000), the best educated (40 per cent had attended graduate or professional schools), the most likely Protestant (58 per cent), and the most likely Republican (43 per cent) of the occupational groups surveyed.[1]

Yet, one characteristic of employers is noteworthy in that it suggests a similarity with, and not a contrast to, the remaining occupational groups. Twenty per cent of the employers stated that they had been active in some civil rights group in the past two years, as compared with 16 per cent of the combined responses of the other groups. Since these latter groups are more racially mixed than is true of employers, this finding tends to support our conception of employers as fairly typical of the white middle-class, "nonracist" American who holds a key slot in a white middle-class "nonracist" American institution—members of that diffuse fraternity indicted by the National Advisory Commission for their support (either inadvertently or by failing to bear witness to what might be) of the existing racial patterns in the United States.

EMPLOYERS AND THE PROBLEMS IN THEIR CITIES

In common with other occupational groups sampled, employers see one of the most serious problems facing their cities to be Negroes. The control of crime, the prevention of violence and other civil disorders, and race relations generally were considered "very serious" by 64 per cent, 50 per cent, and 46 per cent of the employers, respectively (Table 18–1). "Finding tax funds for municipal services" ran a close fourth at 41 per cent, though what services employers had in mind was unspecified. Air pollution was considered very serious by a slightly larger proportion of the employers (26 per cent) than was unemployment (21 per cent).

In comparison with the other occupational groups, the pattern is that employers considered each problem listed "very serious" less frequently than did

TABLE 18–1 *Problems in Their Cities Rated "Very Serious," by Employers and by the General Sample (Q 3-Core, in Per Cent)*

	UNIT	
PROBLEMS RATED	EMPLOYERS ONLY	GENERAL SAMPLE (ALL OCCUPATIONS COMBINED)
Control of crime	64	71
Unemployment	21	36
Air pollution	26	33
Race relations	46	52
Providing quality education	35	45
Finding tax funds for municipal services	41	42
Traffic and highways	31	27
Preventing violence and other civil disorder	50	55
Lack of recreation facilities	11	31
Corruption of public officials	9	19
100 per cent equals	434	1,953

the combined sample. The one exception to this pattern is "traffic and highways," which was rated very serious by 31 per cent of the employers and 27 per cent of the other occupational groups. The largest differences between responses of employers and those of the combined sample appear on items reading, "lack of recreation facilities" (11 per cent of employers and 31 per cent of the general sample viewed this as very serious) and "corruption of public officials" (employers were about half as likely to rate this as very serious as was the general sample).

In the main, the question about problems facing their cities suggests that employers are concerned about personal and collective violence of Negroes but see little relation between these acts and the less dramatic activities in which Negroes might engage (such as employment or leisure). Indeed, employers were not only less likely than the general sample to rate unemployment as very serious (21 per cent as compared with 36 per cent), but they themselves were slightly more likely to rate it "not serious" [2] (27 per cent) than "very serious" (21 per cent).

Insofar as employers as a group rate seriously problems in their cities connected directly or by inference with Negroes, it is reasonable to inquire what employers see as the major problems facing Negroes. First, employers were asked to compare Negroes and other groups in their cities with respect to the equality of their "treatment." The response categories in the item ranged over "treated better" (6 per cent), "treated equally" (21 per cent), "treated as other people of the same income" (36 per cent), "treated worse than any other part of the population" (11 per cent). Obviously, employers split on this item (Table 18–2).

TABLE 18–2 *Treatment Negroes Receive in Their Cities, as Evaluated by Employers and by the General Sample (Q 5-Core, in Per Cent)*

TYPE OF TREATMENT	UNIT	
	EMPLOYERS ONLY	GENERAL SAMPLE (ALL OCCUPATIONS COMBINED)
Negroes treated better than any other part of the population	6	10
Negroes treated equally	21	21
Negroes treated as other people of the same income	36	25
Negroes treated worse than other people of the same income	24	26
Negroes treated worse than any other part of the population	11	16
Don't know or no answer	2	2
100 per cent equals	434	1,953

We find that over one-third of the employers view Negro treatment as deriving from their social class rather than from their race, and about one-fourth select the opposite response—race not class. And then we have one-fifth, roughly, who see no difference in the treatment Negroes receive in their cities. The main differences between employers' responses to this item and those of the general sample are that the latter tend somewhat to see Negroes "treated worse" more often than do employers (16 per cent of the general

TABLE 18–3 *Employers Assess Availability of Resources to Negroes (Per Cent Saying Negroes are "As well off" as other groups of the same income and education, Q 6-Core)*

RESOURCES AND SERVICES	UNIT		DIFFERENCE BETWEEN COLS. 1 AND 2
	(1) EMPLOYERS ONLY	(2) GENERAL SAMPLE (ALL OCCUPATIONS COMBINED)	
Educational opportunities	57	48	+9
Employment opportunities	40	31	+9
Treatment by police	55	36	+9
Housing	19	21	−2
Treatment by public officials	58	49	+9
Medical care	59	54	+5
Recreation	58	45	+13
100 per cent equals	434	1,953	

sample and 11 per cent of employers chose this response) and that employers tend to put more emphasis upon the class component than does the general sample (36 and 25 per cent, respectively).

This tendency possibly accounts for the pattern of differences which appear between employers and the other groups when asked to compare Negroes and others "of the same income and education" with respect to services and resources available in the city (Table 18–3). The following proportions of employers rated Negroes "as well off" as others of their class with regard to: (1) educational opportunities (57 per cent); (2) employment opportunities (40 per cent); (3) treatment by police (55 per cent); (4) housing (19 per cent); (5) treatment by public officials (58 per cent); (6) medical care (59 per cent); and (7) recreation (58 per cent). As may be seen from the third column of Table 18–3, the widest contrasts with the general sample occur in the employers' evaluations of recreation, employment and education opportunities of Negroes, on the one hand, and their treatment by public officials, on the other hand. Yet here again, the employers do not appear as a totally heterogeneous group in their perceptions of Negro opportunities: 76 per cent rate Negroes as less well off than others of the same class where housing is concerned, and 49 per cent see Negro employment opportunities as more limited ("less well off") than other groups of comparable backgrounds.[3]

Whatever this heterogeneity may mean in terms of the individual actions of employers in their own firms, it conceivably is related to one of the more puzzling findings: 58 per cent of the employers rate "major employers" in their cities as "leaders in working for equal treatment for all citizens regardless of race or color" (Table 18–4). Though more see elected public officials "like the mayor" in the forefront (74 per cent) or social workers (62 per cent) in this role, in terms of proportions employers rank themselves third, with the fourth slot going to "major retail businesses" (42 per cent). They as often see police as heading the drive for nondiscrimination (34 per cent) as teachers in public schools (31 per cent), or as bankers (32 per cent).

The combined sample is much less likely to rate major employers as leaders than employers are—28 per cent of the general sample do so, as compared with employers' 58 per cent. Of the remainder of the employers, 31 per cent rated major employers as "active but not leaders," and about that number (30 per cent) viewed major employers as either not caring "one way or the other" or as "dragging their feet."

These differences—in how other occupational groups rate employers and among employers themselves—may be due in part to the use of the phrase, "major employer." The *average* firm sampled employed about two hundred persons. Sixty-six per cent had one hundred or more employees, and 34 per cent of the firms represented could be considered major employers. Thus there are some respondents who, when speaking of the leadership of major employers, may be thinking of the activities of their own firms. In contrast, some companies may be located in a city where *one* major employer is so publicly committed to increasing opportunities for Negroes that other employers respond with that one employer in mind. In any event, the variation among employers in their ratings of the larger of their number as leaders in the drive for equality of opportunity is paralleled by the variation in the reported actions of the respondents' own firms in this area. For example, given

TABLE 18–4 *Local Groups Rated as "Leaders" in the Work for Equal Treatment of all Citizens, by Employers and by the General Sample (Q 10-Core, in Per Cent)*

	UNIT	
GROUPS RATED	EMPLOYERS ONLY	GENERAL SAMPLE (ALL OCCUPATIONS COMBINED)
Major employers	58	28
Major retail businesses	42	23
Bankers	32	18
Police	34	30
Social workers	62	50
Elected public officials like the mayor	74	67
Public school teachers	31	34
Homeowners	1	6
Landlords	2	3
Unions	18	22
100 per cent equals	434	1,953

140 | Major Employers and Their Manpower Policies

TABLE 18–5   *Number of Negro Applicants Among Last Twenty Applicants by Skill Level*

	SKILL LEVEL		
NEGROES AMONG LAST 20 APPLICANTS *	PROFESSIONAL AND WHITE-COLLAR	SKILLED	UNSKILLED
Median number (and proportion):			
0–20	0.8 (4%)	0.8 (4%)	5 (25%)
Number of firms equals	(388)	(357)	(363)
Median number (and proportion) for firms with 1 or more Negro applicants:			
1–20	2 (10%)	4.5 (23%)	9.5 (48%)
Number of firms equals	(251)	(225)	(33)
Number of firms reporting:			
No Negroes among last 20 applicants	137	132	33
Per cent equals	(32%)	(30%)	(8%)
Don't know or no answer	46	77	71
Per cent equals	(9%)	(18%)	(16%)

* Number of firms reporting one or more Negro applicants, no Negro applicants, and don't know or no answer equals total of 434.

the question, "Some companies have been going out of their way lately to hire Negroes whenever possible. Is this mainly true, partially true, or not at all true of your company?", 46 per cent of the employers said, "mainly true," 30 per cent said "partially true," and the remaining 24 per cent said it was "not at all true." When we consider that 86 per cent of these men state they personally feel companies in their cities have a social responsibility to provide employment to Negroes and other minority groups, the task becomes that of explaining the variation in what employers are, in fact, doing about that perceived responsibility.

EMPLOYMENT OF NEGROES

Table 18–5 shows the number of Negro applicants out of the last twenty applications the employers reported receiving for professional and white-collar, skilled and unskilled jobs. Three pieces of information are included in the table: (1) the median number (and the median proportion into which that would translate) of applicants who were Negro across all firms; (2) the median number and proportion of Negro applicants for firms which had one or more Negro applicants; and, (3) the number of firms which had no Negroes among its last twenty applicants. In each case, the figures have been computed separately for skill categories.

TABLE 18–6 *Number of Negroes Among Last Twenty Persons Hired, by Skill Level*

NEGROES AMONG LAST TWENTY HIRED *	SKILL LEVEL		
	PROFESSIONAL AND WHITE-COLLAR	SKILLED	UNSKILLED
Median number (and proportion):			
0–20	0 (0%)	0 (0%)	4 (20%)
Number of firms equals	(385)	(350)	(352)
Median number (and proportion) for firms with 1 or more Negroes hired among the last 20 persons hired:			
1–20	1.5(8%)	1.7(8%)	5.5(28%)
Number of firms equals	(204)	(193)	(309)
Number of firms reporting no Negroes among last 20 persons hired	181	157	43
Per cent equals	(42%)	(36%)	(10%)
Don't know or no answer	49	84	82
Per cent equals	(11%)	(17%)	(18%)

* Number of firms reporting one or more Negroes hired, no Negroes hired, and don't know or no answer equals total of 434.

Reading across the first row in the table it appears that the median number of Negro applicants is roughly six times as great for unskilled jobs as for skilled or professional and white-collar (hereafter referred to as "white-collar jobs"). Five out of every twenty applicants for unskilled jobs are Negro; less than one out of twenty applicants for a skilled or for a white-collar job is Negro.

The second row of the table shows the median number of Negro applicants out of twenty for those firms which had one or more Negro applicants, for each skill category. The proportions better than double for white-collar jobs, nearly double for unskilled jobs, and, oddly, better than quadruple for skilled jobs. That this is odd is indicated by the third row of the table: the proportion of firms with no Negro applicants among the last twenty is very similar for white-collar (32 per cent) and skilled (30 per cent) categories, in contrast to the 8 per cent for the unskilled category. One implication of the showing for skilled category applicants is that if the firm gets Negro applicants for these openings it gets them in good numbers, so that whether the firm accepts or solicits any Negro applicants is even more critical for skilled categories than for white-collar or unskilled.

Table 18–6 summarizes the hiring patterns reported by the firms, again, with reference to the number of Negroes out of the last twenty hired in each of the three skill categories. We see in the first row of Table 18–6 that the median proportion of Negroes hired is zero for both the white-collar and skilled categories. Only for unskilled openings would these data indicate that having applied (Table 18–5) makes a difference in the probability of the Negro applicants being hired.

Looking at the second row in Table 18–6 (and thus taking out from our computations firms which had no Negroes among the last twenty hired), we can see in conjunction with the previous table that the ratio of Negroes applying to their being hired is: for white-collar openings, 10 per cent of all applicants as compared with 8 per cent of all hired; for skilled categories, Negroes are 23 per cent of the applicants and 8 per cent of the hired; and, for unskilled categories, they are 48 per cent of the applicants and 28 per cent of the hired. On the face of it, this looks promising because what it says is that *if* the firm recruits Negroes and *if* the Negro applies and *if* his application is for a white-collar job, his chances of being employed are close to certainty. Something apparently is jamming the system, however, judging by the third row: 42 per cent of the firms report no Negroes among the last twenty persons hired for white-collar jobs, with 36 per cent reporting no Negroes among the last twenty hired for skilled level openings. In fact, the Negro applicant has about one chance in four of being hired for these latter jobs. Prospects rise again for unskilled openings, for here the Negro applicant has around a 40 per cent chance of getting (or of taking) the job.

The final table in this series, Table 18–7, shows the median proportion of the firms' employees who are Negro in each skill level. One per cent of white-collar employees, 2 per cent of skilled workers, and 20 per cent of the unskilled are Negro in the firms over-all. The second row illustrates yet again how these figures are depressed by the relatively large numbers of firms which report no Negroes applying or being hired. When firms with no Negro employees are taken out, the median proportion Negro at the white-collar level is 3 per cent; at the skilled level, the proportion also triples to come up to 6 per cent. The unskilled level is not depressed in this manner because the bulk of the firms do have Negro employees in these slots.

If there is a trend discernible in these data, a very crude way of detecting it would be by comparing the number of Negroes being hired with the number now employed, as was done for the number applying and the number being hired. Repeating this procedure, we see that whereas the median proportion of current white collar employees who are Negro is 3 per cent (Table 18–7), the median proportion among those being hired for these slots is 8 per cent (from Table 18–6), *if* the firm hired any Negroes for these positions —and 42 per cent did not. For skilled workers, Negroes are 8 per cent of those being hired as compared with 6 per cent of the currently employed, a less dramatic but similar pattern. Unskilled Negro workers are holding their own in these firms as well: 28 per cent of those being hired and 20 per cent of the currently employed.

There is nothing startling in the finding that the representation of Negroes is skewed in the direction of unskilled jobs. Still, the three tables taken to-

TABLE 18–7 *Proportion of Negro Employees in the Three Skill Levels* *

PROPORTION NEGRO EMPLOYEES	SKILL LEVEL		
	PROFESSIONAL AND WHITE-COLLAR	SKILLED	UNSKILLED
Median proportion:			
(0–100%)	1%	2%	20%
Number of firms equals	(396)	(390)	(391)
Median proportion for firms with 1 or more Negro employees:			
(0–100%)	3%	6%	20%
Number of firms equals	(295)	(330)	(367)
Number of firms reporting no Negro employees	101	60	24
Percent equals	(23%)	(14%)	(6%)
Don't know or no answer	38	44	43
	(9%)	(10%)	(10%)

* Number of firms reporting one or more Negro employees, no Negro employees, and don't know or no answer equals total of 434.

gether do allow us to speak a little more directly to the question raised initially about shifts in the occupational structure and how these shifts may occur. For what these data suggest are:

1. Despite the employers' statements that Negroes are not qualified, by and large, for white-collar jobs and are qualified for lower level jobs, the gap between Negro and white would appear to be closing for white-collar and skilled Negro applicants and holding constant for Negro applicants to unskilled openings.

2. Judging from the data on applications received, openings for unskilled jobs are being advertised effectively to Negroes, in contrast to openings for jobs above that level.

3. One way of interpreting the data would indicate that the Negro applicant has a zero probability of being hired for either a white-collar or a skilled level job. As we have seen, this finding is confounded by the high proportion of firms that placed no Negroes in these vacancies. The analysis thus far suggests that the Negro has a good chance of being hired, *if* the firm hires Negroes. To put it differently, the Negro who gets to and through the application stage apparently competes effectively for white-collar and skilled level job vacancies. Hence it may be that one of the more stringent handicaps facing Negroes in the marketplace could come under the heading, "information disadvantage."

If so, we will want to discover how the information and selection system works for our firms generally, on the simple assumption (to be tested more fully later) that to the extent the system relies heavily upon personal contacts and influence the system will leave on the periphery those whose friends are not somewhere in the center.

TABLE 18–8 Channels of Recruitment Used for Professional and White-Collar, Skilled, and Semiskilled and Unskilled Openings (*Percentage of firms reporting "yes" to use of each channel*)

	SKILL LEVEL			
CHANNELS	PROFESSIONAL AND WHITE-COLLAR	SKILLED	SEMI-SKILLED AND UN-SKILLED	DIFFERENCE BETWEEN COLS. 1 AND 3
Want ads in newspapers	83	78	66	+17
Labor unions	8	28	26	−18
State employment services	64	65	71	−7
Private employment services	84	52	30	+54
Asking current employees for referrals	73	70	71	+2
Signs posted outside plant	7	11	15	−8

NOTE: 100 per cent equals 434.

To approach this roughly, we have analyzed three segments of data. First, employers were asked whether or not they utilized a given set of recruitment channels to advertise their openings (Table 18–8). Secondly, the employers were asked which of the channels used was most effective in bringing in applicants with the desired qualifications (Table 18–9). Finally, an item was included to get at differences in the criteria personnel people might apply to applicants for the upper and lower level openings (Table 18–10).

Table 18–8 tells us that the methods used for recruitment are a motley combination of direct advertisement and of screening devices. On the one hand, we find want ads—information available to all but the illiterate—widely used. For both white-collar (83 per cent) and skilled level jobs (78 per cent), ads are among the most frequently cited of recruitment methods. This does not confirm that want ads are the most *frequently used* method, only that they are a *generally used* method of advertising openings. (Indeed, the same caveat must be respected in interpreting the other frequencies in the table.) Since this is the case, it seems reasonable at a preliminary stage of analysis to turn our interest around somewhat and ask, "What is the most *consistently* used channel across, rather than within, skill levels?"

Where the differences in proportions of employers using a channel to recruit white-collar and semiskilled or unskilled labor are small, that channel could be defined as consistently used. Conversely, where the gap is wide across skill levels, the recruitment strategy could be considered more geared to the type of employee sought—and, hence, less consistent. To illustrate what this technicality might actually mean in the job search, we could take the case of a person without a job: where should he start looking for one?

Our data indicate (Table 18–8) that if the unemployed person is not certain what skill level he should aim for, his best bet would be to ask employed people he knows about openings where they work. For, asking current employees for referrals is the method most consistently used (by employers) across skill levels—a difference of 2 per cent from the top to bottom level jobs. On the other hand, if our unemployed person aims for a white-collar job, his first stop should probably be a private employment service, where he may or may not be told the location of advertised openings. By our definition, private employment services represent the least consistently used source, favoring top-level jobs by a difference of 54 per cent.

The two methods—the most and the least consistently used by employers—have a common characteristic. Both are "filter" recruitment methods, and the knowledge of openings they yield for an unemployed person will be conditioned by (1) his access to gainfully employed acquaintances, or (2) the extent to which he impresses the intermediary at the private employment service that he is what the client has in mind.

If our candidate has neither friends who would know of openings nor attributes that look marketable to the agency interviewer, his next best bets, according to Table 18–8, are to read newspaper want ads and to register with his public employment service.

To see how effective employers rate these various paths to employment, we turn to Table 18–9. This table reveals that want ads are ranked first in effectiveness both for skilled labor (42 per cent) and lower-level recruitment (35 per cent) and are, in fact, a very close second in rank (33 per cent) for filling white-collar vacancies.

The first rank for the top jobs is given to private employment services at 36 per cent, 3 per cent higher than the rating of want ads for this white-collar

TABLE 18–9 *Frequency with Which a Recruitment Channel Was Rated the "Most Effective" for Professional and White-Collar, Skilled, and Semiskilled and Unskilled Openings (In per cent)*

CHANNELS	SKILL LEVEL		
	PROFESSIONAL AND WHITE-COLLAR	SKILLED	SEMISKILLED AND UNSKILLED
Want ads in newspapers	33	42	35
Labor unions	0	9	8
State employment services	4	7	17
Private employment services	36	13	4
Asking current employees for referrals	11	15	20
Signs posted outside plant	1	1	2
Walk-in applicants *	2	2	5
Recruitment at colleges *	6	0	0
Don't know or no answer	7	11	9
434 equals	(100)	(100)	(100)

* Recruitment channel volunteered by respondent as "most effective," not on the original list in question 5.

category. The asking of current employees for referrals would appear to increase in effectiveness as the skill level of the opening declines: 11 per cent of the employers rank this as "most effective" for white-collar openings, with 20 per cent so ranking it for semiskilled or unskilled recruitment. The public employment service is not generally considered effective unless the opening is for the lower level job. We see that the private employment services outrank the public for skilled as well as for white-collar recruitment. More specifically, employers are nine times as likely to consider private agencies more effective for skilled labor recruitment, with the pattern reversing for lower level jobs, where state employment services are four times as likely as private to be so ranked (17 per cent as contrasted with 4 per cent). Yet even at the lowest level, we find employers place slightly more confidence in the efficacy of referrals from current employees (20 per cent) than in the public employment services (17 per cent).

Asking employers their most effective recruitment source does not necessarily yield information about the most effective employment channel for the unemployed. In that employers presumably define "effectiveness" by the frequency with which they use a channel (coverage) in relation to the result that frequency obtains (impact), what we have summarized in Table 18–9 is a derived measure of effectiveness. To accurately evaluate a method (from the point of view of the unemployed), we would need the same separate pieces of information the employer had in his head when he calculated for us the costs and benefits of the various recruitment channels. This we do not have. Yet a later and more detailed analysis may enable us to approximate what is pertinent to our interests if we relate favored recruitment sources to the actual frequency with which Negroes apply to the firm.

The evidence supporting the hypothesis of an information disadvantage at this point is mixed. The effectiveness of want ads is high in rank, and this does represent a direct recruitment method. Still, one could turn the figures around in Table 18–9 and show that 67 per cent of the employers do not consider it the most effective means of white-collar recruitment, 58 per cent do not consider it the most effective one for filling skilled openings, and 65 per cent rank other methods as more effective in the search for semiskilled and unskilled labor.

An alternative hypothesis might be that Negroes are not qualified for openings, that they are not being prepared for upper level jobs by institutions outside the occupational structure. Table 18–10 summarizes the criteria employers say they apply in selecting from among applicants to each of three skill levels. We see that previous experience is the factor considered most important in the evaluation of white-collar applicants (93 per cent), previous experience is about equally as important as recommendations in evaluating applicants for skilled level openings (80 and 81 per cent, respectively), with recommendations considered the most important tool for screening applicants to the unskilled category (68 per cent).

The pattern in Table 18–10 suggests that if these criteria are the tools

TABLE 18–10 *Factors Considered "Important" in the Selection of Employees from Among Applicants, by Skill Level of Applicants (Per Cent of employers saying "very important" or "somewhat important" shown here)*

SELECTION FACTOR	SKILL LEVEL		
	PROFESSIONAL AND WHITE-COLLAR	SKILLED	UNSKILLED
Previous experience	93	80	50
Recommendations	87	81	68
Performance on tests of ability	75	68	47
Age	41	33	34

NOTE: 100 per cent equals 434.

most often used for evaluation, and if these are applied objectively to candidates within skill categories, the respects in which Negroes or anyone would be most at a disadvantage would relate to jobs they have had and people they have known, rather than to their mental or physical capacities ("ability testing" and "age" in the table).

Or it may yet be, as employers and others report, that there is quite simply a dearth of Negroes to fill slots which require of any applicant a high school diploma or a college degree. Competition among firms for the Negro Ph.D. is fabled. Yet recent estimates are that between 1963 and 1966, our educational system produced about 100 of these, so that at that rate it will be a number of years before we can accumulate enough of these types to test out competing theories as to the nature of employment barriers facing Negroes. At this point in time, we can inquire why it is that firms which have one or more Negro employees in higher level slots are those firms to which the better qualified Negroes are applying.

Part of the answer may lie in the perceptions men who set or administer hiring policies hold with regard to "potential problems" with Negro employees. Table 18–11 shows the proportion of employers who agree ("strongly" or "slightly") with a series of statements—mostly derogatory—on what Negroes would be like if one did hire them in any number. Sixty-four per cent of employers agree that Negroes are apt to be less well trained than whites, "so hiring many Negroes will either decrease production or increase training costs." Slightly over half (51 per cent) agree that Negroes would upset production schedules due to their higher absenteeism rates. About one third (30 per cent) of the employers would expect increased theft and vandalism to accompany the hiring of many Negroes. Roughly one fifth (22 per cent) would agree that the involvement of Negroes generally in civil rights activities might predict agitation and trouble for the company that employs them with frequency, while about the same proportion would expect production costs to rise because "Negroes generally tend not to take orders and instructions as well as whites" (19 per cent).

TABLE 18–11 *Perceived Potential Problems Associated with Hiring Negroes (Per cent of employers who "Agree Strongly" or "Agree Slightly" with the statement)*

	AGREEING
Negroes are apt to be less well trained than whites, so hiring many Negroes will either decrease production or increase training costs	64
Negroes are apt to have a higher rate of absenteeism, therefore hiring too many Negroes may upset production schedules	51
Since Negro crime rates are generally higher than white crime rates, hiring many Negroes could easily lead to increased theft and vandalism in the company	30
Since many Negroes have been involved in civil rights demonstrations and acts of civil disobedience, by hiring too many Negroes you risk bringing trouble makers and agitators into your company	22
Negroes generally tend not to take orders and instructions as well as whites and, therefore, to hire too many of them may raise costs of production	19

NOTE: 100 per cent equals 434.

Altogether, this table indicates that employers as a group expect most Negroes to be less well trained and less reliable than whites. Yet all but 20 per cent rate Negroes as "trainable," if we may thus interpret the low frequency with which employers agree that Negroes take instructions poorly.

We do not know at this point how these perceptions of the Negro labor market tie in with the recent experiences employers have had with Negro applicants. This is one of the directions we will go from here. We do know that 41 per cent of the employers had no Negro applicants or did not know the number of Negroes among the last twenty persons applying to their firms for white-collar jobs. Forty-eight per cent report no recent experiences with Negro applicants for skilled level openings. We can surmise then that the potential "Negro employee" is for a large number of our employers an applicant seeking laborer's work.

SUMMARY

1. Most employers do not see unemployment as a serious problem in their cities and, perhaps more importantly, most are less likely than other occupational groups to rate unemployment as a serious problem.

2. Many employers do not see Negroes as operating under special handicaps, other than those which would derive from class in general.

3. A majority of the employers see the private sector (employers, retail businesses, bankers) as *now* in the forefront of the movement for equality to treatment for Negroes; other occupational groups see the movement quite differently.

4. Many employers apparently view Negroes not only as unqualified but actually as high-risk candates for openings.

5. Virtually every employer agrees that the private sector has a social responsibility to provide jobs for minority group members.

6. Employers split most sharply over whether their own firms are actively promoting that ideal.

In brief, employers as a group tend to see Negroes as simply not qualified —by preparatory institutions or by past employment experiences—for good jobs. But whether or not the firm recruits Negroes for these jobs would appear to be an important factor distinguishing firms which find qualified Negroes from those that do not.

NOTES

1. Each contrast cited in this article refers only to the overall figure for other occupational groups and not to a specific comparison of employers with any one group as would be the case if employers' education were compared with, for example, that of social workers.
2. The "not serious" category is not otherwise reported or tabulated for employers.
3. "Less well off" is neither tabulated nor reported elsewhere in this article.

19

Toward Understanding the Hard-Core

NATIONAL ASSOCIATION OF MANUFACTURERS

[*The Urban Affairs Division of the National Association of Manufacturers has as its principal responsibility assistance to member companies in opening up employment opportunities for minority groups. It does this chiefly through canvassing the nation to discover the successful experiences of employers, which it documents and publishes as case studies which other employers might find helpful. It has also published a handbook,* Effectively Employing the Hard-Core, *which synthesizes and makes generally available the techniques which have been found to work. The following exerpt is from the*

From National Association of Manufacturers, *Effectively Employing the Hard-Core,* 1968, pp. 7–8.

introduction. Further materials on manpower recruitment and development may be found in Part IV.]

In order to maximize the chances of developing a successful program to employ the hard-core, it is imperative that there be sensitivity to the target population with whom the company will be involved. If a program is to make sense, it is important that the staff responsible for its implementation start with an open mind, a determination to put aside preconceived notions, and a desire to gain real understanding of the problems and difficulties that confront the disadvantaged members of our society. Programs which ignore the realities of hard-core life risk failure. To be aware of these realities is a first step toward launching an effective effort.

What are these realities? The undereducated, unskilled, chronically unemployed poor person tends to live in a different world from the one we inhabit. And the impact of his world colors all of his actions and reactions when he comes into contact with the industrial world. This fact is stressed because any attempt to understand the behavior of disadvantaged persons coming into our plants is contingent upon the ability to step out of our own frame of reference and grasp the impact that living in poverty has on individuals.

Most of us find it difficult to appreciate the extent to which the minority-group person living in a white man's world suffers damage to his self-respect, dignity, and sense of manhood. Without spelling out how this damage comes about, it is important to bear in mind that the toughness, the surliness, the indifference of some disadvantaged persons is a mask that is worn for protection. Underneath that mask there is often hurt and anger.[1]

When the hard-core individual comes to work for a company, he may feel that he is at least initially, on foreign soil. Much of his subsequent behavior relates to his underlying fear that he will be seen as someone different and apart—and therefore likely to be rejected.

A case in point: The manager of a small company likes to be on a first-name basis with all of the employees. However, a young Negro woman working in the plant insists on calling him by his last name. This puzzles him because he has tried to be a decent employer, treating everyone alike, and yet he feels this one employee is rebuffing him. She senses his awkwardness and, unable to cope with the situation, tries to keep out of his way as much as possible. The manager, not knowing what to do, checks with a long-time Negro employee who says, "Somehow we even have misunderstandings with the white man who is for us." He explains that this young woman has only recently arrived from the deep South, and she is not about to call *any* white employer by his first name. He adds that he knows that she likes her job and appreciates working for an employer who treats Negroes fairly. His final word to the manager is, "Just relax. You be you and let her be her. You've got to understand and respect what she has lived through. In time she'll get to understand that you're for real. Then maybe she sees past Mr. Whitey—and then you're Ted."

The disadvantaged worker is often reticent to communicate his doubts to his foreman out of fear that if he admits he doesn't understand what he is supposed to do he will be subjected to ridicule and possibly the anger of his boss. If the foreman, due to pressures upon him, hurries his instructions to the new worker so that they are only partially understood, this can be the beginning of the end. Rather than request clarification, the hard-core person may plunge ahead, knowing that he is stumbling, yet too frozen inside to stop himself.

Unless staff members are sensitive to this kind of basic difficulty in communication and at least at the outset meet the disadvantaged worker *more* than halfway, they will one day soon scratch their collective head and wonder why that "quiet guy" who seemed to want the job suddenly stopped showing up at work.

Another reality that must be understood in dealing with the hard-core is the strong sense of failure that pervades their lives. Not to do so is to miss a significant building block that goes into the structure of the disadvantaged person and that can help to explain his sometimes puzzling behavior. To the hard-core, arriving at the age of nineteen, twenty-nine, thirty-nine, or more and still reading on a third- or fourth-grade level, with a work history consisting of jobs such as dishwasher and janitor, unable to adequately support a wife, let alone a family, is to have lived with a bitter taste of failure and a deep sense of worthlessness.

If success breeds success, failure breeds failure. Again the disadvantaged person is conditioned. To fail is his lot. At the same time, trying desperately to hold on to his self-respect, he will resort to a variety of stratagems in order to avoid another failure experience. If this is how he sees the job, he is likely to feel that he can better live with himself by rationalizing quitting than to risk being fired for not measuring up.

A further reality concerning the hard-core is their different approach to time. Many of them have not learned to relate to its importance. We, on the other hand, tend to live by the clock. Since there is so much to accomplish, we are usually very conscious of the passage of time. And, of course, our plants of necessity run by the clock. However, our urgency about time is often alien to the person with little work experience who lives from one day to the next on a kind of survival basis. He may well be puzzled by our concern about punctuality. But this puzzlement can be modified if we build in procedures and incentives to counteract the conditioning that led to his basic attitudes.

NOTE

1. A company executive has pointed out that physical examinations of over 1,000 hard-core applicants seeking employment at his plant revealed the rather startling finding that the most common ailment reported by physicians was hypertension.

20
In the Matter of Allen-Bradley Company
OFFICE OF FEDERAL
CONTRACT COMPLIANCE

[*One way in which the federal government has sought to open up job opportunities for minority groups has been to require business firms with which it contracts to pursue a policy of nondiscrimination in hiring. The following decision by a panel convened by the Office of Federal Contract Compliance of the United States Department of Labor illustrates the difficulties of determining what positive actions such a policy requires.*]

RECOMMENDED FINDINGS AND CONCLUSIONS

This panel, having considered the entire record and the briefs herein, files the following recommended findings and conclusions, pursuant to rule 14 of the rules of procedure herein.

Findings

1. The Allen-Bradley Company, hereinafter referred to as the respondent, is a Wisconsin corporation engaged in the manufacture of a variety of electric motor controls and electronic components. Its main office and facilities are located in the City of Milwaukee.

2. Respondent has contracted and continues to contract with departments and agencies of the United States Government. These contracts, pursuant to Executive Order 11246, contain the following "equal opportunity" clause:

> The Contractor will not discriminate against any employee or applicant for employment because of race, creed, color, or national origin. The Contractor will take affirmative action to ensure that applicants are employed, and that employees are treated during employment, without regard to race, creed, color, or national origin. Such action shall include, but not be limited to the following: employment, upgrading, demotion, or transfer; recruitment or recruitment advertising; layoff or termination; rates of pay or other forms of compensation; and selection for training, including apprenticeship.

Findings and Opinion of Panel, Office of Federal Contract Compliance, U.S. Department of Labor, Docket No. 101, Dec. 17, 1968.

3. Respondent's work force has grown considerably in the past fifteen years. It had approximately 6,500 employees as of March 7, 1968, most of whom were drawn from the Milwaukee metropolitan area.

4. Respondent employs a large number of people on unskilled or semi-skilled jobs. Such jobs could be filled by persons with relatively low skills or by persons capable of achieving the necessary skill after a short training period.

5. Respondent does not ordinarily use newspaper advertisements, employment agencies, or other referral services to secure applicants for employment.

6. Respondent fills job openings from a large pool of applicants who have previously walked in to its offices and filed applications for employment. Respondent receives approximately 18,000 applications from walk-ins each year for the approximately 1,500 jobs that become vacant each year.

7. Respondent had for many years a policy giving preference to applicants who were friends or relatives of employees. That policy was terminated prior to July 16, 1968, the date the Notice of Hearings was issued in this proceeding.

8. Respondent's employees, like other employees, have a natural tendency to recruit others for employment by word-of-mouth, a tendency that was reinforced by the friends and relatives preference, by respondent's relatively attractive working conditions and fringe benefits, and by the terms and consequences of respondent's collective bargaining agreement.

9. Respondent apparently hired its first Negro employee in 1952. As of March 7, 1968, it employed thirty-two Negroes or less than one-half of one per cent of its work force.

10. The Negro community in Milwaukee has increased about fourfold since 1950 and now numbers approximately 87,000, or 11 per cent of the Milwaukee population and 8 to 9 per cent of the population of the Milwaukee metropolitan area.

11. Respondent's plant is located roughly two miles from the center of the predominantly Negro residential area. Public transportation is available from that area to the plant.

12. Respondent's image within the Negro community is that of an employer which discriminates against Negroes on the basis of race or color. Respondent did not seek to change this image of its employment practices.

13. Respondent, with rare exceptions, has not used the facilities of various agencies in Milwaukee which have been attempting to encourage Negroes to seek employment or to upgrade their employment in the Milwaukee labor market. Respondent has rejected requests by government representatives that it utilize such facilities in order to increase the flow of minority applicants.

14. Respondent has a recruitment system, one which relies primarily on walk-ins and word-of-mouth communication. That system tends to perpetuate the racial composition of its work force.

15. Respondent's employment practices were not attacked as discriminatory prior to the government's letter of May 23, 1968, which was the first

step in the institution of this proceeding. During the compliance reviews, the government charged respondent only with a failure to take affirmative action by utilizing sources of minority applicants.

16. Respondent did not discriminate against any individual applicant for employment or any individual employee because of race or color.

Conclusions

1. Respondent has been and is a government contractor and subcontractor subject to the requirements of Executive Order 11246.
2. The government made reasonable efforts, through conference, conciliation and persuasion, to secure compliance by the respondent with its affirmative action obligations under the "equal opportunity" clause in its government contracts.
3. The affirmative action obligation may, under proper circumstances, require a government contractor to do something more than to avoid overt discrimination.
4. Respondent's failure to take some affirmative action to broaden its recruitment base and increase the flow of minority applicants was, given the circumstances involved herein, a violation of the "equal opportunity" clause.

RECOMMENDED DECISION AND OPINION OF PANEL

This proceeding arises under Executive Order 11246,[1] which requires all nonexempt contracts with the United States Government to include certain provisions relating to equal employment opportunity. The Allen-Bradley Company, respondent herein, has entered into such nonexempt contracts. Those contracts contain an "equal opportunity" clause, which provides, in part, as follows:

> The Contractor will not discriminate against any employee or applicant for employment because of race, creed, color, or national origin. The Contractor will take affirmative action to ensure that applicants are employed, and that employees are treated during employment, without regard to race, creed, color, or national origin. Such action shall include, but not be limited to the following: employment, upgrading, demotion, or transfer; recruitment or recruitment advertising; layoff or termination; rates of pay or other forms of compensation; and selection for training, including apprenticeship.

Pursuant to the provisions of the executive order and the rules and regulations thereunder, the Director of the Office of Federal Contract Compliance (OFCC), in the United States Department of Labor, notified the respondent, by a letter dated May 23, 1968, that the respondent had failed to discharge its obligations with respect to equal employment and that the government proposed, among other actions, to terminate existing government contracts and subcontracts with the respondent and to bar it from future contracts pending respondent's compliance with those obligations. That letter also advised the respondent of its right to a hearing on the charges involved. In response to the respondent's timely request for a hearing, dated May 31, 1968, this proceeding was instituted by a Notice of Hearing issued on July 16, 1968, providing for a hearing in Milwaukee, Wisconsin, beginning on August 20, 1968, before this panel,[2] designated by the Secretary of Labor pursuant to 41 CFR 60-1.26(b) and 60-1.27. This panel held hearings on August 20, 21, and 28, 1968. In accordance with post-hearing rulings by the chairman of this panel, the parties simultaneously submitted to this panel and to each other proposed findings and supporting briefs, approximately sixty days after receipt of the transcript, and, approximately two weeks after said submission, simultaneously filed reply briefs.

The Charges, the Amendments Thereto, and the Issues Herein

The Notice of Hearing, in effect, charged the respondent with discriminating against employees and applicants for employment because of their race, and also with failing to take "affirmative action" to ensure that persons are recruited, hired, and treated during employment without regard to color. Those charges were amplified by more specific allegations of a continuing course of conduct by respondent which included the following elements: (1) Respondent has been relying primarily on its work force, which has been more than 99 per cent white, and on its reputation as a desirable employer, to secure applicants for employment. (2) Respondent has been giving preference to friends and relatives of its employees in filling vacancies. (3) Respondent has been discriminating against Negro applicants through its hiring standards, including its use of pre-employment tests. (4) Respondent has been failing to use employment sources that primarily serve the Negro community and to take other action to neutralize its image in the Negro community as an employer that discriminates in employment against Negroes.

During the course of this hearing, the foregoing charges were clarified and modified in the following respects: First, the government made it clear that it was not charging, and had not prior to this proceeding charged, that the respondent had discriminated against any individual who had actually applied for employment with, or had been employed by, the respondent. Second, the government withdrew its charges with respect to the respondent's hiring standards, apparently because the requirement of conciliation efforts imposed by the executive order had not been satisfied. Third, government counsel, in reply to a question from this panel, stated that if the respondent's policy of preferring friends and relatives had been terminated prior to the Notice of

Hearing (July 16, 1968), that policy would "not properly be before this Panel."

It is not disputed that respondent has secured most of its applicants for employment and most of its new employees from walk-ins, who are overwhelmingly white, and that respondent had refused to comply with the request of the Office of Contract Compliance that it use the services of various job-referral agencies that primarily serve the Negro community. Accordingly, a determination of whether the respondent is in violation of its obligations under the "equal opportunity" clause turns on the resolution of the following issues:

1. Did the respondent terminate its "friends and relatives" policy prior to July 16, 1968, the date of the Notice of Hearing?
2. Even though such termination occurred, is the legality of that policy or its consequences a factor to be considered in determining the steps required of respondent in order to discharge its obligations under the "equal opportunity" clause?
3. Under the circumstances properly before this panel, did the respondent's reliance on walk-ins, coupled with its refusal to utilize sources of applicants serving minority groups in an effort to attract more Negro applicants, constitute either "discrimination" against Negroes or failure to take "affirmative action," in violation of respondent's "equal opportunity" obligations?

Respondent's Policy of Preferring Friends and Relatives

As background for resolving the controversy as to whether and when this policy was terminated, it is useful to describe the content and implementation of that policy and the pertinent discussions and correspondence between the government and the respondent that occurred prior to the issuance of the Notice of Hearing.

The undisputed evidence shows that as of April 27, 1967, the formal statement of the respondent's employment policy provided, in part, as follows:

> As in the past it will be our policy to show preference in hiring to relatives and friends of Allen-Bradley employees. If two candidates for a job have nearly equal qualifications, preference will be shown to the relative or friend of the Allen-Bradley employee.

As the first step in the implementation of that policy, receptionists in the respondent's employment office asked applicants whether they had a friend or relative among respondent's employees and noted any such friend or relative on employment applications.

Robert L. Brown, a Contractors' Relations Specialist in the Department of

Defense, had in 1967 been charged with reviewing respondent's compliance with its obligations under Executive Order 11246. Brown testified on direct examination that respondent, in June of 1967, had rejected his request to abandon the friends-and-relatives policy. But, on cross-examination, Brown conceded that he was not aware of any written communication from the government to the respondent that had condemned that policy. Furthermore, Sam Hay, the respondent's labor relations manager, testified unequivocally that Brown had never condemned the friends-and-relatives policy as discriminatory and had never requested its discontinuance. Hay's version is supported by the fact that a letter dated June 16, 1967, from Roscoe B. Ballard, Acting Director of the Contract Compliance office, in recommending action by the respondent required under Executive Order 11246, did not mention the friends-and-relatives policy.

Hay's version also gains support from evidence concerning subsequent compliance meeting on September 27, 1967, at which the government was represented by Brown and Frank W. Fager, Acting Chief, OFCC, Defense Supply Agency (Chicago office), who was Brown's superior. Brown testified that that meeting had been concerned with deficiencies in the respondent's performance set forth in the letter dated June 16, 1967, from Ballard to the respondent. That letter, as indicated above, did not mention the friends-and-relatives policy. Brown first testified in effect that only the deficiencies set forth in the letter had been discussed at that meeting but then testified that the company had been asked, but had refused, to discontinue the friends-and-relatives policy. Hay testified, however, that Fager had not requested the respondent to terminate the friends-and-relatives policy but had requested only that the respondent omit a reference to the friends-and-relatives policy in statements of its employment standards sent to various schools and colleges and other outsiders. Hay's testimony is supported by subsequent correspondence between the respondent and the government. A letter dated November 20, 1967, from Douglas Stark, the respondent's employment manager, to Fager referred to changes in the respondent's hiring procedures made at the government's request, of which the respondent had advised Fager during the meeting of September 27, 1967. That letter stated, in part:

> When *transmitting* the Company's equal employment policy *to an outside source,* there has been omitted any reference to the company policy of hiring friends and relatives of Allen-Bradley employees. (Italics supplied.)

The fair interpretation of that letter is that the company would abandon only the advertising of its policy and not the policy itself. Nevertheless, no evidence was presented of any objection by the government to respondent's proposed change.

This panel has concluded that Hay's unequivocal testimony about the meeting on September 27, 1967, is supported by the implications of the pertinent correspondence and must be accepted.

The evidence about subsequent meetings concerning respondent's compliance also fails to establish a request by the government that respondent abandon its friends-and-relatives policy, prior to the government's letter of May 23, 1968, which was the first step in the initiation of this proceeding. The evidence showed that Peter Giannini, Deputy in the Defense Contract Administration Services, Chicago Region, who had been Fager's superior, had held a compliance meeting with the respondent on February 8, 1968. During the hearing before this panel Giannini was asked, and given an opportunity, to review the file, in order to pinpoint any occasion when the respondent had been asked to eliminate the friends-and-relatives policy. He was, however, unable to do so.

The friends-and-relatives policy was brought up again during a meeting in April, 1968, in Washington, D.C., between respondent and government. In that connection, Hay testified as follows: Early in April, just prior to that meeting, respondent had ended that policy and had instructed its employment interviewers to give no effect to an applicant's having a friend or relative among respondent's employees. Hay had advised government officials during the Washington conference that the policy had been terminated, without specifying any date. Even though that policy had never been questioned by the government, it had been terminated because the respondent had foreseen that it might raise an issue and because the need for it had ended, and not because it had been discriminatory.

Despite the claimed termination of the policy in April of 1968, the undisputed evidence showed that the principal receptionist in the employment department had continued to indicate on application forms whether an applicant had a friend or relative in the respondent's work force. In explanation of this apparent discrepancy, Hay testified as follows: Respondent's interviewers, who do the hiring, had in April, 1968, been instructed about the abandonment of the policy, but the receptionist had apparently not been so instructed. Respondent's supervisors had noticed that the applications continued to show notations about friends and relatives and had, accordingly, instructed the receptionist in June, 1968, to eliminate any questions and notations about friends or relatives.

There was no evidence conflicting with that explanation or suggesting that after June, 1968, the prohibited question had been asked or that the friend-or-relative point had been noted on an application form or had entered into an employment decision by respondent.[3] Notwithstanding the question raised by the delay in fully implementing the termination of the friends-and-relatives policy, the government has not suggested, and the panel does not see, any reason for doubting Hay's explanation. Accordingly, the panel finds that that policy had been terminated prior to July 16, 1968, the date of the Notice of Hearing.

As already indicated, government counsel stated during the hearing that, if the friends-and-relatives policy had been terminated prior to that date, it would not properly be before this panel. That statement was, it may be noted, consistent with the emphasis on conciliation reflected in §209(b) of the Executive Order and was wholly unqualified. The government in its Reply Brief contends, however, that "present practices . . . which perpetuate the effects of the past discrimination violate the [Executive] Order just as effectively as new affirmative discriminatory conduct."

The thrust of that contention is not entirely clear. But insofar as it requests this panel to determine whether the disputed policy was "discriminatory," that contention is inconsistent with the government's unqualified waiver during the hearing. On the other hand, that policy probably affected the composition of respondent's work force and the image of the respondent in the Negro community. Such consequences are relevant without regard to their legality and, accordingly, can properly be considered by this panel in connection with its disposition of the other issues raised herein.

Respondent's Operations, Work Force and Recruitment Methods

We turn now to the principal issue raised by this case, that is, whether respondent violated its obligations under the equal-opportunity clause by the combination of the following recruitment policies: (1) almost exclusive reliance on walk-ins as a source of applicants for employment and (2) refusal to use employment sources that primarily serve the Negro community and to take other action designed to broaden respondent's recruitment base in an attempt to attract a larger number of Negro applicants. It is not disputed that the government has sought by conciliation to broaden respondent's recruitment base. Accordingly, the validity of respondent's recruitment methods, under the executive order, is ripe for determination.

As background for that determination, it is necessary to review the evidence (which is undisputed) concerning the respondent's operations, work force, and personnel practices, the Milwaukee labor market, and various agencies seeking employment opportunities for Negroes, among other groups, in Milwaukee.

The respondent, which was founded in 1909, has its main office and facilities at 1201 South Second Street in Milwaukee, Wisconsin, and manufactures a variety of electric motor controls and electronic components, ranging from relatively simple mass-produced items to extremely large and complex hand-wired products.

The respondent had apparently not hired a Negro until 1952. It hired its next Negro employee about ten years later, when its work force had doubled and consisted of approximately 6,000 employees. As of March 7, 1968, respondent employed approximately 6,500 workers in its Milwaukee facility, most of whom were drawn from the Milwaukee metropolitan area. Of that complement, thirty-two employees, or less than one-half of one per cent, were Negro. Between 1964 and 1967, respondent had hired approximately eighty-six Negroes as permanent or temporary employees.

The Negro community in Milwaukee has increased almost fourfold since 1950 and now totals approximately 87,000, or 11 per cent of the total Milwaukee population of approximately 776,000, and approximately 8 to 9 per cent of the population of the Milwaukee metropolitan area. Respondent's plant is located approximately two miles from the heart of the predominantly Negro residential area. There is public transportation from that area to respondent's plant.

About half of respondent's jobs are unskilled or semiskilled jobs that could be filled by persons with relatively low skills or by persons who could achieve the necessary skills after a short training period. Respondent disclaimed any discrimination on grounds of race and attributed the small number of Negroes in its employ to its high employment standards, which are, according to respondent's explanation, designed to secure employees with the following capacities: the ability not only to perform entry jobs but also to progress to more exacting work; the ability to shift to various jobs, in accordance with changing production needs; the ability to perform effectively with relatively little supervision.

The respondent generally does not use newspaper advertisements, employment agencies, or other referral services to secure applicants for employment. Respondent appears to have a reputation as a desirable employer and is able to fill openings from a large pool of applicants, who walk in and file applications with respondent's employment office. Respondent holds applications on file until vacancies occur and then subjects them to a preliminary screening and a telephone check with previous employers. Thereafter, those applicants still considered eligible are asked to report to the respondent's offices for tests and interviews. Then a hiring decision is made. Each year approximately 18,000 applicants walk in and apply for the approximately 1,500 jobs that respondent fills each year. Out of 500 applications selected at random from the total filed during a recent six-month period, eighty contained a "friend or relative" notation.

This panel takes "judicial notice" of the tendency of employees to recruit applicants by word of mouth.[4] That tendency was reinforced by the respondent's relatively attractive working conditions and fringe benefits, by its friends-and-relatives preference, and by the provisions of its collective bargaining agreement. That agreement provides for promotions and transfers on the basis of seniority when skill and ability are substantially equal and when promotions and transfers on that basis are reasonably practical. That agreement also requires the respondent to advise the union whenever it fills a job by hiring a new employee rather than by complying with a request for transfer by an existing employee. Although no testimony was offered as to the operation or significance of these provisions, they are, as respondent suggests, similar to clauses found in many collective agreements. Such clauses in general operate to increase the likelihood that existing employees will be informed of job openings at their place of employment; and it is a justifiable inference, which this panel draws, that the provisions of respondent's collective agreement had the same kind of effect.

Respondent administered its word-of-mouth and walk-in recruitment system without any overt discrimination against any person who applied for a job. Nevertheless, respondent's reliance on that system was accompanied by the maintenance of a preponderantly white work force despite substantial increases in the percentage of Negroes in the Milwaukee labor market and the large number of relatively low-skill jobs in respondent's plant. This panel takes "judicial notice" of the tendency of such recruitment systems to perpetuate the racial composition of a given work force. Segregated residential and social patterns typically result in denying to Negroes and other minorities the information about job openings disseminated by white workers among their friends and relatives, who are typically white. Such friends and relatives in turn transmit such information through a network of communication from which Negroes are generally excluded.[4]

In view of the foregoing considerations, it was to be expected that respondent's pool of applicants, like its work force, would be preponderantly white; and the foreseeable result materialized. In recent years, Negroes have averaged between 1 and 2 per cent of both the total applicant pool and new hires.

That negligible proportion of Negro employees presumably was a factor in shaping respondent's image in the Negro community as an employer which discriminates against Negroes, and that image in turn reduced the number of applicants. Although the testimony that the respondent had such an image was clear and undisputed, it should be observed that some of that testimony imputed racial discrimination to a "majority of companies." Respondent's image may, accordingly, have been created in part by the deep malaise of distrust between the races. Nevertheless, respondent's practices played an important role. The head of respondent's employment department testified in public hearings in 1964 about the respondent's friends-and-relatives preference. Newspaper accounts of those hearings reported that testimony and also reported that of the nine firms appearing, the respondent had the lowest percentage (0.06 per cent) of Negroes in its employ. Furthermore, respondent's receptionists, by asking applicants about their friends and relatives, contributed to that image. Finally, the record is devoid of any evidence that respondent sought to change the image of its employment practices held by Milwaukee agencies engaged in referring Negroes to jobs or to advise those agencies that its friends-and-relatives preference had been abandoned.

An image does not, of course, necessarily reflect reality. Indeed, it must again be noted that there was neither evidence nor even a charge that respondent had discriminated against individual applicants or employees. But there has plainly been at least a "credibility gap" that probably operated to discourage qualified Negroes from applying to respondent for employment.

Various agencies in Milwaukee have been attempting to encourage Negroes to seek and to upgrade their employment throughout the Milwaukee labor market. Such agencies include the following: the Milwaukee offices of the Wisconsin State Employment Service (WSES), the Milwaukee Inner-City Development Project (ICDP), the Congress of Racial Equality (CORE), the Negro-American Labor Council, the Milwaukee Urban League, and the National Association for the Advancement of Colored People Youth Council. A brief reference to the undisputed evidence concerning the activities of some of these agencies will illuminate both respondent's opportunities for "affirmative action" and the problems that such action may present.

The WSES serves the entire community and not merely minority groups. Nevertheless, nonwhite applicants for employment constituted 22 per cent of the total number of people using the services of WSES during the first seven months of 1968. That figure, which is approximately twice the percentage of the Negro population, reflects both the higher rate of Negro unemployment and WSES' "outreach programs," designed to recruit and to train the unemployed and underemployed among minority groups.

The ICDP engages in similar activities. Although some of its facilities are located in predominantly Negro residential areas, this agency also seeks to match job applicants and openings without regard to race or creed.

CORE since 1967 has organized job fairs directed primarily, but not exclusively, at aiding unemployed or underemployed Negroes. Those job fairs are preceded by seminars for representatives of participating employers as well as for applicants for employment. Such fairs have several interrelated purposes: to bring jobs and applicants together, to educate all concerned in the special problems that may attend the employment of members of minority groups, and to narrow the "credibility gap" that discourages members of minority groups from applying because they are skeptical of protestations of equal employment. Job seekers, with a broad variety of skills, and over a hundred employers, not including the respondent, participated in such fairs held during 1967–1968. CORE has also sought to secure agreements from employers to hire a specified number of employees from minority groups, within a specified period.

The Milwaukee Urban League maintains and circulates a registry of individuals, including those with professional training, who are seeking jobs. About a hundred employers, not including the respondent, have utilized its listings during 1965–1967, and about 300 persons have annually been placed in jobs through its services.

The NAACP Youth Council seeks jobs for Negroes, the elimination of "discrimination," the achievement of what it considers fair and just wages and working conditions, and agreements for "preferential or quota hiring" where work forces are predominantly white.

The respondent, with rare exceptions, has not used the foregoing facilities, has not participated in their programs, and has rejected requests of government representatives made prior to the Notice of Hearing that it utilize those facilities in order to increase the flow of minority applicants.

The Respondent's Practices and the Charge of "Discrimination"

The Notice of Hearing, as indicated above, challenged the respondent's actions and omissions on two distinct, if related grounds: First, the respondent has been guilty of "discrimination"; second, it has failed to take the "affirmative action" required by the executive order. As a consequence of the narrowing of the issues during the hearing,[5] both the charge of "discrimination" and the charge of failure to take required "affirmative action" fundamentally rest on the same contention, namely, that the respondent failed to utilize sources of minority applicants. Such utilization would have cured the alleged discrimination, predicated on respondent's almost exclusive reliance on walk-ins, and would also have cured the alleged failure to take required affirmative action. For the reasons that follow, this panel deems it inappropriate and unnecessary in this proceeding to resolve the issue of whether the respondent's practices and omissions involved "discrimination," as distinguished from a failure to take "affirmative action."

As respondent has urged, the government failed to attack any of the respondent's employment practices as "discriminatory" prior to the letter of May 23, 1968, which was the first step in the institution of this adversary proceeding. Previously, the government had expressed concern only about respondent's failure to take "affirmative action" by utilizing sources of minority referrals. It is, accordingly, doubtful that the government has discharged its obligation to attempt to secure compliance by conciliation and discussion.

Questioning of the adequacy of the government's compliance efforts may, on the surface, appear to involve hair-splitting. For the government in its charges, as in its earlier compliance efforts, is relying on the same basic failure by respondent and is requesting essentially the same curative action. Respondent cannot, accordingly, fairly claim surprise about the alleged deficiencies in its performance; nor can it fairly claim a lack of an adequate opportunity for self-correction.

Nevertheless, respondent, under the circumstances of this case, can fairly claim that it was entitled to be apprised during compliance efforts of the rationale for the government's demands. "Discrimination" on racial grounds involves moral, and possibly legal, implications different from those raised by a failure to take "affirmative action." [6] Furthermore, "discrimination" involves a much higher potential for misunderstanding and provocation in the highly charged atmosphere of an urban center. Respondent's objection to the government's shift of position cannot, accordingly, be dismissed as a meaningless technicality.

Although the question is not free from doubt, this panel has concluded that in the circumstances of this case, it would be inappropriate to consider the government's charge of "discrimination," as distinguished from its charge of the breach of respondent's affirmative action obligation. In that connection, it should be observed, first, that each of the two separate charges made by the government rests fundamentally on the same contention, that is, respondent's failure to utilize minority referral facilities; and, second, an assessment of that failure under the affirmative action obligation will, in the panel's view of this case, have no adverse impact on the basic purpose of the executive order and will, at the same time, avoid the difficulties raised by respondent's objection to the shift in the government's rationale.[7]

The Affirmative Action Obligation

Respondent has urged that the duty of affirmative action imposed by the equal opportunity clause requires only that a contractor take steps to insure that any action it takes effectively avoids the overt discrimination proscribed by that clause. As a corollary of this contention, respondent urges that if, and only if, a contractor recruits or takes any of the other actions enumerated in that clause, he must do so without regard to race or color. Respondent then assumes that it has no recruitment system and, on that basis, urges that it "has no obligation to create out of whole cloth a recruitment system, much less an obligation to create one utilizing minority group employment agencies for the ultimate purpose of enabling the Company to increase its number of Negro employees."

The fundamental assumption on which respondent's argument rests, that respondent has no recruitment system, manifestly cannot be accepted. The record makes it clear that respondent had a recruitment system. It had approximately 1,500 jobs a year to fill, and, like any other employer with such needs, it had a system and machinery to fill them. That system, to be sure, relied almost exclusively on walk-ins. But respondent established machinery to handle that pool of applicants. Respondent arranged for interviews of those applicants and, when jobs opened up, for the screening and processing of their applications.

Respondent's recruitment system, as shown above, operated to attract a pool of predominantly white applicants. Such a result was a foreseeable consequence of the fact that respondent's employees were predominantly white and of the tendency of such employees to act as de facto employment agents largely within their own racial group. That tendency, as already indicated, was reinforced in this case by the requirements of respondent's collective agreement and by respondent's prior practices, including its friends-and-relatives preference, which helped to create within the Negro community an image of respondent as an employer which engages in overt discrimination against Negroes. Even if respondent initially had not been specifically aware of the probable and actual consequences of its informal recruitment system, those consequences were brought home to it by the government's efforts to bring about positive action to diversify the racial composition of those entering the respondent's recruitment stream.

In view of the foregoing considerations, even if respondent's affirmative action obligation with respect to recruitment were contingent on respondent's engaging in some recruitment activity, it is plain that that contingency was satisfied and that it was incumbent upon the respondent to discharge that obligation.

This panel has concluded that, in the circumstances of this case, that obligation required the respondent to take some action designed to broaden its recruitment base. That conclusion rests on the history, the language, the purposes of the equal opportunity clause as well as the procurement regulations spelling out the affirmative action obligation. Before developing those considerations, one point must be made clear. The affirmative action required herein does not involve quota-hiring or preferential hiring based on race.

Executive Order 10925, issued by President Kennedy in 1961, added the affirmative action obligation to previous executive orders dealing with non-discriminatory employment by government contractors. The pertinent language of Executive Order 10925 was retained in Executive Order 11246, issued by President Johnson, which is the basis for this proceeding.

Some light on the purpose behind the requirement of affirmative action included in President Kennedy's order is shed by the Final Report to President Eisenhower by the Committee on Government Contracts, under the chairmanship of then Vice-President Nixon, which was issued in 1960. That report in listing "Examples of Progress" referred specifically to an employer that "had broadened its recruitment sources to encourage more Negro applicants." Furthermore, that report highlighted the need for positive action that went beyond the avoidance of overt discrimination.[8] The preamble to President Kennedy's 1961 order also emphasized the federal executive policy of encouraging by "positive measures" full equality of employment opportunity.

Such general hortatory language does not, of course, resolve constructional issues such as those here involved. But the mood reflected by such language cannot be ignored in dealing with the issues posed by the language of a substantially contemporaneous executive order.[9]

The equal opportunity clause first provides that a contractor "will not discriminate against any employee or applicant for employment because of race," and so on. Then it provides that a contractor "will take affirmative action to ensure that applicants are employed . . . without regard to race. Such action shall include . . . employment recruitment, or recruitment advertising." [10]

The language of the affirmative action clause, coming, as it does, immediately after the no-discrimination pledge, suggests that the former clause requires a contractor to do more with respect to applicants than to see to it that a Negro who actually applies for employment is not rejected because of his race.[11] The precise scope of that additional duty is, as the respondent urges, not without its difficulties.[12] But it is unnecessary to deal with those difficulties in the circumstances of this case.

Procurement regulations have made it clear that contractors in the same general position as respondent are required to take action to broaden their recruitment base. Regulations issued by the General Services Administration on October 6, 1966,[13] provide in part as follows:

> (3) Applications for employment should be objectively solicited from recruitment sources which reach all members of the community regardless of race, color, creed, or national origin, e.g., advertising as an equal opportunity employer through newspapers and other public news media (see § 1–12.810 of this title).
>
> (4) Contractors should take all actions necessary to insure that there are no barriers to the employment of minority group members. Such action should include, where necessary, positive steps to convince minority groups in the community that the contractor does provide equal employment opportunity. In this connection, contacts with minority group organizations, Fair Employment Committees in the community, and schools and colleges attended by minority group members should be considered.
>
> (5) Contractors should employ procedures for handling of applicants which are compatible with equal employment opportunity. In this regard, employee referrals or "walk-ins" require particular attention, since these recruitment procedures are most susceptible to discrimination. Employees tend to refer friends from their own racial and ethnic backgrounds and, therefore, if few minority group workers are already employed, few minority group workers are likely to be referred. With regard to "walk-ins," the entire recruitment program is strongly dependent upon the attitudes of guards and receptionists and can thus be easily frustrated.

Those regulations, like the government's request in this case, are wholly compatible not only with the language, but also with the purpose, of the affirmative action provisions. Those provisions were designed to bring about the encouragement of members of minority groups historically victimized by overt discrimination, so that they would take advantage of the new employment opportunities opened up by the prohibition of such discrimination by the first sentence of the executive order. Plainly, that purpose would not be realized in fact if recruitment systems were not accompanied by recruitment measures designed to promote applications by members of minority groups, among other groups. Plainly, neither members of minority groups nor the community would benefit from the elimination of overt discrimination if members of minority groups did not apply for jobs because of fears, albeit unjustified fears, of overt discrimination or because of lack of knowledge of job opportunities. Where, as in this case, the underlying purpose of the executive order is threatened by such fears, generated, in part at least, by a contractor's course of conduct, action by a contractor to broaden his recruitment base is fully justified by the affirmative action duty.

Respondent urges four broad contentions against an interpretation that would require the respondent to take some affirmative action designed to increase the flow of minority applicants. (1) Such an obligation would be "based solely on race" and would, accordingly, be "constitutionally suspect." (2) It would be based on an interpretation of the affirmative action obligation that would involve such imprecise standards as to be wholly inappropriate for a contract. (3) It would contravene Title VII of the Civil Rights Act of 1964 and the Fifth Amendment. (4) It would also involve Presidential action beyond the scope of the President's constitutional authority.

This panel is manifestly not authorized either to pass on the broad constitutional issues raised by respondent or to interpret the Civil Rights Act of 1964, as such. Nevertheless, insofar as one of several competing interpretations would avoid genuine constitutional difficulties or meritorious claims of repugnance to related legislation, such constitutional and statutory issues would properly be before this panel as aids to construction. We have, however, concluded that even if respondent's contentions raised substantial constitutional issues, or substantial issues under the Civil Rights Act of 1964, there would be no warrant for an interpretation of the equal opportunity clause that, in the circumstances of this case, would bar the government from requiring respondent to take some action to broaden its recruitment base. Accordingly, there is no justification for further consideration of the constitutional issues by this panel. We shall, however, deal with respondent's statutory and contractual contentions because they have a more direct and more significant impact on the precise form of the affirmative action and the procedures for delineating it, to be considered in a later portion of this opinion.

In contending that the action requested by the government would contravene Title VII of the Civil Rights Act of 1964, respondent points to the fact that some of the referral agencies whose representatives testified at the hearing serve minority groups exclusively. Accordingly, respondent urges, those agencies violate Section 703(b) of Title VII, and respondent would be a participant in such a violation if it utilized their services.

Respondent has, however, not been requested to utilize any particular recruitment agency; it has been asked only to take some action to broaden its recruitment base. There are, moreover, agencies in Milwaukee, such as WSES, that are free from any racial exclusiveness and that raise no problems under Section 703(b). Respondent has not manifested a greater willingness to utilize such agencies. In any event, there is nothing in the Civil Rights Act of 1964 that supports respondent's far-reaching contention that any action designed to add members of minority groups to its predominantly white pool of applicants would violate that statute. On the contrary, the acceptance of that contention would frustrate the underlying statutory purpose of promoting equal employment opportunity. It would, moreover, condemn a variety of programs adopted by, or sponsored by, the federal government to promote reaching out to underutilized minority groups, among other groups, in order to bring them into the recruitment stream and thereby to promote equality of employment opportunity.[14]

The far-reaching and perverse consequences of the respondent's approach will be clarified by consideration of the following hypothetical situation: An employer for a long time has filled his open jobs by employing graduates of a predominantly white vocational high school, which is adjacent to his plant, and by employing other walk-ins, who are predominantly white. Although the employer has never overtly discriminated against Negroes who applied, very few have applied, and his work force is more than 99 per cent white. The employer, desirous of broadening his recruitment base by attracting qualified Negroes, as well as whites, advises the placement office of a predominantly Negro high school that he would welcome applications from qualified Negroes, among others, and would consider all applications without regard to race, and so on. Plainly, the utilization of a predominantly Negro high school would, under the circumstances involved, not constitute a racially one-sided recruitment program, in violation of the Civil Rights Act. On the contrary, it would advance the purposes of that Act by neutralizing the racially one-sided consequences of a walk-in system. And so it is with the affirmative action requested by the government in this case.

There remains for consideration respondent's contention that an interpretation of the affirmative action obligation requiring the respondent to broaden its recruitment base would import such great uncertainty into that obligation as to make such an interpretation wholly incompatible with the idea of contract. To support that contention, respondent inquires whether a contractor, in order to increase employment opportunities for Negroes, must take affirmative action to relocate his plant or to initiate a training program. We need not consider that parade of horribles. The affirmative action here involved is of an entirely different character. It requires only a modest supplementing of a racially one-sided recruitment system. Its cost promises to be relatively small. Its general nature and its justification were clearly set out in procurement regulations. The pertinent details might have been clarified by compliance discussions if respondent had conceded the existence of some obligation to diversify its recruitment stream. The possibility that other cases may present more difficult issues of interpretation does not undermine the interpretation clearly appropriate under the circumstances of this case.

Given those circumstances, it is worth noting that neither the difficulty of uncertainty in general nor the particular difficulty of this case is avoided by adopting respondent's suggestion that the applicable rubric is "discrimination" rather than "affirmative action." As already indicated, experienced and responsible commentators have disagreed as to whether recruitment systems such as respondent's constitute "discrimination." Such suggestions undermine respondent's claim that there is "simplicity and definiteness" in the "concept of effective nondiscrimination," whereas there is amorphous uncertainty in a concept of affirmative action that goes beyond an obligation not to discriminate. Whatever the relative uncertainty of those two concepts in other circumstances or their overlap in some situations, the uncertainty factor under the circumstances involved here does not operate against this Panel's interpretation of "affirmative action."

The Details of the Required Affirmative Action

This proceeding, like the antecedent compliance efforts, has been concerned with the question of whether respondent was required to take *some* action to broaden its recruitment base and to neutralize its image as an employer which discriminates against Negroes—and not with the details of any action that might be required. This panel lacks the detailed knowledge required for developing, in the first instance, the details of a program of affirmative action appropriate for this case. Nevertheless, this panel does deem it desirable to set forth, first, the objectives that such a program should, if practicable, attempt to achieve and, second, various steps that might be taken to achieve those objectives.

Those objectives are the following: (1) to increase the flow of minority applicants for employment with the respondent; (2) to advise members of minority groups, among other groups, of respondent's hiring practices, so that their applications could receive timely consideration; (3) to remedy the respondent's image as an employer which discriminates against Negroes; (4) to avoid excessive expenditures by the respondent; (5) to avoid possible exacerbation of racial tensions by action that would imply job openings when none exist; and (6) to avoid any implication of quota or preferential hiring based on race.

The foregoing objectives might be achieved by one or more of the following steps, among others: (1) a clear announcement by respondent to all its existing employees, to the general public, and to the Negro community that respondent's friends-and-relatives preference has been eliminated; (2) utilization of the Wisconsin State Employment Service or other referral agencies that refer Negro applicants, among others, on a nondiscriminatory basis; (3) recruitment through radio, television, or newspapers of general circulation, which reach substantial numbers of Negroes, among others; (4) recruitment through such media appealing primarily to members of Negro groups; (5) utilization of schools or colleges serving substantial numbers of Negroes, among other groups.

It is the view of this panel that respondent and the OFCC should attempt, in the first instance, to determine what specific forms of affirmative action will achieve the objectives set forth above. Accordingly, this panel recommends the following procedure:

1. The OFCC and the respondent be directed by the Secretary of Labor to attempt to agree on an appropriate program of affirmative action, within fifteen days after the Secretary of Labor notifies the respondent that he has adopted the substantive recommendation made by this panel.

2. If agreement is not reached within that period, this panel or another

panel constituted by the Secretary of Labor be authorized to hold a hearing for the purpose of recommending to the Secretary of Labor an appropriate program of affirmative action on the part of the respondent, as well as the sanctions to be imposed, within the framework of the executive order, for respondent's failure to take the particular affirmative action to be required of it.

This panel recognizes that the procedure that it proposes involves further delay with respect to a general problem whose urgency needs no elaboration. But that delay is justified by the novel issues raised in this case, by its procedural posture, and by the fact that this is the first case arising under the equal opportunity clause that has proceeded to this stage.

Boyd Leedom
Bernard D. Meltzer (*Chairman*)
Richard Mittenthal

NOTES

1. 30 Fed. Reg. 12319 (Sept. 24, 1965). The rules and regulations issued pursuant to this order are set forth in 41 CFR 60-1.1 through 60-1.64. This order superseded Executive Order 10925 [26 Fed. Reg. 1977 (March 6, 1961)], as amended by Executive Order 11114 [28 Fed. Reg. 6485 (June 22, 1963)], which also required the inclusion of the same "equal opportunity" clause required by the current order. The current order abolished the President's Committee on Equal Opportunities, which had administered the immediately preceding orders, and delegated its functions to the Secretary of Labor. The Secretary in turn delegated certain functions with respect to the implementation of the order to the Director of the Office of Contract Compliance in the United States Department of Labor. [See 30 Fed. Reg. 13441 (Oct. 22, 1965).]
2. This panel consists of Boyd Leedom, Bernard D. Meltzer (Chairman), and Richard Mittenthal.
3. The absence of such conflicting evidence takes on added significance because of a prehearing ruling made by the chairman of this panel in response to the government's Motion to Amend the Notice of Hearing. That ruling provided that the government's motion would be granted unless the respondent complied with requests for information made by the OFCC after the issuance of the Notice of Hearing and directed the parties to advise the chairman of noncompliance. No such advice was received.
4. See generally, Blumrosen, *The Duty of Fair Recruitment Under the Civil Rights Act of 1964*, 22 Rutgers Law Review 465, 477 and references cited therein (1968); S. 5–12.805–51(5), Federal Procurement Regulations, issued by the United States General Services Administration, 31 Fed. Reg. 13337, 13341 (Oct. 14, 1966).
5. See *supra* [155–156].
6. It should be noted that commentators have expressed doubts that hiring practices such as those involved here constitute discrimination. See M. Sovern, *Legal Restraints on Racial Discrimination* (1966), p. 43; Winter, "Improving the Economic Status of Negroes through Laws against Discrimination: A Reply to Professor Sovern," *University of Chicago Law Review*, 34, 817, 823–824 (1967). But see Blumrosen, *op. cit.* Furthermore, pertinent regulations issued by the General Services Administration do not speak clearly on that question, stating: "Contractors should employ procedures for handling of applicants which are compatible with equal employment opportunity. In this regard, employee referrals or 'walk-ins' require particular attention, since these recruitment procedures are most susceptible to discrimination. Employees tend to refer friends from their own racial and ethnic backgrounds and, therefore, if few minority group workers are already employed,

few minority group workers are likely to be referred. With regard to 'walk-ins,' the entire recruitment program is strongly dependent upon the attitudes of guards and receptionists and can thus be easily frustrated" [§ 5–12.805–51(5), 31 Fed. Reg. 13337, 13341 (Oct. 13, 1966)].
7. The government's brief is open to the construction that the affirmative action obligation is essentially "remedial" and would, accordingly, be activated in this case only if respondent's filling of its open jobs by relying on walk-ins and word-of-mouth referrals were held to be "discrimination," in violation of the first sentence of the equal opportunity provisions. But the government's brief also implies that the affirmative action obligation may be activated even in the absence of "discrimination." This panel would not feel bound by the "essentially remedial" approach to the affirmative action duty even if the government had adopted that approach unequivocally.
8. Its first conclusion was: "Overt discrimination, in the sense that an employer actually refuses to hire solely because of race, religion, color or national origin is not as prevalent as is generally believed. To a greater degree, the indifference of employers to establishing a positive policy of nondiscrimination hinders qualified applicants and employees from being hired and promoted on the basis of equality.

"The direct result of such indifference is that schools, training institutions, recruitment and referral sources follow the pattern set by industry. Employment sources do not normally supply job applicants regardless of race, color, religion or national origin unless asked to do so by employers."
9. Cf. *Universal Camera Corp. V. NLRB,* 340 U.S. 474, 487 (1951).
10. The equal opportunity clause is set out in its entirety, *supra* [p. 154].
11. See Sovern, *op. cit.,* p. 142.
12. Respondent points to the provision that affirmative action "shall include, but not be limited to . . . layoff or termination; rates of pay . . . ; and selection for training." In criticizing what it terms "the government's view" that the affirmative action duty requires more than effective nondiscrimination, respondent urges that that view applied to layoffs, for example, raises substantial difficulties, including the possibility of layoffs on the basis of race. One may conclude, as respondent suggests, that all that is required with respect to layoffs is effective nondiscrimination, including action to instruct supervisors responsible for determining who is to be laid off about the obligation to avoid "discrimination." But the problems that arise in the context of layoffs are likely to be essentially different from those that arise in the recruitment context. For the member of a hitherto disfavored group who is laid off has seen some evidence of equal opportunity in his initial employment. On the other hand, the situation is wholly different for members of such groups who have been deterred from even entering the recruitment stream by a contractor's negative image, shaped in part by nepotistic policies adopted by the contractor. These two situations require different forms of affirmative action to achieve the basic policies of the Executive Order, and interpretations responsive to those functional differences are entirely appropriate. [Cf. *NLRB v. Hearst Publications, Inc.,* 322 U.S. 111, 124–125, 129–130 (1944)].
13. 31 Fed. Reg. 13337, 13341 (Oct. 13, 1966).
14. See, for example, Report of National Alliance of Businessmen, 69 LRR 246, 248–249 (1968).

21
Help Wanted ... Or Is It?

U.S. EQUAL EMPLOYMENT OPPORTUNITY COMMISSION

[*The United States Equal Employment Opportunity Commission was created to administer Title VII of the 1964 Civil Rights Act, which bans job discrimination based on race, color, religion, sex, and national origin. In 1968 it held four days of hearings in New York City "to explore why companies producing so large a share of the city's and the nation's goods and services were producing so little equal employment opportunity." The following reading is drawn from its report of those hearings.*]

Employment discrimination at the white-collar level is a national problem, but the Commission chose to begin its investigation in New York City, where the problem is most clearly illustrated and has its widest impact.

New York's two and a half million white-collar employees represent the largest body of such workers in any American city; they hold two-thirds of New York City's jobs reported to the EEOC in a variety of predominantly white-collar industries. As the nation's financial capital, New York offers hundreds of thousands of white-collar positions in banks, insurance companies and stock brokerages. The various communications industries centered in New York not only provide broad-scale white-collar employment but deliver the news and entertainment that form America's image at home and abroad. Finally, as headquarters for many corporate giants with national and international operations, New York has significant impact on employment policies and practices operating far beyond its geographic boundary.

Paralleling the wide spectrum of job opportunities is the city's uniquely high concentration of minority workers; New York's population is approximately 18 per cent Negro, 10 per cent Puerto Rican and 25 per cent Jewish. Its pool of working women represents well over a third of the labor force. Yet all these groups have been consistently ignored by the city's white-collar employers—despite the increasing pressure of their labor needs.

EVIDENCE OF EXCLUSION

Out of 4,249 New York establishments reporting to the Commission on their 1966 workforces, 43 per cent did not have a single Negro employee at the

Help Wanted . . . . Or Is It?, United States Equal Employment Opportunity Commission, Washington Government Printing Office, 1968.

white-collar level; 46 per cent did not have a single Puerto Rican at this level.

Fifty-six of 100 major corporations headquartered in the city had not a single Negro manager—together these companies had a managerial staff of 12,665 employees. Forty-eight of the 100 corporations, with a combined managerial workforce of 8,857, reported not a single Puerto Rican so employed.

Seven of the top fifteen industries employ women as less than 10 per cent of their managers; five have less than 10 per cent women professionals; seven have less than 10 per cent women technicians; and seven less than 10 per cent women salesworkers. All of these industries, however, employ women in at least 47 per cent of their clerical jobs, and half report over 75 per cent female clerical staffs.

One of the three leading radio-TV networks reported that Puerto Ricans made up 1 per cent of its total workforce—in a city where they represent 10 per cent of the population.

A major airline had only one Negro pilot out of 800. . . .

The leading twenty-one law firms together employed one Negro and one Puerto Rican among their 1,282 attorneys. Four of the twenty-one firms totally excluded Negroes at even the lowest clerical level; five similarly excluded Puerto Ricans.

This pattern of exclusion is clear and repetitive; it exists at every level through every New York industry. But equally clear, and equally important, are the breaks in the pattern—the few concerned employers whose vigorous equal employment opportunity programs stand vividly against the failures of the vast majority. Their existence undercuts the excuse for widespread failure. Despite the myth that "qualified minority candidates just don't exist," firms committed to nondiscriminatory employment are finding and hiring and promoting Negroes, Puerto Ricans and women on a regular basis in increasing numbers.

When two of the top nine banks in the city report thirty-one Negro managers and four other banks have none, the employment practices of the latter must be called into question.

When three banks in the city each report minority workers as 20 per cent of their clerical workforces, yet the 100 corporations, with presumably comparable clerical needs, have hired minority clerical workers in less than 8 per cent of these positions, more is at work than any shortage of qualified minority clericals.

A small number of companies have launched determined and creative programs to recruit minority applicants and promote existing minority employees; such programs have uncovered a significant reserve of minority talent.

The same is true in the case of women. When women represent a quarter of the managers and over half the professionals in the periodical publishing industry, yet 100 major manufacturing and service corporations report women as only 3.8 per cent of their managers and 4.7 per cent of their professional employees, it is not women's ability but employers' will to use that ability which varies so dramatically.

The Chase Manhattan and the Chemical Banks of New York reported that minority applicants represented one-third of their 1967 hires. The New York Telephone Company has more than quadrupled its staff of minority managers —from 85 to 400 in the past five years. Equitable Life Assurance Society employs 136 Negro salesmen—an occupation which has remained "lily-white" in most major corporations.

PORTRAIT OF THE EXCLUDED

These few success stories belie the myth of the nonexistent qualified minority applicant. If he appears elusive to other employers it is the logical product of industry's continued refusal to acknowledge his presence. Many businessmen, indeed, have been oblivious even to his conspicuous absence.

Until recently no member firm had placed a Negro employee on the floor of the New York Stock Exchange; the managing partner of a major brokerage house had not noticed this fact until it was pointed out at the EEOC Hearings.

Such clear unconcern reinforces the minority job seeker's distrust of private industry. His own efforts, and the experiences of his friends, in attempting to penetrate the job market, have generally been both limited and abortive. Past rejection and on-going resistance by the business community have turned many minority job seekers toward the public sector in their pursuit of a fruitful career. Negroes represent 20 per cent of federal white-collar employees in New York City; they hold roughly the same percentage of white-collar positions in the municipal government. Yet private employers city-wide could fill only 5.2 per cent of their white-collar jobs with Negro candidates and the 100 major corporations utilized Negro white-collar workers at only half that rate.

The employment records of New York City's nonprofit institutions also contradict private employer myths. The nonprofit agencies utilize the talents of minorities and women in every white-collar occupation at rates consistently higher than the 100 corporations under EEOC study. Their employment rate for Puerto Rican white-collar workers is double that of the private corporations; their rate of Negro employment at this level is three and one-half times higher.

With personnel needs only one-eighth those of the 100 corporations, the nonprofit agencies have a record for minority employment which, even in absolute terms, outstrips the private employers'. These agencies employ half as many Negro managers, four times as many Negro professionals and one and a half times as many Negro technicians. Roughly the same ratios apply in their employment of women.

While the 100 corporations are so large that they employ about one-fourth of New York's white-collar office workers, their impact on the minority labor market is considerably lighter.

These corporations employ one in three of New York's officials and managers, but they account for only one in seven of the city's Negro officials and managers. They employ one in four of all professionals but only one in nine of the Negro professionals. They employ one in three of the city's technicians but only about one in six of the Negro technicians.

Clearly, qualified minority workers are available in New York City—and the supply is being successfully tapped by the government, the nonprofit agencies, and the few private employers committed to equal employment opportunity.

Beyond the pool of experienced minority manpower available to industry is the sizable body of young minority graduates produced by the city's high schools and colleges. While many employers faithfully schedule an annual recruiting visit to Howard or Fisk University, too many overlook the year-round resources of their own community.

There are more than 15,000 Negroes and Puerto Ricans enrolled in undergraduate courses at the City University of New York, representing 13 per cent of the undergraduate enrollment and 20 per cent of new admissions. They make up one-fourth the enrollment of the city's community colleges, all of which offer training programs in a variety of white-collar skills. There are, in addition, many thousands of minority students in private colleges in New York and across the country. In the greater New York metropolitan area alone, 32,000 nonwhites have completed four or more years of college. Approximately 100,000 minority youngsters are currently enrolled in the city's public high schools, three-fourths of them in academic and one-fourth in vocational high schools. They represent a body of trainable potential which industry, in its current labor shortage, can ill afford to ignore.

Employers repeatedly reject the minority applicant on the grounds of his "inexperience"—and so perpetuate his exclusion. Yet those same employers frequently hire inexperienced white candidates on their potential and have traditionally developed the abilities of existing personnel. Most secretaries, bookkeepers and accountants are produced through internal promotion and employer-sponsored training. Most managers and as many as a third of all engineers do not have formal training for their occupations. The majority of New York employers has liberally extended the standard of qualifiability—to all but the minority applicant.

TECHNIQUES OF EXCLUSION

American industry has developed toward the minority job seeker a broad range of discriminatory responses—some calculated to exclude, others with less conscious design but the same ultimate effect.

The most blatant exclusionary device, the refusal to consider any minority candidates, still functions in New York and across the country. Frequently it reflects the prejudice of lower-level employees rather than the policy of company executives, but regardless of the source, its effect on the minority candidate is identical and conclusive . . .

Employers who have developed successful programs to increase their minority workforces point to a second discriminatory factor in the employment process—the various "unseen" barriers which pervade industry's personnel selection procedures. These employers emphasize that special attention must be given such forms of "institutionalized discrimination" which routinely disadvantage the minority job seeker. Entry requirements, designed to channel the right person to the right job, have often excluded qualified minority applicants who fail to meet irrelevant and arbitrary criteria. Tests constructed to guide personnel decisions have become in themselves the decisive factor—and rigid cutoff scores eliminate applicants of high work potential.

Again, the hiring process has sometimes been transformed from a business decision to the vague product of social pressures—based on untested assumptions about "customer reaction" and "community tradition."

Finally there are the forms of circumstantial exclusion—where no specific company policy operates against the minority candidate, but the total effect of company action is to discourage his application and maintain an all-white workforce. The image projected by most New York firms is a white image—from the makeup of current personnel, to content and placement of commercial and classified advertising, to the focus and methods of recruiting. With a few exceptions, New York industry has ignored the minority presence. This oversight has had the predictable effect on minority individuals seeking to enter the business community.

Minority job seekers assume their application is unwelcome—and the solid white wall they confront at the personnel office reinforces their assumption. The absence of any minority employees above the blue-collar level gives them little reassurance about their own future with the firm. The consistent picture projected by company advertising—where white models portray white employees serving satisfied white customers—does nothing to contradict their opinion.

Companies trying to broadcast the message of equal employment opportunity to a skeptical minority community may fail to realize how clearly their actions have been communicating the opposite—and how deeply the old message has penetrated.

By now, new policies may not automatically produce new results. The history of exclusion can be corrected only through positive efforts at inclusion. Such efforts must be visible *and credible* to the minority community.

The EEOC hearings produced much testimony on the difficulty of finding and hiring qualified minority workers; they also produced a small but highly significant number of success stories—companies where a determined effort was made, and where it paid off. Each employer's program was constructed to meet his own needs, but all contained certain similar elements.

Over the course of the four days, various specific approaches were described; several factors were repeatedly presented as crucial to the success of each company's program. The experiences of these companies provide the business community with a valuable body of information on the creation and guarantee of meaningful equal employment opportunity.

REMOVING THE BARRIERS

Companies constructing effective EEO programs recognized that their attention must be directed to two problems: the creation and enforcement of new policies, and the credibility of those policies within the minority community. While the two are clearly linked and must be handled simultaneously, they merit individual consideration and concern.

At the foundation of any new policy is the company's firm *and explicit* commitment to visible progress in minority participation. Various companies recommended that a written statement of policy be circulated by top management throughout every department, and that it be particularly stressed for employees with personnel responsibility.

The Senior Vice President of Chemical Bank of New York, Mr. Harvey Basham, Jr., indicated that such a step was fundamental to his company's progress:

> What limited success we have had I attribute to one thing—this has not been a one-man enterprise or a two-man or a three-man. . . . Over the years major attention has been paid to person-to-person communication throughout the whole bank so that everyone was aware of the problem; everyone was aware of our approach to the problem and of how we were doing.

"How the company is doing" is at the heart of any successful program, and communication must therefore work both ways; in circulating to employees the company policy and procedures and in reporting to management their enforcement and effect. Mr. Basham went on to discuss the periodic reports which the personnel department submits to the executive staff, and the meetings held between division heads and personnel department representatives to exchange further information.

A systematic reporting process, by directly monitoring EEO progress in each area, clearly facilitates the enforcement of this policy, *but it must not stand in place of enforcement*. Various companies testified to complex reporting systems involving field offices and monthly review but failed to use these reports to effect meaningful change.

Reports of quantitative progress must be evaluated by management and acted on with as much concern as analyses of sales trends or production schedules. Employees should be held accountable for their performance in this area as in every area of company concern, and the sanctions against violation of company EEO policy should be as stringent and as permanent as any other.

22
Implementing Equal Employment Policy Throughout a Large Corporation

NATIONAL CITIZENS COMMITTEE
FOR COMMUNITY RELATIONS

A leading "equal opportunity" and "plans for progress" employer discovers that it is not doing as good a job as it thought and beefs up its affirmative action program by shifting responsibility from personnel to line supervision with staff responsibility in every division.

> We talk to ourselves and everybody tells us what great people we are because we make nice contributions and we spend all this time on committees and so forth, but somehow it isn't getting down to the grass roots in Watts. What they really think of us makes our face red—(DWIGHT R. ZOOK, *Manager Corporate Personnel Services, North American Aviation*).

North American Aviation has considered itself and is considered by others as a leader in employment of minorities. Its minority employment statistics have mounted. The company has worked hard to convey to the minority community that it is an equal opportunity employer, and has participated in many advanced programs. However, when the company broke down its overall minority employment by jobs, departments, and geographical areas, "it really has been an eye opener . . . to see how little we've accomplished . . . in some areas, even though . . . overall we look as good or better than anybody," said Mr. Zook.

Public relations policy was also found to be missing the mark with a considerable part of the Negro community:

> As far as our Anaheim plant out there in Orange County, they don't consider us the great employer of minorities. They consider us merely as part of the Orange County area, a community that has a reputation for excluding minorities. This idea is generated and re-generated in the Watts area community, so what-

---

From a *Report of the Business-Civic Leadership Conference on Employment Problems,* Chicago, Ill., June 5–7, 1967, Part II, "Case Studies" (Washington, D.C.: U.S. Government Printing Office, 1968).

ever good image of North America we have is completely lost. This kind of thing we have to work on and see what we can do to change.

Reorganization of Equal Employment Program to Involve Line Supervision

As Director of Corporate Personnel Services, Mr. Zook has implemented North American equal employment policy through personnel operations. However, he recognized that not enough progress was being made and could not be made until top management gave the program more *priority* and better organizational implementation throughout the company's operations.

> Better than a year ago I got the president of our company, who has a very good attitude basically but has a lot of other problems facing him, to give this problem priority attention. He issued directives that greatly re-emphasized our program.

TOP-MANAGEMENT COMMITTEE FOR EQUAL OPPORTUNITY AND AFFIRMATIVE ACTION CREATED AT THE CORPORATE LEVEL

North American's president appointed a top-management committee composed of vice-presidents of all major functional groups (engineering, sales, public relations, contracting, and so on) to function as a policy and decision-making Committee for Equal Employment Opportunity and Affirmative Action. A similar top-management committee was set up in each major division. Each vice-president assigned a staff assistant to work on affirmative action; these assistants form a working committee. Each major division has one full-time equal opportunity staff member whose responsibility is to get the program going through the line supervisors. Some specific activities include: the review of qualifications of minority employees already on the payroll; the review and analysis of minority employment statistics to see where employment is weak; and the review of discrimination complaints.

A minority advisory committee with Negro, Mexican-American, and Oriental representatives was appointed by management and the various unions. It has no authority to handle grievances but serves as a communication link, informs management committees of "mistakes," "misunderstandings," and "tells us what is not being done." This committee has produced some real "eye-openers," Mr. Zook said.

Results

The stepped-up program is too new to have produced marked statistical results. Mr. Zook believes that the great gain is the shifting of responsibility from personnel to line supervision because this is where changes can be made, particularly in promotions. He states: "Personnel can bring minorities into jobs, into training, but unless something is done beyond that, that is where they will stay for the most part. That has been the experience of my company, and I would bet most other companies. . . ." Following are a few examples of how the new approach is working.

SUMMER YOUTH EMPLOYMENT PROGRAM

For the past two years North American has hired more than 1,000 youths each summer and has received high praise for this program. But when statistics were broken down by division and function:

> Lo and behold, in some of our largest divisions, where we had hired hundreds for the summer we had zero Negroes, and in one or two divisions zero Mexican-Americans. Why is this so? Because we just let nature take its course. In summer employment or full-time employment, the people that get the jobs are people from families of influence. There were many, many summer employees who were sons and daughters of supervisors and vice-presidents. . . . This year we went back and in those divisions where we had zero, as well as all others, we have had from 20 to 25 percent higher minority employment. . . . The only way we were able to do it is to go right out there (to Negro neighborhoods) and recruit and hire in that location. We couldn't just open the door and wait for them to come in. . . . We did encourage our minority employees to do some referring. It would seem amazing that in a division where you already had 10–15 percent minority that you didn't have any minorities coming in for the summer program. Well, it was because the supervisors and other employees with influence got there first.

INTEGRATION OF DIVISIONS IN THE SOUTH

North American has divisions in Texas, West Virginia and other Southern locations where the local employment pattern is exclusion of Negroes.

> In one case it was the union policy to keep them out and they so warned us. Well, we had to go against the so-called "local policy." . . . In another case the local power structure was referring all applicants and it tended to be all white. In both of these situations, we moved right in, took the bit in our teeth and without being difficult or obnoxious, we got as good a record (of minority employment) in those two locations as anywhere else in our company, partly because there is a large percentage of Negroes that live there and also these two particular divisions had a large proportion of entry level training type of jobs. . . . We have made some of the best progress in West Virginia (putting Negroes in supervisory positions) where we are supposed to have all of the attitudes and traditions against that kind of thing.

ASSISTANCE ON TRANSPORTATION AND HOUSING NEEDS OF MINORITY EMPLOYEES

North American has contracted for bus service to enable Negro ghetto dwellers to get to its plant in one outlying suburban area and has worked successfully to get adequate housing for Negro employees in another such area. In both cases, the company has retained and increased its minority employment because of these efforts.

Part IV BUSINESS AND THE POVERTY SECTOR

Cities are not the gathering place of the poor—the poor are simply more evident there, with their concentration in slums and ghettos; nevertheless, about half of those who are defined as poor in the United States are to be found in metropolitan areas. It is this density of the poor population which—aside from considerations of morality—makes it politically necessary to deal with their problems.

Business does not commonly get drawn into problems of the poor as such, except insofar as these involve employment problems. (Part V on manpower training and development will deal more extensively with the employment process.) But business is very much affected by the implications of policies adopted for assisting the poor, such as are explored in this part.

A   *The Urban Poor*

23
Where Are the Poor?

JOINT ECONOMIC COMMITTEE
OF CONGRESS

The location of the poor by degree of urbanization is sharply defined in Table 23–1 and Fig. 23–1. About half live in metropolitan areas of 50,000 or more and about half live in smaller cities and in rural areas.

It is significant, in terms of policy design and execution, that the poor are not scattered evenly relative to the total population. The large metropolitan areas containing 64 per cent of the total population comprise only 47 per cent of the poor. The other 53 per cent are in areas likely to be less prepared in staff and resources to carry out specialized poverty programs.

TABLE 23–1 *Location of the Poor in Terms of Population Density Based on March, 1965, Survey of 1964 Annual Cash Incomes*

	TOTAL POPULATION		POOR POPULATION	
	MILLIONS	PER CENT	MILLIONS	PER CENT
Total	189.9	100.0	34.3	100.0
Nonfarm	176.6	93.0	29.9	87.2
Inside standard metropolitan statistical areas:				
Central city	58.6	30.9	10.1	29.2
Outside central city	62.6	33.0	6.3	18.1
Outside such areas, nonfarm	55.4	29.1	13.5	39.9
Farm (almost entirely outside such areas)	13.3	7.0	4.4	12.8

SOURCE: Special tabulations by U.S. Census Bureau.

From *Federal Programs for the Development of Human Resources*, vol. 1 (Joint Economic Committee, 89th Congress, 2nd Session, 1966).

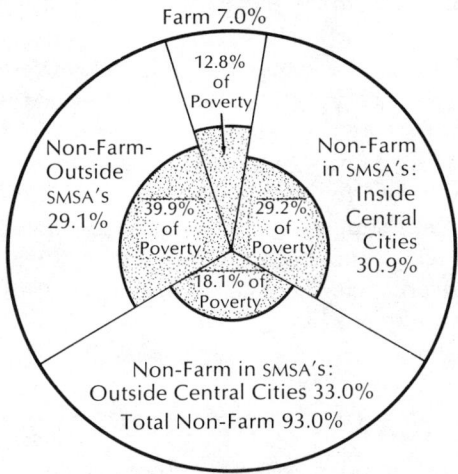

Fig. 23–1. Total and Poor Civilian Non-Institutional Populations Compared

24
Who Are the Poor?

SENATE COMMITTEE ON LABOR
AND PUBLIC WELFARE

When the poverty program was first proposed in 1964, the poverty line was drawn at $3,000 for families and $1,500 for persons living alone. Since then the Social Security Administration has developed and the Office of Economic Opportunity and other federal agencies have adopted a poverty index which relates to family size and differentiates between farm and nonfarm families. This index has as its core the economy food plan, developed by the Department of Agriculture, which provides total food expenditure of 75 cents per person per day in a four-person family (1966 prices). The index adds twice this amount to cover all family living items other than food, and makes annual adjustments to allow for rising prices. Farm families are assumed to raise part of their food supply, and their poverty index, including nonfood expenditures, is placed proportionately lower than for nonfarm families. By this measure, the poverty line for a nonfarm family of four is $3,335 and for a four-person farm family is $2,345.

• • •

WORK EXPERIENCE OF THE POOR

Since three-fourths of the poor are in families headed by a person under age sixty-five (illustrated in Fig. 24–1), it is important to know to what extent employment provides them their foundation for economic security.

In 1966, the work experience of the heads of these 4.6 million families was as follows:

3.0 million had male heads, of whom 1.5 million worked the full year, 1.0 million worked part of the year, 0.5 million did not work; 1.6 million had female heads of whom 0.3 million worked the full year, 0.5 million worked part of the year, 0.7 million did not work. This is illustrated in Fig. 24–2.

Thus, two out of five heads under sixty-five of poor families worked full time, all year round; but still their families were impoverished. They were unable to rise above the poverty line because of low wages, large families, or a combination of the two.

Another one-third of these family heads under sixty-five worked part of

---

Excerpts from *Toward Economic Security for the Poor* (Subcommittee on Employment, Manpower, and Poverty of the Senate Committee on Labor and Public Welfare, 1968).

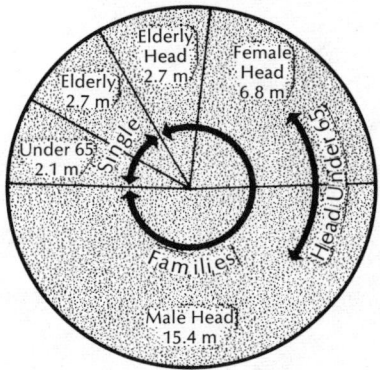

Fig. 24–1. Poor Persons, by Household Type, 1966 (in millions)

the year or in some instances part time all year round. They were unable to find full-time work or not able to hold a job full time because of ill health, family responsibilities, or some other reason. Age was a factor; for among male heads who worked, 62 per cent of those under fifty-five worked full time compared to 42 per cent of those fifty-five to sixty-four.

Altogether 3.3 million poor family heads under sixty-five worked full or part time. This amounts to 72 per cent of such poor families, which shows clearly that they are trying to work their way out of poverty. Furthermore, 1.2 million of these families had two or more wage earners during the year but nonetheless remained poor.

At the same time there were another 1.2 million poor families headed by persons of working age who did not work at all during 1966. Of these, 468,000 were men and 741,000 were women. Of the men, 292,000 were ill or disabled, and 176,000 did not work for other reasons, such as attending school or not being able to find a job. Of the women, 85,000 were ill or disabled, and 656,000 did not work mostly because of family responsibilities, although a number were in school or had other reasons for not working. Thus, of the 1.2 million working-age heads of poor families who did not work in 1966, about one-half had child-care responsibilities and another one-third were ill or disabled.

In addition to the 4.5 million persons under sixty-five who head poor families, the poverty population includes 2.1 million working-age adults who live alone; 509,000 of them are between the ages of fourteen and twenty-four, 743,000 are twenty-five to fifty-four, and 872,000 are fifty-five to sixty-four. All told, two-thirds are at the beginning (fourteen to twenty-four) or at the end (fifty-five to sixty-four) of the normal working ages. In comparison, only 30 per cent of the family heads are in these younger and older age groups.

190 | *Who Are the Poor?*

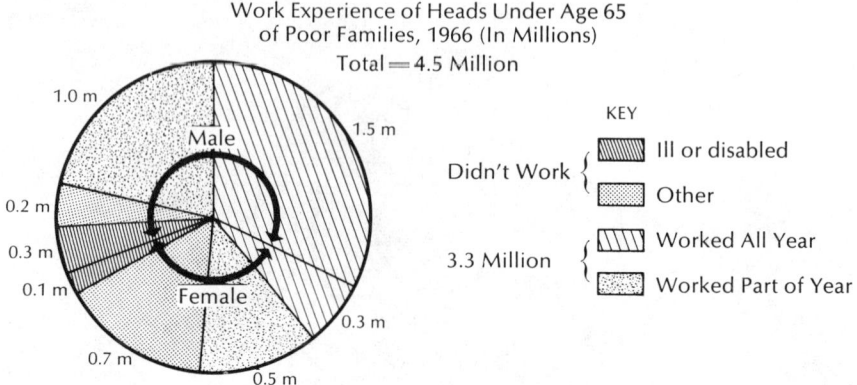

Fig. 24–2. Work Experience of Heads Under Age 65 of Poor Families, 1966 (in millions)

In 1966, 1.3 million of the 2.1 million poor single persons of working age were employed at least part of the time. Of these, 426,000 worked full time for forty to fifty-two weeks, and the others worked less. Of the 850,000 who did not work, 290,000 were ill or disabled.

MAIN GROUPS OF THE POOR

In summary, the poor can be divided into four main groups in devising ways to lift them out of poverty:

The elderly poor: They number 5.4 million. Some can work and want to, but for the majority better measures of income support are needed.

Working-age adults who can work: Counting family heads and persons living alone, there are from 5.3 to 6.0 million, depending upon how many female heads would choose to work, plus some of the wives and other adult family members who want to work. For them job creation, skill development, day care assistance, and job placement are the main remedies.

Working-age adults who cannot work because of ill health, disability, or family responsibilities: This group includes nearly 500,000 disabled persons who are family heads or live alone, and a sizable portion of the more than 600,000 nonworking female heads. Like the elderly, they need income support.

Children in poor families: They total 12.5 million. For them education of the highest possible quality is essential if they are to escape poverty as adults.

From this analysis, then, emerges the broad outline of a strategy to eliminate poverty in America: employment, income support, and education. Underlying these three main thrusts is need to improve the capability of local communities to reach and serve the poor and to carry out effective programs which deal with byproducts of poverty, such as ill health, substandard housing, legal injustice, and the other social ills which afflict the poor. In this report particular attention is given to employment and income support, which are the major ways of achieving greater economic security for those who are now poor.

B *Approaches to Alleviating Poverty*

25
Policy Issues

ANTHONY DOWNS
Senior Vice President, the Real Estate Research Corporation of Chicago

[*The Committee for Economic Development is an organization composed principally of business leaders with a sprinkling of educators. In its own words, it "has been at work on problems of the nation's metropolitan areas for nearly a decade, and during that period has published a number of significant studies that remain classics in their field. These include supplementary papers, such as Raymond Vernon's* The Changing Economic Functions of the Central City *and Robert C. Wood's* Metropolis Against Itself, *and Statements on National Policy, such as* Guiding Metropolitan Growth *and* Raising Low Incomes through Improved Education.*"*]

The following excerpt is taken from a supplementary paper prepared for CED's Subcommittee on Problems of Urban Poverty.

The purpose of this paper is not to recommend policy but to present those factual findings upon which sound policy recommendations can be based. The findings . . . raise a number of policy issues which, I believe, should be fully deliberated before final judgments can be made and before specific policies can be formulated. These issues are:

1. Since over 40 per cent of all poor persons in metropolitan areas cannot be expected to become economically self-sustaining, significantly improved and enlarged programs of public assistance—especially added income—are the only way to remove them from poverty. These programs could stress direct income supplementation under administrative rules, which would be far simpler and less dependency-reinforcing than present welfare programs. Such income assistance could take the form of family allowances, a negative income tax, a guaranteed minimum income, or some combination or variations of these schemes.

2. Provision of about 570,000 additional new jobs for adult men in metropolitan areas, and about 190,000 additional new jobs for adult women, and linkage of existing poor unemployed adults to those jobs, might eliminate nearly all unemployment among such adults in those areas. If these jobs paid reasonably well (about $1.60 per hour or more for the head of a four-person household) and were full-time all year around, filling them with unemployed poor adults could lift about 15 per cent of all the metropolitan-area poor (2.27 million persons) out of poverty. Because of the low skills and poor

---

From *Who Are the Urban Poor?* (New York: Committee for Economic Development, 1968).

work-habits of some of these adults, many of these added jobs might have to be linked to on-the-job or other training programs.

3. Upgrading the earnings made by presently-employed adults who are still below the poverty level could eliminate nearly one-third of all metropolitan-area poverty—or more than twice as much as results from unemployment. Such upgrading could require steadier work, higher minimum wages, faster advancement, better on-the-job training, and a variety of other practices. Some of these practices could be carried out by private employers now, but most would be adopted more quickly and in greater quantity if there were government incentives.

4. Since over 40 per cent of all poor persons in metropolitan areas are children under eighteen, breaking the "vicious circle" of potentially self-perpetuating poverty will require greatly improved educational efforts, especially in central city low-income areas. Developing new approaches to educating poor children might be just as important in such improvement as added funding.

5. Basic institutional changes in low-income areas will be required if there is to be an effective attack upon urban poverty. These might include new credit-buying laws, easier availability of mortgage financing, improvements in the quality of city services, altered requirements for low-skilled jobs, less stringent bail practices, better transportation linking low-income central-city areas and suburban job centers, more just compensation and relocation practices by federally-supported agencies, less "creaming" by agencies designed to serve the poor, and revised welfare practices.

6. Costly programs will be needed if there is to be any effective attack on urban poverty. The cost of eliminating poverty or even reducing it significantly would have to be borne by society as a whole. The amount involved would depend upon exactly what remedies are adopted, and to what degree, but it could exceed $5.0 billion per year (not counting any extensions to poor persons outside metropolitan areas.) [1]

7. Poverty in metropolitan areas imposes a disproportionate financial burden upon central-city governments. This might be offset by some form of outside financial aid not dependent upon local property taxation.

NOTE

1. The total "poverty gap" for the United States in 1966 was approximately $9.83 billion. That is, this amount of income supplementation would have been necessary to lift every one of the 6.086 million poor families and 4.821 million poor unrelated individuals above the poverty threshold appropriate to each. About 51 per cent of all poor persons lived in metropolitan areas, so the metropolitan area "poverty gap" for 1966 was approximately $5.0 billion. This figure may be too high because it does not take into account possible increased earnings through greater employment. But it may also be too low because it does not include payment of training expenses associated with such employment. We assume these two errors cancel out. The true cost of eliminating urban poverty may be higher, however, because of the institutional changes required to keep poverty from reappearing and perpetuating itself as in the past.

26
Creating Employment Opportunities

SENATE COMMITTEE ON LABOR
AND PUBLIC WELFARE

Every American who is able and willing to work should be guaranteed a job which pays a living wage.

To the fullest extent possible, jobs should be available through the workings of the private enterprise system and normal operations of government as it provides public services and facilities. But as necessary, public funds should be used to provide additional public service employment in sufficient volume to close the gap between the number of existing jobs and the number of persons who are able and willing to work. There should also be a full range of manpower training opportunities so that all who wish to work may acquire the necessary skills, and women who seek employment should be assured of adequate day care facilities for their children.

By guaranteeing jobs, training, and day care programs to all who are able and willing to work, poverty in America could be reduced by almost three-fourths.

In pursuing this goal, creation of employment opportunities and job skill development are two main emphases which must be pushed simultaneously. Training people for nonexisting jobs is futile, but to create jobs without giving the unemployed and underemployed the required skills is just as short-sighted. . . .

ECONOMIC GROWTH

The foundation for efforts to provide better employment opportunities for the poor must be national economic growth of significant magnitude. Without sufficient economic growth not enough jobs will be created in the private sector (where most workers are employed) to keep up with the growing population, to replace jobs eliminated because of technological change, and to make headway with the backlog of unemployment, which is still not as low as it should be.

• • •

Excerpts from *Toward Economic Security for the Poor* (Subcommittee on Employment, Manpower, and Poverty of the Senate Committee on Labor and Public Welfare, 1968).

JOB GAP

Policies to stimulate national economic growth and programs to encourage area economic development cannot take hold soon enough or in sufficient magnitude to produce enough jobs for all who are able and willing to work. For the foreseeable future far too many people will be unable to find full-time work at living wages.

What is the size of the job gap? No one knows for certain, but a reasonable estimate can be made from data provided by the Bureau of Labor Statistics. To get the best understanding of the problem one should not rely on a snapshot of unemployment on a particular day or month but rather should examine the situation over the course of a year. To do this requires the use of 1966 data, but the unemployment rate has not changed greatly since then and the labor force has not grown too much to distort the picture. Altogether the number of jobs needed to end long-term and hidden unemployment was about 3.4 million in 1966, summarized in Table 26–1.

TABLE 26–1

	MILLIONS
Unemployed in 1966 and looked for work:	
27 weeks or more	1.0
15 to 26 weeks	1.7
Hidden unemployed: wanted to work but did not look at any time	0.5
Undercount (Negroes and others missed in surveys)	0.2
Total	3.4

Recent surveys indicate that there is every reason to believe that the total in 1968 is about the same.

In addition, during 1966 another 8.7 million persons experienced unemployment ranging from one to fourteen weeks in 1966. Moreover, the Department of Labor estimates that the labor force is growing at a rate of 1.4 million persons per year, and new jobs are needed to absorb these new workers.

There are, of course, always a number of jobs vacant as persons resign or are fired, new jobs are created, and persons with the necessary skills cannot be found. No one knows for certain how many available jobs there might be at any one time, but estimates tend to place this figure around one million.

Although data on unemployment and on job vacancies are not readily comparable, the difference of 2.4 million suggests the magnitude of the job gap. This is the lower limit, and it can and perhaps should be raised by considering the needs of those who are unemployed for less than fifteen weeks and another sizable group of persons who are working only part time because they cannot find the full-time jobs they desire. Nevertheless, the subcommittee will use the figure of 2.4 million as a conservative estimate of the job gap.

CLOSING THE JOB GAP

... Unemployment can be substantially reduced through effective skill development and job placement programs, but these activities cannot do the total task alone because there presently are not enough jobs for which to train all the unemployed. For that reason, the subcommittee is convinced that a major new program is needed to provide jobs for those who cannot otherwise find work.

• • •

Massive Public Service Employment

The subcommittee, therefore, has developed a massive program of public service employment. Such a program should begin as soon as possible. Three hundred thousand jobs should be created during the first year of the program, 600,000 the second year, and 1,200,000 the third and fourth years.

The jobs to be created should be socially useful and not merely makework. Studies by the National Commission on Technology, Automation, and Economic Progress show that there are over five million potential jobs to meet currently recognized unmet needs. The jobs should pay at least the minimum wage and should be ones which provide opportunity for future advancement up a career ladder or lateral movement to related jobs in the regular economy. For that reason the public service employment program should have a built-in training and job placement activity. To the extent necessary, counseling, health care, and other supportive services should be available to the participants.

The program should be designed to provide considerable flexibility as it is carried out in different communities around the nation. It should be operated so as to have rapid application, but to achieve long-range benefits it should be linked to existing skill development and job placement programs.

Public service employment to close the job gap would have immediate benefits for those who are put to work. It would enable them to get off welfare and out of poverty, to support their families through employment, and to gain greater self-respect. It would also benefit the public as a whole through the performance of socially useful work. Since these new earners would be spending more for food, clothing, housing, and personal services, local businessmen and their employees would share in the economic gains. Through a multiplier effect, public service employment would create more jobs in the private sector, which would further contribute to closing the job gap.

Incentives to Private Employers

To complement a public service employment program, there should be special incentives to private employers to get them to recruit, hire, and train the unemployed poor. Such efforts are underway with the JOBS program (Job

Opportunity in the Private Sector) under the auspices of the National Alliance of Businessmen. To the extent that federal assistance is being provided, it comes from manpower programs, but with higher per capita costs than previously, reflecting the greater needs of the unemployed poor who are now being reached.

• • •

MINIMUM WAGE

While work is a major route out of poverty, full-time employment is no guarantee that a family will not be poor if wages are inadequate. This was clearly shown in 1966 when 1.8 million families had family heads under sixty-five who worked all year but the family was poor nevertheless. Another 140,000 poor families had heads sixty-five and over who worked full time the whole year, and 426,000 persons living alone worked the full year forty weeks or more but were poor. For some, family size was a factor since it takes more money to support eight, ten, or twelve persons than four or five, but the major factor was low wages.

In 1966, the period for which the latest data on family income is available, the national minimum wage was $1.25 an hour. Working forty hours a week, fifty-two weeks a year yields only $2,600 at this rate, and many persons received less in work not covered by the minimum wage.

On February 1, 1967, the basic minimum wage was raised to $1.40 an hour for persons previously covered. Workers in hotels, eating, and drinking places, hospitals, nursing homes, laundries, and on farms who were not previously covered were brought in at a minimum wage of $1 an hour. As a result of the higher basic minimum and expanded coverage, about 4,500,000 workers received wage increases averaging 12 cents an hour. This was accomplished without any significant economic disruption.

On February 1, 1968, the basic minimum wage was further increased to $1.60 for 33 million nonsupervisory workers and to $1.15 for 8,500,000 workers recently provided coverage. An estimated seven million workers received increases averaging 16 cents an hour. All of the newly covered workers except farmworkers will go to $1.60 an hour by 1971, and the minimum wage for farmworkers will leave off at $1.30 an hour next year.

For an employee who works forty hours a week, fifty-two weeks a year, the $1.60-an-hour minimum wage will yield $3,328 a year. This is almost up to the poverty line for a nonfarm family of four ($3,335), but it will not enable a large family to escape from poverty.

The subcommittee believes that there should be further increases in the minimum wage until it reaches $2 an hour for all workers at the present price level, and higher if inflation continues.

Minimum payments for the publicly sponsored employment program recommended in the previous section should be tied to the national minimum wage. By offering publicly sponsored work at this wage level, pressures will be exerted on low wages for work not covered by the minimum wage. A by-product might be that for certain work now considered undesirable the wage will have to be raised above the minimum in order to attract workers. The gains from such wage competition would tend to benefit the poor and be another means of attacking poverty.[1]

SKILL DEVELOPMENT AND JOB PLACEMENT

Components of a Comprehensive Community Manpower System

To some degree, all of the necessary major components of a sequence of skill-development and job-placement services now exist. They tend to be fragmented as they are administered by various agencies, but they constitute the building blocks from which a more complete system can be constructed.

RECRUITMENT

To reach the unemployed poor it is necessary to have employment offices conveniently located in urban neighborhoods where the poor reside and in readily accessible sites in rural areas. Many neighborhood residents will come to these offices on their own, especially if they hear of others who have obtained assistance there. Some can be brought in only through outreach activities which go to the hanging-out spots and door to door, and field staff who live in the neighborhood can often do the most effective recruitment. Referral from other agencies and organizations, particularly those in close touch with the poor, is another method of finding recruits.

The basic public source of employment recruitment during the past three decades has been the United States Employment Service. Over the years, however, the Employment Service has tended to become employer oriented, and in the process of trying to shed an early "unemployment" image has developed large, impersonal offices in downtown locations. However, beginning with some experimental and demonstration projects under the Manpower Development and Training Act, a reversal of this trend was started. This was followed by the establishment of Youth Opportunity Centers, and the assignment of personnel to neighborhood offices opened by community action agencies. More recently a human resources development program has sought to extend special services to disadvantaged adults as well as youth. While further progress is needed, the Employment Service is heading in the right direction. . . .

INTAKE, ASSESSMENT, AND ORIENTATION

Once at the employment center, individualized service is required to assist the applicant in obtaining a placement in training or work best suited to his personal needs. Testing sometimes helps, but many of the standard tests are often not suitable since they require reading and verbal ability beyond the present capability of the applicant. Thus, the traditional general aptitude test battery (GATB), developed and used by the United States Employment Service, has come to be administered with greater flexibility, and new techniques have been originated, such as work sampling whereby the applicant actually has a tryout in varied work tasks.

Counseling is an essential part of the process. This is done both individually and in groups, and the latter has come to be practiced in orientation sessions lasting from one to four weeks. Out of this process comes an employability plan which relates individual needs to available opportunities for training and work. As this plan is carried out, personnel from the employment center continue to assist the applicant until he has obtained stable employment.

In the newly established employment centers serving the unemployed poor, interviewing, testing, and counseling is done by the employment service-community action team. The general policy is to permit the Employment Service to be the "presumptive" sponsor of these services; that is, to have the first option, and to bring the community action agency or one of its delegate agencies into the picture when the Employment Service is unwilling or unable to participate. In practice, the Employment Service generally provides placement interviewers, job developers, and some counselors, and the community action agency provides nonprofessional neighborhood workers, additional counselors, and supportive services.

Group counseling to provide information on how to find a job, what employers expect, grooming, and related matters has evolved into regular orientation sessions. These are now becoming a central feature of the Labor Department's concentrated employment program.

WORK EXPERIENCE

For some of the applicants, the first need is to gain some actual work experience. This is particularly true for youthful applicants, who may have never held a job or at best have had spotty employment records; but some adults who have suffered long-term unemployment may require a period of work experience before they can move into job-skill training programs or be placed in jobs. Moreover, in many localities, public service work is needed to fill the job gap between the number of existing jobs and the number of applicants who want to work.

The kind of work should vary. Some persons should be placed in work crews where they can have close direction, the counseling of a skilled supervisor, and the experience of working with others. Other persons can be placed in individual assignments, particularly those which have career possibilities. For a small proportion, sheltered workshops are necessary. In all instances, the work should have a built-in training component and to the extent feasible should lead to opportunities in regular employment.

• • •

BASIC EDUCATION

Those of very low educational attainment need literacy training and fundamental education, particularly in English and mathematics. Because of previously unsatisfactory experience with school, many do better in informal situations which differ from the traditional classroom. For most, basic education seems to be most successful if it is woven into other work and job-skill training programs, for then the application of what is taught is more apparent and relevant. In some instances, individual or small-group tutoring can be a valuable part of a basic education program.

• • •

JOB-SKILL TRAINING

Because most of the low-income unemployed lack the necessary skills for many of the available jobs, some form of job-skill training is a prerequisite to employment. These are persons who did not learn a skill in school and who have not had enough of the right kind of work experience to acquire skills which are in demand. Two basic forms of job-skill training have evolved: institutional and on the job, sometimes in sequence or in combination.

Institutional training gets its name because it is conducted in school buildings, workshop classrooms, or similar settings apart from the place of work. Such training might be carried out in a vocational school in late afternoon and evening, in a skill center specially designed for this purpose, in scattered shop-instructional units, or on the premises of a private employer, but apart from regular production.

On-the-job training is conducted at places of work, such as factories, offices, retail shops, and public agencies, actually performing productive work. When most successful, the trainee stays on as a regular employee at the end of training. In some instances, trainees spend part of the day in basic education or institutional training, or they might have such training first and then move to full-time, on-the-job training. This combined program is known as "coupled" training.

Job-skill training is scattered among a variety of programs. The first and still the basic program was established by the Manpower Development and Training Act of 1962 (MDTA). In the beginning, primary attention was given to retraining family heads displaced from established jobs by technological and economic change, but over the years, as economic growth caused the employment picture to brighten, the program has shifted to serve greater numbers of the disadvantaged. In 1966 three out of four family heads in institutional training had earnings covered by social security of less than $3,000, while only two out of five OJT family heads had such low incomes.

MDTA institutional training was originally conducted mainly in vocational schools after hours, but in recent years special skill centers have been developed. The community action program [CAP] has also assisted in the establishment of skill centers, especially through the funding of opportunity industrialization centers.

Both MDTA and CAP have also developed preapprenticeship programs, in large part to assist youths from minority groups to enter apprenticeship in various trades. On-the-job training has been a major feature of MDTA, and the proportion of trainees enrolled in this phase has grown each year. More recently the "coupled" program was developed to combine institutional and on-the-job training. On-the-job training has always been contracted with employers, and in June 1967 an experimental program of contracting "coupled" programs with private firms was initiated. The Labor Department is currently trying to extend this approach in a program which would give private employers greater incentives to train and hire the unemployed poor. . . .

JOB DEVELOPMENT AND PLACEMENT

The payoff of the entire process, of course, is placement in steady jobs which pay living wages. Here the full realm of private and public employment opportunities must be tapped. This will take, in addition to the routine operations of employment agencies, special efforts to enlist the cooperation of private employers and public agencies. Placement can often be facilitated by getting employers involved in the training program, ranging from curriculum design to the assignment of instructor-supervisors who will stay with the trainees when they move into regular jobs. Public agencies can develop new careers which offer employment opportunities with a future in community service fields. Ties with fair employment programs can help training and placement programs gain access to previously closed job opportunities.

Job placement seems to be the weakest link even though it is the most important. This is a result of many forces. As was noted in the previous chapter, racial discrimination in employment is widespread and many of the unemployed poor are minority group members. Most private employers are reluctant to hire the hard-core unemployed, who often have spotty employment histories, and in many instances police records. Moreover, sometimes entry requirements are higher than the job demand. Employers hire for productivity and profit and not for a social concern, and to date economic incentives have been too low or nonexistent. Public agencies have barriers, too. In particular, the civil service systems of federal, state, and local governments are far more rigid than is necessary to preserve the principle of merit hiring. At the same time many newer agencies with a concern for employment, especially, community action agencies, have not established effective relations with employers, and the Employment Service, which has the employer contacts, is only slowly coming to the aid of the unemployed poor.

• • •

SUPPORTIVE SERVICES

Throughout the sequence of skill-development and job placement services, community manpower programs must deal with certain social-psychological factors which prevent many of the unemployed poor from obtaining and holding jobs. Certain poor people seem to be committed to a particular style of life which prevents them from coming out of their geographical areas of friendship groups if required to do so to obtain employment opportunities. Some even fear success in training programs because they would then enter new job situations which are strange and unsettling and thus a break from the accustomed way of life. There are those who are beset with problems of consumer debt or other legal difficulties, and this interferes with their efforts of skill improvement. Many have health problems.

Thus, a full array of supportive services is required. Continuous counseling during training and for a period on the new job is needed, and this can be accomplished both by professional counselors and by trainer-coaches who are specially trained for this task. Health services, legal services, consumer education, and a host of other individual services should be provided, not necessarily in the employment center itself but at least conveniently available. And as was pointed out in the previous chapter, day care is needed for children of mothers who seek training and employment.

A host of supportive services have been made available, generally through the efforts of community action agencies. At best, an employment center is functionally a part of a neighborhood services system which ties together existing social services and new activities initiated as part of the poverty program. This mobilization of community resources has been a major contribution of the community action program.

FOLLOWUP

Lastly, there must be followup to assure that training graduates achieve success on the job. This might include a push to get new workers to work regularly and on time as they try to break the long habit of irregular employment. It might consist of continuing supportive services. Certainly for working mothers it will require ongoing day-care programs.

A concern for followup has developed in many of the neighborhood employment centers as they have come to realize that the unemployed poor need continuing assistance as they enter the world of work. This has tended to be a function of community action agencies and their delegate agencies, often performed by neighborhood workers.

More recently trainer-coaches have been hired, sometimes by employers, sometimes by other agencies, to stay with trainees and new workers until they have become properly acclimated to their new jobs. This is another innovation being promoted by the concentrated employment program.

• • •

Community Manpower Systems

The goal should be to have a complete community manpower system in each labor market area throughout the United States. This would mean each metropolitan area and each rural development district. Ideally, planning and implementation machinery in the labor market area would make it possible to prepare and carry out an annual plan which would guarantee a job at a living wage, or paid training leading to employment, to everyone who is able and willing to work. Thus, the community manpower system would have an appropriate mixture of training activities, public service employment to fill the job gap and necessary supportive services. This mix would vary from one community to another, and within a community it would be modified from year to year and within a program year to respond to changing local conditions. An area with a labor shortage would place very heavy emphasis upon training while an economically depressed area would need a greater reservoir of public service employment.

Most of the federal support for the community manpower system should come in a single, annual package through a prime sponsor, which would delegate many of the operations to other agencies. However, the federal agencies handling the funds would need to reserve the right of independent funding to worthy local programs which for some reason or other are excluded from the overall package, such as activities run by private businesses, grassroot organizations, and other worthy groups not part of the system.

If provided enough resources, this comprehensive local program could make good on the promise of a job or paid training to all seeking work. Those covered by unemployment insurance could turn to this system even while receiving unemployment benefits, and when such benefits are exhausted they could rely upon the guarantee of job or training for income support as well as an opportunity to obtain employment. It seems to the subcommittee that federal support to the long-term unemployed in this manner would be preferable to extended benefits under the unemployment compensation system.

These community manpower plans would together form the basis for state and regional plans. They would be major building blocks for a national plan for manpower training and full employment. Through a system of advanced planning and forecasting, subject to necessary revisions later, a national plan could be fitted into the budgetary process of the federal government. Annually Congress would receive estimates of the resources needed to provide a job for everyone able and willing to work and to decide whether sufficient resources could be allocated to achieve that goal. Furthermore, a national manpower plan would consider what skills are required to achieve national goals, as identified from time to time.[2]

NOTES

1. For a different appraisal of the value of the minimum wage, see the comment by Sar Levitan, p. 206.
2. Further materials on manpower training and development will be found in Part V.

27
Minimum Wage Legislation: A Limited Tool

SAR A. LEVITAN
*Center for Manpower Policy Studies,
George Washington University*

Low wages are a major aspect of poverty. Nearly three of every ten poor family heads and a tenth of all the poor unrelated individuals worked at a full-time job during the whole of 1963. This raises the question whether positive government action to raise minimum wages would be an effective means to combat poverty. The federal government and many of the states have already answered this question in the affirmative.

• • •

Economists appear to be less than fully agreed on advice to policymakers on the impact of minimum wage legislation upon employment and disemployment. In the final analysis, the economist's conclusion will depend upon which he believes deep down in his heart to be true and he will be able to marshal facts to support his conclusion.

In general, those who favor substantial raises in minimum wages base their arguments on social and humanitarian objections to substandard wages and on an economic need to widen the base of consumer purchasing power. Opponents retort that minimum wage legislation extends the evils of governmental interference with free market forces and that arbitrary meddling with the determination of minimum wages may cause disemployment and, therefore, achieve the opposite of the objectives intended by the proponents of minimum wage legislation.

Even most proponents would agree that minimum wages should not be raised more rapidly than average wages in American industry. There is little precision in measurement of productivity trends in low-wage industries affected by minimum wage legislation, but probably the most reasonable assumption is that the rise of productivity in these industries is no greater than in the rest of the American economy. If this is correct, it would indicate that boosts in minimum wage legislation should be limited *at most* to the rise in cost of living plus average increases in productivity. This rule of thumb suggests implications for federal minimum wage policy in the short run. During

---

From "The Poor in the Work Force," printed by permission of the Task Force on Economic Growth and Opportunity, Chamber of Commerce of the United States, the third report of the Task Force on the Study of Poverty, *The Disadvantaged Poor: Education and Employment* (1966), pp. 304, 308–309.

the first four years following September 1961, the effective date for the latest amendments to the Fair Labor Standards Act, average wage rates in manufacturing, exclusive of fringe benefit costs, rose by about 15 per cent while minimum wages have been boosted by 25 per cent. This fact alone should possibly indicate the need of exercising caution in considering any further increases in minimum wages over the next few years, assuming the continuation of recent trends in overall productivity and consumer prices. Moreover, the most acute unemployment problem we are now facing is found among teenagers who normally enter the labor force in lower-paid jobs. Additional boosts in minimum wages might thus tend to impede further the hiring in covered jobs of young new entrants to the labor force. But some have questioned whether concern over possible adverse affect on youth employment should be a controlling factor in raising minimum wages. They point to the fact that widespread poverty among heads of families who work on full-time jobs suggests that for millions of adult workers statutory minimum rates are not only entry wages but determinants of income throughout their lifetime. Cogent as this argument might appear, it leaves unanswered a more basic issue, namely, whether as many low-paying jobs would remain if minimum rates were raised above levels justified by the productivity of the affected workers. At best, therefore, it would appear that minimum wage legislation is only a limited tool in the war on poverty.

28
Private Enterprise Participation in Antipoverty Programs

STEPHEN KURZMAN

NEIGHBORHOOD YOUTH CORPS AND ADULT WORK EXPERIENCE PROGRAMS

Under the 1964 Economic Opportunity Act the Neighborhood Youth Corps (NYC), delegated by Presidential order to the Department of Labor, was originally designed as an entirely governmental and nonprofit-operated work experience program for unemployed, disadvantaged youths aged sixteen through twenty-one years. Its basic emphasis was on encouraging potential

---

Report prepared for the Subcommittee on Employment, Manpower, and Poverty of the Senate Committee on Labor and Public Welfare, appearing in *Examination of the War on Poverty,* vol. 1 (1967).

dropouts to remain in high school and on encouraging unemployed dropouts to return to school. In both cases the technique used was to provide on-the-job experience at the minimum wage—in the case of students, part time, and in the case of dropouts, full time—but in both cases exclusively in the public or nonprofit sector.[1]

The express goal was not only to make disadvantaged youths more employable, either directly or through a return to high school, but to augment the manpower of labor-short public and nonprofit agencies, particularly in public hospitals and schools and in governmental offices and recreation facilities.[2]

• • •

Federal assistance to NYC amounts to 90 per cent of cost and the local sponsor, which is now often a community action agency, is required to match with 10 per cent. A popular program, NYC has grown from an initial size of almost 278,000 enrollees, more than 65 per cent of whom were in school, during the first, partial fiscal year, 1965, to 394,000 in fiscal 1967, including 177,000 in the summer program. The budget in fiscal 1966 was $271 million and in fiscal 1967 was $325 million.

Clearly these figures reflect vastly larger numbers of people than any other manpower program. But . . . the effectiveness of the NYC program so far in vocational training and ultimate job placements . . . has been questioned. It has been argued that the public and nonprofit sponsors have tended to employ the enrollees for only six to nine months in menial tasks in which the training content and advancing employment opportunities are very low. . . . A recently published study,[3] financed by the [Labor] Department, concluded from a sample of 1,988 out-of-school enrollees that 59 per cent were working, or were in the armed services, in school, or in training when contacted five to fifteen months after they left NYC projects. The 35 per cent who had jobs or were in the armed services were being paid an hourly wage of $1.54 and were working an average 38-hour week. Forty per cent of those now working had found jobs through their own efforts. . . .

In the 1966 EOA amendments the Congress broadened the NYC provisions substantially in order to authorize private profit-oriented sponsorship of NYC projects. Dropping the earlier language relating to public work and conservation, the new provisions call for "part-time employment, on-the-job training and useful work experience" for dropouts and students from low-income families, "combined where needed with educational and training assistance, including basic literacy and occupational training designed to assist individuals to develop their maximum occupational potential." [4]

• • •

Under the amendments the Director is authorized to enter into agreements with "other than public or private nonprofit organizations" to pay reasonable training costs but not wages paid to enrollees for services performed. As in the case of MDTA-OJT, the employer is required to pay the minimum wage to the trainees. In addition, the amendments authorize testing, counseling job development, and referral services to youths through private, profit-oriented companies as well as through public and nonprofit agencies.[5]

• • •

Two of the new adult programs are limited to public agencies and some, at least potentially, are available to private employers. The new programs consist of:

1. Operation Mainstream under section 205(d) of the Economic Opportunity Act, added by amendment in 1965, which provides conservation and beautification work in small towns and rural areas for chronically unemployed poor adults, especially the aged. This is operated entirely by public or private nonprofit agencies under a $36.5 million budget for fiscal year 1967.

2. New Careers Program under EOA section 205(e), added in 1966, which offers subprofessional community betterment work in cities for chronically unemployed adults. Also currently budgeted for $36.5 million, this program may include contracts with profitmaking companies.

3. Special Impact Program under part D of title II, EOA, added in 1966, provides neighborhoodwide work experience and training projects in a few neighborhoods having especially high concentrations of the unemployed. Budgeted for $25 million, the program includes contracts with profitmaking companies as well as grants to public or private nonprofit organizations.

• • •

The Special Impact Program has so far developed one $7-million contract, for jobs and training for 2,700 persons in the Bedford-Stuyvesant area of Brooklyn, N.Y., over the next two years. The four-part program is designed to include:

1. Renovation of a warehouse in the area to provide a new community building. The eighteen-month project will seek to employ 100 area building trades craftsmen at union wages and provide work-training opportunities for an additional seventy-five unemployed or underemployed youths.

2. An industrial development and job-creation program which will seek to attract about twenty-five business enterprises to the area and create 1,000 to 2,000 new jobs. An estimated 650 of the persons filling these jobs will require MDTA-OJT.

3. A community rehabilitation planning program to provide work training for forty students and forty unemployed and underemployed youths, job opportunities in community planning and rehabilitation programs, and twenty-four entry level jobs in public and private community agencies.

4. A community home improvement program which will seek to provide jobs for thirty-four unemployed and underemployed craftsmen at union scale rates and work-training opportunities for 272 youths. The two groups will form teams to help renovate the exteriors of about 750 homes in the area. The entire program will be administered jointly by two nonprofit corporations, one composed of local leaders, the other of prominent businessmen. Also involved more or less formally will be a city agency, the Bedford-Stuyvesant Manpower Center of New York City's Human Resources Administra-

tion; a CAA [Community Action Agency], the Youth-in-Action Community Action Agency; a state agency, the New York State Employment Service; and the Bedford-Stuyvesant Open Industry Center, a nonprofit organization created to operate the new community training centers. The businessmen's corporation, among other tasks, will seek to persuade major New York banks to create a pool of funds to provide mortgages for individual homeowners, who generally are unable to obtain financing in such deteriorated areas, in turn because of the unavailability of fire insurance in such areas, among other reasons.

Clearly the opportunity for business involvement is greatest in programs such as this, where the express purpose is to achieve that involvement. . . .

The short experience so far indicates that the CAA's in most of the cities are so nonprofit-oriented, with such a relatively strong representation of ministers, social workers, and other nonbusiness types, that they have little rapport with the business community. Such CAA's have had to be prodded even to invite key industrial leaders to serve on their policymaking councils. And they have had to be convinced that the businessmen deserve a responsible role in the policymaking process, much as local officials have had to be prodded to give the poor a similar role in the process. Neither can be given only the role of a functionary. In some cities the CAA is unable to reach this accommodation or the business community itself is too diffuse and unorganized to be reached through a few key industrial leaders.

• • •

COMMUNITY ACTION PROGRAM

Community action agencies under title II-A of the Economic Opportunity Act are required to be public or private nonprofit agencies.[6] Consequently, little of the CAP $451 million budget is allocated to contracting with private industry except under the research and demonstrations provision, which has no such limitation.[7]

. . . Hundreds of private companies have contributed large sums of money, goods, and equipment to various CAP components such as Head Start, opportunities industrialization centers (OIC's), training centers established under title II, and the Upward Bound college orientation program. Important as these voluntary contributions are, they do not imvolve a significantly different engagement with the problems of poverty by the companies from their pre-war-on-poverty charitable contributions, although their donations to CAP are more useful than other charitable donations because they often supply the 10 per cent local contribution that is matched by 90 per cent CAP funds.

A common surface participation of business in community action programs is through businessmen serving on CAA boards or councils. OEO has not furnished the number of such business members on the boards of the more than 1,100 existing CAA's, but some business representation appears to be present in a majority of cases. How meaningful that participation is, and what impact it has upon the shaping of the substantive programs of the CAA's toward further business involvement, is unknowable at this point. . . .

A few examples of business contract participation in CAP are suggestive of potentially much wider private enterprise participation of the type toward which this study is directed. One is a series of contracts let by Head Start for training by companies of nonprofessional personnel of CAA's in fiscal and management skills. . . . Such contracts with private industry could be extremely useful for the training of poor people to serve in CAA roles for which trained poor people are often not now available, and could thus indirectly strengthen the effectuation of the policy of maximum feasible participation of the poor in community action programs.

● ● ●

One large company has voluntarily initiated, without governmental assistance, its own series of community action programs in the rundown neighborhood near its plant. Seeking to make a measurable impact on a small geographic area, but with no business interest in or experience with the housing field, the company nonetheless entered into a joint venture with the public housing authority to redevelop seventy decaying, mostly abandoned mansions into 210 low-income apartments. The company's role was to encourage the project by paying 40 per cent of the interest cost, which in the company's view was a relatively small investment. The beneficial impact on the neighborhood is said to be very substantial.

Similarly, CAP has funded a small number of nonprofit housing development corporations (HDC's) which have drawn in industrial and banking contributions, sometimes with and sometimes without expectation of a return on their investments, for redevelopment and renovation of slum dwellings. Of four examples given by OEO three involved private investments of this nature totaling, respectively, $15,000, $60,000, $150,000, and approximately $2 million. In two of these, the smallest and largest, the companies involved have major commercial interests in the housing materials field. A third involves a large trade association of companies in that field. The largest investment, $2 million, is expected to be recovered from rents by a company which has used its investment as a well-publicized laboratory for "instant renewal," the overnight refurbishing of tenements through a massive installation of prefabricated units. In two cases the private funds were used as seed money, either to begin an operation during the period of processing of an OEO grant application, as in one case, or, as in another, combined with OEO funds as a matching fund for much larger Federal Housing Administration insurance commitments.

● ● ●

The company which was mentioned above as having initiated a voluntary housing rehabilitation project also established an information services center at which neighborhood residents are counseled and referred to appropriate agencies. The center costs the company approximately $60,000 per year to maintain and staff. The staff was recruited from the neighborood and was trained by the company and sent through various city agencies to see where and to whom they would be referring people. The center has been in operation for a year and now handles 700 visitors each month. In order to help develop indigenous movement, the center staff has helped form block organizations.

NOTES

1. Former secs. 111, 112, and 113.
2. Sec. 111 made coequal with improving the employability of dropouts and potential dropouts, the purpose of enabling "public agencies and private nonprofit organizations (other than political parties) . . . to carry out programs which will permit or contribute to an undertaking or service in the public interest that would not otherwise be provided, or will contribute to the conservation and development of natural resources and recreational areas."
3. Study by Dunlap & Associates, Inc., released by the Department of Labor in June, 1967.
4. New secs. 112 and 113. A few experiments in this direction had been made by NYC by linking with MDTA in two coupled projects in Rochester, N.Y., and Newark, N.J. in fiscal years 1965 and 1966. This was expanded to seven cities in December, 1966. These experiments generally involve four hours' attendance daily in NYC work-experience programs and four at MDTA institutions. The emphasis in the MDTA training is basic or prevocational education and not skill training. In order to make this meaningful the Labor Department has formally proposed to modify Child Labor Regulation No. 3 under the Fair Labor Standards Act to permit fourteen- and fifteen-year-olds to work during school hours. Under the proposed modification the employer will certify as to the hours of work and that the work will not interfere with the student's health or well-being, and his school principal will certify that employment during such periods will not interfere with his schooling.

   The 1966 amendments also broadened eligibility to include ninth through twelfth graders even if they are younger than sixteen.
5. New sec. 114 (c).
6. Secs. 202 (a) (4), 204, and 205 (a).
7. Sec. 207.

29
The Negative Income Tax
MARTIN SCHNITZER

[*In recent years interest has been growing in the idea of a minimum standard of living or level of income, achieved through some form of income supplementation such as family allowances or a negative income tax.* Fortune *reported in July, 1968: "A lot of businessmen are becoming intrigued by negative taxation, including the corporate executives on a special New York State panel that recently completed several months of study of possible changes in the welfare system. In April this group, headed by Joseph C. Wilson, chairman of Xerox, and including among its members such business notables as Arjay Miller, vice chairman of the Ford Motor Co., and Joseph L. Block, chairman of the executive committee of Inland Steel, sent to Governor Rockefeller a report indicating that it 'leans' toward a negative income tax."*

Professor Martin Schnitzer of the Department of Business Administration of the Virginia Polytechnic Institute was commissioned by the Joint Economic Committee of Congress to undertake a study of guaranteed income programs in a number of countries. The following excerpt is taken from that study.]

Negative income taxation refers to the payment of a cash grant to families or individuals whose incomes are below a specified minimum income level—the amount of payment depending on the negative taxable income and the negative tax rate. However, any proposal for guaranteeing a certain minimum income must ultimately come to grips with what that income should be. And that, naturally, turns on a definition of "poverty" and a definition of a "decent standard of living." In the United States, the poverty definition which is frequently used is that of the Social Security Administration, which has set the line between poverty and nonpoverty $3,130 for a family of four, $1,540 for nonfarm individuals, $2,190 for farm families, and $1,080 for farm individuals. Also commonly used as a definition of poverty is the $3,000 minimum set by the Council of Economic Advisers.

The principle of the negative income tax is not new. In 1946, the noted economist, George Stigler, stated that: "There is a great attractiveness in the proposal that we extend the personal income tax to the lowest income brackets with negative rates in these brackets." [1]

Milton Friedman, eminent University of Chicago economist, advocates

From *Guaranteed Minimum Income Programs Used by Governments of Selected Countries* (Joint Economic Committee of Congress, 1968).

negative income taxation as a way to lower the cost of welfare statism. He would substitute it in considerable part for the whole set of existing transfer payments and subsidies, thereby achieving a less costly and more unitary welfare system, as well as preserving individual rights presumably denied under current systems.[2]

The most popular approach suggested for guaranteeing a minimum income is based on the measure of income deficiency which is the difference between what an individual or family actually makes and a specified minimum income level, such as $3,000. This difference, or gap, would be made up in total or part by cash payments by the federal government. To accomplish this objective via negative income taxation involves the shifting of the present tax system into reverse through the use of negative tax rates which would be applied to the amount by which actual income falls below a minimum level. This differs from the present tax system in only one respect. Under the present system, either a person owes something or he owes nothing. Under a system of negative income taxation, the government would owe something to individuals with incomes below the specified minimum level.

FRIEDMAN PLAN

Negative income taxation can assume a variety of approaches. One approach, advocated by Milton Friedman, would utilize unused tax exemptions and deductions. Under the current tax system, a family of four has exemptions plus standard deductions equal to $3,000, and if it receives exactly this amount in income, would pay no tax.[3] Negative taxable income is $3,000. If family income is less than $3,000, a negative tax rate is applied to the difference between it and the allowable exemptions and deductions. The amount of the tax rate is set at 50 per cent of the unused exemptions and deductions. If, for example, the family earned nothing for the year, it would receive 50 per cent of its unused exemptions and deductions, or $1,500. Payment of 50 per cent of the difference, instead of the full amount, is designed to retain incentives to earn more—incentives which would be lost if a 100 per cent rate were used.[4]

Table 29–1 illustrates Friedman's negative income tax proposal.

RIPON PLAN

Another approach to negative income taxation would rely on a system of standard income allowances based on the number of persons in a family. For example, a standard income allowance of $1,500 would be given to each adult in a family, $1,500 to the first child, $1,000 to the second child, $600 to the third, $400 to the fourth child, with a limit of $6,000 for any family. The use of the standard income allowance means that a minimum income level is flexible because it depends on the number of persons in a family. If the family consists of two adults, the standard income allowance is $3,000; if

TABLE 29–1

	EXEMPTIONS AND DEDUCTIONS	TAXABLE INCOME	TAX RATE (PER CENT)	TAX	INCOME AFTER TAX
Total income before tax:					
0	$3,000	−$3,000	50	−$1,500	$1,500
$1,000	3,000	−2,000	50	−1,000	2,000
$2,000	3,000	−1,000	50	−500	2,500
$3,000	3,000	0			3,000
$4,000	3,000	+1,000	14	+140	3,860

NOTE: Family of four; existing exemptions and standard deduction; existing rates on positive income.

the family consists of two adults and two children, the income allowance is $5,500.[5]

The difference for a family between its present income and the standard income allowance to which it would be entitled, would be called the poverty deficit for that family. The size of the deficit would depend on whether or not welfare payments would be counted as personal income. This would depend on the objective of negative income taxation—to replace or to supplement welfare payments. The negative tax would be levied on the deficit. Assuming a negative tax rate of 50 per cent, a single adult would receive $750 (50 per cent of the standard income allowance of $1,500). For a family of four, the relationship would exist as given in Table 29–2.

TABLE 29–2

	DEFICIT FROM— STANDARD *	NEGATIVE INCOME TAX	TOTAL INCOME
Earned income:			
0	$5,500	$2,750	$2,750
$500	5,000	2,500	3,000
$1,000	4,500	2,250	3,250
$1,500	4,000	2,000	3,500
$2,000	3,500	1,750	3,750
$2,500	3,000	1,500	4,000
$3,000	2,500	1,250	4,250
$3,500	2,000	1,000	4,500
$4,000	1,500	750	4,750
$4,500	1,000	500	5,000
$5,000	500	250	5,250
$5,500	0	0	5,500

* The standard income allowance for a family of four would equal $5,500.

LAMPMAN PLAN

A third approach involves the use of decreasing negative income taxation as income rises.[6] The subsidy determinant is the income deficiency gap between earnings and a nonpoverty level of income, instead of a base of unused exemptions and deductions (Friedman plan). The negative tax rate would also vary as the amount of earned income changes, instead of being a fixed negative rate. For example, the rate could vary from 50 per cent to zero, the actual rate depending on the difference between actual income and the nonpoverty income level. For example, assume an earned income of zero and a nonpoverty income level of $3,000. The maximum negative tax rate would be 50 per cent and the guaranteed income would equal $1,500. For an earned income of $2,000, which is $1,000 less than the nonpoverty income level, a lower negative tax rate would apply. Assume a negative tax rate of 25 per cent. The subsidy would amount to $250.

The Lampman proposal is shown in Table 29–3.

TABLE 29–3

	AMOUNT BELOW NONPOVERTY LEVEL	NEGATIVE TAX RATE (PER CENT)	SUBSIDY	AFTER-TAX INCOME
Earned Income:				
0	$3,000	50	$1,500	$1,500
$500	2,500	45	1,125	1,625
$1,000	2,000	38	760	1,760
$1,500	1,500	33	495	1,995
$2,000	1,000	25	250	2,250
$2,500	500	25	125	2,625
$2,800	200	25	50	2,850
$3,000	0	0	0	3,000

TOBIN PLAN

A fourth approach would utilize the same principles as the preceding plans, but would make modifications with regard to basic allowances and tax rates. This approach starts by allowing a family head $400 for each person in the household, if the family has no income, and until family size reaches a certain level.[7] As income increases, the Government takes back a part of the subsidy. A family would be allowed to keep two-thirds of any new income, and the remainder would be used to reduce the amount of the subsidy. For example, for a family of four, the original allowance is $1,600, and if it earns no income, it keeps the entire amount. However, if the family earns $900, the subsidy is reduced by one-third, or $300, and the total income received would be $2,200 ($900 earned and $1,300 subsidy). If the family earned $2,000, the subsidy would be reduced by $667, and the total income received would be $2,933. As family income increased, the government subsidy would decline by a fraction of every dollar of additional family income. In the example above, a family would keep two-thirds of every dollar it made, and in essence repay the remaining one-third out of the income supplement. This is tantamount to being in a 33 per cent marginal income tax bracket. At some specified income level, the income supplement would cease and a family would pay taxes. The family of four, with an income supplement of $400 per head, would pay no taxes until earned income and the income supplement were equal to $4,800.[8]

This approach can be illustrated in tabular form (see Table 29–4) by presenting a schedule of income allowances for a family with two children. The allowance is $400 per person.

Any negative income tax plan must respond to two conflicting pressures. (1) the need to raise the poor all the way to an acceptable standard of living; and (2) the desire to maintain incentives for them to seek employment.

TABLE 29–4

	ALLOWANCE OR TAX	INCOME AFTER ALLOWANCE OR TAX
Earned income:		
0	$1,600	$1,600
$1,000	1,367	2,367
$2,000	933	2,933
$3,000	600	3,600
$4,000	367	4,367
$4,800	0	4,800
$5,000	−280	4,720

The latter pressure is presumably resolved through the provision in the tax system of payment of only a part of a family's deficit; that is, the difference between its actual income level and a defined minimally acceptable income level. As a result, an individual receiving negative income tax payments would have some incentive to earn additional income. Whether this would actually be the case is debatable, but a premise that most guaranteed income schemes have in common is that payment of the full deficit will stultify incentives to work, while payment of part of the deficit will not penalize incentives.

A variant of the negative income tax approach involves the use of tax credits for the payment of taxes. The 7 per cent investment credit, for example, provides a credit against the current year's taxes amounting to 7 per cent of the expenditures on capital goods. Such a credit was adopted by the United States government in 1962, following its adoption in other countries.

A tax credit can be applied to incomes as well, and could be used to reduce the level of poverty in the United States. An approach suggested by Earl Rolph would rely on two features—a system of flat sum credits which would be given to all families, and a proportional tax with no exemptions.[9] The tax liability per family would be positive or negative depending on the amount of the credit and the size of family income. To compute the positive or negative tax liability, the formula, $T = Yr - Cu$, would be used. T represents net tax liability, Y is taxable income, r is the tax rate, C is the amount of the credit, and u is the number of credits per family.

For example, assume a proportional tax rate of 30 per cent and a tax credit of $500 per person a year. To compute the tax liability, the tax credit would be multiplied by the number of persons in the family and subtracted from the tax rate applied to taxable income. A family of four with an income of $20,000 a year would pay $4,000 a year in taxes ($6,000–$2,000), whereas a family of four making $3,000 a year would be paid $1,100 ($2,000–$900). A range of rates is illustrated in Table 29–5.

TABLE 29–5

Income *	NET TAX	DISPOSABLE INCOME
0	– $2,000	$2,000
$1,000	– 1,700	2,700
$2,000	– 1,400	3,400
$3,000	– 1,100	4,100
$4,000	– 800	4,800
$6,000	200	6,200
$10,000	1,000	9,000
$20,000	4,000	16,000
$50,000	13,000	37,000
$100,000	28,000	72,000

* Assumes a family of 4, a tax rate of 30 per cent, and credits of $500 a person.

In order to properly appraise any negative income tax proposal, it is necessary to determine the cost involved. A prime determinant of costs lies in the nature of the present income distribution. As of March 1966, 7,998,000 families had less than $3,000 of income, and 4,731,480 individuals had less than $1,500 of income.[10] The combined income of this group would have to be $31 billion in order to reach the so-called nonpoverty level. The actual income received by the group amounted to $20 billion. The cost of filling the gap would depend on the plan and negative rate selected.[11]

The cost of a guaranteed income would depend upon the following factors:

1. The definition of a poverty line to be used in enacting a plan. Is the poverty line to be a flat amount, say $3,000, for all families, or will the poverty line range with the number of persons in a family? Also, will there be al-

lowances for differentials in the cost of living between urban and rural families and individuals?

2. The rate of negative income taxation used, assuming that this approach is preferable to the family allowance. It is assumed that the rate would be 50 per cent of the difference between actual income and the desired minimum income level. The rate, however, could be a sliding rate which diminishes as actual income approaches the minimum income level.

3. Whether present transfer payments will be maintained or eliminated. Obviously if the current system of welfare payments is eliminated, then much of the cost of a guaranteed income program will be counterbalanced by the savings in terms of welfare expenditures. However, if the guaranteed income is superimposed upon existing welfare programs, the cost will be considerable.

4. The proportion of those eligible who would take advantage of the guaranteed income plan.

Estimates of the cost of a guaranteed income vary from $8 billion to $25 billion a year based on the type of plan used, the negative income tax rate involved, and the degree to which existing welfare programs are reduced or eliminated.

NOTES

1. George J. Stigler, "Economics of Minimum Wage Legislation," *American Economic Review*, XXXVI (1946), 365.
2. Milton Friedman, *Capitalism and Freedom* (Chicago: University of Chicago Press, 1962), pp. 190–195.
3. The taxpayer could use actual deductions and have a higher negative taxable income.
4. Milton Friedman, "The Case for the Negative Income Tax: A View from the Right," Chamber of Commerce of the United States, *Proceedings of the National Symposium on the Guaranteed Income*, (December, 1966), pp. 49–55.
5. Ripon Society, "The Negative Income Tax," *Ripon Forum*, III, No. 4 (April, 1967), 6.
6. This approach is the Lampman approach. For more comprehensive detail see Robert J. Lampman, "Negative Rates Income Taxation," an unpublished paper prepared for the Office of Economic Opportunity (August, 1965).
7. This approach is advocated by James Tobin. For a more comprehensive presentation see James Tobin, "The Case for an Income Guarantee," *The Public Interest*, No. 4 (Summer, 1966); and James Tobin, "Income Guarantees and Incentives," Chamber of Commerce of the United States, *Proceedings of the National Symposium on the Guaranteed Income* (December 1966), pp. 45–48.
8. Earned income would amount to $4,800. One-third of this amount is $1,600, which would eliminate the supplement.
9. Earl R. Rolph, "The Case for a Negative Income Tax," *Industrial Relations*, Institute for Industrial Relations, University of California, 1967.
10. U.S. Bureau of the Census, *Current Population Reports*, p. 60, No. 51 (January, 1967), pp. 1–2.
11. This is computed as follows: 8 million families times $3,000 equals $24 billion, and 4.7 million individuals times $1,500 equals $7 billion.

30
The "Poor" and the "Broke"

ELI GOLDSTON
President, Eastern Gas and Fuel Associates

Unless you personally have been poor, it is practically impossible to distinguish between what I would call "the poor" and "the broke." My family, back in 1930 and 1931, were very poor, but it was a condition of our purse. We simply did not have money. Our poverty could be cured by the prescription which Professor Milton Friedman of Chicago has suggested, merely by the application of money. This sort of purely financial poverty is no longer a serious problem in our affluent society. It is the people who are "broke" who remain a problem, and, indeed, a threat, to our society. Being broke is not a matter only of the purse. It is primarily a matter of the spirit, and all the money Professor Friedman recommends can be poured over a person who is broke without really making any difference. What a broke person needs is education, vocational training, a job opportunity and some sympathetic restoration of his faith in society and in himself.

From an address before the Harvard Graduate School of Business, May 16, 1968.

31
"In a Welfare Center on Eighth Avenue": A Welfare Recipient's View of Welfare

JULIUS HORWITZ

In a welfare center on Eighth Avenue I sat down next to a Negro man in his late thirties. His name was Mr. Mitchell. He wore a leather jacket. His slacks were neat. He had a strong quiet face. His eyes studied the room. They had

From "In One Month, 50,000 Persons Were Added to the City's Welfare Rolls," *New York Times Magazine* (January 26, 1969), by permission of the *New York Times* and the author.

focus; they did not stare inward, which is what you usually see in a welfare center—row after row of people unable to see the world around them or to feel they have a place in it.

I said, "I'd like to talk to you about welfare. What it does for you. What it doesn't do. What kind of hang-ups welfare has for you. Is that all right with you?"

He looked at me for an instant to see if I was out of focus and then he said, "Sure."

"What do you think of welfare?" I asked.

"It's like being in bondage," he said, as though he had spent a lifetime thinking about it. "You can survive, but that's about all. I feel they should abolish welfare. The kids grow up on welfare with the attitude that everything should be free and easy. With parents that work, the kids are different, they look different, they think different, they see things ahead of them, they're moving toward something real in this world. The kids I see on welfare in the neighborhood around the West 140's are looking for a handout. It's killing them. I see kids of ten and eleven and twelve on dope. They have babies when they're twelve and thirteen. They're pulling down whatever the rest of the black people are pulling up. These kids need leadership. They need it bad."

"How would you give it to them?"

"Nobody ever asked me that before," he said. "But welfare should let a man in the house. Forget the rules. If he's the kind of man you see around the blocks in Harlem he can't make enough money to take care of a family. But he makes some money. He can't take on the responsibility for a whole family. Some men can't face that kind of responsibility. It drives them away. But let them face whatever responsibility they can take and they might stay on."

"Would it drive you away?"

"No, it wouldn't," he said. "I don't have any children yet but one is on its way. It won't set me running. I wouldn't leave my kids. I take that seriously, having kids."

"What about the men you talk to, what kind of reasons do they give for leaving their children?"

"They say they don't make enough money. They say they don't have enough money for themselves if they have to give to the family. They never grew up in families where they saw a father giving money to the family. They don't know what it means to support a child. They never saw it done. They grew up without support. You can tell the guys who never saw their fathers. Something is cut out of them, like they don't belong to anyone, like everyone is an enemy. They produce babies but they never had any training to be a father. They never saw it done, being a father. They never come around to see their babies, most of them. You got a lot of guys that need to be made into fathers."

"Why are you here today, sitting in a welfare office?" I asked. "You look like you can make out."

"I can. I got on welfare in August because the place where I was working on 38th Street closed down. Then I had to go into Harlem Hospital for two weeks. When I came out I needed money to pay the rent that was due on my apartment. You don't get a chance to save for emergencies on $84 a week. But now I found a job with the Board of Education. I'll be starting work next Monday."

"Then why are you here today?"

"Just to ask them for some money to buy working clothes. I need some winter clothes for this new job."

"Will the job pay you much money?"

"It'll pay me less than what they say a poverty wage is here in New York City. I'll get $2,800 a year for a six-hour day. That's less than poverty. But I need a job. And I got it. After that stay in the hospital I can't take the kind of jobs I used to be able to handle."

"When did you come to New York City?"

"In September, 1957."

"Do you remember how you came, why you came, what made you give up your home in the South?"

"That's something you don't forget," he said. "I was doing construction work in Columbia, S. C. I was making $1.50 an hour. I thought I could make more money in that same trade in New York. Some of my family was living here. I had some cousins, aunts, an uncle. I had a long talk with my mother about going. She said it was my decision. The South was getting worse. The court decisions made the whites begin to go by the rules, and they made all the rules go against you.

"I got on a bus and came to New York. I thought I could go right into construction work. I learned I had to get into a union first. No union would take me. I got a job in a restaurant I didn't want to do. I kept getting jobs I didn't want to do. There was no job I wanted to stick to because I knew that construction was my real job.

"That happens to a lot of guys from the South here in New York. They come knowing what they want, but nobody in this city wants to know it. That sets you drifting. You keep drifting. One day you find out that the only thing out there for you is welfare. Without welfare you have to kill or steal just to keep alive. I never thought I would end up needing welfare."

"Now that you're on welfare, what would you like it to be like for you?" I asked.

"Welfare should be quick, swift. They should have people working here who can immediately size up a person, then know what to do for them, real quick, to get them off and going again. There should be no more suspicion about money, thinking people are cheating. The important thing is to get people moving. But these people who work here are all blind. They don't look at you. They don't know you or want to know you. They want to keep things moving for themselves, not for you. They're supposed to be here working for you, not for themselves."

32
Poverty or Planning

LEON KEYSERLING

[*In the paragraphs below, a former chairman of the Council of Economic Advisers takes the view that a war on poverty cannot be successfully mounted without more comprehensive national planning.*]

What I have said really boils down to the conclusion that the kind of war against poverty we should be waging requires much more planning and coordination at the national level than we have thus far been equipped or willing to undertake. The creation of a special agency to deal with the poverty problem, while not undesirable, in a larger sense reflects the ad hoc and improvised nature of all our basic national economic and social programs. This means not only that we are starting too slowly but also that in many respects we are off in the wrong direction. Under the Employment Act of 1946, we ought to be developing long-range goals for the pattern of our civilian labor force, with due regard for the priorities of our needs; for maximum production, which would take account of qualitative as well as quantitative factors; and for the distribution of purchasing power that would support these other ends. We should then be adjusting our national economic and social policies to these goals.

This degree of planning would not force the government into novel fields of activity, nor in itself would it change the balance of responsibility between private enterprise and government (although some changes in that balance may indeed be desirable). It would merely introduce into our national policies the degree of rational planning that is now commonplace in large business corporations. It would merely carry forward the express mandate of the Employment Act itself. And it would merely be a move toward that new balance of flexibility and decision, experimentalism and consistency, short-range response and long-range efforts which the free societies must develop if they are to maintain their position and leadership in the world.

The full article appeared in *The Nation* (June 7, 1965), under the title "Poverty and the Economy," in a Symposium with four other economists, "Our Enemy at Home—Poverty."

Part V BUSINESS AND MANPOWER DEVELOPMENT

It is generally agreed that the way in which business can make its most direct contribution to the solution of urban problems is by opening up a larger number of better jobs. Its activities in this respect help to reduce the incidence of poverty and racial discrimination and contribute to the economic base of the cities. Of course, business is limited in what it can accomplish on its own. It can invent and innovate, research and develop, improve its own production and marketing processes, but its contribution of more jobs—in the aggregate—depends very much on the state of the economy as a whole. Government economic policy is the key.

But even within this limitation there is much that business can do both to make people more employable and to improve their productivity once they are employed. It is this subject which will be explored in Part V. The training and development of workers also involves business with the educational process, which we shall examine in Part VI.

A *The Need for Jobs*

33
The Need for Jobs
JOINT ECONOMIC COMMITTEE
OF CONGRESS

TESTIMONY OF SENATOR FRED R. HARRIS

Of a total of two million unemployed persons and some ten million underemployed persons in the nation presently, the most difficult to reach and bring into the main current of the American economy are 500,000 hard-core unemployed, who, in the Commission's words, "live within the central cities, lack basic education, work not at all or only from time to time, and are unable to cope with the problems of holding and performing a job. A substantial part of this group is Negro, male, and between the ages of approximately eighteen and twenty-five." The Commission cited a 1966 Labor Department study showing that while the nation-wide unemployment rate was 3.8 per cent, the unemployment rate among sixteen- to nineteen-year-old nonwhite males in the major ghettos was 26.5 per cent, and among sixteen- to twenty-four-year-old nonwhite males, 15.9 per cent.

• • •

A lot of people in this country believe that most poor people are different from everyone else in that they do not aspire to decent, steady jobs which provide good wages and a future. I think that simply is not true. Poor people in this country are just like anyone else—they have the same values, whether they want to have them or not. They think about careers and jobs that lead to something, just as we members of the middle class do. I held menial jobs, as many of you did, when I was growing up, but I doubt if you could have gotten me interested in such jobs if I had known that I was going to be condemned to working at them for the rest of my life.

One example I have cited before helps to dispute, I think, the myth that most poor people will not work, or do not want to work. In Watts, after the riot there in 1966, the Aero-Jet General Company—doing what I hope many more private companies will now do—established a core-city employment center, a military tentmaking factory. That plant initially advertised for seventy-five jobs. They now, I think, employ 425 people, but initially they hired seventy-five. For those first seventy-five positions, 5,500 people applied. I have heard more recently that companies publishing similar advertise-

---

Testimony of Senator Fred R. Harris (Oklahoma) and Representative James C. Corman (California), both members of the Kerner Commission, during the Joint Economic Committee's Hearings on the Kerner Commission Report, 1968.

ments in Pittsburgh and Detroit have been simply inundated with applications from ghetto residents.

But it is also true, as I think we all know, that a person from a disadvantaged or deprived background, or someone who has been without work for a long period of time when he was looking for work, is often deeply damaged in some way—personally and psychologically—and, thereafter, the mere offering of job opportunities will not necessarily bring him back into society. He frequently loses something of his motivation and self-confidence and his self-image.

• • •

The problem of job motivation is deep and complex and I do not think we know nearly enough about it. But I feel sure that any effort to employ the hard-core unemployed must include extensive training programs, not only to provide unskilled persons with the ability to perform in an economy which continues to increase its demands for sophisticated skills, but also to try, at least, to overcome the debilitating effects of deprived backgrounds or of being out of work for a long time.

• • •

If an employment program is to be successful, we members of the Commission felt that "the previously hard-core unemployed trainee or employee must believe that he is not being trained for or offered a 'dead end' job. Since, by definition, he is not eligible even for an entry level position, he must be given job training. He must be convinced that if he performs satisfactorily after the training period he will be employed and given an opportunity to advance, if possible on a clearly defined 'job ladder' with step increases both in pay and responsibility."

I think two additional factors are very important in any job program. First, we simply have to coordinate these wildly fragmented and ineffective training programs that we have started in recent years. It is literally impossible to find out, as the Commission tried to do, how many job training slots of various kind are filled and how many are unfilled in any given city.

In Los Angeles—and I just pick that city out of the air—I think it would take two or three weeks to find out how many of the job training programs and manpower development programs have vacancies; the problem is that the administration of those various programs is fragmented, in a city as large as Los Angeles, among perhaps 500 separate public and private agencies of all kinds. And so we say to a fellow who already does not have very much self-confidence in himself—"Well, you just sort of walk around about 500 different places, and maybe when you contact enough of them you will be able to get into some kind of training program."

Reorganization and coordination are essential. I think that has simply got to be taken into hand. We are making some beginning steps, largely experimental now, within the new concentrated employment program, but they have to be expanded and made systematic.

The second essential is that these training programs must produce a real job. One city I visited last summer, as we Commissioners walked singly and in pairs anonymously around the ghettos of this country, had been running a very extensive training program, but had not been able to obtain jobs for the people that they trained. And I do not know altogether whose fault that was. Probably the training centers had not made the proper job surveys; maybe they had not secured sufficient support from private employers to begin with; maybe their training was in obsolete skills. There was some discrimination involved as well. And then perhaps the jobs were simply not there to begin with in many instances.

Whatever the reason, program officials told us that they had more than 500 names of people who had gone through these training programs but who still were not able to get jobs. And they said that these were young kids who were now out there on the streets, more hostile than before, more depressed and pessimistic than ever, who were saying to everybody, "Listen, it's just another hustle; when you go through that job program, you're still not going to get a job."

And that is why the Commission was very interested in private employment with some kind of subsidization, either through tax incentives or direct payments, that would link the training with an actual job. We can do a far better job on that than we have done in the past.

TESTIMONY OF REPRESENTATIVE JAMES C. CORMAN

As you know, the present deterioration of urban life prompted the President to create a National Advisory Commission on Civil Disorders. As a member of that Commission, I became aware of the tragedy which has befallen a substantial number of our nation's youth. Ill educated, and without salable skill, these young people are unable to secure employment. Without a stake in the existing social structure, they have become hostile to authority and thoroughly embittered. These people are often at the core of the social unrest gripping our cities. The Commission found that young Negroes, aged fourteen to twenty-four, are "responsible for a disproportionately high share of crimes in all parts of the nation. In 1966, persons under twenty-five years of age comprised the following proportions of those arrested for various major crimes: murder, 37 per cent; forcible rape, 60 per cent; robbery, 71 per cent; burglary, 81 per cent; larceny, about 75 per cent; and auto theft, over 80 per cent." We must take action to reclaim these individuals, both for their own sake and for the sake of American society.

The past seven years, for some Americans, has been a period of great economic progress and affluence. Yet, in spite of this surge of economic growth, the unemployment rate for Negroes in 1967 was more than double that for whites. For Negro teenagers, the situation has not perceptibly improved since 1961. In 1961, the unemployment rate for Negro teenagers was 27.6 per cent; in 1967, it was 26.5 per cent. The 1968 manpower report of the President . . . states that:

No inroads have been made into the extremely serious problem of nonwhite teenager joblessness. While the unemployment rate for white teenagers dropped as the economic climate improved, among nonwhite teenagers the rate in 1967 was actually higher than in 1960. One out of every four nonwhite teenagers was unemployed in 1967, almost 2.5 times the proportion for white teenagers, whereas in 1960 the ratio was less than 2 to 1.

This problem will be compounded, because the number of nonwhite young people expected to enter the labor force by 1975 will be even greater. It is estimated that the number of nonwhite workers will increase by 26 per cent, while the number of young white workers will grow by only 18 per cent. The search for jobs will be made even more difficult, because employers will be seeking larger numbers of workers whose education and training have equipped them for positions in a highly technical economy.

The problem which is before us now is one of utilizing neglected human resources. People without jobs are people without basic economic security, self-sufficiency, or self-respect. Employment is the only longrun solution which can allow an individual to become a contributing member of his society, and not merely a recipient of its charity. Any other help we provide will only be temporary. Thus far, there has been little evidence that Negro teenagers do not want to work. Whenever job programs are announced, they turn out in large numbers to find the jobs are not there. In Oakland, for instance, a job fair attracted 15,000 people—250 were placed in jobs. What we have found is that Negro teenagers would not accept dead end employment —jobs that pay little and promise no advancement or training.

. . . I do not think there are any of us who did not go through a period of his life where he had a menial job to do for a little wage. But each of us knew that it was temporary. It was a step toward something much better. For the young Negro who looks at the adult males around him and sees that they never moved out of those positions, it is quite a different thing.

They want to be part of the affluent America they see depicted on television, and will no longer be content to be trapped behind a broom. What we must now undertake is a program which will reach the alienated youth of the ghetto. We must no longer tolerate job programs which merely make work, or programs which promise employment and then fail to deliver. These endeavors have only produced a cynicism which views our efforts as a cruel hoax. What we need are jobs—jobs which provide training at work while paying a living wage—jobs which promise advancement.

● ● ●

While I favor the involvement of the private sector, I am not in favor of offering tax credits. Admittedly, the 7 per cent incentive credit for investment in new equipment and machinery has been highly successful as a technique for reaching a large number of individual enterprises. I do not believe this tax incentive would be sufficient motivation for employers to undertake massive programs of job training. The advisory commission estimates that the total annual cost to an employer per hard-core trainee would vary from

$3,000 to $5,000. The assumption of training costs, supportive services, and the cost of marginal productivity during the training period would demand a far greater financial incentive than presently proposed tax credits offer. Business, preoccupied with achieving the highest possible economic yield, cannot be fully responsive to social goals. Private enterprise cannot be asked to assume the sole burden of coping with the social and health problems of these workers, as well as securing adequate transportation, the lack of which hampers the chronically unemployed.

There is also the danger that business will only desire to take those workers who can be most easily trained, and will leave behind those who lack basic education and a record of stability. From the point of view of the federal budget, there is a difference in a tax credit and an appropriation. The argument is made that the tax credit device avoids the burden of administrative "red tape." It also denies the government the opportunity to monitor the selection of the trainee and the kind and quality of training received. Leaving these decisions solely to the conscience of the taxpayer is irresponsible. It would result in maximum cost and minimum return.

The government must enlist the aid of the private sector in providing on-the-job training and work experience for existing jobs. But the government itself must provide the initial contact, counseling and placement, and assume the financial cost involved in rehabilitation. Such rehabilitation will involve literacy training, and education in dress, appearance, money management, and work habits. Special attention must also be given to motivation and to worker incentives. Training allowances, such as offered under the Manpower Development and Training Act are necessary. The trainee must be convinced that after a satisfactory period of on-the-job training, he will be offered a steady job, which will allow him to improve himself.

There is no doubt that such training and rehabilitation will be expensive. It is estimated that the cost-per-job will run from $3,500 in the private sector to $4,000 to $5,000 in the public sector.

This may mean that a tax increase will be necessary, and it may require a reshuffling of national priorities, but this is a task which cannot wait. It would be a terrible mistake in economic judgment to consider the plight of the unemployed as the price for fiscal soundness and price stability. We must not forget that every dollar spent will produce a human return far greater than the original financial investment.

A brief summary of the accomplishments of the Job Corps and Manpower Development and Training Act testifies to this fact. The profile of the average Job Corps enrollee describes a school dropout; most likely educationally retarded at the time he left school, lacking in employment skills and opportunities, and probably a draft rejectee. Out of the 65 per cent who had jobs, 60 per cent made less than $1.25 per hour. Eighty per cent had not seen a doctor or a dentist in the last ten years. Sixty-three per cent came from homes where the head of the household was unemployed and 39 per cent from families on relief.

As of May 1, 1967, some 75,410 youths had some Job Corps experience.

Of these youths, 52,985 found jobs, entered the military service or returned to school. Seventy-six per cent found jobs, 10 per cent joined the service, and 14 per cent returned to school. Those who sought work found that they could obtain better jobs at better wages. The average wage per hour was $1.71 compared to the $1.19 previously earned. Of those working, 39 per cent had received wage increases. Assuming the average Job Corps graduate made $1.71 an hour for the rest of his working life, and worked for forty years, he would pay back the government a total of $11,200 in income taxes.

It is not meaningful to compare the cost of rehabilitating a Job Corps youth to the cost of sending the average child to school. What we are doing here is to make up for years of neglect in the areas of education and health. It is not surprising that the youths served by the Job Corps must receive much extra education if they are to become productive members of society.

The manpower development and training program has also made a significant contribution in training the unemployed and underemployed. The MDTA has helped between 175,000 and 225,000 low-income persons in a period of less than four years. Eighty per cent of the institutional trainees, and 50 per cent of the on-the-job trainees who were heads of families, in training in 1966, had previously earned less than $3,000 per year, or had received no wages for the last full year of employment before training. The Labor Department estimates that for the cumulative period of August, 1962, to December, 1967, 76 per cent of those receiving institutional training were employed at the time of last contact, and 78 per cent were in training-related jobs. Through January 30, 1967, the median pretraining earnings of persons enrolled in MDTA was $1.44 an hour. The median posttraining wages were $1.74 an hour. The Labor Department estimates that the average trainee repays the government for the expense of his training in taxes in about two years. He then goes on in his working life to repay the public's investment in him many times over.

Surely it makes more sense to make an investment now and avoid the risk of spending many times the amount in terms of welfare handouts to each unemployed individual and his offspring. Far less will be spent than will otherwise be needed to control the antisocial or criminal behavior which may develop. Not to incorporate an alienated individual into the mainstream of society will be more costly than the $7,025 spent per Job Corps enrollee, or $900 to $1,000 spent per MDTA trainee.

● ● ●

We are still far from the day in which each American who desires to work will be assured of a chance to make his own way. But this is no reason to state complacently that nothing further can be done. Our experience with existing programs for job training indicates that while we are not always successful, progress is being made. The reports of those who have studied both the job market and the current problems of American society make clear that a greater effort must be made in this direction. We must make that effort, and must give new meaning to the promise which this nation offers each citizen.

B *Business Response to Government Stimulus*

34

The Job Corps and Manpower Development and Training Programs

STEPHEN KURZMAN

[*Stephen Kurzman was commissioned by the Subcommittee on Employment, Manpower, and Poverty of the Senate Committee on Labor and Public Welfare to analyze the relationships of private enterprise to antipoverty programs, including manpower training programs. Portions of his report dealing with the Job Corps and with On-the-Job Training under the Manpower Development and Training Act are reprinted below.*]

JOB CORPS

The largest single business involvement in Economic Opportunity Act programs—and probably in all federal antipoverty programs—is in the Job Corps, the residential vocational education and training component of the Economic Opportunity Act for unemployed high school dropouts, ages sixteen through twenty-one, from low-income families. Of the current $1.6 billion OEO budget, $212 million is allocated for Job Corps centers out of a total Corps budget of $303 million. Approximately $147 million of the centers budget, or almost 70 per cent, is for contract management of centers by private profitmaking companies. There is an additional $7 million in contracts with private enterprise for OEO support functions, notably accounting, auditing and legal services, research and evaluations, and training.[1] Some portions of the latter two items are allocable to the Job Corps and probably should be considered nonhousekeeping items along with the $147 million for center management, bringing the total private enterprise share of Job Corps nonhousekeeping budget up to almost $150 million, or approximately 50 per cent of the total Job Corps budget.

This substantial dollar involvement is even more striking when viewed against the operational pattern of the Corps. The largest number of the 119 centers currently operating (91) consist of conservation centers operated entirely by public agencies, the Departments of Agriculture and the Interior, and in a few instances by the states. These centers, which are located in national or state parks, are small and house only about one-third of the 36,000

From *Examination of The War on Poverty*, vol. 1 (Senate Committee on Labor and Public Welfare, 1967).

youths currently enrolled in the Corps.[2] And the emphasis in the conservation centers is predominantly on conservation and basic education and less on job training than in the remaining twenty-eight urban centers.

The bulk of the Corps job training effort is, therefore, in the twenty-eight urban centers, consisting of ten large men's, sixteen smaller women's, and two small special centers. At the present time, twenty, or more than 70 per cent, of these twenty-eight urban centers are in the hands of private enterprise under contracts for general management. Nine of the ten men's centers, nine of the sixteen women's, and both special centers are under contract to private companies. The remaining urban centers are contracted to nonprofit institutions, consisting of two universities, two YWCA's, two educational foundations, and one national women's sorority.

The gross amount of private profit involvement in the urban centers is in reality even higher, because in two cases a nonprofit institution is operating a center in conjunction with a profitmaking company which has a major subcontract; and in two instances which will be discussed at another point, a nonprofit which operates two centers relies heavily upon industrial involvement without formal subcontracts. Widespread subcontracting to companies by the contractors themselves, both with and without formal Job Corps approval is reported, but it is difficult to quantify. The bulk of this is probably for housekeeping functions performed by small companies, although Corps officials contend that it includes training functions as well as supplies. The example most often mentioned is the food service contractor at one center which is also the trainer in the food service course for the enrollees at that center. At another company-operated center there is a major subcontract with a transportation school in cooperation with a union in the transportation field. The percentage of profit involvement is lowered, however, by the fact that in five cases, profitmaking companies with prime contracts have subcontracted with universities.

Business domination of the Job Corps experiment in residential job training was in part planned by the Congress and OEO, and in part unplanned. The idea of creating residential work centers for the unemployed on government conservation projects was a throwback to the Civilian Conservation Corps of the 1930's. The premise was threefold: to pump consumer money into the depression economy, to reduce the pressure of masses of the unemployed from the cities, and to provide manpower for needed public work. Revived in the late 1950's and early 1960's in a variety of bills, its scope was narrowed to youth, since the unemployment rate among youth was then two and one-half times the rate among other age groups. And the emphasis now was upon training and especially experimenting with the motivational improvement hoped to be gained by removing ghetto youths from their disadvantaged environments during an intensive period of basic education and work training. Hearings were held on these measures, including a Presidential message in early 1963, but final action was not taken on them. Proposals were made to broaden the idea to cover vocational training in urban areas as well, but the focus remained on public service jobs, and industry itself was not mentioned as a source of management or training.[3]

When the President's Task Force Against Poverty, an ad hoc committee created early in 1964 with both government and nongovernment members, began the process of drawing together program ideas for the proposed war on poverty, the concept of contracting with nonpublic agencies for the management of the urban centers was apparently first adopted. But there was a strong difference of opinion among the task force members as to whether contracts should be let exclusively to universities, experienced in administering large, residential, educational installations, or exclusively to industry, experienced in operating large, complex projects of all types under defense and space contracts with the government and in training their own employees, or to a mixture of both. Neither was experienced in converting hard-core, functionally illiterate youths into employable workers, but the governmental sector, the only remaining alternative, had obviously so far failed with this group, at least given only the resources that sector had been given.

The representative on the task force of a large, diversified defense contractor, which had developed a rapid training method for its own employees, is credited with having presented forcefully the virtues of involving industry and the likelihood that industry would be willing to undertake the job. Most of the governmental representatives are said to have opposed industrial involvement or at least to have questioned whether business would be willing to participate. The result was a compromise, with the general understanding that a balance would be sought between contracts with universities and contracts with industry.

Very little of this debate appeared during congressional consideration of the economic opportunity bill, which as finally enacted in August 1964 provided only the most oblique authorization for contracting with private enterprise and certainly in no way encouraged such participation. Section 103(a) of the act authorized OEO to "enter into agreements with any federal, state, or local agency or private organization for the establishment and operation, in rural and urban areas, of conservation camps and training centers." Only by the absence of the word "nonprofit" before "private organization," which otherwise appeared in similar phrases throughout the act,[4] was it indicated that contracts with companies were not prohibited. Section 103(b) was only slightly more explicit in authorizing education and vocational training of enrollees "where practicable" by "private vocational educational institutions or technical institutes where such institutions or institutes can provide substantially equivalent training with reduced federal expenditures." The committee reports in both Houses were also vague on this point, making it clear only that the conservation camps were to be governmentally run and that the urban centers would use surplus federal installations.[5]

What happened when OEO opened its doors surprised almost everyone. A few proposals had been submitted, by profit and nonprofit organizations, even before the act was passed, and an avalanche of proposals followed. Almost all were from profitmaking companies. During the two years of new center growth, before Congress levelled off the program, some 116 proposals were submitted to OEO and approximately 75 per cent of these came from private industry. Contrary to the expectations of the public members of the task force and most members of the OEO staff, the university world did not respond to the challenge and the industrial world did. Moreover, in the competition for the existing twenty-eight urban and special centers it is obvious that the industrial proposals were superior in most cases because the companies won most of the prime contracts. But even among those that did not win contracts, industrial firms submitted two-thirds of the proposals adjudged substantially acceptable under the review procedure set up by Job Corps.

• • •

They were able to prepare and submit proposals more quickly, perhaps because industry has more development funds available than the universities. It is estimated that preparation of a proposal cost from $15,000 to $150,000 and often involved a large investment of high-level managerial time and travel. In many instances, particularly in the cases of large industrial proponents and those which won contracts, the companies had prior government contract experience. The nonprofits had less experience and what experience they did have was with research grants, which are usually prepared by individual faculty members and do not require elaborate cost analysis. The nonprofits often had to have their proposals resubmitted after long consultation with the General Accounting Office over accounting procedures and property and inventory control, which are the daily concerns of the industrial community. During the contract negotiations it also became clear that the companies were far more experienced with vocational training as distinguished from academic education. They could more quickly break down jobs so that they could be handled by the manpower at their disposal. And, surprisingly, they were far more flexible about terms and conditions than the universities. It is reported that in a number of instances universities submitted abbreviated proposals and demanded extensive capital improvements on campus. There were also instances in which industrial firms threatened to walk out of negotiations or did so and never returned, but it is reported that this happened more often in the case of the nonprofits.

. . . In five of the twenty instances in which prime contracts were awarded to companies, major subcontracts were also awarded to nearby universities, and in two of the eight cases in which nonprofits were awarded the prime contracts, major subcontracts were also awarded to companies. These combined awards were the result of OEO's judgment that there was a fairly close balance between the two competitors. OEO would then ask the proponents to merge their proposals so as to utilize the unique capacities of both. . . . Again it appears significant that industry was given the major management role in the majority of the seven cases of joint management. The Tongue Point, Oreg., center, which began as a men's center and has been converted to a women's, is represented as typical of the joint relationships. Although the University of Oregon has the prime contract and operates the former naval base as an extension of its campus, Philco-Ford has a major role as subcontractor in providing the vocational training. . . .

It is not surprising, in hindsight, that the industrial proposals were more reassuring than the nonprofits', in view of the residential nature of the Job Corps experiment and therefore the size and scope of the contracts being let. The men's centers, on the average, have 1,750 enrollees and over 700 in staff, and involve an annual contract of almost $12 million. They require, day and night, all week, full support: housing, clothing, feeding, health services, recreation, and discipline, in addition to imaginative efforts at motivational counseling, basic education, and vocational training. Undertaking the sole responsibility for such an installation—particularly without any models to rely on—is a major commitment for any institution no matter how large, and a small or even middle-size company is unlikely to have sufficient managerial capability to afford delegating the top talent necessary to manage a men's center.

Accordingly, no company which is not at least in the over $100 million annual gross receipts class has yet received a men's center contract. Significantly, though, small- and medium-sized companies comprised more than half the companies which sought such contracts.[6] Furthermore, more than one-quarter of the proposals submitted by small and medium companies were rated acceptable in program content by the Ratings Review Board. Presumably companies of all sizes might be able to make a useful contribution to the program if there were a channel to utilize their level of managerial capability.[7]

The women's centers provide a somewhat less formidable challenge since they average 500 enrollees, 200 in staff, and an annual contract of $4.3 million. Yet these awards have also been to the largest companies. Again, slightly more than half of the companies applying were in the small and medium bracket.[8] And the proportion of these applicants having acceptable proposals was somewhat higher than in the case of the men's centers.[9]

. . . Although the managerial investment required was great, the capital investment involved in these proposals was small, since the land and improvements for the urban centers were provided by the federal Establishment. Consequently the ability to obtain large credit advances or otherwise provide capital was not a significant factor distinguishing between large, medium, and small companies. What swung the Job Corps reviewers to the largest, most diversified companies, as compared with both the smaller companies and the universities, was the ability of the big companies to draw upon a wide variety of resources in order to solve an undetermined number of unforeseeable problems. A majority of the large companies submitted proposals acceptable in program content; a minority of smaller companies and nonprofits did so.[10] Undeniably, too, there was the political benefit of using the prestigious names of the biggest companies.

• • •

These developments suggest a general trend of satisfaction, on the part of both OEO and the companies involved, with business management of the urban centers and a parallel dissatisfaction with university and other nonprofit management. There are some contraindications, however, which should be mentioned. As the Congress presses increasingly harder to reduce the cost of Job Corps training, OEO believes that the pressure is building especially against the industrial contractors. Many are complaining that the innovative and experimental aspect of their work cannot be maintained if costs are to be pressed down still further. They also argue that adequate food and other living conditions, which are blamed in part for some of the early disorders in the nonprofit-run centers, cannot be maintained with lowered costs. And in Job Corps headquarters the reflection of congressional pressure is in uniformly high praise for the one remaining nonprofit, the Gary Center, run by the Texas Educational Foundation, which has also been awarded a contract for a women's center in Texas. By the one standard which pervades the Job Corps today—man-year cost—Gary is uniquely successful. Its cost figure is the lowest of the urban centers.[11]

However, the range of cost from center to center is very wide at this point in time, and the distribution of profit-run and nonprofit-run contractors is random on the cost scale. Size seems to be the most important determinant of cost, with the largest centers having the lowest cost. Gary is the largest center, with over 3,000 enrollees. Furthermore, the Gary example is a complex one, which involves a high degree of business involvement.

Prior to the enactment of the Economic Opportunity Act, the Texas State Department of Education had submitted a similar application to the Vocational Education Division of the United States Office of Education, which was not funded there. After enactment of the antipoverty bill, with strong Presidential and gubernatorial support—which many Job Corps officials consider a key element if not the crucial one—the Texas Educational Foundation, a State-supported nonprofit organization, was created under the leadership of a former state superintendent of schools and given vigorous backing from the business community and the state education department. The industrial community in the state was "galvanized" into action, as one official puts it, and itself established an entity, Opportunities, Inc., consisting of fourteen of the largest companies in Texas and 100 smaller firms. Opportunities, Inc., at first had a formal subcontract with the foundation and subsequently became an adviser to the center. During the organizational period a number of companies lent business managers and were reimbursed only for their salary cost.

What seems most important about the relationship is that the businessmen appear to take their advisory role seriously, particularly in two crucial areas of center operation: job training and placement. Opportunities, Inc., established a board of visitors consisting of the top vocational training men in each of the member companies. The board visits the center at least every three months and an effort is made to insure that the companies represented on it have had experience themselves with the particular skill training the center is currently engaging in. What is most important, the suggestions of the board about ways to improve the training are apparently adopted by the center staff. And the board is invited in by the staff to help deal with specific problems. This kind of broad business impact on the content of center training activity is obviously very valuable and difficult to match with a single industrial contractor or even with one or two business subcontractors. It may be significant for the success of this effort that the companies involved in Opportunities, Inc., are generally not competitive with one another in the business arena. Also, the companies apparently view the center as a free laboratory experience from which they, too, can gain. An attempt is being made by OEO to institute similar business visitor teams in three or four other centers.

The second impressive feature of the Gary experience, its high placement record, is also attributable heavily to its business component and not necessarily to the fact of its nonprofit structure. Each of the companies in Opportunities, Inc., is committed to hiring enrollees who complete segments of training. It is becoming apparent, as placement data are beginning to be collected, that the longer a corpsman's stay at a center, the better his chances of obtaining and retaining employment and the higher his hourly wage, as well as the lower the cost of training him. By having the companies which are likely to hire also involved in the operations of the center, it is easier to bring home to the enrollees the importance of staying in the center. This appears to be the case with Gary, whose placement rate is 84 per cent, which is one of the highest for the urban centers.

• • •

There has been much criticism of the Corps on the ground that, by offering higher salaries, it has pirated educational personnel from the public school system and thus weakened that already undernourished basic source of education and training. OEO has not compiled a statistical answer to this, but the indications are that, ironically, the nonprofits are more guilty of pirating from the schools than the profit-making contractors. One company estimates that, although less than 5 per cent of the center staff came from the company, most of the remaining staff are from private companies or social service agencies, and not from the public schools. For vocational trainers the companies seek skilled people out of the shop, who have had current on-the-job experience and who can interact well with ghetto youth. Bakers teach baking, auto mechanics teach auto repair, and many are recruited from small shops. Similarly, for coaches and counselors, who usually comprise half the nonmanagement personnel, the companies turn to a great variety of sources, including retired military personnel. And for basic literacy training, they are also looking beyond the schools, particularly for those who have had experience in working with the disadvantaged. In one case a company reports that, in order to attain a 25 per cent nonwhite center staff, it had to recruit widely outside the state in which its center is located because there was almost no nonwhite population there.

The nonprofits, however, have been less able than industry to reach out for managerial talent, either from their own ranks or from industry generally. Not only does a large diversified company often have the advantage of having the needed engineering, accountancy, and other talent in its ranks or working for one of its divisions or subsidiaries, but the companies are also more willing than universities and other nonprofits to go outside their own ranks to hire such managerial personnel on a short-term basis when this is necessary. The universities are in part hampered in doing this by their traditions of tenure and retirement. Also, to some extent the universities tend to treat the centers they run as living laboratories for their own campuses and this, too, tends to lead to the involvement of university personnel. Where they did go outside their institutions some universities are reported at first to have given one-year contracts to their personnel; the companies do not make such commitments. In sum, OEO has become convinced that the industrial contractors are capable of hiring good educators but the universities have difficulty in hiring good managers.[12]

• • •

The OEO staff concludes that the companies also have an advantage in hiring nonmanagerial personnel because they have a better grasp of the people needed for the training task since they constantly hire blue-collar workers for their assembly lines. The universities, on the other hand, appear to have difficulty in adjusting, both to the educational level and the numbers of people involved.

One further development in the Job Corps also indicates a significant shift toward private enterprise. Job Corps contractors have increasingly built a kind of on-the-job training into their programs by arranging informally with local business concerns to give work experience to corpsmen who have advanced well in training, usually on a part-time basis. Beginning with one men's center, a number of the contractors have sought to do this in order to supplement the realism of the work experience that the centers themselves attempt to provide, to increase motivation by showing the relevance of the center training, to establish contact with a potential employer and thereby increase placement potential by adding some actual experience to his qualifications. The contractors have themselves developed the program, where it exists, by contacting the employers directly, and it appears to be motivated essentially by a desire on the part of the contractors to improve their center placement records. Although they do not have the responsibility for placement under their contracts, it is significant that the contractors nonetheless feel that their enrollees' placement record reflects upon the contractor's performance. It is also significant that the contractors believe OJT will in fact improve the enrollees' placement chances.

• • •

An unfortunate problem with OJT is resistance from the Labor Department, which insists that the enrollees be paid the minimum wage in addition to the allowance they receive, in order to equalize with wages paid to youths enrolled in the Labor Department's MDTA-OJT program. OEO at first argued that the corpsmen were receiving both subsistence in kind—including lodging, clothing, food, and medical and dental services—and a $30 to $50 allowance and therefore in net effect were receiving at least $60 per week; and that paying additional amounts to those enrollees on OJT would discriminate against conservation corpsmen who generally do not have OJT available to them. What underlies the conflict is the fear of the Labor Department that employers will reject MDTA-OJT programs in favor of Job Corpsmen because in the former the employer must pay the minimum wage and is reimbursed only for his training costs, usually $25 per week. OEO is, of course, sensitive to the charge that it is providing free labor to employers. However, if the Corps begins to insist on payment of minimum wages by the employer, the program may be throttled because employers may not feel that they are receiving sufficient productivity from the corpsmen to warrant full wages. This may call for some subsidy to employers along the lines of the MDTA-OJT training cost allowance, to compensate them for the lower productivity and the cost of training.

• • •

The question of conflict will be more serious when the Neighborhood Youth Corps begins to implement its new authorization for OJT with profit-making employers under the 1966 Amendments to the Economic Opportunity Act. Here the problem of overlapping is a very real one because, although the NYC program also involves longer periods of OJT than thirty days, it recruits virtually the same disadvantaged youthful population as the Job Corps.

Common to all these programs is the highly troublesome difficulty of having three different programs each contacting the same group of employees and seeking OJT slots for the same level of trainee. Almost every businessman interviewed for this study stated that multiple contacts by OJT and placement officials of different programs was a serious problem and discouraged many businessmen from participating in any program.

• • •

The history, growth, and relative performance of private enterprise in the Job Corps have so far been the foci of this analysis. In part, the discussion has been an assessment of the government's interest in this development. Business motivation and interest must also be considered.

The most obvious business motivation—profit—is not an adequate single explanation of the response of a significant number of companies of all sizes to the opportunity to manage Job Corps centers. The true profit margin to the companies under these contracts is difficult to compute, but it appears to be less than other types of government contracts or other forms of diversification would yield. By administrative decision made after some early consideration of fixed fee contracts, the major Job Corps contracts are all of the cost-plus-fixed-fee type now common in government-industry relationships where, as in this case, costs are difficult to predict. Also by administrative decision the maximum fixed fee for a prime contract has been set at 4.7 per cent of a fixed cost.[13] This is often compared with fixed fees of at least 6 per cent on space and defense contracts, with some reported as high as 8 per cent. How the 4.7 per cent figure was determined has not been explained.

The crucial test of profitability is not only in the fixed fee percentage, however, but also in the definition of cost. And, although companies continue to seek higher fixed fees, their major emphasis in negotiation is on what constitutes allowable costs. The Corps began by using Defense Department procurement regulations and has now shifted to the civilian "Federal Procurement Regulations." Under these regulations cost for purposes of determining fee consists of direct cost and indirect cost, the latter computed by estimating the portion of the company's total general and administrative overhead which is attributable to the performance of the particular contract. Three examples furnished by OEO indicate that indirect cost amounted to 4.25 per cent of direct cost for one company; a range of 2 to 5 per cent of direct cost for another company, which had several contracts; and 3 per cent for a third.[14]

Since the average men's center contract is for almost $12 million, the average fixed fee amounts to roughly $500,000 per year. One way of looking at the resultant profit to a company is that, if it was interested in creating a new educational division, which would require a substantial increase in its general overhead, it could recover that overhead out of the indirect cost under the Job Corps contract and have as well both its $500,000 profit and the resultant new division. One OEO official half jokingly calls this a 50 per cent profit.

Another way of looking at the figures is that the contractors are making no capital investment in plant and therefore are earning 4.7 per cent without risking any capital. The land, physical plant, and equipment at the centers are federal property, or in some instances leased by the federal government, whereas under defense contracts the contractor usually must furnish the plant and recover its investment after the fact. The company's investment in a Job Corps center is only its personnel and the wages it must advance for the two-week or one-month period required to process its vouchers for reimbursement. From this viewpoint, it has been suggested, the real profit is 10 to 14 per cent.

The view of the companies is quite the opposite. On a short-run profit basis, they argue, they would never have gotten into center management contracts. The 4.7 per cent fixed fee is less than half their normal profit in many cases. The investment of managerial talent more than counterbalances the absence of capital investment. And OEO's disallowance of costs, which generally amounts to 1 to 2 per cent of claimed costs, means that a company's profit margin is cut twice: Once in computing its fixed fee and a second time in not reimbursing it for the costs it has incurred.

However significant the short-run profit margin may or may not be in itself, it seems clear that, without at least this much reimbursement of costs or profit, the companies would not be as interested in undertaking these contracts as they apparently are. An interesting measure of this factor is that even the so-called nonprofit contractors sometimes demand and receive an "incentive" in the form of a "management allowance" beyond reimbursement of direct and indirect costs. Since the management allowance apparently may be as high as the fixed fee under the profitmaking contracts, the total cost to the government in the case of nonprofits which receive the allowance is the same as in the case of the business contractors. Where general and administrative overhead is even higher for a nonprofit, as has reportedly been the case occasionally, the total cost to the government is greater than in the case of a company contractor.

The conclusion to be drawn from this is that some businesses, and in many cases the academic world as well, can be induced to make managerial investments in antipoverty efforts, even on a major scale, so long as—and perhaps only so long as—their out-of-pocket costs are reasonably well covered. To assure this, some margin of apparent profitability must be built into the formula for recovering costs, perhaps more to offset the disallowances on costs than for any other reason.

What has been said so far is that, as a short-run profitmaking proposition, business interest in center management contracts is not entirely explicable. However, the fact that costs are reasonably reimbursed appears to be a highly important factor, because it takes a company's investment decision out of the charitable contribution or community chest category and into the realm of business choices. The businessmen interviewed stress that the significance of this shift within the corporate decisionmaking structure should not be underestimated. Different decisionmakers are involved, usually; different standards are applied to the choices; different limits are placed on the size of the potential investment; and different explanations are given to boards of directors and stockholders. All appear to favor a deeper and larger commitment if the decision is based on business rather than solely charitable grounds. . . . If short-run profit does not adequately explain business interest in the Job Corps, does long-term profit do so? . . . The factor of long-term profitable growth, over the next decade at least, appears to be a major incentive to industrial involvement. It has been said so often that its meaning has almost been lost that education is now the greatest growth industry.[15] Several different markets are in the process of development and these are seldom sorted out expressly by the contractors. All stem from the apparent inability of the present public educational and vocational training and employment systems to meet the national goal of nearly universal matching of manpower to satisfying jobs, particularly for minority groups and others who are disadvantaged by reason of physical or mental handicaps or age. With the expected increased growth of population and vastly increased density of urban population, the inadequacy of existing systems is sure to be even more deeply felt as time passes.

Industry first senses this inadequacy in the shortage of trained manpower for its own commercial needs. This appears to be most severe in the lower and middle levels of technical skill as automated equipment is introduced into manufacturing, transportation, distribution, and marketing. It is also sharply increasing in the service areas, especially health services and education itself.[16] Some of the Job Corps contractors are themselves readily identifiable as companies in manpower shortage or potential shortage fields.[17] The expertise they can develop for their own in-house training functions may well be an important inducement to them. One company mentions another related benefit to its own manpower picture: the Job Corps acts as an excellent screening mechanism for its candidates for top-level management. This type of direct self-interest is not necessarily confined to the largest companies. As equal employment opportunity legislation is enforced more widely, the ability to train minority group members is becoming increasingly necessary for companies, middle-sized as well as large. . . .

A second long-term motivation for business contracts with the Job Corps is suggested. . . . In most instances the service industries are too fractionalized to undertake a Job Corps center prime contract or, perhaps, even a subcontract. But, while auto repair shops may not sign Job Corps management contracts, they might—if their shortages become severe enough —contract with an industrial training firm to have the skilled workers supplied to them. At least one of the present contractors sees this as a potential market and is actively developing itself as an industrial trainer of personnel for other companies for a fee. A related commercial role is that of training companies to do their own training. Again the same contractor is leading toward this field and has been awarded a further Job Corps contract to train corpsmen to become instructors in conservation camps.

A third commercial or long-term profitmaking potential is the marketing of hardware: teaching machines, audiovisual training devices, programed curriculums, books, and films. Again, the heavy incidence of electronic equipment manufacturers among the contractors has been widely construed as suggesting that this is a major motivation. However, the experience so far has apparently not yielded a great deal in this direction. One contractor is experimenting with instant-replay television for group counseling, but this is not so much a new technology as a technique of using an existing technology. Another contractor indicates that the restrictive patent policy being applied by OEO discourages development of new hardware. Another states flatly that the product is not hardware but the much more difficult product to package: technique, especially the technique of building an environment in which motivation can be instilled.

One highly important factor in the market potential of both hardware and technique in this field is the demand abroad, particularly in the less-developed countries. If the United States has such a large demand for these products, after years of investment in public education, the potential demand in less-developed countries is enormous. The contractors interviewed stressed this as an important long-range market for which they hope to be able to compete, in part because of their Job Corps center management experience. Having run such an enterprise gives them credentials in the field with which companies lacking that experience would find it difficult to compete, both domestically and abroad. Clearly this motivation is a powerful incentive to produce a successful record and coincides exactly with the public interest.

• • •

The most elusive of all motivations is corporate image. Despite the value it is given popularly, it is often, one suspects, in reality only the public veneer placed over the concrete commercial motivations which have been discussed. Whatever it is, it does not appear to be a significant factor for companies undertaking the management of Job Corps centers. Most of the commercial contractors do not, for example, exploit their Job Corps involvement in their national advertising. There have been reports that some companies have actually avoided publicity about their involvement because of their fear that if disturbances occurred on or near their centers, their corporate images would be hurt far more seriously than they would have been helped by the favorable publicity. Perhaps the most important reason for industrial reluctance is the generally held belief that the Job Corps is not a popular antipoverty program, as compared for example, with Head Start. In fact, just the opposite of the companies using the Job Corps to improve the companies' images, OEO is now seeking to use the contractors' images to improve the Job Corps image with the public and with the Congress. At a meeting of contractors called by OEO in Austin, Tex., in February, 1967, for example, a resolution in favor of the objectives of the Job Corps program was signed by the contractors and released to the press.

Finally, there is the complex network of human motivations which are responsible for charitable contributions or social service. These may well in some cases overlap some of the commercial motivations already discussed. Apparently some of the initial industrial proposals were in response to highly personal appeals to individual corporate officers by the President or the Director of OEO. And there have been occasions where personal publicity has been given by OEO to individual corporate officers at least partially in order to reinforce their influence over their companies' intention to remain in the program.

However, there would seem to be far more direct involvement of business management in the solution of social problems where the profitmaking interest, even if it is diluted, is somehow involved in the corporate decision to participate. The Job Corps operates on a contract basis and business has shown a substantial interest in its contracts in spite of all the risks involved in a new and highly demanding social experiment. Although there are reports of companies which have threatened to drop out, so far none has. There may be no cause and effect relationship, but the facts appear to substantiate the expressed feeling that the businesslike relationship of the contractors with the Job Corps gives the companies a firmer and more direct stake in its success, one with which they are highly familiar, than would an appeal only to their charitable and noncommercial interests. As has been noted, a different level of corporate decisionmaking seems generally to be involved than would be for charitable contributions. And certainly under Job Corps contracts a far greater number of corporate personnel are directly involved in helping to solve the problems of the poor than would have been had there been no Job Corps contracts.

Whether the Job Corps experiment in residential work training, an attempt to restructure the trainee's entire environment, and, as a result, his motivation, is worth the large public investment is not the question assigned to this study. But the history and development of the experiment to date do suggest some conclusions about the potential of business involvement in large-scale manpower training programs:

1. Companies of all sizes, in reasonably large numbers, particularly in the electronics equipment manufacturing industry but also in other manufacturing and service areas, are willing to undertake cost-plus-fixed-fee contracts for manpower training even on a massive scale.

2. Their motivation appears to be a complex mix, with long-term profit through diversification the most significant for the larger companies and shortrun profit somewhat more important for the smaller firms.

3. One of the most important inducements is the degree of control the companies are given over the experimental aspects of the program. As cost pressure increases, business interest may weaken because of the impact on experimentation and on company control over program.

4. Because of the relatively small number of urban centers, the potential of business involvement has only begun to be utilized even among large companies with government contract experience, which have significant advantages over other companies for projects of the size of residential centers. Smaller companies could make a larger contribution to the program if there were a greater number of smaller centers (which is unlikely because of cost) or if there were more subcontracting, particularly for assistance on management, training and placement, a technique which has been used with telling effect at Gary.

5. The companies' ability to handle such operations, relative to nonprofit institutions, appears to be good, particularly in management. Evaluation of the longrun relative vocational training impact must await better measurement bases and more data for the Job Corps as a whole. But the indications are that industrial contract involvement does improve training and placement as well as management.

6. There are indications that industrial involvement under contract tends to produce still greater involvement of the contracting companies with solving the problems of poverty, both in placement within their own companies and in seeking out additional contracts and other useful involvements.

7. The Gary experience shows that a nonprofit structure can be made to work successfully with a large enough infusion of business expertise and concern. In that case the primary spur to wide business involvement appears to have been political and, as such, may be difficult to replicate elsewhere. A profit incentive might well bring to bear elsewhere the consortium of a wide variety of businesses which appears to be so useful at Gary.

8. One completely untapped potential area for contract involvement on training is that of private vocational schools. It is highly anomalous that the only significant impetus to private involvement in the original act, in section 103(b), was the reference to private vocational schools and institutes and this appears to have been wholly unused to date. Even with public education systems, vocational and otherwise, a contractual relationship for the orderly interchange of personnel and, perhaps, plant and equipment might be sought.

9. The spontaneous development of on-the-job training as a supplement to residential training is highly significant and should be encouraged, systematized, and brought into a unified program along with the OJT components of MDTA and the Neighborhood Youth Corps. The loss of OJT opportunities for corpsmen or competition among these programs for OJT slots would be very unfortunate.

10. Greater emphasis should be placed upon combined residential and nonresidential centers near the urban core, in order to maximize OJT, to provide increased opportunity for subcontracting with smaller companies, and to afford corpsmen the continued support of center personnel after they leave the center. The combinations should operate in both directions, with some enrollees living all or part time at the center and on OJT in the city, and some living at home and training at the center.

11. Based upon the results of experiments with combined residential and nonresidential centers, considerations should be given to an ultimate fusion in one administration of the Job Corps and the Neighborhood Youth Corps so that the selection of enrollees for each can be made more rationally than it now appears to be and so that the connections of the two programs with business will be made jointly and with maximum effect.

MANPOWER DEVELOPMENT AND TRAINING PROGRAMS

The second largest business involvement in federal antipoverty programs, in federal contract dollar terms, is in the On-the-Job Training program under the Manpower Development and Training Act of 1962 (MDTA-OJT), which is administered by the Department of Labor. That this major business participation is again in the manpower training field is a reflection of the close relationship between long-term profit and industrial manpower needs which has been discussed in regard to the Job Corps.

The history of MDTA-OJT is in some respects the reverse of that of the Job Corps. Originally the MDTA program was designed during the late 1950's as an attack on unemployment through classroom job training and retraining in the public vocational education system. State vocational education departments, administering technical high schools and institutes geared to youth, had received federal aid since 1917 under a series of acts and had become a powerful and highly independent political force.[18] The primary intention of the proposals was to add new federal funds to the system for the training of unemployed adults. The funds were also to be used as a lever to bring the training process more closely into mesh with the job identification and placement facilities of the state departments of labor, which have jurisdiction over the federally financed but state-administered employment service system. The emphasis was on more effective matching of training to jobs, with both training and matching done exclusively through public agencies.[19] Just as in the case of the Job Corps, the initial impetus was toward using governmental agencies exclusively.

During congressional consideration of the bills, a drive to bring industry into the training process was successful, and the expectation appeared to be that the program, originally funded at approximately $100 million, would be split equally between classroom training in public vocational schools, funded by the Department of Health, Education, and Welfare, and on-the-job training, funded by the Labor Department.[20] On-the-job training was to be given by private companies in their own plants and shops, with the employer paying wages to the trainee and receiving reimbursement for the training costs under a contract negotiated at the local level. The innovative concept behind OJT was training for a particular job by the employer himself, who presumably knows what training he wants his prospective employee to have had, rather than training in a public institution for employment in general and then seeking through the public employment service to match the trainee to an employer and a particular job.

Here, the parallel with the subsequent Job Corps development is importantly broken, because as has been discussed, while the Task Force Against Poverty compromised on a balance in the Job Corps between the profit and nonprofit sectors, the Congress virtually ignored private enterprise in the Economic Opportunity Act of 1964 and actually weighted the Job Corps heavily toward public and other nonprofit development by insisting that 40 per cent of the enrollees be in public conservation camps. With MDTA, on the other hand, the Congress made quite clear its intention to involve business significantly in the manpower training process.

Yet, even with the strong congressional emphasis on OJT in the original MDT Act, the percentage of business involvement in the program has grown very slowly and the expected balance between the public and private sectors has been reached only in the last few months, almost five years after the original enactment. In 1963, the first full fiscal year of operation, only 6 per cent of MDTA trainees were in OJT. With repeated congressional insistence, the OJT portion was increased to 12 per cent of trainees enrolled in 1964, 19 per cent in 1965, and 29 per cent in 1966, represented in the last calendar year by 67,800 trainees. There has been a growing involvement of individual firms, from 400, mostly small companies, in 1963, to 2,084 so far in 1967. . . . Over this period of growth, it has become obvious that the congressional insistence on expanding OJT as distinguished from traditional public classroom instruction, was fully justified by the results. The record of initial placements is far higher for OJT trainees, 93.1 per cent of completers over the first three years of the program, than it is for institutional trainees, which averaged 73.6 per cent for the same period. OJT is also considerably more successful in achieving placements related to training, 88.3 per cent as compared with 60 per cent during the three-year period.[21] So far the Labor Department has not compiled reliable figures on the long-term job retention of trainees, but some samples are reported to indicate that OJT is more successful on this scale as well. A problem has been poor compliance with a requirement that the contractor file a series of followup reports three months, six months and one year after completion of training.

The difference in cost per trainee is also highly favorable to OJT, but primarily because of the living allowance which is paid out of public funds to institutional trainees and is not paid to the wage-earning OJT trainees. Current institutional cost per trainee is $1,886, or twice the OJT federal cost.[22] As will be discussed further, the differences in characteristics between the institutional and OJT trainee populations should not be disregarded in evaluating the large advantage OJT appears to have on all these scales. For example, all the institutional trainees are unemployed to begin with, whereas, although the Labor Department has not made available any breakdown on this, it is clear that some substantial proportion of OJT trainees are already employed and are being upgraded in skill.

• • •

Several factors are responsible for the slowness of the growth of the OJT program in spite of clear congressional intent and a better placement and cost record. The first and most obvious is the resistance of the public vocational education system to inroads into its share of the funds. Each state has a joint board of vocational educators and state labor department representatives which generally screens all but the smallest applications and presents them for final review and funding to the Department of Health, Education, and Welfare or the Department of Labor, whichever is relevant. Only applications for ten or fewer OJT trainees are approved at the regional Labor Department level. In most cases, therefore, public agencies have control at the state level over the mix of public and private applications which are ultimately approved. And the state boards have tended to favor the public vocational education system.[23]

• • •

Even at an earlier point the system has been relatively uncongenial toward business involvement. The MDTA-OJT program is administered in the field by representatives of the Bureau of Apprenticeship and Training (BAT) in the Labor Department's 152 field offices in every state. The primary function of the BAT is to encourage employers and unions to establish joint apprenticeship programs, which are an early form of OJT. Such programs are generally limited to unionized companies where both management and labor are sympathetic to the hiring of lesser skilled employees at a starting wage usually one-half the going wage. Apprenticeable trades usually require a relatively higher skill level as compared with OJT occupations. Consequently,

MDTA-OJT programs are inherently only somewhat competitive with apprenticeship. Unlike apprenticeship at least in form, OJT programs do not require union approval before they can be instituted, although in operation this difference tends to disappear.[24] The difference in cost to the employer may be substantial, since apprenticeship permits a lower wage for a period of as long as four or five years on a gradually rising scale, whereas MDTA-OJT is seldom more than one year and, on the average, is between twenty and twenty-six weeks. Under MDTA-OJT the employer is required to pay no more than the minimum wage and is reimbursed for his training cost, which has now stabilized at $25 per week per trainee in the case of smaller contracts and less in the case of larger ones.

However substantive the conflict between apprenticeship and OJT may or may not be, the fact remains that the primary function of BAT personnel is the encouragement of apprenticeship, and the OJT function has been grafted on to that Bureau's work with less than complete enthusiasm. One, admittedly imprecise, measure of the result is that in 1966 there were 67,800 OJT trainees and 240,000 registered apprentices.

• • •

The result of this relative lack of emphasis is that the OJT program is not brought to the attention of employers in great numbers as it should be. It requires little selling to make it attractive to employers, apparently; but it does require systematic efforts to reach the business community, town by town and city by city, with effective information about the availability of the program and its benefits to employers and to the community. . . . The Bureau's own contract study published in 1964 indicates that the opportunities to stimulate new training, not now being done by industry, are enormous. Its survey concluded that only one establishment in five had some type of formal training, even including safety programs, which accounted for more than half the participants in those training programs which did exist. Only a small fraction were in training for a particular skilled trade. Plumbing the extent of business interest requires considerable informational, if not necessarily promotional, effort since the universe of potential employer contractors is enormous. There are more than 3.3. million employers of one or more employees in the United States, and reaching them even to assess their interest in OJT for one or more trainees is a vast undertaking. It is noteworthy that the Labor Department has no funds whatever expressly for this purpose and, with the exceptions to be discussed, depends primarily upon company-by-company contact by BAT personnel, whose chief function, as has been noted, is to contact employers and unions in order to stimulate apprenticeship programs. Somehow, BAT has nevertheless reached or been reached by a total of more than 4,000 employers since MDTA enactment.

• • •

In OJT, just as in the case of the Job Corps, the employer-contractor is receiving funds out of the federal Treasury, and as a result the entire network of federal accounting and auditing requirements is imposed. The paperwork burden thus becomes a material factor for all but the largest employers. Even if a small employer should learn of the program and seek to utilize it, the bookkeeping involved often offsets the benefit of having one or two employees trained.[25] Because of complaints about this, the Labor Department has now simplified its contract and report forms, but there is still a widespread belief among businessmen, in companies of all sizes, that the paperwork requirements of the Labor Department are unreasonably stringent. . . .

Another technique for easing the accounting burden on small business is through pooled training agreements, under which a number of employers with similar manpower needs form a group which receives the OJT contract. Some part-time classroom or "vestibule" training may be built into the plan, perhaps given by the group in the shop of one of the members. MDT pays the group for the rental of space and the instructor's salary. The instructor may supplement the classroom training, which may take a part of each week, by visiting the trainees in the shop during the rest of the week. Each employer pays the wages of its employee-trainees. The group together share the application and report filing for the entire project.

This is the pattern followed in the pilot trade association contract between BAT and the National Tire Dealers Association, which has trained or is training a total of 650 men in twenty-eight such pooled programs among its members. The association itself identifies a city, or area within approximately a forty-mile radius of a city, in which a number of small tire dealers need retreaders. It then organizes a group and sets up a classroom in one shop in a centralized location. The usual group consists of eight to ten employees, each seeking to train from one to four employees. The classes, which average twenty to twenty-five trainees, spend six hours a week at the central shop receiving vestibule training from the instructor, and the remaining thirty-four hours a week in their respective employer's shop, visited by the instructor in rotation. The dropout rate is approximately 20 per cent. Most of the trainees were employees of the employer prior to the initiation of the OJT program. Completers are usually promoted to higher level jobs at higher wage rates than before and make room for new, less-skilled employees to be hired, according to the association.

• • •

As the pressure has increased to include larger numbers of the disadvantaged in both MDTA programs, there has been a corresponding need to add institutional supplements to the OJT experience. An effort was begun in 1966 to move 58 per cent of OJT trainees through an initial period of classroom prevocational training in so-called "coupled" programs. The result has not been entirely satisfactory since many of the same rigidities built into the institutional program have simply been transferred to OJT. The vocational education authorities and the Department of Health, Education, and Welfare regional office must be brought in and must also approve the plan. And industry found that the institutional training was still not particular-job oriented. The worst problem is that the particular industrial need for workers may not wait three months until the courses are over.

To resolve these difficulties a number of alternative techniques are being explored. One involves vestibule training of the type described above, in which the company's instructor gives a type of inplant classroom training during part of the week and then follows the trainees on the job site. This is costly because of the loss of the trainee's time to the employer for four or six or eight hours during the week. Another is for industry to train instructors to do the prevocational training in the schoolroom, in order to make classroom training more relevant to the ultimate job. This technique is usually unfeasible because of a Labor-HEW dispute as to whether the company can be reimbursed for the loss of its instructor during his time at the vocational education school. HEW has preferred instead to use the funds to send the vocational education teachers to school for further training. A third technique is to have the public school instructor follow the trainees into the plant after the month or months of public classroom training are ended.

What these techniques reflect is primarily an attempt to provide additional support for disadvantaged OJT trainees, who gain obvious benefits from actually working with equipment and being paid wages for it, but who may be defeated by other aspects of a new and competitive work situation. An even more intensive effort at support has been pioneered in a demonstration project in Chicago called Jobs Now, in which an evaluation was made of the factors leading to OJT trainee retention. Based on a sample of twenty companies who had each hired approximately sixty Jobs Now trainees, the study concluded that there was a high correlation between job retention with very much or some "high support" and job loss with very little or no high support. The ten companies rated "very much" or "some" high support retained 82 per cent of their trainees. The ten rated "very little" or "none" had a 28 per cent retention rate. High support consisted of the following elements: communication from the "top"; buddy relationship; give special consideration and attention to Jobs Now trainees; share information with Jobs Now staff; special training for Jobs Now trainees; Jobs Now staff invited to enter premises and talk with trainee or personnel of company; knowledge of the Jobs Now program and of high support.[26]

These elements of largely psychological support are not in themselves difficult to provide. The problem is that companies are normally not prepared to provide them. Businessmen interviewed stressed that companies know well how to train employees to handle their jobs and do so all the time whether formally or not. But they contend that because businessmen are production-minded and have in the past not concentrated on employee work attitudes, companies do not know how to provide the supportive elements. In one example given, a mobile recruiting unit brought in from a center city slum some 300 to 400 trainee recruits but within two days on the job, without supporting help, only a few were still on the job. Just as the Job Corps is an effort, as one contractor describes it, to provide a "substitute parent" for the disadvantaged youth, MDTA-OJT contractors are increasingly seeing the need for assistance with helping the disadvantaged trainees adjust to the work situation. Such assistance will require extensive efforts to recruit counselors and coaches, particularly from groups which have had experience with working with the disadvantaged or from the ghetto itself. . . .

• • •

Once again, with MDTA-OJT as in Job Corps, the intensity of business involvement is very much affected by cost. Few if any companies will undertake OJT programs without some reasonable compensation for out-of-pocket costs. Philanthropy would not be a sufficient motive, as one company representative put it, to overcome the paperwork and auditing burden which comes with dealing with the government. Consequently, even the largest companies accept federal reimbursement for training costs, even when it is only a fraction of the company's real cost. Clearly there is no opportunity to make a short-term profit with a cost-reimbursement but nonfee contract. The only incentive to undertaking such a contract is long-term profit of the varieties discussed above in regard to the Job Corps.

It is possible that enough companies may not be stimulated to undertake OJT for the disadvantaged on a cost-reimbursable basis even with the expansion of allocable cost to cover supportive services. Some short-term profit may have to be built into the contract. On the face of it there is no real distinction between operating a residential training center for a fee under a government contract and operating a nonresidential training center for a fee under a government contract. The argument that the trainee is producing and therefore bringing a profit to the employer has not defeated the concept of federal reimbursement for training cost, so long as the employer pays the trainee the minimum wage. By the same token, if the trainee is so disadvantaged as not to be at all or only marginally productive during the training period, it may be defensible to give the employer a fee to compensate him for that loss of productivity. . . .

It may be relevant to the choice of additional incentives that a number of companies interviewed, which do not have OJT contracts, indicated a widespread belief among businessmen that the content of training under such contracts would be directed or controlled by the federal government and that the method of training their employees was too important to their profitable operation to permit them to surrender control. As in the case of similar preconceptions regarding auditing and paperwork, it is important to bring home to employers that there will be no control by the federal authorities over the content of training. Whether the new experiments with supportive service will affect this remains to be seen, but the indications are that the companies will still be responsible for developing curriculums for basic literacy training as well as for the vocational training they have always shaped under OJT. Nonetheless, there is a wide area of business which apparently so much fears the possibility of governmental meddling in what are considered to be managerial prerogatives that it will avoid any contractual subsidy arrangement, no matter what its form. It is possible that a tax credit would have a greater likelihood of success with some of the companies in that category.

• • •

The conclusions from this analysis of the MDTA-OJT program are as follows:

1. On-the-job training stimulated by the cost reimbursement method under the MDT Act appears to be a highly effective tool for training and placing the unemployed and underemployed in satisfying jobs. Job retention figures are not yet available in reliable quantities and should be obtained through a followup system not dependent upon contractors. But the initial placement figures are in themselves far better than in institutional or residential programs and are at least as good if discounted for differences in trainee characteristics.

2. Whether the OJT technique will succeed relatively as well as the trainees are drawn increasingly from the disadvantaged poor is not yet clear, but there are indications that it will, if and only if the necessary additional supportive services can be provided.

3. Business interest in, and involvement with, on-the-job training is widespread and growing rapidly, but at this point only a small fraction of the potential has been reached and a far greater effort is necessary to reach it effectively, particularly in regard to the disadvantaged.

4. The present size and location of the federal effort, in the Bureau of Apprenticeship and Training, are not adequate to the necessary expansion of the program, particularly if other programs—such as the Job Corps, the Neighborhood Youth Corps, and a series of new adult work experience and training programs—begin developing OJT programs of their own as they have now been authorized to do. Multiple contacts with the same companies by representatives of different programs is highly discouraging to employers even if on the merits the programs are not competitive and provide different types of workers or different contract terms. Congressional requirements of coordination, by themselves, will apparently not eliminate duplication of contacts with industry and one subagency should be given the responsibility for this. A logical choice would be the federal-state employment services, since contact with industry to place the unemployed should be their focus. Unfortunately the services as they are presently organized do not in all states constitute a sufficient center for all OJT promotion for the federal government. A single OJT subagency should be created for the purpose of using one set of personnel in the field to contact business and industry on behalf of all federally assisted OJT programs. Other important resources from this point of view would appear to be the Department of Commerce, the Equal Employment Opportunity Commission, and the Plans for Progress program, and effective liaison with these agencies should be explored as a means of reaching private enterprise systematically and comprehensively.

5. A much broader promotional campaign should be mounted to bring the availability of the program to the attention of companies of all sizes and in a

systematic way to the attention of trade associations, social welfare groups, and community action agencies, both as a route to individual companies and with a view toward negotiating pooled training contracts. The advantages of pooled training are manifest and should be explored with companies themselves, particularly those which have sought Job Corps contracts, as well as with trade associations and other existing groups.

6. The promotional effort should seek to overcome the misconceptions about the MDTA-OJT program by stressing the simplicity of the paperwork and report filing, the limited audits required, and the lack of control exerted over the content of job training. At the same time it should also offer assistance in providing curriculums for vestibule or other classroom training and examples of experience gained with various types of supportive assistance to trainees.

7. Supportive services, including the cost of training counselors and instructors of disadvantaged trainees, should be allowable costs where employers agree to accept applicants without regard to the "preferred nominee" selection process.

8. Consideration should be given to authorizing cost-plus-fixed-fee contracts for OJT for the most disadvantaged unemployed, particularly where training is pooled for a number of companies. Consideration should also be given to authorizing a corporate income tax credit for investment in training the most disadvantaged unemployed, in those instances in which companies do not elect to contract for federal assistance.

9. Greater delegation should be made to regional offices to approve smaller OJT contracts, including those with coupled prevocational training. The existing authority is not being utilized fully and should be expanded.

10. One avenue of private participation which should be tested is contracting with private employment agencies, for a fee, to place disadvantaged workers in OJT situations.

11. The recent increased use of coupled institutional and OJT has exposed the public system far more widely than before to the training needs of the private sector. In four instances public vocational education agencies have contracted with private profitmaking vocational or business schools. In one case a company seeking an OJT contract for the disadvantaged is contemplating contracting with public vocational schools. While the $10 million vocational work-study program is limited to public employers, a relatively small part-time cooperative training program, which has been in effect for many years, provides federal assistance for half-time vocational high school matched to half-time employment in private industry. The cross-fertilization of the public vocational sector and industry should be greatly expanded and HEW's mandate in this regard should be considerably strengthened.

NOTES

1. OEO has submitted to the subcommittee figures indicating that in the three months

ending March 31, 1967, seventy-four Job Corps contracts out of ninety-nine were let to industrial firms, the contracts with the latter totaling $22,570,000. These figures were not broken down as between housekeeping and nonhousekeeping functions.
2. Sec. 110 of the 1964 act required that 40 per cent of the enrollees be in conservation camps. In 1966 this was changed to 40 per cent of male enrollees only.
3. See, for example, "Hearings, Senate Subcommittee on Employment Manpower, Youth Employment," S. 1, 88th Cong., first session.
4. See, for example, sections 112, 202(a)(4), 311, 603(a)(1), of the Economic Opportunity Act of 1964, Public Law 88–452.
5. H. Rept. 1458, S. Rept. 1218, 88th Cong., 2d sess.
6. Twenty-six of the forty-six profitmaking companies and trade schools which submitted proposals were small—under 500 employees—or medium sized (a well-known name but in the $5 million annual gross class).
7. Seven of the twenty-six received a rating of 2 or above. Interestingly enough, four of the nineteen large companies (over $30 million annual gross) which submitted proposals were given unacceptable ratings.
8. Of the forty applicants for women's centers, twenty-two were small and medium sized.
9. Eight of the twenty-two received a rating of 2 or above. Again, five of sixteen large companies who sought women's center contracts were given unacceptable ratings.
10. Five of sixteen nonprofit applicants for men's centers were rated 2 or higher; but interestingly, eighteen of thirty-seven such applicants for women's centers received a 2 rating or higher.
11. For example, Gary's operating cost per corpsman per year is $4,600, the lowest of the men's centers, the highest of which is almost twice as high. The average is $5,600 to $5,800. The cost of the smaller women's centers is higher than that of the men's, and that of the less complex and less vocationally oriented conservation centers is lowest of all. The statutory maximum, added in 1966, is $7,500 per enrollee per year. Deducting $1,600, the OEO figure for direct enrollee costs such as enrollee pay and allowance, dependent allotments and enrollee travel, the contractors have $5,900 to work with. Another factor in cost is length of stay, with the cost per enrollee decreasing with longer periods of training. The average now is six months, as compared with OEO's original expectation that it would be one to two years.
12. It has not been verified statistically, but there is a general impression that the OEO headquarters staff, and particularly the Job Corps staff, has also been recruited increasingly from industry.
13. OEO reports that fixed fees are higher under contracts involving less than total center management. Examples submitted include 7 per cent under a $214,000 contract for analysis of the OEO medical processing system; 5 per cent under a $53,480 contract for professional architectural and engineering services at a women's center; 6½ per cent under a $41,987 contract for development of vocational curriculums for several conservation camps; and a $5,727 fixed price contract for weekly poster programs at all conservation centers. OEO also points out that these higher fee contracts tend to be with the smaller companies.
14. By way of comparison, one nonprofit's indirect cost is reported to have amounted to 15 per cent of direct cost.
15. See, for example, *Business Week* (December 19, 1964), pp. 23–24; John McHale, "Big Business Enlists for the War on Poverty," *Trans-Action magazine* (May–June, 1965); "Trying Two Approaches in Job Corps Training," *The National Observer* (Feb. 21, 1966); Gerald Grant, "Automated Devices Will Speed Learning," *Philadelphia Inquirer* (July 3, 1966).
16. See, for example, "Report on Manpower Requirements and Resources" (October–November, 1966), Bureau of Labor Statistics and Bureau of Employment Security, U.S. Department of Labor, especially pp. 12 and 14; "Projections 1970: Interindustry Relationships, Potential Demand, and Employment," *Bulletin 1536*, Bureau of Labor Statistics, U.S. Department of Labor.
17. A curious sidelight on this is that OEO at the outset informally discouraged contractors from hiring corpsmen from their own centers, apparently on the theory that it might be vulnerable for providing trained employees to the companies at the government's expense. Out of the sample of 12,000 placements which has been re-

ferred to, fifteen industrial contractors with the Job Corps nonetheless hired a total of 100 corpsmen. Fortunately, the policy has this year been reversed, and contractors have been encouraged in a written memorandum to hire corpsmen. As more current placement figures are obtained it will be interesting to see whether the amount of self-hiring by contractors increases significantly.
18. Smith-Hughes Act of 1917; Vocational Education Act of 1946 (George-Barden Act); Vocational Education Act of 1963. The first two acts provide a total of $57 million per year; the last adds $581 million per year. The business impact on these programs is discussed at another point.
19. S. Rept. 651, 87th Cong., first sess., especially pp. 2 and 7.
20. Secs. 204(a) and 303(b), Public Law 87-415; H. Rept. 1416, 87th Cong., second sess., pp. 13 and 16-17; hearings, "Employer Encouragement for On-the-Job Training," Senate Subcommittee on Employment and Manpower, 89th Cong., first and second sess., pp. 1-2; hearings, "Fiscal 1968 Labor-HEW Appropriations," House Subcommittee on Appropriations, 90th Cong., first sess., pt. 1, p. 125.
21. These are averages for fiscal years 1964, 1965, and 1966.
22. Hearings, "Fiscal 1968 Labor-HEW Appropriations," House Appropriations Subcommittee, 90th Cong., second sess., pt. 1, p. 160.
23. One reflection of this is that as of Feb. 24, 1967, only 57 per cent of the fiscal year 1967 funds allocated state-by-state for OJT had been obligated, while 85 per cent of the institutional funds allocated had been obligated (Hearings, Labor-HEW appropriations, House Appropriations Subcommittee, 90th Cong., first sess., pt. 1, fiscal 1968, p. 157).
24. Under sec. 205(b) of the act, local labor-management advisory committees give applications under MDTA a preliminary screening and delays have been attributed in some instances to union resistance. (See hearings, Senate Subcommittee on Employment and Manpower, 89th Cong., first sess., pp. 197-198.)
25. A great deal of testimony to this effect was heard by the subcommittee at its hearings, 89th Cong., first and second sess., "Employer Encouragement for On-the-Job Training."
26. This example and others similar to it in Philadelphia and Los Angeles are discussed in detail in the contract report submitted to the subcommittee by Arnold Nemore.

35

The Job Corps—A Cost-Benefit Analysis

OFFICE OF ECONOMIC OPPORTUNITY

[*The Office of Economic Opportunity prepared a cost-benefit analysis of expenditures under the Job Corps Program, for submission to the Joint Economic Committee.*]

From the Joint Economic Committee's publication, *Federal Programs for the Development of Human Resources*, vol. 1 (1966).

JOB CORPS PAYBACK PERIOD

Using conservative assumptions, the government's investment will be matched by the increased earnings of a graduate in 5.1 years. This is a computation based upon earnings alone. If other social costs (public assistance payments, law enforcement, and so on) generated by these same youth had they never been in Job Corps, were included, the period would be reduced considerably below the 5.1 years.

TABLE 35-1

1. COSTS:		
(a) Total costs at steady-state $7,765 by 45,000 man-years		$349,000,000
(b) With average term of nine months, this provides for enrollees		60,000
(c) Assumed number of graduates		50,000
(d) Steady-state costs per graduate ($349,000,000 divided by 50,000)		$6,980
(e) Success rate assumed for graduates *	per cent	80
(f) Cost per success ($6,980 divided by 80 per cent)		$8,725
2. BENEFITS:		
(a) Average hourly wage per successful graduate		$1.60
(b) Assumed annual employment per successful graduate	hours	2,000
(c) Average annual wage per successful graduate		$3,200
(d) Average hourly wage before entry		$1
(e) Assumed annual employment before entry	hours	1,500
(f) Average annual wage before entry		$1,500
(g) Earnings gain		$1,700
3. Earnings payback period ($8,725 divided by $1,700): Time required for enrollee earnings to equal government cost	years	5.1

* Success is defined as holding a good steady job, going back to school or into military service. A good job is defined as semiskilled or better. For purpose of this calculation, all successful graduates are treated as if they were in jobs.

[*In the same publication, staff of the Joint Economic Committee comment on the foregoing figures.*]

The OEO response provides an abbreviated cost-benefit analysis for the Job Corps program. On the basis of a cost of $6,980 for each graduate and a success rate of 80 per cent, OEO esimated a unit cost of $8,725 for each successful case. Assuming further that the successful Job Corps graduates would have increased their earnings by an average of $1,700 a year, from $1,500 without benefit of the program to $3,200 after completing it, the incremental earnings in five years would about equal the cost of Job Corps training.

Such an analysis is incomplete as to both costs and benefits. Among costs, it omits foregone earnings during the training period, however negligible these might be; secondary or indirect costs not charged to the particular program; and training plant outlays. Among benefits, the analysis apparently omits offsets for outside subsistence costs that would have been incurred during the training period; possible reductions in public assistance payments and other welfare expenses; and resultant reductions in costs of law enforcement, delinquency, or crime. The estimates for increased average earnings after training are modest assumptions rather than studied projections, and the calculations might justifiably consider the discounted value of lifetime increases in productivity. Also, the estimated average cost for successful graduates (those who hold a good steady job, return to school, or enter military service) includes all the costs for those who drop out before graduation or do not "succeed" after graduation; that is, the reckoning assumes that "failures" produce no benefits to offset any part of the costs incurred for them.

36

Job Corps Evaluation

COMPTROLLER GENERAL OF THE UNITED STATES

[*In 1969, following the advent of the Nixon Administration, the Comptroller General of the United States, pursuant to a provision of the 1967 amendments to the Economic Opportunity Act of 1967, evaluated the programs for which that Act provided. His conclusions with respect to the Job Corps follow.*]

1. Through Job Corps institutionalized training, corps members have had an opportunity to develop, to varying degrees, work skills and good work habits and to further their academic education. These corps members have also received benefits in a number of areas, such as health and social and psychological development, which are generally not subject to precise measurement. Also, after Job Corps experience, many corps members have obtained good employment, returned to school, or joined the Armed Forces.

On an overall basis, however, it appears that Job Corps has achieved only limited success in fulfilling its primary purpose of assisting young persons who need and can benefit from an unusually intensive program, operated in a

---

Review of Economic Opportunity Programs (Washington, D. C.: U. S. Government Printing Office, 1969).

group setting, to develop their capacities for work and social responsibilities. Our views are based in large part on our findings with respect to post-Job Corps employment experience and related economic benefits of corps members, the unfavorable retention rate of corps members, and problems relating to program content and administration which have existed.

2. On the basis of studies by our contractor and ourselves relating to post-Job Corps experience, it is questionable whether Job Corps training has resulted in substantial economic benefit thus far for those youths who participated in the program. Our tests showed that employment and earning power were somewhat greater after Job Corps experience than before.

It appeared that the increased employment and earning power among those included in our sample can be attributable, for the most part, to the greater employability of youths due to the process of growing up and to higher employment and wage levels. This increased employability and earning power also appeared to be associated with the length of stay of corps members at the centers; those who were graduated were the most successful.

It also appeared that Job Corps terminees had not done materially better than the other eligible youths who had applied to enter the program and then chose not to participate.

3. Factors limiting the success of Job Corps are many and vary in degrees of importance. One of the most significant factors was the short length of stay by corps members. Given the overall achievement level of the entering youths, even the most viable program can hardly be expected to have dramatic results if the youths cannot be induced to remain at the centers long enough to benefit from the training. The effectiveness of the program in meeting its objectives of assisting young persons who need and can benefit from an intensive training program is highly questionable for the large number of youths who remained at the centers for only short periods of time.

4. Weaknesses in the policies and procedures under which the program has been administered have detracted significantly from program success. According to Job Corps estimates, direct costs per enrollee man-year were $6,600 for fiscal year 1968. Considering both the direct and the indirect costs for those centers in operation as of June 30, 1968, enrollee man-year costs for fiscal year 1968 were $8,300. Although costs of this magnitude are required to operate the program and it has been in existence for over four years, there existed a number of major problems of administration including: (*a*) a need for improving the recruiting and screening procedures. A significant portion of Corps members have not met the qualifications generally considered necessary or desirable for participation in the program and the alternatives of enrolling applicants in other less costly, and possibly more suitable, training programs apparently were not always considered; (*b*) a need for improving the administration of the vocational and academic training programs and for establishing minimum graduation criteria which would provide assurance that graduates possess the minimum requisites for successful employment; (*c*) a need for strengthening the counseling system at each of the centers to more fully assist Corps members in making the social, educational,

and vocational adjustments necessary to become self-supporting members of society and to provide a means by which Corps members could be encouraged to remain at the centers for a sufficient period of time to acquire the skills necessary to obtain and hold jobs; and (*d*) a need for the centers to improve their records and reporting systems in order to obtain accurate and meaningful information about individual Corps members and program operations as a tool for evaluating the effectiveness of the centers' various activities.

We have considerable doubt as to whether conservation centers can be expected to provide the intensive training contemplated in the act. . . . To establish intensive vocational training programs at each of the eighty-two centers in a number of vocational areas for the 100 to 250 corpsmen enrolled at each of the centers would appear to be quite costly. Moreover, it is questionable whether a sufficient number of qualified instructors could be obtained to provide such training at the generally remote and isolated conservation center locations.

In summary, it is probable that a valid need can be documented for residential training of the type envisioned in Job Corps for a certain number of youths whose needs, because of environmental characteristics or because of geographic location, cannot be well served through other programs operating in or near their home communities. We have doubt, however, that, in light of our findings and the cost of this type of training, the resources now being applied to the Job Corps program can be fully justified. Our doubt in this regard is especially applicable to the conservation center component of the program, particularly in consideration of the significant changes which appear necessary in this component to upgrade its effectiveness in achieving training program objectives.

37

Report of the Secretary of Labor on Restructuring the Job Corps (1969)

[*Following the Comptroller General's report, Secretary of Labor George Shultz made recommendations for reorganizing the Job Corps, the essence of which are contained in the following excerpt.*]

The Job Corps was established, at least in part, as an experiment in reaching, teaching, and training the hard-core youth—a task that the regular established programs were not then prepared to handle. Since then, however, a number of new manpower programs, specifically designed to meet the education and training needs of young, disadvantaged people have been fashioned. . . . If the objectives of the Job Corps, and indeed of our total manpower program, are to be realized, a major reshaping is necessary.

• • •

The first major change is to make the Jobs Corps an integral part of a comprehensive manpower system rather than continue it as another, essentially separate, program. This can benefit both Job Corps and the other manpower programs, which now generally lack intensive residential-support services. Integration will facilitate improvement of recruitment, screening, and selection practices, with material reduction of inefficient recruiting and unwarranted screening-out. The Job Corps has often received a lesser priority in overall manpower programs; that will be changed. Refinement of selection criteria can help us to identify those who have a special need for residential services as against other alternatives.

If the Job Corps were to use available community manpower services, such as Concentrated Employment Program, Job Opportunities in the Business Sector, Manpower Development and Training Act, Neighborhood Youth Corps, all program elements would be more relevant and more readily accessible to most of the Job Corps' target population. More attention will be given to a planned sequence of integrated services. *In effect, by coupling the unique residential services of the Job Corps with each of the on-going programs we will multiply the effectiveness of all our efforts. . . .*

The second major change is to direct part of the Job Corps resources to new organizational forms, particularly smaller inner-city or near-city residential centers. Examination of the past, rather rigid forms in which Job Corps has been structured suggests the need for greater flexibility. Assignment away from the home community is necessary or useful for some enrollees but not all. Use of a variety of new center models will generate a greater responsiveness to the differential needs of the target population. Smaller centers, located in or near cities, can recruit, train, and place youth entirely within their home state or urban area. They can serve young people who need residential support but are unwilling or do not need to move to a distant area.

Such centers will do a better job with delinquent youth, more difficult to handle in large camps and often unwelcome in strange communities. They can be developed as multipurpose facilities; they could, for example, provide unwed young mothers (a group particularly needing residential support) with combined day-care and residential assistance for both mother and child. They can, in general, better draw on the full range of local community resources.

• • •

The Department is now running three of these inner-city residential support efforts (one for boys, two for girls) for NYC enrollees. Experience at the boys' center initiated in New Haven two years ago indicates that high-risk NYC youths living in a special residence are less likely to dropout, have fewer brushes with the law, and a better subsequent employment experience than a comparable group which did not receive such residential support. After six months, average weekly earnings of graduates from the New Haven center increased by 80 per cent, while the control group's earnings declined by 29 per cent, largely because of poorer work habits. Arrests of graduates were cut in half while those of the control group rose by 22 per cent. Half of the residents elected to return to school full time.

• • •

Several types of residential centers are required, depending on the special needs of each selectively identified segment of the target population.

1. *Comprehensive regional residential skill training centers* will be retained for those for whom full-time residence away from home area and family is necessary. These centers will provide manpower services to youth from sparsely populated rural areas which cannot support such programs. Four men's centers and eleven women's centers are proposed.

2. *Conservation centers in rural areas* will be operated for youths needing remedial education (reading below sixth-grade level), skill training in less complex occupations, and who seek outdoor-work careers. The program should lead more directly to placement in skill training or some specific occupational employment. The centers should also be used for brief summer outdoor work experience for some inner-city residents. Twenty-seven conservation centers should be retained.

3. *Near-city residential centers* will be opened for those for whom work-week residence away from home is desirable, with work-training geared to the specific occupational needs of the area served. Ten such centers should be opened.

4. For youths unwilling or not needing to leave their city, two types of *inner-city residential support are desirable.* One is a training *facility with attached residential support* which provides training in one or several skills, for both residents and nonresidents, while placing some of the former in courses already available at other training facilities in the area. Five medium size centers are recommended. *The other type of support is a small residence with no training facilities* of its own, serving simply to provide residential support for those who need it and are enrolled in area training programs. Such support is designed particularly for high-risk youths who ordinarily have high dropout rates from training programs because of home and family problems. It is suggested that fifteen small centers be developed.

The private sector's involvement must be expanded in both quantity and quality. This may be provided by better relating financial returns for private operators of centers to their performance. More effective ties will be explored with the National Alliance of Businessmen's program. The good start made on involvement of organized labor in providing trade and preapprenticeship training to corpsmen should be expanded, with emphasis on continuing union support during the formal apprenticeship period after graduation from Job Corps.

C *Experience under Private Manpower Programs*

38
Transferability of Manpower Programs

ARNOLD NEMORE

[*The Subcommittee on Employment, Manpower, and Poverty of the Senate Committee on Labor and Public Welfare commissioned several studies, among them the one which is reprinted in part below.*]

With the growth of the federal government's manpower responsibilities, there has been a search for local programs to serve as prototypes for broader federal support. Jobs Now (Chicago), the Opportunities Industrialization Center (Philadelphia), and the Management Council for Merit Employment, Training, and Research (Los Angeles) have been recognized or suggested as models which might be widely emulated. The fourth program, the Neighborhood Adult Participation Project (Los Angeles), illustrates the attempt to implement a very popular idea—the development of subprofessional jobs for the poor in public and private service agencies—which has become a major goal of manpower programs funded under the Economic Opportunity Act.[1] Although not successful, the program's experience provides valuable lessons for future efforts. In all of these cases, therefore, it is important to gain an understanding of these programs and to assess the extent to which they are transferable.

Many factors contribute to a successful local program, some readily evident, others subtle. Although several individual ingredients common to each of the successful programs were identified, it is the proper combination of factors based on local needs which has been responsible for success. Consequently, a priori judgments as to the potential transferability on a broader basis are hazardous.

In each successful program there was strong policy and administrative leadership. This key leadership or the sponsoring organization also had a long-term community involvement which provided a base of power and broad community support. This broad base of power and support has been effectively used and is, in large part, responsible for the programs' success. In addition, in each case there has been a period of development and growth during which staff has been "weathered," community interest and commitment solidified, and adaptations made to meet unexpected problems and changing conditions.

Subcommittee of Employment, Manpower, and Poverty, *Examination of the War on Poverty* (Washington, D.C.: U.S. Government Printing Office, 1967), Vol. 2.

The involvement of the business community has held the key to the success of each program. Although the techniques used to mobilize this involvement differed, all of the successful programs recognized the critical nature of the business commitment and devoted considerable time and resources to assuring or gaining their commitment and support. However, even in these successful programs which have had business support, except for a few firms, the amount of industry resources which have been actually allocated has been small when measured either in terms of the magnitude of the problem or the resources available to the business community. Even business leaders who are community leaders and see the relevance of these programs to individual firms have had difficulty in implementing their commitments or in getting other companies to offer the kind of support necessary to assure the success of the endeavors. While racial disturbances or riots cannot be called an essential ingredient for business participation, in each of the cities they provided the impetus for mobilization of previously latent business support. Considerably more time and resources must be devoted to the task of involving business in manpower programs and to making this involvement meaningful.

In light of the continuing search for instant success and quick replication, there has been in the past a tendency to affect a "quick and dirty" transfer of programs from one city to others. This most often has been without an examination of the reasons or the conditions necessary for success and an assurance that these conditions exist in the new location. It is, therefore, not surprising that significant difficulties have been encountered when this technique was used. Unfortunately, some of those involved in the original success of programs encourage this approach and only in the case of Jobs Now did the leadership raise hard questions when discussing transferability or further expansion of their program.

JOBS NOW

Jobs Now is a Chicago experimental and demonstration project working with hard-core, gang-oriented youth, funded by the Department of Labor and operated by the YMCA. It is a departure from the usual approach which considers preemployment training essential to placing an unskilled unprepared youth on a job. Though less than a year old, it has become a model for much of the concentrated employment program now being undertaken by the federal government in nineteen cities and two rural areas around the country. Although new, the program is built directly on the YMCA's three-year experience with the JOBS (Job Opportunities through Better Skills) program and indirectly on its long-term working relationship with other voluntary agencies, on its ten years' work with youth gangs and its seven or eight years' work with employers.

The effective utilization of these existing resources and experiences has been instrumental in the success of the project. Through the advisory board and board of managers of the YMCA, the project has had access to and support from some of Chicago's most prominent business leadership. Through its working relationship with Chicago's voluntary agencies, Jobs Now has gained their support and has been able to knit together the efforts of thirty-eight of these agencies. From its JOBS project, the Y has been able to put together a trained staff which has the confidence of and is well versed in the problems of "hard-core" youth while at the same time being knowledgeable about industry. Helped by the tight labor market conditions prevalent in Chicago during the past several years, the Jobs Now project, with able leadership, has put together a program which shows that there are many among that group of youth whose habits and attitudes are most dysfunctional for our world of work who can be enticed and helped to make the transition to the world of work. However, its most important product is the change in attitude which has begun to take place in the youth community and, more importantly, in the business community.

History

The development of the Jobs Now project was precipitated by the outbreaks of violence in Chicago during the summer of 1966. Although the YMCA had been operating the successful JOBS program since 1963, this and other programs had failed to attract many of the "status" gang members who were involved in the violence. These gang members could not be interested in training or low-status jobs with little money—they wanted jobs which paid at least $2 an hour and which promised some "chance for the future."

In a series of meetings spearheaded by Edwin Berry of the Chicago Urban League, Frank Cassell, Director of the United States Employment Service, and Roger Wilkins, Director of the Community Relations Service, it was decided that the Advisory Board of the YMCA should be asked to take the responsibility for coordinating an employment program aimed at serving the hard-core gang youth. The board agreed to coordinate the project and to secure the support of their respective companies and the business community, which was necessary to assure the project's success. In addition, contact was made with Chicago's youth gangs which gave their blessing to the project and agreed that its facilities were neutral territory and, therefore, off limits for gang fights. Initially, twenty-nine voluntary agencies—it has grown to thirty-eight—were involved and the project was announced in September 1966. Most of the original Jobs Now staff was recruited from the JOBS project. In late September, less than three weeks after the announcement of the project —during which time there was staff recruitment, a week of intensive human relations training, and a complete remodeling of the physical facilities to be used for intake and orientation—the first group of 96 clients was referred from the cooperating public and private agencies throughout the city. Every second Monday since September another group of approximately 100 has started the two-week orientation.

Recruitment

Recruitment for Jobs Now is done by a number of public and private agencies which have outreach among gang-oriented youth. Each agency has a specific quota for each intake period, as well as a responsibility for certain services and followup activities. Its staff is responsible for giving a complete explanation of the program to prospective clients, and for accompanying the client to the center on the first day. The only characteristics which make a client ineligible for the program are (1) under seventeen years of age, (2) obvious mental retardation, (3) narcotic addiction or alcoholism, (4) more than four months pregnant, or (5) has a pending court date.

On the first day, the reception staff, which consists of ten people on loan from the Illinois State Employment Service, registers the clients, most of whom are males, and makes what arrangements are necessary to see that those eligible—most are—receive training allowances. The reception center staff is also responsible for interviewing the clients, accumulating personal information, administering tests, and assisting the employment staff in matching clients with available jobs.

Operation and Counseling

After registration there is a brief explanation of the two-week program, an introduction of leaders and counselors, and a tour of the center. The student then receives his schedule. Half of his day is spent with counselors in one-to-one counseling sessions and in human relations training; that is, guided group discussions in which the clients are encouraged to express themselves freely and to learn from the comments and experiences of other members. These sessions try to focus on understanding of their attitudes, values, and standards, as well as those of employers and the society in general. In addition to fostering the development of verbal communications skills, the sessions lay the groundwork for transition to the world of work. Daily classes and practice sessions in grooming, personal hygiene, and money management and transportation as they relate to the world of work are also a part of the clients' day, as are sessions on completing employment applications and being interviewed. Whenever possible, field trips are made to companies employing Jobs Now clients, and employers and appropriate agency people visit the center to conduct lecture-discussion sessions.

During the orientation, each client receives a physical examination (when minor problems are encountered arrangements can often be made to remedy them) and is tested (GATB for dexterity and the nonverbal revised Beta for IQ). There is daily telephone followup on absentees—two absences a week lead to a client being dropped—and biweekly meetings with the referral agencies.

Matching and Followup

During the orientation, each client is assigned to a team which consists of two job developers, two or three coaches, a reception center staff person, a counselor and a teacher. Prior to the completion of the cycle, the client will meet with his team at least twice to discuss the jobs available, his interest, capabilities, character, and personality in relation to those jobs. On the basis of these sessions the client is referred to a job. On the second Thursday of the orientation, the client is assigned to the coach who works with employees of the company to which he is being referred. In addition to accompanying him to the initial employment interview, the coach maintains regular contact with the client and, if appropriate, with his family, on the job, in the client's home, at the Jobs Now center, or wherever the particular situation demands. If the client has a serious financial problem, is involved with the police or courts, or is absent or late to the job, the coach will attempt to provide advice, support, and assistance. This can include getting the client up each morning, providing an emergency loan, or accompanying the client to court. In some companies the coach has access to the personnel department or to the employee the company has assigned as a buddy to the Jobs Now client, and in this way the coach may learn about absenteeism or other problems.

Weekly reports are submitted by coaches and job program developers on all clients to maintain a record of their progress. They also provide the basis for the followup on all Jobs Now clients conducted after each two-week orientation. In addition, coaches have begun to invite all their clients to the center on a weekly basis for group sessions, to explore the experience of others, and to develop solutions for minor problems.

Job Development

The key to the success of the Jobs Now program rests with the ability to develop high support jobs in industry where the severely disadvantaged youth can bridge the gap between the world of the gang and the world of work. The responsibility for developing such jobs rests with the employment staff which serves both the JOBS and Jobs Now projects.

The first contact with a company is through a letter from Mr. C. Virgil Martin, chairman of the YMCA's Advisory Board, and president of Carson, Pirie, Scott & Company, to the company's president. This briefly explains the Jobs Now idea and asks that the president meet with one of the people on loan from industry to Jobs Now. Almost all will provide some access to the company—in about half the cases the president will make himself available, otherwise he sets up an appointment with a vice president or industrial relations director. During this interview, the attempt will be made to show the company the advantages of becoming involved in the program. The company will be asked to (1) drop the requirement of a high school diploma, (2) evaluate police records on an individual basis, and (3) waive aptitude testing. This is done with the understanding that the project will be selective in referring clients and will provide a continuing followup on those employed. If the response is positive, as it is in almost all cases (a positive response can be a sign of genuine interest or it can be lip service—on the first interview it is treated as the former), the job developer will then call upon the appropriate personnel people in order to determine the nature of the jobs available for the project's clients.

He will also try to develop the company's interest in a high support program—preferential treatment which communicates to the new employee the company's desire to keep him and give him a second chance, if necessary, to become acclimated to his new environment. The features of a high support program include: (1) provision of jobs which have definite potential for further development and promotion; (2) assignment of a "buddy" from among the company's employees whose support will complement that given by the coach and who will feed to Jobs Now staff information, particularly on activities which are detrimental to the employee's job performance and which if uncorrected would result in dismissal; (3) communication to all levels, especially to firstline supervisors, of the nature of the program, the firm's commitment and the need to provide encouragement for the employee until he has adjusted to his new environment; (4) provision of special orientation which will acquaint the employee with the company's rules and standards and will make clear what is expected of him and what he can expect from the company; (5) access by the coach or job program developer to individuals in the company who can report on the progress of new employees. It is unlikely that any particular company will offer to incorporate all these features. However, if the job developer is convinced of the commitment, he will contact the company on a regular basis to determine the availability of jobs and will work with the personnel people in referring potential workers. He will also introduce the coach to the appropriate company personnel and will continually attempt to open lines of communication that will improve understanding and implementation of the company's commitment and that will facilitate discussion of all facts pertinent to the employee's adjustment.

Jobs Now has established a seminar center for helping employers prepare their employees, many of whom lack the necessary experience with hard-core youth to be comfortable in dealing with them, to provide high support. In two five-day sessions about three months apart, participants are helped to understand, predict, and anticipate the behavior of hard-core gang youth and to develop techniques for relating to them. More recently, the job program developers have begun to work with employers to explore steps which must be taken to develop careers for JOBS and Jobs Now clients. Most employers feel this experience will help them provide better career opportunities for all employees.

Staff: Nature, Development, and Training

The staff consists of (1) a reception center staff, (2) orientation staff, (3) supplementary services staff, (4) employment staff, and (5) administrative staff. The reception staff of ten people is on loan to the project from the Illinois State Employment Service. The orientation staff consists of the teachers and counselors who have been recruited from traditional channels as well as from ex-Peace Corps types. The nucleus of the supplementary services staff is the coach who has between four and seven companies and may receive as many as five to seven new clients per two-week cycle. The range of clients handled by any one coach ranged from about six for a new coach to more than fifty for one experienced coach. This was the case even though it was agreed that twenty was the maximum which a coach could effectively handle. Most of the coaches who have been hired from the JOBS project, while lacking professional training, have often had experience as detached workers or gang leaders and have proven ability in communicating with gang youth. In addition, the Cook County Department of Public Aid has provided a caseworker in the center to aid with aid to dependent children and general assistance claims.

The employment staff, which services both JOBS and Jobs Now, consists of four individuals on loan from cooperating companies—three full time—plus a seasoned staff of job program developers. The lend-lease personnel are usually from middle management in their companies and have had some experience in special employment problems. The job program developers are the most seasoned staff (range from two to four years with JOBS or Jobs Now). Most have had some college training or industrial experience. Some attempt is being made to prepare coaches to become job program developers.

Finally, there is a small administrative staff which provides leadership, administrative, and statistical services. The predominance of Negroes in all phases of the organization is in keeping with the preponderance of Negroes among those whom the program serves.

Company Experiences

The experience of several companies points up some of the problems and opportunities. The first, a major financial institution whose president was very much committed to the success of the program, is an excellent illustration of high support. Its commitment to keep Jobs Now clients employed was impressive.

The direct responsibility for the program was delegated to a young assistant vice president of personnel who, taking his clue from the strong support given by top management, has made a personal commitment to the program. He has employed all his ingenuity to make it work and the eight Jobs Now clients initially hired are all still employed.

He attributes this success to (1) a good coach who established good rapport with the supervisors in the organization and stopped in frequently to see them, (2) the communication to department managers of the nature of the program and the strong management support, and (3) the approach which he and department managers took—they accepted the challenge and adopted a philosophy of strict discipline and high support. He noted that most of the eight had at one time or other done something for which they would have been fired had they not been Jobs Now clients. Most often tardiness or absenteeism was involved. Even though a large employer, he felt that eight or nine employees were about as many as they could handle under high support. He expects to make the Jobs Now clients regular employees in six to eight months and to bring in new clients to fill the vacancies. He was most proud of two cases. One involved a sixteen-year-old male who had lied—said he was eighteen—in order to get into the program and was not discovered until the employer received notice from the school system that it was in violation of the law. Although lying is grounds for immediate dismissal, since the youth had shown some ability for the work (his only problems were absences and lateness), the matter was discussed with top management officials and cleared with regulatory agency people, who approved a part-time (four-day) job with attendance at continuation school. He is still working part time and has become a very good employee. He has been promoted but still returns to his old job when needed. Although he did not like his initial job operating a machine for checking empty envelopes, his production rate was two or three times that normally obtained.

The second case involved an eighteen-year-old male who, from the beginning, felt uncomfortable in a white-collar institution. Although his aptitude was considered good, after several days he indicated to the personnel man his desire to quit. When asked why, the youth indicated the lack of money for busfare. The personnel manager offered to arrange a daily payment for busfare. He then said he was afraid of being beaten by his friends who kidded him about his "fancy" dress. He was told that locker facilities could be made available for changing clothes. Although not taking advantage of either offer, the employee returned to work and his attitude seemed to improve. However, a couple of weeks later he failed to report to work and indicated to his coach his desire to quit. The coach and client went to the office of the personnel manager who expressed the need to determine the reason for leaving in order to complete his records. The employee was unable to supply a reason for leaving. After a long discussion with the coach and personnel manager, the youth agreed to stay on and his performance has improved to the point where he is soon to be regarded as a regular employee.

The personnel man concluded with the thought that if Chicago businessmen used the ingenuity which they display in handling technical, marketing, and production problems they could hire and keep employed every hard-core gang youth. "It wouldn't be an easy job, but neither is running a successful business."

The experiences of several other companies illustrates the barriers which must be hurdled before Jobs Now type clients become acceptable. The first case is a large company involved with the construction industry. Here the president of the company has made a commitment to the program but the personnel department has not been able to implement it. The personnel department director is quite young and, although obviously impressed with the Jobs Now program, has been unable to hire any clients recommended by it. The first client referred had been above average in intelligence, appearance, and motivation. His handicap was a conviction for manslaughter.[2] The personnel man, although satisfied with the interview, felt he could not hire the client because he would come in contact with female clerical personnel who would be very much upset if this murder conviction were to become known. Several months later he was still bothered by this decision and seemed relieved to learn the client had obtained employment and was doing well. Several other youth had been referred but had not been hired. Although impressed by the sincerity of the personnel man, it was obvious he was searching for the ideal Jobs Now client—comparable to the instant Jackie Robinson. He was unprepared to deal realistically with those whom Jobs Now serves.

Another major company which has publicized its commitment to the program took a number of Jobs Now clients. However, it refused access to the coach because it felt its personnel people could handle any problems. Although Jobs Now was unhappy with this arrangement, it accepted the placements. The results have been unsatisfactory and the company has not taken any clients for the past several months. Half of those hired are no longer with the company and half of those remaining were to be downgraded. It was doubtful whether those to be downgraded would remain. Here again, the company's unwillingness to recognize very real handicaps among Jobs Now youth and to deal realistically with them threatens to curtail its involvement in the program.

Evaluation

During the first thirteen cycles (September, 1966, to May, 1967), 1,119 individuals had enrolled in the Jobs Now program and 99 had repeated the two-week orientation. Of this number, 308 (27.5 per cent) are currently employed and 90 (8 per cent) are in school, training or the armed services. This represents a 35.5 per cent success rate. Of the remainder, 312 (27 per cent) were terminated during orientation and 102 (9.1 per cent) withdrew after the orientation. The remaining 29.6 per cent were awaiting re-referral or had been assigned to a new coach (see Tables 38–2 to 38–4). Given the experimental nature of the program and the population which is served (see Table 38–1) the 35 per cent success rate is commendable. However, it should not be forgotten that the program does not represent the answer for the majority of hard-core gang youth. In fact, the difficulties of expanding the program in Chicago have been well recognized by the Jobs Now staff. When

TABLE 38-1

CHARACTERISTICS OF THOSE COMPLETING ORIENTATION	NUMBER	PER CENT
AGE:		
17	273	32.8
18	232	27.9
19	138	16.6
20	82	9.9
21	37	4.5
22 to 25	43	5.2
26 plus	26	3.1
POLICE RECORD:		
Arrest record	266	32.0
No record	457	55.0
Juvenile record	91	11.0
No information	17	2.0
EDUCATION:		
Nongraduate	24	2.9
Elementary school graduate	744	89.5
High school graduate	56	6.7
Some college	7	.09
RACE:		
Negro	815	98.0
Caucasian	8	1.0
Other	8	1.0

	Average
Test scores	
Beta IQ	95
GATB:	
Finger dexterity	85
Manual dexterity	97
Motor coordination	99

offered the opportunity to significantly expand, they chose to limit expansion to 25 per cent (to 125 per cycle) because of staff size, but more importantly, because employers have not been providing the needed high-support jobs for more than this number.

The quality and dedication of the Jobs Now staff and leadership, the continued high level of evaluation and the attempt to modify the program and to make it responsive to the needs of the clients is impressive. The quality and availability of data is also heartening.

The company experiences indicate both the strong dependency of the program on the commitment of business and also the significant difficulties business has in coping with the Jobs Now type of client. The importance of high support was verified by a profile study of a group of sixty clients who have remained in employment for a long period of time and of another group of

TABLE 38-2 *Currently Employed*

MALES—246	
Placed by Jobs Now (78.9 per cent)	194
Found jobs on own (21.1 per cent)	52
AGE:	
17 (34.9 per cent)	86
18 (24.0 per cent)	59
19 (17.9 per cent)	44
20 (10.2 per cent)	25
21 (4.9 per cent)	12
22–25 (6.1 per cent)	15
26 and over (2.0 per cent)	5
Total	246
FEMALES—62	
Placed by Jobs Now (80.6 per cent)	50
Found jobs on own (19.4 per cent)	12
AGE:	
17 (19.4 per cent)	12
18 (24.2 per cent)	15
19 (14.5 per cent)	9
20 (19.4 per cent)	12
21 (8.0 per cent)	5
22–25 (9.7 per cent)	6
26 and over (4.8 per cent)	3
Total	62

NOTE: Salaries: Males, average, $79.71, range, $50–$154; females, average, $67.11, range, $50–$113.

sixty who had been unsuccessful in retaining a job. The study (see Table 38–5) shows that the most significant difference was whether or not the company in which they were employed was a "high-support" company.

The success experienced by the first employer with high support, without which most of the Jobs Now clients would have been fired before they had a chance to adjust, gives one hope that answers may yet be found for the hardcore gang youth. A strong commitment by top management is probably an essential element in this high support, for without it supervisors would be unable or unwilling to make the accommodations necessary to draw the new employees into the system.

Only two major areas of the program are open to serious criticism—the job matching process and the relations between staff and employers. In matching clients with jobs, each client is assigned to a team and is, therefore, limited to the jobs of two or three job developers whom it is felt can handle

TABLE 38-3   *Termination*

DURING ORIENTATION	
Poor attendance (78.6 per cent)	245
Underage (4.8 per cent)	15
Refused program (2.9 per cent)	9
Incarcerated or court appearance pending (5.1 per cent)	16
Physical problems (1.9 per cent)	6
Domestic problems (3.2 per cent)	10
Miscellaneous (3.5 per cent)	11
Total terminated during orientation	312
AFTER ORIENTATION	
Unable to locate (33.3 per cent)	34
Needs special training (2.9 per cent)	3
Refused program (21.6 per cent)	22
Incarcerated or court appearance pending (17.7 per cent)	18
Physical problems (5.9 per cent)	6
Domestic problems (2.9 per cent)	3
No reason given (15.7 per cent)	16
Total terminated after orientation	102

about fifteen companies. Although the procedure is justified on the grounds that it is essential for the team approach which is the heart of the program, it is difficult to justify, considering the problems faced by clients, a procedure which does not provide each client with the widest choice of jobs.

The relation of staff to employers seems somewhat haphazard. Much of this may be due to the great overlap between the coach and the job program developers in dealing with employers. Some coaches have excellent rapport with employers and their workers, while others have no ready contacts within their firms. This is the case even though the coaches are available to the company on request and are to initiate at least one contact per week with each company. This may be the result of the heavy load of clients carried by some coaches, but seems more likely to result from their backgrounds. Some have no previous experience dealing with employers and feel the major part of their job revolves around dealing with the client in his "home" environment. Whether the coaches' relationship with the company is the result of or the effect of a high-support program is not known, but the question is worth exploring.

Other criticism may stem from the fact that the project is still very new. It does not seem to have adequately exploited those employers who developed good high-support programs as salesmen and advisers to other employers. It has not learned how to effectively handle companies which have become disenchanted or show signs of dropping out. It has not developed strong backup

TABLE 38-4 *Pending Rereferral (Total, 276)*

Recent referrals (2.9 per cent)	8
Referred and not hired (31.5 per cent)	87
Hired but did not report (1.1 per cent)	3
Unemployed (see below) (35.2 per cent)	97
Never referred (7.6 per cent)	21
Refused referral (6.2 per cent)	17
Recycled (10.1 per cent)	28
Referred to other program—not accepted (0.7 per cent)	2
Did not report for employment interview (4.0 per cent)	11
Wants part-time work only (0.7 per cent)	2

UNEMPLOYED

	MALE	PER CENT	FEMALE	PER CENT
Quit (29.9 per cent)	27		2	
Fired (56.7 per cent)	45		10	
Laid off (13.4 per cent)	11		2	
Age of unemployed:				
17	36	43.4	5	35.7
18	26	31.3	2	14.3
19	14	16.9	4	28.6
20	1	1.2	0	0
21	3	3.6	0	0
22 to 25	2	2.4	1	7.1
26 and over	1	1.2	2	14.3
Total	83		14	

support for coaches necessitating that all new and difficult problems must be brought to the director or assistant director. Finally, its training for coaches does not adequately prepare those who have had no contact with business to take on this job.

Many of these criticisms have been recognized by the project and work is underway to overcome them. Their success in doing this can be illustrated by many examples but one must suffice. It was discovered that the second day of orientation was the day on which the largest withdrawal from orientation occurred. By holding an assembly during the final period of the first day, by bringing the clients into contact with the entire staff during the first day, by seeing that referral agencies more clearly explained the project and by clarifying any questions during the first day, the number of withdrawals on the second day was cut approximately 40 per cent.

TABLE 38-5 *Characteristics of Successful and Unsuccessful Males and Females*

	AGE	EDUCA-TION	IQ (BETA)	MARITAL STATUS	POLICE RECORD (PER CENT)	NUMBER OF PREVIOUS JOBS	LENGTH OF TIME IN PREVIOUS EMPLOYMENT (MONTHS)	FIRST PLACEMENT BY JOBS NOW (PER CENT)	HIGH OR SOME SUPPORT (PER CENT)	LOW OR NO SUPPORT (PER CENT)
MALES										
Successful	18.5	10.0	96.0	Single	54	4	5	72	96	4
Unsuccessful	18.8	9.8	93+	do	51	4+	4	86+	63	37
FEMALES										
Successful	18.3	10.8	95.4	do	11	3+	4	83	76	24
Unsuccessful	18.6	10.2	95.0	do	21	3	4	97	14	86

Transferability

The major factors responsible for the results achieved by Jobs Now are: (1) availability of an experienced private agency which had long-term community involvement and support and which had the trust of both the business and youth communities; (2) availability of an experienced staff (from the JOBS project) and capable administrative and policy leadership; (3) access to and cooperation of the business community achieved through the strong personal participation of a number of prominent business leaders; (4) tight labor market; (5) general community and political support.

Even with all of these factors present, the Jobs Now staff, as indicated earlier, chose to limit expansion to 25 per cent. The moral may be that this type of project can only be operated on a limited basis, at least until employers can generally be persuaded to provide a larger number of high support jobs needed to assure success.

Thus, although it may be possible under ideal conditions to transfer this program on a small scale, it cannot now be looked upon as an answer to the problems of hard-core disadvantaged youth. However, the use of Jobs Now as a model to serve those among the unemployed who are more employable is worth exploring since good results may be possible at lower costs to the government than those offered by existing programs. Even here the commitment of resources by business will be essential.

In the estimation of the Jobs Now staff, if a private agency with good business and community ties and support could be found, it would take from three to six months to recruit, train, and season a good staff, and about one year to develop a good industrial program for high support jobs. At this point it would be operational and its success would then hinge on the continued willingness of industry to supply high support jobs.

OPPORTUNITIES INDUSTRIALIZATION CENTER

The Opportunities Industrialization Center, a self-help training and "human revitalization" program founded in Philadelphia in 1964 by the Reverend Leon Sullivan and the Negro Ministerial Association of Philadelphia, has achieved widespread recognition for its results in preparing and placing the hard-core unemployed. Reverend Sullivan, the charismatic and energetic minister of the 4,000-member Zion Baptist Church, has been the moving force behind OIC. The OIC approach combines the grassroots support of those being served with the support of local businesses which donate cash and equipment and employ OIC graduates. OIC relies heavily on motivational training designed to produce the will to succeed among many previously considered unemployable. Recently an OIC institute was established in Philadelphia to provide technical assistance to communities across the country interested in drawing upon the OIC experience in developing their own programs.

History

The antecedents of OIC date to the citywide youth community and employment services program, which Reverend Sullivan and others, who recognized inactivity among youngsters as a major cause of juvenile delinquency, formed to counteract the unemployment among this group. During its first five years the program interviewed more than 35,000 minority-group youngsters, but was able to place only about 5,000. Two major obstacles hindered employment of these young people: (1) discriminatory hiring practices in industries that traditionally shut out minority-group workers, and (2) lack of skills and training necessary to meet the requirements of industry.

Subsequently, Sullivan and 400 other Negro ministers organized a very effective selective patronage campaign—consumer boycott—against a number of Philadelphia firms to enforce demands for increased employment of Negroes. As the boycotts helped open doors for the Negro, lack of skills and training again kept many of the unemployed from filling the newly available jobs.

Sullivan and his associates moved to correct this situation. Early in 1963 they drew up a program for training and motivating the unemployed. The support of the community was enlisted for volunteer services, acquisition of necessary equipment and materials, and fund-raising. Arrangements were made with the city to rent an abandoned police station in North Philadelphia for $1 per year, and in January 1964, the first training center was opened in this facility.

The Mystique

One of the most unique aspects of the OIC Philadelphia program is its mystique and missionary fervor. During the early stages the need for a readily identifiable image for the program was recognized. Even before OIC was fully operative, an all-out campaign was launched to sell the motto "We Help Ourselves" and to establish communitywide recognition of the OIC decal— the "golden key to opportunity."

Reverend Sullivan has been able to maintain communication with both the business community, which applauded the bootstrap approach to dealing with a problem, and the Negro community, which was badly in need of citywide leadership that was optimistic and projected self-pride. Recognizing the ability of the communications media to sustain enthusiasm at a high level, he has skillfully handled much of the public relations work himself and has been able to infect the community at large with the favor and enthusiasm of the movement.

In the process, Sullivan has become somewhat of a messianic figure in the

Negro community. His picture hangs on the wall of each training center, enrollees do sketches of him during their training breaks, and the first question to a visitor is generally, "Have you met Reverent Sullivan—isn't he wonderful?" This reaction is not limited to the Negro community, but was evident during meetings with the Chamber of Commerce and with others. It is further reinforced by the recognition which Sullivan has earned in the white community. In 1966 he received the Philadelphia Award, and this year the William Penn Award of the Chamber of Commerce.

Finally, the mystique builds on the community's view of the program as their own. This is encouraged by constant use of the motto "We help ourselves" and by intensive fund raising efforts in which everyone is encouraged to give to OIC, even if the contribution is limited to a few pennies. The OIC staff itself uses a voluntary payroll deduction system to donate, usually from $1 to $5 to the program per payroll period.

Operations

INTAKE

A majority of clients are reached through the house-to-house and neighborhood recruitment work of seven subprofessional recruiters, themselves graduates of the OIC program. Recruiting is also done through conventional channels, that is churches and settlement houses, and referrals are accepted from other agencies.

Although the program is open only to those between ages eighteen and fifty-five, counseling is provided for all who seek it. At the intake session the staff counselors, each of whom handles eight to ten persons per day, attempt to determine the educational background, employment record, health and emotional state of the prospective client. On the basis of this, a prospective training program is selected and, because OIC cannot provide training allowances, the method of support is decided upon. If necessary, the counselor will attempt to find immediate employment for the client, urging him to enroll in an evening program, or will refer him to MDTA for training not offered by OIC, or to the Pennsylvania State Employment Service, which maintains an office in the same building, for further help.

After this initial counseling, the client receives a one-day orientation before being assigned to the feeder program. The orientation, after covering the philosophy of OIC and explaining the program and what it can do for the client, stresses the need for self-improvement and for viewing oneself with dignity and the importance of each individual's contributions to society.

FEEDER PROGRAM

The basic features of the program are: counseling, prevocational training, motivation and attitude development, employment (if needed), and referral to OJT or vocational training in OIC branches, or to other social agencies for additional help. Depending on the needs of the individual, the program may range from two weeks to three months.

On entering the program the client is assigned to a counselor who will follow him through the feeder process, relating to him in all its phases. This is part of the unstructured "buddy" system which is used to motivate trainees. Another part involves trainees in assisting others in the program, thereby giving them a greater sense of participation and importance. Thus, if a trainee is absent from class without explanation, the counselor will ask one of the absent trainee's friends to call on him and to find out if there are any problems.

The counselor also observes how his clients verbalize and relate to others in class and other situations. Aptitude, reading, math, and IQ (paper and pencil) tests, although their validity is questioned, are also used as counseling devices. Trainees are encouraged to accept their limitations, if any, and will receive as much remedial work as necessary before leaving the program.[3] In addition to remedial work in arithmetic and communications skills, the trainee is assigned to classes in minority history, grooming and self-presentation.

Recently a male orientation program, designed to increase OIC holding power among men, was introduced. The withdrawal rate in this special program has been 17 per cent, which compares favorably with a 20 per cent overall withdrawal rate. Previously the withdrawal rate for males was somewhat higher than the overall rate.

Prior to referral to another OIC branch for vocational training, trainees are given a tour of the physical facilities and meet with the instructors and branch counselors for an orientation session.

VOCATIONAL TRAINING

OIC is licensed as a private trade school and offers twenty-seven courses ranging in length from nine weeks to six or eight months. These courses generally prepare the trainees broadly rather than for a specific job. In contrast to the feeder program, where counselors and instructors have college degrees, vocational instructors must have at least two years journeyman experience (most have more). While vocational competence is a prerequisite, commitment to the program and ability to communicate with clients is the first priority. Some subprofessionals as well as VISTA and local volunteers with skills in the area are used as teaching aids. Branch counseling and guidance deals with day-to-day problems as well as with the psychological problems involved in readying the trainee for separation from OIC.

Industrial advisory boards, set up for each vocational area, provide continuous feedback to the program, review curriculum, advise teachers and indicate what equipment and levels of training are necessary. Representatives of management, technicians and job developers serve on these boards, which range in size from five to ten persons. The industrial advisory boards have been a useful tool for maintaining industry interest and for monitoring industry needs. In spite of this, the impact of fast-changing technology on training and equipment has been a continuing problem. For example, last year OIC bought ten machines for a power sewing class which this year are obsolete. The machine tool operation faces the same problems. Fortunately, industry has responded by donating a good deal of modern equipment.

Currently the training director is exploring the use of audiovisual education for remedial and vocational training of functional illiterates.

JOB DEVELOPMENT

OIC's job development specialists, who originally worked out of each branch, are now centralized and assigned to work with the branches for greater efficiency. Most of their time is spent coordinating job openings with the training specialists and counselors in the branches through their "job ready" [4] lists. Many employers now recruit through OIC and there are generally more jobs available than can be filled. OIC has arranged to refer extra openings to the Pennsylvania State Employment Service.

The industrial advisory boards have been very useful in drawing potential employers to the OIC program and, when necessary, in coming up with openings for which clients have been trained. OIC is cautious about job placement, seeking employers with a stable labor force who offer fair and equitable wages, understand the program, and are willing to give OIC clients time to adjust.

Support and Services

OIC, Philadelphia, has received good support from other agencies, in particular the Pennsylvania State Employment Service (PSES) and the Department of Public Assistance (DPA) as well as from industry. The employment service maintains an office in one of the OIC branches, and has a large facility in the building housing OIC's central office.

The Department of Public Assistance recently contracted with OIC to provide additional allowances (up to a maximum of $150 monthly) for OIC trainees receiving public assistance. The allowances are to include child care costs, car fares and lunches, and incidental expenses. While the DPA budget covers about 250 trainees this year, OIC is hopeful that training allowances can be written into future governmental contracts. Most OIC officials admit that the lack of an allowance has been the major handicap to reaching many of the hard-core unemployed, in spite of the challenge this presents to the idea of self-help.

OIC clients are still handicapped by lack of health facilities. While the attempt is made to have all clients get a physical examination at one of the community health centers, a good health program is lacking. OIC counselors have referred some clients to the Pennsylvania Department of Vocational Rehabilitation, which will provide glasses, emergency dental work, and other services to those who cannot otherwise be trained. OIC has also been able to provide limited services of a psychologist and psychiatrist.

Local industrial support has generally been enthusiastic, in part because the program initially did not rely on federal funds. The National Association of Manufacturers and the National Chamber of Commerce have also endorsed the program.

In Philadelphia, the vice president of a national company that has hired a number of OIC trainees in various divisions related that the trainees have worked in well and have had no greater adjustment problems or greater turnover than other employees. Although his company approved of the "Job Ready" concept, they felt the greater emphasis on "human investment" than on training was appropriate. He was hopeful that OIC would get interested in management trainee programs since many companies have great difficulty in finding qualified minority group workers to fill these slots. His company is assisting OIC in other areas of the country.

Another company found OIC trainees "highly motivated." When they needed a number of welders, they were able to assign their instructors to train OIC recruits in OIC facilities since OIC had no welding class instructors available at the time.

Many believe that employers have really "bent over backward to make the program work, whereas ten years ago they wouldn't have bothered with these people." Reverend Sullivan's moral persuasion, the tenor of the civil rights movement, the emphasis on the war on poverty, and the 1965 riot in Philadelphia have all been helpful in getting employers to support the OIC program.

The greatest criticism of the OIC program has come from the vocational education people, who carry on a running battle with the organization. As one OIC official states, "They laugh at us and say we don't know anything about training. We laugh back and say you don't either, but at least we're honest." There is also a feeling of resentment and jealousy between MDTA people and OIC, which both sides are quick to justify.

Evaluation

The OIC program has been a positive force in Philadelphia, even though one may question the use of certain techniques. While OIC is widely heralded as a manpower or training program it is in reality a multipurpose program. The value of the program lies much more in the impact it has had on the Negro community and on Philadelphia in general than on its placement record. The strength of OIC is not in its manpower components. Its success can be traced to the dynamic leadership of Reverend Sullivan and to his ability to organize the Negro community and win the support of the community at large.

The feeder program represents the most innovative feature of the manpower effort and has been quite successful in producing an individual with a positive self-image and a desire to be trained. It has also been quite successful in its use of VISTA volunteers as both instructors and counselors.

Training is probably strongest in those courses geared to specific companies and industries with a continuing and growing need for trained manpower rather than in courses where the market is flexible or seasonal. These industries are also the most likely to provide strong industrial advisory boards, to donate modern equipment, and to help provide experienced teachers.

Objective evaluation is rendered almost impossible by the lack of data on clients and on placements, the confusing and conflicting nature of placement data, and the inadequate followup of trainees after placement. The quality of available data is as bad as has been seen for a program which has been in operation as long as OIC. The unusual mystique under which the program operates had not been conducive to internal evaluation and the low priority given to data can be seen by the minimal resources devoted to this function.

Although OIC is widely thought of as reaching the hard-core unemployed, the indication that 20 to 30 per cent of the day students and most of the evening students hold jobs while in the program suggests that OIC performs its greatest services for the underemployed.

Two followup studies of OIC trainees have been attempted, one based on job placements for the month of February, 1966, the other on 166 trainees enrolled in the Germantown branch power sewing course during 1966. OIC has recognized the insufficiency of these followups and has developed an "Operation Followup" procedure to complete records on representative samples of former OIC trainees. To service trainees after placement and through followup, OIC estimates an additional forty employees will be needed.[5]

OIC's flexibility and willingness to experiment have proved valuable. The "Job Ready" concept best exemplifies this flexibility. Others are the industrial advisory boards and the ability to gear resources toward the immediate needs of industry, if the skill acquired has a continuing value. OIC experiments to cut down on class absenteeism—most common on Mondays and Fridays—by offering free breakfasts to trainees on those days and holding centerwide assemblies featuring well-known personalities are also interesting.

Finally, two new programs may have some bearing on OIC's future direction. The adult armchair education program (AAE) is a pre-prevocational program that meets in the home for those who do not feel ready to come to OIC. Through this program, OIC hopes to motivate and encourage people in the atmosphere of the home and neighborhood surroundings, while providing basic adult education skills, and to develop indigenous leadership and participation in community activities. Two hundred and fifty homes have been organized into AAE centers, but no data is available on the number who have entered this program and have gone on for further training at OIC. Some local politicians are eyeing this setup with suspicion, since it provides a base for political organization.

The second new program is "Progress Plaza," a major Negro-built-and-operated shopping center which will serve as a training center for Negro entrepreneurial talent. In addition, retail establishments will be staffed and serviced by OIC vocational trained personnel.

OIC-LOS ANGELES

Los Angeles was a target for the OIC Institute (then the OIC Extension Institute) from its inception in November 1965.[6] In dealing with Los Angeles, Reverend Sullivan admitted uncertainty because of (1) fragmentation of leadership in the Negro community, and (2) the political ties between the emerging leadership and the mayor. However, the Ford Foundation was persuaded to provide seed money. In doing so it imposed two conditions: (1) the training function would be developed and supported by the Los Angeles branch of the American Society for Training and Development, and (2) job development and placement would be carried out in conjunction with the management council. The tripartite structure was a distinct departure from the Philadelphia prototype, although the heavy reliance on the local Negro clergy for leadership was not.

The history of OIC-Los Angeles has been marked by crisis. It started under a stigma of political opportunism and it has never rid itself of this image. Since the majority of the Negro clergy who were involved in the program were out of touch with the Negro community and had little community support, the board has never provided leadership and has been severely hampered by factionalism. The formerly all-ministerial board has been changed a number of times and currently only three of its members are ministers. The staff, suffering from lack of clearly defined leadership, has been torn by antagonisms and crippled by insecurity. After the resignation of the first executive director, which was accompanied by charges and countercharges, OIC-Los Angeles was unable to find an executive director within the community. After operating for a number of months without a director, a Philadelphia OIC consultant who has worked with the project from its inception was chosen as director. This decision to select an outsider elicited great dissatisfaction on the part of some elements in the Negro community.

In light of these administrative and organizational problems, it is not surprising that little attention has been given to technical problems. Thus, some excellent machine tool equipment obtained through the federal government in late 1966 was still not in use for training purposes six months later. As of May, 1967, the entire vocational programs seemed in a state of disarray. Almost no training was available which could attract and hold males. Although no data was available from OIC, the December, 1966, SDC study indicated that of 450 trainees transferred from the feeder program, 200 (45 per cent) were in training, 175 (40 per cent) had dropped out and 75 (15 per cent) had been placed.

The feeder program which has operated quite separately from the vocational program seemed in somewhat better technical shape, although the staff seemed to be suffering from low morale. Using SDC study data (December, 1966), of 900 registered students, 450 (50 per cent) had completed the program, 125 (14 per cent) were in training—half had stopgap employment as well—25 (3 per cent) had been placed and 300 (33⅓ per cent) had dropped out. As in Philadelphia, a principal reason for dropping out was lack of financial support.

The recent changes probably cannot help but improve the program, but there is real doubt as to whether OIC can overcome its bad start and poor image. It has failed to find strong leadership or to attract broad community support. Although there is a real need in the Los Angeles Negro community for a self-help program which could produce self-respect and dignity, OIC-Los Angeles has failed to reach or make an impact on this community. Finally, its funding situation is still tenuous.

Transferability

OIC-Los Angeles points up many of the problems which may be encountered as attempts are made to transfer the program to other cities. While OIC has been a positive force in Philadelphia, it is essential to penetrate the public relations and the mystique in order to develop realistic expectations of results when the program is transferred. Not having fully accomplished this, the feeling remains—in part strengthened by exposure to OIC-Los Angeles and discussions with others knowledgeable about OIC operations in other cities—that without a Leon Sullivan who can marshal the support of all segments of the community behind a self-help effort that reflects the needs and ideas of those being helped, the manpower phase of the program will be similar in nature to traditional manpower programs and its results will be dependent on the same factors as for other manpower programs. . . .

The OIC Institute has maintained that initially there must be grassroots interest in the program—which they refer to as the "OIC movement"—and that it cannot be imposed upon the community by, for example, a chamber of commerce. As in Los Angeles it has relied heavily on the initiative of local Negro clergy, assuming that since these men have traditionally been the communication link between the Negro and white communities they have a headstart on some of the problems to be encountered. When a local group has approached the institute, staff is sent into the community to seek potential business support, assist in mobilizing community enthusiasm and resources, and help in fundraising efforts.

The ability of potential local candidates for leadership positions and their rapport with the business and indigenous communities is tested by institute staff, who visit everything from poolhalls to Kiwanis Club luncheons. This appraisal would seem to indicate at least some recognition by the OIC that the man who heads the program is as important to its success as the program itself. Unfortunately, it is not easy to find a man of the caliber and status necessary to put over an OIC program who is willing to withdraw from whatever his energies have previously been channeled into and put full time into the OIC effort.

OIC has once again pointed up the potential of a self-help program, especially for improving motivation and for instilling a sense of pride in a previously downtrodden group. Traditional programs have had the greatest difficulty in this area. Thus, rather than transferring the entire OIC program, some consideration should be given to transferral of those activities which precede vocational training with a referral of clients to existing programs. Followup and counseling by the referring agency might be continued during the entire period. In addition, some of those features which help the individual adapt during the vocational training—establishment of an internal "buddy" system, giving higher priority in selecting instructors to the ability to communicate with trainees, greater availability of counseling for day-to-day problems, and so forth—should be infused into the existing training programs. While selling the value of self-help features to the established programs would be most difficult, since it would require changes in traditional ways of doing things, the rewards are worth exploring. Perhaps the OIC Institute could add this function to its activities.

THE MANAGEMENT COUNCIL FOR MERIT EMPLOYMENT, TRAINING, AND RESEARCH

The Management Council, which is broadly representative of the Los Angeles business community, has received significant national prominence and has been suggested as a model for business participation in advancing the practice of merit employment. Relying almost exclusively on the personal influence and commitment of Chad McClellan, the Management Council has succeeded in getting employers to open their doors to qualified minority group workers and to conduct positive recruitment efforts in the poverty areas of Los Angeles. It has also made it difficult for those employers who did not seek to hire minority group workers and who were simply looking for excuses.

History

Immediately following the Watts riot in August, 1965, the Los Angeles Chamber of Commerce appointed a rehabilitation committee of seven members chaired by H. C. (Chad) McClellan. The committee, after assembling the essential facts, decided it would stay out of the controversies over probable causes of the riot and possible remedies for the situation, leaving these to the newly appointed McCone commission.

Since unemployment stood out as a prime cause of the trouble, the committee concentrated its efforts in this area. It invited the presidents of 100 major corporations to a meeting where it was pointed out that a number of the unemployed within south central Los Angeles (curfew area) could meet the demands of industry. It then undertook to work with these companies and with the state employment service to match existing jobs with the unemployed within the south central area who possessed the skills needed by industry. Their efforts drew praise from the McCone commission, which recommended that a permanent organization be set up to continue the work of the committee.

In March, 1966, ten leading business organizations, including the California Manufacturers Association, Downtown Businessmen's Association, Industrial Council of the City of Commerce, Los Angeles Chamber of Commerce, Los Angeles Junior Chamber of Commerce, Merchants and Manufacturers Association, National Association of Manufacturers, Southern California Hotel and Motel Association, Southern California Restaurant Association, and the Western Oil and Gas Association, cooperated in the formation of a nonprofit public service corporation, the Management Council for Merit Employment, Training, and Research. Its stated objectives were: (1) to coordinate activities of employers in employment, training, preemployment training and research; (2) to coordinate and utilize all possible resources that will bring together applicants, jobs, and training opportunities irrespective of race, religion, and nationality; (3) to utilize and develop research projects and data on projections and changes in the labor market, job availability, and manpower availability; (4) to advance the practice of merit employment in which individuals are considered for employment, training, and promotion on the basis of individual affiliates and qualifications, irrespective of race, religion, and nationality.

Funds for the corporation came from the John Randolph Haynes and Dora Haynes Foundation, the Ford Foundation, and the aerospace industry. The 1966 budget of the Management Council of approximately $60,000, however, represents only a portion of the resources devoted to the endeavor.

While continuing to work with the initial companies, McClellan, ably assisted by his executive director, Murray Lewis and a small staff, began to enlist the cooperation of additional companies. At present (May, 1967) there are 201 reporting companies and approximately 2,600 cooperating employers. In addition to the south central area, the Management Council has channeled resources to the east Los Angeles area (predominantly Mexican-American) as well. At the request of Governor Reagan, the Management Council is now in the process of assisting other communities throughout California in establishing a council responsive to local needs and patterned after the Management Council.

Operations

The Management Council does not operate programs. It does not place workers nor does it train them. Its role is to clearly communicate to the business community the nature of the problems faced by minority group workers and to act as a catalyst in inducing activities which will bring together workers and jobs. To accomplish these goals it indicates that it has worked to do the following:

1. Coordinate with the California State Employment Service and the Los Angeles Urban League and other community agencies in implementing the

goal of bringing together jobs, training opportunities, and applicants irrespective of race, religion, and nationality.

2. Coordinate with and provide counsel and guidance to the Opportunities Industrialization Center for the training and placement of the unemployed.

3. Coordinate and provide counsel and guidance for the skill centers (such as some within the provisions of the Manpower Development and Training Act) for training and placement of the unemployed.

4. Coordinate with the Los Angeles City schools, county schools and state department of education on training programs, encouragement of education, and preparation for job opportunities for individuals irrespective of race, religion, and nationality in accordance with their maximum potential.

5. Coordinate with the Bureau of Apprenticeship and Training (federal) and the Division of Apprenticeship Standards (California) for on-the-job training programs and apprenticeship programs.

6. Coordinate with other federal, state, and municipal agencies whose activities are related to employment, training and preemployment training and research.

7. Coordinate with all segments of the minority community to (*a*) encourage training and education to prepare for job opportunities in accordance with maximum potential of individuals to absorb such training; (*b*) furnish information about job opportunities; (*c*) present periodic reports to the minority community on progress achieved.

8. Gather and disseminate information to business and industry on the various resources, agencies, and organizations that exist in the community—who they are and what they are.

9. Provide counsel and guidance to business and industry on merit employment procedures, practices, and developments.

10. Plan and conduct education programs, seminars, and conferences on various facets and developments in the area of merit employment and training.

11. Coordinate, develop and carry through meaningful research programs in accordance with the objectives of the Management Council.

12. Prepare brochures, pamphlets, and newsletters for broad dissemination to business and industry on activities of the Management Council.

13. To coordinate with various communications media—TV, radio, and newspapers—for adequate interpretation and dissemination of information on activities of the Management Council.

Its effective work with the California State Employment Service has helped to improve the service's image among employers and has gotten employers to use the newly established service centers in Watts and other areas for direct recruiting of minority group workers. Its work with the Los Angeles City schools and others involved in the establishment of the MDTA multioccupational skill centers has meant a much better liaison between the centers and employers. The survey which the council helped conduct among business helped get a curriculum more attuned to the needs of employers. Its brochure, "You Too Can Be A Winner," has also been helpful to school counselors and others in selling Negroes and other minority groups on preparing for and seeking careers in business.

The council has recognized its role as a bridge between the business community and the minority community and has worked with and supported other agencies—public and private—who seek to improve the picture for minority group workers.

Evaluation

The Management Council is an asset to Los Angeles. In a city into which massive federal resources have been poured and where politics seems to guarantee that few programs will work well, the council has made a positive impact on the employer community. After the Watts riot, many worried and upset businessmen wondered what could be done. The Management Council focused this anxiety of the business community on the problems of hiring qualified minority group members and these energies have been well spent.

Chad McClellan is a prominent and successful man who wields a good deal of influence in the Los Angeles business community. His substantial personal commitment to the philosophy and involvement in the direction and activities of the council are certainly key factors in its success. Those in Los Angeles who have long fought for equal employment opportunities for qualified Negroes and other minority group members have found Mr. McClellan a staunch and powerful ally. The council has utilized many techniques—from public service spot announcements and appearances on television to needling and cajoling in private discussions—to help open employer's doors to qualified minority group members. Thus, some employers after evaluating their requirements for a high school diploma for entry level jobs have substituted completion of training at a skill center or appropriate experience while others are now willing to examine police records on an individual basis before deciding whether they disqualify a worker. Thus, while the Management Council still has not made a major positive impact on the minority community (particularly for reasons mentioned below) and recently has received some criticism from minority leaders, the results of its endeavors are becoming known in the minority community. This can be in part seen by the backlog of applicants awaiting training at the MDTA skill centers.

The major criticisms of the Management Council is its use of numbers.[7] The council has reported that between September 1, 1965, and September 30, 1966, over 17,000 workers from south central Los Angeles (riot and curfew areas) have been hired by the 201 reporting companies working most closely with the council. The number was obtained by asking each reporting company the single question—how many minority group workers from south central Los Angeles (defined) were hired by you during a specified period? Although some attempt was made to screen out temporary and part-time employment, the 17,000 plus is the result of adding the numbers obtained from each company. Although there are serious technical problems with such a survey and there is obvious duplication caused by individuals who moved one or more times during the thirteen-month period, the greatest problem is that since the number is not comparable or related to any other number, it has little meaning. There are no data on the number of hires by the reporting companies of minority group workers from the south central area for prior periods nor are the characteristics of those hired available (except for a sample study of 100 workers).

One cannot even tell from the number reported by an individual company how many benefited from the efforts of the council. In light of the small staff of the Management Council, the minimal resources devoted to the provision of data is not surprising. In determining whether additional funds and staff time should be devoted to improving this data, the question must be asked as to whether the resources would not be better spent on programmatic efforts. While some data is needed for internal evaluation (simple quarter-to-quarter comparisons for each company might provide a simple and useful tool), the release of numbers for external use invariably leads to the "numbers game" approach. Thus, for new councils it is recommended that simple data be collected for internal evaluation purposes, but that they not be made available to the public. The Los Angeles Management Council might well find that discontinuing public announcements of total numbers would result in an improved image in the minority community.

A council-sponsored sample study [8] had indicated that at least the initial efforts of the recruitment done at the Watts Service Center by employers contacted by the council did not result in employment of the hard-core unemployed. The median age was 25.5 and only 25 per cent were under twenty-one or over forty-five. The median education was 11.5 years and only 22 per cent were not high school graduates and none had less than eight years of education. Most were long-time residents of Los Angeles and only 17 per cent had police records (10 per cent convictions), while 28 per cent came from families with incomes below $3,000.

Most of those who have been hired thus far through the efforts of the Management Council have been the cream of the crop, that is, they are in the prime age group, and have had some experience and have some skill. The staff of the council supports the view that only recently have the "hard core" begun to feel the impact of their efforts. However, the large numbers of placements made through the efforts of the council have led many to indicate that the problems of Watts are well on the road to being solved. The council staff does not believe this and has made some effort to place their endeavors in a proper perspective. However, some, for political reasons, have ignored these statements and the misuse of numbers is resented by the minority community. Although McClellan has often indicated that the Management Council cannot do the job alone and that more funds should be put into training and other activities, the linking by Governor Reagan of a request to McClellan to make his effort statewide, with the announcement of the closing of many of the state's multiservice centers left many with the opposite impression. This was particularly unfortunate since it raised doubts in the minds of those in the minority community who were gaining confidence in the efforts of the Management Council.

Transferability

The Management Council feels strongly that it can transfer its program to other communities and has prepared the following ten-step agenda for doing so:

1. Develop a structure representing the top business leadership of the community. This organization to provide the essential impetus and drive in mobilizing the resources of industry in an action program of bringing together jobs and the unemployed, particularly the disadvantaged.

2. Develop a comprehensive list of the employers in the area including the name of the president of the company and the chief personnel officer. Learn if possible the number of people employed by each firm.

3. Ascertain to the extent possible the minority population in the area and concentration of residents.

4. Develop necessary procedures with the Department of Employment local officers so that management and staff in the Department have a clear concept and understanding of their responsibility to make competent evaluations and referral of unemployed individuals with respect to needs of industry.

5. Arrange for a group meeting with the chief executive officers of the companies who should participate in the program. This meeting will provide an opportunity for a face-to-face discussion of the meaning and significance of the program. The meeting will be primarily geared toward a request for their cooperation in utilizing the unemployed among the disadvantaged who could meet the job needs of the various companies.

6. Convene a meeting of personnel officers so that they are aware of the contribution they can make in their operating capacity toward a success of the program.

7. The program, if it is to succeed, requires a sustained intensive followup. There should be followup by personal letter to the chief executive officers, as well as the personnel directors whose cooperation will be requested.

8. Continuing followup procedures by letter, telephone, and in person in order to enlist to the maximum extent possible the support of the various companies.

9. An inventory to be made of the training facilities and resources of the community. Are they adequate to meeting the needs, particularly of those who need to be brought up to a level of employability through remedial education, et cetera.

10. Coordination with existing community, minority, and governmental agencies in the area is a vital ingredient to the success of the program.

There is no doubt that the philosophy behind the Management Council—that among the unemployed in any ghetto there are many whose skills are valuable to employers and that some grouping of business interests can help improve the process whereby the workers and employers are brought together—can and must be transferred. The technique for translating this philosophy into action—a substantial investment in time by an influential business leader(s)—is also transferable.

While each community surely has such business leaders, the difficulties in finding such a man, who will lend not only his name and influence but who will devote his time, and surrounding him with a competent staff, are apparent. While there may also be significant technical problems based on the varied needs of communities, these problems could be overcome by a top flight executive. Thus, similar efforts in most communities will probably be hamstrung by the inability to find a business leader who will make what amounts to a full-time commitment to getting a Management Council started.

NOTES

1. This fourth case is not reprinted here [Editor].
2. This conviction illustrates the multiple problems of poverty. The client was one of four youths involved in a gang killing. The other three, with competent legal assistance, were freed, but this youth was convicted and served several years. It had been ascertained that he did not have a gun at the time of the killing.
3. Although there is a formal length for each course, the individual's time in a specific course will be determined by his ability to master the work.
4. "Job ready" lists are based on the recognition that the regular required course length may be covered by some trainees in a shorter time than specified, while others may need more time to master a skill. Therefore, trainees are placed when they can handle a skill with competence rather than on the basis of having completed a formal timetable.
5. Additional staff is also needed in the regular program where, for example, the ratio of counselor to client is generally one to fifty.
6. Much of the early history has been obtained from the "Los Angeles OIC: An Organizational and Operational Review," Systems Development Corp. (December, 1966).
7. A look at the experience of the Merit Committee in Chicago, an industry sponsored group with much the same purpose as the Management Council, shows that much of the problem with numbers can be avoided. Each company which joins the Merit Committee must file a confidential report (which is not even available to the Merit Committee staff) of current minority group hiring and employment with a well-known accounting firm. Each year another report is filed. During its first year 216 companies which had a total of more than a half million employees, of whom about 100,000 were minority groups members, reported hiring 14,000 minority group employees. This represented a 10 per cent increase from the previous year. During its second year, the number of reporting companies will be expanded to about 1,200.
8. William H. Reynolds, "Experience of the Los Angeles Employers With Minority Group Employees," Graduate School of Business Administration, University of Southern California (March, 1967).

39

Employing the Disadvantaged: Inland Steel's Experience

RALPH CAMPBELL
Cornell University

Effective management, like politics, is the "art of achieving the possible" rather than the theoretically ideal. But just what is possible when one attempts to convert ghetto-bred, gang-oriented youth into useful industrial citizens? Some clues may be provided by the experience of the Inland Steel Company.

Impelled by a strong civic consciousness and needs generated by a tight labor market, Inland has absorbed into its mills and offices a significant number of parolees, gang leaders, and "disadvantaged" youth. The effort has included formal programs and informal practices (that is, individuals have been given a chance because of the intercession of such persons as parole officers, priests, rabbis, and ministers).

Results have been mixed. They range from highly encouraging to downright disappointing depending on the particticular approach and on the criteria used for evaluation. When the ratio of retentions to hires range from near 0 to 85 per cent among three plants participating in the same program, interesting questions arise as to causative factors.

THE RYERSON WORK EXPERIENCE AND TRAINING PROGRAM

The program, which evokes great pride among Inland's personnel staff and which to date appears to show the greatest promise, is a Work Experience and Training Program initiated in 1965 in the Joseph T. Ryerson and Son, Inc., plant, an Inland subsidiary since 1935, located in the Lawndale (West Side) area of Chicago near the scene of 1966 riots.

The original plan was to take inner city high school dropouts in groups of twelve, provide a week of off-the-job orientation followed by twenty-four weeks of combined training and work experience (six hours of work and two hours of classes daily). The prime requisite for admission was that the individual must be unqualified for a job; that is, Ryerson would not have hired him if normal employment standards prevailed.

From *Issues in Industrial Society*, Vol. I, No. 1 (1969), published by the New York State School of Industrial and Labor Relations.

Key individuals in the development and operation of the program during the first year were Robert Szrom, industrial relations manager of Ryerson who had transferred from the Indiana Harbor works in October, 1964, and Fred Erickson of the nearby Sears YMCA. The two apparently made a good team. "I'm an industrial relations man, not a social worker," Szrom explained. "Sometimes I had a little static from Fred Erickson. All in all this was probably good for the program. I cooled him down. He wound me up. We had no guidelines," recalls Szrom. "We simply developed the program from scratch." [1]

Forty-eight individuals, referred by various community agencies, were interviewed for the first program. "We tried to sell each person in the first interview," Mr. Szrom said, "but we wouldn't let him decide at that time. We told him to come back in two days. We saw this as a rough test of motivation." Thirteen did not return. One turned down the opportunity in the first interview. Three were overly qualified and the staff referred them for full-time employment. One was eliminated because his ability to read and write was too low, two could not be hired because they were under eighteen years of age, and six were screened out for physical reasons, including size—"you just can't put a 125 pound man in some jobs in the steel industry."

Orientation was conducted at Shellbourne, a facility at Valparaiso, Indiana, owned by a Catholic lay organization. The program was quite informal with periods of free talk (that is, anything the trainees wanted to talk about), a layman's version of sensitivity training, and discussions of work discipline and performance. Much of the discussion was generated by open-ended questions such as: "If you were running the company, what qualifications do you think you would need?" Sometimes there were debates on such topics as whether it is fair to ask for one's race on a job application. A small amount of time was devoted to elementary skill training such as micrometer reading. Sports activities (basketball, volleyball and, in winter, skating and tobogganing) were scheduled.

The main thrust of the orientation was to help the staff "get to know the boys" and to acquaint the trainees with someone to whom they would feel free to say "I've got a problem." It was also geared to giving each youth an identity with the group and providing him with some understanding of why it was necessary for him, once employed, to be on the job regularly.

At the end of the orientation the participants were placed in combined job-training. Erickson conducted the daily two-hour class sessions devoted primarily to mathematics, reading, writing, and minority history. Each youth's immediate supervisor assumed primary responsibility for him during his six hours on the job. At the outset there was a staff meeting called by the General Superintendent. At this meeting there was a fulsome discussion of the problems to be expected with regard to attendance and work performance. Supervisors were told to "be lenient in the beginning and tighten up as the program progresses."

Originally the youths were paid $1.25 an hour as a starting rate with periodic reviews; some received a raise as a result of reviews and others, of course, did not. In either case the trainee was told why. The starting rate was subsequently raised to $1.75 an hour. "We found from experience that this was about the rate necessary to match what a youth could earn by hustling in the gang, assisting in the 'numbers game' etc.," says William Caples, vice president for industrial relations and a prime mover in many of Inland's civic activities and personnel innovations.

When a trainee was absent, Szrom was usually called in. On one occasion, he recalls, a participant was sent to the Cook County jail for $270 worth of traffic violations to work off his fine at $5 a day. "We let him stay for a week," Szrom said, "and then went down to talk, 'Do you want out,' we asked. 'Yes!' We replied that it would not come easy. We finally reached an agreement that he would pay us back out of his weekly salary. He didn't graduate but he did pay us back before he left. He could have been fired or he could have quit before we were repaid. On one occasion he left work without any notification. For all we knew he could have been lying dead under a pile of steel. I called him in and said, 'If you do it again, you've had it! If you have an urgent need you can get permission.' A few weeks later he did it again. I was going to fire him. The manager of the service department said he had come a long way. 'Give him another chance.' I told the trainee that as far as I was concerned he should have been fired but he was being given another chance because of intervention of the manager. Two days later he did it again. He knew that this time he would be fired for sure. So I say he quit. Erickson and I wondered if he really wasn't afraid of succeeding. Here he had only a week or two to go. Then, for the first time, he would have moved into a full-time job with steady income. Maybe he was afraid of falling back!"

Only five of the first group survived the Work Experience and Training Program. One was drafted into military service, two quit for other employment. Four terminated voluntarily and involuntarily for other reasons than military or another job.

A second group of trainees were processed during the latter part of 1966. Six out of twelve were graduated to full-time employment. Classes for the second group were taught by Joseph Kubica, who had served on the staff of JOBS (Job Opportunities through Better Skills). Szrom left the program during the latter half of the year; Kubica took over direction of the program.

In 1967 it was decided to run the project on a continuous basis. Experience with this approach suggested two difficulties: (1) a new trainee found it difficult to establish communications with the group and felt left out, (2) this approach did not give the operating supervisors who were responsible for integrating the trainees into the work group any "breathing time." Szrom points out that the program actually confronts the supervisor with a dual system of operations, that is, regular supervision and treatment of the trainees who are given special consideration. Not only does this require extra time and attention for the trainees, but it also involves problems with the rest of the work group. For example, some of the regular employees complained that the company was buying safety shoes for the trainees so "why not us?" The General Superintendent replied, "Fine! If you are willing to work for $1.25 an hour as they are, we'll buy your safety shoes too." This response seemed to satisfy the complainants.

RYERSON'S RESULTS

A detailed analysis of the training results of the three programs conducted through 1967 is shown in Table 39–1 and the status of the fifty-four trainees as of November 6, 1967, is shown in Table 39–2.

Results may be evaluated in terms of at least three separate criteria: (1) meeting labor force needs of the company, (2) converting "unemployables" into successful job holders, and (3) efficiency, that is, cost of attaining results.

Meeting labor force needs: Table 39–2 shows that only eleven individuals of the fifty-four trainees were still working at Ryerson. From the viewpoint of filling job vacancies then, the ratio of retentions to hires is disappointing.

Converting "unemployables" into successful job holders: With reference to this criteria it might be said that success is attained each time an individual who might otherwise live on welfare rolls or live a life of delinquency is

TABLE 39–1 *Summary of Training Results*

	PROGRAM I	PROGRAM II	PROGRAM III	ROW TOTAL OF ALL PROGRAMS
Graduated to full-time at Ryerson and still employed	1	4	6	11
Graduated to full-time at Ryerson and quit	1	2	1	4
Graduated to full-time at Ryerson and discharged	0	0	1	1
Graduated to full-time and left for military service	2	0	0	2
Still in training	0	0	4	4
Completed training but were unable to graduate to full-time at Ryerson	1	2	4	7
Left while in training to enter the military	1	0	0	1
Quit training for other employment	2	1	3	6
Terminated both voluntarily and involuntarily for reasons other than those of the military and another job	4	3	8	15
Failed to begin training after orientation	0	0	3	3
	12	12	30	

Number of trainees in all three programs—54

TABLE 39–2   Current Status of Trainees

CURRENT STATUS	PROGRAM I	PROGRAM II	PROGRAM III	ROW TOTAL OF ALL PROGRAMS
Total number now in military service	4	2	0	6
Total number now working at Ryerson	1	4	6	11
Total number referred for training and placement elsewhere	1	1	9	11
Total number last reported working elsewhere	3	2	9	14

NOTE: These categories are not mutually exclusive since some of these people are referred to placement elsewhere and are also shown under total number reported working elsewhere.

added to the labor force. In this sense the results seem more encouraging. Tables 39–1 and 39–2 show four youths still in training, eleven working at Ryerson, six in military service and fourteen last reported working elsewhere —a combined total of thirty-five out of fifty-four with nineteen unaccounted. There is, of course, no way of knowing what might have happened to the six in military service and the fourteen reported working elsewhere had there been no Ryerson Work Experience and Training Program. There is also no way of knowing the impact of the program on individuals who failed to complete the training. For example, Szrom points out that while Trainee H was fired for having a whiskey bottle in his locker, he later suggested to his brother that he explore the possibility of getting into the program. "Something positive must have happened to him," said Szrom, "or he would not have urged his brother to try the program."

Efficiency: What Price Success?: In the case of the Ryerson Work Experience and Training Program the investment per individual finishing the training is $3,180. This figure is determined by taking the $57,200 total cost for the program over a two-year span and dividing it by the number of graduates.

Table 39–3 shows a striking difference in results attained in the North Plant as contrasted with the Center and South Plants. Later we will look at probable causes for these variations, but it should be noted here that the cost *per graduate* would have been sliced in half if the success rates for the entire project to date had even approximated those of the North Plant for the third program.

Figured in the costs are such items as teacher's salary, a pro-rated salary for the part-time project coordinator, transportation to and from the place of initial orientation, and safety shoes, gloves and wages of the trainees. Some question might be raised about including the full amount of wages since there is some benefit from the work performed by the trainees. All are employed on regular jobs, rather than made-work but they do not perform at the level which would normally be expected of an applicant hired through routine em-

TABLE 39–3 *Results of Third Program by Plant*

	NORTH	IP&G	CENTER	SOUTH	TOTAL
Number of trainees assigned	8	1	7	11	27
Number graduated to full time at Ryerson	5	1	1	1	8
Number now employed at Ryerson	5	1	0	0	6
Number still in training	2	0	1	1	4
Number who failed to graduate to full time at Ryerson	1 (12.5%)	0 (0%)	5 (71.4%)	9 (81.8%)	15 (55.5%)
Per cent of trainees who have been through training and are now working full time at Ryerson (does not include trainees still in training)	82.6	100	0	0	22.2

ployment procedures. Offsetting the work contribution of the trainees is the extra supervisory time needed for special attention and for handling problems arising with the regular work force as a result of what some of them consider to be partial treatment of the trainees. In any event, success *cannot be bought cheaply.*

The high input required may account partially for Inland's lack of success with Jobs Now, a program in which youth are inducted into the regular work force after only *two weeks'* orientation. Jobs Now was an outgrowth of a project known as JOBS (Job Opportunities through Better Skills), funded by the federal Office of Manpower Automation and Training, and initiated in October of 1963. JOBS was designed to train currently unemployable youth (many functionally illiterate) to reach the necessary educational level for employment, to develop the attitudes required for employment, to acquire some job skill experience, and finally to be placed in employment. As finally developed, the program included several thousand youths who were given eighteen full-time weeks of basic education, *on the average,* followed by as much on-the-job training as was needed. Many individuals actually required from thirty to forty-five weeks of training.

As a result of the Lawndale riots in the summer of 1966, Frank Cassell, now assistant to the President of Inland Steel and then on a two-year leave from the company with the Department of Labor, met in Chicago with Mayor Daley and a number of the community leaders to determine what emergency measures might be taken. Specifically, Cassell was interested in exploring what might be done in two weeks instead of the many weeks required by the JOBS program. With the cooperation of Joseph Block, chairman of the board of Inland Steel, the meeting was held at Inland's corporate headquarters. It was decided to take the more hardened dropouts. Many with police records, and give them two weeks of orientation by a special staff under the direction of the YMCA. A number of community agencies, including the Chicago Association of Commerce and Industry, cooperated in sponsoring the project. Following the orientation period individuals were to be placed in jobs and a counselor from the Jobs Now staff would follow up each individual and maintain liaison with the employing companies.

Twelve applicants were referred by Jobs Now to the Ryerson Works of Inland. Despite the company's role in the establishment and sponsorship of the Jobs Now program the results of the Ryerson participation were, in Szrom's words, "disastrous." Two of those referred were rejected for reasons of weight; two failed to secure work permits because they were under age; and of the eight who started with the company, none are employed now. The average length of service of those eight individuals was 2.8 months. One was fired during the probationary period; one quit for a second job giving three days notice to the company; and one quit to move out of state. One was a good worker but was often absent and was finally fired under a company policy which calls for termination of employment when an individual fails to report for three days without notifying the company unless there are extenuating circumstances. One other individual was discharged for failure to report; one quit after three days because he felt the work was too hard; one quit during the shift (his supervisor noted on his personnel record that he was often absent and had turned in a poor performance and consequently should not be rehired.); one entered military service.

This total lack of success comes as a curious phenomenon in a company which was a prime mover in the establishment of the Jobs Now program, and which, perhaps more importantly, has a long tradition of civic consciousness and humane personnel practices under the leadership provided by such former board chairmen as Edward L. Ryerson, 1940–1953; Clarence B. Randall, 1953–1956; and Joseph I. Block, 1957–1967.

• • •

REASONS FOR JOBS NOW FAILURE

From written reports and from interviews with both Inland and Jobs Now representatives, it appears that a complex of factors may be causative: (1) length and type of training; (2) nature and status of the work performed; (3) the interpersonal environment of the workplace; (4) relationships between key personnel of the company and community or governmental agencies who recruit and/or provide orientation and training; and, of course, (5) the motivation and attitudes of the trainee.

Graney questions whether too much is expected of the Jobs Now approach to prepare ghetto youth for industrial life adequately. "Two weeks of orientation is not going to change attitudes to the extent that these people are happy with rules and regulations and a new way of life," he says. "Many of them are similar to the old frontiersmen, the mountain people. They value freedom. They don't like to be forced to report for work everyday, to show up on time. The real job has to be done at the work site over a long period of time.

"We are making the mistake of forcing them to be what we want them to be too quickly instead of finding out what they want to do and can do best and somehow getting them employed in that capacity in work that is meaningful and which hopefully will lessen their bitterness and apathy. We have a great responsibility to make them realize that they are wanted and to treat them as ordinary employees. Have the programs accomplished this? We may lose them; but, if we train them in skills that are marketable, they will go to another and another job and hopefully keep on one."

Joseph Ehrenberg, executive director of Jobs Now, echoes somewhat the same theme. "Our kids aren't just like everybody else," he says. "If they were they'd be working. They have to break habits that are dysfunctional in a work force. They also have to overcome feelings of failure and alienation.

"To say we aren't giving them preferential treatment is not true. We are! When we give this advantage, however, there's a response. Our kids go much further in adapting their habits and feelings to get an entry level job than most companies are willing to go in adapting their requirements." [2]

Ehrenberg would agree that two weeks of orientation would not change habits. Success of Jobs Now clients depends heavily on the kind of support the employing company gives them on the job during the period of adjustment. "High support" includes effective communication by a socially conscious top management to make its ideas known throughout the organization—particularly at the level of first supervisor, the representative within the employing firm who makes the trainee his personal responsibility—and also includes access for the Jobs Now "coach" to the trainee on the job and to key personnel of the company.

Ehrenberg points out that Inland is not identified by Jobs Now as a high-support company, but he adds that part of the problem with the Jobs Now project at Ryerson may stem from unfortunate experiences with the "coach" assigned. This coach apparently made three different appointments with the personnel director at the Works and failed to keep any of them; he also failed to see that clients took birth certificates with them for job interviews, a necessity because of age requirements for employment. "Our coaches," Ehrenberg says, "must manifest concern for the problems of business." This sort of empathy is difficult to attain because Jobs Now is staffed by Negro youths who were brought up in the ghetto. Such persons identify readily with the clients, a necessary attribute; but they are not readily comfortable in a business atmosphere.

Ehrenberg feels that more adjustment of behavior on the part of business is required and that this will only result from a true "confrontation" of the business community with the ghetto. He points out that to date only one personnel director has taken the trouble to go through the Jobs Now Center. Government support is needed, he agrees, but adds that bureaucratic government and voluntary agencies frequently create barriers to confrontation instead of facilitating it.

"For one thing," he points out, "most bureaucratic agencies are not set up to help temporarily and immediately. We recently had a case of a young man twenty-two years of age who had just served a term in a house of correction for the third time. He has nothing. He can go back to his Northside home and get in trouble again. He needs $200 to $300 for suitable clothing and an equal amount for suitable housing until he can get a job and be productive. He needs another $100 for medical treatment. There is nowhere we can go to get this kind of help.

"For years government has been involved," he concludes, "but it has been involved in the wrong way."

The length of training and orientation and the problems of relationships, however, are not factors which can explain the striking differences between the results obtained in the Ryerson Work Experience and Training Program for the three participating plants. In his final report on the program, Kubica states: "Of trainee success rates by plant, the major differences between the training provided in other plants and that in the North plant is that trainees are made part of teams operating machines (which is rarely possible in the other plants), and thereby feel that they are really receiving training and doing productive work. This raises their self-esteem and allows the release of greater ego commitment to the job."

He points out that trainees who are given training on machines tend to succeed while those given jobs such as sweeping or cleaning up tend to fail. "Machine training is especially important," he says, "because it teaches trainees to pace themselves at the production rate of experienced workers." Kubica concludes that "The inplant training is the single, most important component of the program and largely determines success or failure of the trainees."

Training for such jobs as stock clerking, according to Kubica, requires "inordinant amounts of supervisory attention." He explains this as follows: "We have found that reading skills are difficult to raise significantly during the training period, but that much progress can be made improving math skills. This prevents us from taking trainees with extremely low reading ability and preparing them to become, for example, stockmen. However, almost all trainees can be trained to become operators of sheet shearers, coil slitters and other machinery, the operation of which does not require high verbal skills." [3]

The problems of status, the meaning of work, and the climate of the work place are also emphasized by Ehrenberg. He cites two banks in Chicago which "have done a fantastic job." He attributes their success not only to high support but to differences between white-collar and blue-collar occupations. Blue-collar jobs he contends are more and more purely routinized and involve higher pressure. "Work in the factory," he says, "is far less meaningful. There is higher pressure for the production with red-necked supervisors doing the pushing." He points to one example of a youth who left a factory job paying $2.86 an hour to work in a bank at $1.85. The motivations and attitudes of the individual were underscored by Graney:

> I feel that if you are not careful you run into one-shot deals, emergency programs that don't get at the real problem. I feel we don't understand the Negro. He is undergoing a metamorphosis where for the first time he has power. Hatred of whites is coming to the surface. And the Negro has good reason for this hatred. He wants to be a good American but in his own way. We must encourage this and encourage them to correct their deficiencies.
>
> When we speak of the hard-core disadvantaged we know what we are talking about in a general but not a specific sense. Some Negro youths may be happy with their lot. It may be the sociologist who's not happy. We have to be able to determine the personality makeup of the individual, is he motivated toward upward mobility or not? If he is, industry can and must give him a job and improve his weaknesses while he is employed at a regular job.
>
> If we are teaching we have to teach at the pace of the student himself, not the average student. The football coach must use a system tailored to the skills of his players—whether they are fast or slow. Each disadvantaged person has to be treated individually—this is a most difficult task and places a tremendous burden on industry. However, the burden is a national one and no organization is better fitted to dealing with it than businessmen who are interested not only in the success of their company but also their community.

Graney also emphasizes the importance of interpersonal relationships. "*Accept* and *tolerate* are not appropriate words," he says. "We must demonstrate that we are *eager* to be friends. The key to success in upgrading the academic ability and the skills of the disadvantaged is how well the trainer interpersonalizes with the disadvantaged. If he doesn't, the program will fail. This takes time and patience."

DIMENSIONS OF THE PROBLEM

While the Inland Steel experience is not conclusive in any quantifiable sense it does dramatize some of the dimensions of the problem.

Take a large manufacturing company with economic and technological need for work discipline and performance; imbue its top management with a liberal dose of social responsibility; now mix into the work force a dash of ghetto values and street gang philosophy. *What have you got?* Apparently not much—unless you add other ingredients. Habits and attitudes bred in the ghetto normally won't mix with industrial requirements. Something extra is needed to change "unemployable" youth into permanently employed persons.

The experiments of Inland Steel and the entire Jobs Now program suggest that the something extra includes at least the following:

1. First and foremost a sympathetic and understanding set of interpersonal relationships. This need not include all persons on the job but should involve top management, the personnel staff, the immediate superviser, and notably

one person who serves as "buddy" to the disadvantaged individual, someone within the organization to whom he can, and will, turn for help, counsel, and moral support.

2. Placement in a job which will be meaningful *to him* and satisfy his need for status. It probably has to be at least equal to the status he enjoys in the street gang. In this sort of placement, personnel interviewers are crucial, according to Ehrenberg. "They have been paid to screen out," he says, "now they have to be trained and induced to screen in."

3. A sufficient period of training and orientation and counseling. Part of the orientation has to be provided on the job to help the individual adjust his habits and attitudes to the work environment. Some adjustment of the work requirements are also needed in the early stages of employment. Where orientation, as in the case of Jobs Now, is shared by the employing firms and an outside agency there must be a close and understanding relationship between the key staff members of each.

Three basic questions are raised by the Inland experience:

1. Can industry, which must compete to be profitable, be expected to bear the high cost of providing appropriate motivation and conditions for the transition from street gang to industrial life? It appears that no one company or small group of companies can absorb the cost. Industry-wide sponsorship and financial support and/or government subsidy seems necessary.

2. Where will we find appropriate liaison personnel to bridge the gap between the ghetto and the world of business and industry? Individuals who can be comfortable and effective in both worlds are hard to find. They cannot be effective if they identify too closely with either the ghetto or industry, yet they must be able to identify with both. George J. Yoxall, manager of personnel and training for Inland, points out that in the "detached worker" program in Chicago, where individuals from social agencies worked with gang members in the ghetto, the most effective workers are ghetto-bred Negroes who have had college exposure and who have a good understanding of both lower- and middle-class values.[4] We will have to find improved ways of locating and training such persons and determining what inducements are needed to put them to work at such tasks. "We have a problem of determining," Graney says, "which Negroes can lead, will lead, do lead every day. They, in turn, need a good deal of coaching, encouragement, and status so that they in turn can be the recruiters, the trainers, and the counselors for business."

3. Finally there is the question of whether all disadvantaged persons can be absorbed directly into the work force, even with significant amounts of orientation. It is not clear whether all such individuals will respond to a situation where they are initially given favored treatment and discipline is gradually tightened. Work groups cannot be relied on to give support to individuals who are being treated with partiality. Nor is there any reason to suppose that the pride of some individuals will not prevent their working in groups where they are singled out for most favored treatment. Perhaps we need way stations, a type of "sheltered workshop" where individuals, all of whom are

disadvantaged, can learn to accept work discipline.

The results achieved by the North Plant in the Ryerson Work Experience and Training Program [5] are encouraging and point to some of the ingredients which make up that "something extra" required if we are to absorb ghetto youth into the work force successfully. But the outcome of the various approaches utilized by Inland suggests that to wipe out hard-core unemployment requires more experimentation, insight, sympathetic understanding, time, and money than industry generally has been able or willing to provide up to this point.

NOTES

1. Most of the information for this article, unless otherwise noted, was derived from interviews on January 18, 1968, with Messrs. Szrom, Graney, and Ellis, personnel representatives of Inland, whose titles are shown in the text. All quotations from these three gentlemen were made during the course of these interviews.
2. All quotations from Ehrenberg are from personal interview, January 19, 1968.
3. Report of Kubica to W. T. Hensey, Ryerson Works director of industrial relations, Joseph T. Ryerson and Son, Inc., November 6, 1967.
4. Interview George J. Yoxall, Ithaca, N.Y., March 7, 1968.
5. Tables 39–1, 39–2, 39–3 from Kubica report, *op. cit.*

40

Private Industry and the Disadvantaged Worker

E. F. SHELLEY AND COMPANY

[*The Urban Coalition commissioned E. F. Shelley and Company, consultants, to undertake an inquiry as to the successes and failures of business involvement in recruiting and training low-skilled minority-group members, especially Negroes. This manpower role had been stimulated both by The Urban Coalition itself and by the National Alliance of Businessmen. At the time field work for this study was completed (November, 1968) these programs had had perhaps a year of effective operation. The introduction to this study indicates its scope.*]

From a study by E. F. Shelley and Company, *Private Industry and the Disadvantaged Worker* (New York, 1969).

The major findings and recommendations of this report are based on an analysis of the questionnaire response of 224 companies with a total work force of over 8.7 million and field visits to sixty-four of these companies with a total work force of over 4.1 million. It should be noted that the survey is limited to selected urban areas and large scale enterprises. . . .

THE EXTENT OF THE COMMITMENT

While the emergence of private industry into the field of human resource development is of great significance, the effect of this effort to date on the overall problem of the unemployed and underemployed must be viewed in perspective. Although unemployment is currently at a very low ebb, the average unemployment for 1968 was still approximately 2.8 million people, including one million adult males, one million females and 800,000 teenagers. Also included are approximately 400,000 persons who have been unemployed for fifteen weeks or longer. And the unemployment rate among Negroes, although it dropped during the past year, is still twice that of whites. These statistics are necessary to give some context to the private industry programs.

From the data returned by the surveyed companies, less than 10,000 recruits can be identified as receiving special training. While publicized figures indicate that industry has hired over 100,000 "hard-core" nationally, it is beyond doubt that this figure includes a large percentage of persons who would have been hired whether the term "hard-core" existed or not.

Many corporate officials, while generally sympathetic to the National Alliance of Businessmen's purposes, were highly critical of what they regarded as "the phony numbers game" in which the NAB engages. They pointed out that the pressure to report numbers of recruits was resulting not only in companies' reporting as hard-core personnel whom they would have hired anyway but also in rewarding companies with higher turnover by enabling them to report more recruits.[1]

It is clear therefore that industry is only beginning to reach those in need of jobs. Further, if the "hard-core" definition is interpreted in its broadest context to include "poor persons who do not have suitable employment and who are . . . subject to special obstacles to employment," the effort has barely made a dent in reaching the over 5 million heads of families living in poverty.

FINDINGS AND RECOMMENDATIONS
Factors Affecting the Level of Corporate Commitment

CORPORATE MOTIVATION

Findings. The primary motivation behind most firms' hard-core hiring and training programs is the need for new sources of workers in a tight labor market. If and when the need for workers slackens so will industry's performance. Also playing an important part in companies' involvement are pressures from several sources, including government equal opportunity units, the National Alliance of Businessmen, and community agencies such as the Urban League, NAACP, and antipoverty groups.

Corporations also express the opinion that a climate of social unrest generated by a deprived urban minority is not good for business, and this understanding generally provides a context for more direct needs and pressures.

Recommendations. The ultimate success of private industry training programs is most closely tied to the tight labor market. The federal government must therefore adopt a policy of assuring full employment if the gains currently being won by minority groups in the private sector are not to be swept away by overall increases in the unemployment rate. The details of such a policy, which may well include the concept of the government as an employer of last resort, should be developed and put into operation as quickly as possible.

FACTORS INHIBITING CORPORATE ACTIVITY

Findings. Economics, location and corporate structure are the greatest inhibiting factors to company involvement. Company divisions operating on thin profit margins usually aren't participating in special minority hiring programs; but when they do, normally no structure is given to their efforts. Companies with most operations in the South or in noncentral city locations have the lowest record of change in employment procedures. Highly decentralized companies, especially conglomerates, normally show weak involvement with major exceptions in some retailing firms.

Recommendations. The present pattern of industry participation places primary emphasis on companies with central city locations, while the primary expansion of private employment opportunities is occurring outside of the city —especially in suburban locations. It is therefore unrealistic to expect that the problem of unemployment and underemployment among urban minorities can be permanently ameliorated without broader participation by private industry. National and local groups should increase and concentrate their efforts to pressure firms outside of central city locations to share the load of training—either by establishing ghetto feeder plants or by providing more effective transportation to outlying areas. At the same time federal and state pressure to enforce equal employment opportunity provisions must be intensified in such areas.

In order to partially overcome corporate reluctance growing out of economic conditions, companies should be encouraged to approach training and upgrading programs as a research and development effort to meet long-term needs, rather than as a short-term profit and loss matter.

TOP-LEVEL CORPORATE COMMITMENT

Findings. An initial commitment by top management is mandatory for a successful program. Beyond this, continued followup—usually by the delegation of responsibility to a high-level person with full-time authority in minority hiring and training—through regular and extraordinary channels of communication provides for the most effective programs. This effort is best attended by regular contact with the minority community.

Recommendations. Since without high-level commitment private-industry programs are doomed to failure, top corporate officials must be kept vitally involved in NAB, local coalitions, and other volunteer groups if their interest in the current effort is to continue. As part of this participation, these officials should be encouraged to appoint a high-level person with overall program responsibility, establish at least one full-time staff position to deal with day-to-day operating problems, and get personnel into ghetto neighborhoods to establish relationships with local organizations and broaden their understanding of the community's dynamics.

UNION INVOLVEMENT

Findings. Labor unions have not been directly involved in the development or implementation of most programs. Most local union officials are adopting a wait-and-see attitude, reserving judgment until program impact on such issues as seniority and promotion become clearer. However, where the union is strong and where the company plans noticeable changes in training procedures, there has been participation in planning, especially in lengthening probation periods.

Recommendations. Labor unions should be involved in program planning and implementation, at least when hard-core training programs can affect collective bargaining agreements or when a significant upbeat in minority hiring can arouse its membership. When labor contract provisions are too inflexible for lengthened training and increased support services, ghetto plants, vestibule training centers, or separate nonprofit corporations should be established to provide the necessary training structure.

COWORKER RELATIONSHIPS

Findings. Thus far, most programs have not developed to the size to arouse white employee hostility, but many employers expect trouble when qualified white workers are turned away or when a significant increase of unskilled black workers is evident.

On the other hand, black militancy appears to increase as new minority employees become more secure in the plant situation. Demands include a greater union voice, more upgrading opportunities, and alterations in seniority provisions since blacks are primarily the work force most vulnerable to layoff.

Recommendations. Given the current climate of racial hostility among low-income whites and the inclination toward racial separatism among blacks, effective means of combating these problems on a short-range basis within an industrial environment have not been devised. What can be recommended, however, is corporate awareness that such problems can arise. Companies can prepare for these eventualities by developing soundly conceived program structures with built-in advancement opportunities and by establishing channels of communications with white- and black-worker leadership.

• • •

Program Costs

Almost all businessmen contacted during this survey were enthusiastic about their companies' programs and the efforts of private industry to deal with minority-group employment problems. However, almost unanimously, they qualified this enthusiasm, noting that private industry's activities must be carried on within the free enterprise, profit-motivated economic system. That is, expenditures for such programs should be voluntary and should not hurt a company's competitive position. This type of attitude places several strictures on industrial activity in this field.

Perhaps the primary issue to be faced is what portion of the company's resources should be given over to this effort. However, it is not easy to make generalizations on resource allocation since only 93 of the 224 operating or contemplated programs surveyed were able or willing to provide cost information. Of those which did, over 63 per cent are receiving federal funding and, as shown in Table 40–1, the training costs are generally higher when the government is involved.

The inability or reluctance of firms to furnish cost data may be ascribed to several factors. Many firms, particularly those which have relatively unstructured programs, have found it difficult to set a price on such intangibles as loss of productivity and increased supervision time. One firm, in attempting a cost study of straight OJT operations for minority employees, found that the program did not cost more than its normal training effort. Lack of information is also a result of company policies which do not permit the release of financial data except to recognized government agencies. Several corporate executives contacted were somewhat suspicious of this study's aims and were not willing to release specific cost figures. Finally, in at least one case, a company official described his firm's MA-3 (government) contract as "a real sweetheart." If this is more than an isolated incident, companies will naturally be loath to release such information.

Among those firms which had available cost figures, no consistent ap-

TABLE 40-1 Program Costs (By Funding Source)

	TOTAL		GOVERNMENT FUNDED		COMPANY FUNDED	
	NO.	PER CENT	NO.	PER CENT	NO.	PER CENT
Under $10,000	11	12	3	5	8	23
$10,000 to $49,999	19	20	4	7	15	44
$50,000 to $99,999	10	11	7	12	3	9
$100,000 to $499,999	29	31	23	39	6	18
$500,000 to $999,999	12	13	10	17	2	6
$1,000,000 and over	12	13	12	20	0	—
TOTALS	93	100	59	100	34	100

proach as to what should be included was found. The government's guidelines for program cost seemed to form a convenient takeoff point for estimating costs; but the rationale of how these guidelines were initially arrived at is unclear. A sampling of the costs claimed by companies indicated that at least on the surface training for similar jobs is costing substantially dissimilar amounts. Without more detailed analysis on the exact functions associated with the job as well as the skill levels of the trainees (a task which this survey was unable to undertake), conclusions on these differentials would not be meaningful. Table 40-2 indicates the cost range reported per trainee.

• • •

Some companies can afford to spend substantial sums on programs which, at this stage, might be characterized as a risky research and development effort. Others work within such a narrow profit margin that any minor displacement in the marketplace jeopardizes the financial integrity of the com-

TABLE 40-2 Program Cost Per Enrollee (By Funding Source)

COST RANGE	PROGRAM RESPONSES		COMPANY FUNDED		GOVERNMENT FUNDED	
	NO.	PER CENT	NO.	PER CENT	NO.	PER CENT
Under $500	12	12	9	25	3	5
$500–$999	10	10	7	19	3	5
$1,000–$1,999	23	24	13	36	10	17
$2,000–$2,999	15	16	3	8	12	20
$3,000–$3,999	22	23	2	6	20	31
$4,000–$4,999	9	9	2	6	7	12
$5,000 and over	6	6	0	—	6	10
TOTALS	97	100	36	100	61	100

pany or one of its divisions. Several examples were found during this survey of large multidivisional companies which have extensive hard-core activity in some of their divisions and almost none in others. It was explained that all divisions were expected to show a profit and that it was unreasonable to expect a company division which was under constant pressure because of poor profit margins to make substantial investments in this type of training operation.

The staff visited at least two divisions, however, which operate at a loss within very profitable companies; and yet because of serious worker shortages have mounted sizable hard-core training programs through the use of MA-3 money. In both instances company officials credited the NAB for alerting them to the availability of Labor Department funds, thereby allowing them to train needed workers with relatively little company investment.

NOTE

1. For example, almost one-fifth of the total hard-core hires which the NAB announced recently can be attributed to one major manufacturer. Field reviews disclose, however, that the overwhelming majority of the people reported by that company had been hired through the regular personnel mechanism, received no special training, and just happened to fit some aspect of the NAB hard-core definition. To be sure, a small but potentially significant group of the firm's new employees were receiving special training.

41

A Look at the Disadvantaged Employer

FRANK CASSELL

[Frank Cassell was given leave from his position as Assistant to the President of Inland Steel Company to serve for two years as Director of the United States Employment Service of the Department of Labor. It was in this latter capacity that he gave the speech which is reprinted below.]

Society is asking a great deal from employers and their spokesmen when it says, "employers must change their recruitment and selection techniques so

---

Address at the Business-Civic Leadership Conference on Employment Problems, Chicago, Ill., June 5–7, 1967.

that they do not screen out an individual on the basis of his school record and work experience, but rather, attempt to determine his potential and to help those who lack necessary qualifications to become qualified." This is a far cry from the concept, so long accepted, that corporate responsibility for good citizenship required provision of jobs, paying taxes, and involvement in community good works.

Even as late as 1951, corporate gifts to educational institutions were challenged in the now famous Smith case.[1] Certain stockholders of the A. P. Smith Manufacturing Company objected to the company's contribution of $1,500 to Princeton University. They contended that the company should not use corporate funds except in the furtherance of its business needs and to create profit for its stockholders. The judge, in ruling against the stockholders said:

> I cannot conceive of any greater benefit to corporations in this country than to build, and continue to build, respect for the adherence to a system of free enterprise and democratic government, the serious impairment of either of which may well spell the destruction of all corporate enterprise. Nothing that aids or promotes the growth and service of the American university or college . . . can possibly be anything short of direct benefit to every corporation in the land.

That industry recognizes the benefits it receives through financial contributions to colleges and universities is demonstrated by the fact that such contributions grew from an estimated $43 million in 1950 to $225 million in 1963.[2] The benefits are in terms of meeting its needs for college educated and trained personnel. But what about the uneducated and unskilled segment of our population—the unemployed poor? What benefits accrue to employers such as Xerox Corporation which has found, in its pioneering effort to recruit and train a group of such individuals, that the costs exceeded by four times the cost of "normal" hiring and training practices?

M. A. Wright, current president of the United States Chamber of Commerce, recently commented on this problem as follows:

> . . . The social cost of poverty is not fully measured by . . . statistics or the privation they suggest. Today, in varying degrees, the desperation and frustration that result from poverty contribute to ill health, to deteriorating citizenship values and understanding and to other factors that can weaken our society. The social cost of poverty must also include the goods and services that are not produced because of the unemployment and low productivity of the poor knowing nothing but the cycle of poverty—a cycle extending in some cases back for generations—far too many of the poor have little incentive for expecting a better life, or for that matter, going out and working for a better life." [3]

Recognition of these costs to society has prompted Xerox and many other employers throughout the United States to accept the challenge of investing time, money, and effort in breaking this cycle of poverty for the several million whites, Negroes, Indians, Spanish-Americans, and other Americans who are so trapped. Many employers have embarked on this course of action on their own; many have done so with the assistance of government financing. In the process, these employers have learned that most people, when given the opportunity to work, want to work. They have learned that most people who are unemployed are employable; that most of the untrained people in our country are trainable; that most uneducated people are educable! Furthermore, employers have learned that their investment in working with these people, whom they formerly ignored, has resulted in gaining valuable new employees and opened a new labor market resource. The following examples demonstrate these points.

The Texas Division of Champion Papers decided, late in 1966, to restructure certain of their entry-level jobs by waiving requirements such as high school education and passing a battery of aptitude tests. Nine individuals were hired on this basis. They turned out to be "exceptionally good employees," according to W. W. Kethan, employment supervisor. As a result of this experience they hired seven more. These people also proved to be exceptional employees. As of May, 1967, twenty-four people were employed, three of whom have already been promoted to higher skilled jobs.

The Diebel Manufacturing Company, in 1964, hired for the first time, employees from among Spanish-speaking and Negro groups. In 1967, about 10 per cent of their employees were Negro and 18 per cent were from other minority groups. The company instituted formal in-plant training programs to upgrade these people, including classes in English. A number of them are already well started on the ladder of higher-skilled jobs and supervisory positions.

Hundreds of other exciting, successful case histories of employer experiences in the hiring and training of minority-group individuals, formerly considered unemployable, have been documented by the National Association of Manufacturers in their STEP [4] reports, the United States Chamber of Commerce in a motion picture [5] and in their monthly news bulletins, the National Industrial Conference Board,[6] the United States Employment Service, and other governmental agencies, trade, and professional associations. Every employer and every person concerned with assisting employers in becoming involved with providing jobs for the unemployed poor of minority groups should study these reports to learn what special efforts need to be undertaken to bring such individuals into the mainstream of our economy.

Some people might consider these efforts and attendant expenses an undue burden on employers. They might even expect me to describe these employers as the "disadvantaged employers." They are wrong. When I think of disadvantaged employers, I have in mind a radio and TV manufacturing company in Chicago which recently reported an overall rate of turnover of 98.5 per cent for all males in lower-level factory jobs. As a matter of fact in some job categories the rate of turnover runs from 105 to 186 per cent. This company also has other personnel management problems, with both minority-group and nonminority-group employees. This company is disadvantaged, in my opinion, just as much as are the disadvantaged unemployed poor.

Basically, the disadvantaged employer hasn't come of age in utilizing modern personnel management practices in terms of the requirements of today's technological demands and the needs of his employees as recognized by social scientists. Professor Douglas M. McGregor of the Massachusetts Institute of Technology commented on this fact over ten years ago when he pointed out that most employers think of manpower resources in the same way as they think of physical and financial resources. He suggested, instead, that the essential task of management ". . . is a process primarily of creating opportunities, releasing potential, removing obstacles, encouraging growth, providing guidance." [7]

When Professor McGregor was talking about creating opportunities in the work setting of the plant and office, he was thinking of *all* employees, not just opportunities for the uneducated and untrained. Few companies fully understood the implications of his concept. But, as management has applied itself and in the 1960's become involved in hiring and training and utilizing individuals whom they wouldn't have hired in the 1950's, they have and are learning many lessons applicable to all their employees. This has become the big payoff, far outweighing the extra costs incurred in conducting special recruitment and training programs conceived initially to tap previously unused sources of new manpower.

As one example, is it not reasonable to assume that an employer who redefines entry-level job requirements so that they have relevance to the job to be done is, in fact, a "hard-headed businessman?" By eliminating unnecessary requirements, he is in a better position to find people to do the job at a higher level of performance than a person who is overqualified for the job. We have known for a long time that overqualified people are a major reason for high turnover rates, job dissatisfaction, low productivity, and poor morale. Show me a company with a large number of overqualified people on the job, and I will show you a disadvantaged employer! Eliminating irrelevant requirements for entry-level jobs is one of the basic techniques that employers have used in hiring the uneducated and untrained unemployed poor! At first glance it appeared as though this technique was solely for the purpose of providing jobs. Actually, the technique is a pure and simple matter of saving money now wasted due to high personnel turnover rates!

As another example, there is ample evidence that employees usually relegated to low-level, dead-end, or menial jobs because of traditional hiring and promotional practices can be trained and educated for higher-skill-level jobs. When given the opportunity, they have proven their potential! With this fact in hand, many employers are expanding their in-plant educational and training programs for all their employees in order to provide more growth opportunities within the company. "Pirating" of skilled employees from other employers is not only expensive but becoming more and more difficult in today's labor market. Therefore it just makes good "dollars and cents" practice to look for the potential in presently employed personnel and to provide the opportunity for this potential to develop. Show me a company which hires and places minority-group individuals in menial and dead-end jobs, without providing opportunities for skill-upgrading, and I will show *you* a disadvantaged employer who is not tapping the potentials of many of his other employees!

The Board for Fundamental Education has demonstrated, through their in-plant basic education courses, that within a period of several months they can raise the reading, writing, and arithmetic levels of illiterate adult employees by two and three grade levels. The steel industry, with a grant from the Labor Department, has initiated such a program using the Board's techniques for 1,600 employees in two cities.

The point I am making is that those employers who have involved themselves with hiring, placement, education, and training of individuals usually considered as unemployable or minimally employable—and this includes the physically and mentally handicapped, older workers, people with police records, and so on—are learning lessons about people which will have a tremendous beneficial impact on their personnel management policies and practices in toto. These employers will have a better workforce and a better competitive position in the marketplace because they have a better workforce.

I consider as disadvantaged those employers who announce themselves as "equal employment opportunity employers" and then sit back and wait for qualified minority-group individuals to apply for jobs in their companies. These employers fail to recognize that other, more committed employers are *seeking out* qualified individuals, regardless of race, color, creed, and so on. Furthermore, it is almost axiomatic that such employers will have involved themselves in the educational systems of their communities in order to help assure equal educational and training opportunities for all youth. Working with and in the schools, these employers are getting "first crack" at the best qualified students in the graduating classes! The longer the "sit back and wait" employers do not become involved in improving their communities and their schools, the more disadvantaged they become in competing for and attracting the kind of employees they need to stay in business.

I consider as disadvantaged the employer who, rather than become involved personally in resolving the problems of the unemployed poor, looks to somebody else to do so. He pays ever higher taxes to keep people in prisons, ghettos, hospitals, and on the welfare rolls, at the same time loudly protesting his tax burden and increasing crime rates and welfare rolls. He moves his plant to the suburbs and complains about the shortage of manpower available to him, but is unwilling to arrange for transportation from the inner city where the labor supply exists. He hasn't learned any lessons from such companies as Montgomery Ward and Sears, which have stayed in the city, have improved their warehouse, office, and store facilities so as to prevent their neighborhoods from deteriorating, have provided jobs for the residents in these neighborhoods, and have increased their sales to inner-city residents.

The disadvantaged employer is one who hasn't yet learned how valuable and productive the physically handicapped, mentally handicapped, and older workers can be if provided special training. This employer knows that other companies have utilized such individuals to good advantage and profitably, but he is both unwilling to change his traditional attitudes and to seek assistance in his hiring, training, and placement from such organizations as the Employment Service, Equal Employment Opportunity Commission, vocational rehabilitation agencies, Plans for Progress, Goodwill, and others with special expertise and staff who are eager and willing to help employers with their employment problems.

There are other lessons concerning better utilization of individuals which disadvantaged employers ignore or are unwilling to experiment with. Among the most dramatic lessons we are learning about young people from minority groups who are placed in employment for the first time, is that they require supportive services not usually available from the employer. The Jobs Now program in Chicago has demonstrated that disadvantaged individuals need on-the-job coaching provided by Jobs Now counselors. Where employers permit these coaches to visit the new employees on the job, the employees stay and progress. If the coaches are not permitted, there is a high rate of discharge or voluntary disemployment. Yet, many employers resist the idea of permitting "outsiders" in their companies to assist their employees to become better employees!

By now the outlines of the composite disadvantaged employer are clear. He is just as much disoriented to the mainstream of our economy and his community as is the disadvantaged individual brought into the "big city" from a rural pocket of poverty in Appalachia. The disadvantaged employer may have even wrapped himself in the virtuous cloak of respectability of nondiscrimination in his hiring and promotion policies. He may even be contributing funds to civil rights movements. But he has neither provided opportunity for disadvantaged individuals to work for him, nor provided himself the opportunity to learn from such individuals how to better develop the human resource potential of his company and his community.

Employers, in the pursuit of economic ends, have always attempted the fullest possible development and utilization of available resources—material, financial, and human. However, with respect to manpower, for too long we have been concerned with "management" rather than "development." It is now becoming clear that development of human resources starts long before the individual becomes an employee, is an on-going process, and is as much affected in the office, store, and plant as it is by education, housing, transportation, and other amenities of our communities and the nation. As long as an employer thinks in terms of managing personnel, he will be "disadvantaged." The employer who applies his ingenuity and perseverance to the problems of human resources development will not only enhance his materialistic achievements but at the same time will bring more and more of our citizens closer to the "good society" Americans have proclaimed as the goal of our nation. We may be certain of one thing in the pursuit of this goal—the fewer disadvantaged employers in that society, the greater will be the number of advantaged individuals.

It is interesting to note that the United States Chamber of Commerce has established a Human Resources Development Division, and that the United States Employment Service has recently redefined its mission as that of human resources development. The day is not too far distant when many employers will be organizing "Human Resources Departments" to replace outmoded "Personnel Management Departments." Working together, government, business organizations, and employers will succeed in their efforts to assure meaningful and productive employment for all, to the fullest extent of each individual's ability.

NOTES

1. *The A.P. Smith Manufacturing Co. versus Barlow, et. al.*, 97A. 2d. 186, affirmed 98A. 2d. 581, New Jersey.
2. The National Industrial Conference Board, *Industry Aid to Education*, (New York: 1965).
3. M. A. Wright, "Private Enterprise and the Great Society," paper presented to Chicago Association of Commerce and Industry, Chicago, Ill., July 28, 1966 (mimeographed).
4. Solutions To Employment Problems.
5. "Tale of Four Cities."
6. The National Industrial Conference Board, *Company Experience with Negro Employment* (New York: 1966).
7. Douglas M. McGregor, "The Human Side of Enterprise," *Proceedings of the Fifth Anniversary Convocation of the School of Industrial Management*, Massachusetts Institute of Technology, Cambridge, April 9, 1957.

D *A Skeptical View*

42

Toward Greater Industry and Government Involvement in Manpower Development

SAMUEL M. BURT AND
HERBERT E. STRINER
W.E. Upjohn Institute for Employment Research

Who is there among us who will not applaud the growing numbers of board chairmen, presidents, and other top executives who are pledging themselves and their companies to employ the so-called hard-core unemployed youth and adults of our nation? This outpouring of social conscience is proof that many of our country's leaders are dedicated, more than ever, to making it possible for all Americans to become full participants in the mainstream of our economic, social, and political life.

The fervor, excitement, and enthusiasm of the meetings at which these pledges are made, however, are rarely matched in the meetings of the personnel managers, office managers, plant superintendents, and foremen who must do the hiring, training, upgrading, and promoting of the disadvantaged chronically unemployed and underemployed. Even when the social conscience of managers and supervisors matches that of the head of their company, these people cannot suddenly shift gears from *managing personnel* and take on the unprecedented task, for most of them, of *developing the potential* of the persons whom they supervise and direct. As they attempt to carry out the pledges of their top executives, they soon learn that they are operating in uncharted areas foreign to the "business of running a business." There are just too many problems involved in developing a package of services for the hard-core unemployed which includes outreach for recruiting the disadvantaged, restructuring job duties, providing remedial and compensatory education and counseling services, eliminating traditional testing and other pre-employment screening-out practices, providing special training programs and new kinds of promotional ladders, and arranging for "buddies" and "job coaches" to help the trainees adjust to the day-to-day requirements of the world of work.

Furthermore, many of those assigned the responsibility for developing such a packaged program quickly learn that their company has provided little or no funds to cover the costs of the program, including new incentives—material and otherwise—to foremen and supervisors. With production quotas

---

From a Staff Paper of the W.E. Upjohn Institute for Employment Research, 1968.

and business as usual, middle management and frontline supervisors of the company soon recognize that they have become involved in a social service program within the company which they or their company is ill-prepared to undertake, and which their company is either unable or unwilling to finance on a massive scale commensurate with the magnitude of the problem, quantitatively as well as qualitatively. Even when the federal government subsidizes the company for its special efforts and expenditures, what usually emerges is little more than an experimental and demonstration project involving a handful of disadvantaged and/or hard-core unemployed individuals.

Despite the difficulties and costs encountered, many employers in the private sector of our economy, with or without federal government subsidization, have been and are engaged in such experimental programs. What has been learned from the more successful programs has been widely disseminated in case studies and meetings by a variety of national business and industry associations, magazines, and government agencies, as well as university and foundation research reports. Also, newspapers and popular magazine articles, books, and television programs have played a role in publicizing the efforts of employers in resolving the problems of the hard-core unemployed. Unfortunately, there has been insufficient recognition by the manpower planners and the policymakers of our nation that:

1. There is considerable duplication of the companies named in the various published reports—the actual number of companies involved is extremely small and relatively infinitesimal when compared to the number of corporations and major employers in the United States.

2. The number of hard-core unemployed individuals hired, trained, and promoted in any particular company case study is very small compared to the total number of employees in the company.

3. The cost to companies per disadvantaged individual trainee is extremely high in terms of remedial education (not skill training) and social services; it is prohibitively so for most companies in terms of a long-range continuing activity as a regular part of their personnel programs.

4. Even though there has been wide dissemination of case-study reports of successful experiences in the hiring and promotion of disadvantaged individuals, employers continue to consider any such efforts on the part of their companies as experimental.

5. Few employers are providing upgrading and promotional opportunities and programs for their employees who require special and remedial services for both entering into and retaining initial jobs.

6. While many employers have hired and are still hiring disadvantaged individuals from minority groups, many other employers are involved primarily as the result of governmental pressures to eliminate discriminatory hiring practices.

7. Except for some special experimental programs, the individuals included in company programs have usually been "creamed" from the existing pool of the unemployed and underemployed.

The time has come for a change in the continuing pattern of employers engaging in experimental and demonstration projects, each learning *de novo* what others have learned about hiring, training, promoting, and providing compensatory and remedial services for the hard-core unemployed. To correct this situation, assistance and guidance must be provided to employers by government agencies whose staffs have acquired knowledge and competence in the field of working with the hard-core unemployed. Beyond this, government agencies must begin to view themselves as major employers and to "practice what they preach" to nongovernment employers in terms of seeking out and providing meaningful job opportunities to the unemployed.

Over and above these remedial efforts of government and industry, there must be a massive joint undertaking by both these segments of our economy to eliminate those conditions in our country's elementary, secondary, vocational, and higher education schools which permit an individual to be disadvantaged when he enters the labor market.[1] When quality education and training are available to all the youth of our nation, "equal employment opportunity" in its fullest and finest sense will become a reality and a way of life for this nation.

THE PROBLEM

The past and present inequality of educational and training opportunities for our citizenry has enmeshed the employers of our nation in experimental remedial programs for the hard-core unemployed. To understand this, let us examine, even though briefly and perhaps superficially, what the hard-core unemployed bring to the job and what the employer finds it necessary to do in order to develop the potential of such individuals as productive members of his work force.

The intensity of the unemployment problem of the hard core can probably best be understood from the question asked by concerned employers: "How do I go about hiring and training uneducated, unskilled, untrained, and unmotivated individuals?" It might be enough to point out that the employer probably has a number of such employees already on his payroll, but this doesn't help him much in doing something constructive about either his present group or those unemployed individuals whom we want to bring into the mainstream.[2] Possibly the first thing to be done is to help him understand something about the nature of those individuals considered hard core.

The Disadvantaged

Elliot Liebow has a poignant description of a hard-core group in his study of Negro streetcorner men.

> When we look at what the men bring to the job rather than at what the job offers men, it is essential to keep in mind that we are not looking at men coming to the job fresh, just out of school perhaps, and newly prepared to under-

take the task of making a living, or from another job where they earned a living and are prepared to do the same on this job. Each man comes to the job with a long history characterized by his not being able to support himself or his family. Each man carries this knowledge, born of his experience, with him. He comes to the job flat and stale, wearied by the sameness of it all, convinced of his own incompetence, terrified of responsibility—of being tested still again and found wanting.[3]

The picture is much the same for adults of other minority groups who, lacking in education, skills, and training, are living out a frustrated existence within a vicious cycle of failure. This is a notion foreign to many people, particularly those who have experienced some success. This same cycle of failure also plagues school dropouts and even high school graduates who have obtained only menial, low-paying jobs. What the employer must understand is, first, that the typical hard-core unemployed is not unemployable—he is chronically unemployed; and second, the cycle of failure must be broken by inserting a successful job experience that offers opportunity for the individual to utilize to the fullest his capabilities and desires. Realistically speaking, isn't this exactly what most people in the United States want from their jobs? "If you want to see some really motivated people, take a look at a guy who is having his first chance to make a living wage," [4] stated an employee relations executive in a recent report on the hiring of the chronically unemployed.

Providing a decent job opportunity at decent pay is certainly a basic motivational factor. Assuming, however, that such an opportunity is provided, there are other problems which must be overcome. Some of the problems are minimal since the employer has had experience in solving them when dealing with other than hard-core unemployables, for example, orienting trainees to the unfamiliar environment of a shop or office, or teaching specific job skills. Despite this experience, however, there are differences which have not been previously encountered. These differences are well described by the president of the Chrysler Corporation in commenting on his company's recent experience with a small group of hard-core trainees:

> Training the hard-core unemployed—even for factory work—is more difficult than imagined and there are no overnight solutions . . . it can involve teaching a man how to catch the correct bus, or how to get up in the morning, or getting him glasses so he may learn enough reading for simple jobs. . . . These people . . . have to be taught the letters that spell common colors so they can read the instruction cards that tell them to put a blue or green steering wheel on a car as it comes down the assembly line. . . . They must learn simple addition so that they can count boxes of parts they take off a supplier's truck. . . . Some sign an "X" for their names. . . . We have had to overcome fear and resentment, hostility and a history of failure.[5]

While the report goes on to describe the successful adjustment of these trainees after a comparatively short period of training—particularly the development of attitudes which have resulted in staying on the job—it is quite evident that the number and extent of the problems presented the employer in dealing with the hard core is a "package" too unwieldy for more than a handful of the largest companies in the country. Frank H. Cassell, former director of the United States Employment Service, and now a management consultant, sums up the problem as follows:

> The job-holding ability of gang members, school dropouts, and the underprepared is generally poor in relation to the regular work-force. . . . Many such people lack staying power in training programs, preferring a job *now* with money to spend *now*. Their expectations are often unrealistic in terms of their background. Merely creating jobs will not correct this; the creation process in the absence of a job retention effort ends in more failure for both the individual and the employer. . . . What may be understandable behavior to the sociologist, is to the employer laziness and lack of responsibility; he cannot condone this. . . .[6]

Fortunately, the number of individuals posing this "package of problems" requiring a "package of remedial social service programs" is comparatively small, estimated variously at from 250,000 to 2,000,000 in an economy that produces a million and a half new jobs per year. While the estimates include urban and rural hard-core unemployed—whites, Indians, Negroes, Spanish-speaking groups, and so on—the general public and most employers tend to think only of Negroes as comprising the hard core, most of them suffering the full gamut of deficiencies described above. As unrealistic as is this stereotype, there is no question as to the need of remedial education and social services for all trainees with a disadvantaged background, particularly those who are characterized as the hard-core unemployed.

The Employer

The experience of a number of employers who have been involved with the hard-core unemployed indicates that the cost of training one person can range from $2,000 to $5,000 or more. The current MA-3 (Manpower Administration) program of the Department of Labor offers up to $3,500 per trainee if the employer will provide for one year of training and promotional opportunities plus the remedial education, counseling, and other supportive services that we have learned must be provided the trainee in order to assure his job-holding power long enough to bring him well into the mainstream of our labor force.

It is expected that with the help of the National Alliance of Businessmen (NAB) a sufficient number of employers, with or without government subsidy, will pledge at least 100,000 jobs for the hard core by June, 1969, and another 400,000 by the middle of 1971. While the "pledge goals" will probably be met, there is considerable question as to whether the nongovernment subsidized pledges will really provide meaningful jobs. Furthermore, many businessmen involved in the NAB effort characterize it as a nationwide "United Fund" campaign complete with the hoopla, rhetoric, and trappings of pledge meetings and collection and reporting of pledges at the local, state, and national level. Furthermore, there are questions as to the meaning of the reported figures. There is evidence that many of the jobs pledged are either menial, low-paying, dead-end jobs, or at levels too high as yet for the hard core to handle. Nevertheless, a number of employers are seriously engaged in this effort, and many others are casting about for practical ways and means to be involved.

To what extent are such programs meeting the real needs of our nation's hard-core unemployed? An indication of the gap between what is being done and what needs to be done is found in a recent report for Washington, D.C., where it is estimated that less than 10 per cent of the unemployed will have jobs made available to them.[7] We can be pleased about this 10 per cent group, assuming that none of these jobs are dishwashing in a lunchroom, but we cannot ignore the continuing problem of the remaining 90 per cent. Even if the number of the hard core is open to question, reports from other major cities and rural areas indicate a severe gap between their number and the availability of decent jobs with decent pay.

There is also the question of what happens to the trainees, such as those included in the aforementioned Chrysler program, who, trained for specific jobs, lose their jobs in a layoff occasioned by a drop in production. Can they "sell" their minimal skills to other employers? How far can employers in the private sector be expected to go in developing human resource potential while they are committed to the philosophy and practice of hiring people when needed and discontinuing employment when the people are not needed? So long as American industry and business continue this practice as a general way of doing business, the specter of unemployment must haunt all of us, particularly those in the semiskilled and operative jobs—the very jobs for which most of the hard core are being trained.

• • •

Even large companies with highly sophisticated personnel departments have not exhibited any real know-how in working with the hard core, nor do many of them offer the package of remedial services needed by such trainees. Some of the companies, such as Westinghouse, have established a separate educational corporation to deal with the government and the hard-core trainees. Employers strongly feel, however, that education is the province of the educators and that counseling, medical, and family-problem services are the province of social service and health and welfare agencies. Even those employers who have successfully utilized remedial basic-education organizations, such as MIND, Inc., and the Board for Fundamental Education, find themselves involved in programs and activities too expensive and too unrelated to their business to warrant continuing involvement to the extent needed to make more than a dent in the employment problems of our nation. "Looking over what is being done to employ the poor in private industry," stated William L. Batt, Jr., in a recent article, "we can fairly conclude that more efforts are being started now than ever before, but they are still very small indeed in relation to the need." [8] What is required is an effort commensurate with the magnitude of the problem, realistically attuned to the manpower needs of employers and based on factors which will motivate employers to become involved in a major way in the fundamentals of human resource development and utilization. An examination of these motivating factors may well point the direction toward greater industry involvement in the manpower development program of our nation.

NOTES

1. While not within the province of this discussion, the need for industry and government to work together in correcting inequities in health services, housing, and so on, for minority groups is obvious.
2. It has been observed that as employers obtain experience in working with trainees recruited from among the "hard-core unemployables" they are learning invaluable lessons in improving the effectiveness of their entire work force.
3. *Tally's Corner* (Boston: Little, Brown, and Company, 1967), p. 53.
4. *Business and the Urban Crisis,* A Special Report (New York: McGraw-Hill Book Company, 1968), p. 6.
5. "Jobless Training Begins With ABC's," *The New York Times,* June 16, 1968, p. 52.
6. "Realities and Opportunities in the Development of Jobs," *Business and Society,* VIII, No. 2 (Spring, 1968), p. 25.
7. "Burgeoning Training Centers Barely Dent Joblessness," *The Washington Post,* April 4, 1968, p. C 13.
8. "Incentives to Private Employers," prepared for presentation to the National Association for Community Development Conference, Washington, D. C., May 21, 1968.

43

The Nature of the Job Problem and the Role of New Public Service Employment

HAROLD L. SHEPPARD

[*In light of the above skepticism concerning corporate efforts at manpower utilization, a colleague of the two preceding authors at the W.E. Upjohn Institute for Employment Research argues that government must undertake the assignment.*]

From a Staff Paper of the W. E. Upjohn Institute for Employment Research, 1969.

... It is highly probable that the private sector—even with the best of intentions—cannot find enough jobs in its various production and commercial service activities to employ all the youths, men, and women with whom we are all concerned.

At the same time, there is a need for more workers in what has been called "public service employment." Unfortunately, this need has been obscured by the use of such terms as "government as employer of *last* resort," which implies that such employment should be advocated and provided only *after* private enterprise has failed to employ everyone; that these jobs with government agencies are only temporary, pending the rise in demand for workers in private enterprise; and that such jobs are not very desirable for the individual or useful and worth while to the community.

But government is more than an employer: more accurately, its function is to provide services to citizens—such as education, health protection, national defense, park and recreation facilities, waste disposal, water services, construction and maintenance of highways and other transportation facilities, police and fire protection, etc.

In living up to these and other obligations, the government obviously employs persons in jobs which are vital to the functioning of the society and the economy. The main point here is that *the need for the services to be provided is the underlying justification for public service employment.*

Part VI BUSINESS AND EDUCATION

Education is generally regarded as a public responsibility. The system of public instruction, from grade school through the state university, is the backbone of the educational system in the United States. Even private educational institutions are given public subsidy.

More recently we have begun to recognize the educational role which business firms also play, partly through support of schools in financial and substantive ways and partly through programs of their own devising. In this part we examine first some of the needs and potentials of business involvement with public education and then the educational functions which business firms might themselves assume.

A *Working with Public Schools*

44
Bridging the Gap from School to Work
MANPOWER REPORT OF THE PRESIDENT

The persistence of high unemployment among young people throughout the nation—despite the inauguration of new education, training, and job programs for youth—has led to public concern over the adequacy of the entire range of institutions that normally serve as bridges between school and work. A substantial review of the problem and much soul-searching have begun among all those in American life who have a responsibility for preparing youth for their adult activities of earning a living and raising families, or for helping them enter fields of work where they can acquire the wherewithal for productive and satisfying lives.

• • •

THE PROBLEM

The essence of the problem is reflected in the paradox that emerges from the following two propositions: (1) the United States keeps larger proportions of its children in school longer than does any other nation, to insure their preparation for lifetime activity; yet (2) the unemployment rate among youth is far higher here than in any other industrial nation and had been rising sharply until the introduction of the government's youth programs over the last four years.

Unemployment rates among youth, while highest for those in low-income minority-group families, are substantially higher in all income groups than those considered desirable by any concept of acceptable unemployment rates that has been developed in our nation. Thus, youth in the fourteen- to nineteen-year-old bracket from families with incomes of less than $3,000 have unemployment rates of 17.4 per cent, an extraordinarily high level. But even youth from families with incomes of $10,000 and over have unemployment rates of 7.7 per cent—rates that are about double the national average and quadruple the rates of adults.[1]

The differentials between youth and adult unemployment rates have persisted despite marked improvements in the overall employment situation. Examination of the character and dimensions of youth programs undertaken in the last four years, of the rise in youth unemployment rates before that, and of the demographic and economic factors at work suggests that the introduc-

---

From *Manpower Report of the President* (1968), pp. 111–123.

tion of these special programs has been a key factor in keeping youth unemployment rates from rising even further in relation to adult rates.

• • •

The youth for whom bridges to work are now most adequate are those with the intensive preparation provided by professional training at the college level or beyond. For them, careers are virtually assured and unemployment is at or very close to minimum levels. In fact, in many specialties there are numerous opportunities open for people with professional training. But sizable proportions of all other groups of youth—high school dropouts, high school graduates, and college dropouts—face serious uncertainties as they leave the academic world and begin the work for which school was to have prepared them.

The tremendous advantage college graduates have in entering the world of work can be seen from the unemployment rates for young adults. In March, 1967, for example, twenty- to twenty-four-year-olds with a college degree had an unemployment rate of only 1.4 per cent, compared with 5.3 per cent for those with a high school diploma, and a completely unacceptable 10.5 per cent for those who had completed only eight years of school.

Vocational preparation at the secondary and postsecondary levels has been progressively strengthened, however, under the impetus of the Vocational Education Act of 1963. This act has made possible extensive improvements in both the quantity and quality of vocational education offerings, which should mean better job preparation for many youth.

• • •

WAYS OF IMPROVING THE TRANSITION PROCESS

Perception of the school-work gap and of ways of bridging it is naturally colored by the vantage point from which it is regarded. Those involved with school administration have been concerned that the preparation given young people in school be improved so that it can ease their transition into work and reduce youth unemployment rates. Those in the manpower agencies concerned with the cadres of young people who continue to enter the labor force, from school systems that will require many years for improvement, think youth should be helped, where necessary, by new and special training facilities designed to equip them for available jobs. Those who work directly with youth in the process of transition—counseling and placing them as they graduate or drop out of school and advising them on job and training opportunities and on the special work and work-training programs open to them—are particularly concerned about improving the mechanics of the transition. Those involved with youth who are making the transition from rural to urban areas are concerned also with the problems of residence and cultural change and with the wide range of information on occupations needed by those who are leaving rural areas.

Indeed, a strong case can be made for a variety of approaches: (1) Improvements in the educational system and great expansion of cooperative education programs to prepare young people better; (2) special programs to take care of the approximately 6 million school dropouts expected to seek work opportunities without adequate preparation over the next decade; (3) improvements in the process of communicating occupational information to young people while they are in school and putting them in touch with jobs and additional training opportunities as they come out; and (4) improvements in early employment experience, by adding to this experience new opportunities to learn.

At the present time many high school graduates and dropouts do not receive any guidance or counseling. Eight out of ten school dropouts have never had counseling by school or employment office officials about training or employment opportunities, and four out of ten high school graduates have never had such counseling (see Table 44–1). There are no school counselors at all in 13 per cent of the nation's secondary schools and in 90 per cent of its elementary schools. And only Massachusetts and the Virgin Islands meet the Office of Education's basic standard of one counselor for every 300 students.

Even smaller proportions have been exposed to supervised work experience while in school. Among out-of-school youth in 1963, only 7 per cent of high school graduates and 3 per cent of dropouts had such work experience.[2]

The Employment Service's part-time, cooperative school program—under which regular Employment Service counselors come into the schools to test, counsel, and take applications from those not planning to go on to college—reaches about 50 per cent of the high schools and about 75 per cent of all high school seniors. Unfortunately, however, it reaches a much smaller pro-

TABLE 44–1 *Proportion of High School Graduates and Dropouts Who Had Received Job Guidance or Counseling* *

RECEIPT OF JOB GUIDANCE OR COUNSELING	PER CENT DISTRIBUTION	
	DROPOUTS	GRADUATES
Total	100.0	100.0
Received guidance	22.4	56.1
School counseling only	17.1	37.8
Employment service only	4.2	4.9
School and employment service	1.0	13.4
Never received guidance	77.6	43.9

* Data relate to persons sixteen to twenty-one years of age in February, 1963, who were no longer in school, were not college graduates, and were in the civilian non-institutional population.
NOTE: Detail may not add to totals due to rounding.
SOURCE: U.S. Department of Commerce, Bureau of the Census.

portion of the students who drop out of school, and in many cases the degree of contact with the outgoing student is far too superficial.

• • •

Some notable attempts have been made to give more personalized and intensive counseling to individuals, as in schools that provide a full range of guidance services beginning at seventh grade, in the skill centers financed under the MDTA, and in the efforts of the Employment Service to deal with potential dropouts at several continuation schools. These experiences suggest that, with improved guidance materials available throughout the junior and senior high schools and intensive work by counselors knowledgeable about the practical employment situation existing for students coming out of school, some inroads can be made into present youth unemployment rates. These experiences also point to the overwhelming importance of full cooperation and joint action by the local education agencies and the local Employment Service.

Innovative experiences have also taken place under the Vocational Education Act and in special MDTA training courses that expose students to the realities of work life rather than merely to academic situations. The development of more cooperative education programs, even under academically oriented curriculums, has meant that increasing numbers are exposed to work situations that make abstractions come alive.

These experiences suggest that substantial improvements in educational curriculums and more linkages to the reality of the work world will help substantially to improve the preparation of youth. While advocates of general or college-bound preparation still argue with those who want to see more work content introduced throughout the school curriculum, there is growing agreement on several points: (1) that curriculums can generally be enriched by material drawn from real work situations; (2) that all students should be given much more information concerning career paths and opportunities, and much earlier than is now usual; and (3) that the vocational school program should offer opportunities for students with a far wider range of interests and abilities to try out vocationally oriented curriculums and go on not only to jobs but also, increasingly, to higher education—either directly or after periods of employment. In any case, the secondary education system in this country must strive to reach the point at which all youth who receive a high school diploma but do not go on to further education are adequately equipped to find and keep a meaningful job.

There have also been suggestions on other points that need further exploration. It has been proposed, for example, that the schools themselves assume increased responsibility for the actual job placement of their graduates. The exercise of such responsibility would expose the schools to industry and should result in improved and more realistic curriculums and guidance services. It is argued that it makes no more sense for the schools to be unconcerned about what happens to their graduates than it does for an automobile manufacturer to pay no attention to the sales of his products.

How this concern is reflected in new programs becomes an important matter. The government's manpower services are already coping with some of the problems of transition by finding jobs for young people through the facilities of the Employment Service (in particular, through the Youth Opportunity Centers and the Cooperative School Program), as well as by projecting the future needs of the economy and its occupations as a base for educational, training, and curriculum planning. A potentially serious problem in having the schools handle placements is that the knowledge of job opportunities required for a satisfactory placement extends far beyond a school district or even a labor area, and calls for the information network available to the Employment Service system. Furthermore, the government is inevitably concerned about problems of duplication and coordination that might result from newly awakened realizations of need, at a time when there are already recognized shortages of qualified personnel in both the schools and the manpower services.

Solutions to this range of problems by cooperative effort between school systems and Employment Service offices have been worked out in a number of cases and can be carried further, as they have been in other countries such as Sweden and Great Britain. In Sweden, the school system and the employment service each finances half of the cost associated with youth placement activities. In Great Britain, a cooperative relationship has been developed over many years, with responsibility allocated for both guidance and actual job placement. As part of this program, a special Youth Employment Service has been created to deal with youth both in school and as they come out seeking jobs.

EXPERIENCES OF OTHER NATIONS

The problem of youth unemployment in this country takes on added dimension when contrasted with the situation in Europe—a contrast in many ways revealing, but also in many ways deceptive.

Unemployment rates for youth in other nations, particularly the western industrialized nations, are for the most part noticeably lower than for youth in this country. Sweden and France, for example, have youth unemployment rates one-half to two-thirds lower than the American rates. English rates are far below the American ones. While part of this difference can be attributed to a generally tighter European labor situation, a major factor is the highly developed man-job matching apparatus. The youth employment situation in these countries is apparently characterized by a relatively quick entry of youth into jobs following school, an extensive training structure, and a great variety of "apprenticeable" trades through which youth can make a start in the world of work.

In assessing these seeming successes, one should keep in mind that there are some basic structural differences between these countries and the United States—a fact that makes it very difficult to choose what would work as well here. For one thing, the percentage of youth receiving vocational education is much higher in Europe than in the United States, where in 1963–1964 only about 19 per cent of the fourteen- to seventeen-year-olds received vocational education. This contrasts to a range among countries recently studied by the Department of Labor, which begins at 21 per cent (of the fourteen- to seventeen-year-olds) in the Netherlands and extends up to 58 per cent (of the fifteen- to seventeen-year-olds) in West Germany.

These figures reflect a heavily structured status system for entry into jobs —the kind of system that has been traditionally rejected in the United States. Here, the ultimate educational goal—still not fully realized—is to open the broadest and highest level of opportunity for everyone. But this goal is far from being accepted in the countries of Europe. This very aspect of the European practice, moreover, is now a source of dissatisfaction in the European nations themselves. Serious review is underway in several countries with respect to their educational systems, what they lead to, the limited opportunities they afford to youth, and the limited lifetime real incomes that result. Part of this review has been occasioned by concern over inadequate economic growth and the inability of the nations to cope with United States and other foreign drains upon their professional and technical manpower resources.

Contrast with the European situation, perhaps more than any other single factor, suggests that the school-to-work gap in the United States is the result in part of the high educational and flexible career sights that have been set here. The contrast also points up the general failure—as reflected at least in the United States teenage unemployment rates—to bring reality to as high a level. This means that the essential task posed by the school-to-work problem in the United States is how to create a bridge that would bring youth into jobs more directly, and thus reduce their unemployment rates to acceptable levels. But the problem also involves getting them into jobs that are not below their potential, that are not routine jobs into which they are forced for lack of any alternative. The problem is how to make real the now unfulfilled promise of the American educational and opportunity systems.

The much higher educational sights for youth here than abroad are reflected dramatically in the differences in how long youth attend school. In the United States nearly 94 per cent of all fourteen- to seventeen-year-olds are in school, as compared with a range of 56 to 65 per cent for the same age group in several European countries. In recent years, however, a number of these countries have planned to raise the age level for compulsory education. Austria has introduced a ninth year of required schooling; Belgium plans to extend its school-leaving age to sixteen by 1968; and Sweden recently extended schooling to age sixteen. France is lengthening required schooling from age fourteen to age sixteen as of 1968, and the French Planning Commission envisions that, by 1970, 40 per cent of all seventeen-year-olds will be in school. The United Kingdom is also contemplating an extension from fifteen to sixteen years of age.

• • •

Employers in the United States rely heavily on the school system to educate young people in basic skills presumed to be needed for work and—except for the small group of apprentices—do little to insure that the schools actually prepare students for the world of work. They respect the competence and independence of educators, though they often complain about the products they get from the schools.

Schools and employers at this point have similar value systems. The student who drops out, gets low grades, or gets in trouble with the police is in trouble both in school and in getting a job. This creates a circular process: when schools and plant employment offices close doors, they also help to break down self-confidence, and this, in turn, makes it difficult for a youth to overcome the special barriers he faces. Employers naturally prefer experienced and mature youth. High school graduation and school achievement records, as well as minimum age requirements, are generally used for sorting out those who, it is assumed, would not be satisfactory workers. Fragmentary evidence from Employment Service orders indicates that jobs in the United States are as tightly closed to youth on the basis of chronological age as they are to older persons. Whether better methods can be found for judging and developing maturity (a matter that is becoming more and more important in approaches to training) and overcoming lack of experience is an additional question that needs exploration.

Much further study is needed, as well, of the kinds of preparation given to youth, in relation to the kinds of jobs they actually obtain. At this point, data on the relation of education to later work experience are limited to the general relationships between levels of education, parental support, and lifetime or eventual earning capacity. There is as yet no valid information on the more subtle relationships important for the development of public policy and programs—between amount and quality of schooling, kinds of curriculum, and extent of counseling or guidance, on the one hand, and success in overcoming the initial hurdles to job entry on the other. To some extent the longitudinal studies of school and work experience now being sponsored by the Department of Labor, under the Manpower Development and Training Act, and other studies sponsored by the Office of Education will illuminate this question. But more detailed analysis of linkages between particular kinds of school experience and first entry into the job market will be needed.

Whether high unemployment rates for youth will continue because youth is trying out, and can afford to try out, a variety of jobs is another question to be explored. Past explanations of high youth unemployment have often tended to emphasize the "trying out" character of the process. Clearly, job quits contribute to youth unemployment to some degree, but such "voluntary" unemployment in itself needs further assessment. To the extent that this reflects youth searching for job experience, the question might well be raised whether this searching—and the development of realistic expectations concerning the need for preparation—could not be made a part of the education process. At present, this searching occurs at a time when young people are on their own and their education is presumed to have been completed. The in-and-out process between education and work now takes place only in a limited number of situations, such as the Antioch plan.

At the high school level, it would be useful also to gage the impact of part-time employment, while the youth is in school, on his ability to adjust to regular employment once he is out of school. Perhaps a more extensive program of part-time jobs for youth who are in school but who do not plan to pursue higher education would be fruitful. . . .

CONCLUSIONS

. . . While it is recognized that a great many of the factors mentioned need much further exploration, certain general conclusions can be reached on the basis of present knowledge concerning the character of the steps that can be taken to narrow the gap between school and work:

INCREASING KNOWLEDGE ABOUT THE ENVIRONMENT
OF WORK WHILE IN SCHOOL

1. We can insure that every school child has more knowledge about the world of work than is now the case. Preparation for occupational selection should begin not later than the junior high school level because of the social, emotional, and physical changes taking place in the students at this time. This should be a process of increasing knowledge—not of forcing premature decisions. There is need for professional and subprofessional counseling far beyond that which now exists, curriculum revision and new curriculum materials to begin the process of world-of-work exposure, and vast expansion of knowledge about work through teaching aids, television, or direct exposure to real-life occupational situations.

2. Whatever one concludes about the merits of broad versus occupationally oriented education, it is clear that more occupational curriculums offered at high school and post-high school levels should be expanded. These curriculums should be based on the "broad cluster" concept, as part of broad-based education, to permit both the opening of more options than are now available and the prospect of career ladders in these options.

INCREASING OPPORTUNITY FOR YOUNG PEOPLE IN SCHOOL TO
GAIN ACTUAL WORK EXPERIENCE

1. Even before entry into the job market, the student should have maximum opportunity to explore his abilities and preferences in the real world. The tryout period should take place during school years rather than afterward. There should be a vast expansion of cooperative work opportunities that will open new horizons. Work experience, in fact, should become a meaningful part of preparation for career development and life at several stages of youth—not only at the final professional internship stage. The interaction of classroom instruction and practical exposure should be planned to

develop the highest level of capacity possible for each young person at the time of his entry into the job market, whenever that occurs. These work activities should be accompanied by supportive counseling—the kind of counseling that may well be the most important in the practical process of launching youth on a career.

2. The great desire of young people to be involved in meaningful activities in our Nation should be matched by expanded development of opportunities for voluntary service, both during school years and afterward. Academic credit should be given for such activity, and the Nation's voluntary organizations should be assisted to develop such opportunity.

INCREASING PARTICIPATION OF BUSINESS AND OTHER PRIVATE GROUPS IN THE EDUCATION WORLD

1. There should be vastly more involvement of people from the working world (businessmen, supervisors, labor officials, professionals, and Employment Service and other public servants) in the process of education—through exchanges of various kinds, or simply the direct contribution of the time of personnel.

2. There should be vastly more two-way interchange—especially over summers or other vacation times—between professionals in the world of education and the world of industry and employment.

3. There is a need for industry to develop new forms of training, and new kinds of training for supervisors, in the techniques of introducing young people—including disadvantaged and minority youth—into the new world of work. For too many youth, this world is one of unsympathetic supervisors and fellow workers. Such programs could involve educational upgrading in plants, placing school personnel in plants, and use of various forms of educational release time, with resultant lessening of dependence on school classrooms as the sole places of organized instruction.

NOTES

1. These data, the latest available on unemployment rates of teenagers by family income, are available only for teenagers fourteen to nineteen and relate to teenagers who were family members, other than head of the family, and were unemployed in March, 1967. Family income is for 1966.
2. These statistics relate to cooperative educational arrangements between schools and industry. In addition, since 1963, the Neighborhood Youth Corps has provided hundreds of thousands of parttime employment opportunities to poor children to enable them to remain in school.

45

Uplifting Vocational-Technical Education

U.S. CHAMBER OF COMMERCE

The Task Force paid considerable attention to public school vocational-technical education in the course of its study. In many communities public school vocational-technical education suffers apparently for two main reasons. First is what Dr. J. Chester Swanson, in his paper for the Task Force, calls the "image" factor. Vocational-technical education, in the minds of many, is a second-rate, second-class kind of education. Our modern society has not placed proper emphasis on, and in many cases has not even recognized, the important part craftsmen and technicians play in this technological age. Over the years, school systems have often placed their failures in vocational-technical courses. Schools have segregated vocational from academic students. Equipment is often obsolete, materials are scarce and teachers are often ineffective. Other teachers within the school system hold the vocational courses in low esteem.[1] Thus, to quote Dr. Swanson, "the vocational program has become the exit vestibule for incompetent students, an area for second-class citizens."

On the other hand, some school systems have been so intent on improving the image and statistical performance of their vocational programs that they have raised eligibility requirements to unrealistic levels. On occasion, jobs have gone vacant because unnecessarily high eligibility requirements have kept prospective students out of the appropriate vocational program.

The second reason why vocational-technical education suffers is that courses are insufficiently related to actual labor market conditions; courses often prepare people for jobs that either do not exist or are disappearing. As John H. Fischer, President of Teachers College, Columbia University, points out, "schools have adhered too long and too closely to concepts of [vocational] curriculum and organization developed forty years ago." [2] In some places, courses are still centered around woodworking and mechanical drawing at a time when the economy needs—and compensates well—mechanics, computer operators, electrical appliance repairmen, welders, tool and die makers, carpenters, lathe operators and a host of other highly respectable skills. As Dr. Swanson points out and as the Task Force learned first hand during field trips, schools do not generally know what jobs are available in a community. Schools do not generally know of the changing skills and knowledge require-

---

Printed by permission of the Task Force on Economic Growth and Opportunity, Chamber of Commerce of the United States, the third report of the Task Force on the Study of Poverty, *The Disadvantaged Poor: Education and Employment,* © 1966.

ments of many job opportunities. Less is known about the number and kinds of job opportunities that may be available in the future when today's younger students complete their educations. Without current and projected information about the labor market, schools cannot design and carry out effective vocational-technical education programs. To the extent the schools fail to prepare their graduates for jobs, the image of vocational-technical education deteriorates. A vicious circle effect emerges. As one panelist told the Task Force, the single most effective way to uplift the prestige of vocational-technical education and promote incentives for people to enroll is for vocational education to demonstrate success in leading people to well paid and respectable jobs.

Effective vocational education is pivotal to the alleviation of poverty. Few jobs remain that require no training or skills. For every scientist and engineer half a dozen or more technicians and craftsmen are needed. And the men who build, test, try out, adjust and repair equipment are as vital in an industrial economy as the scientists and engineers who create. Graduates of vocational-technical training are in great demand by industry and business. In a recent survey by the Chamber of Commerce of the United States, 90 per cent of the local chamber of commerce executives reported that their members have been voicing concern about the shortages of skilled manpower.[3]

Public schools can improve today's vocational-technical education. To do so, school administrators and educators must recognize the important place vocational-technical education can play in preparing youth to earn a living. For years, many schools have assumed only the responsibility of teaching the basic skills of reading, writing, and arithmetic, plus subjects required for admission to college.[4] In many places, there is a need for a thorough restructuring of the educational program to make effective vocational-technical education an integral part of the public school program through high school and beyond.

To achieve this, educators should take the initiative, inviting the interest and involvement of business and industry. Businessmen can help design vocational-technical education programs by keeping education officials thoroughly informed about current and anticipated job markets and about changes in the skills and knowledge needed by the economy. Businessmen can help by lending their own experts to help the school system train vocational-technical teachers. Businessmen can help by providing up-to-date equipment to schools or advising school officials about new equipment being introduced in industry. Businessmen can help by taking an active interest in placing graduates of vocational-technical training in jobs immediately upon graduation. Businessmen can help by insisting that vocational-technical schools publish periodic reports on their graduates' success in finding jobs for which they were trained or in entering apprenticeship and advanced training programs for which the schools qualify them. Finally, businessmen can help by promoting more and better vocational-technical training high schools and junior colleges wherever they are needed.

It is in the interest of businessmen to involve themselves actively in public school vocational-technical education. To the extent that public schools can turn out people ready for employment, businessmen are saved training expenses. In many cases businessmen are saved taxes that would be necessary to meet welfare and law enforcement problems often associated with undereducation and unemployment. Remarkable progress has resulted where business has taken an active part in vocational-technical education.[5]

NOTES

1. Eugene P. Foley, "The Negro Businessman: In Search of a Tradition," *Daedalus*, Winter 1966, pp. 109, 112.
2. *Target: Employment* (Washington, D.C.: Chamber of Commerce of the United States, 1964).
3. *Loc. cit.* These are but a few examples.
4. See, the Special Supplement of "Washington Report," of the Chamber of Commerce of the United States, May 12, 1963.
5. A few examples, Dallas, Tex.; Denver, Colo.; Kenosha, Wisc.; Los Angeles, Calif.; Pittsburgh, Pa.; San Diego, Calif.

46
Business Involvement in Public Education—the Detroit Experience

Michigan Bell and Chrysler Corporation

[*The Detroit Public School system has welcomed the cooperation of business firms in improving the quality of its educational offerings. Among the most active of its industrial collaborators have been the Michigan Bell Telephone Company and the Chrysler Corporation.*]

From a letter of an official of the Detroit Public Schools (1968):

All programs were developed through the joint planning of educators and representatives from the business community. There has been no attempt on the part of the business community to dominate public education for its own purposes.

As educators, it is our responsibility to determine if a program offered by industry can make an appropriate contribution to education. On this basis certain so-called cooperative programs with business organizations have been rejected.

NORTHERN HIGH/MICHIGAN BELL: AN EDUCATIONAL PARTNERSHIP

Michigan Bell's general employment supervisor, Edward N. Hodges III, conceived the idea of an "educational partnership" as a dramatic demonstration of the concern of business for the quality of inner city education. "A social contribution and an investment in Detroit's future" is the way Michigan Bell Board Chairman William M. Day put it. Northern High was chosen for the program because of its significant location in the central city near the 1967 riot area, and the fact that it had previously been the target of student unrest. It embodied to a high degree all the implications of the word "disadvantaged."

The purpose of the partnership is to help students prepare for the world of work and to aid the faculty in enriching the education provided by the school. Manpower resources, managerial skills, technical assistance and training facilities of Michigan Bell have all been tapped to help achieve these goals.

Programs carried out to date at Northern have been determined jointly by school and company representatives. Many projects have been undertaken at the specific request of school personnel. Fresh ideas are constantly being discussed with the result that bold, new steps are being taken toward a truly significant relationship.

Understandably, in its first year of operation the direct effect of this unique program was felt by relatively few Northern students, but in subtle ways it influenced the lives of all of them. And it offered solid grounds for hope that when the full, exciting potential of this partnership is realized, "advantaged" will best describe every graduate.

Activities at Northern

COMMERCIAL ART EXPOSURE

For a firsthand look at commercial art as it is used in the telephone industry, art students made visits to Michigan Bell's telephone directory art section. The students met company artists who discussed the communication effects and business use of art. Professional techniques and procedures were explained. During the summer, the head of Northern's Art Department was employed in this art section. His commercial art experience will be shared with future students.

EMPLOYMENT READINESS

This is a special course taught by a Michigan Bell employment manager to most of Northern's seniors. It was made part of the economics curriculum

---

From "Northern High/Michigan Bell: An Educational Partnership," prepared by Michigan Bell, 1968.

and referred to by the Social Studies Department Head as "practical economics." The course taught the basics of job hunting: how to fill out job applications; proper grooming for job hunting; how to take employment tests; and how to conduct yourself in an employment interview. Employment readiness made it possible for students to explore the entire process of applying for a job. Through the technique of role-playing, the students stimulated actual situations they might encounter.

NORTH CENTRAL ACCREDITATION BOOKLET

In May, 1968, Northern High had its periodic seven year visit by the North Central Accreditation Committee. High school accreditation procedures require extensive studies of curriculum, plant, equipment, personnel and related matters necessary to a school's continued accreditation. To assist Northern's administration and faculty in this vital area, Michigan Bell printed a special booklet prepared by school personnel for accreditation purposes. Since the booklet fully describes the entire school operation, sufficient copies were printed as an informational aid to present and future Northern staff members.

SCHOOL NEWSPAPER STAFF

Student staffers of "The Northern Light," the school newspaper, spent a day with Michigan Bell's newspaper and magazine staff to observe how the company handles its publications. The students saw how the content of a publication was determined, the layout procedures, photographic selection and printing processes. Following the visit, the school newspaper staff published a special community edition describing the educational partnership.

RETAILING PROGRAM

Two of the company's marketing representatives worked with the retailing instructor as part-time lecturers, revealing to students the larger world of marketing as distinguished from "store" retailing. On several occasions, individual students accompanied marketing representatives as they made regular calls on Michigan Bell business customers. These trips gave the students an opportunity to observe marketing in action. The retailing instructor described the impact of this experience on her class as "unbelievable, great, tremendous!"

DATA PROCESSING CLASS

Classroom instruction in data processing was supplemented with a special program developed by Michigan Bell's Comptroller's Department. A computer expert from Michigan Bell served as part-time instructor, lecturing on computer concepts and demonstrating the company's use of data processing. In addition, students were able to visit the company's computer facility for firsthand experience, and to consult with computer personnel.

BUSINESS EDUCATION CONSULTANT

A Michigan Bell employment supervisor spends one day per week at Northern serving as a business education consultant. She works closely with the business education department and occasionally teaches classes on a part-time basis. In addition, she serves as an aide to Northern's counselors in providing students with job information.

LECTURES ON ENGINEERING CAREERS

To assist Northern students interested in an engineering career, a Michigan Bell engineer lectured in science and mathematics classes on opportunities in that field.

PROJECT THIRTY

Thirty girls (twelve recent graduates and eighteen returning students) began work in late June on a special clerical project for the company's Plant Department. These girls, all with business education training, transcribed certain records necessary to Plant operation. The girls were on the company payroll, receiving the regular wage of newly hired clerical employees. All the work was done at Northern under the supervision of two Northern teachers hired for the summer.

PROJECT TEAM (TELEPHONE EXPERIENCE AND MOTIVATION)

This was a ten-week Saturday training class in basic telephony taught at Michigan Bell's Plant Department Training School. Senior boys participated in the program, during which they received a training allowance of $2.05 per hour. Most of the boys were hired by Michigan Bell as full-time craft employees upon graduation and satisfactory completion of the course.

CO-OP EMPLOYMENT

Under the school's co-op program of half-time study and half-time employment, twenty-eight Northern students worked at Michigan Bell. They were employed as switchroom helpers, keypunch operators, stenographers, test center clerks, and in a variety of other clerical assignments. This experience gave students the opportunity to see the business world while still in school. It also provided them with a chance to earn while learning, and perhaps will ease the transition from school to job for those students who do not plan to attend college following their graduation.

EMPLOYMENT AFTER GRADUATION

Seventy-seven 1968 Northern graduates applied for and received full-time employment at Michigan Bell. It should be noted that while the company is assisting the faculty to prepare Northern students for the world of work, Michigan Bell is not using the partnership for the purpose of developing a future pool of Bell employees. The primary aim is to provide help that will enable Northern's graduates to qualify for entry level positions throughout the general business and industrial market.

CHARM COURSE

As an after school project, a Michigan Bell supervisor who is also a freelance model conducted a charm course for tenth-grade girls. The seven-week course dealt with grooming, make-up, deportment, speech and related subjects.

SPEECH IMPROVEMENT

To aid the English Department in its speech improvement program, a Michigan Bell teletrainer unit was made available for full-time use. This unit, consisting of two battery-operated telephones hooked up to a tape recorder, is used to acquaint students with the type of speech expected of employees in the business world.

STUDENT HANDBOOK

Similar to the accreditation booklet but aimed at student orientation was a handbook prepared for Northern students. The company printed the handbook which contains information on the school's facilities, curriculum, student clubs and activities as well as general information about Northern.

OFFICE PROCEDURE ANALYSIS

At the request of the principal, a Michigan Bell supervisor from the Comptroller's Department made a week-long study of Northern's clerical office procedures for the purpose of streamlining and improving record keeping, business machine use and the work flow of the massive amount of school paper work. As the result of her study, the supervisor was able to make a number of recommendations for the general improvement of the total clerical process.

SCHOOL SWITCHBOARD OPERATION

To improve the flow of telephone traffic in and out of the school, the company was requested to provide switchboard training to the student office assistants. Special training on Northern's switchboard was given not only to the part-time staff but to the adult full-time office workers as well.

BASIC ELECTRICITY AND ELECTRONICS COURSE

During the first year of the educational partnership, Northern High did not have a course in electricity and electronics. At the request of the school's vocational education department, Bell technicians developed a five-week course on the subject. Michigan Bell training personnel built the laboratory equipment and wrote most of the text material for the course, called "Exploring the World of Electricity." Portions of the course were used in Project 60. Northern now offers an electricity class of its own, and "Exploring the World of Electricity" is available should the instructor want to make it part of the regular course.

CULTURAL ENRICHMENT

As a contribution to cultural enrichment for Northern students, Michigan Bell provided transportation and tickets for English Honors and drama students to attend a performance of the Detroit Symphony Orchestra and plays at Oakland University's Meadowbrook Theater and the Detroit Institute of Arts.

ATHLETIC "HALL OF FAME"

At the request of one of the school's athletic coaches, Michigan Bell is assisting in the establishment of a Northern High "Hall of Fame." To encourage school pride and further develop esprit de corps, the coach is assembling a large photographic display of school athletes. The company's photographic department has taken large individual pictures of all team members participating in the five competitive sports at Northern. These pictures will be the beginning of a school "Hall of Fame."

STOCK MARKET LECTURES

At the request of the economics instructor seeking to provide curriculum enrichment through outside expertise, a Michigan Bell employee, who had been on the Board of Directors of the National Association of Investment Clubs and who has had considerable experience in the field of stock transactions, lectured to senior economics classes on stock market operations.

PROJECT 60 (A SPECIAL SUMMER PROGRAM)

Northern's counselors were requested to recommend sixty tenth- and eleventh-grade students whose grades did not measure up to their potential. These students were invited to participate on a voluntary basis in Project 60, a program designed to provide a half day of concentrated remedial education in English and math, and a half day of vocational training. Three of Northern's top teachers were hired and one Michigan Bell supervisor was loaned to plan and teach the six-week summer session.

In their vocational classes, the girls studied clerical procedures and the boys studied basic electricity. All students received an attendance bonus of five dollars per day. Classes were held in a modern parish building of a northwest Detroit church, and bus transportation was provided from Northern High to the church and back each day. Students also toured various Michigan Bell offices and other work locations to encourage them to finish school and get better jobs.

Although conclusive results of this unique summer program will be some time in coming, comparative testing of students was done on the first and last days of the session. Test scores showed students had raised their mathematics and English grade levels an average of half a year, with grade level improvement of two years not uncommon. Hopefully, the teachers benefited also. They were given free reign to innovate and try new teaching techniques which, if found effective, may find a place in regular school classrooms.

DEBATE TEAM SUPPLEMENTAL ASSISTANCE

To aid in the development of Northern's debate team, the company financed the attendance of three debaters to a two-week summer seminar at Michigan State University. The seminar was a special program conducted for high school students of speech and debate.

Summary

Coordinating and implementing these projects has been the work of two Michigan Bell Personnel Department employees, William T. Rice and Jean M. Alfsen. Both have become familiar faces at Northern High, where they find out what help is needed, and at the telephone company, where they find either solutions or problem solvers.

Of the progress made by the "educational partnership" thus far, Dr. Leonard Sain, former principal of Northern Senior High School, and now assistant to the superintendent, Detroit public schools, had this to say: "The pioneering relationship that was inaugurated between Michigan Bell Telephone Company and Northern Senior High School has pointed the way for business and industry to have a meaningful relationship with our school systems. I am enthused with the results and the potential of this relationship and congratulate Michigan Bell Telephone Company for having the foresight and the courage to initiate this cooperative effort."

NORTHWESTERN HIGH/CHRYSLER

. . . I would like to tell you, in general terms, what we at Chrysler think this kind of program *should* and *should not* concern itself with. It should aim at a constructive combination of the facilities and the expertise *you* have with the facilities and expertise that *we* have. It should not try in any way to displace or supersede existing, effective methods or approaches. It should attempt to build a bridge between the world of the classroom and the world of work. It should *not*—in the effort to build this bridge—encourage an overemphasis on vocational education.

It should be designed to equip young Detroiters to get jobs with industrial companies of all kinds. It should not be designed to provide a captive source of trained manpower for Chrysler alone. It should emphasize the importance of motivating *individual* students through teacher-student relationships. It should *not* be treated as a program for mass producing industrial trainees.

From "Northwestern High/Chrysler," remarks by Lynn Townsend, Chairman and Chief Executive Officer, Chrysler Corporation, at a meeting of the faculty of Northwestern High School, May 21, 1968.

Objectives of the Northwestern/Chrysler Program

The proposal of the Chrysler Corporation is intended to develop between Northwestern High School and the Chrysler Corporation a relationship of mutual cooperation wherein the competencies and resources of both would combine to provide a broader and deeper educational program for the students of Northwestern.

Chrysler's industrial facility and personnel can offer possibilities to expand the educational offerings at Northwestern so that the following objectives might be achieved more effectively: (1) additional cooperation and work experiences in office and industrial skills; (2) employment and job application guidance and training; (3) provision of specialists to inform students of the nature of the world of work and the preparations required to be successful in it; (4) special classes and seminars to develop the specialized skills required by industry particularly for apprenticeship programs; (5) implementation of specialized programs by providing equipment which would enhance the training of students in these programs; (6) establishment of employment services to directly assist Northwestern students in gaining employment after graduation.

Recommendations

The following is a list of proposed recommendations which Chrysler Corporation might undertake in behalf of Northwestern High School.

1. Make available for consultation and advice appropriate specialists to work with Northwestern faculty members to review and advise on curriculum content as requested. This could involve such areas as chemistry, physics, mathematics, auto mechanics, metal shop, drafting, typing, and so on.

2. Make the fullest possible use of Northwestern co-op students in typing, filing, auto mechanics, and so on, to provide modest work experience wherever Chrysler vacancies can be converted into co-op placement opportunities.

3. Maintain a Chrysler Corporation "Interviewing Employment" service *at Northwestern* to the extent necessary to (a) interview and place all recent Northwestern graduates who are unemployed or refer them to other appropriate employers through the CDC-New Detroit Placement functions; (b) provide an "in-house" experience for students to learn to cope with application forms, tests, interview procedures, and so on, or to make actual applications for work as they approach graduation; (c) make available a continuing source of information on job availability and job requirements for counselors, teachers, and students as needed.

4. Recruit the volunteer services of about 200 interested supervisory and professional personnel who would donate one hour per week to counsel with students designated as potential drop-outs concerning the realities of the world of work and the values of good education and dependable work habits.

This would presuppose one or two sessions with Chrysler volunteers to discuss counseling techniques and close coordination with Northwestern administration.

5. Provide Chrysler Corporation personnel to serve as guest lecturers before student groups as a part of normal school activities. This could run the gamut from a research engineer lecturing on applications of new technology before classes in chemistry and physics to a current Chrysler Apprentice talking to a male student group about the qualifications for and broad range of opportunity in automotive skilled trades.

6. While opportunities for summer work experience are restricted by law in machine-shop type industries, a limited number of work-training type experiences could be made available, subject to Chrysler Corporation's ability to provide an appropriate Training Subsidiary, to (a) conduct two six-weeks sessions (twenty-five students per session) on automechanics for youths between their junior and senior years; (b) conduct two similar sessions for interested youths to coach them in subjects which would assist them to pass an apprenticeship qualifying test upon graduation. This approach aims at increasing the number of youth who could qualify for an apprentice training program in conjunction with a junior college in the area and would enable the student to earn forty-seven of the sixty credits needed to complete the junior college associate degree program. Beyond that, the Chrysler Corporation's Tuition Refund Plan would finance any additional college course work leading to a degree in a job related field of study. Opportunities for in-service training and the tuition refund provision would be available to girls as well as boys who become Chrysler Corporation employees.

7. Donate to Northwestern specialized type of surplus equipment available in the Corporation which would support teaching programs in the school.

8. Work cooperatively with Northwestern faculty and administration in the testing and application of teaching techniques utilized within Chrysler Corporation as they may have application in the Northwestern program.

The administration of the above recommendations, subject to the approval of the Detroit Board of Education, would be coordinated through the Chrysler Institute of Engineering and Related Academic Affairs Department of Chrysler Institute.

Concluding Statement

The Chrysler proposal gives substance to industry's commitment to the community and to the education of young people in particular. The proposed services will supplement Northwestern's efforts to help students to perceive the relationship between what happens in school and what awaits them in our complex technological society. There is every reason to anticipate that this joint effort will result in higher aspirations and achievement among Northwestern students.

47
Business Amid Urban Crisis
NATIONAL INDUSTRIAL
CONFERENCE BOARD

In cooperation with the School Volunteer Project of the Massachusetts Council for Public Schools in the underprivileged sections of Boston, Raytheon provides six staff specialists to spend three to six hours a week (during the school day) to advise and assist classroom teachers in Dorchester High School in physics, chemistry, mathematics, astronomy, and technical writing. They also work with school administrators and faculty and with guidance personnel in improving school curricula and motivating students.

Philadelphia Gas Works, too, has employee-teachers. "Twenty-two of our key executives serve as nonpaid instructors in the public school system with the sanction of the company and on company time, thus giving an added dimension of business experience to two Philadelphia junior high schools dealing with seriously disadvantaged youngsters," says the company's public relations manager.

From National Industrial Conference Board, *Studies in Public Affairs*, No. 3 (1968), p. 41.

B *Education within Industry*

48

Innovation in Education

A. WRIGHT ELLIOTT
Vice President, National Association of Manufacturers

It is all too easy to be bound to the past, to use *only* experience as our guide, to set our standards for future programs with caution, based empirically upon what seems to have worked fairly well before. But this we cannot, must not, do. If we must choose between caution and daring, between moving too slowly or with too much speed, then we *must,* I think, move on the side of boldness.

Perhaps a few brief examples are in order. We must be willing to look at new technologies in the educational field, fully recognizing that the adaption of these new concepts will threaten some of our existing educational institutions. But when a nation as great as ours has within its population 25 million functional illiterate citizens, it seems to me that we can ill-afford the luxury of waiting for the traditional education system to come around to that point where it widely adapts new educational technology. We must not only use the new technology but, indeed, we must apply it within different learning environments, even if this means in some instances converting factories into classrooms.

From an address before the Congress of American Industry, 1968.

49

Remedial Education

E. F. SHELLEY AND COMPANY

Approximately three-fifths of the 128 firms with some program experience indicated they provide remediation for new recruits. Firms training recruits for white-collar positions almost always require some specific educational attainment and yet also add a basic education component to the program.

From the report, *Private Industry and the Disadvantaged Worker* (1969), prepared by E. F. Shelley and Company for the National Urban Coalition. The survey was limited to large-scale enterprise in major urban areas.

TABLE 49–1 *Number of Hours of Remedial Education Supplied by Companies*

NUMBER OF HOURS	TOTAL COMPANIES		COMPANY FUNDED COMPANIES		GOVERNMENT FUNDED COMPANIES	
	NO.	PER CENT	NO.	PER CENT	NO.	PER CENT
Varies	6	(8)	3	(9)	3	(7)
1–10	3	(4)	1	(3)	2	(5)
11–25	3	(4)	2	(6)	1	(2)
26–50	8	(10)	4	(12)	4	(10)
51–100	19	(25)	11	(32)	8	(19)
Over 100	38	(49)	13	(38)	25	(57)
Totals	77	(100)	34	(100)	44	(100)

The response to the questionnaire indicated that those firms making the most substantial effort toward remediation are being reimbursed, at least partially, by the Department of Labor's MA-3 program. Over 64 per cent of the firms receiving federal funds reported a substantial remedial program, more than half of these being over 100 hours of remedial work. This is in contrast to only 40 per cent of the company-funded programs whose basic education program is usually of more limited scope (one-third of these are under 50 hours). As one business executive said, "I've already paid for this education twice—through corporation taxes and personal income taxes—why should I pay for it a third time?" (see Table 49–1).

Besides the availability of federal funds, the data in Table 49–2 infer that the certification procedures of the federal program may encourage or force companies to employ persons with less educational background and more need of remediation services. Of the more than 1,700 trainees reported in federally funded programs, 77 per cent never finished high school as mea-

TABLE 49–2 *Trainee Educational Achievement (by Funding Source)*

EDUCATIONAL ACHIEVEMENT	TOTAL		COMPANY FUNDED		GOVERNMENT FUNDED	
	NO.	PER CENT	NO.	PER CENT	NO.	PER CENT
Grades 1–6	218	7	53	4	165	9
Grades 7–9	681	22	241	19	440	25
Grade 10	601	20	193	15	408	23
Grade 11	515	17	222	17	293	17
Grade 12 or beyond	985	32	574	45	411	23
No formal schooling	51	2	2	—	49	3
Totals	3051	100	1285	100	1766	100

sured against 45 per cent of the trainees in company-sponsored programs who finished at least twelve grades of school.

Educational methods used by the companies surveyed vary greatly. They range from intensive professional classes to do-it-yourself, home-study programs. Classes are taught by local high school teachers, trainers from remedial education firms, or education specialists. In approximately 52 per cent of those reporting, the companies' own personnel operate the basic education component. In one-fourth of these cases company staff run the program in conjunction with private educational consulting firms or a local board of education.

The location of the instruction varies. Classes are held on company premises, in public schools, at antipoverty agencies, and in the specially designed facilities of private training agencies. In at least one case, a tenement basement in the heart of the ghetto serves as the remedial education facility.

Data on the exact structuring of the remedial programs could not be derived from the questionnaire, but on field visits the staff found the instruction appendaged to the workday in a wide variety of ways. For example, companies may pay trainees full entry level salary for the class time, pay a small stipend, or provide only transportation and lunch money. Some companies provide no remuneration at all for time spent on basic education. Most of the companies surveyed conduct classes in remediation on a part-time basis, pulling the recruits off the job. When the special hiring effort does not include a structured training program and is solely on-the-job training, remedial education is often held for one or two hours before or after the regular workday. When this is the case, attendance is normally mandatory for government-sponsored programs and voluntary for company-financed programs. Several firms have made use of the pre-employment remediation service which is given by local Opportunities Industrialization Centers. The OIC effort requires that a trainee reach a certain reading level for remediation before he can be certified as being "job-ready."

Forty-eight per cent of the companies delegated the responsibility for basic education instruction to an outside agency or company. Staff review of remediation training packages indicated that when outside training resources operate the program, the length of instruction is usually considerably longer and more highly structured than are company-run programs.

It was found that when the instruction is job-related and uses materials such as selected newspapers and periodicals indigenous to the recruit's neighborhood, it is far more successful than lessons structured more in the manner of conventional academic environments. Without reference points and materials with which the recruit can clearly identify, trainers have indicated that the remedial phases of all training programs tend to bore the trainee.

50
Basic Education: Case Studies
NATIONAL CITIZENS COMMITTEE
FOR COMMUNITY RELATIONS

[*In 1967 the National Citizens' Committee for Community Relations held a three-day conference in Chicago at which employers and civic leaders from a number of cities exchanged experiences in "Putting the Hard-Core Unemployed into Jobs." The following cases are taken from the report which bears that title.*]

BASIC EDUCATION: MIND

A company finds that 32 per cent of its employees cannot qualify for changing jobs, and ends up marketing a basic education course for other companies.[1]

Corn Products Company went into the education business when it discovered that 32 per cent of its 2,700 employees, many of them good workers, were by today's standards, functionally illiterate and unable to master the company's changing technology. Some of these employees were hired fifteen, twenty, or twenty-five years ago when there was no qualification for hiring except ability to handle the job. Many had worked their way up to more difficult jobs that were still manually related. Some were high school graduates who had forgotten their basic education; others had never had much education.

The company asked supervisors to recommend good workers to be considered for a program that would improve basic skills to the point where they could compete for new jobs opening in the plant. Working with MIND (Methods of Intellectual Development, a pilot program originally sponsored by the National Association of Manufacturers), employees were tested to find their current levels of reading, writing, and arithmetic. Thirty-eight people in the first project averaged a little above third-grade level in reading and writing, a bit above-fourth grade in arithmetic. The MIND project recommended 160 hours of classroom work to bring these workers up four grade levels in their basic skills.

Classes were held two hours a day, four days a week, after working hours on the employees' own time. The company did not pay the employee for attending. Due to work-scheduling difficulties, the average employee-student in the first project did not get the full course that was programmed. But an average increase of three and a half years in mathematics, somewhat less in reading and writing, made the company very happy with the results. A second program is now under way with fifty-nine more employees.

Staff and Budget

Allen Vinson and two "monitors," not trained teachers but women with deep interest in individuals and able to help them make progress, constitute the staff of the company education program. The cost is estimated at about $200 per trainee. Expenses consist of the salaries of the three staff members, teaching materials, and some special furniture to make comfortable classrooms.

Some Interesting Byproducts

1. The local school system was so impressed by the results of the first basic education program that Vinson was asked to try the same techniques with a regular school class. A group of ninth graders were bussed to the Corn Products plant for 35 minutes of instruction daily, for a total of 23 hours. The average grade increase was about 1.5 grades; one student jumped 2.6 grades. Says Vinson: "It can be done effectively with school systems. The school is interested, but they do have to be shown the way."

2. Following Mr. Vinson's initial work with NAM's "MIND," Corn Products Company has now taken on this project as a subsidiary activity and is marketing it to other companies as a commercial venture.

3. The Campbell Soup Corporation in cooperation with the union and the Chicago Board of Education also has developed a basic education program for company employees. The Board of Education supplies teachers and materials, but the program is conducted on company premises. This company has found that workers who will not go back to school will participate in such programs.

BASIC EDUCATION: TRAINING EMPLOYEES FOR BETTER JOBS

As requirements for jobs call for more skill, many companies are finding that employees who have been with a firm for many years cannot be trained for jobs involved in new processes because they simply don't know how to read, write or do arithmetic well enough. School drop-outs and graduates from poor schools present the same problems. Basic education may be the answer, and many companies find it works best when courses are conducted right on company premises.[2]

The Board for Fundamental Education designs special courses to meet individual company needs. With 1,000 hours of instruction the program can take a person from zero grade level through high school equivalency. The course is usually divided into units of zero through four; grades four to eight, and eight to twelve.

Example

The Diamond Alkali Company in Deer Park near Houston, Texas, had a real shortage of "trainable" people. The Board for Fundamental Education developed a basic education program for employees in the unskilled labor pool, whose average age was forty-two and whose written and arithmetic skills tested at approximately third grade level.

Classes were held three evenings per week, two hours per session for twenty weeks. Employees attended on their own time after working hours. Their attendance was purely voluntary. Originally, nearly all of the workers in the unskilled labor pool wanted to enroll, and the company had to select twenty for the pilot program. After fifteen weeks—approximately 150 classroom hours—eight of the men passed a test qualifying them for promotion to beginning jobs in the progression ranks. Ultimately, almost all of the men passed the tests and are now in the skill training program. The company is now running classes for the remaining men in the unskilled labor pool. The students were given the usual two employment tests required for promotion into entry jobs in the progression rank. One important change was made in the usual procedure; if an employee passed one of the two tests, he was considered eligible for entry into the skill training ranks while he continued his education. The immediate success of passing one test gave greater incentive than if the employee had to pass both. Eventually, all passed both tests.

The Board for Fundamental Education, a nonprofit organization, has conducted in-plant basic education courses for about 80,000 people. Dr. Blackburn says firmly: "The place to train people is in the world of work." He finds:

> Motivation is almost as important as actual training for an individual who has failed at everything he has touched. The company can create a learning situation in which the trainee-student feels an identity with the company and its growth. The individual will participate in a company program, whereas he would not return to the inconvenience of the public school. Having the program in-plant, he might, even though it's not guaranteed, find himself in a better job paying more money.

EDUCATION: HELPING VOCATIONAL SCHOOLS MEET BUSINESS AND INDUSTRY NEEDS

Three years ago Pittsburgh surveyed its vocational education program. The survey showed that less than 6 per cent of the total student body was attending five vocational schools, and that less than 1 per cent of these students were Negroes. Now the city has totally reorganized its vocational program, with businessmen serving on key advisory committees and subcommittees.[3]

First Step

Pittsburgh combined its vocational schools where possible with adjacent academic high schools. To get sixteen comprehensive high schools, existing facilities were remodeled and re-equipped, and curriculum was radically revamped. All students in these schools now have an opportunity to get a far broader range of courses related to current business and industry needs.

The tenth and eleventh grades in these schools are used to diagnose and evaluate the aptitudes of students and to advise them on specific courses to prepare them for employment during the last two years of high school.

Counselors advise on both academic and vocational training needs. Special in-service training was needed to prepare existing counselors for this expanded role.

Example

Formerly in vocational education, a teacher would say, "Give me the boy for half a day and I will teach him what he needs to go out and get a job in a machine shop (or become a plumber or bricklayer)." Today, there are thousands of new job fields opening up and a more comprehensive kind of counseling is needed. "In the health field, for example, of every 100 jobs only eleven are physicians; the rest are nursing aids, laboratory technicians, and a whole range of jobs that need certain kinds of preparation and require different kinds of personal aptitudes," said Dr. Olson. He believes the counselor should be able to advise the student which field he seems most suited for and what training to take.

The Pittsburgh school system has reorganized its vocational curriculum with the aid of advisory committees including business and industry representatives. An overall advisory committee provides program guidance in view of total needs of the city, and subcommittees advise in special fields. About eighty craft committees are represented by 600 industrial, civic, and other leaders who give specific program guidance and direction.

The school system is concerned about giving students a more comprehensive total education because it is impossible to know today what specific job requirements will be in a few years. In the *work-experience* programs [so-called Distributive Education (DE)] the school system has for the first time gotten a sizable number of Negro students to participate because it is giving related training in school *before* students go out on jobs. For example, sales and merchandising training are given before students go to jobs in stores. There are now almost 200 Negroes (and 350 whites) in work-study situations, where previously there were practically no Negroes.

NOTES

1. Reported by Allen Vinson, Supervisor Training and Development Programs Corn Products Co. Argo, Ill.
2. Reported by Dr. Cleo Blackburn, Director Board for Fundamental Education.
3. Reported by Dr. Jerry C. Olson, Director Occupational, Vocational & Technical Education Pittsburgh Public Schools, Pittsburgh, Pa.

51
Upgrading Manpower—Whose Responsibility, What Responsibility?

NEIL W. CHAMBERLAIN

Industry problems, like contagious illnesses, tend to spread. One problem which seems to be epidemic at the present time is manpower. . . . With only a few minutes of reflection, we could probably put together a sizable catalog of reasons why this should be so, but there is no point in discussing these preliminaries extensively here. Let it suffice to remind you of just three reasons.

The first reason is the tight labor market. . . . The second reason is just the converse—the number of those who form the hard core of our unemployed remains unpleasantly high: younger people who are adjusting to, sometimes resisting, and often excluded from the world of work; minority groups, especially Negroes, who, if not discriminated against, are no longer satisfied with the occupational leavings; functional illiterates who cannot be accommodated. . . .

The third reason for industry's manpower fixation arises in part from the fact that its people at all levels, right up to chief executive, are facing a world of rapid change and obsolence. . . . The consequence of this escalation of the rate of knowledge accumulation and its application is the need for more frequent enrichment of the knowledge base in industry, either by importing freshly trained minds or updating the old ones. . . . There is

---

A talk before the general membership of the American Iron and Steel Institute, New York, May 22, 1969.

much more that might be said on this subject, but I am going to move along very rapidly with the main theme, omitting most of the embroidery. . . .

Consider the colossal magnitude of what must be contended with. First (at least first in the order of the hierarchy of needs) you now find yourself in the business of basic education. If people grow to adulthood unable to read, write, or figure, that has now become an industry problem. Those who question whether this should be so simply miss the point. Whether we believe that the fault lies with the educational system which should be corrected, or with family background, urban environment, or whatever, the fact of the matter is that for as far as we can see into the future people will be growing up in this country who are unequipped with the basic skills for living in our kind of society. Just as President Truman used to say of the president's office, you can now—with respect to this problem—say of your own: "The buck stops here." For whatever reason the education deficiency exists, the problem lands at industry's doorstep, and society has now agreed that industry should not shut the door on this unwanted waif. It is, so to speak, now "your baby."

A number of companies, recognizing this fact, have themselves gone into the business of providing basic education for other companies who do not want to staff themselves for the job. This is simply a question of how the job can best be done. And a good deal of disagreement still exists over how much of the expense for this social service should be assumed by business and how much society should subsidize, simply a question of who picks up the check. About who is to do the job, there is little question. You are elected.

A second type of training is one which is more traditional—vocational and job-related training, both on the job and in the classroom. All of you have been engaged in this, to varying degree, for years. Many of you are now expanding and refining your activities in this field. There is no question that many advances can be made, and difficult problems remain to be resolved, most notably the relationship between industry and the public schools. Let me simply hazard my own prediction that industry will become increasingly involved with the vocational offerings in junior and senior high schools, on a participatory as well as an advisory basis, and probably also with vocational instruction for adults in special classes sponsored by the community and the federal government.

One aspect of vocational training which deserves some intensive consideration is apprenticeship, a hoary institution much in need of rejuvenation and modernization. In many ways it is reminiscent of the now obsolete tradition of "reading for the law" as a preparation for that profession, in contrast to the more systematic, specialized, concentrated, and content-full law-degree programs which have replaced that practice.

Consider briefly the characteristics of most present apprenticeship programs. A young chap, usually of minimum age eighteen, with minimum education of high school or its equivalent, indentures himself for four years, during which time he spends 144 hours a year in correspondence school, tradeschool, or company classes; the rest of the time he learns by doing, presumably under the eye of skilled journeymen and his foreman. At the end of that time he comes out an electrician, machinist, carpenter, pipefitter, toolmaker, or welder. The question which a number of people in industry (and some in the unions) are now asking is whether such a program is primarily intended to force a young man to serve time rather than to provide a genuine learning experience. Are four years really needed to learn the trade? Or if four years is to be the term, do they constitute as much of an educational experience as they really could be? There are a number of possibilities.

Suppose that a young man is not obliged to take a four-year program through to completion as a condition of attaining some status labeled "journeyman." Suppose, instead, we recognize that for certain kinds of jobs involving a craft, completion of a one-year program may be all that is needed, while for other assignments a longer period of instruction would be required. Instead of the arbitrary requirement of serving *time* as a condition of attaining some formal status, we might think of jobs as having educational or training prerequisites of varying duration and content. The length of time in apprenticeship would then depend on the particular craft content of the job in question. A limited period of apprenticeship at an early stage of a youth's career might be followed by a second period later, and perhaps a third, as necessary, further along. At each stage optional related instruction of a nonvocational nature might be made available, so that those whose curiosity is aroused as to the physics, chemistry, technology, or even the history relating to their craft would be given the chance to build a broader education on the occupational base. Even if only a few responded to this possibility, it would be worthwhile encouraging them. In the process we might learn something of value about the relationship between education and vocation, something about which we have been decidedly ambivalent. The sponsorship of such related programs will be discussed later.

Or suppose that we set up the content specifications for journeyman status but attach no requirement of a *period* of indenture. Whenever the apprentice satisfied the specifications of the craft, he would be granted his journeyman's label. Apprentices would earn their status in a period of time that accorded with their efforts and ability.

Again, suppose that, instead of confronting a young man of eighteen with the prospect of four years of indenture (the very term is more suggestive of servitude than of "mind-expansion," to use a term now more frequently employed in another connection), that same young man were confronted with the possibility of a four-year program which went *beyond* the state of knowledge of most practicing journeymen. The possibilities are suggested by Republic Steel, which in its Industrial Education Institute has been experimenting with a variety of specialized courses of instruction. In the area of Electrical and Electronic Maintenance, to take one illustration at random, it offers a four-year program for people who are holding full-time jobs. This program begins with basic electrical concepts in the first year and proceeds through successively more complex subject matter to solid-state logic systems, computers, and automated process control in the fourth year. The same kind of educational program could be adapted as a substitute for traditional apprenticeship.

Let us imagine a little further. We can readily grant that certain educational courses may have certain job or experience prerequisites. Before an employee could proceed to course work in automated process control, there might be certain work experience which would be indispensable to his understanding what he was studying. If we move along this line, we find ourselves conceiving of a man's career as a constant interplay of work and study. Attainment of the journeyman status would not be viewed as a plateau of achievement but as a temporary base where experience could be gained, qualifying one for more demanding assignments relating to newer technological developments, which would require further study. From another point of view, the notion of a four-year apprenticeship at the start of one's career, during which are absorbed the basic knowledge and craft practices which are to stand one in good stead all one's journeyman days, would give way to a more contemporary conception of the need for continuing instruction if one is to stay on the frontiers of his craft. The journeyman who finds his knowledge inferior to that of the most recent graduate from improved apprenticeship programs might be encouraged, by appropriate inducements, to undertake some of the same study as the apprentice whom he supervises in more traditional matters.

It would take some doing to work out a system which would meet all the objections which can be expected from foremen, employees, unions, and perhaps yourselves, but some fresh thinking with respect to apprenticeship is very much needed. Innovation, when it comes, will undoubtedly affect many more than the relatively limited numbers now benefiting from apprenticeship programs.

One problem lies in the difficulties which firms sometimes encounter in providing the varieties of experience or training even now required for apprenticeship. More cooperation within industry is obviously needed. I see no reason why numbers of companies, cutting across industry lines, cannot mount joint apprenticeship programs. Within most communities, employers, by pooling their facilities, can add greatly to the learning potential of the community's working population. This is especially necessary in the case of smaller companies, whose own resources may be inadequate to mount an existing type of apprenticeship program, let alone an improved one, but who in combination with other employers in the area could put together a superior offering. Indeed, even large companies are not immune from this problem.

Whether jointly or individually mounted, is there a danger of overtraining employees, of companies winding up with too many of their people having gone further in their skill development than the jobs available will give an outlet to? I am not very much concerned about that possibility. In this area, as shall be discussed more fully later, companies are not likely for long to be in a position to do only what is good or comfortable for them. A company which finds itself with a labor force trained beyond its immediate needs must either update itself as a company or be prepared to lose some of those employees to other companies which can use them. Business firms no less than individual employees need updating and redirection from time to time if they are to remain relevant within a changing context. In this respect I suspect that, as in Say's law in economics, supply will create its own demand. The availability of more highly trained individuals will stimulate the growth of those employers who know best how to use them. In any event, we are a long way now from having an excess of highly skilled employees. Why delay in undertaking to meet a clear and present social need for fear that we may be too successful in our efforts? . . .

Industry's manpower involvements are not limited to basic education and vocational training. I need only remind you, without elaboration, of the extent to which most companies have established or participated in programs for executive development. These have ranged all the way from systematic attempts to improve a manager's technical, administrative, and interpersonal competence to seminars which are designed to increase the individual's awareness of his social and economic environment and the changing role which business plays in that changing context.

Along with executive development, companies have supported professional advancement. Firms which recruit postgraduate engineers and scientists have learned the importance of encouraging them to keep their professional interests lively and current through such devices as periodic in-house seminars, participation in academic programs, and released time for the pursuit of independent research.

These varied educational activities occurring within industry reflect the growing acceptance of a concept which has come to the fore within the last decade—the notion of education as a lifetime or continuing affair. For years we listened complacently to commencement speakers who told graduating classes that they were just embarking on the great adventure of learning and that high school or college had simply been the preparation for a never-ending pursuit of knowledge. But the thought, however valid, seemed more grandiloquent than significant and seldom motivated a behavioral response. Now the situation has changed. Within the short space of a decade we have been moving to accept, both intellectually and programmatically, the view that an individual's career will be subjected to relentless pressures for updating, and that the individual who wishes to avoid the unhappy state of personal obsolescence, in which he gradually resigns himself to the fact that he is becoming more and more irrelevant to society's functioning, must accept as a necessity the continuous feeding of his mind and the continuous exercise of the muscles of his imagination.

But along with this spreading realization has come recognition of the fact that in maintaining his intellectual vitality and keeping his stock of knowledge current the individual cannot always go it alone. Learning has become a more complex process, and the acquisition of some of the new knowledge often requires more formalized instruction. Certainly if the individual's investment of effort is to have a richer return, it is often necessary and almost always desirable for him to be exposed to another person already expert in the subject and to have access to laboratory equipment or teaching aids.

These two considerations—first, the importance of continuous learning, and second, the need for more formal programs to facilitate that learning—pose a challenge to industry which I do not think it can very well avoid, and one which I think it should not even try to avoid. Industry (if by that term we encompass private economic activity generally) is in effect the "campus" of most of our adult population, and at the same time it is industry which has within its own ranks the largest pool of professionally trained people who are not already occupied as educators. Just as the skilled journeyman and the foreman now provide instruction to the apprentice (even though in a manner which can be criticized as inefficient), so can we conceive of people with particular expertise at all levels within the company serving as teachers for others within the company who are interested in acquiring the knowledge and skills which the experts can impart.

This is not such a remote idea as it may seem at first encounter. A number of companies on the American scene are already moving down this path. If one looks ahead to the 1970's and assumes a rate of social change no greater than has characterized the 1960's, one might reasonably predict that the business corporation will emerge as an increasingly significant part of the educational establishment in quite a literal rather than a metaphorical sense, and that its educational functions will embrace, more fully and more systematically, the full range from basic to postgraduate professional education. The programs that it will offer and the methods that it will adopt will be more closely related to the offerings of the "regular" educational establishment, from public schools through community colleges to national universities.

It is by no means a wild flight of fancy to conceive that our major corporations, in carving out their educational roles, will develop their own philosophies and styles, so that a Xerox Corporation, for example, may be the business equivalent of MIT; United States Steel may become industry's Carnegie-Mellon Institute; General Electric may fancy itself as a new Harvard. (I won't venture to guess what corporation might aspire to Columbia's place in the educational spectrum.) In similar vein a smaller company may adopt an educational philosophy reminiscent of, say, Williams College or Antioch or Swarthmore. Firms need not actually mount educational operations on the same scale as a university or college in order to reflect an educational philosophy, and the notion that a business firm can and should think along these lines is relevant to a firm of any size, however small. Nor do I mean to imply that entirely new educational policies might not also find an industry sponsorship.

If we are serious about lifetime or continuing education, it cannot be made the sole responsibility of our present educational establishment. It will be possible only if we bring into use resources which are not now being employed for educational purposes—principally those which are to be found in our business corporations. It is not at all surprising that so many major companies see education as a field ripe for development and have set up divisions or subsidiaries for this line of activity. In some cases their interest centers on assisting education in existing schools. In other cases their concern is principally with preparing or upgrading people for jobs in industry. But in still other instances they view themselves more broadly and experimentally as part of the learning process (however that comes to be defined) even if not yet conceiving of themselves as actually an educational establishment or their programs as in any sense a curriculum. Where their entrepreneurial venturing may take us is still problematical, but I feel reasonably certain that we are moving towards a much more integrated relationship between corporate- and school-sponsored education. In the future, an individual may move easily and frequently between job and classroom, and the classroom may be located in his own plant, another company's offices, a public school or community college, or an institute for advanced learning.

There are some outside the business world who vehemently oppose such a development. The basis for their opposition is entitled to respectful consideration. They are concerned that if business comes to play so significant a part in the nation's educational process, the educational process will be subverted to business ends. Business will have an even more pervasive influence on the way our citizenry think and reason and will use that influence to perpetuate and entrench social, economic, and political dogmas favorable to its own interests.

I readily admit the reality of that danger, as I suspect many of you will. But there is another possibility. In our affluent society we may learn to look on economic activity not as *dominating* our personal lives and our institutions but as *part* of a larger whole. The job which engages us need not swallow our lives but become one ingredient of a richer life. From that perspective, work can be made an instrument for self-development. Granting that most jobs will always contain their measure of boredom, frustration, and unpleasantness, they can also be made part of an educational process. Our objective would be to link work with intellectual advancement.

If this seems a bit fanciful, may I suggest that the kind of job structuring and educational activity already taking place in our business firms would have seemed no less fanciful to the manager of less than a hundred—even fifty—years ago? Why should we deride the possibility that the institution which now occupies so much of the time and effort of our people—the business firm—cannot be adapted and modified so that it becomes a major instrument for social renewal? Is it beyond our ingenuity to channel its capabilities for social betterment along lines other than simply the production of goods? Have we become so obsessed with the virtues of specialization that we must restrict a firm's function to efficient production of goods without respect to the effects on those engaged in the production process? Have we become so enamored of the idea of individuals as human capital that we cannot conceive of investments in them which have their effect in ways other than increased productivity?

If you react uneasily to questions like these I can understand your reaction. It is one thing to say that all institutions must change, business no less than any others. It is another thing to discern or chart the direction of change. To suggest that the corporation, organized for one essential purpose—production—should now reorganize itself in such a way as to perform an additional function—education in the broadest sense—opens up a host of thorny problems relating to management and profitability, corporate control, and even survival. It seems far safer to leave things as they are, to accept no more change than society forces on this institution.

That may indeed be the case, but it is also possible that these finite lives we lead would be invested with a great deal more zest and satisfaction if we created our own challenges rather than simply reacted to those posed by others. Even so, I do not underestimate the risks and hazards that would be run in the process of moving along this uncharted path.

One of those risks would be to place the firm in the same parlous positions as our colleges and universities now face. Students are now demanding a larger role in determining their own education. Some of their demands are extreme to the point of denying the validity of any teaching function, placing student in the role of instructor. But the thrust of their position is clearly in the direction of more self-determination, a principle to which our culture is generally dedicated. The insistence is that their education be relevant in their own terms. They understand what cannot be denied, that education embodies the values of a society, and they want more to say about those values.

As business firms become more and more involved in the educational process, can they escape these same challenges from those whom they educate? If business becomes more closely integrated into the educational life of the nation, will it not be subjected to the same insistence on employee participation in determining the forms which corporate education takes? Does management have some immutable prerogative to decide for itself how its employees will be trained? Can it control the values which underly its educational programs?

When management speaks of education and training, it usually talks in terms of "manpower" programs. The term is telling. It conceives of its endeavors in this area as related to the more effective development of its employees as production inputs—manpower. Can a particular program be justified? Yes, if it leads to cost reduction or quality improvement or an expanded sense of identification with company goals. The right economist will even figure a return on the investment involved.

This approach is a sophisticated step down the road from paternalistic concern with an employee's welfare. It provides the rationalization for an expanded set of company-financed programs benefiting the employee in the act of benefiting the employer. But it is still a long remove from company-sponsored training and education programs in the design of which employees and the public have a significant voice.

It requires no prescience to observe that we live in a time of ferment. Even if we confine our attention to our own society, we encounter on all sides serious questioning of our established institutions. The upcoming generation challenges all conventions. The distinction between liberty and license seems to have been obliterated. Students confront their universities. The blacks demand sweeping reforms. Political parties are divided, and religious bodies face rebelliousness and schism. Even the army must come to terms with an insurgency in its ranks.

It would be reassuring if we could sweep these unsettling movements under a philosophical rug, hoping that with the passage of time they can be forgotten. I doubt that any of us believes that to be likely. But if that is so, reflect for a moment. What special providence gives industry immunity from the passions of our time? When the rebellious youth and the assertive students are employees on your payroll, will they be satisfied to be looked on as manpower? Will your programs for the improvement of their skills and minds be accepted willingly because they add to productivity and hence to their earnings? Or will the yeasty ferment still be at work, but now *inside* your institutions?

In short, industry is not likely to face the issue of *whether* it should change, but *how*. In this area we have been discussing—training and education—with all the progress that has been made in the last decade, the time is ripe for a more searching and systematic examination of where industry's opportunities and responsibilities lie.

52
Don't Ask the Employer . . .

SAMUEL M. BURT AND
HERBERT E. STRINER

[*A different view of the role of business in the educational process is offered by two economic analysts in the following excerpt.*]

Employers' concern with the proper preparation of youth for jobs in their offices and plants has long been demonstrated through their involvement with

From *Toward Greater Industry and Government Involvement in Manpower Development* (W. E. Upjohn Institute for Employment Research, 1968), pp. 9–11.

colleges and schools in cooperative work-study programs. Such cooperative programs at the high school level have made it possible for students throughout the country to attend school part of the day and perform work for which they are paid in plants and shops the remainder of the day. Many employers have now extended these programs, or have initiated new ones that are specially designed for minority-group young people with disadvantaged backgrounds. And more and more employers are becoming involved in a new spontaneously originated program of "adopting" a particular high school in their community in order to improve the total educational program for all the students. The employers arrange for their professional, technical, and supervisory staffs to serve as part-time teachers; provide in-service training to the school instructors; conduct demonstrations of new techniques, products, and equipment for the students; and hire the students on a part-time basis for work in their offices and plants. These "adopt-a-school" employers are interested in making the school more relevant to the world of work, in improving the educational program of the school, and in motivating young people to stay in high school and even go on to further education. The employer expects that, sooner or later, some of these students will become his employees.

Where public schools and colleges have failed to provide the amount and type of manpower needed, employers *have supported and will support* other educational and training institutions, programs, and instrumentalities. In recent years we have seen the growth of area vocational-technical schools, junior and community colleges, technical institutes, Opportunities Industrialization Centers, labor union-operated schools, private trade schools, and programs designed to prepare youth and adults to produce on the job at a high rate of effectiveness in a minimal period of time. All of these institutions and programs (except the labor union schools and the private trade schools) have been made possible by increased taxes, of which the major burden is in one way or another on employers. Even the union-operated schools and training programs are paid for by special funds collected by the unions from employers as negotiated in labor-management contracts.

In contrast to this immense outlay of funds and time in support of education and training programs by employers outside their plants, a 1964 Department of Labor study found a comparatively small number of formal in-plant skill-training and upgrading programs being conducted for a very small number of employees. The great majority of such in-plant programs were, and still are, short-term safety training programs and executive development programs for foremen, supervisors, and executives. The truth of the matter is that most skill training in private industry is conducted informally and that few employers have any idea of the costs of training their employees. It is obvious that most employers much prefer, and will support in terms of money and time, educational and training programs to meet their manpower needs (either generally or specifically but preferably specifically) conducted by some institution, agency, or organization other than their own, outside their plants and offices. (This preference for somebody else to provide companies with skilled manpower extends to letting other employers do the training and then "pirating" the skilled personnel.)

These generalizations are not made as a criticism: they are simply a fact of life in the world of business and should be recognized as such by the manpower specialists responsible for planning our cooperative government-industry manpower development programs. The planners can learn a great deal about education-industry cooperative efforts from educators who have long been involved in developing such programs. There is also much to be learned from educators involved in educating and training physically and mentally handicapped (disadvantaged) people and placing them in jobs.

The lesson is really simple—provide a program which will supply the employer with the kind of people he wants, and the employer will support it both financially and through a personal involvement—but don't ask the employer to turn his plant and office into a social service agency or an educational institution. He is paying taxes to the government and is contributing huge sums to educational and charitable institutions to provide such services. He will readily admit that the present programs are inadequate and must be changed. If he can be persuaded that any particular new program or programs will do the job more effectively, he will support them either by paying additional taxes or by increasing his contributions.

Part VII BUSINESS AND URBAN ECONOMIC DEVELOPMENT

Civic organizations and local chambers of commerce have long been active in trying to promote the economic development of their communities. In recent years urban economic development has come to focus on something quite different. It is concerned chiefly with efforts to resuscitate the decaying inner cities, areas which often incorporate or are adjacent to the cities' slum and ghetto areas.

How this can best be done has been the subject of numerous conferences and papers. Proposals vary all the way from using a private-enterprise approach, encouraging business firms to see potential profit in a rebuilding operation, to treating the inner city as an underdeveloped area and providing it with infusions of capital and technical assistance. Obviously these approaches need not be alternatives but can be combined and made complementary. This part explores some of the possibilities.

A *The City as a Market*

53
The Private Side of Public Business
NEIL W. CHAMBERLAIN

DECENTRALIZING SOCIAL OBJECTIVES

Scarcely a country in Western society is not contemplating a relative expansion in social services in the years ahead—not in response to any governmental desire for added power but in response to needs felt by society itself, insofar as the political process can register such an expression.

It has been customary to think of this as a movement from the private sector to the public sector, but this is necessarily the case only in a demand sense, not with respect to supply. By definition it constitutes a movement from private to social consumption, but it does not necessarily connote a movement from private to public production. A business firm can produce for governments no less than for individual consumers. If business comes to look on governments as *markets,* and to recognize that social demand provides an opportunity for developing wholly new product lines geared to those markets, then its field of operation is expanded. Opportunities are opened for research and development leading to new kinds of products and services.

Once this is realized, attention can be directed to ways of making this new market for private business ventures as effective, competitive, and innovative as possible. One area for examination is the relative roles of central and local governments in the provision of social services. We had occasion earlier to observe that central governments were coming to play an increasingly dominant role in this respect. The atrophy of local governments has been remarked by a number of observers in different countries. There has been good reason for the more important role of the central government in providing social services. In a national economy standards of social services can hardly be left to local administrations, with widely varying degrees of fiscal and professional competence. So central governments have become the collecting agents for revenues and the disbursing center for expertise. It is logical enough.

But to the extent that there is an increasing centralization of governmental provision of social services, the less satisfactory a market does this become. Even when the government buys rather than produces, it appears on the scene as a monopsonist; business firms are invited to compete against each

From *Private and Public Planning* (New York: McGraw-Hill Book Company, Inc., 1965), pp. 206–210. © 1965 by McGraw-Hill, Inc. Used with permission of McGraw-Hill Book Company.

other for such contracts as the central government lets; the successful bidders become more heavily dependent on the central government as a buyer, more subject to its influence, more clearly drawn in as a subunit of its own extensive organization. Moreover, centralization of decision making contributes to loss of adaptability to changing or varied circumstances. There is an almost exact parallel here with the weaknesses of corporate centralization.

If we regard local governments as the equivalent of corporate departments or divisions, then there is the same gain to be had from decentralization in the one case as in the other. But aside from the increased efficiency that comes from decentralization, there would be a further gain for which there is no parallel in the corporate case, arising from the fact that decentralization of public-service functions to local governments would be chiefly with respect to a *purchasing* rather than a *producing* function, thus helping to create a market rather than expand a hierarchy.

The central government could continue to collect and redistribute revenues and could specify minimum standards to be met in the provision of the social services for which revenues were allocated. These would constitute the premises binding on local governments and guaranteeing that the specific objectives of the economy as a whole were reasonably met. But within these premises local governments would be free to exercise their discretion, to innovate and experiment in line with local preferences.

From the point of view of building a market for the private provision of public services, the important consideration is that there would be a proliferation of purchasers of the same type of service, as a large number of local governments would form the demand side of the market in contrast to a single central government. Private suppliers would cease to become dependent on any one government: the loss of a contract in one locality might be compensated by the gain of a contract in a different locality. We could presume that with a growing but diffused demand for such services, the number of firms competing would also increase. What would be the difference to a firm whether it sells its product to individual consumers, to other corporations, or to local and state governments? Thus more buyers and more sellers would help to create a more competitive market, with all its attendant advantages. We need only accept—could we not say welcome?—a variety in the provision of social services in respects which do not threaten system objectives.

The number of types of services for which local governments could contract, in line with certain prescribed national standards, is probably much greater than we sometimes tend to think. There is no reason why it could not extend to general education, recreation and youth development programs, health, housing, and cultural activities. At the level of the state or province it could include highway construction and some regional redevelopment activities.

One important consequence of such reorganization of public markets would be that it would encourage business firms to direct their research and development activities to social as well as individual wants, to develop new product lines more nearly meeting public needs, thus expanding their own potential investment outlets. The result would be to harness private initiative and innovation in the service of organized society no less than of the individual.

The potentialities are suggested if we consider public education in the United States as a prototype. This is carried on as a state and local function (but without national standards). Architects, construction firms, furniture and equipment suppliers, and textbook publishers, among others, compete among themselves in this specialized and diffused market. Local governments do not supply these goods and services themselves but purchase them from private profit-making institutions. In particular, the flow of improved textbooks to the school market is directly traceable to the competition of publishers to best each other, and the result is more varied and updated instructional materials than if the schools—or a central ministry of education—undertook to provide this important ingredient of the educational system on their own initiative. One might reasonably argue that overall educational objectives might be better served if minimum national standards were provided for, but even with that modification the same principle of local discretion in meeting national standards would permit the operation of an effective market.

Thus private and public objectives can be made more compatible by improving the market relationship of the public to the private sector. An increase in the public budget designed to provide more adequately for social services and investment would carry no more adverse connotation to private business than a decision by consumers to put more of their expenditures into, say, housing than clothing. One early example of such a business reorientation is provided by the Reynolds Metals Company, which in 1960 established a subsidiary, Reynolds Aluminum Service Corporation, headed by a former United States housing administrator, primarily to contract for construction projects in urban renewal programs. Such business ventures may encounter difficulties at this early stage of market organization, but this is entrepreneurship in the pure Schumpeterian sense of opening up a new market.

"PRIVATIZING" PUBLIC OBJECTIVES

There are, of course, some public services which cannot be disaggregated to the local level. These must be carried on by the central government directly. Included in this category are national defense, technical assistance to foreign countries, development of transportation systems other than road transport, noncommercial research programs, resource development, underseas and space exploration, and certain forms of power development.

In the case of such activities, public and private objectives can be brought closer together by what may be termed the "privatizing" of public objectives —the contracting with private enterprise for their development and operation. There is seldom any reason why the government need carry on such activities itself, even if its initiative is required to set them in motion.

The extensive system of contracting which has been developed by the United States Department of Defense is indicative of how reliance can be placed on private firms for the effectuation of public programs. Even the conduct of research and development with an eye to the more effective meeting of public needs can be undertaken, on a competitive basis, by private corporations. It would be interesting to see, for example, what varied proposals a half-dozen large firms might come up with for the economic provision of more suitable transportation between the cities on the United States East Coast, from Boston to Washington. Whatever system was selected could then be privately constructed under government contract, and arrangements made for its private operation—either on a subsidized ownership or management fee basis. The important consideration is that from start to finish it would rely on private inventiveness and organization to provide a public need. In the process the economy would make more effective use of one of its prime assets—its private business firms.

Such a system of economic administration by contract—something which the United States has pioneered and brought to a more advanced state of organizational effectiveness than is generally appreciated—is even the potential basis for a new type of economic system. It differs from historic capitalism, which stressed private organization to meet private wants, with the latter assumed to be overriding. It differs from socialism, which relies on public organization to meet both public and private wants, with the former assumed to take precedence. The system of administration by contract depends heavily on private organization to meet both public and private needs, neither of which has any special claim to dominance but which can be mixed in any proportions desired. Its advantage lies in the dispersal of authority throughout society, accompanied by an instrument for its effective coordination for the achievement of system goals. It permits the realization of public wants without a concomitant expansion of the governmental establishment. It encourages private initiative by offering it a wider scope for its application.

54
Does Business Have a Future?

J. WILSON NEWMAN
Chairman, Dun & Bradstreet, Inc.

NEW INITIATIVES BY BUSINESS

Social progress requires material achievements. And these achievements require the very type of management of new technologies and human resources that business has developed. Who has more experience and talent for the kind of cost-benefit analysis required to solve problems such as pollution than the private corporations which developed such techniques?

The purpose of business has always been to answer human wants. Whether these wants are for candy-striped toothpaste and wrinkle-free dresses, or traffic systems and pollution control equipment, nine times out of ten business can do the job more efficiently than government or any other institution.

The common ground of people questioning business leadership today is the conviction that the priorities of our society have changed and the businessman *by nature* is not motivated to do anything about it. But I see encouraging signs that some businessmen are making radical adjustments in their concepts of the market that may prove the critics wrong.

1. Recently, Ford Motor Company announced it has set up a center to study total transportation problems, including urban development, regional planning, population shifts and economic trends. Among its purposes is to find out where and how—and *if*—the automobile has a long-range future in answering the needs of society.

2. Xerox Corporation has swung its great technical talents into a thoroughgoing study of education—digging into the roots of things like learning processes and curricula to find out how age-old techniques can be changed and made more effective with the help of new behavioral technologies.

3. The Radio Corporation of America, working with teachers at Stanford University, has just launched a new computer-based instructional system aimed at improving and personalizing the educational process in schools and colleges.

4. General Electric Company has formed a Community Systems Division to plan and engineer new cities from the ground up.

From J. Wilson Newman, "Does Business Have a Future," *MSU Business Topics* (Autumn, 1967), pp. 16–21. Reprinted by permission of the publisher, the Bureau of Business and Economic Research, Division of Research, Graduate School of Business Administration, Michigan State University.

5. Four aerospace firms in California are making systems analyses of the state's needs in three critical areas—waste management, transportation records handling and criminal processing.

Another promising initiative from the private sector has been the development of proposals for creating non-governmental corporations financed by public funds that can draw on business management and technology in finding solutions to society's problems. A prominent example is the Corporation for Public Television which was recently proposed to enrich the nation's cultural and educational life through a fuller use of television technology and talents. Others have been proposed to direct large-scale urban renewal programs.

A $100 BILLION MARKET

The recent initiatives by private enterprise on these social fronts are by no means confined to the biggest giants of industry. Business firms of all sizes, often encouraged and aided by business organizations such as the Chamber of Commerce, are beginning to sense, and respond to, a new market in which I believe business *can* play a vital role.

It will be the toughest market business has ever tackled. Bringing a new product to consumers is child's play compared with the political and social problems that the businessman meets when he enters a field like urban rehabilitation.

But the market—the human need—is there. Over the scant thirty-three years left in this century:

1. The potential market for private enterprise to rehabilitate slum housing in our cities, so they can be ready when dramatic population changes make us an almost completely urban society, is several trillions of dollars;

2. The potential market for new aids to education in our schools and colleges and homes is several hundred billions of dollars. Here again, population changes are radically changing our environment. Shortly, half our population will be under twenty-five, and it has been estimated that by the end of the century every other person in the country will be either in the process of teaching or being taught, as we educate and re-educate ourselves to keep up with change;

3. The potential market for private enterprise solutions to the problems of air and water pollution is roughly put at $300 billion.

Altogether, I can foresee a total market averaging out as much as $100 billion a year over the rest of this century to lift the smog, clean the rivers, rebuild the cities, unsnarl the traffic and educate and re-educate the young and old of our society.

GOVERNMENT INCENTIVES

These staggering numbers measure needs of people. More important than monetary rewards for business, they represent a giant opportunity for private enterprise to renew its leadership in American life and gain the wholehearted support of the public on a higher scale than ever before.

If business doesn't take up the challenge of this market, who will do the job? The federal government, three years after proclaiming *its* plans for building a Great Society, today is encountering crises of organization and management in almost every domestic program.

Billions of dollars of federal aid have been turned loose for federal, state and municipal agencies, offices and departments. But one thing government has learned from this experience is that answering human needs today is far more complex than merely funneling money from one group to another. It is complex because—whether it involves rebuilding a city or retraining a worker—it requires sophisticated knowledge of the very technologies and techniques that business has developed.

Government's proper role, therefore, is not to try to *do* the job. Rather, as suggested in the 1967 report of the Joint Economic Committee of Congress, it is to "act as a catalyst which stimulates and energizes the private sector to attack the nation's social problems."

Just as the government assembles capital for private enterprise to create nuclear ships, supersonic planes and satellites, so it must devise bold *new* incentives for business to tackle equally complex social problems.

This can be done not only through increased direct loan assistance when investment capital is not available in the private sector, such as provided for in the Public Works and Economic Development Act of 1965, but also through new legislative devices such as guarantees to private lenders, rebates for interest paid to private lenders and tax credits against the cost of worker training programs.

Equally important in improving the climate for business to venture across this new frontier is the need for government, and our educational institutions, to take a more enlightened view of profits.

We have always been willing to pay to get things done well in this country, and to provide incentives for enterprise. Profits are not merely an end in themselves—the reward for providing goods and services efficiently—but are in fact the lifeblood of the risk-taking enterprise, enabling it continually to improve its research, its job opportunities and its performance, which of course means providing better answers to the needs of its market. . . .

We businessmen must realize that the phenomenal success of the business system has produced not only great wealth, but also great problems such as congestion and pollution, noise and even suffering for large numbers of people unable to adapt to the pace of change. Many thoughtful people therefore are questioning our qualifications to find solutions to the new needs of man. To them, we have become under business leadership a buck-hungry nation, a gigantic anachronism in a post-money society.

I believe that the businessman today must find a way to apply the profit motive and the spirit of competitive enterprise to the fulfillment of the new desires of society. Money, after all, has never been more than a measure of price and debt, though we have fallen into the habit of using it to express values for nearly everything.

55
Subsidies Are Needed

ANTHONY DOWNS
Senior Vice President, Real Estate Research Corporation of Chicago

People with the greatest need for new or improved housing have far too little money to pay for it. Over thirty million Americans live in poverty as defined by the Office of Economic Opportunity. Many of these people live in the most inadequate housing units, which are not necessarily defined as substandard by the Bureau of the Census. The Census definition depends largely upon whether or not a unit has plumbing. Circumstances like overcrowding that are far more important are not taken into consideration.

The fact that people currently living in such housing cannot afford anything else means that provision of new or rehabilitated units for them will require major subsidies. Merely reducing financing costs through a program of below-market-interest-rates (as is included in the 1968 Housing and Urban Development Act) will not bring the price of new housing within the financial reach of lower income families. For example, a housing unit that costs $12,500 (including land) and has 100 per cent financing over thirty years at zero interest would require a monthly payment of $35. Moreover, there are costs to homeowners beyond the loan payments; these additional operating expenses would amount to at least another $35 per month. The minimum annual cost of such housing, therefore, would be $840, or 25 per cent of an annual income of $3,360. That is slightly above the 1967 poverty level for a four-person household. None of the 30 million people now in poverty can afford new housing, therefore, even at zero interest.

PRIVATE ENTERPRISE CANNOT DO THE JOB ALONE

The significance of this conclusion cannot be overestimated, particularly in light of current political declarations. Having rejected the myth that government could solve all of our urban problems, many leaders have now embraced the equally false notion that the job can be done by private enterprise alone. The above example clearly demonstrates the absurdity of such ideas. It is indeed desirable to have the free enterprise sector of the economy assist in

From "Problems in Financing Urban Redevelopment," *Savings and Residential Financing*, the 1968 Proceedings of the annual Conference on Savings and Residential Financing, sponsored by the United States Savings and Loan League.

solving the problems of housing and urban development. But private enterprise cannot solve, or even seriously affect, the low-income housing problem without major government subsidy.

No one expects private companies to build aircraft or missiles or to design rockets or satellites purely because doing so is in the national interest. We pay such companies billions each year for their efforts. Exactly the same thing has to be done if we expect to improve our urban situation. We are trying to overcome a nationwide social problem and the costs should be borne by society as a whole.

Some kind of government subsidy will be necessary if the persons currently living below the poverty level and in substandard housing are to be provided with decent units—that is, if such families are not going to be forced to devote 40, 50, or 60 per cent of their incomes to housing. Such subsidies would not have to cover the total cost of the housing because private capital could be attracted so long as a return comparable to that of a competitive investment were assured.

If the obstacles to real estate investment mentioned earlier could be overcome, a subsidy approximating $800 a unit would probably suffice. The annual cost of subsidizing 600,000 units would, therefore, be about $480 million, which does not seem like very much. The annual subsidy cost for the six million units projected for the next ten years would build up to $4.8 billion by 1980, however. That looks considerably larger. Nonetheless, if changes are to occur in the urban housing situation, we are going to have to accept the necessity of government subsidies. Private enterprise simply cannot solve the problem without assistance.

56

Good Housing Can Be Good Business

ELI GOLDSTON
President, Eastern Gas and Fuel Associates

Our subsidiary, the Boston Gas Company, has a perpetual franchise to serve a large part of Greater Boston, including the Roxbury area, which is Boston's black ghetto. Until this year, it was a pretty poor area for a gas utility to serve. Many of the apartments were boarded up because some tenants had

---

From an address at the Harvard Graduate School of Business Administration, May 16, 1968.

TABLE 56–1. *Projected Financial Consequences of Boston BURP Program to Boston Gas Company and Eastern Associated Properties Corp. 3,000 Rehabilitated Units, Total Cost $36 million*

FIVE-YEAR SUMMARY

Cash Out

Underground Facilities, Meters, etc.	$450,000	
Partnership Interest, 10% of Total Equity	360,000	
Total Investment		$810,000

Cash Return

Gas Revenue @ $450,000/Year, Five Years	2,250,000	
Less Cost of Gas @ $280,000/Year, Five Years	1,400,000	
Gross Margin @ $170,000/Year, Five Years	850,000	
Less Income Tax @ 48%	410,000	
Net Income from Sale of Gas, Five Years		440,000
Tax Savings; 10% of Partnership Tax Losses for Five Years	830,000	
Tax Rate	48%	
Tax Saving for Five Years		400,000
Total Cash Return		840,000

moved out and taken along the bathtub, toilet and lighting fixtures. Very few of the people used gas for anything but cooking, and each gas stove was on a separate meter. The bills were small, the handling expense was great, and the bad debt percentage was huge because people moved so frequently.

We discovered at the end of 1967 that the federal government, through the Federal Housing Administration of HUD, was considering an immense housing demonstration program for this area. But to make the demonstration possible a substantial amount of working capital was needed above and beyond the government mortgages. By acquiring limited partnerships in the major development firms that had been selected by the FHA, we were able to specify gas heating, gas water heating, and gas clothes drying as well as the original gas cooking. Furthermore, one meter would handle each complete apartment house, and the landlord would pay the bill. The government financing, large volume use, and method of landlord billing justified the Gas Company in offering the low public housing gas rate to the project. In a period of less than one year, 3,000 dwelling units are going to be rehabilitated and one-seventh of the Negro population of Boston significantly better housed. At the same time, Boston Gas Company will have acquired the largest single additional gas load in its history, and the parent company will have gained the "tax shelter" advantages of real estate depreciation. Together these gains make economic dollars out of social sense—we're doing well by doing good.

We think that many features of the Boston formula will be copied elsewhere. The federal government agencies assigned special expediters from

Washington to the Boston offices. The city collaborated in planning relocation. Small-scale contracting firms took on the rehabilitation. The large gas utility supplied working capital and some specialized financial and federal income tax expertise. This public and private cooperation in the urban housing field will mean that Boston, by the end of the current year, will have the best housed Negro population of any major city.

Of course, there were a lot of problems. Because of the size and speed of the program, there was a minimum of communication with residents of the area. The relocation problem had been underestimated. A perfectly legitimate demand developed for the residents in the community to get "a piece of the action." They objected to the fact that the program was entirely in the hands of outside owners and developers. We set about to try to find solutions for these problems, and I believe we have made a good start.

Of all our activities in the past few months, perhaps the most significant and satisfying has been our help in putting together an all-black commercially motivated rehabilitation team which has been awarded FHA guarantee mortgages for a one million dollar project as part of the demonstration program. This is the first such award in FHA history. It is important to realize that men who are capable of undertaking such an enterprise can be found in any major city if you look for them; men who are interested in genuine business opportunities, and have the capacity to become part of the mainstream of American economic life.

The all-black Boston development team is headed by Thomas Sanders, the star basketball player, "Satch" Sanders, of the Boston Celtics. He is a graduate of New York University in the field of business administration. The group was organized as Thomas Sanders Associates. Sanders, with an income from sports, can use the tax shelter offered by real estate investment and has a genuine personal desire to help out in the Roxbury area where he lives. Samuel L. McCoy and Jack E. Robinson are Roxbury real estate men who became part of Thomas Sanders Associates, and the participating construction firm was headed by Lester Clemente, a local builder. This group, for all our assistance, is very genuinely on its own. We have merely coached from the sidelines to help them through the intricacies of FHA legal requirements and applications and the complexities of double declining balance depreciation as it affords "tax shelter." We also encouraged them to engage an experienced FHA developer on a consulting basis. In taking on a million-dollar eighty-three-unit rehabilitation project, these black businessmen are really getting "a piece of the action." This is the way to help the Negro ghetto get good housing and also to help the Negro community stay in the mainstream of American life—by offering an opportunity to Negro businessmen to do it themselves. There is continuing validity in the ancient Chinese saying, "If you give a man a fish, he will feed himself once. If you teach him to fish, he will feed himself all his life."

GOOD HOUSING CAN BE GOOD BUSINESS

Now we didn't start out on this Roxbury housing matter as a charitable venture. It was a business opportunity related to the fact that society is in the process of giving the Negro community a better economic break. This means that the Negro market is becoming an immensely more attractive market. It also means that you must, as an elementary matter of business knowledge, learn an awful lot about the problems and the potentials of doing business in this market.

If you are creative, . . . this is one market where you can combine profit, social purpose and the fun of significant involvement. Here is the real challenge for the modern business manager.

A security analyst suggested to me the other day that any firm which is not planning ahead for the business opportunities and problems which will be created by the shift of funds from Vietnam to the urban crisis is a bad citizen and is probably a bad investment.

When the war in Vietnam ends, our society, under the new economics, is going to pump an awful lot of money either into space or into the cities. The temptation is to pump it into space, where all the troublesome problems of relocating people and racial strife do not exist—or at least, they do not as yet exist. But where there are no people, there are no votes. So I think the more likely place for society to make this huge investment will be, somehow or other, in our core cities.

BUSINESS MUST GAIN KNOWLEDGE OF AND SENSITIVITY TO CENTRAL CITY PROBLEMS

We won't be capable of doing this unless American businesses start now to gain the knowledge of and sensitivity to the problems of the central city, recruiting and upgrading Negro employees to help with the job. The day is gone when white society can take from the Negro community and give very little back. There just can't be all white milkmen, all white mailmen, all white utility employees serving a militant black society. There just can't be all white landlords, all white builders, all white craftsmen, seeming to dominate the housing of the black community.

Here is the great challenge that you soon will be facing. You are returning to your firms, as I have said, and they will be expecting you not only to be better technicians but also to be better judges of the appropriateness of your firm's goals.

Calvin Coolidge used to say, "The business of America is business." Well, for the type of creative business managers Professor Bliss has tried to develop you into over these past sixteen weeks, the old Coolidge saying has got to be rephrased to say, "The business of business is America."

57
The Opportunity in Rehabilitation
UNITED STATES GYPSUM COMPANY

United States Gypsum Company sees the development of a major market for the whole building industry. Company plans are to acquire direct, meaningful experience in rehabilitation projects, carefully review and analyze this knowledge, and then eventually present a working guide for the whole building industry. Low-cost products and systems are being developed, along with suitable techniques to bring greater economy and speed to rehab construction without sacrificing durability and appearance. Naturally, as with other technological advances, such materials and methods might be expected to be of value to other areas of the building industry.

Rehabilitation could be an important new activity, a vital new aspect and function of the building industry, and one essentially independent of new construction. The industry has been subjected to seasonal and cyclical fluctuations for many years, particularly where residential starts are concerned. This problem is industry-wide, affecting everyone, from stockholder to drywall applicator, to some degree. If rehabilitation does nothing more than help to stabilize employment and incomes on a year-round basis, it will have made a major contribution to our industry.

If rehabilitation can be achieved efficiently, while yielding marketable rentals for low-income tenants, the interests of government, tenants, and the building industry will be served.

HANDICAPS TO REHABILITATION

In the few years since Congressional enactment of rehabilitation programs, a variety of problems have become apparent. Possibly, the greatest handicap to rehabilitation is its relative newness. The following are other significant considerations.

1. While present government programs provide incentives for builders and contractors, even greater encouragement is required. If contractors and builders can be motivated to enter rehabilitation, they can realize many benefits from this immensely large potential market, particularly more stable business incomes and employee earnings and the opportunity to diversify their building activities. Contractors and builders are becoming increasingly interested

---

From *Rehabilitation: A New Look for Vintage America,* an interim report from United States Gypsum (1967).

in the possibilities. Attempts are being made to simplify programs and ease the many headaches to contractors involved.

2. There is a lack of expertise on the part of government agencies. FHA field offices are often unfamiliar with rehab, and processing is complicated by red tape. This may be because federal programs are mainly new programs involving a new kind of activity. No one is more aware of the necessity of upgrading the nation's housing stock than the federal government. Therefore, it is expected that improvements will be made to implement these programs, and that their local offices will become increasingly knowledgeable and flexible in dealing with rehabilitation.

3. There is a shortage of products and systems specifically related to rehabilitation projects. Likewise, there is little present research and development devoted to rehabilitation. Faster, more economical materials and methods are vitally needed. It is in this area that building materials manufacturers, such as United States Gypsum, can make their greatest contribution.

4. Government support is necessary. Frequently, the financial condition of people in blighted areas is such that rehabilitation cannot be accomplished effectively without rent subsidies, grants, and long-term mortgages.

5. Building codes and standards, which generally presuppose new construction, are not necessarily appropriate to rehabilitation work, and meeting these regulations often increases project cost and time. While there is little reason to believe that codes will be revised to accommodate rehabilitation, there is some experimentation here, and there have been instances where codes were waived.

6. There is lack of experience in rehabilitation on the part of contractors. It is estimated that there are no more than forty or fifty building contracting firms in the country having the understanding and skills for this work. Yet, far more contractors are needed.

Federal and local government—as well as private interests—are determined to make rehabilitation feasible and workable, and are working to create effective solutions for these problems. United States Gypsum has been working to increase knowledge of the process of rehabilitation and to create better methods and products for this specialized type of construction. As new products and better, more useful means of using them become available from USG, this information will be made available.

58
The Business of Education
NATIONAL INDUSTRIAL CONFERENCE BOARD

To help meet the challenge of better education for more people, General Electric and Time, Incorporated, have formed General Learning Corporation as a joint venture. Among its activities is operating a Job Corps Center in Clinton, Iowa, for the educationally disadvantaged. The company believes that methods and techniques which it and other federal Job Corps contractors learn may have broad application and usefulness in raising the educational level of disadvantaged citizens.

Job Corps administration is but one of several business-based efforts to improve education. (Job Corps contractors receive cost plus fixed profit.) Others include Lockheed's contract with a California school system to evaluate teaching techniques and equipment and its contract program to retain Mexican-Americans in school. North American Rockwell has a proposal, now under consideration by the Unified School District of Sacramento, California, to develop a long-range master site and facilities plan for the school district. The plan would be designed to alleviate the social impact of *de facto* segregation.

One of the companies working on new teaching devices is Ford Motor, which has been developing a line of electronic training and demonstration aids for use at various educational levels. Ford's communications and electronics division has produced a large-scale, computer-assisted instruction system, which is being installed in a number of high schools in Philadelphia on an interconnected basis. In this system, each student interacts directly with the computer complex by means of his own console containing a TV screen, a keyboard, and other devices.

From *Business Amid Urban Crisis* (National Industrial Conference Board, 1968), p. 42.

B *Economic Development of the Ghettos*

59
Developing Business and Entrepreneurs in the Ghettos

SAR A. LEVITAN AND
ROBERT TAGGART III

[*A skeptical view of the possibility of redeveloping the economy of the central cities and of newly developing the economy of the ghettos is presented in the following excerpt.*]

There is no way to compare the profitability and viability of businesses operating in central cities with those of suburban or rural firms. The handful of ghetto subsidiaries recently established by the large corporations is only the "tip of the iceberg." However, for the purpose of attracting new firms, the experience of those which have recently located is important. To date, the experience generally has not been favorable and the business environment of ghetto areas does not seem to be profitable.

Three of the most highly publicized efforts by big business are Aerojet-General's Watts Manufacturing Company, E. G. & G's Roxbury plant, and IBM's plant in Bedford-Stuyvesant. The Watts plant began operations in 1966, producing tents on a $2.5 million defense contract. Despite a $1,300 per man training subsidy from the Labor Department and $1.5 million in Department of Defense set-aside contracts, Aerojet has lost several hundred thousand dollars. Recent attempts to diversify have been unsuccessful and the work force has been cut from 500 to 300. The problems are clear-cut: in the first year, 1,200 had to be hired to maintain a work force of 500; and the company estimates that its training costs were closer to $5,000 per man than to the $1,300 paid by the Labor Department to offset the extra costs of hiring and retaining ghetto residents.

E. G. & G's metal fabrication plant in Roxbury encountered similar difficulties. Despite a $575,000 training grant, the plant was $75,000 in the red in 1968, and anticipated a loss of $250,000 in 1969. In addition, the company has experienced considerable difficulty in finding and retaining managerial talent for this operation.

IBM's experience has been more favorable and it has operated without government subsidies. The Bedford-Stuyvesant plant produces computer components that are used by IBM, and it produces them more cheaply than out-

---

Paper prepared for the Community Self-Determination Steering Committee meeting, Washington, D.C., April 17, 1969.

side suppliers. However, IBM has produced the components at a lower unit cost in its other plants, and the internal guaranteed market disguises many profitability questions.[1]

No doubt, some of the recent corporate efforts have suffered from birth pains and ghetto plants may prove more profitable in the future. But it is also probable that if these plants do not get out of the red soon, some plants will be abandoned, thereby discouraging other ghetto locations.

THE INDUSTRIES TO BE ATTRACTED

While specific firms that are to be induced to locate in central cities must be selected on a case-by-case basis, some overall desirable characteristics can be gleaned from experience. The best candidates are larger manufacturing firms, though most recent efforts in central city development have concentrated on retail trade, service industries and small manufacturing firms. There are several reasons to concentrate on attracting larger manufacturing firms besides their greater impact due to size and viability. First, employment in selected services has continued to expand in the central cities. Second, it is not likely that the shift of retail and wholesale employment to the suburbs can be reversed. Retail trade is consumer-oriented and has followed consumers who are moving to the suburbs. While the population of central cities increased by 1 per cent from 1960 to 1968, the corresponding rise in suburban rings was 18 per cent. Compounding demographic changes are shifts in shopping habits. Consumers who formerly traveled to the central city now patronize suburban shopping centers, and this pattern does not appear likely to change. Finally, since the payroll per employee in central city manufacturing is lower than that in the suburbs, the city probably has its comparative advantage in manufacturing employment.

There are some obvious limitations to the numbers and types of manufacturing enterprises which can be attracted to the central city. Plants which require ready access to natural resources, consume large quantities of water, create severe nuisances or hazards, or require large tracts of land are not suitable for location in central cities. Even more significant, but often overlooked, is the fact that there are a limited number of new, expanding or relocating firms. Between 1958 and 1963, the annual number of new plants was only around 3,500. One-quarter of these were in the chemical processing industries whose plants are generally unsuitable for central city location; about two-thirds employed less than twenty and would have little impact upon the community; and a substantial number of these 3,500 were firms which located within or moved out of central cities.[2] A rough estimate would place the total annual number of new plants with more than twenty employees suitable for central cities at less than 500. Competing for these businesses are suburban areas with many relative advantages, and rural areas, which in many cases have an even greater claim than central cities on the basis of need. Given the limited supply of new plants and the demands from other areas, the potential impact of central city development programs should not be overestimated. Considering the fact that between 1958 and 1963 the twenty largest cities alone suffered a net loss of 850 manufacturing plants, the immediate prospects of revitalizing central city economies through attraction of manufacturing establishments are not particularly good.

Within these aggregate constraints relating to the numbers and types of plants which can be attracted, development efforts should concentrate on firms which will require the least inducement to locate in central cities relative to their impact. One particularly thorny question in development efforts is the relative emphasis that should be placed on quality compared to quantity of employment. If job creation is the major goal, inducements should favor labor-intensive industries. On the other hand, if the low income of the working poor is considered more critical, then subsidies should focus on highly capitalized industries which can use the unskilled. In practice, the choices will not be clear-cut and the demand for new industry will exceed supply, but it is better that the goals be explicitly stated rather than developed by default.

THE LEVEL OF THE SUBSIDIES

Experience with federal subsidies has supplied only limited insights into the extent of incentives needed to affect locational decisions. Federal programs to aid depressed areas since 1961 have offered subsidized loans and grants for the construction of public facilities needed to improve the infrastructure of the areas. However, the economic conditions that led to job deficits in depressed areas have apparently not responded to the limited inducements offered by the federal government. The efforts under the Area Redevelopment Act and its successor the Economic Development Act, have not had a discernible impact upon the conditions which the legislation sought to ameliorate.

Since 1966, the federal government has subsidized a number of plants in ghetto areas with antipoverty and manpower funds. The Labor Department has contracted with firms to cover the differential costs of training the disadvantaged. Although central city development was not a specific goal of these programs, several firms opening branch plants have sought and received funds. Since "differential training costs" are not explicitly defined, the size of a grant is negotiated and is presumably an inducement to open a plant rather than a reimbursement for measurable training costs. As examples, Control Data Corporation, with a one-million-dollar training grant, opened a 110-employee plant in Minneapolis' Northside; AVCO Corporation started a 220-man printing plant in Boston's Roxbury section with a $1.1 million grant; and Xerox established a 100-man electric transformer and metal stripping plant in Rochester with a $446,000 grant. Spokesmen for the corporations have claimed that the government subsidies did not fully cover the differential costs of training. CDC president, William Norris, for instance, estimated that its one-million-dollar subsidy would cover only 15 per cent of its total costs of hiring and training the disadvantaged.[3]

In addition to these activities, eight firms have been subsidized through the Special Impact program to locate "in or near" ghetto areas. These grants are not tied to training programs, since the industries are low-skilled. To move within commuting distance of the ghetto and to hire disadvantaged workers at $2.00 per hour, the eight firms received $3,000 per projected employee or $1.00 for every $6.50 of capital investment.[4] Special Impact funds have also supported several local groups seeking to attract businesses to ghetto areas, including the Bedford-Stuyvesant Restoration Corporation. Its efforts and those of other experimental community development corporations have so far produced few results. For the most part small businesses, which will have little impact on ghetto employment or income, have been started.

Not all firms locating in ghettos seek federal assistance. The IBM case is especially instructive. In June, 1968, the company opened a 300-man plant in Bedford-Stuyvesant to produce computer cables. This decision was made by IBM's president, Thomas J. Watson, despite a projected $500,000 annual loss over several years. Watson's membership in the Development and Services Corporation, which was concerned with economic development in Bedford-Stuyvesant, was crucial to the choice of location. Since most location decisions are made by top management—one study found that in fifty-one out of sixty-nine cases examined, the decision was basically that of one man.[5] Reaching top corporate executives may be the key to increasing the number of central city plant locations.

• • •

THE POTENTIAL

The effect of black capitalism programs on ghetto income depends first on the success of black-run businesses. There are strong reasons to believe that they will not be very profitable. The firms that would be acquired under all but the most radical black-capitalism proposals would be small and located in the ghetto, and their chances for growth and profitability under any management would be limited. There is also a lack of trained managers among Negroes. For instance, in 1966, there were less than 15,000 black proprietors and managers,[6] and the federal government employed, in 1967, only 4,700 Negroes with an annual salary in excess of $12,000.[7] While this group has expanded, and though it is not the complete universe from which black businessmen will be drawn, it is clear that a shortage exists and that this would be an immediate constraint on any large-scale program of ownership transfer, whatever arrangements are made to carry out such a program. Black companies would have to compete for black talent and the demand already greatly exceeds the supply. And, the chances of blacks learning managerial skills en masse are very small. Moreover, a persuasive case can be made against channeling too great a proportion of emerging Negro executive and administrative capability into running business enterprises. There are other possibly more pressing needs for these resources.

Even if Negroes achieved equality of ownership, and their businesses were as profitable as others, the aggregate effect would not be large. Profits are only a small part of total income. A 2 per cent increase in wages and salaries would have more effect on the total income of the average Negro than a 100 per cent increase in profits.

Proponents of ownership transfers have claimed that keeping profits within the ghetto will have a multiplier effect, since they will be re-spent and generate further income for ghetto residents. The income multiplier is a measure of the total amount of income generated within an area by income accruing to its residents. If this multiplier could be increased, the total income of the area would also increase. Keeping profits in the ghetto would enlarge the multiplier as claimed, but the amount of increase is very small since profits are a small proportion of total income. Based on data for Philadelphia, a city-wide multiplier of 1.30 would increase to about 1.33 if all the profits earned on residents' purchases were added into the income flow. The change would not greatly improve economic conditions of city residents, and for smaller areas within the city the effect would be even less since for smaller areas the multiplier approaches one. Thus, programs to give blacks proportionate ownership are likely to have little effect on their income and would do little to improve the economies of the central city.

NOTES

1. Allan T. Demaree, "Business Picks Up the Urban Challenge, *Fortune* (April, 1969), p. 174.
2. Management and Economics Research, Incorporated, *Industrial Location as a Factor in Regional Economic Development* (Washington, DC: US Government Printing Office, 1967).
3. "Business Attack on Poverty: Training the Untrainable," *U.S. News and World Report* (March 18, 1968), p. 63.
4. Westinghouse Learning Corporation, "Preliminary Report on the 1968 Special Impact Programs," prepared for Office of Economic Opportunity (January 30, 1969, mimeographed).
5. L. T. Wallace, "Factors Affecting Industrial Location in Southern Indiana 1955–58," *Research Bulletin*, Purdue University Agricultural Experiment Station, Lafayette, Ind. (August, 1961), p. 8.
6. U.S. Equal Employment Opportunity Commission, *Equal Employment Opportunity Report No. 1, Job Patterns for Minorities and Women in Private Industry, 1966* (Washington, D.C.: U.S. Government Printing Office, 1968), p. 10.
7. U.S. Civil Service Commission, *Study of Minority Group Employment in the Federal Government* (Washington, D.C.: The Commission, 1967), p. 5.

60
A Million Tiny New Businesses

HAROLD F. CLARK
Professor of Economics, Trinity University

I am all in favor of helping the American Telephone and Telegraph Company, General Motors, Standard Oil Company of New Jersey and other big companies grow and provide more jobs. But what is needed more than almost anything else to help the poverty group is at least a million very tiny new businesses. Many people will say this is impossible.

A high fraction of these new businesses would be providing services at a competent but simple level. There are probably millions of families that would like to have their houses cleaned once a week or on odd Thursdays or even Mondays.

One businessman and two helpers might be the company, providing cleaning and many other services. The business man would work along with the two workers and provide close supervision of the work. There are yards to be taken care of, fences to be fixed, minor repair jobs to be done. There is the annual house cleaning to be done. There are meals to be cooked on special occasions, or on Thursdays or Sundays. There is clothing to be repaired, laundry to be done occasionally. There is the need for a little help when minor illness strikes the family. All of these services are available for the very high-income families and at very high prices. Household help has disappeared for the great mass of American families and has probably disappeared for good.

The work still needs to be done. The people have the money to pay for it. The jobs are there. Many of the people in the poverty group could provide many of the services. A new type of very small business man is needed to get the worker and jobs together.

This little businessman will have a hard time dealing with workman's compensation, social security deductions, minimum wages, and all the other regulations. He could not keep the records if he did know about them. Education and training might help a little. It may well be that we are creating unintended barriers to starting small businesses that may be hitting the poverty group very hard.

There are many reasons for supporting a minimum wage, but there is little doubt that it is an additional barrier to many people in the poverty group get-

---

Printed by permission of the Urban Action Clearinghouse, Community and Regional Resource Development Group, Chamber of Commerce of the United States.

ting a job. This is especially true of the young worker or the worker with little or no special skill.

One of the kinds of education that is most needed is to give people in the poverty group the simple skills that are necessary to do many of the jobs that are available in these service fields. There is a great potential demand for these services if they can be packaged and marketed in a manner acceptable to the average-income family.

61

The Resources Aren't There

BERTRAM M. BECK
Executive Director, Mobilization for Youth, New York City

Even a half-century ago, the immigrant poor of America shouldered their way into our economy and our politics through many ports of entry. The Irish and the Italians built railroads, highways, and skyscrapers. Those ports are now closed . . . closed by the conspiracy of "credentials" that ranges from union cards to racist hiring practices. Thus the lion's share of the American dream is walled-in by our own complacency, our habits of success, our myopic optimism, our anxiety to live the good life that our grandfathers were denied.

Having said that, let me briefly cover the three of the usual "solutions" propounded by manpower experts in recent years to the employment crisis. The first is the "industry into the ghetto" argument—which calls upon the American industrial establishment to move pieces of its production capacity into the central city where it can take advantage of the resources of manpower available there. *I see no serious evidence* that the private sector of our economy is prepared to do anything of the sort except on the most token basis. American industry considers the ghetto a high-risk area, incompatable with the standards of their business. American industry is not, with some exceptions, prepared to engage in the kind of sensitive, unique skill training operations required to qualify many of the ghetto unemployed for productive labor. The spectre of "credentials" reappears—the habits, the standards of a lifetime are not about to disappear and be replaced with surge of uneconomic morality—it isn't going to happen and we must look elsewhere.

Statement before the Joint Economic Committee of Congress, in *Employment and Manpower Problems in the Cities: Implications of the Report of the National Advisory Commission on Civil Disorders* (1968).

A second "solution" often advanced is the creation of jobs by the institution of public works projects by the federal government. Forgive my cynicism —the Kerner Report was published four months ago—the Kerner Report unequivocally nailed the central city crisis to vast unemployment. There is not now, nor has there been, any credible evidence of a will on the part of the Congress or Administration to create such public works projects in response to what the Kerner Report has described as a national emergency. It is not a matter of money—it is a matter of will. When this country was paralyzed by a depression three decades ago, our meagre public resources were mobilized into a positive program of rebuilding the nation, both its property and its people. *There is no less a crisis before us now.*

A third "solution" is one for which I have much enthusiasm but little hope. That is the belief that the poor themselves can, in the ghetto, build their own viable economy based on local industry, cooperative economics and self-determination. It is the nature of all men to survive even the most degrading environment. And in the ghetto, particularly in the black ghetto, the determination to govern his own institutions and build his own economy and life-style, is now the first commandment of the new, articulate black militant. The stridency of his voice is an excellent measure of our failure—and I intend to help this home-made economic and social upheaval in any way I can. But make no mistake; it is a poor alternative made necessary by our failure of will, our unbending credentials—our national selfishness. To be candid, this movement towards self-determination cannot do much in the way of altering the inexorable facts spelled out in the Kerner Report. The resources simply aren't there. But it *can* help to transform the black American into a formidable political and economic force which we can never again ignore.

C   *Promoting Black Capitalism*

62
An Entrepreneurial School

BERKELEY G. BURRELL
President, the National Business League

This is a dollar society, a business world, a profitmaking culture that places the highest premium on success in the business of profitmaking. Every man in this country is measured by his peers on the basis of his relative economic success.

The news vendors on the street corners are respected and looked up to by their peers because they are in business for themselves. The captains of industry, the high and the mighty of the world of business enjoy the greatest degree of admiration, indeed, adulation, as a result of their profitmaking skill.

All along the path from the corner news vendor to the top corporate executive, each and every businessman is revered by the small sample population that knows him primarily because he is in business. Every strata of our society holds the business functionary in great high regard and accords him an inordinate amount of respect.

In the light of these facts it would seem that only elementary commonsense would be required to point up the need for an entrepreneurial class of indigenous citizens. Not only has this nation not seen the need but it is resisting all efforts to point it in that logical direction. The determined effort, with very few exceptions, points in the direction of corporate plantationship, not interracial partnership.

There seems to be a kind of steel net cast over us that galvanizes and magnetizes us into one direction and one direction only. And that direction is the principle of black men working for white men, not with them. And that pattern leads to further chaos.

And I have said it before and I repeat it here and now, you do not need any particular degree of extrasensory perception to predict that the residue of this hated plantocracy will be destroyed by this generation of angry black youth who are determined to assert themselves as men.

These strong, proud young people are not directly bent on destroying our nation but they are hellbound to establish their own identity, to master their own destiny, and to make those same positive contributions to our society for which white men have seen their names emblazoned in this history book. Un-

---

Statement before the Joint Economic Committee of Congress, in *Employment and Manpower Problems in the Cities: Implications of the Report of the National Advisory Commission on Civil Disorders* (1968).

fortunately unless access to power in the business system is provided for them, they will indirectly destroy whatever they can of it, until it is opened to them or until they are suppressed into concentration camps.

In place of this downward dehumanizing spiral we suggest the committee rearrange its thinking, to the extent of redefining both the Kerner Report's assumptions and even the assumptions of the joint committee as it operates under the assumptions of the Employment Act of 1946.

The fact is that in 1968 merely a "useful job" is not enough to "fully utilize the human resources" we are talking about. The committee must accelerate its redefinition of public policy about "employment" to mean "employment in upwardly mobile careers" and "employment as potential managers in businesses that provide access to a stake in the capital accumulation system." That is where the action is in American society and unless the black man obtains the opportunity to qualify there, unless he obtains access to the wherewithals to compete in business, et cetera, not just equal job opportunity but access to equal participation in business, we will still be imposing on black men the subtle steel net of slavery, an advanced form of it to be sure, but one which he is still but the instrument in the hands of another and not "his own man."

To be quite specific, one of the first priorities to be rearranged in the federal establishment after the committee develops its thinking as suggested above, is to fund an experimental entrepreneur school for the explicit purpose of developing effective entrepreneurial education programs. Today entrepreneur education for the disadvantaged is scandalously neglected both by federal agencies and public and private educational institutions.

• • •

We do not want the image of whites always controlling jobs and money, rather we want to establish a new class of owners, managers and proprietors who will act as catalyst for the minds of our very young, and point them toward the excited enrichment of careers in the world of business. In the process, we will create jobs that do not currently exist which should cut down the resistance to sharing now prevalent in many areas of the majority community.

We seek to forge a greater balance of power by joining multiracial talent in the vigorous pursuit of profits that will yield a sense of worth, of dignity, of positive value as we expand job opportunities and create economic vibrations that do not and cannot otherwise exist.

A new plant in a ghetto is fine so long as the ghetto residents own at least part of it, manage most of it and exercise some degree of meaningful control over its future.

The National Business League has chartered a course of action for our central cities that can yield to our nation the highest possible benefits at the lowest possible cost. We call our program Project Mainstream. It involves the rapid revitalization of our cities by involving the inner city residents in a determination of their own destiny; we would do this by creating a total new cultural environment within the heart of the ghetto.

We have developed what we call a modular core that we would place in the heart of every ghetto in our fifty-odd chapter cities. Within this new core we would create new economically stratified housing environment, a new diversified shopping environment and a new governmental services or civic environment. During the process of physically erecting the core, we would involve every element in our moving vibrant community. We would train the able bodied in skills that are marketable as they rebuild an area they can identify as their own. We would create a class of entrepreneurs by the merging of white resources with minority capability. We would maximize the benefits of governmental social programs by making them productive of meaningful social benefits.

• • •

Look around us in this country today and observe the tiny, infinitesimal number of black businesses that are involved in the nation's business. Simple proportional mathematics will tell us that there should be ten times the number of successful minority businesses that we have today. How else can the ghetto develop natural leadership based on legitimate power?

But few and far between are those elements of our society that are willing to believe that we have the training and the mental capability to succeed.

63

The Opportunity Industrial Center Program

REV. LEON H. SULLIVAN
Chairman, Opportunity Industrial Center, Philadelphia

Unfortunately, perhaps the most significant manpower program in America has been hidden by most people who ought to know some of the facts about it. It has been reported to some minimal extent in the press, and there are some administrators and executives in the federal government who know about it. But for some reason the real significance and impact of the program has been hidden from the Congress. . . .

The program I make reference to is OIC, the Opportunity Industrial Cen-

---

Statement before the Joint Economic Committee of Congress, in *Employment and Manpower Problems in the Cities: Implications of the Report of the National Advisory Commission on Civil Disorders* (1968).

ter program, a program created out of the black community, led largely by the black community, a program that was not begun by the government, is not an agency program, is not a bureaucratic program, but is a program in the true American tradition—of the people, by the people, and for the people. It was initiated in an old abandoned jailhouse in Philadelphia in January of 1964. This program was begun with nickels and dimes from people in the black community, in the concentrated communities rather than the ghetto, for we abhor "ghetto," we abhor it. And my people do not think they live in ghettos. . . .

From these men and women, black men and women, and boys and girls, tens of thousands of dollars was raised, to initiate OIC, the Opportunity Industrial Center. This was before there was an OEO. This was before there was any effort expended as far as the Department of Labor is concerned, for these kind of indigenously created and initiated programs.

Yet on our own, by the hundreds and then by the thousands, black men and women in Philadelphia began to build OIC.

Our first partnership was with industry—because we did not believe it was possible to develop a manpower program without the full partnership of industry. Therefore, we went to industry, to assist us in structuring our curriculum, to assist in securing equipment, to screen our instructors, and to be sure that jobs were available to our people when our people had concluded training.

This was significant, gentlemen, in that in January of 1964 very few industries in America had begun to open their doors to black men and women of the concentrated community. There was only tokenism on a very broad and general scale. And yet industry, by evidence of the support it began to give to an indigenously created program, said in Philadelphia and in Delaware Valley—If men and women are training, then we will see the jobs are available.

At first many of us did not believe it. We said "We will see, if you put your jobs where your mouth is." So we began training.

Most of the people who came to us did not finish high school. Most of the people who came to us were in poverty categories. Many of the people who came to us were from jails, from all kinds of conditions, walking in the streets, doing many things to keep alive. . . .

Two distinct phases of OIC distinguish the program. First was skill development. But skill development was only incidental. There are thousands of institutions in America that can provide skill development to black and white people—the academicians, institutions, the technicians. But we developed skill because we wanted a man to have a minimum skill—so that the excuse of industry could not hold up by saying "You have no skill."

The next and most important thing we did was to develop a program of attitude—self-habilitation, I called it—the process of self-habilitation. This was the first self-habilitation prevocational program in America. All programs that have occurred in manpower dealing with prevocational training were patterned after this program begun in the black community, OIC.

The attitudinal program called the feeder program was made out of necessity. After a month I found that putting a man behind a machine to teach him a skill was not enough. Therefore, we developed the feeder, the attitudinal prevocational program, to prepare men for skilled training.

Two weeks to three months, men and women were in the attitudinal training program, feeder training programs. Here men learned the basics again of reading, writing and arithmetic, although we did not call it that. So I called it communications skills and computational art. Therefore, the language of computational skills that now you find in your schools and your technical institutions and in your universities is traced to the black community of Philadelphia, where I created the term, communications skills and computational art.

The first programs in America institutionalized to teach minority and African history were in OIC. I did it because I wanted black men to be proud of what they were. A colored woman does not have to be blond to be beautiful, and a black man does not have to be white to be smart. I wanted him to be proud of what he was, to stand on his own feet, and to realize that genius was color-blind. Therefore we taught African-American history. In addition to that, we taught Italian-American history, Irish-American history, Appalachian-American history, Chinese-American history, so that our people could see that every man had a sense of value and respectability in our American society, so that a man could respect himself first, and others next, because if a man respects himself, he does not have to hate you any more.

People who have been a part of violent movements came to OICs by the hundreds, and their total lives have been reconstructed. Women who had been walking the streets for a living, women who had been in jails, men who wanted to tear the country down, had come to OIC, and had become some of the most positive productive citizens in Philadelphia.

It is not what I say that will prove what I say. You should see what I say.

But no one believes it. For example, there are those who say OIC is "creaming." I think creaming was created somehow synonymously with the development of OIC, because there are those who perhaps felt that in OIC, a massive manpower program in the black community, we do not have the sense or capability to take people who had been out of jobs and make them available for productive employment. So they say these people cannot be what you call hard-core people, you must be creaming—until they come to see, and they find people in the seats of OIC, many of them never had jobs in their lives. They have been on relief. . . .

Each year we save the Commonwealth now more than $2 million that would have gone into relief checks. We saved the money from relief checks, as much as we used to operate the program. The money saved in relief checks in Philadelphia amounts to more than we put into putting the program on. . . .

OIC's are now developed in seventy-five cities on pennies and nickels and dimes, on shoestrings—while billions of dollars are being poured into manpower programs that do not reach us at all. Programs that can be seen, led by black leaders in this country—I mean the real black leaders of this country—are crying for support. We are having programs in church basements, in shanties, on street corners, under trees in this country. OIC. And yet billions of dollars are being spent in sophistication, rather than implementation of programs to reach the heart of the person who needs the work most. . . .

I am a preacher. I am not a theoretician, I am not an academician. I am a black man who knows that either I will do something to help my people to be lifted and raised, or by 1988 one-half of the black community in America will be on relief. We will become a government's people, rather than a people's government. It will mean that the whole life will depend upon what the government and the President want to do with me. And I do not want that. I do not want a government to tell me what to do, to structure my life. I do not want it. I want to be self-dependent on my own right.

Another thing I want to say is—you talk about jobs, creation of jobs. Black people can create jobs where they are in their own communities. Help us develop skills, and we will rebuild our own inner cities.

General Motors and General Electric—they are not the only ones with sense enough to know how to create jobs. We have got brains, too. We can create economic development ourselves for the good of America. Not just for black men, but for all Americans. Not that we want people to give us jobs, even now.

I want to have the capability to create my own jobs. Six hundred thousand corporations in this country of size, and a very few controlled and owned by black men. I want to create corporations. I don't want to shine the shoes, I want to make the shoes. I want to make dresses, not buy them. My people want not just to be the consumers, the beggar, we want to be producers. We don't want you to build housing for us. We will build it for ourselves, and you, too. We will build them together. There you have a problem with the labor unions. That is a whole new sermon I won't go into right now.

The thing I am saying is there is a movement on foot here, a massive movement of self-habilitation in America; black men who are saying—the cry is not "Burn, Baby, Burn" but "Build, Brothers, Build." The new cry is "Build, Brothers, Build."

What we need, though, is support from manpower committees and councils, from the Congress, to say to the Department of Labor—"Look at OIC, and give OIC a chance to prove or disprove what it can do." And I think this will happen. You give us a chance. Give us a $100 million a year on the basis of what we are doing, come and see what we are doing. And we have not lost a penny that I know of. Might have. But $100 million a year. Eighteen months after we get $100 million, I will double it in income to the community. In ten years—I did this on the plane—I figured it out—in ten years, with a $100 million a year—it will still be a baby as far as manpower is concerned—we will develop our manpower, we will develop the capability, we will organize the community militantly toward training and retraining, and productivity—within ten years, with a $100 million for ten years, I will add to the American economy $24 billion. I will add $13,750 million in new wages, and I will save the relief rolls in America $10,800 million that would go in relief checks. I will save the economy of this country $24 billion.

If you think it cannot be done, go to the Chamber of Commerce and ask their economist, because they have been there too, and they said I save more than that. But I am giving you a minimal calculation.

In other words, gentlemen, you have in your hands an egg. Either you can crack it or else you can hatch it. But it is up to this government.

64

Discussion of the Statements of Berkeley G. Burrell and Rev. Leon H. Sullivan

JOINT ECONOMIC COMMITTEE
OF CONGRESS

CHAIRMAN PROXMIRE. I would like to start with Mr. Burrell. If Mr. Sullivan would like to comment—you gentlemen have similar approaches, and similar ideas. They are different in some respects.

I agree wholeheartedly with your basic theme of the importance of Negro ownership and Negroes being in business for themselves. This to a very great extent is a business society. It is a lot of other things too, but it is a business society, and we consider the businessman as a leader, in many ways the important economic leader in our society. So I think what you plead for and suggest is enormously appealing.

I wrote a book about four years ago called *Can Small Business Survive?* The conclusion was that to survive it is going to take a great deal more ability as well as more capital. Small business will need to have people who are much more competent in recordkeeping and so forth than many small businessmen have been.

As you know, the survival prospects for small business in this country are not good. The average small businessman who goes into retailing lasts six months and fails, or sells out—he often sells out at a loss.

So that it is tough. And it needs all the studies—and there have been a

---

Joint Economic Committee of Congress, *Employment and Manpower Problems in the Cities: Implications of the Report of the National Advisory Commission on Civil Disorders*, 1968.

whole series of studies—on the needs of small business. Number one, it needs capital. But number two, it perhaps needs even more ability, training, experience.

So that I think that you are making an excellent appeal. I think what you say makes all the sense in the world. But I just wonder if the entrepreneur school that you talk about can really get it moving with sufficient speed and on a sufficiently comprehensive basis to do the job unless we also look at this from the standpoint of providing training and education at many levels. After all, the best businessmen are men who have had jobs elsewhere, who have learned to be good by working for somebody else for a while. Some come out of school and start their own business, but not very many. Usually they work for five or ten years at least, develop managerial qualities and abilities, have gone through the tough hard experience of competing with others, done well in working for somebody else, and then started their own businesses.

So that what you feel is necessary to be done in addition to establishing the entrepreneurial school, to provide a real opportunity for the black man, to own his business in the kind of substantial way that you and I agree he does not now.

Mr. Burrell. Well Senator, I think looking at some of the experiences of the world we miss, for example, the opportunity in America to approach the economic development of the inner city in much the same way that you approach the development of Africa, for example—there you pump in whatever capability is needed—if it is financial resources, if it is the managerial capability of whites, that has to be there.

In our own community we can look around us and find out that American business has joined hands with every conceivable kind of person in this world except the black man in the pursuit of profits, here in America.

So in the normal process of profitmaking, the training that you talk about could be the kind of experience that is needed. I would agree that as time passes, as each minute passes, businesses become more capital intensive. Well, if that is true, then large amounts of capital are indicated.

I do not think I have said today in my testimony, or in any other of my public policy statements—have I seemed to indicate we are talking about the startup of a number of marginal businesses that are expected to feed on its own uneconomic community. But I am simply suggesting more significantly that we establish the kind of viable businesses that can compete in an open society.

A mistake that a lot of people make is that as they hear the plea of the National Business League to create within this country the kinds of businesses that I am now suggesting, they simply look at me, a black man, and I suppose their assumption is that I am talking about the creation of a number of very small businesses. I am not. I am suggesting that the businesses could be made viable and large enough to compete in an open society.

Chairman Proxmire. Let me just ask. You had your business experience. I think I have seen you on television.

Mr. Burrell. I am afraid so.

CHAIRMAN PROXMIRE. A gentleman who has a very successful business, or at least has had. So you know yourself the very serious problems of business management, and how you do not easily come by a man who can run a successful small business these days. What kind of experience did you have before your started your own business? Did you start it yourself directly; is this the only employment you have had?

MR. BURRELL. I have had government experience, but I certainly did not have a background of business. I had the desire and the determination not to work for anybody after coming out of World War II. So I started with a hundred dollars and went into the dry cleaning business—not knowing really too much about it. I had the experience of having run a rather large drycleaning plant on an Army post. But my experience there was just yelling and screaming and keeping people working. I did not know anything about the business at all.

The point I make is that I started and made all the normal mistakes. I took all the wrenching steps necessary. I did not have the help of people who told me—who could have told me I was about to make a mistake. I made them. I think many small businessmen in this country have done exactly that, white or black.

I am simply suggesting that blacks need the right to fail as much as any other person in this country. And that right to fail seems to be somehow elusive. There is no one at this point in time who seems interested enough to join hands with potential black capability and teach them the necessary ingredients of operating a business. There are some small efforts being made right now within our own organization. We run a program of management training and assistance.

CHAIRMAN PROXMIRE. I would think—I do not mean to interrupt—I would think that your proposal dovetails very well with Mr. Sullivan's experience.

MR. BURRELL. It does.

CHAIRMAN PROXMIRE. And that these two should work very well together. They are both aimed at the same purpose. Mr. Sullivan's would perhaps involve a somewhat greater number of people. But certainly the people who have developed the self-habilitation, and then the skill, and then the work experience, would be the natural people to work into your entrepreneurial school, and then work on to developing their own businesses.

● ● ●

MR. SULLIVAN. Could I say something on that, please?

CHAIRMAN PROXMIRE. Yes, sir.

MR. SULLIVAN. I agree. I can see how they could dovetail. We have already developed a manpower and economic development school. I have done it with private resources. I am building Progress Plaza, which is a $2 million shopping center in Broad Street—not personally, but a community corporation—people put $10 a month down, thirty-six months, and we raised a quarter of a million dollars, in developing this Progress Plaza. On the site I am developing an entrepreneurial training school, being built right now, in which I am going to train 200 entrepreneurial managers a year.

CHAIRMAN PROXMIRE. Is this in Philadelphia?

MR. SULLIVAN. Yes. And with these entrepreneurs, I am going to use these men to go into establishments. I am already developing several factories—not for me—I do not get anything out of it—in which I will be training men to go into these smaller businesses, and small factories.

CHAIRMAN PROXMIRE. OIC is doing this?

MR. SULLIVAN. OIC is a nonprofit institution. This is what I call Progress Enterprises, which is another nonprofit group.

CHAIRMAN PROXMIRE. I see.

MR. SULLIVAN. Now, the Ford Foundation gave me money for the entrepreneurial school, and I raised a hundred thousand on my own, just from my own friends and people of my church.

CHAIRMAN PROXMIRE. I was just going to ask you that. I do not mean to interrupt. But I would like to know if you could tell me how much foundation money, private money, industrial money of various kinds, how much local or state money or if, and how much federal.

MR. SULLIVAN. No state or federal money at all. This first training program I am using no federal money. I am talking about the entrepreneurial development and training school.

CHAIRMAN PROXMIRE. You have foundation money?

MR. SULLIVAN. From Ford. And I raised a hundred thousand dollars myself. I am going to train 200 men for businesses in Philadelphia, in the precise Philadelphia area—not only for our own creative businesses but for supermarkets, and other enterprises. I can see how on a national scale, Mr. Burrell, you ought to talk to my men. I think you have something here—Senator Proxmire is saying here—maybe we can work out something.

But I think we are on the threshold of something here that can really mean something.

Frankly, it is my ambition to train a thousand entrepreneurs a year. And I will do it with or without the government. I am going to do it anyway. If I have you, I can do it faster.

• • •

MR. BURRELL. This country is going to have to face up to the fact that black men must participate in what we know as the free enterprise system. This is what the movement is all about—it is the lack of participation in this free enterprise system that makes people say—since we do not see blacks participating, let us destroy the system. Those of us who are a part of it know that the system works, that probably America, the free enterprise system of America is the best system in the world. But it has to be preserved long enough to fit blacks into it.

• • •

MR. RUMSFELD. I can remember sitting in a conference where Margaret Mead recommended that we have a year of compulsory service for every young person in our country. A very liberal professor who had been active in the poverty program made the comment that her proposal made his flesh crawl. Everyone wondered why. He said:

> I am for national service, but once you make it compulsory, and pretend that the government has the wisdom to organize and order the lives of every young man and young woman in this country for a year, into something productive, on behalf of society, you are destroying the whole concept of it, and the government does not have that wisdom.

This leads to my question about your program.

Is it possible that part of the strength of your program is that it is not being corrupted or bureaucratized or frustrated by the government involvement to the extent that others have—it has not suffered the plague of the sophistication to which you refer?

MR. SULLIVAN. I think there is no question about it, sir. I think that if we are permitted by government agencies—and there were attempts made to come in and bureaucratize the program, and take it over—I perhaps would have had more money in it, but less effectiveness. I have maintained the indigenous leadership, role characteristics of the movement, because I think it is on that basis that it has been successful. I think the people look at it as being their program. They do not look at it as being a government program.

They do not look at it as being a poverty program. It is a poverty program. I get money from the poverty program. But they do not see it like that. They see it as theirs, OIC belongs to them, with the support of the government. I think that is one reason, one of the big reasons it has succeeded. And maybe one of the big reasons I have not gotten more support.

• • •

CHAIRMAN PROXMIRE. I would like to have you and Mr. Burrell comment on a problem that has plagued many members of Congress, and divided Presidential candidates and others recently, and that is the deep difference between those who think we must de-centralize the cities—that is do our best to persuade people not to live in these concentrated communities, and persuade them to move to the suburbs, the argument being that the economic fact of life is that there is greater increase in jobs in the suburbs than people, and especially the blue-collar jobs. But all kinds of jobs are in the suburbs. There are good solid economic reasons for it, one of them being that the land is much less expensive, of course, in the suburban areas, and second being we now have a transportation system that enables us to take advantage of that, with highways all over the place, and with trucking transportation. That this is a clear, definite, continuing economic fact of life. And to try under these circumstances to, some people say, gild the ghetto, or concentrate in these already congested areas, is noneconomic, won't work very well. But on the other hand, you have the problem which Senator Kennedy put to Senator McCarthy in that debate on Saturday night: "Are you telling me you are going to move 10,000 Negroes to Orange County in the next few months; and if you don't, what are they going to do in the next few months? How are they going to solve their problem?"

In other words, theoretically it might be fine to say move to the suburbs. Practically, how do you accomplish this, and is it worthwhile to accomplish?

MR. BURRELL. Senator, you just sailed up my favorite stream!

I think that we have a lot to accomplish by way of making the pie larger, so that you can divide the slices greater. In our present growth pattern we have a certain size pie, and nobody seems to be willing to cut it any thinner. I think you would agree that the revitalization of the urban centers must be the next frontier of activity in this country. If that is true—and it must be true, because we simply cannot continue to permit our cities to become increasingly black, further deteriorated—a lot of activity is going to have to occur within the central cities in order to make it livable for anyone who wants to live there. In other words, the tax base continues to flee to the suburbs, and it leaves this uneconomic core in the center, living on the most valuable land that the country has. The reverse of that is that you say the jobs are fleeing to the suburbs, and they certainly are. They are following the money. The development of enterprise around the beltways of this country means that you do not have people living there who can accept the blue-collar job. So why don't we approach it both ways. . . .

Here we are, the uneconomic central city, trying to solve our own problems. With what? Yet we must get away from the economics of despair, and the attitude of scarcity and cutback in this economy, and look at where the new units are for growth. I leave it to the economists to tell me where the mortgage money is going to come from to build in the numbers that would be required, numbers of housing that would be required—and I would suggest that there are many job opportunities attendant to that kind of revitalization. If Leon will help when the time comes to take on the unions—and that is going to have to be done, because somehow Negroes are going to have to participate all along the line in the revitalization of our urban cores in the planning, in the development, in the actual construction, in the construction trades.

The day of the old line master carpenter is gone. We have subcontractors that do all kinds of things. Subflooring is done by the subcontractor. You do not need a degree in electrical engineering to pull wires through a conduit. You do not need six years of apprenticeship to learn how to nail a piece of board up on a wall. These are the new opportunities that could be created, and a lot of money is going to have to be spent in doing it. Negroes are not going to have an opportunity to build an Israel as the Jews did, and to develop the kind of pride in Israel that they developed. But they can have a stake in re-creating their own communities, and from it will come the kind of pride that we are all looking for within the black community.

We can solve a lot of problems therefore simply by beginning to approach the problem of how you revitalize our urban centers. You will give people then the opportunity to earn the money that it will take to crack the white picket fence that surrounds our central cities, and those who want to move there can, there will be a free movement in this country that has to occur. Any other programs that we are talking about leave America divided at its foundation, which is its economic base, and this is where we are going to have to reach. There is going to have to be a commitment on the part of the Congress, on the part of whatever administration, and somebody better send the message to the Bureau of the Budget that Congress should not be frustrated in its attempts to revitalize our centers and provide these kinds of opportunities.

D *Governmental Encouragement of Small Business Enterprise*

65
Small Business Loan Program
STEPHEN KURZMAN

Two EOA [Economic Opportunity Act] programs, the title IV small business loan program and the title III-A rural loan program, are relevant to this study since they consist of governmental credit extensions to private enterprise, in the first to small businesses in ghetto areas and in the second to low-income farm families, for the express purpose hopefully of making these otherwise private economic units self-sustaining. To the extent that they include management assistance these are also manpower training programs.

The small business loan program was originally administered under the Small Business Administration by delegation from OEO. Since enactment of the 1966 EOA amendments, the program has been administered directly by SBA. SBA construes its authority to make economic opportunity loans to two classes of small businessmen: low-income persons living in poverty; and persons lacking equal opportunity who are above the poverty level but cannot qualify for SBA's regular business loans. Both groups can borrow up to $25,000, depending on the type of business and their needs, for as long as ten, and in some cases fifteen years. The interest rate is 5½ per cent except in designated depressed areas, where it is lower.

SBA divides its economic opportunity loans into categories corresponding to the two groups of eligible borrowers. EOL I is the loan program for low-income persons living in poverty and is described by SBA as an expanded version of the original economic opportunity loan program. EOL II is a new program which began in November 1966, for the second group, those who have suffered from lack of opportunity and as a result have not had the chance to compete in business on equal terms.

Figures for fiscal year 1967, to April, 1967, indicate that of 3,469 outstanding loans, 3,014 were under EOL I and 455 were under EOL II. The total amount outstanding is $24,311,000, consisting of $14,526,000 under EOL I and $9,785,000 under EOL II. The average amount of approved EOL I loans has been $8,900; the average EOL II, to those above the poverty line, has been expectably larger, $13,800. The average length of loan has been six years. Both programs include direct loans from SBA: participation loans, in which part is lent by SBA and part by a bank or other lending institution;

From "Private Enterprise Participation in the Antipoverty Program," a paper commissioned by the Subcommittee on Employment, Manpower, and Poverty of the Senate Committee on Labor and Public Welfare and published in *Examination of the War on Poverty*, vol. 1 (1967).

and guaranteed loans, in which a bank loan is guaranteed by SBA. Again predictably, a considerably higher proportion of EOL II loans than EOL I have been participation or guaranteed loans, in which private profitmaking institutions must rely in part on the economic stability of the borrower. However it is noteworthy that a total of $351,000 was lent by private institutions in participation and guaranteed loans despite the fact that borrowers under both EOL I and II are by definition unable to obtain commercial credit.

In terms of ultimate economic success, the liquidation or default rate of EOL I loans since the inception of the program has been 8 per cent. An additional 14 per cent of EOL I loans have been considered delinquent. The EOL II loan program is too new to evaluate in these terms, particularly since in most cases initial payments are deferred for a period of two or three months.

On a comparative basis with SBA's regular loan program the EOL I loans are clearly less successful, with a total of 22 per cent delinquent or in liquidation, as compared with 15 per cent in those categories for regular SBA loans over the same period. Again, however, the percentage difference is not nearly as great as might be expected considering the risks involved in many small enterprises in disadvantaged areas. The higher liquidation and delinquency figures for EOL I loans reflect the need for extensive management assistance and other types of support for small businessmen in disadvantaged areas. Originally such support was given to EOL applicants only by forty-four small business development centers (SBDC's) which were CAP-funded nonprofit outstations in urban centers through which loan applications were forwarded to SBA for processing. Whatever value the SBDC counseling program may have been, it was decided by the Senate committee in its report on the 1966 EOA amendments that the split of authority between CAA's and SBA was not working and that the $5 million per year which had been authorized for grants to SBDC's should be disbursed by SBA, not by CAP. The ultimately enacted amendments did not so provide, however, and while the loan program was shifted to SBA, the new section 402(b), which for the first time explicitly authorized grants to establish SBDC's, nonetheless referred to OEO and not to SBA.

The result has been an administrative snarl over how many federally assisted offices will be available to promote EOL's and to provide management and other counseling to borrowers in disadvantaged neighborhoods. Once it received direct responsibility for the loan program, SBA in November 1966, expanded its coverage by offering EOL loans and counseling for the first time through all of its seventy-three regional and branch offices. Since then there has been considerable uncertainty as to whether OEO will continue to fund the forty-four SBDC's. OEO's position is that it will do so only if CAA's request their continuation. In view of the ever-increasing budgetary pressure on CAP funds, there is a danger that the CAA's may elect to use the $5 million for other purposes and close the SBDC's. This would be highly unfortunate, since SBA regional and branch offices, while a worthwhile additional set of intake sites, are generally in downtown locations and not in the disadvantaged neighborhoods, in which SBDC's are often more strategically located for the purpose of the EOL program.

Along parallel lines a privately sponsored nonprofit group created by two social action agencies, the Interracial Council for Business Opportunity, has been providing Negro businessmen with free management assistance since 1963, primarily through the donated personal time of successful white businessmen at all levels of management. ICBO now has offices in four cities and is seeking to reach with consultative help some 1,000 small businesses each year, especially in service industries, which it sees as the field of greatest opportunity for small business. The cost of counseling is estimated to be about $80 per client. ICBO is just beginning to assemble a privately sponsored loan fund, with which it hopes to make bank-guaranteed loans to Negro-owned small businesses. Efforts are also being made to improve and standardize the quality of volunteer counseling and obtain regular progress reports on clients' progress.

ICBO seeks to provide a continuous source of managerial support for the Negro small businessman. By comparison the SBDC efforts are more oriented toward loan-application processing and paper preparation than toward the kind of support ICBO believes is crucial. Consequently, it would be highly desirable if the two efforts could be carried forward in tandem, with SBDC's and SBA field offices providing the necessary information and assistance on EOL loan applications, and ICBO—and perhaps other nonprofit, or even for-profit, organizations as well—providing supportive and managerial services, under contract, with OEO if necessary. To permit contracts with profitmaking consulting firms for this purpose would require amendment of section 402(b) of EOA, which authorizes grants to or contracts with only public or private nonprofit agencies for counseling.

In addition, the availability of some private banking participation in EOL loans suggests that pooled arrangements, like those being developed among banks for housing rehabilitation, might be stimulated in order to expand the private participation in small business lending by spreading the risks among a number of institutions.

66
Promoting Small Business Through Government Procurement

SENATE SELECT COMMITTEE
ON SMALL BUSINESS

Statement of Hon. Robert C. Moot, Administrator, Small Business Administration

The focus of the Small Business Administration (SBA) in the government-wide attack on the hard-core unemployment problem is on the development of small business entrepreneurship for resident citizens in urban and rural poverty pockets. The creation of small business concerns which are owned, managed and operated by low-income individuals and the award of federal procurement contracts as an initial input in these firms can be an important contribution to the winning of the war on poverty.

We are of the view that while SBA's regular procurement assistance programs can assist significantly in this effort, it is also necessary to make use of the SBA prime contract authority set forth in Section 8(a) of the Small Business Act.

Section 8(a) of the Small Business Act declares it to "be the duty of" SBA, and SBA is empowered whenever it "determines such action is necessary" to enter into procurement contracts with other federal agencies on such terms and conditions as the parties agree. SBA, not being itself a producer of supplies or services, is authorized by Section 8(a) (2) to subcontract to others the performance of contracts it has obtained under Section 8(a) (1). Section 407(a) of the Economic Opportunity Amendments of 1967 further directs the Administrator of SBA to see that federal procurement is placed in such a way as to further the purposes of Title IV of the Economic Opportunity Act of 1964 as amended.

The history of the Small Business Act and related legislation indicates that the chief objective of Section 8(a) was to enable existing small business firms to expand and grow or new small firms to enter into being. The decision to implement Section 8(a), which heretofore had not been activated, was made

---

From *Federal Procurement Activity and Hard-Core Unemployment*, Hearings before the Subcommittee on Government Procurement of the Senate Select Committee on Small Business (1968).

pursuant to the President's directive of October 2, 1967, in which he announced the launching of a major test program which has among its goals the encouragement of new enterprises combining the resources of big and small businesses. The passage of the Economic Opportunity Amendments of 1967 and the direction given the Small Business Administration in that legislation is altogether consistent with the Presidential guidance.

The volume of government procurement has an important and continuing economic and social impact upon the country. Federal procurement is big business and, as such, affects the careers and livelihood of millions of people, of whole regions, whole industries and whole sections of the country. And as big as it is, federal procurement is not as large as the aggregate of state and local government procurement. Government procurement, at all levels, accounts for more than 15 per cent of the Nation's Gross National Product.

As a member of the President's aforementioned test program, SBA assessed its authority and capabilities with a view toward making a meaningful contribution to this test program. During the development stage it became clear that the solution to the problems of the hard-core unemployed involved more than just the creation of jobs. It was evident that, in order for minority and low-income citizens to become a part of the economic mainstream of American life, business ownership opportunities have to be established in their communities. Further, such business opportunities needed to be provided in enterprises of relatively substantial scope, not just small retail sole proprietorships. We, in SBA, felt that by focusing our attention on this ownership aspect of the total problem, we could make our greatest contribution.

To do so, we called upon all of our resource tools, financial, management, technical, as well as the authority vested in us by Section 8(a) of the Small Business Act. To date we have helped to establish or expand eleven small business concerns, all of which employ the hard-core unemployed and most of which are owned and managed by minority citizens. We have negotiated, to date, three prime contracts with the Department of Defense and, in turn, awarded four subcontracts to minority-owned small business firms. One of the three prime contracts, for $137,500 with the U.S. Army Ammunition Procurement and Supply Agency, Joliet, Illinois, calls for the production of two and one-half million sets of powder bags made from light duck material. This item met the general criteria we established for the selection of items to be considered for Section 8(a) use in assisting in the development of minority-owned businesses and the employment of hard-core unemployed. These criteria are: (1) that the item be of a non-sophisticated nature; (2) that it represent a continuing requirement of the procurement agency so that possible additional contracts could be negotiated; (3) that there be either a relative shortage of suppliers for the item, or that the item not represent a significant part of the annual buy by the procurement agency.

The purpose of these criteria are obvious. It is not the intention of SBA to use 8(a) where it would unduly penalize other small firms which had previously bid on these items.

To produce these powder bags our industrial specialists located an existing minority-owned manufacturer. This small firm, located in Chicago, Illinois, employed twenty minority people. While the owner had limited capital resources, he is a man of excellent reputation and we worked out an arrangement whereby advance payments through a controlled account will enable his firm to expand its facilities and hire thirty-five additional minority employees. There is sufficient leadtime for production and delivery to enable the company to set up a training program and develop the skills of the new employees. With this expanded facility, and an improved capital position resulting from the performance of this contract, the company's owner is confident that he now has the basis for a more profitable and expanding enterprise.

Another contract was negotiated with the Defense Supply Agency for 50,000 wood pallets. A subcontract award in the competitive price range was then made to the Fairmicco Company, a newly formed minority-owned enterprise in Washington, D.C. This is a unique development, embodying the essential aspects of an industry-government cooperative approach which, SBA feels, contains the essential ingredients for successful economic growth in a ghetto area. In this instance, the Fairchild Hiller Corporation, a large successful company, committed itself to work with a local community group to establish a facility in a concentrated hard-core unemployment area in Washington, D.C. The Fairchild Hiller Corporation assigned a key executive and other staff members to provide the leadership necessary to plan the project and guide it through the initial stages of development. Prominent Negro community leaders were brought into the plan at its inception and have worked closely with the large business concern, the District of Columbia government, and several government agencies in bringing this conception to fruition.

The government input to date in this project includes funding for personnel training by the Department of Labor, as well as a subcontract from the Small Business Administration. The initial contract input—the wood pallets—will serve to train and develop employee skills in the wood-working trade. It is contemplated that following the pallet contract, wood-working items requiring more advanced skills will be produced—if necessary, from additional 8(a) contracts. Concurrently with its development of a wood-working capability, Fairmicco, with the assistance of Fairchild Hiller, will begin setting up an electrical assembly unit. SBA, with the cooperation of the United States Army Electronics Command, Fort Monmouth, New Jersey, will contract for some nonsophisticated electrical cable assemblies and will provide this work as an initial subcontract input for the electrical assembly production operation.

A third prime contract has been negotiated by SBA with the Department of the Air Force, Lackland Air Force Base, San Antonio, Texas. The requirement is for troop-issue pastries and is estimated to amount to approximately $1 million annually. The subcontract plan here is to award a sizable portion of the contract to an existing producer and the remainder of the contract to an expanded minority-owned bakery in San Antonio. The existing producer employs about 85 per cent minority employees. This producer is not interested in expanding his own facility to take care of the increasing volume required by Lackland. He has agreed to assist the new small minority-owned bakery in developing the capability to take over the expanded requirement. Besides providing the contract input for the minority-owned and operated bakery, SBA has agreed to provide a loan of $33,000 to upgrade the bakery premises to meet the quality standards of the Air Force. It is contemplated that a minimum of fifty hard-core unemployed will be hired and trained as a result of this contract.

SBA is in the process of considering and negotiating a number of other 8(a) prospects. The small businesses which have been aided under this new program which combines all of SBA resources will employ about 1,000 hard-core unemployed. Even more important is the ownership of substantial businesses in urban slum areas by resident citizens and the community pride and involvement which result from economic accomplishment. These new enterprises export goods and services outside of the ghetto areas and bring income into the community for growth purposes.

In addition to financial assistance and the newly developed Section 8(a) tool, SBA's regular small business procurement assistance programs are called upon to support not only our efforts under that Section, but also to assure that small businesses, especially those located in urban areas of high concentration of unemployed or low-income individuals, be provided maximum opportunity to participate in government procurement awards. We now have eighteen "Procurement Center Representatives" (PCRs) working on the small business set-aside program and other functions relating to the prime contract function. We are budgeting for full implementation of this program during fiscal year 1969 when we hope to implement Congressional intent at government purchasing offices with a total of forty-five PCRs covering on a full- or part-time basis 104 procurement installations, which account for approximately 65 per cent of the total federal government procurement dollar.

These SBA PCRs can be of specific help to small firms in the ghetto—they can guide these firms in selling to the government, they can help them with the problems at purchasing installations and, very importantly, they can assure that these firms receive the opportunity to participate in government contracting. Relative to our 8(a) program, the PCR has been, and will continue to be invaluable in screening and locating items suitable for the SBA 8(a) input and, generally, in assisting in our negotiations with procurement installations.

An important source of government procurement input into the ghetto areas may be via the normal subcontract route. About half of the dollars spent with prime contractors are, in turn, spent by the primes through subcontracting with other suppliers. SBA, in cooperation with the Department of Defense, is working with the major prime contractors to encourage them to subcontract to small business. Our voluntary subcontracting program has grown from 1963, when there were twenty-five major prime contractors involved, to this current fiscal year when the total number of primes working with us will be seventy-five. These seventy-five primes account for approximately 60 per cent of total Defense contract awards.

Our subcontracting program staff is also being utilized in our 8(a) program to assist in finding appropriate and capable small business sources in or near the ghetto areas, and they are encouraging the prime contractors to subcontract with these firms. It is also our aim to encourage, as required by Section 406(b) (5) of the Economic Opportunity Amendments of 1967 the placement of subcontracts by major businesses with small business concerns located in the areas herein under discussion. The cooperative and mutually beneficial relationship we have established with these major primes will be, we believe, a contributing factor to the increasing interest shown by these companies in working with us in this respect.

We believe that a successful pattern for development of job opportunities in the ghetto area has evolved. There are many paths and methods which can be successfully used. We are using several. Deputy Administrator Howard Greenberg is personally directing the implementation of a program which will have SBA teams housed in target areas and working with community citizens to develop substantial business enterprises owned by residents. In addition, Associate Administrator Irving Maness is personally working with big business concerns in the development of small business, urban area projects. The following features, we believe, are significant in the SBA approach.

1. Local community involvement is an essential feature in the development of a practical ghetto program. Community leaders insist on having a role in determining the type and nature of assistance that is directed toward them.

2. It is not simply jobs that people in the ghetto area are looking for. They want to develop skills which will provide a degree of labor mobility to assure them an opportunity for long-term meaningful employment. These people resist menial tasks which will perpetuate their unskilled status.

3. The minority groups whose members form the bulk of the hard-core unemployed want an opportunity to own and manage the businesses which are to be established in their areas. The initiative and direction for carrying out this program must rely on a meaningful coalition of government (federal, state and local), industry, and the target area community.

Discussion

SENATOR JAVITS. May I just say, by way of comment, that I think you are a good man, an able man. I must say, however, in all fairness to you, and what you are trying to do, that if we are going to accept this pace as the best the Small Business Administration can do, then I look for the worst—not only in 1968, but in 1969 and 1970, and 1971 and 1972, and as far as I can see ahead. We simply must—and this is not only for you, but for us, and for American business primarily, which has not yet stirred itself to get into this —I do not care how many alliances they belong to. But it really is going to be incumbent upon all of us to bestir ourselves in this critical program if we are ever going to permit the small business community to exercise its full capacity to deal with the ghetto problem. Really, with all respect, sir, if we are going to go at this pace, seven cities, fifteen cities, three teams, December to March through April, to even find out who is going to do what in the private business field—it is going to be just ghastly, and you can just write it off, except for what the cities and the states can do themselves.

Statement of Dan A. Kimball, Chairman, Executive Committee, Aerojet-General Corp., El Monte, Calif.

Private industry as you know has been asked by the government to train and employ the disadvantaged in hard-core unemployment areas. Resources of the government are being directed toward this program. But there must be a far greater team effort and less restriction if we are to enjoy any meaningful long-range success.

Equaling this task of uncommon magnitude is the very real responsibility of sustaining an appropriate employment level in the plants and businesses established in the rural and urban poverty areas. To me, there could be no greater defeat than be forced into a major layoff because suitable business could not be directed to such plants. My company, which operates Watts Manufacturing Company in the Watts district of Los Angeles, has deliberately limited expansion of this activity for just this reason. It would be a tragedy to train a work force from an unskilled labor pool only to lay them off because we lacked contracts.

In order to avoid layoffs once poverty area plants have been formed and operating, all procurement agencies of the government must take into consideration these additional factors in awarding contracts for goods and services that could be produced in poverty area plants.

All government agencies should recognize that in general small businesses do not have the financial ability, nor the management depth to establish facilities in hard-core areas. It is imperative that the Small Business Administration be encouraged to negotiate more contracts under the provisions of section 8(a) to not only small businesses, but to other small subsidiary operations that have been located in hard-core areas by larger companies.

The Small Business Administration could do much in this area to encourage companies to establish facilities in poverty areas, generating employment for the hard core.

At this point, Mr. Chairman, I would like to discuss briefly the Watts Manufacturing Company, which is a subsidiary of Aerojet-General Corporation. After the riots of 1965 in Watts, it was obvious that jobs had to be created for these citizens. We began talking with Negro leaders in Watts, and governmental leaders as well to see how Aerojet could help. In July of 1966, Vice President Humphrey called an informal meeting of Los Angeles aerospace contractors and urged them to provide job opportunities for these disadvantaged citizens.

Watts Manufacturing was incorporated in August of 1966. The president of the company is a Negro business leader who resides in the area and who is well aware of the problems of the community.

When Watts Manufacturing was started, we didn't have any business. Finally, we were successful in obtaining a contract for the production of large canvas tents for the military services. Now we also do some wood and metal work. With the full knowledge that a single product line, such as tents for the armed services, is at best a hazardous reed on which to hold, the other divisions of Aerojet responded in a meaningful way by subcontracting work in both woodworking and metal working to the Watts Manufacturing Company. We are expanding these product lines as rapidly as possible.

We have a capital investment of $1.3 million in Watts Manufacturing, all from Aerojet. The labor force of approximately 438 is almost entirely from the Watts district. There were 5,000 applicants for these few hundred jobs. And there are another 25,000 people in the area available to be trained for employment.

When we employed these people, there were no restrictions, except that they were able and wanted to work. We didn't care if they had police records or whether they ever held a steady job before. They had to be trained.

Initially, we had our problems. Training was slow, because some employees had not worked in five years. Absenteeism initially was high. But we have resolved many of these problems and the operation is today running rather smoothly.

Our greatest concern today is an adequate workload to sustain this work force.

I would like to point out that our experience in poverty areas is not limited to Watts.

Two years ago, my company invested $3 million to organize a manufacturing plant at Batesville, Ark., where there was a persistent labor surplus. Here again, we trained native people in the region to do ordnance work. They have done a fine job, and the cooperation of the city and state agencies has been excellent. Today we employ 1,000 people there.

Last year we established another plant at Camden, Ark., where today we employ another 1,000 people. We did not face so many training problems in the rural poverty areas, since most of the people we employed had some previous work experience. We feel that it is extremely important to establish facilities in rural areas, because this helps to prevent the migration to the already crowded urban areas. In fact, we have been successful in attracting some employees back to Arkansas who previously worked in urban industrial centers such as Cleveland and Detroit.

Here again, however, the concern is to keep a reasonable level of employment—avoid layoffs.

In attracting business and industry to rural and urban poverty areas, private industry must go a bit beyond conventional methods of doing business. It seems appropriate to me that agencies of the government should do likewise; that the procurement offices give every consideration to business and industry, large or small, in providing employment for the hard-core unemployed.

Discussion

SENATOR MONTOYA. . . . Do you think that government procurement can be genuinely effective in helping companies like Watts to get started?

MR. KIMBALL. I think you can get it started that way.

SENATOR MONTOYA. Well, is it your feeling, Mr. Kimball, that if the government would assist these so-called big corporations, provided they established in hard-core unemployment areas, do you think that they would be willing to go to those areas?

MR. KIMBALL. I am sure they would. I am sure a lot of the companies would. Now in our case, we decided if we waited to get help from the government we would never get the job done, so we established the business first and then got an order.

Statement of Stanley Ruttenberg, Assistant Secretary, U.S. Department of Labor

I am disturbed by the fact that the establishment of businesses in which minority individuals become the small entrepreneur, and that business in turn has to rely upon a defense government contract to remain in business, might be good at the outset. But it worries me terribly as to what the social ramifications and repercussions are going to be down the road if that company sticks to and is solely dependent upon a defense-type contract to remain in business.

Have we done a real service for the individual?

Now, if somehow, by using the defense procurement technique to get them into business, they somehow may be diversified and receive business from the rest of the nondefense economy, all right. But I am worried. I just refer to the Aero Jet experience in the Watts Manufacturing Company in California. They established a business on the basis of a contract to produce tents for the Armed Forces. The Armed Forces no longer needed tents. Aero Jet then had 250 people employed in the Watts Manufacturing Company wanting to know what to do next. They had to search for, and they finally did get, another defense contract. It is an excellent idea; the Aero Jet Watts manufacturing plant is a wonderful idea. But I just raise this caution, which worries me no end.

Discussion *

REPRESENTATIVE CORMAN. I have two problems with the tax incentive for locating industry in ghetto areas. Again, as I say, a tax credit is a public ex-

---

* (From *Employment and Manpower Problems in the Cities: Implications of the Report of the National Advisory Commission on Civil Disorders,* Hearings before the Joint Economic Committee of Congress, 1968. The Lewisohn statement which follows returns to the Hearings of the Senate Select Committee on Small Business, 1968.)

penditure, so far as all the other taxpayers are concerned. The effort to bring industry back to the ghetto seems to me in the long run to perpetuate the condition which we are trying to eliminate, and so I have grave misgivings. If the effort is fairly short-ranged and involves little investment, then the tax incentive isn't going to be much of an incentive. The tentmaking operation in Watts, for instance, is a project that is not anticipated to have any long life.

But to think of attempting to bring industry back into the central cities, it seems to me, just from the point of simple planning, is a bad thing to do.

But beyond that, to say to Negroes in America, all right, stay where you are; you are really where we want you to be; we will send you some jobs, just seems to me to be a step backward, and a bad one.

Statement of Richard Lewisohn, Administrator, Economic Development Administration, City of New York

The problems of selling to government are staggering for the ordinary small businessman. To compound these problems by using procurement to spark new businesses—to boot, new businesses hampered by the frustration and pain of ghetto life. . . . Well, we are taking on quite a chore.

The City of New York is willing to try. And I am sure the federal government is, too. But let's know what we are getting into.

For one thing, most levels of government are required by law to let contracts to the lowest responsible bidder. These laws automatically eliminate many small businesses, which cannot compete with the bigger fellows both from the point of view of price, and the point of view of ability to deliver on a contract.

It costs more to live in a city, so wages are higher. This fact alone widens the cost differential and makes it more difficult for a small city manufacturer or distributor to be competitive.

Second, there are the problems of specifications and terms of contracts. Much of this language, perhaps unnecessarily, is too complicated and tricky for the small businessman, especially a newcomer—that is, even if he can find out which contract is available and when.

Third, the requirements for financial responsibility are far too stringent for the average tiny business, let alone one started in a ghetto.

Fourth, these tiny businesses cannot afford to operate for the length of an entire contract before payment. In New York City, payments delayed for ninety days after contract satisfaction are not uncommon.

Fifth, few tiny businesses can command the depth of managerial and technical experience that will enable them to conform to the contract-fulfillment requirements of government.

These "obstacles," gentlemen, will not vanish with the twinkle of a kindly eye. If our purpose is the generation of business and jobs for minority groups, we will have to change a good many of our procedures and much of our thinking. We may even have to retrain some of our purchasing personnel, or at least provide additional personnel whose task it is, principally, to strengthen a firm's ability to serve the public interest.

We in New York have been pondering these problems and believe we can overcome them to a large degree.

In order to do so, however, we will require the assistance of the federal agencies which help the small—or I should say, tiny—businessman.

We will be recommending certain changes in legislation, primarily at the state and local levels. We feel strongly that the federal government must not carry the entire burden; it is imperative that the local governments and the private sector do their share.

1. The key problems we face together in creating or expanding ghetto-based businesses are the low-bid requirements. While federal "set-aside" provisions and Section "8a" SBA prime-contractor rights can be administratively interpreted in some cases to incubate businesses, we might as well face up to the limitations right now.

The small ghetto-area businessman is simply not equipped to compete with the most efficient manufacturers.

The laws of the City of New York are more inflexible in this regard than those of the federal establishment.

But we believe that we can enact special city legislation to provide a degree of resiliency. For the moment we are planning to ask special legislative approval of *individual* contracts to enable us to make awards to small manufacturers in poverty areas *at prices higher than those of the lowest responsible bidder*. Provided, of course, that certain conditions of public value are met, such as location, size, employment density and composition.

We know that objections will arise from other bidders. But we also believe that overriding social benefits will accrue from fuller employment, business investments in ghetto areas, and the partial employment of some people now receiving public assistance. We are willing to face the objections, considering the compelling nature of the social problems. I believe your legislative and administrative recommendations should also look the tiger in the eye.

2. As to the second problem—complicated specifications and promulgation:

The city's purchase offices plan to work together with community installations to systematize and simplify these matters, so that market opportunities for the tiny ghetto-oriented business are clearly delineated well in advance. We shall have a number of people working on what we call contract "translation." People who can tell an incipient businessman—"Here's what you can do for the city"; "Here's what you need to do it"; "Here's how you do it."

I suggest that each major agency of the federal establishment needs a senior staff member assigned to this task in cooperation with the special work being done at SBA, a man whose job it is to sniff out a likely contract for an incipient business, and to make small-business sense of it. While other men, in

SBA, in the cities and states, are sniffing out likely businessmen and helping them meet the requirements.

3. As to the third problem, financial responsibility, most small manufacturers or distributors, who are already in business or who will start up in business as a result of our joint efforts, will require special treatment with respect to their financial responsibility. Obviously their balance sheets will not be ones that pass muster by normal standards.

The various governments involved must be willing to approve on the basis of *anticipated* results rather than past performance. We in New York City plan exactly such a standard. Of course, this problem will be somewhat alleviated by current New York Coalition (our local branch of the Urban Coalition) efforts to provide equity financing and expert assistance.

4. As to the fourth problem, it is my understanding that the SBA has the ability to make partial payments against delivery of government contracts.

Efforts must be made to expand the use of this privilege in order to enable small manufacturers to pay current bills, both for payroll and for materials, while producing goods to be delivered against contracts. Other levels of government must make similar provision if they wish to encourage small manufacturers to supply the needs of either the cities or the states.

5. And now the fifth problem—assistance: In New York we propose to set up centers to be manned jointly by personnel from the city government, the federal government, community "corporations," and the New York Coalition. These centers will be concerned with the problems mentioned in this text. Government procurement schedules will be studied in depth and pruned to eliminate items which are not practical to have manufactured locally. Feasible "opportunities" will be rephrased so as to be easily understood by nontechnical people. Negotiations will be carried out on behalf of the new manufacturer, combined with financial assistance in many instances, and particularly with technical and managerial assistance for production problems, marketing and sales difficulties, and administrative and fiscal questions. When the manufacturer finally starts to produce there will be personnel on hand to be certain that the first production runs meet specifications and that controls are installed so that the whole production run is up to standard.

What we are proposing to do essentially is to bring together, *in the communities,* the city, state, federal and business expertise being developed to create managerial and enterpreneurial skills in poverty areas.

We ask the federal government to provide business opportunities, personnel, financing, and information. We will ask the state for purchases and financing, especially for the legislative changes which will permit this form of purchasing. The city's contribution will consist of personnel, administration, financing, and business opportunities. We, too, must provide the necessary legislation.

And finally, the private sector, with its tremendous technical skills, purchasing power, and marketing know-how, must *provide not only staff and financing*, but also commit itself to purchasing a percentage of its requirements from small businesses in the poverty areas. Private businesses, as well as government, should set aside a percentage of their purchase requirements.

The various levels of government must clarify their position as well. Section 8a procurement efforts have numbered only a few and must be expanded drastically, including awards that require a prime contractor to set up a new minority business. The federal government must make a conscious effort to put more dollars into set-aside contracts for labor surplus areas. The cities must recognize their obligation to the poverty areas and amend their inflexible regulations involving purchasing of goods and services. States and the federal government must require risk pools, both for insurance and bonding purposes, to enable small contractors as well as manufacturers to participate in government construction and other service contracts. Or reduce cash-deposit requirements which can bring bidding in the reach of the tiny minority contractor. Even unions must recognize the problem and relax certain of their contractual requirements.

If all these things are done and if every member of our society will assume his or her share of the burden, only then will we be in a position to make a dent in the serious poverty area problems of unemployment and under-recognition.

67

GHEDIPLAN (Ghetto Economic Development and Industrialization Plan)

DUNBAR S. MC LAURIN

[*In December, 1967, the Deputy Administrator for Community Relations of New York City's Human Resources Administration requested Dr. Dunbar S. McLaurin, a Negro economist, to develop a plan which would put the City's financial power behind the development of the ghetto areas. The result was the GHEDIPLAN, which is outlined by the author below.*]

From *Federal Procurement Activity and Hard-Core Unemployment*, Hearings before the Subcommittee on Government Procurement of the Senate Select Committee on Small Business (1968).

INTRODUCTION

The events of the past several summers have produced convincing proof that traditional approaches to urban crises are woefully inadequate and that something new must be developed. It is equally clear that this something must be based upon creative economics, with a generous and imaginative application of the sociological lessons we have learned in the slums. The Ghetto Economic Development and Industrialization Plan, or GHEDIPLAN for short, is an attempt to meet that need.

This plan has been written and developed against the compelling events of the last hot summer of 1967, and against the shadows cast by the impending summer. At this time, the nation has not begun to comprehend the full impact of the Report of the President's Commission on Civil Disorders. But what is apparent is that we cannot long provide the vast sums recommended by the Commission, if as a dole. Yet the nation itself cannot be sustained, it is apparent, unless something approaching the recommended order of magnitude is applied to the problem. The problem can only be solved by making the economies of the ghettos productive and self-sustaining. This is what the GHEDIPLAN seeks to do.

The social agony of the slums is but the symptom of an underlying and basic pathology of economic sickness. Until the ghettos have a sound economic basis, the social service dollar is only a financial palliative at best—a Band-Aid, an aspirin, or a "Compoz" pill. It has taken a long time and many hot summers to reach this truth. The word "Economic" in the Economic Opportunity Act has finally attained the respectability that it should have had all along.

Now, however, economic development of the ghettos is of the highest domestic priority. Poverty experts now realize that unless ghetto residents own their businesses and have a stake in the economy, it is easy for them to rationalize that what they are burning and looting belongs not to them but to absentee white owners and is fair game.

Senator Jacob Javits of New York has dramatically stated the case:

> Though he is tragically mistaken, the slum Negro sees himself as having no stake in the economic life of his community and no realistic possibility of becoming part of it—hence there is no community morality against destroying it.[1]

The weakness in most ghetto economic development plans, which now abound, is that they do not view the ghetto as an entirety, and they therefore are basically piecemeal, sociological, and cosmetic in their approach to the problem. None comes to grip with the immediate economic problems of: (1) transferring ownership from absentee owners to local minority owners in an orderly manner, thereby strengthening the local population; (2) diversifying, strengthening, and expanding the economic base so that it can compete in the wider economic mainstream; (3) increasing the "ghetto national product" by increasing the number of ghetto-owned industries that *produce,* as opposed to the present businesses that merely *distribute* "foreign" goods and services.

Inadequate Philosophy of Other Plans

The failure to view the problems of the underdeveloped ghetto economy in the same way that we view those of an underdeveloped nation has led to several inadequate plans—all based upon an inadequate philosophy—about the requirements for true economic development of these areas.

There are five basic false assumptions underlying this philosophy.

First: That only research is needed to develop ghetto businesses. This false assumption has resulted in a rash of "plans" which, when distilled, provide for nothing more than the collection of data about ghetto businesses. Many of these businesses fail even before the statistics are compiled. Research *is* needed, but a study or a diagnostic survey does not produce economic development. It is, at most, a tool.

Second: That high unemployment is the real economic problem of the ghetto. This false assumption is bottomed on the belief that if more people worked there would be more consumers, and ghetto businesses would therefore flourish. What is overlooked, however, is that these businesses are rarely *owned* by ghetto residents. Hence another rash of "development plans," which are nothing more than programs to train, retrain and break down employment barriers.

Full employment is a desired goal and must be vigorously pursued, but it alone will not insure a healthy, viable minority business community. The Negro had full employment on the plantation. Yet it insured only the economic growth of the white owner. New industry is needed in the ghetto. Manpower training is vital. Discrimination must end. But these are not the true routes to economic growth.

For without ownership and control of production and distribution, employment means little. The Negro remains a straight man for the flow of money through him directly back into the white community. The minority business community must be helped to diversify and develop its capacity to own and control the economic mechanisms; to retain the money once it is earned, and to circulate the money within the community.

In the "real" world outside the ghetto, a dollar that is worth only a dollar is a losing dollar. A plan to develop the ghetto economically must look beyond mere full *employment.* The goal must be full *self*-employment. The ghetto must not only help provide full employment, it must also determine the multiplier effect use of money in the community and participate in the basic economic decisions that underlie a sound economy.

Third: That ghetto economic development requires only the provision of long-term, low-interest loan money. The theory is that only the lack of capital prevents the survival and expansion of the otherwise marginal and high-risk ghetto businesses.

Fourth: That the provision of management training, together with sufficient capital, is a sure-fire solution to the problem. All that is needed additionally, the theory goes, is some professional guidance about tax practices, and in the maintenance of ledgers, inventory systematizing, purchasing, store layout, etc.

These last two assumptions constitute perhaps the oldest and most traditional approach: provide the ghetto businessman with capital and training, and, ipso facto, the problem is solved. This approach is the "old fur coat" theory, based upon the radio commercial: "Don't remodel your old fur coat; you will still have an old fur coat."

It is apparent that if every minority businessman was thoroughly trained in bookkeeping, inventory control, layout, and so on, and if each was given a small loan, the economy of the ghetto would hardly move upwards an inch. The result would be a community of clean, neat, tidy—but still marginal—shopkeepers with a minimum economic output. In short, we would still have "an old fur coat."

The "old fur coat" approach has failed in minority economic development, largely because it itself is based upon a fifth false assumption.

Fifth: That the minority businessmen have the same problems as their white counterparts and that remedies and legislation designed for the white community can be applied intact to the ghetto small business community.

The small businessman in the white community operates within a framework of mutually supporting larger businesses and industry. Unlike the minority businessman, he is an integral part of a fluid and mobile economy, in which he can move upwards and outwards in response to the interactions of the free enterprise system, and according to his own entrepreneurial ability. He is a member of a network of business and social relationships that are alien and unavailable to his minority counterpart but that constantly stimulate and offer him happenstance unearned opportunities. He has a heritage of business tradition and of easy availability of capital and technical know-how unknown to the ghetto. Growth is a natural consequence of this heritage; it is expected of the white businessman. And the rules and regulations of the game are designed for and by him.

On the other hand, the ghetto businessman has no such advantages, and no such opportunities. He operates within the high-walled framework of a closed economy. His access to the outer and larger business and industrial world with its opportunities, challenges, and stimuli is as nonexistent as if he were in a remote, underdeveloped country.

And therein lies the challenge. As long as plans for the economic development of the ghettos are based upon the foregoing false assumptions, they will continue to fall far short of what is necessary. The problems of the ghetto economy must be viewed the same way as the problems of an underdeveloped nation are viewed: as an entity and as an interlocking whole. This is the basic approach of the GHEDIPLAN and the essential distinction between this plan and its predecessors.

The "Underdeveloped Nation" Philosophy of the GHEDIPLAN

When the ghetto is viewed as an underdeveloped nation, an entirely different perspective of the problem is gained.

When the United States helps underdeveloped nations, it concentrates on extending the free enterprise system. The United States wants these nations to have a favorable balance of trade and applies hard and soft money theories in lending money at fair interest rates.

The goal is to create businesses and industries that will use local resources most productively. A central banking system, insurance networks and other instruments of capital accumulation are established. Favorable tariff rates are set so they can trade with us, and production machinery as well as consumer items are sold. The goal, then, is to establish a balanced, diversified and self-supporting economy that will generate capital and support a stable, friendly society. Enlightened and selfish dividends are sought, for only a stable economy can support a society that is free of political upheavals and friendly to us.

The parallel lesson for New York City is that ghettos are indeed impacted underdeveloped "nations." As long as their economies are unproductive, unstable and unable to support their inhabitants in dignity, they, too, will breed riots and upheavals. To eliminate our Watts, Newarks and Detroits, the cities' underdeveloped ghetto-nations must be given the economic tools with which to build stable, sound economies.

A final and fundamental similarity between the economic philosophy underlying both the GHEDIPLAN and aid programs for underdeveloped nations is that of "nationalism," the local ownership of the economy and the control of its destiny. This concept reflects the universal feeling that dignity, opportunity and a sense of economic independence are vital energizing elements for the development of a young economy, whether in the ghetto or in an underdeveloped nation.

This, then, is the philosophic background for the GHEDIPLAN. It seeks to establish the machinery with which to restructure the ghetto economy as we would restructure an underdeveloped nation. The plan would diversify the ghetto, create new businesses and industries, and interlock the whole into a mosaic with itself and with the presently "foreign" outer white community. It is not a plan to attack one sector timidly. It seeks to look at the overall ghetto picture and to utilize available municipal resources to create a whole new economy in the ghetto. This economy will be strong enough to participate in, compete with, and become an integral part of the national economy, contributing its own part to the gross national product, instead of being a "colonial" underdeveloped appendage.

It is only by this method that the separate *economic* division of the nation

—a serious division that is similar to the social and political division about which the Commission on Civil Disorders warned—can be avoided.

Against the backdrop of the times, nothing less seems worth trying. Nothing less will do. The fate of this nation depends upon the solution of the problems of the ghetto economy.

SUMMARY

GHEDIPLAN seeks to end poverty by creating a strong locally-owned economy. The prime target is not the small service business. Emphasis is placed on large-scale business and industry that will have a productive economic impact. Ghetto communities sadly lack indigenously owned businesses that are large enough to be productive and to provide significant employment. For example, statistics compiled by the Interracial Council for Business Opportunity show dramatically the absence of such large scale firms: New York City has a Negro population of about 1.1 million, yet only about twelve Negro-owned or managed enterprises employing as many as ten persons.

Thus the creation of ten viable new enterprises, providing substantial employment and capitalized at $1 million each, would do more for the ghetto economies than 1,000 additional tiny businesses capitalized at $10,000. However, heretofore no machinery has existed for the broad economic development of the ghetto community through the creation of such large enterprises that require greater funds.

The Basic Requirements

In creating the plan, these following basic requirements were considered:

1. It must be able legally to use public funds to generate financing for developing private profit-making businesses without actually spending these funds.

2. It must be able to use the City's purchasing power as a generative factor without dislocating City procurement activities.

3. It must harness the ghetto's private initiative, profit motives and business instincts.

4. It must be broad enough to be capable of real community improvement and central planning.

5. It must be designed to attract broad support from the community, the City, bankers, local and outside businessmen, and federal agencies, including the Small Business Administration and the Office of Economic Opportunity.

6. It must be self-generating, so the businesses and industries that are created will eventually become healthy enough to compete in the general economic structure, once the pump-priming process is finished.

The Goals

The plan seeks to remove the causes of poverty in the ghetto, not only by creating or helping individual businesses, but by developing the community's entire economy as a working entity and as a whole. In short, the entire economy is treated like an underdeveloped nation as far as feasible. To achieve this economic growth without the need for large grants or at a great cost to the City, a new and creative use of the City's present fiscal, purchasing and administrative resources is required.

The plan consists of the following components: two *tools,* and six *machinery* instruments. The tools are the guaranteed market and guaranteed financing. The machinery instruments are: *administrative* (the Office of Minority Development); *operative* (Small Business Development Centers plus two "conduit corporations"—Local Development Corporations, and Small Business Investment Companies), and *supportive* (the private economic consultant firm, and the Small Business Administration).

The Tools

GUARANTEED MARKETS

The City would establish "guaranteed markets" for ghetto businesses and contractors by setting aside for the ghettos roughly 10 per cent of its one-half billion dollar annual expenditures for purchases and small contracts. This would pump an additional $50 million in purchases of goods and services into the ghettos. This would trigger an additional $50 million from the private sector and from federal and state governments, for a total guaranteed market of $100 million.

As presently structured, however, minority small business communities cannot supply this demand, because they do not have the right type or the right size businesses. It is therefore necessary to diversify and restructure these economies by creating new businesses or expanding existing ones. Such a vast undertaking requires (1) ample capital and (2) technical know-how and management training. These requirements are supplied by the creative use of existing City resources, via guaranteed financing and the machinery components.

GUARANTEED FINANCING

Guaranteed financing would be achieved by using the City's aggregate $20 to $100 million day-to-day demand deposits to encourage banks to lend money to, or invest in, minority businesses and industries.

The City recently started depositing a portion of these funds in banks that agreed to lend to ghetto businessmen. But this system has not worked because the deposits are merely backed by general promises to lend, and these bank promises cannot be policed effectively. Moreover, this "unlinked policy" is isolated and provides no overall backup resources for the borrowing businesses such as the GHEDIPLAN provides, and the banks are therefore hesitant to participate.

GHEDIPLAN would extend and change the present unlinked policy. Each deposit would be *linked* to a specific commitment by the bank to lend or invest an agreed-upon amount. The line of credit thus established would be the ghetto's guaranteed financing, and the plan is designated the Link-Deposit Plan.

The Administrative Machinery

THE OFFICE OF MINORITY ECONOMIC DEVELOPMENT (OMED)

OMED would be the City agency that organizes and catalyzes the entire plan. It would represent the City in administering, implementing, and operating the plan, and would generate guaranteed financing and guaranteed markets with City resources.

The Operative Machinery

THE SMALL BUSINESS DEVELOPMENT CENTERS (SBDC'S)

SBDC's are quasi-governmental, community-based economic development centers that will recruit, organize and spawn the ghetto conduits. Initially operational and administrative, they will provide training, planning, technical aid and community coordination. SBDC's now exist and are operating under HRA. There would be one SBDC in each ghetto area.

THE LOCAL DEVELOPMENT CORPORATIONS (LDC'S)

An LDC is a conduit to convert City link deposits into medium- and long-term "brick-and-mortar" capital. These conduits will gain leverage of up to nine to one by securing matching federal funds. They are private, community-based and community-controlled. There would be one LDC in each community. Eventually, the LDC would be the economic planning center of the community, providing management and technical training and establishing businesses.

THE SMALL BUSINESS INVESTMENT COMPANIES (SBIC'S)

An SBIC is a conduit to convert City link deposits into equity or venture capital. By securing matching federal funds, it will gain leverage of up to three to one. SBDC's are flexible enough to provide technical training and to be community-based, with one for each community, or it may be centralized with community branches and a common board.

The Supportive Machinery

THE PRIVATE ECONOMIC CONSULTANT FIRM

The firm would provide technical and professional know-how for establishing the plan. It would provide backup for management and technical training and would design and establish the two community "conduit corporations," the LDC's and the SBIC's.

THE SMALL BUSINESS ADMINISTRATION (SBA)

The federal SBA provides monetary leverage to both the LDC and the SBIC conduits through matching federal funding of up to nine to one. It provides a wide range of direct and guaranteed loans and of back-up technical services, advice, and materials.

NOTE

1. Congressional Record S10554, 1967.

E *Private Encouragement of Ghetto Business Enterprise*

68

Rochester Business Opportunities Corporation

U.S. CHAMBER OF COMMERCE

[*In Rochester, N.Y., a number of community leaders and business firms have sought to foster business development in ghetto areas through the medium of Rochester Business Opportunities Corporation, a nonprofit organization funded by private business. The story is told in the following article.*]

PROGRAM DEVELOPMENT

Early Actions

The events leading to the formation of Rochester Business Opportunities Corporation (RBOC) began with a riot in Rochester during the summer of 1964. As one business leader puts it, "All of us since then have said 'what can I do?'" Community tensions continued unresolved, and during 1966 became focused in a controversy between a militant community group, the FIGHT Organization, and the Eastman Kodak Company, which is headquartered in Rochester. That initial confrontation, over job training and employment, was resolved in 1967 and led to a series of continuing discussions between FIGHT and Kodak aimed at talking out various community problems.

Kodak had already begun to look into the area of assisting Negro entrepreneurs when that topic was broached in their discussions by FIGHT. The community group suggested Kodak establish a plant in the inner city to be owned and operated by ghetto residents on the model of the Watts Manufacturing Company, established in Los Angeles by Aerojet-General.[1] Kodak felt that such an approach had less applicability to Rochester, where transportation to a job was not a major problem, and after consulting with various outside persons and groups—such as Daniel Moynihan and the National Business League—announced a small business assistance plan of its own on November 17, 1967. This plan involved the formation of a community development corporation to finance small businesses, with Kodak undertaking to buy products from the new companies and to provide technical assistance. The Kodak proposal identified four new business opportunities which company personnel had identified as workable and from which the company might purchase products or services.

Reprinted by permission of the Urban Action Clearinghouse, Community and Regional Resource Development Group, Chamber of Commerce of the United States.

While Kodak was exploring on a confidential basis, the Rochester Chamber of Commerce also was developing a business assistance program. The Chamber had conducted a poll of its membership, modeled after a poll suggested by the United States Chamber at the 1967 Annual Meeting, and had found a wide consensus that businessmen should provide leadership in solving community problems. In designing an action program to implement that mandate, the Executive Committee met with a group of inner-city leaders and found high interest in the idea of promoting locally-owned small businesses. The Chamber had already formed a committee on business development and had held conferences with local banks when it learned of the Kodak plan, which heretofore had been kept confidential.

Leadership

Chamber officers and Kodak officials met to discuss joining forces, and they subsequently called a luncheon meeting to introduce their plans to leaders of the Rochester business community. Here it was learned that other companies were also working on similar projects. The community development corporation idea appeared to be the proper approach to provide a common vehicle for all the parties to pool their efforts.

A Steering Committee was formed to select board members, and a twenty-eight-member Board of Trustees was chosen representing industry, banking, and the Negro business community. A decision was made to exclude representatives of the FIGHT Organization on the ground that the new corporation should be "business based."

On January 26, 1968, the trustees met for the first time, elected officers, with William Maxion of the Case-Hoyt Corporation named as President, and announced the formation of RBOC. At the second meeting, on February 19, a policy statement was issued . . . , John L. Blake was appointed as RBOC General Manager, and doors were opened for business. Blake, a Negro, took a leave of absence from his post as training coordinator of the Ritter-Pfaudler Corporation to join RBOC.

The Rochester Chamber has continued to play a key role in RBOC's operations, and has converted its library into an office for the Corporation. Being in the same building, the Chamber staff provides a wide variety of informal technical services for RBOC; and the Executive Vice President, Worth Holder, serves as a key liaison with the business community. That informal liaison is further assisted by the fact that several members of the Executive Committee of the Chamber sit on the RBOC Board.

Corporate Organization

RBOC is structured as a nonprofit membership corporation with no stock issued. Contributions to it are tax deductible as "business expenses," and an affiliated organization—the Rochester Opportunities Foundation, Inc.—has been set up in order that gifts to it from churches, foundations, and other charitable institutions will be tax deductible under New York law. The RBOC charter has purposely been drawn in a flexible manner so that the Corporation could act as a Section 502 development company or as a Small Business Investment Company under the Small Business Administration Law, and thereby take advantage of federal financial assistance.

Capitalization of the Corporation has been directed by a Finance Committee under C. Peter McColough, President of Xerox Corporation. An initial operating budget and loan fund was fixed at $250,000.00, then a formula was worked out to raise that sum from Rochester's major businesses based on a company contribution of $2.00 for each of its employees. A letter of solicitation from Mr. McColough was sent out on April 3, and each RBOC trustee was assigned three or four companies on which to follow up, using a simple pledge card . . . This solicitation had the important added effect of spreading the word about RBOC. News reports which accompanied the letter generated most of the applications RBOC received in the first six months.

PROGRAM OPERATION

Policy

RBOC serves both new and existing businesses in the inner city. Although a greater economic impact is typically achieved by establishing a new business with a substantial employment and sales potential, the Corporation feels it cannot ignore the "little man" who may have only a mom-and-pop kind of business. In every case, the idea is to produce a fully competitive business, and RBOC officials feel that their program could be damaged in the eyes of the Negro community if it is associated with business failures. The potential or existing entrepreneurs with whom the RBOC deals are certainly among the better educated and more skilled members of the Negro community. It is recognized that this program is no replacement for efforts—in areas such as education, jobs, and housing—which deal directly with the hard-core disadvantaged.

When evaluating a new business opportunity, whether suggested by someone coming in off the street or researched and developed by one of the major corporations, a flexible set of criteria is applied. Typically, the new business must (1) require small initial capital; (2) be labor intensive and have a low engineering content; (3) involve equipment which is not too technical for the kinds of inner-city people who hopefully will be employed; (4) be owned, operated, and staffed by Negroes; (5) be located in the inner city; (6) be able to start operations relatively soon (six to twelve months); and (7) offer a product or services which will have a broad potential market, including, if possible, the opportunity for industrial accounts which RBOC might arrange. There is no strict requirement that insisted businesses hire hard-core people, but that is certainly encouraged. As one businessman helped by RBOC put it, "I am aware that I have some special responsibilities."

There has been a conscious decision to handle press matters in a low-key fashion, issuing a release only when there is some particular accomplishment to announce. Company officials do not want to oversell the community or raise false expectations concerning what they know will be a long-term project.

Forms of Assistance

RBOC assistance takes four principal forms: (1) financial aid; (2) technical assistance and advisory services; (3) purchase commitments by established corporations for products of assisted businesses; and (4) research and development of new business opportunities.

FINANCIAL AID

RBOC provides financial help to its clients both from its own resources and by helping to arrange bank and SBA loans. From its own capital, the Corporation makes or participates in loans, loan guarantees, and equity investments. Its loans may be for plant, equipment, or working capital and are subordinated to those of other lenders, even to the SBA. Its interest charges are generally set at the going commercial rate. Typically, its equity investments will be given in situations where the owner of a new business does not, himself, have capital of his own; the Corporation would "close the equity gap" by buying stock sufficient to give the new business something approaching a proper investment base. RBOC officials are talking about working out arrangements, in appropriate cases, whereby the Corporation can pass the stock it acquires in a business on to the employees of the business in order to broaden the community stake in the enterprise. The Corporation also helps arrange business and personal insurance protection for inner-city entrepreneurs.

Most often, RBOC will try to arrange a package financing plan involving itself, a bank, the SBA, and, where possible, the individual businessman. By equity investment, technical assistance, and industrial purchases of the borrower's products, RBOC provides the kind of underpinning that allows Rochester's banks to take on these higher risk loans.

One banker identified as the most important element in RBOC the tie-in of major corporations with the future of the assisted business—that these major companies, with established national reputations, had put their prestige on the line and would not allow the borrowers to fail. It is not planned, however, to ask any of the major firms which work with RBOC to provide direct loan or other financial guarantees to assisted businesses. Whatever may be the implicit corporate backup, loan guarantees stand on RBOC's own capital resources.

The involvement of local banks, by having bank presidents on the RBOC board and through close staff relations with RBOC, is crucial. The banks now provide the personnel to do basic financial analysis and to package loans with the SBA. The attitude of local bankers is important—they do not feel that they are being asked to make bad loans, many of which will fail, but rather to take on certain higher risks which are going to be made to work.

In most cases, loans will be given at existing interest rates. The departure from usual practice is that these loans are being made at all, when better prospects are available, and that they are made for longer terms than is commonly allowed. Moreover, it is broadly agreed that the efforts of RBOC have led banks to do more on their own with inner-city clients, where RBOC is not involved.

TECHNICAL ASSISTANCE

Advisory and technical services of two basic types are provided on a continuing basis to assist businesses. On the one hand, by working through the Rochester Chamber and existing businesses, and by contacting professional groups like the Harvard Business Club and the CPA Association, RBOC has compiled a large list of volunteers who can be brought in on a case. The SBA management counseling program known as SCORE, using the volunteer services of retired businessmen, is also available. If anything, there are more such volunteers than can now be used. For some of these volunteers, such as CPA's, it is expected that the initial relationship with an assisted businessman can grow into a paying client arrangement later on.

Somewhat broader technical assistance is given new business opportunities which have been researched and developed by a major company like Eastman Kodak or Xerox.

For example, in the case of a plastics products company, Kodak did the basic feasibility studies and is now providing in its own facilities the technical training on plastics molding to the owner-operator of the business (who was formerly a chemist at Kodak). In this case, Kodak and the new businessman involved have planned an entire course of technical and business training which Kodak will provide free of charge. The trainee is paid a salary during this process by his own company, which has already been funded and has working capital, although it is not yet operating.

In another case, where the Rochester Urban League is sponsoring the formation of a new business which Kodak researched, the School of Business Administration of the University of Rochester is providing some of the business training.

PURCHASE COMMITMENTS FOR PRODUCTS

An innovative type of assistance which is being provided through RBOC is the arrangement of industrial and other purchasing accounts for the products and services of assisted businesses. This kind of guaranteed market for a new or existing business is often the key to getting a project going. Over time, however, the assisted business is expected to branch out to other purchasers, some of which RBOC may help him find.

In many cases, the industrial purchaser will provide technical assistance to the supplier which acts as a kind of quality control for the purchaser. The purchasing arrangements are based on competitive prices—if any subsidy is involved, it comes through the provision of free technical assistance from the purchaser or RBOC to the producer which allows him to absorb higher start-up costs without sacrificing competitive pricing.

RESEARCH IN NEW BUSINESS OPPORTUNITIES

Thus far, all the established corporations represented on the RBOC Board of Trustees have been asked to examine their purchasing requirements to find possible markets for inner-city suppliers, and most of the new business opportunities developed by these corporations have been based on such a potential purchasing arrangement. RBOC plans shortly to set up a marketing committee which will distribute to the established business community a list of the products and services offered by RBOC-assisted firms, in an effort to further strengthen the market for these firms.

Operating Procedures

Since RBOC presently has a staff of only three persons—including John Blake, his accounting-trained assistant, and a secretary—much of the actual case work is done on a volunteer basis by participating businesses and banks.

For applicants who come in for assistance on their own initiative—the referrals and "walk-ins"—RBOC staff does an initial feasibility check, often with the help of volunteer CPA's. After this basic data is prepared, the case is referred to the Business Development Committee of the Board of Trustees for a weeding-out process. Typically, the case will be assigned to a member of the Board, who, using the resources of his own firm as necessary, will do a more sophisticated analysis and market study. The Negro members of the Board of Trustees are particularly useful in providing information at this stage on the reliability of the applicant and on business conditions in the inner city.

Cases which pass this initial muster, together with the new business ideas which have been developed by established corporations, are then passed on to the Appraisal and Investment Committee where a further separation takes place and from which a project is taken to the banks for funding. These procedures are highly flexible and are varied on a case-to-case basis as the situation demands. . . .

Community and Government Relations

RBOC's community contacts and relations have developed informally and by word of mouth. The only "formal" link with the inner-city community is through the membership on the Board of Trustees of several inner-city businessmen who are, themselves, involved with a number of community service groups. Through these men, and as a result of several newspaper stories which have appeared in the local press, the word has gotten around about the availability of RBOC services.

While no formal ties have been established with community groups, referrals are coming in from the local Urban League and the Human Relations Council; a meeting with local antipoverty agency officials is planned, although RBOC officials already feel they have as much business as they can handle.

Perhaps because of the lack of a formal liaison with community groups, some elements—notably the FIGHT Organization—are said to feel that RBOC is a creature and tool of the big corporations. FIGHT would prefer a community development corporation which is inner-city owned and managed and which serves to establish larger manufacturing eneterprises which were employee-owned, but thus far FIGHT has not actively opposed RBOC projects.

In fact, FIGHT and the Xerox Corporation in July invited RBOC to participate in establishing a manufacturing company which is being funded in major part by a federal grant under the JOBS (MA-3) program of the Department of Labor. . . .

Governmental involvement at the state or local levels has been virtually nonexistent, and seems unnecessary. The federal government, through the SBA, has been involved as a partner in many of the financing arrangements worked out by RBOC, and an SBA field representative spends one day a week in Rochester working with RBOC clients and referrals (he also spends a second day in the Rochester Chamber working with the public at large). University involvement has thus far been relatively slight, and could probably be expanded.

PROGRAM EVALUATION

Key Factors in Success

The single greatest success factor in the RBOC equation has undoubtedly been the participation of the business community, including its leading figures, from the very outset. These men have brought their own prestige—and the reputations and resources of their companies—into the effort in a sufficiently massive way to allow RBOC to overcome its problems as they come along. Particularly important in this regard have been the willingness of top business figures to take a leading rather than a supporting role, and their willingness to deal with RBOC affairs themselves rather than delegating problems and attendance at meetings to company subordinates.

A second key factor is the use of the corporate purchasing device which provides the inner-city businessman with a sure market during the initial start-up period and helps him to get bank financing. This device is particularly effective where it is coupled with a kind of on-the-job training for the entrepreneur in the plant of his purchaser-sponsor. This gives the purchaser a built-in quality control and offers the new operator a type of intimate technical and management training that probably cannot be duplicated by the use of volunteers on the basis of a few hours a week.

Other key factors enumerated by different participants are: the involvement of inner-city businessmen on the Board who evaluate applicants and ideas on the basis of direct experience; the fast start which RBOC got by using initial donations to complete action on several cases within a few weeks of opening its doors (this was thought to have convinced the Negro and business communities that RBOC was a serious effort and to have helped in the solicitation of funds); the large resources of volunteers willing to provide technical assistance; and a press policy of not overplaying initial results or of soliciting applicants before the Corporation was ready for them. . . .

One problem which has already arisen is the difficulty in finding capable inner-city people with the basic qualifications to become entrepreneurs. There are probably more business ideas than eligible businessmen at this point, and training efforts may have to be intensified.

NOTE

1. Aerojet-General Manufacturing Company, Los Angeles, Calif., formed a subsidiary called Watts Manufacturing in the Watts district of Los Angeles. The new company employs over 200 residents to make tents and other easily assembled equipment for military purposes. Unskilled, unemployed persons are hired without regard to previous police records. They are trained in basic skills necessary for production.

69
Restoration: A Profile of Economic Development

ALVIN N. PURYEAR

In recent months, there has been increasing discussion and debate on the most meaningful ways to fully assimilate minority groups—Negroes, Puerto Ricans, American Indians and Mexican Americans—into the American Economic System. Such phrases as "Black Capitalism," "A Piece of the Action," "Economic Self-Determination," and "Inner City Economic Development" are familiar to anyone who has even a passing interest in the problems now facing America. In the discussion that follows, we will examine one of the most effective economic development programs in the country. We will also look at the role which graduate business students might play in this economic development effort.

Among Ghettometrians there is some question as to whether the Bedford-Stuyvesant section of Brooklyn, New York, is the country's largest ghetto or *only* number two after Chicago's South Side. In any case, it is certainly one of the nation's most depressed areas as is illustrated by the following statistics. Crowded within Bedford-Stuyvesant's 600 blocks, which stretch over nine square miles, are approximately 425,000 persons, a population which would place it among the thirty most populous cities in the nation. Ninety-two per cent of its residents are black or Puerto Rican. Its infant mortality rate is nearly twice that of the national average. The area's juvenile delinquency rate is double that of New York City. Seven out of ten children of high school age drop out before graduation. Unemployment and underemployment total about 27 per cent. Nearly one-third of the area's families live on annual incomes of $3,000 or less.

Despite this desolation, there is very real basis for hope. In Bedford-Stuyvesant a substantial number of the residents live on tree-lined streets in solidly constructed two or three story brownstones, originally built as private dwellings by homeowners. Furthermore, the home ownership rate in the area is remarkably high, thus increasing the potential for the area's reconstruction.

Into this depressed community came the late Senator Robert F. Kennedy in February, 1966. Although he was appalled by the area's physical deterioration and social disorganization, he, too, appreciated the potential for improvement which characterized the community. However, to some residents

---

From *The MBA* (February, 1969), © by MBA Enterprises, Inc.

he represented just one more in a long procession of politicians who walked through their misery into the headlines of the nation's newspapers. Undeterred by such negative responses, he returned in December and announced that the area was to become the testing ground for a bold experiment in community rejuvenation. The people of Bedford-Stuyvesant, in concert with political and business leaders, would guide and control a massive attack on their own economic, social and environmental ills. By May, 1967, the program, backed by New York Senator Jacob Javits and New York City Mayor John Lindsay, was in operation.

IMPLEMENTATION OF THE PLAN

The method for implementation of the task is in itself unique. Directing this urban redevelopment effort are two nonprofit corporations: The Bedford-Stuyvesant Restoration Corporation (Restoration) and the Bedford-Stuyvesant Development and Services Corporation (D & S). Restoration, whose twenty-six board members are local residents, is headed by former deputy police commissioner Franklin A. Thomas, a life-long resident of Bedford-Stuyvesant. *This community-based group initiates and directs all projects and programs.* D & S, whose twelve man board is drawn from the nation's business establishment, is directed by John Doar, former assistant attorney general of the civil rights division of the Department of Justice. The D & S Corporation provides important supportive services to the Restoration Corporation. Both corporations are financed by public and private funds.

In addition to its Economic Development Program, which we will examine shortly, Restoration has developed several other programs over the last eighteen months. Among these are: a *Home Improvement Program* to renovate dwellings throughout the community; a *Vocational Training and Job Placement Program* for the hard-core unemployed; *Neighborhood Restoration Centers* which inform residents about community opportunities; a *Home Mortgage Pool* for insured loans to purchase or remodel one-to-four-family homes; a *Superblock* city plan which creates islands of open space in overcrowded streets; and a *Television Series* which carries news and interviews with residents and local celebrities.

REBUILDING THE ECONOMIC BASE

Restoration's initial programs were designed to provide visible progress to the community. Frustrated by too many unfulfilled promises, residents of areas like Bedford-Stuyvesant usually insist upon and best respond to programs which show quick, tangible results. In anticipation of such demands, Restoration devoted its first major efforts to housing, community centers, employment, and other areas which would have high visibility, clearly recognized successes, and immediate rewards to a broad cross-section of the community.

In July, 1968, Restoration began its Economic Development Program which has three objectives. First Restoration encourages the development and expansion of business enterprises which are owned and operated by residents of the community. This phase of the operation might be described as "Black Capitalism." Second, and of equal importance, Restoration offers management assistance designed to contribute to the operating efficiency of the local businesses. It is in this area that the program may make its greatest contribution to the economic health of the community, for management assistance is predicated on the belief that the difficult task is not financing the business, but maintaining its existence. Third, Restoration encourages enterprises outside of Bedford-Stuyvesant to move part or all of their operations into the area and provide meaningful job opportunities for local residents at every level within the enterprise. During the program's first six months, it was imperative that the bulk of the resources be directed toward the implementation of its first two objectives, local business development and management assistance. What does an analysis of Restoration's implementation of these objectives reveal?

LOCAL BUSINESS DEVELOPMENT

This aspect of the program emphasizes the establishment and expansion of business enterprises owned and operated largely by local residents. The philosophy supporting this approach is that any move at improving a community's economic base must include the development of the residents' undernourished pride of ownership. For pride of ownership is a basic part of the American economic system. While non-residents may occasionally receive aid under local business development, such aid must clearly benefit the residents of Bedford-Stuyvesant.

Restoration began hiring staff for its Economic Development component in July, 1968, and by the end of the year, the staff had assisted twenty-five businesses in various aspects of their operations. Of the twenty-five, twelve can be classified as manufacturing, seven as retail and six as service establishments. With respect to financial aid, Restoration provided loans of approximately one million dollars to these businesses; of great importance, its contributions stimulated banks and private investors to provide a nearly equal amount of capital. It is safe to say that few economic development programs in the country can match these figures in terms of number of businesses or dollar investment over a comparable period of time. Furthermore, Restoration expects to assist another twenty to twenty-five firms over the first six months of 1969.

An important aspect of Restoration's program is that in almost all of its ventures it encourages the participation of the private sector, particularly commercial banks. Traditionally, banks have looked unfavorably upon the "soft" loan market that characterizes the ghetto. At the same time minority groups have never approached the banking community with the confidence that their requests will receive fair treatment. While Restoration desires to stretch its financial resources, this consideration is not as important as the local businessman establishing continuous relationship with banks. To this end, Restoration has aggressively tried to convince banks to make their resources available to clients whom both Restoration *and* the bank see as reasonably good risks. The success of this effort is illustrated by five cases in which the bank's financial participation *exceeds* that of Restoration.

Another aspect of this Economic Development effort is that it encourages the entrepreneur to initiate skill job training for the hard-core unemployed of the area. To induce participation Restoration reduces part of each businessman's financial obligation as he provides job training. To assist enterprises in establishing job training programs, Restoration employed Barry Lemieux, a Harvard-educated development and training specialist, to direct its efforts in this field. The assisted firms expect to employ approximately 550 new employees when fully operational, the majority of whom will be trainees from the hard-core unemployed.

Much of the success of Restoration's local business development effort can be traced directly to its administration by a Bedford-Stuyvesant resident, Richard J. Easton. Like all of Restoration's programs, Economic Development is staffed largely by local residents. For Restoration, early in its history, saw the advantage of employing local professional talent to meet the needs of local people.

MANAGEMENT ASSISTANCE

Restoration feels that the creation and expansion of locally owned businesses are really not unique features of Economic Development. Rather, it believes that any such program can assist in the development of business enterprises if it has the proper staffing of persons trained in such fields as economics, accounting and management, effective contact with financial institutions, and a good working relationship with the community. Instead, the more important task is to provide the means for insuring that local businesses will maintain their existence and grow into financially sound firms able to pump dollars and job opportunities into the community. It is to this very important end that Restoration directs its Management Assistance effort.

Recently many organizations throughout the country have started to stress "management assistance" thus illustrating the importance placed upon the task of helping the minority group entrepreneur to become a successful businessman. This stress on management assistance is a further reminder that a disturbingly high proportion of *all* new business ventures fail in their formative years. The minority group business owner not only faces the normal problems of the small businessman, but carries the added stigma of being black or Puerto Rican. This greatly increases his chances of early failure because of limited financing sources, the inability to serve the broader spectrum of consumers, or racial prejudice.

While Restoration agrees that there is a need for management assistance, its approach in meeting this need differs from those of many other organizations. The dominant view seems to be that management assistance can best be accomplished through a system of volunteers, usually from outside the affected community. While volunteers can play a very effective role in assisting local business development, Restoration questions whether they should be the primary instrument for assistance. In this regard, Restoration uses volunteers and consultants as a secondary source of aid with the ultimate responsibility resting with its own staff.

Restoration's rationale for taking this approach is that the volunteer's time is limited by his other interests. This is true of the majority of volunteers: interested businessmen, retired businessmen, and students, particularly those enrolled in graduate business schools. The chief problem with businessmen volunteers is their necessary preoccupation with their own business careers. Retired businessmen, at first glance, would appear to be a very valuable source of volunteer help. However, the chief limitation of many such men is that much of their involvement is with leisure time activities. Finally, students represent, potentially, an excellent supply of volunteers. However, they face the demands of teachers whose academic and training interests are not necessarily in keeping with the needs of disadvantaged entrepreneurs. Also because students have examinations, papers, and vacations, they often disappear, leaving the client wondering about the degree of their committment. This writer feels that even with these limitations, however, students, and particularly graduate business students, can play a vital role in this effort, a point we will examine later.

Restoration has found a second problem with volunteers as the main source of management assistance. Often minority businessmen do not relate well to this type of "outside" and often paternalistic aid. Such help is sometimes given in a tone of correction rather than assistance toward jointly held goals. These negative feelings are further reinforced by "generalist" volunteers who are often unable to help the businessmen with his immediate problems. Cases can be cited where well-meaning businessmen have attempted to assist businesses involved in such specialized areas as trucking, furniture manufacturing, or shoe repair. Yet while these volunteers are often speaking in general terms, the local businessmen are starved for help in such important and relevant areas as promoting sales, locating skilled talent, or meeting debts. The need for general business assistance can probably be well documented. However, economic development programs should not rely solely on volunteer workers who may not have the necessary skills to meet the particular needs of a businessman.

If not volunteers, then, what? Restoration's answer to this question is unique, in that it decided not to use a "canned" program which might have worked for others. Under the direction of Thomas Greene and Levi Pace, who joined Restoration directly from two large industrial firms, it adopted a "contact man" system for its management assistance activity. In this system each client (businessman) is assigned to a Restoration contact man who is given full responsibility for helping that client until a successful business operation is established.

The contact man is expected to provide a wide range of services to the client. These usually start with assisting the client in preparing a request for funds from Restoration and other lending institutions. Typically, the contact man then assists the client in coordinating Restoration's and the client's activities with a bank, obtaining a business location, and selecting equipment and machinery. In effect, he provides any service which might help a businessman starting or expanding an operation. Once the doors of the business are open, the contact man must increase his efforts. For it is then his responsibility to insure that this enterprise will be a success and add to the economic development of the community. Obviously, the contact man, regardless of his skills, cannot be a jack-of-all-trades and must often go outside of Restoration to seek specialized skills. However, under this approach, even outside assistance, whether from volunteers or paid consultants, is secured under the direction of the contact man.

Because Restoration deals with *individuals* and not with minority groups (an important distinction) every aspect of management assistance is tailored to the needs of that individual and his business. The determining factor is the contact man's evaluation of the client's needs and his using all available resources to meet those needs. These might vary from something as simple as arranging a refresher accounting course to the hiring of a consultant to evaluating a special problem of the client. Restoration's dedication to management assistance is best exemplified by a staff motto: "If we lose a business, we should lose our jobs."

Restoration realizes that even with management assistance through the best efforts of the contact man, there is always the possibility of a business failure. When a business fails it is imperative that the contact man be able to document the reasons for its failure. That is, the contact man must continually evaluate a business, its operations, its management and its market, and record these findings in periodic progress reports. Careful documentation of business failures will often prove quite valuable since it is through analysis of these failures that Restoration hopes to find clues to prevent future failures.

RESTORATION AND THE GRADUATE BUSINESS STUDENT

Graduate business students often ask "Why should I assist in an economic development program?" There are at least two views which explain why graduate business students should feel some responsibility in this area. The first view is related to an observation of Alexis De Tocqueville. He saw that whenever Americans found some problem which afflicted an individual or the community, they—these Americans of the nineteenth century—would rush in to fill the breech. The community would organize itself to replace a burned down barn, to build a schoolhouse or to provide for older persons left alone in the world. It was the lingering characteristic of the American that he would attempt to solve the problem without waiting for a directive from centralized authority. Therefore, if this one American characteristic of helping people voluntarily is still alive and if graduate business students are sensitive to it, then they should feel an obligation to help the disadvantaged community businessmen.

A second and more radical view of why graduate business students might assist is related to the belief that this generation's prosperity is based on the capital accumulations of exploitive past generations. That is, much of this capital accumulation resulted from the wage slavery and the black slavery of the eighteenth and nineteenth centuries. Regardless of this theory's validity, certainly the disadvantaged minority community still feels that while it works the white, or majority, community reaps the benefits. It is probably safe to assume that few graduate business students have any guilt feelings for the past outrages against a sizable portion of this nation's people. However, graduate business students might feel that it is part of their present civic and business responsibilities to assist the minority community.

There remains the question of how graduate business students can assist the economic development programs of organizations like Restoration. Already ruled out is the possibility of graduate business students independently practicing their skills on Restoration's clients. For Restoration believes that the student's many talents can be utilized through a Restoration representative (contact man) rather than through directly approaching the local businessman.

The experiences of a group of graduate business students who were working in New York City are an example of how Restoration's system works. Initially, these students' interest had been in providing consulting services to Restoration's clients. However, an analysis of their resources, including the obviously limiting factor that most attended schools outside of the New York City area, convinced them that their best contribution could be made not as business consultants, but rather in a manner prescribed by Restoration. Therefore, under the leadership of Jerry Clayes, a second-year graduate student from the business school at Notre Dame University, and the guidance of a Restoration staff member, these students assisted substantially in the development of Restoration's very effective management assistance program.

If one accepts the thesis that all volunteers should be used under the guidance of a specialist, then the role of such volunteers is clear. They should offer their services to the professional agency which can best make use of their talents, and not directly to the client. Using and encouraging this approach, Restoration has been extremely successful with its volunteers, both students and businessmen. For they are first screened and then utilized in the way that makes the best use of their talents for Restoration, the client, and the volunteer.

One final point should be made on the role of the graduate business student in this environment. Many graduate business schools now permit students to take a one semester leave of absence to gain business experience through full-time employment. Schools and students might be wise to explore the possibility of making available to students similar large blocks of free time to engage in economic development activities. Certainly one vehicle for doing this is through established programs like Restoration's where students' talents can be directed for the best results for the student and the client.

Is it worth three or four months of a student's time to work full-time in such a program? Yes. For certainly the student will learn from such an experience. He will learn more about the problems of the city and the problems of the small businessman. And since he will probably become a specialist in a corporate giant, this may be his last opportunity to grapple directly with the multivariant problems of the city and small business. In addition to learning, he will also contribute his services to solving one of the major problems afflicting our society. To borrow from Restoration's Management Assistance motto: "If we lose the ghettoes, we lose the cities. If we lose the cities, we lose the country." We cannot afford this loss.

Part VIII BUSINESS AND THE FUTURE OF THE CITIES

What role business will play in solving the problems plaguing our cities depends largely on the manner and extent to which business corporations reconstitute themselves to perform social functions markedly different from those they have performed in the past, and the manner and extent to which government stimulates and supports business in performing a new role. The opinions as to what business can and should do vary markedly. We return to some of the same issues encountered in Part I, as to the nature of business's interest in social problems such as the cities present.

70
The Younger Generation

ELI GOLDSTON
President, Eastern Gas and Fuel Associates

The older generation concentrated on solving its priority problems of world stability and domestic productivity. But, in doing so, its technology and automation blighted the environment and left pools of poverty, particularly among our black population. Now, the younger generation, rather than crediting their elders for preserving world stability and creating domestic productivity, merely blames them for the consequences of large-scale industrialization and calls for immediate improvements in social justice and life's quality. I can remember the happiness in the steel-mill town where I grew up when the men were called back to work in the mid-1930's. We were delighted to see smoke belching from the blast furnaces, open hearths, and Bessemer converters. We really were not sorry to see agonized fish leap out of the waters of the Mahoning River as its pollution was resumed from the waste products of reactivitated pickling pits.

My children and yours want something more than a busy and productive plant. They want an attractive structure which is a good neighbor to its environment. They want the present employees to be paid generously for work which is not only safe but fulfilling. And they want the unemployed, particularly the Negroes, to be introduced immediately into the work force on all levels and, of course, without dismissing, demoting, or even disturbing those already there. If we don't meet these priorities, then many of the younger generation won't work for us, won't permit their churches and schools to invest in us, won't buy our products, and may even decide to occupy our offices. Since the population bulge indicates that the younger generation already outnumbers us and soon will outvote us, we had better pay some attention to these demands.

From Remarks at a Conference on Management and Man in the Computer Age: The Moral Imperative, sponsored by the National Industrial Conference Board, Nov. 14, 1968.

71

Nongovernmental Leadership

JOHN W. GARDNER
Chairman, The Urban Coalition

In our pluralistic society, a great deal of the analytical skill, executive talent, and dynamic leadership necessary to make our society function exists outside government—in the corporate world, in the professional world, in the universities, and elsewhere. A lot of the decisions that centrally affect the life of the community are made outside local government. If it is to be a coherent community, there must be some means of bringing all these segments of the private sector into some kind of sensible dialogue with one another and with the public sector.

In the past, American cities were not without coherence. There was such a thing as an Establishment, in the sense of a more or less comprehensive system of power. The city was held together—perhaps by the first families, perhaps by an old-fashioned political machine, perhaps by the dominant industry. But in most American cities the Establishment has disappeared. And where it remains it is not usually considered an acceptable solution to the problem of governing. So the typical city today is in fragments.

I saw this at first hand when, as Secretary of Health, Education, and Welfare, I had to visit all of our major cities—and many not so major. I found that the typical American city was split up into a variety of different worlds that were often wholly out of touch with one another. The suburbs were out of touch with the central city. Business, labor, and the universities were three wholly separate worlds—as far apart as worlds can be. City Hall was usually out of touch with the ghetto and often out of touch with the ablest and most influential people in the city. Is it surprising that cities so fragmented have great difficulty in solving their problems and great difficulty in even formulating their problems?

The Urban Coalition was formed to cope with the fragmentation, so let me talk briefly about the Coalition. After the riots of 1967, a group of outstanding leaders in American life came together to form the Coalition. The members of the Steering Committee included mayors such as John Lindsay of New York and Jerome Cavanagh of Detroit, business leaders such as Henry Ford and David Rockefeller, labor leaders such as George Meany and Walter Reuther, leaders from the black community and religious leaders.

From an address before the 73rd Congress of American Industry, sponsored by the National Association of Manufacturers, December 4, 1968.

I would emphasize the importance of the coalition principle. We bring together segments of American life that do not normally collaborate in the solution of public problems. Because of the need for such collaboration at the local level, our national organization set out immediately to form local coalitions. We now have thirty-nine. As in the case of the national organization, each local organization includes representatives from a variety of leadership segments in the community—the mayor, business, labor, minority groups and religion. And we encourage the participation of other relevant elements: universities, schools, the press, professions.

The coalition principle requires that minority groups be represented in the effort to solve community problems. And such representation is itself a step toward solving the toughest problem of all: effective dialogue between minority communities and the dominant elements in the city. The problems the local coalitions turn to are fairly predictable. They turn to the things that worry them the most: unemployment, housing, education, race conflict, black entrepreneurship, police-community relations, and so on.

I will not burden you with a discussion of the achievements of the locals, but they have gotten into an extraordinary variety of activities. They have formed venture capital corporations to assist black businesses, launched significant housing ventures, supported important new educational activities such as the Street Academies, set up youth councils, tackled local problems of race conflict, and so on.

How does the Urban Coalition—local or national—differ from other organizations? First, we are not sponsored by one constituency. We are not a businessman's organization, nor a governmental organization, nor a minority-group organization. Our sponsoring constituency includes all significant elements in the community.

Second, we do not focus on a single problem—unemployment, race conflict, good government, welfare—but are concerned with the whole range of problems.

It is precisely this comprehensiveness of constituencies and functions that is our greatest strength, but it also makes it hard for people to understand our role. In this society, everyone is keyed to specialization. When Americans become concerned about the community, they typically join with others of their own group (for example, businessmen with businessmen) to form a special-purpose organization. And this is fine. But the special-purpose organizations proliferate endlessly and still there is no organization designed to pull the whole fragmented community together—until an urban coalition is formed. A fragmented community cannot eliminate the senseless duplication of functions and agencies. An effectively functioning urban coalition can help the community correct that problem.

If the American city cannot pull itself together under local leadership in and out of government, cooperating voluntarily, the federal government will move in and coordinate it from outside. For at least two years there has been talk in Washington of a federal czar for each city. The implications for local autonomy need not be elaborated. There is every incentive for the city to pull itself together voluntarily. And the local coalition can provide the forum in which all of the various elements of the city can accomplish that pulling together.

This larger goal is infinitely more important than all of the specific projects that local coalitions undertake. It is a goal that can never be accomplished by the innumerable single-purpose organizations concerned with employment, education, discrimination, and so on. Nor can it be accomplished in a city that is paralyzed by the rifts described earlier. . . . Once the significant elements in the community begin to work together, once they begin to think as a community and act as a community, all kinds of things are possible. Then they can give city government the kind of intelligent support it needs; they can make the needs of their city felt at the state and federal levels; they can see how all the various federal, state, and local programs fit together; they can provide strong citizen support for federal programs that are working and strong citizen criticism of those that are not working.

Surely you understand the gravity of the problems facing our cities. You have seen the decay of the city's physical plant, you have breathed the polluted air, you have been caught in the snarled traffic, you have read the crime and narcotics statistics, you know of the breakdown in the schools, in the supply of housing, in the delivery of health services, and in the city's fiscal affairs. Any one of these problems can be understood as the product of special circumstances. But taken all together they reflect one powerful reality: most of our cities have lost command of themselves and their future. They cannot appraise their problems. They cannot act to solve their problems. They stand helpless as their future is determined by the multiple, uncoordinated federal programs, trends in migration, the uncontained hostilities of warring groups within the community, or empty circumstance.

To solve the problems of the cities, to reverse the trend toward chaos, to re-create livable and governable communities will be a gigantic task. The worst thing we can do is to dabble with the problems, nibbling around the edges with a little job program here, a little training program for dropouts there, telling ourselves what worthy things we're doing. If we have sense enough to see the enormity of the problems, then we will address ourselves first to the fragmentation and paralysis that are presently making our cities incapable of solving *any* of their problems effectively.

Let me conclude with a word on the role of business. First, a compliment: Of all the various worlds the Coalition deals with—universities, unions, professions, minority communities, local governments—none has been more active and enthusiastic than the world of business. We have received excellent financial support from major corporations. Our national steering committee includes some of the most distinguished names in American business, and they are active participants. In our local coalitions, outstanding business leaders, such as Stephen Keating of Minneapolis Honeywell, have made all the difference in the vitality of the local operations. So my chief message to you is one of thanks.

If I had to give you a word of advice, I think I would bypass the question of what your corporation is doing on such matters as the hiring of the hardcore, and address myself to you as individuals. And I would urge you to interest yourselves—as individuals, mind you—in the workings of your society—your community, your state, your nation. How does it work? How ought it to work? Where is it headed? This great nation was not put together by professors of public administration. It was put together by a planter named Washington, a printer named Franklin, a lawyer named Jefferson, a banker named Morris and others of varied occupations who had made themselves experts in statecraft in order to found a nation. Is it not ironical that very few of our most talented, able, and distinguished Americans today have been guided by that great tradition? Our communities and the nation show the marks of that neglect.

It is characteristic of our system that a great deal of the significant leadership in our society lies outside of government. But today that nongovernmental leadership is rarely an effective voice in the larger issues facing our society. That can and must be remedied. We need, outside of government, an effective body of leaders, local as well as national, who are committed to preserve the vitality and stability of the community, despite the ups and downs of partisan conflict.

Our society has become so complex, change so swift, and the social forces impinging on us so tumultuous that it is almost more than we can manage. If we are to retain any command at all over our own future, the ablest people we have in every field must give thought to the largest problems of the nation. And they do not have to be in government to do so! But they do have to come out of the trenches of their own specialties and look at the whole battlefield!

The nation is in serious trouble. The moment has come for every American to ask, "What can I do?" I recognize that in a society so huge, so populous, and so complex, it is almost impossible to believe that one man can do anything. But if we accept this conclusion, then we become dropouts and defeated men, even though we sit on all the important committees and show up regularly for our golf foursome. If we accept this conclusion, the whole idea of a self-governing society falls apart.

72
The Social Environment of Private Enterprise

NEIL W. CHAMBERLAIN

Perhaps the most striking characteristic of contemporary business is its environment. We have become so accustomed to referring to the atmosphere of persisting pressure and constant challenge surrounding business today that we sometimes take it for granted, as though it had always been there. And of course from one point of view that is correct. Businessmen in every time and place have had to face competition. In a system of free private enterprise, as we view ourselves, competition comes from rival producers. In other systems, whether characterizing an earlier period in the West or present societies under collective control, privileged charters or monopoly positions were or are subject to competition more political than economic, but it remains competition nonetheless, from those who are seeking ways of undercutting an enterprise's temporary advantage.

The pressures on business today are something different from, or in addition to, these kinds of rivalries which take place within a given and familiar social and economic framework. The challenge comes from the necessity of adapting to changes in the social system itself. These adaptations are in part responses to circumstances and phenomena which are changing in an unpremeditated or uncontrolled manner, such as an expanding population or scientific discoveries. But they are also *precipitated* by people who have a different vision of the future and who initiate—through instrumentalities, both private and public—actions which are *intended* to remold the institutions around us.

Obviously I am not speaking of apocalyptic visions or ideological agents. I am talking about people who, whether in business, government or universities, see a potential for improving some aspect of society and who have the temerity, if you will, to believe that they can make the potential a reality. And enough of whom are successful enough to create, for us all, a necessity for constant adaptation, an unrelenting pressure to adjust to frequent and major changes.

Perhaps we in this country are somewhat more accustomed to change than in other more tradition-oriented societies, so that these remarks will be met with indifference. We have had a history of rapid introduction and improve-

From an Address before the American Management Association Annual Personnel Conference, February 6, 1967.

ment of technological processes, for example. Professor Elting Morison of M.I.T., in a recent book, has emphasized the rapidity with which the steel industry developed in this country. What he calls the "American approach" was given concrete expression in "the steady development of bigger machines and labor saving devices" and less concretely in "the prevailing attitude, in what the nineteenth century called 'hustle.' " Morison recounts the story of a British traveler who was so awed by the size and complexity of one of the major steel producers of the 1880's that he opined he would like nothing better than to sit down on an ingot and watch all day, to which one of the company executives retorted that "he would have to go back to England to find an ingot that had been left alone long enough to cool off enough for sitting purposes." The same sense of rapid, forceful change has characterized, at least at one time or another, our transportation companies, both carriers and manufacturers, our coal and oil producers, and our electrical manufacturers, and we could extend the list considerably.

The rapidity of technological change and product innovation is still part of the pressure exerted on business enterprises, forcing them to adapt or become extinct. Indeed, the pace has accelerated in recent years. I will not dwell on the speed with which new technical developments are now occurring—that is too familiar a story to warrant retelling. Let me simply urge the point on your imaginations by asking you, taking a single example, whether there is any doubt in your mind that some form of battery-powered automobile will replace the present version within, say, ten or fifteen years. What tremendous effects that development will have on innumerable companies! Or to bring the point closer to home, reflect for a moment how firmly you believe that your own company will, ten years from now, still be producing the product on which it now chiefly relies, or, if producing it, will be producing it by techniques even roughly comparable to those it now employs. And what changes this will imply for the conduct of your company's affairs.

But the pressures of change to which I first referred are not primarily of a technical or product nature. Partly because the successes of science have induced in us a sense of achievability and partly because of heightened sensibilities to the potentials of change, advanced societies today almost take for granted that we can, if we put our minds to it, solve our major *social* problems by appropriate application of resources. We need only to will the result enough to make the effort. And so, for the last decade or two, we have begun to view our social blights, such as urban slums, agricultural peonage, bad housing, poor health, the destitution of classes like the unemployed and the aged, and even racial intolerance, not as some inevitable human condition but as problems which lend themselves to solutions.

Our confidence is based not on raw optimism or blind faith, but grounded on a conviction that scientific analysis will open doors that have remained shut to previous generations. René Dubos, of Rockefeller University, who is known for his philosophical writings as well as for his scientific achievements in microbiology and experimental pathology, has asserted quite flatly: "Now it can be said that it is possible to achieve almost anything we want—so great is the effectiveness of technology based on the experimental method."

This sense of the perfectability of society into which we have only recently come has not only infected our scientists, educators, dreamers, and poets, but has also gotten into the bloodstream of business, which is beginning to feel heady at the prospect of social reform for a profit. Defense contracts, the designing of immense road systems, space programs, and other similar activities of a type which were relatively easy to accept as a natural basis for business collaboration with government were the "pilot projects" which attuned management to the realization that its product line could include social betterment. And this development is likely to prove a more profound perpetrator of change than any previous forms of business rivalry and even than our already developed sense of the possibility of increasing material productivity. We have suddenly entered on an era when it is the business entrepreneur rather than the utopian who is becoming infatuated with the possibilities of redesigning cities, reorganizing transportation networks, improving educational methods, and expanding recreational facilities.

I do not intend to bestow all credit on business managers for a newly heightened imagination with respect to these concerns. Government officials and academicians were there first. I have stressed the business role in part . . . because it is peculiarly strategic. In the realization of the new social goals, while government must often take the initiative, business must often supply the organizational capacity to effect what is wanted. The consequence has been that we have moved more and more in the direction of blurring the line between what is public and what is private, and have become bolder in experimenting with new organizational forms mingling elements of both—a Comsat Corporation, contractor relationships for specific enterprises ranging from supersonic planes to high-speed railways, agencies like the Atomic Energy Commission and NASA whose function is less to regulate than to coordinate.

We are still so little a distance into this new territory that a great deal of exploration will be going on for a long time. One thing is evident, however —that initiative in such undertakings can come from private business as well as from government. Society in its organized form, that is, as represented by governmental bodies, has become a major and lucrative market whose appetite can be aroused by appropriate corporate investment in specialized research and development and by appropriate marketing tactics.

How does a business firm operate within this kaleidoscopic context? One requirement it is having to come to grips with is a new sense of timing, which involves not only extending its time horizon (something about which we often hear) in order to lay the groundwork now for projects of a protracted nature, but also accelerating the pace at which new developments, once brought about, are reduced to routines and exploited as fully and as quickly as possible before further changes pass them by. This heightened sense of timing has encouraged the spread of more formal and sophisticated planning procedures, which put dates on projected developments and allocate resources to their realization as needed.

Planning means something other than attempted prophecy; it means purpose. Perhaps this should be made plural, since it means very specific purposes, with a program for deploying the firm's organizational assets in order to carry off the projects specified. This means that the firm is not content simply to react to change. It must, of course, do that; but it also seeks, insofar as possible, to control the course of its own development by purposive forward planning.

What the firm does, society, through its several strata of government, also seeks to do. It sets goals for itself—very specific goals, dealing with a wide range of activities—and it seeks to exercise such control as it can to bring about the objectives specified. This is true of democratic as well as authoritarian governments, though the breadth of objectives and the extent of control placed in governmental hands differs markedly between the two forms.

Within a democratic society, government must rely more on persuasion and inducement to secure the kind of performance it must have from its business firms if it is to achieve its goals. Whether we are talking about urban redevelopment or transportation, worker training or improvement of the nation's health, the government of a democratic society can achieve what it wants principally by *inducing* private responses, not by commanding. While we can view business firms as national assets which must be redeployed in order to realize national goals, their redeployment comes chiefly by their consent. At the same time, this independence of the private firm has to be exercised within a social context, which is changing. And firms which fail to fit themselves into the social context and to exercise their initiative in ways compatible with social goals are almost certain to lose out on the rewards.

The spread of systems analysis has helped some management people to realize that not only does their own organization have to be looked at as an integrated unit, a system with its parts functioning in reasonably articulated fashion without too much leakage of overall corporate objectives through misuse of divisional discretion. It is also true that their firm is part of a larger social and economic system, perhaps not so tightly integrated but bonded together enough that they cannot pursue their own objectives independently of larger social goals. And further, management has begun to realize that their own welfare is at least partly tied up with bending their energies, imaginatively, to assist in both designing and realizing the overall social design.

By viewing itself within this systems context, a firm is assisted in its planning activity. And with specific reference to the interests which are uppermost in your minds—manpower planning and labor policy—these can proceed effectively only as a firm attempts to envision the social and economic context within which it will be operating not only next month, but five or ten years from next month. Only by taking a long-term view will a firm be able to plan intelligently in ways which help it to *control* its future rather than simply *react* to changes.

It is the importance of this vision of the future which I most emphasize—the imaginative capacity, the intellectual flexibility, and the managerial courage to look ahead and draw a picture of a society which you *know* will differ in important particulars from the society with which we are familiar today, and to take actions now which will prepare for the changes uncertainly foreseen. It is the capacity to look ahead to a future state which you *wish* to create, and to plot the steps which lead you to that state.

In addition to taking this longer view in order to tackle your company's problems more effectively, it is possible that imaginative analysis, within the area of your own specialization, may suggest programs with a larger social relevance. Conceivably these may have a marketable value, constituting something saleable to society. Even if not saleable, they may constitute approaches, not evasions, to social problems more compatible with business's own interests than the formulas emanating from other sources. Once we have accepted the notion of the perfectability of society, we can be sure that social ills will not long be left unattended, and it is likely to be to business's self-interest to advance prescriptions and methods which will do the job with the least disorientation of present relationships. Business cannot usually do this collectively; it will commonly have to come through the creative work in individual companies whose innovations may attract imitators.

• • •

I can readily imagine that a number of you will protest that social efforts are not business's function, just as a number of my academic friends insist that business should keep its influence out of such social interests. My own position is that we cannot do without the aid of our business institutions in effectuating the kinds of social goals we are now setting for ourselves. My own guess is that we are now in process of building an indigenous economic system which will cast our firms in a different and larger role than they now play. They will be employed more as instruments of social change. And any effort on the part of business to hold back from filling this new role may well mean its default and its relegation to a position of lesser importance in a society which increasingly believes in its own perfectibility.

73
Goals for Urban Development

LYLE C. FITCH
President, Institute of Public Administration

Given the volume of output of which the American economy is capable during the next thirty years, and given the rate of accumulation of knowledge and technological know-how, it would appear that we can, by the end of the century, reach levels of material abundance which few now even dream about. This possibility can be quickly dissipated, of course, by catastrophic war, by spending for other unproductive purposes; or it can be dissipated by outdated viewpoints and by obsolete social and governmental institutions.

At the risk of seeming to repeat old bromides, I urge that the best assurance we have of making good use of our promised abundance is to consider what use we should be making of it, and defining goals for our economic, social, and physical development. There is nothing wrong with the goal popularly ascribed to the typical middle-class college graduate—a secure job, a home in the suburbs, an agreeable wife, and several healthy children—but it will hardly suffice to produce the good urban life. It means nothing at all to the increasing number of people who can look forward to nothing better than living out their lives in the slums and ghettos, and it offers little challenge to many of our contemporary younger generation. It is also blithely innocent of the growing problems created by the pace of urban expansion and the tide of migration from the rural areas into core cities. Problems such as the following are already provoking wide protest and demands for more effective solutions.

1. Air pollution is already a serious menace to health in many cities; even more apparent is the economic cost of stench, airborne dirt, and chemical corrosion. Beginning with cleaning bills, the annual cost to the nation is reckoned in the billions of dollars.

2. Partly because of the extent of water pollution, large sections of the country are already threatened periodically with water shortages which at the least impair comfort and convenience (New York City had to struggle through much of the summer of 1965 short-rationed on air conditioning) and at most force the shutdown of industries. And a society increasingly oriented toward recreation finds some of its most important recreational resources (lakes, streams, and ocean beaches) preempted for use as sewers.

3. Uncoordinated, badly planned and inefficient transportation acts to

---

From *Urban America: Goals and Problems,* a compendium of materials compiled and prepared for the Subcommittee on Urban Affairs of the Joint Economic Committee on Congress (1967), pp. 20–41.

frustrate the economic rationale of cities, which is to reduce transportation and communication costs of satisfying economic wants. It has been a long while since technological innovation has contributed materially to improvement of urban transportation: automobiles, buses, and rail cars are essentially the same vehicles as they were a generation ago, even though mechanical improvements, air conditioning, and radios contribute to comfort.

4. The migration from southern rural areas to northern urban areas continues. The nation's twenty largest cities, in the period 1950–1965, gained 3.2 million nonwhite population while losing 1.2 million white. In several major cities nonwhites are a majority of the population or soon will be if present trends continue. They come to older core areas for the simple reason that core areas possess the obsolescent housing which is the only housing most of the immigrants can afford and, for Negroes, the only housing to which they will be admitted. Meanwhile, the unskilled and semiskilled jobs they might fill in manufacturing and other goods-handling industries have been moving to the suburbs.

5. With their spreading stocks of increasingly obsolescent buildings, many of the central cities begin to resemble the slagheaps of our urban civilization. Even in the great national and regional centers such as New York City, urban renewal, exuberant office buildings, and luxury housing have made no more than a dent on the miles of dreary outworn buildings.

6. The general shortage of housing at rents that low-income people can afford to pay (1) causes serious overcrowding and accelerated deterioration of the housing stock concerned, and (2) poses, in many cities, one of the great obstacles to slum clearance and urban renewal, since there is no way to locate people dispossessed by clearance. Millions of dwelling units are rated as substandard—seriously deficient in one or more respects. Housing construction techniques are still essentially those of a half-century ago, with only minor improvements, and the cost of housing and construction generally mounts disproportionately. Technology is further slowed by archaic building codes supported in turn by fearful labor unions and building supply manufacturers.

7. The costs of crime and delinquency increase geometrically with population growth, with a consequent decrease in the public's sense of security and enjoyment of life (how enjoy life when one's property, person, and very life are continuously under threat?).

Urban planners, administrators, and physical and social scientists have been pointing out other problems not yet so visible as to arouse wide public concern:

8. New suburban developments sprawl formlessly over the former countryside, with little consideration of efficient layout in such matters as relating work, residential and recreational centers, providing for open space (not only for recreation but also for hydrological and climatic control), or simply for preserving and creating beauty.

9. New central city construction repeats the monotonous and inefficient

patterns of the old, with buildings located and constructed without consideration of their function or relationships to other buildings, to transportation facilities, or to residential centers. The most fundamental principle of efficient traffic planning—separation of pedestrian and vehicular traffic—has been little observed. Grand Central Station, with its separation of motor vehicle, pedestrian, subway, and train traffic, and Rockefeller Center, with its grouping of buildings around a central plaza, were the last great innovations in New York City, but there has been little further use of the principles they employed.

10. New concepts of organization and management emphasizing systems approaches—extending the scope of planning and management control of an organization or a project to all the interrelated elements—have been too little applied to urban planning and management. One instance is the failure, until recently, to take account of the relationships between intraurban transportation networks and land-use development, or the essential interdependence of transportation modes.

11. Despite the proliferation of federal urban programs, the federal government thus far has contributed relatively little to urban development *per se*. Thus the amounts laid out for assistance to urban renewals, public housing, community facilities, open space, and pollution control have been largely offset by collections from various programs, mainly insurance premiums derived from housing finance programs. Net federal expenditures on housing and community development in the first six years of the 1960's were in the magnitude of $1.5 billion. Total expenditures on agricultural development and support programs over the same period amounted to some $28 billion; defense expenditures came to $385 billion.

WHAT DO PEOPLE WANT?

Let us accept the propositions that the major development task of the next few decades is raising the standards of urban life, and that without larger goals we shall not mobilize the collective effort necessary to realize our potential. Nonetheless, goals without political substance which can be translated into support at the ballot box are of no avail. So we ask, first, what does the public want enough to vote for and pay for? This question runs into the fact that there are many publics, which want different things. There are different economic classes and groups of different age and family characteristics, racial and ethnic groups, residents of central cities, of high-income suburbs and of low-income suburbs, to mention a few.

Interest in urban goals on the part of the groups trapped in poverty in the slum stems from deprivations about which these disadvantaged people (particularly the Negroes) are flaring into rebellion. (Whether the vintage 1967 riots have been incited by "agitators" is beside the point that gross deprivation makes fertile ground for rebellion.)

When we look behind the riots, the threats, and the other forms of protest, we find demands which on the face of things are entirely reasonable. People want employment opportunities, better housing, better educational facilities, better social environment beginning with neighborhoods free of violence, dope pushers, and vagrants. They want most of all to be treated as dignified human beings, not as inferiors. All of these things reflect existing middle-class values and middle-class opportunities. For the poverty class, wants are defined by what the majority of Americans already have, despite the offbeat values of the subcultures that tend to form in these groups.

Until recently the contemporary generation of poor have not been politically vigorous or articulate because of their low level of education and sense of alienation. They have tended to look to the welfare bureaucracies rather than to political organization for assistance in meeting pressing needs. Political machines and leaders, which once sought the support of the poor with welfare and other assistance, have been cultivating other constituencies, notably the lower middle class. In both central cities and suburbs, political control has tended to be dominated by the middle class, which demands less from government, rather than by the lower class which demands much, but this situation is changing as Negro and other minorities find strength to protest and numbers to gain political strength.

The working and lower middle classes typically have no great personal aspirations which they expect government, particularly urban government, to fulfill. For improvements in their general condition members of the working class tend to look to increased wages and to union organization. They tend not to seek improvement by upward movement, and lacking this motive for education and self-improvement they tend to resist being taxed for education and other public services. They are typical of the group of which Robert Wood has observed: "The great bulk of the urban population neither is conscious of its public needs nor anticipates that urban governments will fulfill them." [1] They particularly resist being taxed for welfare and other services to the poverty groups; we may confidently expect that this resistance will be further stiffened by the recent outbreaks of violence.

The higher echelons of the middle class also are oriented to the market but at the same time are prone to make more demands on government for better education (for which they depend heavily on the public sector) and for various urban services such as transportation, health services, recreation, and other utilities.

These groups are likely to be more keenly aware of the need for special services to the "disadvantaged" than are the working and lower middle classes. But frequently they escape the problem. Many of the middle class, along with the more affluent part of the working class, can and do move to the suburbs where they tend to encapsulate themselves in homogeneous communities walled off against incursion by the poor. (Scarsdale and Levittown are examples of wealthy and working-class suburbs in the New York City area.) Many have no alternative to suburban residence, for the costs of land and construction are tending to discourage the private sector from building residences on anything less than a luxury scale in central cities.

The upper-middle and upper-class groups have even wider choices—they can wall themselves off, more or less, from the city's unpleasantness if they choose to live in cities or, like the middle class, they can flee to suburbia or exurbia. In either case, they are likely to absolve themselves of any responsibility for the core city or its problems.

If this were all of the matter, urban development goals from those above the poverty class might well focus on continuing growth and high-level prosperity, which enable the gradual improvement of living standards over time, mainly through increased purchasing power to be spent in the bountiful market. Physical avoidance of the grosser urban problems, along with the fact that urban and suburban political leadership has been dominated by the middle class, helps to explain the weak response of so many urban governments to growing urban problems. Robert Wood has observed that, "The urban political process is not directly concerned with the provisions of goods and services except when these 'problem solving' activities can be translated into useful resources for the resolution of political conflict or its avoidance, or . . . outright failure of law and order seems imminent." [2] Moreover, various circumstances, of which one is perennial financial stringencies, another unimaginative leadership, and a third the lack of well-defined goals around which to mobilize consensus for positive action, have tended to magnify the power of the negative elements in the community.

The worm in the apple is that the kinds of problems listed above are impeding improvement of middle-class living standards and in part offsetting material gains. In many places some things are getting worse—we are sliding back from levels we had once attained. So while we as a society depend on rising incomes and the market for improvement and the things we want, we are forced to turn to collective action to eliminate things we don't want, such as congestion, pollution, crime and delinquency, and urban ugliness. But this is a negative concept of social action; I suggest that we can do better, and possibly avoid some of the problems which happen to us, if we give more thought to what we want our urban communities to be, say, by the end of the century. Here goals come into the picture.

I think there is increasing acceptance of the notion that national and community goals are essential tools of urban physical, social, and economic development.[3] Goals serve somewhat the same purpose in the public sphere that goods in the shop window serve in the market. They educate, arouse interest, and stimulate action, or support for action. Appreciation of this fact is manifested by political leaders and the public in such efforts as, for example, President Eisenhower's Goals Commission, White House conferences on national policy, and citizens' commissions on goals in a number of cities and metropolitan areas, including Dallas, Phoenix, the Twin Cities, and Los Angeles. The business community is taking interest in urban problems and urban goals; thus the Committee for Economic Development has organized a subcommittee on urban goals, in part for the purpose of lending guidance and support to community efforts.

Aspiration goals may spring from many sources: Existing dissatisfactions, the thinking of people in "leverage positions"—business and political leaders, professional specialists, and so on—and from technological and economic developments. Some aspiration goals stem from development of technical knowledge which makes possible their achievement. Probably the greatest triumph for United States social planning thus far in the twentieth century has been general acceptance, in a generation, of the goal of high-level employment and stabilization. The principal contributing factor was the development of a theory of economic control which would make possible achievement of this goal without unduly impinging on the free market in the process.

I do not think however, that goals can be formulated by taking public opinion polls. People in the large do not spend time pondering what they would like the society to achieve, any more than they spend time thinking of things they would like to have which haven't yet been invented. Goals, like consumer goods, have to be devised and marketed. Public opinion polls can inform the process of goalmaking but cannot substitute therefor. Goal formulation is the job of experts, primarily, and marketing goals is the job of community leadership.

Despite the forces of inertia which today keep so many urban communities in a swamp of mediocrity, some cities and metropolitan areas have developed a public spirit and forward thrust which demonstrate the latent potentialities of local leadership and local cooperation. Thus Pittsburgh cleans up smoke pollution and rebuilds the Golden Triangle; Philadelphia creates a Penn Center; the San Francisco Bay area undertakes to build a billion-dollar rapid transit system; New York City undertakes a broad reorganization of city government to equip it more adequately for the new responsibilities; and New Haven carries forward a wide-ranging program of urban renewal and human resources development. In some cases, the leadership comes from elected officials, in some from the business community, in some from civic organizations. Wide-ranging effective programs, however, usually necessitate the cooperation of all these elements, no matter what the initial source of leadership and ideas. To take one example, the Pittsburgh achievements were made possible by a working partnership between a group of the city's top business leaders, largely Republican, and the Democratic administration of Mayor Lawrence.

GOALS FOR URBAN POLICY

I suggest highest priority should go to two main goals which have already been accepted as objectives of national policy but which have thus far received less than overwhelming support.

The first goal is a decent level of living for all American families.

The other face of this goal is the abolition of dire poverty. I think there is little point in debating with the nitpickers who argue that some people will always be better off than others and that since poverty is only a relative concept we cannot abolish poverty short of absolute leveling. I am referring to poverty which brings hunger and physical discomfort, and social and moral degradation. I mean the poverty implied by the New York City welfare standard, one of the most *generous,* which allows nothing for culture, education, or entertainment (no newspapers, periodicals or books) and for children not even so much as an ice-cream cone per week.

Obviously the goal has many dimensions—it requires more emphasis than has thus far been accorded to factors making for individual productivity— good health, aspiration, and motivation; lifelong opportunities for education and training; jobs for everyone who wishes to work. It requires a national policy to provide adequately for those unable to work—the old, the young, the disabled. It necessitates more social innovation and experimentation with ways of providing decently for the economically stranded without spoiling the incentive to work.

The second goal is continuous improvement of the urban (and rural) environment—as to efficiency, convenience, safety, and attractiveness. Here again there are many dimensions, such as the following:

1. Offering a greater variety of ways of life and opportunities for choosing among them, such as a greater degree of choice as to where one lives and works, as between living in central cities or suburbs, as between living in homogeneous or heterogeneous communities.

2. Freedom from aggression, such as criminal aggression against person and property and such other environmental aggressions as noise, pollution, congestion, and ugliness.

3. Elevation of central cities to be attractive places to live, work, recreate and do business. In the past they have been conceived of largely as centers of commerce and industry, only incidentally as centers of culture and knowledge, and hardly at all as delightful places to live. Nowadays they are in danger of becoming dumping grounds for the socially and economically dispossessed.

4. Planning for metropolitan development outside central cities with specific concern for efficiency and esthetic appeal, orderly relationships between residential, employment, shopping, and other centers, and preservation of open space not only for recreation but also for ecological values.

RESOURCES FOR ACHIEVING URBAN GOALS

In discussing urban goals with businessmen and others, one invariably encounters the reservations, "Yes, but can we afford it?" and "We can't afford everything at once, what should come first?" These questions are pertinent, for even in the affluent society there are not sufficient resources to implement fully, and in a short period, the goals proposed here, including the patching up of defects already discussed. And we can be sure that new goals will suggest themselves, and that new defects will become apparent, as we go along.

If we take a longer view, however, and consider the last third of the twentieth century (1967–2000), the potentialities for goal implementation are enormous. The gross national product, despite several technical shortcomings, is still the best measure of available resources. The value of GNP in 1966 was $740 billion. The average annual growth rate in real GNP in the thirty-seven-year period, 1929–1966, was 3.2 per cent, and the aggregate GNP in that period, in 1966 dollars, was approximately $15 trillion. Assuming a growth rate of 3 per cent in the thirty-four-year period, 1966–2000, the aggregate GNP would be $42.5 trillion (1966 dollars). A 4 per cent growth rate, which many analysts think well within our capacity, would yield an aggregate GNP of $51.5 trillion. The difference, $9 trillion, is equivalent to about thirteen years' output at the 1966 rate. The astonishing magnitude of this difference underscores the importance of a high growth rate to all our other objectives.[4]

With a 4 per cent growth rate and an overall population increase of 40 per cent (the lower Census Bureau projection, which looks reasonable at present) we could accomplish the following by the year 2000:

1. Double average consumption per household. The goal of eliminating poverty would require that we move toward greater equality in consumption by increasing the consumption power of the lowest income groups proportionately more than that of the higher levels. This in turn depends in part on moving toward greater equality of productive capacity by labor force members and more generous income-maintenance programs for those not in the labor force.

2. Provide new dwelling units for all the new households, replace approximately three-fourths of present dwelling units, and provide second dwelling units for 25 per cent of households. Meanwhile, raise quality, as measured by real construction costs, by 50 per cent over 1966 levels.

3. Double, by 1975, the real expenditure on education per pupil while eliminating elementary and secondary school dropouts and expanding college enrollments by 50 per cent.

4. Triple the annual average expenditure, over the thirty-four-year period, on public facilities including transportation, water and sewer lines, recreational and cultural facilities, health centers, hospitals, and so on, with provision for such needs as improved pollution control, development and introduction of new transportation devices (separation of vehicular and pedestrian traffic, new transportation technologies), rapidly growing demands for recreation and culture, and generally higher standards of urban design.

5. Increase the rate of private domestic business investment, as a proportion of GNP, by approximately 50 per cent to allow for developing and introducing new technology, provide new types of consumer goods to meet public and private demand, reduce social costs hitherto imposed on the public (such as air pollution), and replace obsolete equipment.

TABLE 73-1 *Projected Demands on Gross National Product, 1966–2000*

	TRILLIONS
Consumption	$27.2
Housing	1.6
Education	4.4
Urban public facilities	2.0
Business investment (plant and equipment)	7.7
Federal government:	
Defense	2.2
Other	1.2
State and local government (excluding education and public facilities)	3.1
Foreign balance, and unallocated	2.1
Total	51.5 *

* Projections for a population increasing to 280,000,000, with a 4 per cent annual growth rate in GNP.

6. Increase annual federal government nondefense purchases by an average of 4 per cent per year.[5]

7. Increase state and local government purchases for purposes other than public facilities and education by about 4 per cent per year.[6]

Table 73–1 shows the aggregate amounts of gross national product that would be absorbed by these various quantitative objectives in the period 1966–2000.

While a 4 per cent growth rate would supply the demands as projected in Table 73–1, a 3 per cent growth rate would fall $9 trillion short of meeting these projected demands; they would have to be reduced in some degree. But up to a point, lower levels of expenditure on such items as private domestic investment and human resources development (particularly education and training) themselves dampen the gross national product growth rate.[7] Various other assumptions, such as a larger population increase, would somewhat change the detail of the above projection but would not alter the main point: that the nation has the power to achieve within the foreseeable future the goals proposed above, if we measure achievement by present standards. Of course, by the end of the century standards will have greatly risen and we will have new and higher goals.

URBAN PUBLIC POLICY AND URBAN GOVERNMENT

I hold that in the last analysis the impetus for improvement in any urban community must come chiefly from the community itself. Federal and state governments can provide financial and other assistance and a certain amount of stimulation, but only with lively local leadership and citizen participation can a community realize more than a fraction of its potential. Moreover, there are many values and goals which only vigorous urban governments can achieve.

One of the most important objectives is variety and experimentation, along with flexibility in meeting local requirements in ways appropriate to local traditions and conditions. The need for variety and experimentation stems partly from the fact that there is no consensus among urban planners or other urban experts as to what constitutes an ideal city in size, configuration, transportation systems, and other components of urban design. Some experts believe that further deconcentration and lower densities, made possible by the ongoing revolution in communications technology, are the wave of the future; other experts, exemplified by the new housing panel of HUD's 1966 conference on technology at Woods Hole, call for greater densities to facilitate communication and reduce the cost of transportation and other utilities, and promote multiple uses of land devoted to urban purposes.

Many communities have great but unmobilized resources for attacking their own problems, including resources in the private sector which could be put to work on applications of technology and other matters if there were a way of creating the demand therefor. But most urban governments are always fighting holding actions against accumulations of past deficiencies and unforeseen developments. With financial resources perennially strained, there is little left for innovation except in response to major crises. Recently, most innovation has been stimulated by the federal government and by federal grants for housing and redevelopment, highway construction, antipoverty programs, and health and education.

Urban governments are handicapped also by structure. Most are built around the traditional service functions for which they were responsible in the nineteenth century—protection, regulation, health, sanitation, sewage disposal, and some aspects of transportation, education, and various utility services.

Beginning in the depression and continuing at an accelerated pace after World War II, urban governments began perforce to assume additional responsibilities having to do with the physical and economically disabled, with economic development, urban redevelopment and renewal, poverty, and new kinds of relationships with federal and state governments having to do with all of these.

Urban governments have not yet digested these new responsibilities, which tend to be lodged in newly created authorities and special agencies such as housing and redevelopment authorities. Thus the new functions have tended to remain outside the mainstream of planning and decision-making, though intrinsically they are as important to community welfare and as imbedded in community politics as are the old-line service functions. (This fact is being impressed on many urban administrations by the often violent protests of large-city poverty groups against their own deprivation and misery and the inability of the community to supply them with decent housing and amenities or with jobs.)

Many systems of logically related functions cut across traditional departmental lines. For instance, it is now clear that the effective education of children from lower culture home environments may require, in addition to education, the combined resources of welfare, health, police, housing, and other departments which in practice are seldom to be found working together on coordinated programs. Development of efficient urban transportation systems has been impeded by the fact that numerous facilities and controls having to do with the movement of people and goods—private motor vehicles, bus, rail transit, traffic controls, parking facilities and controls, toll and fare systems, and so on—tend to be lodged in many different, uncoordinated agencies.

And finally, the systems way of thinking has long since informed us that some types of urban services cannot be efficiently provided or provided at all by governments of less than metropolitan scale. Transportation, water supply, air and water pollution control, and efficient land-use planning are prime examples.

Commenting on the deficiencies of local governments, the Committee for Economic Development's recent policy statements on *Modernizing Local Government* makes the following observations:

> Few local governments are large enough—in population, area, or taxable resources—to apply modern methods in solving current and future problems. Even the largest cities find their major problems insoluble because of limits on their geographic areas, their taxable resources, and their legal powers.
>
> Overlapping layers of local governments abound—municipalities, townships, school districts, special districts—which in certain areas may number 10 or more. They may all have the power to tax the same land, but frequently no one of them has the power to deal with specific urban problems.
>
> Public control of local governments is ineffective or sporadic, public interest in local politics is lagging. Contributing factors are the confusion resulting from the many-layered system, profusion of elective officers without policy significance, and increasing mobility of the population.
>
> Personnel are notoriously weak. Low prestige of municipal service, low pay scales, and lack of knowledge or appreciation of professional qualifications all handicap the administrative process.

State governments by and large (there are exceptions) have a long history of unresponsiveness to needs created by urban growth, central city obsolescence, migrations from rural to urban areas, and the demands for more services. The Advisory Commission on Intergovernmental Relations in a report of March, 1967, comments that only a handful of states have moved to meet the problems of their urban areas and that state governments are on the verge of losing control over the mounting problems of central city deterioration and the rapid growth of urban areas.[8] Professor Roscoe Martin observes that while states are critical "of the growing practice of direct dealing between

Washington and the cities, which they regard both as a perversion of the federal system and a pointed threat to state sovereignty" the states themselves have displayed little interest in taking action.[9]

PLANNING MACHINERY

By now, most large cities and many metropolitan regions have planning agencies, but these tend to concentrate on certain aspects of physical planning such as the location of highways, water and sewer lines, and other public facilities, and on administering zoning controls and subdivision regulations. Most city planning agencies lack resources to develop new concepts and designs for helping their communities find their way in the future. But such basic work is essential to the goal-making process; without it there is no adequate basis for informing public opinion or stimulating political and other community leaders to push for betterment.

Few are staffed to take full advantage of federal grants now available or to prepare first-rate model cities programs. Little is done to relate planning for commercial and industrial improvement to the needs of slum dwellers. The planning for development of human resources which goes on is generally confined to specialized agencies—education, welfare, and so forth—which deal only with pieces of the problem.

Lacking adequate planning machinery, urban governments predictably will continue staggering from one crisis to the next, continually out of line with the demands of the times. In New York City alone more than a million people live in 40,000 old-law tenements that were outlawed and scheduled for demolition and replacement in 1905. Many more live in other substandard dwellings. The city planning agencies thus far have only nibbled at the problem: there is no grand strategy for providing decent housing for the city's residents in the foreseeable future. And there is even less consideration given to solving the problem arising from the fact that, as in many large cities, the unskilled and low-skilled population congregates in the core while many of the jobs they might fill locate in the suburbs. I do not know how many jobs in the region remain unfilled because of lack of access to people who might fill them, but the figure in Chicago a couple of years ago was put at 35,000.

State planning agencies have been under the same handicaps as urban agencies and (with few exceptions) have had little impact on the course of urban and metropolitan development. The state highway departments, which do substantially affect metropolitan development, have been largely oblivious to planning values not immediately related to moving motor vehicles.

State and urban governments, then, have done little basic planning and introduced little innovation—their bureaucracies and political officials have been resistant to change. Most of the recent spurt of planning activity in these fields has been fostered and financially assisted by the federal government; for instance, through the workable program and other planning requirements posed as conditions for federal aid.

INTERGOVERNMENTAL COOPERATION

The remarkable development since 1930 of federal, state and local cooperation—in education, highways, urban redevelopment and renewal, health, housing, poverty and other areas—has served to motivate state and local governments to do things they would not otherwise have done, and to raise administrative and technical standards. The response to federal grant programs, demonstrated most recently by the scores of applications for model city programs, shows that money is still the best incentive and most powerful energizer in the public as well as the private sector of the enterprise system.

I think that testimony by urban officials before the Congress within the past year has made clear that in their view the leading difficulty with federal programs is not simply with red tape and complexity but with the fact that most are still grossly underfinanced. The urban development goals I have suggested imply much higher levels of federal grants whereby urban governments take advantage of the federal government's superiority as a revenue collector.

If we accept the premises (1) that the primary responsibility for setting and implementing urban goals must rest on the individual cities and metropolitan areas; (2) that most urban communities can marshall more intellectual and economic resources to solve their problems than they have thus far; (3) that urban (and state) governments need to be modernized and better equipped to handle their responsibilities; but (4) that in the urban political arena the forces of inertia tend to outweigh the forces for innovation, I think federal support is justified for state and local innovation in governmental and political arrangements as well as programs. And I believe that encouragement and assistance to urban (and state) governments to improve planning and administrative machinery are better than trying to control every detail of federal grant programs through minute regulations and supervision.

AGENDA FOR MODERNIZING STATE AND LOCAL GOVERNMENT MACHINERY

If states are to participate more effectively in urban development, most need substantial reorganization and reform of administration, planning, and budgeting systems. Here I draw upon the Committee for Economic Development's recently published policy statement *Modernizing State Government* (1967), which lists the following needed reforms:

> Abolition of quasi-independent administrative boards and commissions (frequently they have earmarked funds), insulated from any responsibility for state welfare as a whole.
>
> Concomitantly, centering administrative responsibility in the office of the Governor, and equipping the office with planning, budgeting, and administrative expertise.

Limitation of legislative responsibility to matters of broad policy and budget approval; abolition of legislative budgets and exercise of administrative powers by legislatures or by individual legislators.

Comprehensive merit personnel systems.

Comprehensive budgets covering all funds and expenditure categories; preferably based on program budget concepts (these have been notably unsuccessful thus far for reasons having little to do with their intrinsic merits).

Strict conflict-of-interest laws.

Constitutional provisions affording maximum latitude to local governments which meet reasonable standards of adequacy.

In *Modernizing Local Government,* CED presents an agenda for local government reform which includes:

Reduction in number of local governments by at least 80 per cent, and severe curtailment of overlapping layers of local government ("townships and most types of special districts are obvious targets for elimination").

Limitation of popular election to members of legislative bodies and the chief executive in the "strong mayor" type of municipal government.

A single strong executive: elected mayor or city manager.

Modern personnel systems.

Use of county, or combinations of county, jurisdictions to attack metropolitan problems.

Use of federal (and state) grants-in-aid to encourage local governments administrative reforms, particularly reforms having to do with consolidation and organization to meet metropolitan problems.

A FEDERAL ROLE IN STATE AND LOCAL GOVERNMENT MODERNIZATION?

Although I favor, and consider inevitable, much larger federal grants for urban development and improvement, I am equally concerned about the ability of state and urban governments to make good use thereof. For this reason I have reservations about the formula of the Heller plan distribution of a "national dividend" (a fraction of the annual increase in national output) through the medium of per capita grants to state governments. If federal tax machinery provides the wherewithal for a "national dividend," would it not be profligate to use federal funds simply to bolster up existing inadequate and archaic institutions? If we are going to depend, as I think we should and must, on the decisionmaking and innovational capacities of state and local governments, should we not seek to improve those capacities?

The Congress has attached conditions for administration and performance to many grants, going back at least to the 1930's when state unemployment insurance agencies were required to be under civil service. A few other instances include the design and construction standards required of federal-aid highways; the requirement that federal-aid highways in urban areas of more than 50,000 population be based on a continuing comprehensive planning process carried on cooperatively by state and local agencies; the requirement of general state plans for hospital development as a condition for federal grants for hospital construction; the provision of more general grants for water pollution control under metropolitan wide plans, as opposed to purely local jurisdiction projects; the requirement for comprehensive community planning and the submission of community "workable plans" as conditions of urban renewal grants; the requirement that federal aid community development projects shall be reviewed by metropolitan agencies designated "to the greatest practicable extent" by elected local officials.

While few such stipulations have wrought wonders, many of them have wrought improvements. For example, while many "workable plans" submitted in support of urban renewal applications have been rudimentary and the provisions of many have not been complied with, the requirements have made urban governments more aware of the elements of urban renewal and of the necessity for professional planning than they otherwise would have been.

The instances cited above all relate to specific grant-in-aid programs. Is it possible to establish general standards for planning and administration as a condition of per capita grants or other general grants? Admittedly the task of administering such requirements would be difficult. There is first the job of devising criteria for acceptable standards of administrative organization. Next there is the job of evaluating state and local governments to determine whether they meet established criteria. Inevitably there would be protests from offended state and local interests and congressional protests against adverse rulings.

One possible formula is that set forth in the bill introduced in the House of Representatives by Congressman Henry S. Reuss of Wisconsin in January, 1967. Under the Reuss bill, block grants would be made conditional upon the submission by states of acceptable programs of government modernization; the review and evaluation bodies would be regional coordinating committees and the United States Advisory Commission on Intergovernmental Relations, which would certify as eligible programs reflecting "sufficient stated creative initiative so as to qualify that state for federal block grants." Among the items suggested for consideration in drawing up such programs are: (1) arrangements for dealing with interstate regional, including metropolitan, problems; (2) strengthening and modernizing state governments; (3) strengthening and modernizing local, rural, urban, and metropolitan governments; and (4) proposed uses of federal block grants, including provisions for passing on at least 50 per cent to local governments.

Any general formula that might be established should be related to administrative standards already imposed by other federal grants-in-aid. This leads to the point that the federal government itself is not a model of organization, least of all with respect to urban programs. The scores of urban-oriented programs and grants administered by the Departments of Housing and Urban Development; Labor; Commerce; Transportation; Interior; Health, Education, and Welfare; the Office of Economic Opportunity; Army Engineers; and General Services Administration, and others; still suffer from a lack of centralized planning and direction. Down below, state and local governments are handicapped by the number of, and administrative requirements imposed under, the federal programs ostensibly established to spur, not hog-tie, local initiative. Several coordinating devices established in the last few years have made little impact, and the situation overall is little changed from what it was a decade ago. Obviously more muscular measures, of which several variants have been proposed, are needed.

The prospect of the urban concentrations of the year 2000, as described by the urban land institute, poses still further questions of administrative organization. Two of the great megalopolitan areas projected will be contained within the boundaries of single states (California and Florida), but the metropolitan belts around the Great Lakes and along the east coast will encompass a dozen or more states. Aspects of many of the problems now plaguing metropolitan areas, such as water supply, air and water pollution control, and transportation, will be transferred to the larger areas of the future. The states offer the only organizational building blocks below the federal level for coping with megalopolitan-scale problems. In some cases, they may be able to organize into regional blocks (as through the device of interstate compacts) for dealing with interstate megalopolitan problems. An interesting possible precedent is offered by the Delaware Valley Authority compact encompassing the States of New York, New Jersey, Delaware, and Pennsylvania with the federal government as an equal partner. This may be the megalopolitan counterpart of the emerging federations of municipal governments at the metropolitan level.

I should say at least a word about personnel to man planning and administrative posts in urban governments as well as urban program posts in federal and state governments. This is, of course, the resource in shortest supply. There are, for instance, no more than a handful of people who can direct the preparations of a first-rate model cities program application. It is no secret that New York City, despite the attractions offered by a reorganization of city agencies along modern program lines, relatively high salaries, and vigorous chief executive, has had great difficulty in finding competent people for top staff positions in the human resources administration, housing and development administration, and transportation administration, not to mention posts in the top staff agencies.

In the long run, the shortage of personnel trained for modern urban planning and administration will be alleviated only if the universities assume responsibility for attracting and training many more people, and if urban governments become more aware of the nature of their manpower needs and show a willingness to compete for talent. In the short run, federal assistance for training urban planners and administrators, as in programs backed by Senator Muskie and others, would help to break the logjam.

FOSTERING LARGE-SCALE INNOVATION

There is wide agreement that problems of urban improvement offer the greatest challenge (outside the field of national defense) to innovators of our time. It is offensive to our general notions of progress that many aspects of urban life, for many people, are not improving while some are retrogressing. The lack of progress has a disproportionate impact on people lowest in the income and cultural scale, but no participants in urban life remain unaffected by deterioration somewhere. Everyone endures the irritations of poor transportation and traffic congestion, air and water pollution, noise, lack of recreation facilities, crime and delinquency, and the ugliness of the urbanscape.

The main point is not whether things are better or worse than they formerly were, however, but whether research resources of modern social and physical science and technology have been utilized to the maximum practical extent in the solution of urban problems. The consensus of most physical scientists and engineers, and social scientists, is that they have not been and are not.

Technology, we are assured, can provide means for achieving more efficient, more beautiful, more livable cities. But the engineers, scientists, and designers complain that they have not been given the opportunity to demonstrate what they can do to improve urban environment. This is hardly surprising, because there is little demand for their talent, and there is little demand because much of technology's potential is on the drawing board or in the conceptual or preconceptual stages. (By contrast, the consumer products sold by the private sector are already in existence and are promoted with all the resources of modern advertising.) The politicians and the public can hardly be blamed for failing to demand what does not exist. Somewhat analogous factors impede organizational and political innovation, as illustrated by the slowness to develop machinery for coping with metropolitan-scale problems.

As already implied, technological innovations must depend upon organizational and political innovations, and in many cases innovations in the social sciences as well. So-called systems approaches are an attempt to assemble in packages all the necessary components of solutions to particular problems—thus an urban transportation system involves demographic, economic, physical design, financial, political, organizational, and other policies, all of which depend upon the particular technological approaches selected.

Most of the significant innovations having to do with urban improvement have been stimulated not by state and local governments but by the federal government (sometimes, but sometimes not, pushed by urban government interests). But with the exception of the highway program, the amount spent by the federal government systematically to stimulate urban improvements has been insignificant compared to expenditures for agricultural improvement and support, or for space programs.

OBJECTIVES AND INCENTIVES

Experience thus far indicates that more resources and energy can be mobilized if there are defined generally accepted objectives, and incentives for pursuing them. Four cases are in point:

1. The urban development and renewal programs have been utilized by many cities with some failures but with some notable successes. In the process there has been a great conceptual development (more significant than the physical development that has occurred thus far), and a great improvement in planning standards and in the number and quality of planners employed.

2. The space effort has demonstrated the potential of technology organized under a public program, with the participation of both public and private sectors.

3. The war on poverty has mobilized a great national effort, again with the participation of both public and private sectors.

4. The competition for the site of the proposed giant (200 to 300 Bev) nuclear particle accelerator, involving a construction cost of several hundred million dollars and an annual payroll of some $60 million, drew in all the major regions and many individual states and localities in the United States, who spent millions of dollars preparing their cases.

All of these programs have in common (1) clearly defined objectives and (2) large prizes in the form of federal funds for programs which would galvanize the public sector and furnish incentives for the participation of the private sector. All have in common also the fact that though the objectives were clearly defined the means of achieving them were still to be worked on at the time of their initiation—technological approaches had still to be developed.

A difficulty with most federal urban improvement programs is that they never concentrate enough resources in any one place to demonstrate what an adequately financed "systems approach" can do in any particular field. The model cities (demonstration cities) program, which seeks to concentrate federal grants in limited areas of cities, will inevitably be handicapped by fiscal malnutrition as well as federal red tape; it will end up with some improvements in most areas, no doubt, but with nothing conclusively demonstrated. Much of our experience with federal grant programs recalls the experience of the 1930's with spending: when toe-in-the-water spending programs did not promptly produce full employment and an economic boom, government spending to create demand was written off by many as a failure until the very much larger spending of a defense-war demonstrated that the problem of the 1930's had been simply one of inadequate scale.

I suggest that as soon as the military situation is resolved and federal funds are available, the federal government should make a number of substantial grants for urban improvements in a number of selected fields, each designed to produce a major impact. Project designs would employ systems approaches encompassing both technology (applied science, hardware design, etc.) and all the machinery necessary for planning, making decisions, and implementing the projects concerned. Following are some of the areas in which such large demonstration projects might be run:

1. A comprehensive, integrated intraurban transportation system such as exists nowhere at present.

2. A comprehensive, metropolitan areawide health and hospitals program.

3. A twenty-year housing development plan, taking into account not only the provision of decent housing to all families in the area but also (*a*) the efficient location of housing with respect to employment centers, (*b*) the probable rise in incomes and housing standards over the planning period, and (*c*) feasible approaches to geographic dispersion of minority groups.

4. A metropolitan area recreation development plan to make recreation facilities available to all inhabitants of the area on approximately equal terms.

5. A design for a new town or a system of new towns in a metropolitan area.

Any project for which a large-scale "innovation grant" is made should meet rigorous specifications. For example, the specifications for a transportation plan (transportation breakthroughs are particularly needed) might include the following:

1. The plan should encompass all forms of intraurban transportation—private motor vehicle, bus, rail transit, traffic controls, parking facilities, parking controls, tolls, fares, and fees (or as many of these as would be appropriate for the particular region). There should be provision for integration with interurban transportation facilities through such devices as integrating interstate and other highways into physical development plans, and efficient transportation links between air terminals and other points in the area.

2. A project development plan should encompass a period of twenty to twenty-five years. It should be constructed for maximum flexibility to meet future demographic and economic changes and to take advantage of unforeseen technological developments.

3. The plan-and-program should provide for continuous planning machinery capable of revising plans in accordance with experience gained in developing and operating the system and for keeping transportation and related planning up to date; decision-making machinery capable of taking necessary decisions for implementing various aspects of the transportation plan including highways, streets, parking facilities, bus transportation, traffic controls, and so on, and administrative apparatus. The elements of planning, decision-making and administrative machinery should be parts of the same "system," but each element should be constituted to meet the needs and changing institutional framework of the particular urban area.

4. The plan should also lay out the conventional requirements of a conventional intraurban transportation system in terms of capacity for movement of people and goods, and devise a preferred development plan for meeting

these requirements, with emphasis on employment of improved technologies.

5. The various systems should be integrated economically as well as organizationally, with each transportation mode bearing appropriate costs consistent with overall criteria laid down for the system. Economic specifications should be devised, first to guard against wasting resources on overelaborate or grandiose plans, but more important, to permit maximum freedom of consumer choice.

A transportation plan of the scope indicated would involve drastic changes in local government organization, arrangements between local governments, state highway departments, and the Federal Transportation Department. But the purpose of the innovation grant would be to stimulate this kind of political and organizational innovation as well as innovations in hardware. In this respect, the program would differ sharply from the usual federal grant program, which stays within the bounds of existing political frameworks so as to permit everybody to participate without undue strain.

COMPETITION FOR LARGE-SCALE INNOVATION GRANTS

The certainty that there would be intense competition among cities and metropolitan areas to be selected as recipients of large-scale innovation grants suggests that the grants be made through a series of national competitions and awards for best "plans-and-programs" dealing with various urban needs. The awards would be made, in any specified field, for the best plan and program to be submitted by a government or consortium of governments representing a metropolitan area. The plans submitted should meet specifications laid down, such as those suggested for an intraurban metropolitan transportation plan. To qualify for an award, the competing area should give evidence of its willingness and ability to make any necessary organizational changes.

Such a system of awards would, I suggest, have the advantage of attracting wide-scale attention and interest and of drawing a number of metropolitan areas into competition. The activities involved in competing, and coping with specifications of the kind described, would have a high educational value. The "losers" in each competition would benefit in many ways from the experience of competing. It is probable that meritorious plans which did not win awards would be eligible for federal assistance on a matching or other basis under federal programs that already exist or which would be enacted in the future. The competitions themselves, if successful, would furnish valuable guidance to the Congress in expanding the federal grant program.

Many details would have to be worked out, a few of which are considered here:

Selection Committees

Competition entries should be judged by panels of experts of national reputation in relevant fields, drawn from the universities, industry, and nonprofit institutions. Selection of panels to avoid any favoritism or political influence would be of highest importance in realizing the objectives of the competition. (Experience with the selection of the site for the new accelerator indicates that a certain amount of controversy would be inevitable in any case.)

Financing Research and Planning

Preparation of plans and programs of the scale contemplated would involve, for most communities and most functions, heavy expenditures on research and promotion. Referring again to transportation as an example, preparing an integrated plan and program would entail coordinated work of demographers, economists, city planners, traffic engineers, highway engineers, specialists in urban technology, political scientists, specialists in finance and administration. New hardware (as new types of transportation vehicles) might need to be developed to the point of demonstrating feasibility for purposes of submission as part of the plan. New political arrangements would require time-consuming negotiation, public education, and in some cases legislative action. Private firms should be drawn in. This suggests the possibility of setting up award competitions among private firms for development of various aspects of an overall plan and program, particularly aspects having to do with development of physical technology and systems design. Management consultant firms might be invited to enter competitions for plans for governmental reorganization, financing, and other matters within their competence. The device of competitions has already been successfully employed in several fields, notably architectural design and military and space hardware.

To help finance plan and program preparation, including competitions among private firms, the federal government, following established precedents, might make available research and planning funds for plan and program preparation—some funds already available under such legislation as section 701 of the Federal Housing Act, highway-related research funds provided under the Federal Highway Act, and funds for research on health, education, and various other urban-related activities.

Basically, research funds for award competitions should be part of a more general system of encouraging and assisting work on urban problems, just as the proposed awards system should be only one part of an expanded national effort for urban improvement.

Time Allowed for Plan Preparation

The time required for plan preparation would depend upon the subject matter of the particular competition. In the case of intraurban transportation plans, a period of three years is about the minimum for preparation of a major plan, and the kind of plans contemplated here are considerably more expansive than any undertaken to date. In addition to the preparation of plans per se, a considerable amount of negotiation and political engineering would be necessary to commit the community fairly definitely in advance to organizational and institutional changes. This suggests that transportation plans might require as long as three to four years for proper preparation and presentation. Other functions may require less time, and a few are likely to require more.

Amounts of Awards

One possibility is that the federal government meet the capital construction costs of award-winning plans. Where high operating expenses (or deficits) are likely to be a deterrent, the award might also cover operating expenses (or deficits) for a limited period of, say, five years.

One hundred per cent financing might not go a great distance beyond amounts already available for some kinds of projects, as two-thirds federal financing for development of urban mass transportation, two-thirds for urban redevelopment, 90 per cent for construction of interstate highways, and 50 per cent for primary highways, and various other federal matching grants. In many programs, a major limitation is appropriations rather than the percentage of federal matching.

The absence of any requirement for local matching under the award program would remove incentives for economy, but extravagance might be held in check by making economy one of the criteria for evaluation and by introducing appropriate pricing systems and other devices to make projects such as transportation, water supply, and so forth, more efficient from the economic standpoint.

The awards would have to be very large to produce innovations of the scale required, however. A transportation plan alone for a major metropolitan area might cost a billion dollars or more. But the amounts should be compared, not to what we have been accustomed to spending on urban improvement, but rather to (1) needs, (2) prospective resources as measured by our rising gross national product, and (3) what we are already spending for innovation in other fields, for example, military hardware, space, the SST, and so on.

It seems obvious that no competition could be devised that would cover urban areas as widely disparate as the New York metropolitan region at one end of the scale and, say, Lubbock, Tex., at the other. The kinds of problems confronting urban areas, and optimal solutions thereto, will vary greatly according to size, age, demographic characteristics, wealth, governmental, and

TABLE 73–2

CLASS	POPULATION
1	100,000 to 500,000
2	500,000 to 1,000,000
3	1,000,000 to 5,000,000
4	over 5,000,000

political traditions, and other factors. It therefore would be desirable to divide cities into classes for purposes of an awards program, as in Table 73–2.

Areas under 100,000 are not included: first, because of the large number of such areas; second, because their needs for innovation are generally less acute, and third, because it seems unlikely that they could contribute much of interest to larger areas. For such areas, it might be desirable to establish special awards, perhaps administered by state governments with financial help from the federal government and with competition on an intrastate rather than an interstate basis.

NOTES

1. "Contributions of Political Science to Urban Form," in Werner Z. Hirsch, ed., *Urban Life and Form* (Holt, Rinehart & Winston, Inc., 1963), pp. 108–109.
2. *Ibid.*, p. 107.
3. I distinguish between *aspiration goals, achievement goals,* and *performance goals.* My concern here is with *aspiration goals.*
4. I suggest that the aggregate national output will not be greatly affected by the rate of population increase, within the limits of the projections previously mentioned (the range is 80 to 160 million population increase by 2000). The reasons are as follows:

    (*a*) A larger population would require more funds for the support and education of the population differential, part of which alternatively could be expected to go into private and social capital formation. (On this point see Stephen Enke, "Economic Development Through Birth Control," *Challenge*, May–June 1967. While Enke's analysis is addressed primarily to less developed nations, it has also some relevance for the United States.)

    (*b*) Because the differential between high and low projections would all be borne (except for immigrants) between now and the year 2000, much of it will not be in the labor force by 2000; thus the labor force differential would be relatively much smaller than the population differential.

    (*c*) A relatively high proportion of the differential labor force would come from the low-income, low-culture groups; their productivity in the year 2000 almost certainly would be under average, no matter what we could do in the meantime.

    (*d*) Continued technological progress may keep on depleting the number of jobs for low- and semi-skilled workers, and might make part of the differential portion of the labor force redundant.
5. The crucial element in the federal account is defense-war purchases which were $60 billion in 1966 compared with $17 billion for nondefense purchases. Here I have optimistically projected defense-war purchases at an average of $65 billion a year (1966 prices) for the rest of the century.
6. This is the approximate increase rate in the 1960's, the period of most rapid recent growth.
7. Leonard Lecht's study for the National Planning Association, "Goals, Priorities, and Dollars (the Free Press, 1966), presents a somewhat more elaborate projection of the cost of meeting the main goals called for by the Eisenhower Goals Commission, in terms of the demands on GNP in 1970 and 1975. The amounts required to meet Lecht's projected demands total about 10 per cent more than the projected supply of GNP in 1975, assuming a GNP growth rate of 4 per cent. Lecht's projections differ from the ones presented here in that they apply only to selected single years.
8. Advisory Commission on Intergovernmental Relations, *Eighth Annual Report*, 1967.
9. Roscoe C. Martin, *The Cities and the Federal System* (New York: Atherton Press, 1965), ch. 6.

74

We Are the "Power" Group

IRWIN MILLER
Chairman, Cummins Engine Company

We live in a most remarkable time. For four years there has been almost no unemployment. Wages, even in real terms, are at an all time high. Health is generally the best we have known. Forty per cent of our youth are enrolled in higher education—a percentage four times as great as in Great Britain. Home building, auto production, and consumer goods are all being utilized by a broader segment of the population than ever in history. General public giving to good causes exceeds anything previously known. The list is very long, with each item a new achievement for the nation—for the whole race.

Why then am I assigned for this occasion the subject "Crises in American Life"? How can a period in which we have achieved nearly every one of man's ancient goals be also a period of unease and crisis? Yet it is, and you and I, who are better off than we ever imagined we might be, are nevertheless truly insecure and feel that we are under attack from many directions.

We are under attack from our workers (outrageous wage demands and constant threats of strike). Labor does not seem to understand that improved real wages can in the long run come only from increased productivity. We are under attack from our customers, who resist paying for our constantly increasing costs and steadily narrow our profit margins and hence our capacity to survive. We are under attack from government at every level—increased taxes, increased laws, increased regulations, increased interference. Why does not government understand that unhampered profitable operation of American business will produce more general good and more tax revenue than any other single thing?

We are attacked by our children. Money, jobs, and education come so much more easily to them than to previous generations that they set little value on them and at times appear even to despise them. Had they been forced to begin a career in the 1930's, as most of us did, they would realize the enormous worth of the opportunities which they now take for granted.

We are under attack from educators, who have the nerve to criticize business and at the same time tell businessmen it is their duty to support higher education in ever-increasing amounts.

We are under attack by the church; by the very nations we have helped

---

Address before the 73rd Congress of American Industry, sponsored by the National Association of Manufacturers, December 5, 1968.

most and who try hardest to imitate us; by minorities, who are better off here than in any other nation, and making more rapid progress. There seems to be no end to the list.

But we feel a very early end coming to our patience, to our capacity to persist, and to our good humor—if any still remains. The whole situation is so obviously unnecessary. It is clearly time to crack down, return to common sense, and, as was said so often in the recent campaign, restore orderly, sensible procedure to the society. We do not like the changes we see taking shape, and we feel called to oppose the worst of them insofar as we are able.

Do you know what we are doing? We are making the historic mistake of most powerful groups in history. We are identifying the welfare of the whole society with the peculiar state of affairs which works best for us. Consider the list: Loyalists in early New England, the French aristocracy in the eighteenth century, feudal lords in late Middle Ages, Southern slave owners in the nineteenth century, Spanish monarchy in the twentieth century. Each tried to stop the clock. Each thought they had the sensible answers in a senseless society. Each of these faced a crisis and failed to survive. Is there similarity between their cases and ours, or not?

• • •

It seems pretty clear, I think, that present programs to attack urban decay, school crowding, racial discrimination, lack of job opportunities, air and water pollution, transportation congestion are simply not even keeping us even. In each of these we suffer, month by month, a visible deterioration. The size of the effort required to reverse deterioration, to get for once on top of the problems, to reduce them to manageable proportions within a specified time is very great indeed. It may also be the alternative to catastrophe.

Such a specific national effort is not beyond our power. We have done it before on both larger and smaller scales. In the years of World War II we were willing to allocate half of the gross national product to defeating Germany and Japan. In the 1960's "landing on the moon by 1970" was such a program, and was the means of giving order and sense to the whole space program. A similarly explicit statement of the kind of country we aim to have in 1980, an organized systems approach to get there (with the federal government the "systems manager"), a means of measuring progress against the timetable adopted (for example, a biennial Deprivation Census), an initial massive (war-like) effort for perhaps three to five years (a short time in the life either of an individual or a nation), followed by a sustained effort to maintain the accelerated rate of advance—all these could quite possibly do the job, that is, avert the crisis and permit subsequent progress to keep pace with change. They could do the job in time and even preserve the value of the dollar. If any free nation were to address itself to such an effort during the years just ahead and accomplish its purposes with clarity and economy, it would offer to the rest of the world an example of incomparable leadership. . . .

Such a massive effort is beyond the reach of the federal government alone, in fact, beyond the reach of all governments (federal, state, and local) combined. This may well be the new lesson of our times. Government alone is not big enough to do the job. The character and number of our problems have changed. There are more problems, and they are bigger problems. They interact on each other. They affect everyone promptly and not certain areas only. Government must lead, but it cannot be the sole problem-solver. Its role is to define problems, articulate desired results, and organize, directly and indirectly, the whole potential of the society in a coordinated effort to remake the society and save it from destroying itself.

The potential outside the government is greater than the combined potentials of all our governments by an order of six to one—the potential to invest money, to educate, to provide jobs. The federal government can play the role of systems manager of the whole potential of the society both directly and indirectly. Of the two, its indirect function may be the more important.

Let us take money first, and let us look at taxes, which are government's source of income. Today any system of taxation is by definition a system of incentives. It cannot be otherwise. Individuals, business corporations, labor unions, banks, and investors—all study the system of taxes under which they operate to take maximum advantage of them. Their resultant plans are as often influenced by the potential advantages in the tax system, as by their own nontax purposes and objectives. When, therefore, the incentives in the existing system encourage the development of policies and acts contrary to the national purpose, all the compulsion imaginable can scarcely force a change in a better direction. On the other hand, since incentives are always present, the sensible first act of the systems manager would be to bring these incentives into line with national purpose—to close some doors, to open others.

From the point of taxes, slum property is now the most lucrative real-estate investment a man can make in many cities. But, if he repairs his property to raise it above the slum class, he earns significantly less money on his total investment. Public policy might well consciously reverse this condition and these incentives. Private action would then, of its own choice, begin to work toward the accomplishment of national objectives. Furthermore, this flow of men and materials into areas of national need would not of itself demand such dangerously large sums of federal money and of itself necessarily threaten the value of the dollar. Large federal sums and increased taxes would undoubtedly be required for the period of "massive effort" at least; but to the extent that flows of present funds were rechanneled in the way just described, the burden on taxes and on the government itself would be relieved, and solutions to our problems of crisis would at the same time be greatly accelerated.

All this, of course, is not without a price. Existing incentives might be dropped or diminished. There would be dislocation of present patterns and drying up of accustomed channels of investment. These dislocations and hardships are real; they are painful, and they are inequitable. But to say this is not to discredit the merit and the imperative of needed solutions. We cannot compare a proposed solution against some nonexistent ideal, but rather against the old and imperfect system which has got us where we are and which has begotten critical problems which need urgent correction.

There will be other difficulties and dislocations in the course I am describing: If a war-like effort at catching up is to be mounted, some industries (notably the building and construction industries) will be faced with excess demands. Either the total level of construction would have to be held fixed by restricting some areas while expanding others (I might be restrained from expanding diesel-engine floor space while urban housing and hospital construction are accelerated). Or a wage and price freeze (which itself carries evils, and which horrifies me as much as it does you) would have to be accepted, until the catchup had been accomplished. But this is not all. Money alone will not solve our crisis.

Our institutions, which were made for a simpler time, are not able to function with the coordination, speed, and effectiveness which the execution of prompt plans today requires. It is hard to describe briefly the situation in our various governments which frustrates those within as well as those without: (1) proliferated and overlapping agencies which prevent coordinated solutions; (2) confusion and blurred lines between each federal branch; (3) state boundaries which no longer make sense (business has for some time made its own regional boundaries, and they pay scant attention to state lines); (4) inadequate federal power where swift action is required; (5) inadequate local and community power to have a say in those matters where local interest should prevail.

A very wise businessman has said "organization is reorganization." All the money in the world will not help us in a time of crisis, unless we organize to use our money and our planned efforts effectively.

Our present national reaction (as reflected in much of the press) seems to me dangerously wide of the mark. We express alarm over the growing power of the federal government, and state that it must be curbed and power returned to the people. There is a half-truth here. Local communities truly ought to accept more responsibility for local solutions to local problems and plan, organize, and finance what needs doing. Additional dispersal of power is needed. But this is not all. Every local community right now has powers and capacity to raise money which it does not use. It is waiting until things get worse.

At the other end, we must unite. We are not a collection of autonomous states. Few of us have lived and operated in one region throughout our lives. We are a national people, and, in many respects, we are overdue in organizing as a national people. . . .

Government, however, is not the only one of our institutions which is ill-fitted to serve the present need. Education too has now become dangerously irrelevant. Many of our students, both the responsible and the irresponsible, are trying to tell us this, mainly in ways which are exceedingly repugnant to us. A quotation which I am fond of repeating is Cicero's comment on a friend, "He remained the same, but the same was no longer fitting." And so it is with today's education. I do not wholly support today's youth. I do not like long hair, protests, bad manners, and the rest. Reluctantly, however, I must admit that they are clearly the brightest youth this country, and perhaps any country, has ever seen. Race horses are harder to handle than plow horses, and they are clearly both race horses and hard to handle. We must, however, listen to them when they say that a very great part of today's education seems irrelevant and meaningless to them. We do not have to accept their answers uncritically, but they will and should have some significant "say" in final decisions. To admit to this is not wholly dissimilar from saying that a community must have an appropriate say in community affairs.

Management-labor relations are dangerously obsolete. As each becomes very large indeed, the nation will reach a point where it will no longer tolerate crippling national strikes as a means of settling regularly recurring wage negotiations. If management and labor continue to sit still, blame each other, and remain indifferent to the national interest, then we shall have either national collapse one day or a nationally imposed answer, with which neither one of us will be happy.

I could go on in my account of inadequate, obsolete, irrelevant organizations and institutions: the press and media—their too casual concern for accuracy and determination to make news where there is no news; the institutional church and its increasing similarity to a religious Rotary Club; farm organizations and their unwillingness to seek new ways out of a situation which everyone agrees is thoroughly bad. Then there is the medical profession. The cost of health care in this country is rising faster than any other component of the gross national product. Its quality is not as good as in many other less fortunate countries, and in many areas it is dangerously low. The correction does not call for vast amounts of money, but rather for a change in the system, something that is in the power of the profession to accomplish now. But nothing happens.

What does this all say? To me it says we have an internal crisis which is in nature complex and pervasive and in size and significance ultimately mortal. It could destroy us. It also says that it is not too late to act, though it may very soon be too late. It says further that we cannot act slowly, as usually in the past we have been able to act. We cannot wait for a problem to become clearly desperate and act by bits and pieces. Instead we must act with a speed to which we have never been accustomed. We must act across the board because we have let crises pile up on us, and we must act with a degree of national commitment which in our history we have shown only in times of major war. . . .

This is a business and industry society. We are the "power group," the "lead group," the group which has a chance to set the example. Will we remain content with our relatively pleasant position and concentrate our efforts on a holding operation? If we pursue *selfish* interest, there is no reason to suspect we will not meet the fate of all other power groups in history which pursued selfish interest. Or will we pursue *self*-interest? In clear recognition that we can flourish only in a thoroughly healthy society, will we place national interest above our own immediate advantage and lead the country in a wise, far-sighted attack upon its grave and critical weaknesses? Government, in all probability, will not step out and lead, and I am well aware that for a political candidate to propose seriously what we have just talked about might well be political death for him.

Two hallmarks of the free society of which you and I are so proud are personal liberty and private property. If personal liberty is defined to mean a single-minded concern for the preservation of a maximum amount of personal liberties for me, and if private property is defined to mean a single-minded concern for the preservation of my own personal property and my right to do with it as I wish, then we have wrought nothing new in America. The animals in the jungle have operated according to these principles since life began, and we should expect that we will sooner or later have a jungle here. But, if personal liberty in America comes to mean a fierce concern for the personal liberty of the other fellow and an individual and collective commitment to achieving this, and if private property comes to mean a fierce concern for the private property of the other fellow, especially the weak and disadvantaged, and an individual and collective commitment to achieve this, even at the surrender of some present personal privilege, then we shall have achieved a most remarkable society indeed. We shall have saved ourselves from a perilous time. And we shall have shown the whole world the way out. Because of what and who you and I are, this all begins with us.

75

What Business Can Do for the Cities

FORTUNE MAGAZINE

THE OUTER LIMITS OF UNPROFITABILITY

These public-service operations are an extraordinary new phenomenon in United States business; they are also a principal source of the puzzlement so many businessmen now feel about the extent of their—and their companies'—new involvement in the crisis. In principle, of course, the main objective at

---

From an editorial, courtesy of *Fortune Magazine* (January, 1968).

most companies is generating profits; "profit maximization" is presumed to be what business is all about.

Not everyone agrees that this *should* be what business is all about; and most businessmen can name some companies at which sales volume seems in fact to be more intensely sought after than profits. But still, the prevailing view of the case is that businessmen who don't try to maximize profits aren't really doing their jobs: if they are employed executives, they are subject to dismissal, if they are corporate directors, they are vulnerable to stockholder suits. Even the barely visible dents in profits represented by corporate charity have been assailed by some stockholders. What, then, about corporate "contributions" that take the form of relatively expensive efforts to recruit, train, and hire uneducated slum Negroes? Or about mortgage investments in the slums that yield appreciably less than alternative investments (which are safer besides)? How far can profit-oriented corporations go with such ventures?

The conventional answer to such questions, volunteered many times by public-spirited businessmen, is that in the long run their inclination to perform good works will also serve to maximize their profits—that, in fact, the profits won't be there unless society is sustained by the kind of good works in question. It is an appealing answer and there is a temptation to swallow it whole; the world would indeed be a wonderful place if profits and good works were so neatly laced together. Unfortunately, however, good works are related more easily to costs than to profits, and where there really is a long-term payoff it will presumably benefit not only the corporation that originally shelled out for those good works, but other corporations too, including competitors that poured all *their* resources into mere profit maximization.

A SUDDEN FEELING OF INVOLVEMENT

What it comes down to is this: the public, and many government officials at various levels have now eagerly embraced the idea that private corporations have a unique capability for dealing with the cities' problems. But many in government, and indeed many businessmen, have not yet perceived that we need new institutional arrangements to help corporations use that capability as well as they might. It will not do to pretend that we can create all the jobs and houses we need simply by appealing to the profit motive. Nor will it do to pretend that corporations can make major investments in the cities on a nonprofit basis.

What kinds of arrangements are called for? Several possibilities come to mind. In some cases, presumably, tax incentives and subsidies might be appropriate when there is no other way to get major corporate involvement. Another possibility would be to allow competitors to form industry councils, with immunity from antitrust action, so that all could engage in "public service" operations from the same competitive base. Some kind of immunity from stockholder action might also be considered. Corporations, and their individual officers and directors, should be freed from concern that any special efforts they put forth will entangle them in court with stockholders. We need a great many more working relationships between our executives, our local planners and government officials, and our universities. In fact, we might well try to evolve a concept of our top managers as a major unused national resource—a resource from which society might expect a lot more. The possibility of a management "tithe" for public service is an intriguing one.

If we really are looking to business to provide some leadership in the cities, what may be needed most of all is a change that will require no new laws, but simply some new attitudes. It is a change already taking place in a good many business communities; its main symptom is a suddenly intense feeling of *involvement* with the city on the part of businessmen. It is this sense of involvement that sent James Roche, the new chairman of General Motors, on a pilgrimage to Lansing to lobby for open housing; and got Henry Ford II to go calling personally on a Negro activist in the Detroit slums. Large and beneficial consequences can be expected as more and more business leaders act on the idea that the city is not just a place where one works and, possibly, lives—but is the major component of America.

76

How Deep Is the Private Sector's Involvement?

CHESTER HARTMAN
Professor of Urban Planning, Harvard-M.I.T. Joint Center for Urban Studies

The first issue I would like to discuss with you is the question of the costs of a program run by the public sector versus a program run by the private sector.

In the various proposals I have heard and discussions I have engaged in over the last few months about what has been called unleashing the private sector, I find there is, explicit or implicit, an assumption that somehow if the private sector can be convinced to do the job, we are going to wind up with a much less costly program than might otherwise be the case.

In my opinion this is an untrue assumption and a rather dangerous one, because it tends to postpone the realization we all must come to that at this time we have to be spending billions where we are now spending only millions.

From *Urban America: Goals and Problems,* Hearings before the Subcommittee on Urban Affairs of the Joint Economic Committee of Congress (1967), pp. 192–194.

It seems that in an age where we can, with incredible facility, spend $5 billion for antiballistic-missile systems, several billion dollars on supersonic transports, we still have not been willing to come to the realization that these kinds of billions, billions of government tax moneys, must be spent in solving our urban problems.

I made some estimates . . . that just for solving the housing problem alone we would need somewhere in the neighborhood of $7 to $8 billion a year. The financial realities of our urban problems can't be skirted or wished away by some magic wand called the private sector. The realities are such that the gaps in the housing field between the incomes of people who need decent housing and the cost of producing decent housing are very great and they can only be met through a program of government subsidies.

In the area of economic development and creation of jobs in the ghettos it is quite obvious that the commitment to guarantee profits, the tax credits offered, the reimbursable risks for business corporations that can be convinced to locate in the ghetto are all going to be extremely costly, and we shouldn't pretend there is any magic about a private sector solution.

Second, I have some very deep doubts, based upon my own readings and observations about corporations in the private sector, as to how widespread and how deep and long lasting is going to be the private sector's involvement in the solution of these urgent social problems.

It seems to me it is one thing to persuade a few corporations known to be progressive, a few key executives who are known to be socially responsible, to pioneer in carefully planned experiments, but there are going to be counterpressures from the stockholders and within the organization itself, and I think some of the questions . . . about the internal attitudes of corporations are very relevant here. I don't think you are going to find a mass movement within the corporations themselves toward an altruistic sense of helping out with social problems.

There is also the question of a possible competitive disadvantage that corporations which are willing to put their resources, manpower, and managerial skills into this field of urban problems may find themselves in, vis-à-vis other corporations in the same field who are not willing to risk similar resources in these experiments.

There is the question of corporate image, too. How long will a corporation be willing to get involved in what is essentially a minor part of its operations which can very severely damage its own corporate image through difficulties which may arise in the process of social experiments? We have had instances, in New York, of insurance companies which have been very reluctant to get involved sponsoring housing developments, following their experience in the 1940's and 1950's when these companies found themselves in the position of landlords having to impose rent increases on their tenants; they feared their main business—insurance—would suffer because of this.

In short, my reading of the nature of the corporate beast leads me to believe that its own goals, motivations, and inner dynamics are not consonant with its playing a major role in the solution of social problems.

The third, and last, issue I would like to raise with you is the question of control. I think if we are at all sensitive to the demands coming out of the ghetto right now, possibly the principal issue, if there can be called one single issue that stands out, is the demand of the ghetto residents to control their own institutions, the economic and political forces that shape the community.

On the other hand, the primary feature of the American corporation is its concern with power and control, extremely centralized control to shape a corporate environment conducive to maximizing the profits and competitive position of the corporation. There is bound to be a clash here. That large corporations will include in their decisionmaking processes members of the ghetto community seems to me highly unlikely. And, it seems highly unlikely that they will be sympathetic with many of the key demands of the ghetto. They won't be able to communicate effectively with the people in the ghetto community. Similarly, the imposition into the ghetto of a powerful outside force with its own demands and agenda is going to lead to a great deal of resentment; may lead to very destructive behavior, and is not likely to produce an atmosphere of success. Therefore, I think one of the major issues we have to discuss is the question of who controls what in the ghetto; from this vantage point, at least, suggestions to bring private corporate enterprise into the ghetto seem to run counter to the major thoughts and trends within the ghetto itself.

77

The Corporation in Larger Terms

NEIL W. CHAMBERLAIN

Aside from government itself, the business firm is the dominant institution of Western society, and it is so significant primarily because it represents a form of specialization in the social system. If specialization tends to limit the life of the mind, then business dominance in our society tends to have that effect pervasively. A reasonable case could be made for the proposition that specialization has indeed become characteristic of Western life generally—in the universities at least as much as elsewhere—but there is a monumental differ-

---

From "The Life of the Mind in the Firm," *Daedalus* (Winter, 1969), pp. 139–146. Reprinted by permission of *Daedalus*, Journal of the American Academy of Arts and Sciences, Boston, Mass., Winter, 1969, "Perspectives on Business."

ence between the specialization of fields of learning, none of which dominate our way of life, and the specialization of a form of activity (business) that does in fact dominate our total society.

Because this argument has been made in one way or another by critics whose socialist alternatives have been unpalatable to most Westerners does not excuse us from examining it on its merits. In its simplest form, it reduces to the thesis that it is a crippling limitation on the life of any mind to judge the quality of its play by the single standard of profit.

At a stage of economic development where existence presses hard on resources, and private control over those resources is widely diffused, such devotion to profit as a standard of efficiency is justified. Adam Smith has articulated that position eloquently—so eloquently, in fact, that his words are still being recited even though their relevance has been blunted. Our society is no longer hard pressed for its subsistence, and although economic power is still diffused, economic concentrations have developed in the form of large corporations, distributed throughout society like lumps of fat in a buttermilk batter.

Under such changed circumstances we cannot remain preoccupied with private corporate profit as the ultimate standard by which to test the validity of the activities of the largest part of our population. It is still considered a high economic virtue that our major corporations behave like somewhat softened, but scrimping Scrooges or modest, but misanthropic misers—whose actions are governed only by the test of whether they are efficient in adding to a revenue stream and whose only purposes are limited dispersal to a limited stockholder clientele and reinvestment to maintain or augment the profit flow.

The life of the mind in the firm is hobbled and its vision is blinkered by the constraint to which the business institution is subject within the larger social system. The firm's specialized role is perhaps the greatest limitation on the role of the individual within it. This argument has little or nothing to do with the question of private ownership of the shares of major corporations; that is a separate issue. The argument is concerned with the standards that apply to the conduct of those organizations which give our society its special character. If our major corporations were wholly government-owned, but still applied only the profit-efficiency test to their operations, the result would be the same. The socialist approach provides no solution for this problem; its ideology may be defended or attacked on other grounds, but not in terms of the intellectual freedom that it automatically accords to those who compose its principal economic agencies. There is much to be said for leaving control over our giant corporations in private hands—diffusion of discretion and power is a value not to be given up lightly—if we can broaden the standards by which we judge their activity, if we can free them from a test of efficiency more relevant to the past than to the present.

In speaking of a role not restricted by the pursuit of profit, I am talking about something more than the corporate handout to colleges and community chests. I refer to those activities that a company is particularly geared to perform, but from which it does not expect to reap any reward, on which it may indeed have to spend some portion of its own funds—activities like urban housing, slum reclamation, recreational developments, education and training programs not restricted to its own needs, cooperation with city, state, and federal governments in a variety of programs that could not otherwise be undertaken. The list is limited only by imagination.

• • •

Many people believe that to cast any doubt on the profit standard is to imply, as an alternative, a limitation of managerial direction, perhaps by government regulation. Others fear precisely the reverse: that managers would have excessive discretion to use corporate revenues for a variety of purposes not subject to any social sanction if the discipline of profit maximization were removed. Professor Milton Friedman of Chicago, and Professor Fritz Machlup, for example, question the desirability of giving managers the right to use corporate earnings in any way they see fit so long as it is not actually illegal. What would guide the managers' judgment, they ask, if the standard of profit maximization were diluted with other standards? Investments could be justified by managerial whim, so that scarce economic resources might be channeled into fruitless or quixotic adventures ranging from utopian communities to museums of vintage automobiles. Personal managerial philosophies would be free to find their expression in large-scale corporate grants to the arts, to technical education, to park development without respect to housing needs, or to housing development without respect to park needs.

The Friedman-Machlup argument has two separable strands running through it. If one is to reject it, as I do, it is worth disentangling the two. First, their argument is based on the proposition that because economic resources are by definition scarce, they should not be wasted, and their allocation should be strictly governed by a standard of efficiency. It is further contended that no standard of efficiency has proved so efficacious as unalloyed profit maximization.

Second, their case rests on the political principle that economic power should be decentralized to private hands, but that this devolution can be justified only by restricting the exercise of that power: hence the *specialized* economic role of producing goods and services for sale, under a *systematic* constraint of profit maximization. Whatever a manager can legally do in "turning a buck," or a million bucks, is socially sanctioned as a valid and desirable exercise of power and discretion; anything else is suspect as *ultra vires,* beyond the firm's appropriate role in the system.

Both these defenses are highly questionable. Scarce resources have to be assiduously husbanded by a society on the edge of subsistence, but for a society in some state of material comfort other considerations are at least as relevant. Among these concerns is the life of the mind of its people. If material goods-producing institutions dominate the society, as they do ours, all those whose functional activities are involved in them are subjected to a way of life based on resource conservation—and this without respect to whether resource conservation has actually been tested by the profitability of our large corporations.

The necessity for binding managerial discretion within a tightly woven systematic web involves a matter of faith. Those who would keep the web intact are presumably reluctant to entrust humans with discretionary power. I confess to a greater optimism. The managers of our major corporations *already* possess discretionary power, and I should like to see the field for appropriate exercise of that discretion extended to embrace other activities than those with a profit potential. Such dominant organizations of our times as General Electric or Union Carbide should not be inhibited from a larger role in nonprofit areas. To the extent that we encourage a wider range of corporate activity, we are likely to encourage the accession to business of many of the more imaginative and idealistic minds among the young. I should be willing to take my chances on the kinds of programs that might emerge from those who see the corporation in larger terms. In recent months I have read statements of officials of the Xerox and Polaroid companies asserting explicitly that there must be more to business than the making of a product and a profit. They see the need for the large corporation to use its resources and its powers perceptively in integrating itself more closely with the society by moving on social problems that the front pages identify daily.

There may be irresistible pressures driving us in the direction of greater centralization of power in all organized activity—in governments, universities, businesses. But even if this should prove to be the case, the effects of this process may be partially offset by developing in private hands the capacity to undertake actions as yet associated only with government. It may be worth experimenting as to whether we cannot make ours a livelier, more creative, more daring society by invigorating the private corporate centers of power. We may, in time, develop new standards for judging the effectiveness of such institutions, but I should not want to postpone our experimenting until we have done so. The pace of change is matched too closely by impatience with the lack of change. The corporation is one resource we cannot afford to waste by chaining it tightly to the profit stake, while searching for another more suitable stake to which to anchor it.

Those large firms with their present ambiguous effects on the intellectual life of those who inhabit them have the greatest capacity to move in this direction. By loosening the specialized role of the firm itself, we can invigorate the intellectual climate within which the specialized roles of its employees are performed. Perhaps, indeed, we have become excessively infatuated with systems analysis, in which all the cooperating parts are judged by their efficiency in contributing to the performance of the system as a whole, the system conceived as a machine. Perhaps a more ragged system has its own values in social affairs, granting discretion to the parts to move with some unsystematic purposiveness of their own.

This approach would obviously de-emphasize the role of profit in corporate life, but to de-emphasize is not to abandon. As long as private enterprise prevails, some profit is essential to survival. Moving from the certain discipline of profit maximization to the more flexible standard of simply making a profit would not entirely change the game, but it would require some institutional modifications.

A lower rate of return on its investment will increase what a company must pay for its capital whenever it resorts to the capital markets to finance its growth, and it may have to resort to them more frequently than in the past if its retained earnings decline because of expanded not-for-profit activities. Stockholders who are disappointed because their shares fail to appreciate as rapidly as those of a more profit-oriented company may band together to turn out the incumbent management. Alternatively, if the profit potential of a firm is not fully realized, and this is reflected in a lower value of its shares, it exposes itself to possible assault by a raider bent on realizing the profits implicit in its assets. None of these are minor matters to those responsible for the conduct of a corporation.

Nor are they beyond solution if we are persuaded that there is social value in the effort. A reconsideration of the desirable restrictions on corporate acquisitions of other companies may be required: Perhaps corporate assets should not be used in the purchase of shares of companies in the size range with which we are dealing, with whatever exceptions seem warranted. Corporate taxation could be used to induce the wanted result—perhaps by a marked gradation past some percentage return on investment, perhaps by a lower rate for firms that have put at least some percentage of earnings into other than production purposes.

If there is the intent to encourage such broader corporate activity, we can find ways to protect companies that respond. We need not impose a new system on our corporations; we can encourage independent business action with *ad hoc* devices. In the process, we may find that not-for-profit corporate activity will take on as much glamour and excitement as corporate activity designed for profit, and that part of the challenge of the game will be to effect a satisfactory mix of the two. In such circumstances, the life of the mind in the firm will almost certainly be invigorated.

Skeptics are sure to retort that business firms—even those that are most public in their professions of social concern—do not now undertake as much in this regard as present law permits. To my knowledge, the limit of the 5 per cent rule has not been approached by any major firm. The skeptics ask why one should expect any change of behavior when business has so clearly expressed how it views its interest. They may be right. Business may not modify its social role, but the issue is not closed.

If we play the currently popular game of looking ahead to the year 2000, it is not so fanciful to picture General Electric and IBM, Ford and ITT, LTV and AT&T—yes, even U.S. Steel and General Motors—operating in two broad categories of activities: a profit-making sector in which they continue to exploit change and to probe the social environment purposively for ways in which to improve their earnings position; and a nonprofit sector in which they employ their organizational and productive talents, with appropriate political encouragement and tax incentives, to modify the social environment itself. Each would still decide for itself how much of the latter it would do, but public attitudes and facilitating legislation would presumably encourage bolder actions than are now typical.

The possibility that private companies would, without sanction from the electorate, come to dominate society under such conditions can be faced as a calculated risk. If business abuses its extended powers of initiative, these can then be clipped. Similarly, if big business demonstrates that it lacks the capacity to carry out this new social role, government can assume this function. But the social conscience and social consciousness that would be needed for business to be infused with a new vitality and made an intellectually more stimulating sphere of activity cannot themselves be legislated. They can only be achieved intentionally by the business institutions; at a point in time, enough must realize that to retain their dominant role in Western society they may have to shift their perspective away from profit as a single standard toward a broader set of social objectives.

78
What Is to Be Done?

GORDON P. SHERMAN
President, Midas-International Corporation

Last year our company enjoyed unprecedented prosperity in the fulfillment of its most optimistic predictions and in obedience to modern management principles of our great free enterprise system. Yet, let us frankly admit: By way of our exhaust system products we have "innocently" conveyed into the atmosphere countless tons of toxic gases, and, by way of our recreational vehicles we have helped bring into our waning wilderness the happy but despoiling presence of tourists by the thousands.

This admission is hardly appropriate to the kind of letter a corporation's president sends to its shareholding public, and yet, by these very words, I wish to avoid the sanctimoniousness with which prosperity is usually equated to progress.

From the introduction to the 1968 Annual Report of Midas-International Corporation, by Gordon P. Sherman.

The following pages will assure you that our business is on a steady and admirable course. I confine this letter then, only to wondering aloud how we and other well-intending corporations can bring to our products and practices a total responsibility that addresses the ultimate well-being of our country.

What then is to be done? Let this letter only exemplify what might well be the first step toward this purpose: a break with precedent in the admission that there is no natural consonance between our desire to show present profit and the desperate long-range needs of our people and our environment.

Index

Index

Adams, Sherman, 13–18
adult work experience programs, 209–210
Advisory Commission on Intergovernmental Relations, 483
Aerojet-General Corporation, 52, 228, 396, 428–430, 444
African Methodist Episcopal Church, 129
age structure, population and, 79–82
Albrook, Robert C., 25–29
Alcoa, 25
Alfsen, Jean M., 353
Allen-Bradley Company, 152–171
American Oil Company, 29
antipoverty programs, private enterprise participation in, 207–212, 236–260
apprenticeship: minorities and, 121–127; programs, discrimination in, 112–120, 121–127
Area Redevelopment Act, 398
Argyris, Chris, 33
Armiger, Donald, 114
AVCO Corporation, 398

Ballard, Roscoe B., 157
Basham, Harvey, Jr., 177
Batt, William L., Jr., 329–330
Bay Area Rapid Transit System, 52
Beck, Bertram M., 402–403
Bedford-Stuyvesant area (Brooklyn, N.Y.), 209, 452–459
Bedford-Stuyvesant Development and Services Corporation, 453
Bedford-Stuyvesant Manpower Center, 209
Bedford-Stuyvesant Open Industry Center, 210
Bedford-Stuyvesant Restoration Corporation, 399, 452–459
Bell & Howell, 31
Bienstock, Herbert, 114
"Black Power," 88, 99–100
Blake, John L., 445
Blasier, Robert D., 28
Block, Joseph I., 213, 303, 304
Blough, Roger, 49
Board for Fundamental Education, 319, 329, 362, 363
Boston Gas Company, 388

Brennan, Peter, 118
broke persons, 220
Brown, Holmes, 114
Brown, Robert L., 156–157
Buber, Martin, 32
Budd Company, 52
Burrell, Berkeley G., 406–408, 412–418
Burt, Samuel M., 324–330, 373–375
business: antipoverty program and, 236–260; as "power" group, 496–501; developing, in ghettos, 396–400; development of people as co-aim of, 29–34; disadvantaged workers and, 298–321; education and, 333–375; financial contributions by, 5, 6, 26; future of, 384–386; future of the cities and, 461–511; ghetto business enterprise, private encouragement of, 443–459; government and, 41–53; helping vocational schools meet needs of, 363–364; interests in the city, nature of, 3–53; manpower development and, 225–331; new initiatives by, 384–385; participation in community affairs, 3–21; poverty sector and, 183–223; private, public side of, 47–53; public, private side of, 380–383; racial relations and, 83–181; role of, in public affairs, 5–9, 13–18, 47–53; social conscience of, 25–29; technology and, 42–43; urban crisis and, 356; urban economic development and, 377–459. *See also* industry; private enterprise; small business
businessmen, motivation of, social problems and, 14–15

California Manufacturers Association, 292
California State Employment Service, 292, 293
Campbell, Ralph, 298–309
Campbell Soup Corporation, 362
capitalism: achievements of, 13; black, promoting, 405–418; shortcomings of, 13
Caples, William, 300
Case-Hoyt Corporation, 445
Cassell, Frank, 303, 315–321, 328
Caterpillar Tractor, 28
Cavanagh, Jerome, 464

central cities: color composition of population in, 76–78; population data, 65–69; redeveloping economy of, 396–400
Chamberlain, Neil W., 47–53, 365–373, 380–383, 468–472, 505–510
Champion, George, 46
Champion Papers, 317
Chase Manhattan Bank, 25, 46, 53, 174
Chemical Bank of New York, 174, 177
Chicago Association of Commerce and Industry, 304
Chrysler Corporation, 327, 329, 347, 353–355
CIO, 128, 129
cities, future of, business and, 461–511
citizenship, corporate: attitudes toward, 5–9; practices (table), 7
civil disorders: effect of enrichment policies on, 98–99; future, probability of, 94–95; National Advisory Commission on, report of, 87–103
Civil Rights Act (1964), 122, 167, 168
Civilian Conservation Corps, 237
Clark, Harold F., 401–402
Clark, Kenneth, 129
Clayes, Jerry, 458
Clee, Gilbert H., 47
Clemente, Lester, 390
collaboration, public-private, 15–16, 53
color composition of population, changes in, 69–78
Committee for Economic Development (CED), 28, 194–195, 478, 483, 485, 486
Communications Satellite Corporation, 52
Community Action Agency, 210
community action program (CAP), 202–203, 210–212
community affairs: business participation in, 3–21; employee participation in, 6, 9. *See also* public affairs
community manpower systems, 200–205
community service, business and, 5–6
Comptroller General of the United States, 262–264
construction industry, racial discrimination in, 112–127
contributions, financial, 5, 6, 26
Control Data Corporation, 398
Coolidge, Calvin, 391
Corman, James C., 104–107, 230–233, 430
Corn Products Company, 361
corporations, future of, 505–511
Corwin, Ed, 114
Council of Economic Advisers, 213, 223

counseling, 201, 204
curriculum, reform of, 16
Curtis, Thomas B., 106–107

Daley, Mayor (Chicago), 303
Day, William M., 348
demographic data, 55–82
Detroit, Michigan, business involvement in public education, 347–355
Development and Services Corporation, 399
Diamond Alkali Company, 363
Diebel Manufacturing Company, 317
disavantaged persons: description of, 326–328; employers of, 315–321, 328–330; employing, 298–321; private industry and, 309–315
discrimination: apprenticeship programs and, 112–120; employment, in New York City, 172–177; unions and, 112–120, 121–127
Doar, John, 453
Donham, Wallace B., 30
Downs, Anthony, 194–195, 387–388
Downtown Businessmen's Association (Los Angeles), 292
Drucker, Peter, 45

Eastman Kodak Company, 444–445, 448
economic development: Bedford-Stuyvesant Restoration Corporation and, 452–459; employment opportunities and, 196; of ghettos, 395–403; urban, business and, 377–459
Economic Development Act, 398
Economic Opportunity Act (1964), 207–210, 236, 244, 251, 423
Economic Opportunity, Office of, 189
education: basic, 361–365; bridging the gap between school and work, 336–344; business and, 333–375; business of, 394; entrepreneur, 406–408; inadequacies of, 499; innovation in, 358; Negroes and, 100–101; remedial, 358–360; vocational, 363–364; vocational-technical, 345–347; within industry, 357–375. *See also* schools
Ehrenberg, Joseph, 305–306, 308
Eidson, Bettye K., 133–149
Eisenhower, Dwight D., 165, 477
Elliott, A. Wright, 19–20, 358
employee participation in community affairs, 6, 9
employers: characteristics of, 134–135; city

problems and, 136–140; disadvantaged, 315–321, 328–330; major, manpower policies of, 133–149
employment: creating opportunities for, 196–205; disadvantaged and, 298–321; discrimination in New York City, 172–177; equal, activities concerned with, 125–127; implementation of an equal policy throughout a corporation, 178–181; Negroes and, 90–91, 108–120, 140–148; nondiscrimination policy in, 152–171; public service, 198–199, 330–331; recruitment for, 200; significance of, 89
Employment Act (1946), 223
employment offices, 200–201
entrepreneur school, 406–408, 415
environmental problem solution, business and, 5, 6, 8
Equal Employment Opportunities Commission (see United States Equal Employment Opportunities Commision)
Equitable Life Assurance Society, 174
Erickson, Fred, 299

Fager, Frank W., 157, 158
Fairchild Hiller Corporation, 425
Fairmicco Company, 425
family allowances, 213
family planning, 16
Federal Contract Compliance, Office of, 152–171
Federal Housing Administration, 389–390
Fifth Amendment, 167
FIGHT Organization, 444, 445, 450
financial contributions, 5–6, 26
First National City Bank, 16–17
Fischer, John H., 345
Fitch, Lyle C., 473–495
Ford Foundation, 415
Ford, Henry, 464
Ford, Henry II, 27, 503
Ford Motor Company, 27, 213, 384, 394
Fortune Magazine, 501–503
Franklin, W. H., 28
Freedom Budget, 129
Friedman, Milton, 213, 214, 220, 507

Galbraith, John Kenneth, 26, 36
Gardner, John W., 464–467
General Electric Company, 53, 370, 384, 394, 411, 508
General Learning Corporation, 394
General Motors Corporation, 411

Ghetto Economic Development and Industrialization Plan (GHEDIPLAN), 434–441
ghettos: developing business and entrepreneurs in, 396–400; economic development of, 395–403; private encouragement of business enterprise in, 443–459; racial, formation of, 88–89; resources lacking in, 402–403
Giannini, Peter, 158
Goldston, Eli, 132, 220, 388–391, 463
government: business and, 41–53; inadequacies of, 499; procurement, promoting small business through, 423–434; small business enterprise encouraged by, 419–459
Greenberg, Howard, 427
Greene, Thomas, 456
Griffiths, Martha W., 106, 107
guaranteed income, 213–219

Haggerty, C. J., 123
Harper, John, 25, 27
Harrington, Michael, 26
Harris, Fred R., 228–230
Hartman, Chester, 503–505
Hauser, Philip M., 57–82
Hay, Sam, 157, 158
Haynes Foundation, 292
Head Start, 210, 211
Herzberg, Frederick, 31
Hodge, Patricia Leavey, 57–82
Hodges, Edward N. III, 348
Horwitz, Julius, 220–222
housing: good, can be good business, 388–391; public, 15, 16; subsidies needed, 387–388
Housing and Urban Development Act (1968), 387
housing development corporations, 211
Humphrey, Hubert, 428

incentives: management, for social action, 35–41; necessity for, 15–16, 18
income tax, negative, 213–219
Industrial Council of the City of Commerce, 292
industry: as "power" group, 496–501; developing, in ghettos, 396–400; education within, 357–375; helping vocational schools meet needs of, 363–364. *See also* business; private enterprise
Inland Steel, 213
institutional realignment, 23–53
integration, 102–103

International Business Machines Corp., 396, 399
Interracial Council for Business Opportunity, 422

Javits, Jacob, 15, 427–428, 435, 453
Job Corps, 232–233, 236–250, 394; cost-benefit analysis, 260–262; evaluation of, 262–264; restructuring the, 264–266
job gap, 197; closing the, 198
job placement, 200–204
job training, 16–18, 28, 202–203, 362–363
jobs: importance of, 108–112; nature of problem of, and role of new public service employment, 330–331; need for, 228–233; Negroes and, 90–92, 108–120
Jobs Now, 268, 269–282, 303, 304–305, 320
Johns Hopkins University, 133–149
Johnson, Lyndon B., 50, 52, 85, 165
Joint Economic Committee of Congress: discussion of Burrell and Sullivan statements, 412–418; on location of the poor, 186; on need for jobs, 228–233; on racism, 104–120; on the Job Corps, 260–262
Jonas, Gary F., 35–41

Keating, Stephen, 466
Kennedy, John F., 49, 165
Kennedy, Robert, 15
Kerner Commission (*see* National Advisory Commission on Civil Disorders)
Kerner, Otto, 85
Kethan, W. W., 317
Kimball, Dan A., 428–430
Kubica, Joseph, 300, 306
Kurzman, Stephen, 207–212, 236–260, 420–422

labor policies, of major employers, 133–149
labor unions (*see* unions)
Lampman, Robert J., 216
Land, Edwin H., 31
leadership, nongovernmental, 464–467
Levitan, Sar A., 206–207, 396–400
Levitt, Professor, 39
Lewis, John L., 128
Lewis, Murray, 292
Lewis, Sir W. Arthur, 121
Lewisohn, Richard, 431–434
Liebow, Elliot, 108–112, 326
Lindsay, John, 453, 464
loans, small business, 420–422
Lockheed, 52, 394

Los Angeles Chamber of Commerce, 292
Los Angeles Junior Chamber of Commerce, 292

McClellan, H. C. (Chad), 291, 292, 294, 295
McColough, C. Peter, 446
McCoy, Samuel L., 390
McGregor, Douglas M., 318
Machlup, Fritz, 507
McLaurin, Dunbar S., 434–441
Madden, Carl, 41–47
management, incentives for social action, 35–41
Management Council for Merit Employment, Training, and Research (Los Angeles), 268, 291–297
management-labor relations, 500
Maness, Irving, 427
manpower: business and development of, 225–331; community systems, 200–205; Opportunity Industrial Center Program, 408–412; policies of major employers, 133–149; toward greater involvement in development of, 342–330; program, transferability of, 268–297; upgrading, responsibility for, 365–373
Manpower Development and Training Act, 200, 202, 203, 233, 250–258
Manpower Report of the President, 336–344
Martin, C. Virgil, 272
Martin, Roscoe, 483
Maxion, William, 445
Meade, Margaret, 415
Meany, George, 464
Merchants and Manufacturers Association, 292
metropolitan areas: age structure changes in, 79–82; color composition changes in, 69–76; population outlook (1960–1985), 57–64
Michigan Bell Telephone Company, 347–353
middle class, Negro, 99
Miller, Arjay, 20–21, 39, 213
Miller, Irwin, 496–501
MIND, Inc., 329, 361
minimum wage, 199–200, 206–207
minority groups: apprenticeship and, 121–127; employment discrimination and, in New York City, 172–177; nondiscrimination policy toward, 152–171. *See also* Negroes
Mobilization for Youth, 113–114, 118
Montgomery Ward, 319

Montoya, Senator, 430
Moore, L. W., 29
Moot, Robert C., 423–428
Morison, Elting, 469
motivation, businessmen and, 14–15
Moynihan, Daniel, 47, 89, 444
Muskie, Senator, 488

National Advisory Commission on Civil Disorders, 85, 230; hearings before Joint Economic Committee of Congress on report of, 104–120; report of, 87–103, 132
National Alliance of Businessmen, 17, 26, 28, 123, 309, 310, 311, 312, 315, 328–330
National Association for the Advancement of Colored People (NAACP), 114, 129, 311
National Association of Manufacturers, 149–151, 292, 317, 361
National Business League, 407, 413, 444
National Citizens Committee for Community Relations, 178–181, 361–365
National Commission on Technology, Automation, and Economic Progress, 198
National Commission on Urban Problems, 55
National Council of Negro Women, 129
National Industrial Conference Board, 5–10, 18, 317, 356, 394
Neal, Alfred C., 28
negative income taxation, 213–219
Negro Ministerial Association of Philadelphia, 282
Negroes: apprenticeship and, 121–127; education and, 100–101; employment and, 90–91, 108–120, 140–148; entrepreneurial school for, 406–408; middle class, 99; nondiscrimination policy toward, 152–171; population data, 69–76, 88–89, 91; promoting capitalism among, 405–418; report of National Advisory Commission on Civil Disorders, 87–103; self-determination movement and, 403; self-development and, 99–100; self-help and, 128–130; unemployment among, 90
Neighborhood Youth Corps, 207–209, 244, 250
Nemore, Arnold, 268–297
New Careers Program, 209
Newman, J. Wilson, 384–386
New York City: Bedford-Stuyvesant Restoration Corporation, 452–459; employment discrimination in, report on, 172–177; Ghetto Economic Development and Industrialization Plan, 434–441; Human Resources Administration, 209–210; Human Rights Commission, 116, 117
New York City Building Trades Council, 114
New York State Commission for Human Rights, 115, 116
New York State Employment Service, 17, 210
New York State Urban Development Corporation, 15
New York Stock Exchange, 174
New York Telephone Company, 174
Nixon, Richard, 165
Nixon, Russell A., 112–120
nondiscrimination policy, employment and, 152–171
Norris, William, 398
North American Aviation, 52, 178–181
North American Rockwell, 394

On-the-Job Training program, 243–244, 250–258, 313
Operation Mainstream, 209
Operation Outreach, 126
Opportunities, Inc., 241–242
opportunities industrialization centers, 210, 268, 282–291
Opportunity Industrial Center Program, 408–412

Pace, Levi, 456
paternalism, 41–42
Pearson, Henry G., 29–34
people, development of, 31–34
Percy, Charles H., 15, 31
Philadelphia Gas Works, 356
Pigors, Paul, 33
placement, job, 200–204
polarization, 95–98
Polaroid, 31, 508
pollution problems, 6, 46, 473
poor, the: "broke" and, 220; location of, 186; main groups of, 191–192; urban, 185–192; work experience of, 188–191. *See also* poverty
population: color composition of, changes in, 69–78; data concerning, 57–82; Negro, 69–76, 88–89, 91
poverty, 13, 16; alleviating, approaches to, 193–223; definition of, 213; low wages and, 206; policy issues, 194–195; sector, business and, 183–223; war on, 223, 238. *See also* antipoverty programs; poor
"power" group, business and industry as, 496–501

private enterprise: antipoverty programs and, 236–260; disadvantaged workers and, 298–321; participation in antipoverty programs, 207–212; public role of, 5–9, 13–18; social environment of, 468–472
profits: city problems and view of, 27–28; private initiative for, 19–20
Progress Enterprises, 415
Progress Plaza, 414
Project Mainstream, 407
prosperity, 13
protest, political, place of, 128–130
Proxmire, William, 105–106, 118–120, 412–417
public affairs: corporate involvement, areas of, 5–6; role of business in, 5–9, 13–18, 47–53. *See also* community affairs
Public Affairs Research Council, 18
public assistance programs, 16
Public Works and Economic Development Act (1965), 386
public works projects, 403
Puryear, Alvin N., 452–459

racial relations; business and, 83–181; Joint Economic Committee of Congress on, 104–120; National Advisory Commission on Civil Disorders report on, 87–103; study by Social Relations Department of Johns Hopkins University, 133–149
racism, 104–107
Radio Corporation of America, 384
Randall, Clarence B., 304
Randolf, A. Philip, 121
Raytheon, 356
Reagan, Ronald, 292, 295
realignment, institutional, 23–53
recruitment, employment, 200
rehabilitation: handicaps to, 392–393; opportunity in, 392
Republic Steel, 367
restoration (*see* Bedford-Stuyvesant Restoration Corporation)
Reuss, Henry S., 487
Reuther, Walter, 464
Rice, William T., 353
Richardson, Robert C., 27
Riot Commission (*see* National Advisory Commission on Civil Disorders)
Ripon Society, 214–215
Ritter-Pfaudler Corp., 445
Robinson, Jack E., 390
Roche, James, 503

Rochester Business Opportunities Corporation, 444–451
Rochester Opportunities Foundation, Inc., 445
Rockefeller, David, 53, 464
Rockefeller, Nelson, 213
Roosevelt, Franklin D., 128
Rossi, Peter H., 133
Rumsfeld, Donald, 104–105, 415–416
Rustin, Bayard, 128
Ruttenberg, Stanley, 430–431
Ryerson, Edward L., 304
Ryerson, Joseph T., and Son, 298–309

Sain, Leonard, 353
Sanders, Thomas, 390
Schnitzer, Martin, 213–219
schools: bridging the gap between work and, 336–344; curriculum and, 16; entrepreneurial, 406–408, 415; public, working with, 355–356; vocational, helping them meet needs of industry, 363–364. *See also* education
Sears, 319
Selekman, Professor, 30
Senate Committee on Labor and Public Welfare, 188–192, 196–205
Senate Select Committee on Small Business, 423–434
services, 401–402
Shelley, E. F., and Company, 309–315, 358–360
Sheppard, Harold L., 330–331
Sherman, Gordon P., 510–511
Shonfield, Andrew, 44
Shultz, George, 264–266
skill development, 200–204
small business, 401–402, 412; government encouragement of, 419–459; loan program, 420–422; promoting, through government procurement, 423–434
Small Business Act, 423
Small Business Administration, 420, 439, 441, 447, 448, 450
Smith, A. P., Manufacturing Co., 316
social action, management incentives for, 35–41
social conscience of business, 25–29
Social Security Administration, 188; poverty defined by, 213
society: benefited by job training, 17–18; social objectives of, application of systems-analysis approach to, 20–21

socioeconomic problem solving, business and, 9
Southern California Hotel and Motel Association, 292
Southern California Restaurant Association, 292
Space-General Corporation, 52
Special Impact Program, 209–210, 399
Stark, Douglas, 157
Stigler, George, 42, 213
Straus, George, 121–127
Striner, Herbert E., 324–330, 373–375
subsidies, federal, 398–399; housing and need for, 387–388
suburbs: color composition of population in, 76–78; population data, 65–69
Sullivan, Leon, 282–284, 289, 408–418
Swanson, J. Chester, 345
systems-analysis approach, application of, to social objectives of society, 20–21
Szrom, Robert, 299–300, 302

Taggart, Robert III, 396–400
tax, negative income, 213–219
taxes, 498
technology, business, and, 42–43
Time, Inc., 394
Tobin, James, 216–219
Toynbee, Arnold, 30
training, job, 16–18, 28, 202–203, 362–363
Truman, Harry S, 366

underemployment, 89–90
unemployed, hard-core, 16–18, 25–26, 28; description of, 326–328; understanding the, 149–151
unemployment, 89–90; among youth, 336–344; Negroes and, 90
Union Carbide, 508
unions: apprenticeship and minorities, 121–127; discriminatory practices of, 112–120, 121–127
United Auto Workers, 122
United States Chamber of Commerce, 317, 321, 345–347, 444–451
United States Employment Service, 200, 201, 317, 321
United States Equal Employment Opportunity Commission, 125, 172–177
United States Gypsum Co., 46, 392–393

United States Steel, 49, 370
Upjohn Institute for Employment Research, 330
Upward Bound, 210
Urban Coalition, 26, 113, 309, 464–466
urban crisis, business and, 356
urban development: extent of private sector's involvement, 503–505; goals for, 473–495; innovations in, 489
Urban League, 126, 129, 292, 311
urban renewal, 15

Vernon, Raymond, 194
Vinson, Allen, 362
vocational education, 363–364
Vocational Education Act, 339

wage, minimum, 199–200, 206–207
Wagner Act, 128
Washington Post, 44
Watson, Thomas J., 399
Watts Manufacturing Company, 428, 444
welfare: possible changes in system, 213–219; programs, 16; recipient's view of, 220–222
Western Oil and Gas Association, 292
Westinghouse, 28
West Virginia Pulp and Paper, 26
Whitehead, Alfred North, 45
Wilberforce University, 129
Wilson, Joseph C., 33, 38, 213
Wolchok, Harold, 114
Wood, Robert C., 194, 477
Workers Defense League, 114, 119, 124, 126
Work Experience and Training Program (Ryerson and Son), 298–309
Wright, M. A., 316

Xerox Corporation, 33, 38, 213, 316, 370, 384, 446, 448, 450, 508

Young, Whitney, 14
younger generation, values of, 463
Youth-in-Action Community Action Agency, 210
Youth Opportunity Centers, 200
Yoxall, George J., 308

Zook, Dwight R., 178, 179